FUND RAISING AND PUBLIC RELATIONS:
A Critical Analysis

COMMUNICATION

A series of volumes edited by
Dolf Zillmann and **Jennings Bryant**

FUND RAISING AND PUBLIC RELATIONS:
A Critical Analysis

Kathleen S. Kelly

LAWRENCE ERLBAUM ASSOCIATES, PUBLISHERS
1991   Hillsdale, New Jersey   Hove and London

Lawrence Erlbaum Associates, Inc., Publishers
365 Broadway
Hillsdale, New Jersey   07642

Library of Congress Cataloging-in-Publication Data
Kelly, Kathleen S.
     Fund raising and public relations : a critical analysis / Kathleen
S. Kelly.
         p.   cm. — (Communication)
     Includes bibliographical references and index.
     ISBN 0-8058-0943-0
     1. Fund raising—United States. 2. Public relations—United
States.   I. Title.   II. Series: Communication (Hillsdale, N.J.)
HV41.9.U5K45 1991
658.15'224—dc20   90-3876
                                                                CIP

Printed in the United States of America
10 9 8 7 6 5 4 3 2 1

For George

Contents

Preface

This book was written for scholars of communication and philanthropy, as well as for fund-raising and public relations practitioners. It grows out of my dual sides: a researcher who is fascinated with theoretical explanations and the practitioner. It also reflects my dualism in public relations and fund raising. My degrees are in communication, and I began my career as a public information director. At that time, I did not know what fund raising was and wanted nothing to do with it. But in 1976 I attended one of the first professional development workshops that focused on women in institutional advancement. As we went around the room "sharing" information about our careers, it became clear to me that we were being "cornered" into support functions and that the fund raiser would soon be our boss. It was one of those moments when the proverbial light bulb goes on, and I left the room determined to become the boss—the fund raiser.

For 13 years I specialized in fund raising, serving as director of development for my alma mater, the University of Maryland at College Park, vice president of development and public relations for Mount Vernon College in Washington, DC, and as the associate dean of the College of Journalism and assistant dean for external relations of the business school at Maryland. During the early years while I was directing annual giving programs and planning donor cultivation events, I recognized that my public relations skills were invaluable, but I thought of myself as a *development* officer. It wasn't until I moved into major gifts that I started thinking of myself again as a public relations practitioner, managing important relationships on behalf of my institution.

I was fortunate that during those years I became active in the Public Relations Society of America (PRSA), which helped expand my understanding of public relations. On the scholarly side, I was even more fortunate to be studying at Maryland under James Grunig—the leading theorist in public relations. What my colleagues in PRSA were espousing, Jim was explaining through his theories. What I was practicing also seemed to me to "fit" within those theoretical and applied sides, but it appeared that mine was a voice in the wilderness.

A voice not entirely alone. I shall always be grateful to Patrick Hunt, who, as director of university relations, hired the first fund raisers for College Park and called us his best public relations people. Michael Radock, whose successful career in development and university relations included 20 years as vice president at the University of Michigan, was another voice for me to emulate. Mike is the only practitioner I know who is recognized as a leader by members of both the National Society of Fund Raising Executives (NSFRE) and PRSA. Mike and Pat endorsed my ideas in the early stages of conceptualization and have continued to provide encouragement and support.

To speak with credibility about fund raising, some would say it is necessary to have raised a mega gift of at least $1 million. For that credential and his belief in my approach to gifts, I single out Michael Dingman, chairman of The Henley Group, for special thanks. At our first meeting he surprised me with a gift of stock, and then gave another 1 month later, yielding $2.6 million. To me, Michael will always symbolize the exhilaration and true pleasure of fund raising.

Like the proverbial light bulb that moved me into fund raising in the first place, writing this book has opened a new career path—a full-time faculty position in public relations. My research agenda is a long one, including fund-raising problems, and I look forward to teaching future communication managers, not just about how things are done now, but how they should be done. In this new direction, as in all others, I am strengthened by the love and friendship of many wonderful people: my life partner, husband for 30 years, and best friend, George Kelly, to whom this book is dedicated; my daughter, Jodie, who is a constant source of pride; my mother, Idun Mehrman, who is the most caring person in the world; my late father, Russell, to whom I owe my *chutzpah*; my sister and brother, Julie and Russ; my friends from Minnesota, particularly Barbara, Linda, Julee, Sue, Jean, and Judy; and those in Maryland, including Maitland, Rosemary, Mercy, Peg, David, and Martel, who cheer and endure.

The first version of this book was a doctoral dissertation, which was directed by Jim Grunig. I am indebted to Jim, not only for his scholarly contributions, but also for his confidence in and kindness to me. Likewise, I thank the other members of my dissertation committee for their help in shaping and improving my ideas: Steve Barkin, Eugenia Zerbinos, Frank Schmidtlein, and Rudolph Lamone. Parts of this book have been presented at conferences of PRSA, NSFRE, and the Association for Education in Journalism and Mass Communication. Feedback and comments on the concepts have been promising.

I truly appreciate the opportunity and support I have been given by all.

Kathleen S. Kelly

Chapter 1

A Critical Analysis of Fund Raising: An Overview of the Book[1]

In 1988, tax-deductible gifts to American charitable organizations exceeded $100 billion for the first time (American Association of Fund-Raising Council [AAFRC] Trust for Philanthropy, 1989c). In 1987, these nonprofit organizations received $93.7 billion, which was more than the combined profits of all *Fortune* 500 companies ($91 billion) and if computed as sales, would have placed charitable organizations second on the *Fortune* 500 list, ranked only behind General Motors and more than $17 billion ahead of the Exxon Corporation (AAFRC Trust for Philanthropy, 1988a).

Whether viewed as sales or begging for alms, the "getting" of tax-deductible gifts has reached new heights in recent years. To offset reductions in federal funding during the 1980s and to maximize their share of philanthropic giving, the estimated 800,000 organizations that are categorized by the Internal Revenue Service (IRS) as charities are increasingly hiring fund-raising practitioners and charging them to raise increasingly higher totals of gift revenue ("Reagan years," 1988). Although no reliable statistics are available, it can be estimated that tens of thousands of men and women today carry out fund-raising duties as paid

---

[1]There is no consensus on the correct style for the terms *fund raising* and *fund raiser*. Scholars and practitioners use the verb and the noun as a single word, as two words, or as a hyphenated word, depending on their preference. This lack of agreement is indicative of the little progress that has been made in advancing the field beyond a vocation. For the purpose of this book, *fund raising* and *fund raiser* are expressed as two words, and *fund raising* is hyphenated when used as an adjective.

employees of charitable organizations. One indicator of this growth is that membership in the National Society of Fund Raising Executives (NSFRE) has grown from fewer than 2,000 in 1979 to more than 10,000 in 1989 (NSFRE, 1989).

These fund-raising practitioners conduct prospect research to identify potential donors, plan special events to cultivate donors, solicit gifts by direct mail, phonathons, proposals, and face-to-face meetings; and write and edit publications to report fund-raising results and recognize donors. To help them carry out these duties, practitioners rely on fund-raising principles that have evolved through anecdotal material and studies that have primarily been administrative in purpose. Collectively, these principles form a dominant perspective of the fund-raising function that focuses on how to raise more money without questioning the rationale for the function or its effect on recipient organizations and society. For example, the following four important questions rarely are raised about fund raising:

1.   Are the underlying assumptions of current fund-raising principles valid, or are some of the more important ones misconceptions and "myths?"
2.   Is the relationship between a charitable organization and its donors one of benevolence, business, or pseudo-relations?
3.   How does fund raising contribute to organizational effectiveness?
4.   How and why do charitable organizations practice fund raising in different ways?

Although varying opinions may be offered in response, fund-raising research has made little progress in answering these important questions. Without a theoretical base grounded in the literature of academic disciplines, fund raising traditionally has been ignored by educators as a subject worthy of scholarly study (Simon, 1987). Part-time practitioner–scholars generally have produced research on fund raising that "has been sporadic, scatter-gun, and often pedestrian" (Carbone, 1986, pp. 22-23). Although there has been a dramatic increase of scholarly activity in the domain of philanthropy, fund raising as an organizational function has not been identified as one of the agreed upon problems that define that domain of study (e.g., Powell, 1987). This lack of scholarly interest in fund raising is illustrated by the fact that only 80, or 3%, of the 2,717 research projects on philanthropy and nonprofit organizations identified by Independent Sector over the last 5 years have focused on the fund-raising function (Independent Sector, 1988). In short, the questions just cited can be viewed as major problems of fund raising that have remained unresolved by previous research.

These unresolved problems are, or should be, of great concern to practitioners who are charged to raise billions of dollars with little substantive theory to guide them. Concerned with the growing number of capital campaigns and their skyrocketing goals, some fund-raising practitioners are beginning to question the unrealistic demands being placed on them by their organizations (e.g., Alexander, 1990; Carbone, 1989b). The big-dollar results of fund raising have thrust the function into the public spotlight more so than ever in the past, prompting questions about the "greediness" of charitable organizations ("Carnegie's 'gospel,'" 1989). Frustration and cynicism on the part of donors and public officials are raising questions about professional and ethical conduct that already have resulted in investigations and increased regulations, which one state charity regulator described as an "'unheard of' flurry of activity" ("States modify laws," 1989, p. 1).

Clearly, the time is right for stepping back from the current perspective of the practice and study of fund raising to ask a fifth and critical question:

5.   How can fund raising be explained in a different way that would
     help us more fully understand the current fund-raising behavior of
     charitable organizations?

This book is designed to answer that critical question, as well as those important questions raised earlier. It can be argued that the answers to these questions are crucial to the future of fund raising. Indeed, a reexamination of the dominant perspective and a reinterpretation of the fund-raising function may be critical to the well-being—and perhaps even to the survival—of the nonprofit, or third sector, in our democratic society.

In a departure from previous research, this book takes a critical approach to fund raising. According to S. Hall (1980), critical studies are valuable in advancing knowledge because they focus on "significant *breaks*—where old lines of thought are disrupted, older constellations displaced, and elements, old and new, are regrouped around a different set of premises and themes" (p. 57). Using critical methodology, this book first provides evidence that the dominant perspective of fund raising is inadequate for a full understanding of the function. Drawing from the literature in communication, public relations, management, organizational psychology and sociology, economics, political science, and higher education, the critical analysis brings to light serious flaws in some of the major assumptions on which current principles of fund raising are based.

As a result of these misconceptions and myths, generally accepted explanations of fund raising are rejected as incomplete, misleading, and lacking in explanatory power. Proceeding from that basis, the book's purpose is to shift the public relations paradigm to encompass fund raising. To justify such a shift, fund raising is reoriented to the body of knowledge of public relations, which provides a reinterpretation and a fuller understanding of the function. To support this reorientation, systems theory and the concept of organizational autonomy are employed, and a case is made by systematic, step-by-step processes that lead to a new and different perspective of fund raising. The result is a theory that defines fund raising as a specialization of public relations (i.e., donor relations). Essentially, this immanent critique demonstrates how themes extant in the fund-raising literature can be reinterpreted and reconstructed and how the public relations paradigm can be shifted to develop a theory of fund raising that is, perhaps, radical in comparison to current theories within the dominant perspectives of both fields.

The theory of donor relations developed in this book answers the critical fifth question about how fund raising can be explained in a different way. It also provides tentative answers to the important questions posed at the beginning of this chapter—answers that, in the form of hypotheses, will need to be tested systematically in the field. As presented here, the new theory can only claim to represent an *interpretation* of what theory and research from diverse fields tell us about the nature of fund raising and its effect on organizations and society. Future testing of its hypotheses will shape, revise, and improve the theory to make it more useful for directing the behavior of fund-raising practitioners and for solving the problems they face. Be that as it may, this book represents a significant first step toward a theoretically grounded and fuller understanding of fund raising.

BUILDING THEORY THROUGH STEP-BY-STEP PROCESSES

This book is organized into two preliminary chapters and five major sections. Each section contains chapters, some of which are further divided by subchapters. The book's organization is intended to provide a structure for drawing from diverse fields, such as organizational sociology, higher education, and public relations, while demonstrating a logical interrelationship in the theoretical blocks that support a new theory of fund raising.

This chapter is the first of the preliminary chapters. It conceptualizes the theory of donor relations developed in this book and shows how each of the other chapters builds up to that theory. Chapter 1 concludes by discussing the critical methodology used in this book. Chapter 2 sets the stage for a critical analysis of fund raising by first stating the problem that prompted the book and then by examining the background of the problem as it relates to the fund-raising behavior of American colleges and universities.

The chapters in Part I analyze current perspectives of fund raising by examining definitions, research, and some major assumptions on which principles have been based.

Answering the first question posed at the beginning of this chapter on the validity of fund-raising assumptions, critical statements are made about definitional confusion, sporadic research, and misconceptions and myths inherent in the dominant perspective, which lead to its rejection. The chapters in Parts II through IV then describe the building blocks that develop a new and different theory of fund raising.

First, fund raising is approached in Part II from a macrolevel by examining charitable organizations and their environments. In response to the second question on the relationship between donors and recipient organizations, this section argues that—contrary to conventional wisdom—such relationships are best understood not as benevolent, business, or pseudo-relations, but as an interdependency of groups and organizations within an environment. These fund-raising interdependencies constitute an ongoing exchange process that requires management and negotiation by the charitable organization, especially by those practitioners who manage its fund-raising programs. The concept of autonomy is a central issue in the exchange process in that the power of an organization to determine and pursue its own goals is affected by how successful an organization is at managing its interdependencies. Charitable organizations face a double-edged sword: In order to enhance their autonomy, they must seek external funding to support their institutional goals, but in so doing, they risk losing autonomy by accepting gifts that limit their power to determine goals and the means of pursuing those goals.

Part II then focuses on higher education for an in-depth analysis of the concept of institutional autonomy and the effect of fund raising on American colleges and universities, which, because of their inherent value to society, are generally thought to enjoy a higher level of autonomy than other organizations. Historical and current evidence is presented that demonstrates how institutions of higher education have been and are being shaped and changed by the three sources of private support: foundations, corporations, and individuals. The findings of this analysis are generalized to other types of charitable organizations through the use of selected case studies on how dependencies on donors have changed the missions and goals of social services organizations for the blind, a social welfare agency concerned with juvenile delinquency, and an educational institution for the arts.

As current perspectives of fund raising do not take into consideration the concept of autonomy and its potential loss through the exchange process of fund raising, it is appropriate to answer the fifth question on how fund raising can be explained in a different way by looking to other theoretical frameworks for answers. In Part III, the function of fund raising is approached from a public relations perspective, specifically the public relations theory developed by Grunig (e.g., 1976, 1984, 1989a, in preparation), which is based on the central premise that autonomy is a primary goal of organizations and that the purpose of public relations is to enhance and protect autonomy by effectively managing communication between an organization and the various publics in its environment. Redefining fund raising as the management of communication between a charitable organization and its donor publics, the book shifts the public relations paradigm to encompass the fund-raising function as donor relations.

Approaching fund raising from the microlevel, the generally accepted, four-step process of fund raising (i.e., research, cultivation, solicitation, and stewardship) is reinterpreted as communication programs and activities that are designed to achieve the five communication objectives, or effects, used in the public relations process (i.e., awareness, understanding, belief, favorable attitude, and desired behavior). For example, the solicitation step, which accounts for only about 5% of the fund-raising process (Wood, 1989), is reinterpreted as a communication activity that is designed to achieve a giving behavior from donor prospects through mass media channels, such as direct mail, for lower level gifts and through interpersonal communications, such as face-to-face meetings, for major gifts.

After theoretically grounding fund raising within the paradigm of public relations, Part IV uses current theories from that paradigm as analytical tools to provide a new way of explaining the fund-raising behavior of charitable organizations. Of particular importance, Grunig's (1984; Grunig & Hunt, 1984) theory of public relations models is used to answer the first half of the fourth question raised at the beginning of this chapter on how charitable organizations practice fund raising in different ways. Four historical models of fund raising are identified, and evidence from the fund-raising and philanthropy literature is presented to demonstrate their continued use today by different organizations. The concept of strategic public relations management is used to critique the current principles and practices of measuring fund-raising effectiveness by dollars raised, providing a partial answer to the third question on how fund raising contributes to an organization's effectiveness. Also in response to Question 3, a normative theory on how fund-raising effectiveness should be measured in relation to its effect on autonomy is presented.

Grunig's (1989a; Grunig & White, in preparation) presuppositions about public relations are used to draw analogies that help explain why worldviews about the role of fund raising in society have led to a misinterpretation of the function and to unrealistic demands that threaten organizational autonomy. Whereas the four models of fund raising explain how charitable organizations practice fund raising in different ways, these presuppositions answer the second half of the fourth question by helping to explain why these organizations select the models they practice.

Part V draws together the conclusions of the step-by-step processes, interpreting and discussing results. A set of propositions is expounded from the theory of donor relations to guide the behavior of fund-raising practitioners and to help them solve the problems they face. A major problem of the theory, specifically its low probability of acceptance by scholars and practitioners, is examined and counterarguments are offered. Part V also outlines the theory's implications for research.

Given this overview of how the five sections of the book are connected to one another and how they systematically build a coherent theory of donor relations, this chapter turns to some preliminary definitions of fund raising and public relations and then to an overview of each of the chapters of the book. Chapter 1 then concludes with a discussion of critical methodology.

SOME PRELIMINARY DEFINITIONS OF FUND RAISING

Up to this point, only the term *fund raising* has been used to describe the fund-raising activities of charitable organizations, specifically those programs and activities managed for the organization by fund-raising specialists. Although *fund raising* is probably the oldest concept used to describe the fund-raising activities of charities, many organizations that are defined as such by the IRS, particularly colleges and universities, now use the term *development* to describe those activities—in part because of the negative connotations of *fund raising*. As Payton (1987) said, "There is often a stigma attached to asking for money. . . . [an] unwillingness to 'lower oneself' to the ordinate role of petitioner" (pp. 41-42). Carbone (1987) pointed out that practitioners at academic institutions seem to have a special "aversion" to calling themselves fund raisers and that the use of *development* has caused considerable confusion because colleges and universities have professors who teach "human development," programs in "developmental studies" for underprepared students, and "international development" courses that focus on the economic and social growth of foreign nations.

Such confusion and avoidance have hampered a clear understanding of the fund-raising function and lend support to a redefinition of fund raising as donor relations.

In its *Glossary of Fund-Raising Terms*, the National Society of Fund Raising Executives (NSFRE) Institute (1986) defined fund raising as "the seeking of gifts from various sources as conducted by 501(c)(3) organizations" (p. 40). Development practitioners generally define their role more broadly than *fund raising*, equating the latter term to just one part of the development, or fund-raising, process—that of solicitation. According to Payton (1981):

> To equate *development* with *fund raising* . . . will outrage many who have struggled for years to create a larger vision of the field. In their view, development is both broader in scope and deeper in purpose than simple fund raising would imply. (p. 282)

Through their quest to broaden the fund-raising function beyond solicitation, many practitioners have adopted the term *institutional advancement*, which the Council for Advancement and Support of Education (CASE) advocates as an umbrella term for the organizational functions of fund raising, public relations, alumni relations, government relations, publications, and in some cases, student recruitment and admissions (Carbone, 1987). As Pray (1981) explained, "The word *development* . . . has gone through an interesting transition and is variously used for the whole spectrum of institutional advancement and, latterly, more narrowly, for fund raising" (p. 6).

Self-defining efforts to broaden the development function in colleges and universities have coincided with a movement over the last 30 years to integrate fund raising with public relations and alumni relations, as recommended in 1958 by the predecessor organizations of CASE, the American College Public Relations Association (ACPRA) and the American Alumni Council (AAC) (Pray, 1981). In many colleges and universities, these parallel movements ironically have resulted in institutional advancement offices that today are headed by fund raisers (Kelly, 1989b). Robert Payton, who was the vice chancellor for development and planning at Washington University in St. Louis earlier in his career, questioned this expansion of development over the other organizational functions. Although he had formerly headed "a comprehensive development program" that integrated public relations and fund raising, Payton (1981) said that he now holds a middle-ground view in that the other functions "are not merely subordinate to the central development function of fund raising" (p. 283).

In support of this view, Geier (1981) pointed out in his article, "Public Relations as an Arm of Development," that fund raising is only one of the priorities of the public relations function and that in addition to donors, public relations practitioners have responsibility for developing communication programs for other important publics, such as students and residents of the community. Geier argued, however, that the more traditional separation of the functions of fund raising and public relations leads to disagreements about priorities and "misconceptions about purpose. . . ." Although he—as do other public relations writers—stopped short of defining fund raising as a specialization of public relations, Geier said, "In a well-coordinated institutional advancement program, fund raising can grow out of and become an extension of the public relations–communications effort" (pp. 203-204). In contrast to his own prediction, Leo Geier, who has been a public relations practitioner for various colleges and universities for more than 30 years, is, today, a planned giving specialist at the University of Maryland where he holds the title of associate vice chancellor for university *relations*, but uses his public relations expertise solely in support of fund-raising goals.

In summary, many fund-raising practitioners, particularly those at colleges and universities, have adopted the terms *development* or *institutional advancement* to avoid the negative connotations of the term *fund raising*. In many cases, these practitioners manage departments that include other organizational functions, including public relations. As was touched on earlier and as is developed more fully later in this book, the expansion of fund raising into functions outside of "seeking and accepting gift support" is primarily a matter of historical encroachment that has frequently resulted in subordination of the other functions in support of fund-raising goals.

Therefore, this book uses development and fund raising synonymously to describe the narrower function that manages the purposive process of soliciting and accepting gifts on behalf of a charitable organization. Fund raising/development is not as broad as *institutional advancement*, a term that is only used in this book to refer to departments with responsibility for the various functions outlined by CASE and when discussing the work of other scholars and practitioners.

Following Grunig and Hunt (1984), *public relations* is defined as the "management of communication between an organization and its publics" (p. 6). As so defined, public relations is broader than communication techniques, such as publications, and broader than specialized public relations programs, such as media relations, employee relations, or donor relations. According to Grunig (in preparation), "Public relations describes the overall planning, execution, and evaluation of an organization's communication with both external and internal publics—groups that affect the ability of an organization to meet its goals." As developed in this book, the new theory of donor relations supports the incorporation of fund raising as a specialization within the public relations function and eliminates the need for the artificial umbrella term of *institutional advancement*.[2]

With these definitions of fund raising and public relations in mind, chapter 1 turns now to an overview of each of the chapters of the book that builds up to a theory of donor relations. This third section is introduced with a brief discussion of the book's object of analysis and a defense of its selection of higher education as a focus for special, in-depth treatment.

AN OVERVIEW OF THE CHAPTERS

The purpose of this book is to advance the body of knowledge of public relations by shifting that paradigm to encompass the function of fund raising, allowing a theory of donor relations to be developed. The organizational behavior that is the object of analysis and discussion, therefore, is fund raising by charitable organizations. Although the analysis and its findings are intended to apply to organizations in all six categories of charities as defined by the AAFRC Trust (1989c) (i.e., education, religion, health, human service, arts, culture and humanities, and public/society benefit), the subcategory of higher education is used throughout the book as a focus for in-depth analysis. Thus, an assumption is made that there are enough cross-category similarities in the fund-raising behavior of charitable organizations to support such generalizations.

This is not to be taken as an assumption that all charitable organizations in all six categories are the same, or that motivations for giving to all such organizations are identical. Indeed, distinct differences are emphasized in the book (e.g., chapter 3 on definitions presents a typology of nonprofit organizations drawn from Douglas, 1983, that differentiates eleemosynary charities that traditionally attract altruistic gifts from charities with positive externalities that traditionally attract gifts made for reasons other than altruism). It is assumed, however, that differences in organizational missions and differences in motivations for making gifts supposedly in support of those missions do not restrict generalizations about fund-raising behavior and its effect on organizational autonomy.

---

[2]In accordance with the traditional segmentation of the public relations function by strategic publics, alumni relations and government relations would also be defined as specializations of public relations; whereas, publications would be properly recognized as a communications technique used in support of all public relations programs. As most student-recruitment activities currently handled by institutional advancement offices are support functions (e.g., the production of brochures, catalogs, and videos), these activities would be redefined as product/service publicity carried out by the public relations department, or be reassigned to the admissions office as a function of marketing.

The selection of higher education for in-depth analysis is justified on five bases: (a) its ranking as one of the top categories receiving the most gift dollars; (b) its documented status as a preferred recipient of gifts from wealthy individuals; (c) its employment of the greatest proportion of fund raisers; (d) its rich literature on institutional autonomy; and (e) because as Payton (1987) said, "If philanthropy permeates American life as a whole, it is even more evident in higher education" (p. 9). Second only to religion, which received 46.2% of all charity dollars in 1988, education receives the largest share of gift dollars, 9.4%, or $9.8 billion in 1988 (AAFRC Trust, 1989c). And of that amount, higher education receives the lion's share, according to the Council for Aid to Education (CFAE): $8.2 billion, or 87%, in 1987–1988 ("Gifts to colleges off," 1989).

In addition, colleges and universities, according to Jencks (1987), traditionally have received the majority of major gifts (i.e., those gifts of $100,000 or more), along with hospitals. As is discussed in more detail in chapter 8, Jencks developed a typology of gifts from individuals that separates "giving away surplus" (major gifts) to organizations such as universities from "paying dues" (lower level gifts) to organizations such as churches. Feldstein (cited in Leslie & Ramey, 1988) said that "voluntary support of institutions of higher education by individuals [is] concentrated in the upper income classes" (p. 118). Brossman (1981) cited a 1976 study by the American Council on Education (ACE) showing that 70% of the gift dollars received by colleges and universities come from fewer than 0.5% of all donors. A hypothesis of this book is that unlike lower level gifts that only affect organizational autonomy *collectively*, major gifts can—and frequently do—infringe upon autonomy collectively and individually. Therefore, institutions of higher education provide a "richer" area for the analysis of the relationship between fund raising and autonomy than do other types of charitable organizations that traditionally receive fewer major gifts.

Although not well documented, it is generally accepted that higher education currently employs more fund-raising practitioners than any other category of charitable organizations. According to the National Society of Fund Raising Executives (1988), the greatest proportion of its members (25.6%) work at educational institutions. In addition, Carbone (1989b) found that 41% of the respondents in his study of fund raisers who belong to one or more of the three major fund-raising associations were employed by colleges, universities, and schools, whereas only 25% were employed by medical and health-care organizations, 13% by social service organizations, 5% by cultural arts organizations, and 3% by religious organizations. Carbone hypothesized that "perhaps the rapid expansion of fund raising units in academe means that these institutions now employ four of every ten fund raisers in the nation" (p. 24).

Such a possibility is reasonable, as Carbone (1989b) stated, "It is not uncommon for large, complex research universities, both public and private, to have 50 to 100 staff members involved in fund raising (or institutional advancement) activities. This is particularly true in institutions that have decentralized these functions or that are conducting substantial capital campaigns" (p. 24). In support of Carbone's assessment, the University of Pennsylvania has a staff of 250 employees working on its current $1-billion capital campaign ("Major domo," 1990). Fisher (cited in Brittingham & Pezzullo, 1990, p. 14) estimated that there are about 9,000 full-time fund raisers employed at colleges and universities in the United States and Canada.

Discussion of the last two bases for justifying the selection of higher education (i.e., the richness of the literature on the autonomy of colleges and universities and the historical evidence of the effect private gifts have had on these charitable organizations) is reserved until chapters 7 and 8.

In light of these comments, the overall research question guiding the analysis and theory building in this book can be stated as follows:

> How does systems theory, the concept of autonomy, and the public
> relations paradigm provide a new way to explain fund raising,
> particularly at American colleges and universities?

Chapter 2: The Problem Prompting the Book: A New Function Taking on Greater Importance

The second preliminary chapter that follows this one examines the background of the problem that prompted the book, including the historical evolution of the fund-raising function at American colleges and universities. Two questions are answered in this chapter: (a) Has fund raising for U.S. colleges and universities changed since its early years, and if so, what implications do these changes have on our understanding of the fund-raising behavior of these charitable organizations?, and (b) Is a gift a one-way transfer of resources, or does the solicitation and acceptance of a gift involve two-way considerations that may affect the autonomy of charitable organizations?

Fund raising—as an ongoing set of activities managed by internal specialists—is a relatively new organizational function for public *and* private colleges and universities (Pray, 1981). Before World War I, fund raising was primarily the responsibility of boards of trustees and, before that, of presidents (Rudolph, 1962). Between World War I and II, fund-raising needs of educational institutions were met by periodic campaigns managed by external, commercial fund-raising firms working with trustees and presidents (Cutlip, 1965). It was not until after World War II that fund raising was institutionalized when colleges and universities hired their first internal fund raisers and these new practitioners joined ACPRA and AAC in the early 1950s (Pray, 1981). A serious implication of this evolution is that fund raising moved out of the hands of senior policy-makers and the managers of overall financial resources and into the hands of practitioners who frequently research, plan, execute, and evaluate their function outside the academic mainstream.

In addition, the beginning of this new organizational function occurred during a time that is now referred to as the golden age of higher education—an era of growth, expansion, and unprecedented governmental support (Nielsen, 1985). Through increasing student tuitions, state appropriations, and federal grants, resources were plentiful enough that colleges and universities could continually add new programs in accordance with ideas and innovations prompted by private gifts restricted in purpose. Because an educational institution's mission could be broadly defined, most gift purposes, or gift conditions, could fit comfortably within a college's mission. Reflecting on that period, Pray (1981) said, "The practice at most institutions was to add programs without much reexamination of existing programs" (p. 3).

Starting in the 1970s, economic conditions changed, and today fund raisers are expected to bring in needed funds to replace tuition lost by declining enrollments and/or government allocations. These private gifts are generally expected to be in support of institutional goals, but each new program that is initiated by gifts restricted in purpose encumbers institutional resources for the future and limits the options of a college or university in allocating future operating funds. Commenting on the fact that large gifts frequently "have a hook on them," Boyer (1989), for example, questioned whether it was the donor's or the institution's purpose that was being served when the University of Southern California (USC) recently accepted a $4-million grant from a local real-estate developer to establish a center for real-estate development.

At a time when colleges and universities are increasingly turning to fund raising to generate revenue needed to support core programs, fund raising—as discussed in chapter 14—is being evaluated solely on the basis of dollars raised, with little concern being given to the purposes of the gifts. Therefore, it is conceivable that the appropriate response to Boyer's (1989) question may be that the fund-raising practitioners responsible for managing the solicitation and acceptance of the multimillion-dollar gift by USC were not concerned with whose purpose it served because they, like most fund raisers, are evaluated by the number of dollars they generate, not by the "utility" of the gifts they raise.

In chapter 2, the literature of higher education and current news items from trade and mass publications document the current era of fund raising in higher education that is characterized by a lack of understanding about the fund-raising function, a rising level of gifts—including "mega and ultimate gifts"—by a decreasing proportion of donors, an unprecedented number of capital campaigns with multimillion-dollar goals, a competition for hiring fund-raising practitioners, and incidents of infringement on institutional autonomy and academic freedom by donors and/or fund raisers. For example, a 1989 article in *Fortune* magazine ("B-schools," 1989) reported that Bill Daniels, a businessman and college dropout, has pledged $10 million to the business school at the University of Denver to teach business graduate students "kindness, courtesy, punctuality, cleanliness, proper dress, as well as academic subjects such as ethics and communications" (p. 85). Daniels is quoted as saying: "I guess I'm telling them what to teach. But goddamn it, it's time someone did" (p. 85).

The Denver business faculty would prefer that students learn such skills as part of the overall curriculum, but Daniels, according to the article, "insists that his money be used to establish a separate entity at the business school that will probably be called something like the Bill Daniels Institute for the Enhancement of Graduate Business Studies" (p. 85). Daniels also pledged an additional $1 million to help the business school attract a new dean, raising the available salary from $90,000 to $200,000, which, theoretically, provides Daniels with a powerful voice in governance and operation. Today, Denver has expanded its 2-year MBA program to include more than 6 weeks of non-credit requirements in an "Institute for Professional Excellence." According to the new dean, who believes Daniels was "a catalyst" for desired change, it has not yet been decided whether the additional time will be spent in a pre-program "boot camp," or a "finishing school." Commenting on this fund-raising situation, the *Fortune* reporter ("B-schools," 1989) concluded, "Some universities would find that kind of generosity hard to accept" (p. 85). Yet examples given in chapter 2 indicate that colleges and universities are accepting similar gifts in increasing numbers.

Summarizing this stage-setting chapter, the solicitation and acceptance of a gift, particularly major gifts, clearly involves two-way considerations with strong potential for infringement on a charitable organization's power to control its own goals and operations. In addition, today is an era of limited growth for American colleges and universities—an era in which funding choices must be made. Given the fact that the function of fund raising has its roots in another era with a different economic climate, perhaps for the first time the management of relationships with donors must be examined as a negotiating role for acquiring those resources that have utility for the institution. Finally, the evolution of fund raising from a part-time responsibility of policymakers to a full-time specialization of lay administrators has led to increased levels of fund-raising activity in higher education that, at times, appears unrelated to institutional mission and goals. A lack of attention to the problem as presented in this chapter will likely lead to increased incidences of infringement on autonomy by donors and the possibility that colleges and universities, as well as other charitable organizations, will forfeit most of their power to determine and pursue their goals as they see fit.

Part I: Current Perspectives of Fund Raising: Confusing Definitions, Sporadic Research, and Myths

With the problem presented, the book moves to a critical analysis of current perspectives of fund raising and rejects them as being inadequate for addressing the problem. A lack of precise definitions, specifically ones that account for differences in types of recipient organizations and types of gifts, have contributed to inappropriate generalizations about philanthropy and confusion about the fund-raising function.

Part I opens with chapter 3, which answers the research question: How do current definitions confuse our understanding of fund raising? The definitions of charity and philanthropy are examined and differentiated, based on their historical evolution and current usage. According to Payton (1987), there are two historical dimensions to the third sector: philanthropy, which comes from classical Greece and which is generally described as rational, large-scale efforts to improve the quality of community life in the community, and charity, which can be traced back to its Judeo-Christian origins in the Old Testament. As Payton described the differences, "On the one hand, then, the charitable-religious, and on the other, the philanthropic-secular; the impulsive and personal and direct act of mercy contrasted with the reflective, prudent, planned determination to build a better community" (p. 8).

Also in chapter 3, a typology of nonprofit organizations is given utilizing legal definitions and political concepts developed by Douglas (1983) in his book on the rationale and justification for a third sector. This subchapter provides evidence that the failure to differentiate charitable organizations by legal and political concepts in much of the fund-raising literature has contributed to confusion about the fund-raising function and misconceptions about donor motivation. For example, the altruistic behavior of donors referred to in much of the fund raising literature is related to only one of two subcategories of eleemosynary organizations, a small proportion of charitable organizations to which gifts may be altruistic if the beneficiary is unknown, or which may contribute to one's own utility by the pleasure that comes from helping others when the beneficiary is known.

By concisely defining the different types of charitable organizations, this book approaches fund raising as the purposive solicitation and acceptance of gifts that may be, but most often are not, made for altruistic reasons. It is a conclusion of this chapter that charity best describes fund raising for and "fund-giving" to those organizations that are primarily eleemosynary, and that philanthropy best describes fund raising for and fund-giving to those organizations whose goods and services are defined as positive externalities or public goods (e.g., universities, churches, and public television).

Research on fund raising is sparse and generally of poor quality; it receives little scholarly attention as a serious subject. Chapter 4 answers the research question: Why has previous research failed to provide a full understanding of fund raising? Within this chapter, four sections examine (a) gaps in the research on philanthropy, specifically the lack of scholarly studies on the fund-raising function; (b) the weakness of the research on educational fund raising, which is primarily administrative in purpose with very few introspective studies or basic studies that lead to theory building; (c) the absence of fund raising as a topic in communication and public relations research; and (d) the practitioners' need for research.

As evidence of the critical need for research on fund raising, for example, the first comprehensive bibliography on philanthropy, Layton's (1987) *Philanthropy and Voluntarism: An Annotated Bibliography*, references 1,614 publications, of which only 9 books and 11 articles—or slightly more than 1%—deal with fund raising. In comparison, the bibliography contains 267 articles and books on foundations. In pointing out three primary areas in which far more scholarship is needed—"worrisome gaps"—Layton included fund raising as an area most in need of additional scholarly attention. She explained, "While there is an enormous practical literature on fund-raising, there is almost nothing which examines the phenomenon of 'getting' with the same depth and comprehension that the phenomenon of giving has received" (p. xv). As Payton (1987) summarized, "The perspective of asking is less often examined than the perspective of giving" (p. 41).

A hypothesis of this book—one that is addressed in chapter 4 and more fully in the later chapter on presuppositions—is that the lack of research on fund raising can be attributed to a mindset, or worldview, held by lay people, practitioners, and scholars that fund raising is not conducive to scholarly study and that it is even distasteful. According to Payton (1987), the mechanics of raising money, or the "ordinary business calculation associated with the high aspiration of marshalling funds to help starving children" (p. 133) is of little interest to most people. Payton explained as follows:

> A lot of people don't want to be bothered with the fund-raising, don't like it, find it distasteful, and don't want to be involved with it at all. They want to limit themselves to a "concern for the problem." (p. 133)

After critically reviewing the state of research on the fund-raising function, chapter 4 concludes by discussing a leading spokesperson's perspective of fund raising as an anomaly in higher education—an anomaly that has remained unresolved by previous research, which, alone, provides a strong argument for looking to other paradigms for an understanding of fund raising.

In chapter 5, the following research question is answered: What underlying assumptions of current fund-raising principles are invalid? Four major "myths" are identified and critically analyzed: (a) the myth of unrestricted gifts; (b) the myth of a broad base of donors; (c) the myth of the volunteer solicitor; and (d) the myth of the invisible fund raiser. For example, a generally accepted principle of fund raising is that private support provides the means to independence for charitable organizations, providing "venture capital" for higher education (Kramer, 1980). An underlying assumption of this principle is that the majority of gifts to all charitable organizations are primarily unrestricted in purpose (i.e., gifts may be used to pursue self-determined goals). Although this assumption is widely perpetuated, it is basically false.

As evidence of the strength of this myth, the winning study of the 1989 John Grenzebach Outstanding Published Scholarship Award for research on philanthropy for education is based on the underlying assumption that private support is primarily unrestricted in nature. According to the winning authors, "Unlike appropriations and allocations from government and income from many other sources, voluntary support for colleges and universities takes on relatively unrestricted spending forms" (Leslie & Ramey, 1988, p. 115). The authors said that although the spending of other resources, particularly government funding, is prescribed or at least closely regulated, "much voluntary support may be expended almost without constraint" (p. 115).

Yet, widely available statistics on private giving to colleges and universities prove otherwise. CFAE conducts an annual survey on gifts to colleges and universities that traditionally accounts for approximately 85% of the total given to higher education each year. In 1987–1988, 420 public institutions and 722 private institutions reported total gifts of approximately $7 billion, of which $1.1 billion was given for unrestricted use for current operations and $0.4 billion was given for unrestricted endowment ("Gifts to colleges off," 1989). Unrestricted giving, therefore, totalled $1.5 billion of the total $7 billion raised by these institutions, or only 21% of all gifts.

The statistics are even more revealing when broken down by public and private institutions. Of the total $2.56 billion given to the public colleges and universities in the 1987–1988 survey, only $0.26 billion was unrestricted, or slightly more than 10% of all private support to public institutions ("Gifts to colleges off," 1989). In summary, approximately 79% of gift dollars to all colleges and universities and 90% of those to public institutions in 1987–1988 were restricted in their use.

With such figures available, it is difficult to understand how scholars continue to perpetuate the myth of unrestricted giving (i.e., that private gifts generally provide flexible funds for which spending is not prescribed). It is argued in chapter 5 that the perpetuation of this myth has led to a misinterpretation of the fund-raising function that ignores its "true" effect on organizational autonomy (i.e., if gifts are unrestricted in their use, autonomy is enhanced because gifts provide the means to pursue self-determined goals, but if gifts are restricted in purpose, autonomy may be lost because the wishes of the donors may be incongruent with self-determined goals). By exposing the flawed assumptions of such principles, this book sheds new light on the role of the fund-raising function in managing the solicitation and acceptance of gifts that may enhance or infringe on the autonomy of charitable organizations.

Chapter 5 concludes that the myth of the volunteer solicitor and its corollary, the myth of the invisible fund raiser, are primarily attributable to the historical evolution of the fund-raising function and to the self-interests of commercial fund-raising firms that do not solicit money as part of their consulting service. These myths have hidden the fact that fund-raising specialists, rather than chief policymakers, are currently responsible for managing the solicitation and acceptance of gifts that may or may not support organizational goals. In much the same way, the myth of a broad base of donors has hidden the fact that practitioners are increasingly focusing their fund-raising efforts on donors of major gifts, who, individually, can infringe on organizational autonomy. This myth is analyzed in the context of the current flood of capital campaigns for colleges and universities, and it is concluded that major gifts from a small proportion of donors are increasingly playing a dominant role in the private support of charitable organizations.

In addition to identifying flawed assumptions, this chapter analyzes the perspectives of fund raising as a sales or marketing function and strongly criticizes such perspectives as inappropriate for an understanding of an organizational behavior dealing with donor motivations that encompass more than the *quid pro quo* of the marketplace. It is argued that such perspectives, based on a business mentality, are likely to lead to loss of autonomy by relinquishing control to donors or by bringing about increased government regulations, including changes in the tax-exempt status of charitable organizations and the tax deductibility of gifts to them.

As evidenced by confusing definitions, lack of research, and invalid assumptions, the book concludes that current perspectives of fund raising are inadequate for addressing the problem as stated in chapter 2 and turns to systems theory for a theoretical foundation on which to build a new theory of donor relations.

Part II: Systems Theory and Autonomy: Approaching Fund Raising From a Macroperspective

Chapter 6 opens Part II by approaching fund raising through the framework of systems theory. Specifically, the resource dependence perspective, the norm of reciprocity, the theory of social and power exchange, and Mintzberg's (1983) power theory are applied to fund raising to provide a theoretical explanation of the relationships between charitable organizations and the donors in their environment. In our complex and specialized society, interdependencies between organizations and groups in an environment are managed through an exchange process that involves economic, political, and social resources. Basically, charitable organizations are dependent on external sources for private funding, and these sources are dependent on the recipient organizations for some form of reciprocity. The process is an ongoing one that requires management and negotiation in order to achieve some degree of equilibrium between what is gained for the organization and what is lost in the exchange.

A major concept of systems theory is that organizations strive to maintain their autonomy through the effective management of interdependencies. Grunig's (e.g., 1976, in preparation) theory of public relations, which is grounded in systems theory, is introduced in chapter 6 because of its value in explaining the relationship between managing external relations and organizational autonomy. As stated earlier, a central premise of Grunig's theory is that autonomy is a primary organizational goal and that the purpose of public relations is to enhance and protect organizational autonomy by effectively managing communications between an organization and the various publics in its environment.

Chapter 7 builds on the issue of autonomy within the context of environmental interdependencies by analyzing the relationship between the educational concept of "institutional autonomy" and private support. Because of higher education's special autonomous status and because of the rich body of literature available on institutional autonomy, this chapter focuses on fund raising for institutions of higher education.

Altbach and Berdahl (1981) divide the concept of institutional autonomy into two parts: College autonomy of a *substantive* nature is defined as the power of a college or university to determine its own goals and programs, and college autonomy of a *procedural* nature is the power of an institution to determine the means by which its goals and programs will be pursued. This distinction is critical to an analysis of the fund-raising function in light of the earlier discussion in chapter 2 on the utility of gifts in higher education's current era of limited resources. As Lee (1968) stated, "The common goals of higher education may be almost infinite, but the local *means to pursue them are always finite*, and the nation may be better served if each institution pursues only those goals which are suitable to its requirements, needs, and abilities" (p. 15; italics added).

Assuming that the fund-raising function in colleges and universities shares similarities with the function in other charitable organizations, the chapter draws from the literature of higher education to document that resource dependency relationships with donors can and do infringe upon institutional autonomy. For example, the positive and negative effects of private support are well summarized by Harcleroad (1981), who stated the following:

> Private constituencies . . . can and do have significant impact on institutional autonomy and academic freedom. Much of this impact is positive, supportive, and welcome. However, those that provide funds can affect institutional trends and direction by determining what types of academic program or research efforts to support. . . . Acceptance of grants moves institutions in the direction dictated by fund sources, and faculties are well advised to consider this possibility as the "crunch" of the 1980s and 1990s become greater in more and more institutions. (p. 217)

This chapter moves closer to a theory of donor relations by answering the research question: Why does the concept of autonomy provide a new way to explain fund raising and its contribution to organizational effectiveness, particularly at American colleges and universities? To be effective, charitable organizations must maintain a relatively high degree of autonomy in order to determine and pursue their own goals. Fund raising, therefore, contributes to organizational effectiveness by soliciting and accepting gifts that enhance autonomy (i.e., gifts that are made in support of organizational goals) and by negotiating the conditions of gifts that threaten to infringe on organizational autonomy.

In short, a new way to approach fund raising and its contribution to organizational effectiveness is to consider fund raising as the effective management of a charitable organization's interdependencies with donors in its environment.

Chapter 7 concludes by drawing an analogy between the relationship of donors and recipient organizations and the autonomy lost by research universities through their external funding relationship with the federal government. Staying with the focus on higher education, chapter 8 then analyzes the three primary sources of private support to answer the research question: In relation to institutional autonomy, how do foundations, corporations, and individuals differ in their potential to infringe on a charitable organization's power to determine its goals and the means of pursuing those goals? Historical and current evidence is provided that—contrary to conventional wisdom—funding relationships with all three sources share an inherent potential for loss of institutional autonomy. As is pointed out in chapter 5, the myth of a broad base of donors is based on the false assumption that private support consists primarily of numerous and equal gifts from multiple donors. An important conclusion of chapter 8 is that major gifts—whether from foundations, corporations, or individuals—have the potential, on an individual basis, to infringe on institutional autonomy. This conclusion refutes previous studies that characterize donors, particularly individuals, as a faceless mass that can affect autonomy only on a collective basis. For example, Kramer (1980) concluded:

> The main developments in philanthropic support for higher education in this century have, if anything, increased the distance between the sources of funds and academic initiative and decision making. . . . The growing importance of alumni-giving programs has meant that less rides on the decision of the average donor. . . . academic leadership . . . can rely on the fact that the biases of individual alumni will often be in opposite directions, tending to cancel each other out. (pp. 13-14)

Generalizing beyond colleges and universities, chapter 9 then answers the research question: What evidence can be found to substantiate the hypothesis that all gift sources can cause all types of charitable organizations to change their goals? An analysis of three classic studies is provided in Chapter 9 to document cases of charitable organizations that have changed their mission and goals primarily because of their dependency on external, philanthropic funding sources. One case study is based on social services organizations for the blind that changed their missions and programs in order to attract numerous lower level and major gifts from multiple donors; the second is on a social welfare agency concerned with juvenile delinquency that changed its mission in response to the demands of the Ford Foundation and two government funding sources; and the third case is on a university for the arts that was primarily dependent on one individual for funding.

At the end of chapter 9, the book is able to draw from the findings of the preceding chapters to state three major conclusions:

1. *All* sources of donors—foundations, corporations, and individuals—have potential for infringing on the autonomy of charitable organizations through their gifts;

2. *All* types of charitable organizations—even those eleemosynary charities most closely related to altruistic gifts, as demonstrated by the case study of social services organizations—are vulnerable to losing autonomy during the process of raising private gifts;

3. *All* gifts (i.e., major gifts, individually and collectively, and lower level gifts, collectively, as demonstrated by the chapter on gift sources and by the case study of social service organizations) have potential to affect organizational autonomy negatively.

Summarizing the four chapters in Part II, systems theory and the concept of organizational autonomy provide a new way of approaching fund raising (i.e., fund raising is the management of environmental funding relationships that contributes to organizational effectiveness by enhancing and protecting autonomy). This approach, in turn, provides a strong argument for shifting the public relations paradigm to encompass fund raising. The book moves, then, to Part III and the task of redefining fund raising as a specialization of public relations.

Part III: Shifting the Public Relations Paradigm: Approaching Fund Raising From a Different Theoretical Perspective

In Part III, the function of fund raising is approached from a public relations perspective, specifically the public relations theory developed by Grunig (e.g., Grunig, 1976; Grunig & Grunig, 1989; Grunig & Hunt, 1984). Chapter 10 examines the fund-raising function as a boundary role of a charitable organization in response to the research question: Within the context of systems theory and autonomy, how can fund raising be reinterpreted on a macrolevel as a public relations function (i.e., as a negotiator of organizational autonomy with strategic donor publics)?

One of the strategies an organization uses to reduce its dependence on its environment, according to Robbins (1987), is to create boundary roles, which he described as those roles, like public relations, at the nexus of interaction between an organization and its environment. Adams (cited in Robbins, 1987) said, "Boundary roles are the linkage or mechanisms that organizations create to relieve the threats of uncertainty posed by dependence" (p. 158). As charitable organizations are, to varying degrees, dependent on external sources of private support, fund raisers act as a link to donors in order to relieve threats of uncertainty about the ongoing flow of gifts.

Building on Grunig and Hunt's (1984) four types of linkages that are critical to the survival of an organization (i.e., enabling, functional, normative, and diffused), the book redefines fund raising as donor relations. The concept of linkages explains why organizations have public relations programs targeted for specific publics, such as government, employees, and consumers. According to Grunig and Hunt, charitable organizations "must also maintain a critical enabling linkage with sources of funds if they are to survive" (p. 361). Donor relations, therefore, describes the management of communication between a charitable organization and its donor publics much the same way that investor relations describes the public relations programs of publicly owned, for-profit organizations that are aimed at investors—a public that provides authority and controls the resources that *enable* these organizations to exist.

Boundary roles also can be viewed as functions that buffer an organization from its environmental dependencies. According to Payton (1987), "To practice philanthropy is to engage in a constant struggle with the claims of self-interest" (p. 277). Thus, the practitioners who manage fund-raising programs on behalf of charitable organizations can be properly described as serving in a boundary role through which they reduce environmental uncertainty of donor dependencies and buffer the organization against claims of self-interest. This boundary role is critical to understanding the fund-raising practitioner's key position in affecting organizational autonomy negatively or positively.

In a section of chapter 10, evidence is provided that public colleges and universities may be more vulnerable to infringements on autonomy by private donors than private institutions. Within his theory of social and power exchange, Blau (1986) said that institutionalization (i.e., establishing formal procedures that preserve and rigidify patterns of social conduct and relations) perpetuates the legitimate order and the social values that sustain an organization through time. Therefore, the institutionalization of the fund-raising function can be viewed as a protection against loss of autonomy because relations with donors are less affected by individual practitioners when there is a high degree of institutionalization. Using the resource dependence perspective of Pfeffer and Salancik (1978), Tolbert (1985/1986) found that fund raising was not as socially accepted and defined at public universities as it is at private ones. However, a brief examination of the finances of public and private institutions of higher education leads this subchapter to conclude that 4-year public colleges and nonselective, private colleges are more vulnerable to external control through the fund-raising process than other types of colleges and universities.

Chapter 11 continues the examination of fund raising as a specialization of public relations by answering two research questions: How can fund raising be reinterpreted on a mesolevel, or departmental level, and on a microlevel as a public relations function? In so doing, the book contends that theoretical links between the two functions have been ignored in previous research because public relations scholars have not understood the fund-raising function and those studying fund raising have limited the definition of public relations to techniques and publicity. It is further argued in this chapter that fund raising, as an organizational function, has traditionally been separated from public relations because of the historical models of both functions (i.e., in earlier years, public relations was primarily a publicity function and fund raising was primarily a function that organized armies of volunteer solicitors).

Citing a 1960 psychological study conducted by ACPRA, Pray (1981) said that fund raisers and public relations practitioners represent two distinct styles or functions: the fund-raising specialist who "views his job as meeting certain specified dollar goals within a certain period of time" (p. 4); and the specialist in image building who "views his task as that of acquainting the larger community with the 'image' of the university in order to develop a broader base of financial support *as well as for other reasons*" (p. 4). In his history of fund raising in the United States, Cutlip (1965) identified organization and communication as the two separate elements important to fund raising, but said that public relations' role is traditionally one of communication, whereas fund raising is concerned primarily with organizing or managing programs. Yet Pearson (1989) argued that virtually all current definitions of public relations, including Grunig and Hunt's (1984), which was given earlier, have two elements in common: management and communication.

In short, narrow definitions of public relations and the historical models that are identified in chapter 13 have misled practitioners and scholars into believing that fund raising is a separate or superior function in relation to public relations.

Approaching fund raising from a microlevel, chapter 11 analyzes the processes, programs, and techniques shared by fund raising and public relations. For example, while annual giving is primarily built on mass communication techniques, such as direct mail, major gift solicitation requires the same interpersonal communications that the public relations manager generally uses in legislative relations and in dealing with activist publics. This book contends that fund raising is essentially a communication function and provides evidence in this chapter by comparing the fund-raising process with the five communication objectives of public relations. Fund raisers generally claim that solicitation, in particular, is unique to their function; yet, a solicitation activity designed to affect behavior (e.g., solicit a gift through interpersonal communications or through media, such as telephones) is a communication activity with a communication objective.

Nor are fund-raising programs primarily concerned with behavior objectives. Wood (1989), for example, described major gift solicitation as 25% research, 60% cultivation, 5% solicitation, and 10% recognition. In other words, only 5% of the major gift process is designed to affect donor behavior, whereas the remaining 95% can be related to the other four communication objectives and to the public relations activity of researching relevant, or strategic, publics. As Hawes (cited in Pearson, 1989) summarized, "Communication behavior does not occur *within* a network of relationships but *is* that network" (p. 163).

Although there have been few attempts to include fund raising, or "gift getting," within the public relations domain, there is a related precedent in the for-profit sector where some public relations practitioners have recently integrated "gift giving" within their departments. This analogy, presented in chapter 12, answers the question: Given the fact that little attempt has been made to place fund raising within the public relations paradigm, what evidence can be found to substantiate the hypothesis that fund raising can contribute more to organizational effectiveness as a sub-function of public relations than as a separate function?

In particular, Levy and Oviatt (1989), public relations managers at AT&T, demonstrate why contributions—or philanthropy from the perspective of the provider of resources—add to the effectiveness of corporations when integrated within the public relations function. According to the authors, contributions can be managed to yield economic and sociopolitical benefits for the corporation. They point out, for example, that the economic power of the nonprofit sector, which spends more than $200 billion annually, is a strong reason for utilizing corporate gifts to stimulate and sustain relationships.

As corporate donors are frequently contractual vendors to charitable organizations, donor–recipient relationships can often lead to preference in the vendor selection process. Chapter 12 concludes that charitable organizations can also reap economic and sociopolitical benefits by incorporating fund raising within the public relations department (e.g., relationships with politically powerful donors can be tapped for help in legislative relations). More importantly, this chapter concludes that raising money for the sake of raising money is short-sighted and costly—just as giving away contributions in isolation of other corporate goals leads to waste.

Given this evidence, the following question arises: If fund raising is placed within the public relations paradigm, how do the theories of that paradigm help explain the fund-raising behavior of charitable organizations? For answers to this research question, the book turns to Part IV in which public relations theories are used as analytical tools to complete the building of a theory of donor relations.

Part IV: Using Public Relations Theories as Analytical Tools for Explaining Fund Raising

Leading off Part IV, chapter 13 uses Grunig's (1976, 1984; Grunig & Hunt, 1984) theory of public relations models to identify four historical models of fund raising. This chapter answers the research question: *How* do charitable organizations practice fund raising in different ways? Although practitioners agree that fund raising is practiced differently in different organizations, this chapter represents the first time that theoretical models have been developed to explain those differences. The historical development of the four models of fund raising is traced, and a table summarizing the characteristics of each is adapted from Grunig and Hunt (1984) and presented. For example, the purposes of the four models are as follows: the press agentry model is to propagandize a cause; the public information model is to disseminate needs information; the two-way asymmetric model is to scientifically persuade giving; and the two-way symmetrical model is to reach mutual understanding in donor–recipient relationships.

The fund-raising activities and philosophies of leading historical figures associated with the first three models (e.g., John Price Jones and the two-way asymmetric model) are provided as evidence of the distinguishing characteristics. Chapter 13 hypothesizes that the two-way symmetric model of fund raising is only recently being adopted by a few charitable organizations, although symmetrical concepts of fund raising are identified in the historical literature.

Chapter 13 also provides evidence of the four models today by drawing from the fund-raising and philanthropy literature, answering the research question: Given the four models of fund raising identified historically, what evidence can be found to substantiate the hypothesis that these four models continue to be used by organizations today?

As Grunig and Hunt (1984) explained, the public relations models did not supersede each other by chronological years, but rather public relations evolved through stages toward maturity. Similarly, the emergence of a new model of fund raising did not mean the demise of a previous stage, which explains why all four models are still in practice today.

This chapter advances hypotheses as to which models are currently practiced by charitable organizations and what types of charities practice one of the four models predominately. For example, it is hypothesized that the press agentry model—the oldest fund-raising model—is practiced by approximately 50% of today's charitable organizations that are actively engaged in fund raising. It is further hypothesized that the press agentry model is predominant in national health and social service agencies, and in religious organizations—the recipients of the largest percentage of gift income. Providing evidence of the practice of this model today, Panas (1984) developed tenets that guide and shape the success of securing mega gifts, and many of his tenets are related in the chapter to the press agentry model.

With the dominance of the press agentry model in mind, chapter 14 uses the concept of strategic public relations management to critique the current principles and practices of measuring fund-raising effectiveness by dollars raised. This chapter provides an answer to the research question: What is the relationship between current measurements of fund-raising effectiveness and the overall effectiveness of a charitable organization?

Given the newness of the two-way symmetric model of fund raising, this chapter also develops and presents a normative theory on how fund-raising effectiveness should be measured in relation to its effect on autonomy and on key publics of the organization.

A central concept of strategic public relations is that when practitioners identify issues that are important to their organizations, they segment those strategic publics that are most likely to enhance or limit autonomy in relation to that issue, identify objectives for communication programs, plan and execute those programs, and evaluate the effects of the programs on members of the segmented publics (i.e., whether the programs achieved their set objectives). In their resource dependence perspective, Pfeffer and Salancik (1978) said that effectiveness is an external measure and is a question of sociopolitical support, whereas the ratio of resources used to output produced is efficiency, a quantitative, internal measure. In soliciting and accepting gifts, therefore, charitable organizations should be concerned not so much with the dollars raised (i.e., the internal measurement of efficiency) but with the impact those dollars have on the effectiveness of the organizations as perceived and externally measured by the various groups that are most concerned with its activities (e.g., donors, faculty, and legislators).

The neglect of environmental interdependencies and the concept of autonomy by current principles of fund-raising effectiveness leads to a discussion of presuppositions about fund raising and the resulting argument that the two-way symmetric model of fund raising is pragmatically more effective, as well as being more ethical and socially responsible.

In chapter 15, Grunig's (1989a; Grunig & White, in preparation) presuppositions about public relations are used as an analytical tool to examine worldviews of the role of fund raising in society. This chapter answers the research question: *Why* do charitable organizations practice fund raising in different ways? As emphasized by Grunig (1989a), the understanding of presuppositions (i.e., where theories come from and why there is conflict over them) is a critical, and often missing, step in building and applying theory. Grunig and White described five worldviews, based on assumptions about the social role of public relations, that help explain the presuppositions that shape the practice of fund raising: pragmatic (its social role is to help charitable organizations raise money), neutral (objective view of fund raising that allows it to be observed as an object of study), conservative (its social role is to maintain an elitist socio-economic system), radical (its role leads to social improvement and reform through the transformation of private resources into public good), and idealistic (its social role is to manage interdependence and conflict between an organization and its resource providers).

Evidence of asymmetrical presuppositions that support pragmatic, conservative, or radical worldviews of fund raising is provided, as well as evidence that demonstrates the weaknesses of these underlying assumptions. The literature provides warnings that asymmetrical fund raising—which promises powerful results for the potential good of the charitable organization—can cost money, rather than saving money through the protection of autonomy. For example, Lawson (1988) said. "As difficult as it may be for the enthusiastic fund raiser, some gifts should not be accepted. The ramifications of soliciting and accepting a gift that compromises an institution's mission could undermine future support for years to come" (p. 60).

As the press agentry, public information, and two-way asymmetric models of fund raising are based on asymmetrical presuppositions, chapter 15 concludes by arguing that charitable organizations should adopt the two-way symmetric model of fund raising to effectively manage external interdependencies with foundation, corporate, and individual donors.

In summary, asymmetrical presuppositions generally have led to a dominance of asymmetrical models of fund raising today. These models, which primarily measure fund-raising effectiveness by dollars raised, are supported by principles that are based on flawed assumptions. Current principles do not take into account the environmental interdependencies inherent in the donor–recipient-organization relationship, nor the concept of organizational autonomy. As presented in this book, the theory of donor relations, which encompasses fund raising within the paradigm of public relations, provides a fuller understanding of the fund raising function—one that promises to help fund-raising practitioners and their charitable organizations carry out this important function more effectively and solve the problem outlined in chapter 2.

Part V: A Theory of Donor Relations: Conclusions and Suggestions for Future Research

The final section of the book consists of only chapter 16, which draws together the conclusions of the preceding sections. In addition, this chapter answers the research question: What propositions can be expounded from the theory of donor relations to guide the behavior of fund-raising practitioners and to help them solve the problems they face? For example, the theory of donor relations encourages practitioners to:

- recognize the tensions inherent in the interdependencies of an organization with its donor publics;
- consider potential loss of autonomy as a primary factor in negotiating the purposes and conditions of major gifts and in planning annual giving programs for lower level gifts;
- calculate and communicate the gift-utility *cost* involved in accepting every gift;
- implement and evaluate everyday decisions with a keen awareness of their role in and influence on organizational autonomy;
- prioritize fund-raising programs and activities by institutional agendas;
- decline gifts that are inappropriate to the organization's goals or that will limit the organization's means to pursue its internally determined goals (i.e., gifts that "cost" too much to accept);
- evaluate the results of fund-raising programs, not by dollar totals or by interorganizational comparison, but by how much the programs contributed to organizational effectiveness; and
- research, plan, execute, and evaluate fund-rasing activities with the understanding that donors are not an organization's only public (i.e., in dynamic environments, organizational problems change and strategic

publics may also change so that donors may at times be less important
than other publics of the organization; for example, legislators, faculty,
or students).

In addition, chapter 16 discusses a major problem with the theory of donor
relations, specifically the low probability of its acceptance by practitioners
because of the asymmetrical worldviews of fund raising held by them and by
the chief executive officers and governing boards of their charitable organizations.

Finally, future research directions are explored in response to the question:
How can future research shape, revise, and improve a theory of donor relations?
For example, a quantitative study measuring the loss or enhancement of
autonomy in relation to gifts received would provide statistical evidence in
support or disproof of the central concepts of this theory. In anticipation of
such a future study, chapter 16 presents some sample indicators that have been
developed to measure the effect of fund raising on the autonomy of charitable
organizations. Two such indicators are:

#1   In your opinion, has any organization that you have represented
     as a fund raiser altered its stated mission in order to attract a
     particular gift?

     ☐ No
     ☐ Yes

#2   Which of the following situations best describe the relationship
     between a particular major gift and the change in institutional
     mission that you referred to in #1? (In the case of multiple gifts,
     indicate the appropriate answer for gift #1, gift #2, etc.)

     ☐ Donor funded some or all costs of mission change that
        had previously been evaluated as desirable by organiza-
        tional management.

     ☐ Donor's gift helped determine which of two equally
        desirable directions would be followed by the organiza-
        tion.

     ☐ Donor's gift stimulated discussion on several mission
        options, but final decision was an internal one, not
        related to gift.

     ☐ Donor's gift was directly responsible for modifying or
        changing some aspect of the organization's mission.

     ☐ None of the above.

With this overview of the individual chapters complete, chapter 1 concludes by discussing the use of critical methodology in this book.

USING CRITICAL METHODOLOGY TO BUILD THEORY

As stated at the beginning of this chapter, this book breaks with previous research by taking a critical approach to the study of fund raising. The use of critical methodology in this book is justified on two bases: (a) the lack of critical studies in fund raising, as well as in public relations; and (b) its appropriateness for studying the selected object of analysis.

First, few—if any—scholarly studies have critically examined the behavior of charitable organizations. Yet, fund raising is a $100-billion-a-year function that touches approximately 80% of the adults in the United States, who make at least one charitable contribution each year (Payton, 1987). This economic factor, alone, raises critical questions about the function of fund raising (e.g., Should the practice of fund raising be regulated?). In whose interest should fund raising be practiced?

Or, as Payton (1988b) asked, "Is the marketplace of grants materially different from . . . the publishing competition for readers?" (p. 8). The very fact that such questions are raised should prompt a critical look at the function of fund raising.

As stated earlier, the purpose of this book is to contribute to the body of knowledge of public relations. Fund raising, it must be emphasized, is a function of free speech that is protected under the First Amendment, as recently reaffirmed by the Supreme Court in 1988 ("House panel," 1989). As such, it is deserving of attention by communication scholars, particularly those in the specialty of public relations who deal with the communication of organizations. Yet, as is documented in chapter 4 on research, fund raising has basically been a nonsubject of communication study. Through its selected methodology, this book criticizes the public relations paradigm for its neglect of fund raising and shifts that paradigm to include a theory of donor relations. In so doing, the critical approach contributes to public relations, as well as to its parent field of communication.

Hsia (1988) said that critical studies are needed on every aspect of communication, and Pavlik (1987) has called for more critical research on public relations. Thus, this book responds to the need for a critical approach to fund raising and also addresses the underrepresentation of critical studies in communication and public relations.

Second, it is argued that critical methodology is appropriate for the object of analysis in this book (i.e., the subject of this book calls for a methodology that allows for a broader approach than that provided by other methodologies, such as empirical studies). According to Freire (1970), "The investigation will be most educational when it is most critical, and most critical when it avoids the narrow outlines of partial or 'focalized' views of reality, and sticks to the comprehension of total reality" (p. 99). Critical methodology allows this book to concentrate on building a cohesive theory of donor relations from the conceptual blocks provided by scholars in other fields (e.g., organizational sociology, higher education, economics, and public relations), rather than presenting a narrower theory, or a "focalized view of reality," and then testing that narrower theory through data collection.

The justification for placing theory building first, before testing, is commonly recognized by scholars and summarized by Grunig (in preparation), who stated:

> Too often social scientists leap into the empirical stage of research without thoroughly studying the research and theorizing that has come before. Seldom, therefore, do those social scientists build a solid theory from the building blocks provided by other scholars.

In addition, the purpose of this book (i.e., shifting the public relations paradigm to encompass fund raising) calls for a critical analysis of *current* perspectives in order to justify its placement within a new and different paradigm. Although there has been little effort to critically examine principles, there is evidence in the literature that others believe such an approach is justified. As Pray (1981) said, "Perhaps, we may speculate, the need to reappraise certain basic principles has been obscured by the too-ready acceptance of the 'body of knowledge and practice,' which has grown in our field to have almost the acceptance of law when, in fact, some of it may be merely myth" (p. xiv).

According to Pearson (1989), "Criticism's purpose is to confront uncritical acceptance of what is given as real with what is not given, but might have been given, or might yet be given" (p. 433). Therefore, the methodology selected for this book is an appropriate one for answering the critical question stated earlier: How can fund raising be explained in a different way that would help us more fully understand the current behavior of charitable organizations? Such a critical question is necessitated both by the problem introduced earlier, which is also the focus of the following chapter, and by the lack of rigorous research on fund raising (i.e., it is time to step back from empirical and case studies that are primarily administrative in purpose and raise questions about the rationale for the function, itself, and its effect on charitable organizations and on society).

According to Laudan (1977), problems are the focal point of scientific thought, and theories are the end result. Laudan said there are two different kinds of problems: (a) empirical problems, which are anything about the natural world that needs explanation; and (b) conceptual problems, which are of a higher order of problems. In addition, certain problems, such as anomalies, are more significant than other problems, and a conceptual anomaly is more serious than an empirical anomaly. The problem, as discussed in chapter 2, is a conceptual problem—one that requires theorizing on a higher level than an empirical problem. In addition, fund raising can be viewed as an anomaly, in that the four questions raised at the beginning of this chapter have remained unresolved by previous research. Therefore, fund raising is approached in this book as a conceptual anomaly (i.e., a serious problem of a higher order than an empirical problem).

In contrast, the prevalent view of fund raising is as a set of organizational problems concerned with raising more money, which scholars address by asking empirical questions about how the problem can be solved through various management or communication techniques. Most research is devoted to answering such questions and is, therefore, administrative in purpose (e.g., Burke, 1988). Using a distinction from Smythe and Van Dinh (1983), administrative research seeks to make an organization's actions more efficient, while critical research seeks fundamental change in organizations to meet collective interests.

Fund-raising scholars rarely see their field as a domain for theorizing, which, in part, is attributable to a lack of consensus on the important problems in this area of study. Although most research is devoted to questions of how to raise more money, a few scholars (e.g., Carbone, 1986, 1987; Payton, 1987, 1988c) have identified introspective and conceptual problems as being more important. For example, Payton (cited in O'Connell, 1987) said, "We will improve our performance only if we seek to understand how philanthropy works—and why, so often, it doesn't" (p. 277). Or as Thompson (1987) said, "[Philanthropy] deserves the attention of all of us not merely on issues of the operations of philanthropy but on underlying principles and problems" (p. 137).

Agreement on the most important problems, according to Grunig (1989a), is what defines a domain of study, not agreement on theories. The lack of consensus on the important problems of fund raising, therefore, suggests that fund raising can not be accurately defined as a domain of itself and that other domains should be identified in which to place it.

In agreement with this conclusion, Payton (1988a) called for establishment of a new domain of "philanthropics," which he said would be analogous to economics and politics and constitute a formal field of study "concerned with the organization, methods, and principles of voluntary action for public purposes" (p. 260).

As mentioned at the beginning of this chapter, there has been increased scholarly activity in the area of philanthropy since the late 1970s. Economists, sociologists, political scientists, and historians, among others, have begun to define a domain of philanthropy (i.e., they have agreed upon important problems in this field of study). As is documented in the later chapter on research, the growing literature on philanthropy has virtually ignored the behavior of organizations (i.e., problems about fund raising have not been defined as important by scholars of philanthropy).

In summary, fund raising has not created a domain of its own and has not been included in the emerging domain of philanthropy. Therefore, the shifting of the public relations paradigm to include the function of fund raising is supported by the lack of an identifiable domain for fund raising, and the methodological tools that support such a paradigmatic shift are critical in nature.

Given this defense for using critical methodology, how does the book fit within the parameters of what is defined as a critical study? As interpreted in the policy statement of the inaugural issue of *Critical Studies in Mass Communication* (CSMC), a scholarly journal of the Speech Communication Association (1984), critical studies may be based on original research data, on analysis of an existing body of literature, or on new theoretical arguments. Additionally, such studies are expected to make a critical statement. In comparison to the CSMC policy statement, this book both analyzes an existing body of literature (i.e., fund raising) and advances new theoretical arguments, as well as making critical statements.

In his recent book on research methods, Hsia (1988) adopted Masco's definition of critical studies in communication, saying that such studies challenge established research perspectives, offer an alternative way of seeing the place of communication in society, and connect communication to a wider social order. As outlined in the preceding pages, this book challenges and rejects current perspectives of fund raising and offers a new way of viewing that function as essentially a communication function (i.e., as a specialization of public relations). In so doing, the book approaches funding raising from a macroperspective by explaining how fund raising, as a communication function, affects charitable organizations and the other groups and organizations in their environments (i.e., it connects the communication function of fund raising to a wider social order).

In conclusion, the use of critical methodology in this book is justified because of the scope of the subject studied (i.e., the conceptual anomalous problem of fund raising) and because of the lack of critical research on fund raising and an underrepresentation of such studies in communication and public relations. Critical methodology allows this book to shift the paradigm of public relations to include a theory of donor relations by critically analyzing current principles and by criticizing public relations scholars for their neglect of the communication function of fund raising. It supports what S. Hall (1980) referred to earlier in this book as a "significant break" with old lines of thought, regrouping old and new elements around a different set of premises.

Finally, this book fits well within the parameters of a critical study as defined by methodological experts (i.e., although this book is not based on original research data, it does analyze an existing body of literature and advance new theoretical arguments). The theory of donor relations that results from this critical approach is not weakened by the absence of original data. As Laudan (1977) argued, the acid test for any theory is that it provides satisfactory solutions to important problems, which is of greater consequence than whether the theory is true, corroborated, or well confirmed.

Concluding this discussion of methodology, it should be noted that personal observations drawn from more than 16 years of experience as a practitioner, scholar, and teacher of public relations and fund raising are embedded within the book to illustrate concepts. While adding thick description to the analysis, such "biased" participant observation, as well as the "insider's" orientation, raises questions of objectivity. As pointed out during a seminar on philanthropy (Payton, 1987), however, "firsthand, intimate detailed experience" is often viewed as a desired and positive characteristic to bring to a discourse of ideas, and that without the contribution of "practical experience in real life situations," scholarly dialogue can result in "a great debate about a lot of fallacious views" (pp. 19-20).

Although an "outsider's" viewpoint is characteristic of a critical perspective, Lang and Lang (1983) said that the issue is one of style of research more than the orientation of the scholar (i.e., "whether one develops a broad definition of a problem" [p. 133]).

Turning now to chapter 2, the book states the conceptual problem that prompted it and presents evidence on the background of the problem, including the historical evolution of the fund-raising function at American colleges and universities.

Chapter 2

The Problem Prompting the Book: A New Function Taking on Increased Importance

This second preliminary chapter examines the problem that prompted the book. After stating the problem, chapter 2 addresses two questions related to its background: (a) Has fund raising for U.S. colleges and universities changed since its early years, and if so, what implications do these changes have for our understanding of the fund-raising behavior of these charitable organizations? and (b) Is a gift a one-way transfer of resources, or does the solicitation and acceptance of a gift involve two-way considerations that may affect the autonomy of charitable organizations?

A commonly accepted definition of *philanthropic giving* is the one provided by Boulding (1973), who said that gifts are the "voluntary, one-way transfer of exchangeables" (p. 1). This chapter demonstrates how this definition, and others like it, have disguised the fact that the giver expects consideration in return for the gift, and sometimes, this two-way transfer has serious implications for an organization's autonomy. Focusing on colleges and universities, the literature of higher education and recent news items in the trade and popular publications are used to document the potential of private gifts to negatively affect the autonomy of charitable organizations.

Before doing so, however, chapter 2 turns to the fund-raising and philanthropy literature to sketch the historical evolution of the fund-raising function at colleges and universities in order to demonstrate how changes related to that function have resulted today in a set of ongoing activities managed by lay administrators, who—unlike their predecessors—do not raise gifts as part of overall fiduciary or policymaking responsibilities (i.e., gifts are raised for the sake of raising gifts). Finally, news items are used again to illustrate the current era of higher educational fund raising that is characterized by higher giving totals, larger private gifts—including "mega and ultimate gifts"—by a decreasing proportion of donors, an unprecedented number of capital campaigns with multimillion-dollar goals, a competitive market for hiring fund-raising practitioners, and increasing calls for regulation of fund raising.

These characteristics of the current era, coupled with the implications of the evolution of the function, lead one to believe that the examples of autonomy threatened or lost through the two-way transfer of giving are not exceptions, but warning signs of danger ahead. Chapter 2 opens by stating the problem that prompted the book.

STATEMENT OF THE PROBLEM

According to scholars of organizational behavior, one of an organization's primary goals is to decrease uncertainty by seeking autonomy from its environment (i.e., the freedom to determine and pursue its goals without interference). Yet organizations, particularly those in a democratic society, are interdependent with publics that limit autonomy. Although absolute autonomy is unattainable, charitable organizations seek to enhance opportunities and to minimize threats from external publics, including foundation, corporate, and individual donors, that provide necessary revenue in the form of tax-deductible gifts. Increasingly, fund raisers are hired by charitable organizations, including institutions of higher education, and charged with raising greater amounts of private dollars. These practitioners, guided by current fund-raising principles, raise gifts to meet dollar goals with little understanding of the impact their activities have on organizational autonomy; yet, their role in soliciting and accepting private gifts places them in a critical position for determining the degree of autonomy lost or gained. As $1-million-and-up gifts become more commonplace, it is imperative that fund raising be examined in relation to its effect on organizational autonomy and that a theoretical framework be developed that will explain this organizational function within the context of interdependencies.

BACKGROUND OF THE PROBLEM

In the last few years, the spotlight in educational and other charitable organizations has been on the fund-raising function as it works to bring in much needed revenue for organizations that have rising expenditures and static or decreased funding from other sources. Fund raising has emerged as a relatively new field that for most people maintains a cloak of power and mystery.

"Many faculty members seem to think that the president and vice president for development sit astride a set of pipes through which money flows," stated Ross Webber, who returned to full-time teaching after serving for 5 years as vice president for development at the University of Pennsylvania (cited in "Professors taking," 1987, p. 35).

Fund raisers who have the "power" to raise millions of dollars are sought intensively. According to a 1987 article in _The Chronicle of Higher Education_ ("Pay gap widens," 1987), colleges and universities are continuing to pursue high-priced "stars" to head their fund-raising operations, offering them salaries (average of $65,100 in 1986) that are significantly higher than those of the staffs they supervise.

Yet, there are visible signs that fund raisers, once they are within an organization, are often isolated from the administrative mainstream and academic core. Describing fund raisers as "applied rhetoricians," a communication professor illustrated the distance between faculty members and fund raisers when he said (Trachtman, 1987):

> To most faculty members I know, the world of university advancement is _terra incognita._ They think of the advancement officer vaguely—if at all—as a salesperson and petitioner who haunts corporate and foundation board rooms and is likely, in Emily Dickinson's sly language, to "tell all the truth, but tell it slant." (p. 11)

Echoing these sentiments, Payton (1981) said, "In an academic community ideologically committed to truth and objectivity, there is much about development work that makes the academic soul uneasy" (p. 282).

An article in _The Chronicle of Higher Education_ ("Professors taking," 1987) related the story of fund raisers who got a major donor interested in creating a master's degree program in business management even though their university did not have a business school. Apparently, the fund raisers in question had little comprehension of the process involved in setting up a degree program, prompting a professor of the university to state, "Our development people made claims we couldn't deliver on" (p. 35).

David Lundberg (cited in "Professors taking," 1987), associate dean for faculty development at Tufts University, agreed that fund raisers are often raising money in isolation. "Our development people were going out and fishing for money without a good understanding of the academic side of the university" (p. 35), he said. Payton (1981) had harsh words of evaluation for such fund-raising practitioners, who he likened to real estate salesmen and said, "They neither know nor care about the real work of the institution" (p. 283). In almost the same breath, however, Payton pointed to the awkward situation faced by most fund-raising practitioners on college campuses, saying, "His is not yet an accepted role. He is the newcomer in an ethnic neighborhood who cannot speak the language very well, the new resident in the small town" (p. 283).

Fund raising as an internal, ongoing set of activities is a relatively new function for colleges and universities, and is commonly recognized as such in comments like Payton's. Yet, another commonly accepted perception of fund raising is that it has been an integral part of American higher education since colonial days. According to Cutlip (1965), the first systematic effort to raise money on the North American continent was for Harvard in 1641. How can it be that fund raising has been around for the last 350 years and, yet still is considered "a new resident in the small town" of academe? Obviously, some changes have occurred in fund raising, although the consequences of these changes are not readily apparent in our current understanding of the function as it exists today.

The Evolution of the Fund-Raising Function in American Colleges and Universities

Fund raising as an internal, specialized function of American colleges and universities is relatively new, not well understood, and largely separated from the primary missions of these charitable organizations.

According to Rudolph (1962), fund raising, indeed, began with the formal establishment of educational institutions in the United States, but the fund raisers for these colonial colleges were their presidents, although sometimes clergymen served as paid agents working on a commission basis. Not only does fund raising trace its roots to the colonial period, but both major gifts and annual, or operating, gifts—still the two primary categories of charitable gifts—began at the same time. As Pray (1981) explained, "Capital gifts from a relatively few wealthy benefactors were sought assiduously by presidents and occasionally by a supportive trustee, sometimes sparked by sale of the college name" (p. 1). Annual funds, according to Pray, came through "subscriptions from church members, community residents, or organized friends" (p. 1).

According to Curti and Nash (1965), "Appeals to private individuals for funds were present in the earliest attempts to found colleges in the New World, and most donations in the colonial period were the result of active solicitation" (pp. 4-5). Curti and Nash pointed to John Witherspoon, who assumed the presidency of the College of New Jersey (later Princeton University) in 1768, as an example to describe the fund-raising responsibilities of early college presidents. Witherspoon, they said, raised 7,000 pounds in 4 years through "ingenuity and talent," including a fund-raising mission to Jamaica in 1772, during which he gave an address that the authors quoted:

> President Witherspoon pointed out how over-worked the college's limited faculty was, especially the president. . . . [He] declared that "the short lives of the former Presidents have been attributed to their excessive labours, which is hoped will be an argument with the humane and generous to lend their help in promoting so noble a design." (pp. 35-36)

According to Curti and Nash (1965), a variety of methods were used by colonial college presidents to raise private support. For example, operating funds for Harvard were raised by asking community residents to make an annual voluntary donation of one-quarter bushel of grain or its equivalent in money to the college, and capital gifts for Princeton and Brown Universities, among others, were raised by "selling the location of the college to the highest bidder" (p. 28). Presidents also used honorary degrees as an inducement to prospective donors in the early 1770s. As Curti and Nash explained, "That such an honor might be useful was evident from the experience of Yale College, where a donor had asked for and received an honorary degree in return for a contribution of books" (p. 29).

In summary, fund raising was an integral element in the founding and operations of America's earliest institutions of higher education, and the presidents of those institutions were the primary fund raisers. As Curti and Nash (1965) emphasized, "So important was philanthropy to the existence of the colonial colleges that its solicitation was usually entrusted to high officers in the institution" (p. 32).

The presidential function of fund raiser continued into the 19th century. As Cutlip (1965) stated, "More than one struggling institution of higher education in America was kept afloat in the nineteenth century by the resourceful fund-raising efforts of a promoter-president" (p. 19). As an example, Cutlip described the fund-raising prowess of Colorado College's president, the Rev. E. P. Tenney, who—when the college was out of funds—would "jump the next train for the effete East where by hook or crook he would procure enough money to keep going for another few months" (p. 19).

While acknowledging the primary role of the president in raising private support for America's early colleges and universities, historians of fund raising generally have ignored the transition in governance that took place in these institutions after the Civil War and the implications that this transition had on the fund-raising function.

As documented by Rudolph (1962), Pray (1981), Curti and Nash (1965), and Cutlip (1965), presidents were the first fund raisers for American colleges and universities, whereas members of their external governing boards (e.g., trustees, overseers, or regents) primarily held responsibility for policy and management. However, as emphasized by Duryea (1973/1986) in his historical study of the evolution of university organization, governing boards lost much of their power during the 40 years between the Civil War and 1900—a time of educational revolution when enrollments skyrocketed and universities became departmentalized. By the early 1900s, presidents had become the dominating influence of American higher education—virtually one-man shows, as demonstrated by Charles Eliot at Harvard and Daniel Gilman at Johns Hopkins.

As knowledge became more specialized, professors were increasingly recognized as the only authorities of their respective specializations, which led to their increased control over academic affairs and to professional segmentation. The practical result of growing size and complexity necessitated delegation of policymaking and managerial responsibilities from boards to the president. In addition, the managerial burden of the president brought about the beginnings of an administrative bureaucracy.

There is a correlation between this transfer of power and the evolution of fund-raising responsibility—one that is critical to this discussion. When presidents assumed responsibilities for managing educational institutions, particularly those at universities, trustees retained only broad policymaking power and assumed increased responsibility for fund raising. The transfer of a significant portion of fund-raising responsibilities from presidents to trustees after the Civil War is illustrated by Curti and Nash's (1965) description of early gifts to the University of California. For example, the authors point out that Darius Mills established a professorship of intellectual and moral philosophy at that university "at the suggestion of a friend on the Board of Regents," and that California's most outstanding early benefactor, Phoebe Hearst, began her generous giving in 1891 "and as a regent encouraged others to open their purses" (p. 163).

This era, according to Hall (1987), marked the beginning of "Welfare Capitalism" (p. 12) as an alternative to socialism in the United States. Explaining that business leaders historically were adverse to government solutions and that government at that time was corrupt, Hall explained that "it was incumbent upon the leaders of American business, culture, and charity to work toward a private-sector alternative to socialism" (p. 11). As a result, the boards of charitable organizations became filled with business and social leaders, and, as Hall reported, "Big business and private wealth underwrote the growth of universities, libraries, hospitals, professional organizations and private clubs" (p. 9).

Nowhere was this movement to join capitalistic forces with social goals more apparent than in America's colleges and universities, primarily private institutions. According to Hall (1987), "From 1865 on, the advocates of private power concentrated their energies in two areas: building private business corporations capable of operating on a national scale and transforming nonprofit institutions, especially colleges, into organizations that would facilitate that end" (p. 9). Business people and university presidents sought each other out, until, as Hall said, "Businessmen became so involved with the affairs of the major universities—all of them private—that it was hardly an exaggeration to claim, as Thorstein Veblen did [in 1918], 'men of affairs have taken over direction of the pursuit of knowledge'" (p. 9).

This is not to say that presidents completely stopped being involved in raising gifts, but that after the Civil War trustees and regents took over many fund-raising duties as part of their changed responsibilities as members of a college's governing board. Therefore, until the end of World War I, fund raising was primarily handled first by presidents and then by trustees or regents in a personal search for private gifts as part of their overall policymaking and fiduciary roles. Arnaud Marts (cited in Cutlip, 1965), co-founder of Marts & Lundy—an early and leading fund-raising firm—emphasized the noninstitutionalization of the function when he said that this "personal search for gifts" was "the accepted technique for college fund-raising in America right up to the close of World War I" (p. 10).

In summary, the first critical point in understanding the evolution of the fund-raising function is that until World War I fund raising for colleges and universities was handled primarily by presidents and trustees. It should be noted here that a similar evolution of the fund-raising function took place in other types of charitable organizations. Fund-raising consultant Robert Sharpe (1989) said, "Until the early 1950's, very few charities had professional staff members running fund-raising operations" (p. 40).

As explained by Duryea (1973/1986), an administrative bureaucracy grew out of the increased management responsibilities of the college president after the Civil War. Distinguished by a division of labor, according to Duryea, the bureaucracy that grew in American universities in the latter half of the 1800s was quite different than that of European universities. He said, "In part, it grew out of a relationship with the general society, unique to this country, which imposed on the university the task of securing financial support from both public and private sources and concurrently of attending to public relations" (p. 173).

He pointed out that alumni secretaries were one of the early administrative positions created by the new managerial role of the president, and that the first press bureau appeared at the University of Wisconsin in 1904.

Fund raising was the last of the three primary functions that are now included under institutional advancement (i.e., fund raising, public relations, and alumni relations) to become an internal function of colleges and universities. As pointed out by Duryea (1973/1986), the alumni office was the first to emerge within the new organization, and the Association of Alumni Secretaries (renamed the American Alumni Council [AAC]) met for the first time in 1913 ("Diamond jubilee," 1988). Public relations was internalized at enough institutions by 1917 to allow those practitioners to form the American College Public Relations Association (ACPRA) that same year ("Diamond jubilee," 1988). In his 1942 study, *College Publicity in the United States*, Fine (cited in Rowland, 1983) documented the institutionalization of the public relations function: Four college publicity offices existed between 1900 and 1909, 13 more were added between 1910 and 1919, 83 were added between 1920 and 1929, and 134 were created during the 1930s.

Fund raising did not become an internal function of colleges and universities—including private institutions—until the latter part of the 1940s, or about 30 years after the formation of ACPRA. As Pray (1981) explained, "The development of fund raising for education on a formal or institutionalized basis came, however, with agonizing slowness over the years" (p. 1). It wasn't until 1949, or just 42 years ago, that the first fund raiser joined ACPRA, and by 1952 there were 13 directors of development in the public relations association. Although Pray pointed out that the first alumni fund dates from shortly after the Civil War, surveys by ACPRA in 1936 and 1942 showed that "fewer than half the institutions had such funds" (p. 1). Those funds that did exist before the 1950s were generally managed by the alumni office, although only one-fifth of the respondents to a 1937 AAC survey said they were involved in raising funds for their college ("Diamond jubilee," 1988).

In further support of this fact, Brittingham and Pezzullo (1990) summarized the research dealing with the beginning of internalized fund raising and reported, "With regard to organization, it appears that almost all coordinated and centralized development activity in higher education is less than 40 years old, with only 25 percent of all institutions reporting a centralized development function as recently as 1970" (p. 82).

This distinction of fund raising as a new institutional function in comparison to the other two functions of alumni and public relations is the second critical point in this discussion because much of the fund-raising literature blurs the origins of institutional advancement. For example, Cutlip (1965) credited "the new professional fund raiser" as "an effective stimulus in prodding colleges and universities to put in publicity and public relations departments in the 1920's" (p. 251). Although part of his statement is supported by the pattern of growth in college public relations departments as reported earlier by Fine (cited in Rowland, 1983), Cutlip is not referring to the fund-raising function as we know it today, but to external fund raisers (i.e., the fund-raising consulting firms that conducted periodic campaigns for colleges and universities between World War I and World War II). This lack of distinction between external and internal fund raising is perpetuated in the literature, as evidenced by Hall (1987), who cited Cutlip when stating, "In the 1920s . . . the Community Chests, the YMCA, and the universities all professionalized their revenue-generating operations" (p. 15).

As described in more detail in the chapter on historical models of fund raising, commercial fund-raising firms were started immediately following World War I, with the earliest firms dating from 1919 (Bintzer, 1981; Cutlip, 1965). Much of the impetus for the rise of these fund-raising firms can be traced to a sense of urgency in the United States after World War I to create an alternative to socialism. According to Hall (1987), "The success of the Bolshevists in Russia, the almost successful socialist revolutions in Germany and Hungary, and a wave of radical-led strikes in the United States in 1919 made the creation of such an alternative an urgent task" (p. 13).

Utilizing skills and expertise gained during the war, these external fund-raising consultants managed periodic campaigns to meet the fund-raising needs of charitable organizations, including colleges and universities (Cutlip, 1965). As Bintzer (1981) explained:

> In those days, fund raising for an educational institution was not an integral part of the ongoing management of the institution, Rather, it was undertaken as an "extra" activity whenever the need for additional funds made itself felt. Then the professional firm would be called in to advise and direct the client in his search for the needed funds. (p. 218)

According to Bintzer, "Their success resulted from two conditions: (1) their own well-developed expertise and proven procedures and (2) the lack of any similar (or even remotely akin) expertise within the staff of the client" (p. 217).

Bintzer (1981) neglected to mention another factor in the success of commercial fund-raising firms between World War I and World War II. Although it is fully discussed in chapter 5 on myths and misinterpretation, it must be pointed out here that these external fund-raising firms did _not_ and still do not solicit gifts, largely because most states require charities and "solicitors" to register with a regulatory agency and pay fees or post bond (AAFRC Trust for Philanthropy, 1989a). As Bintzer said, "Counsel will not solicit gifts but will use all his knowledge and powers of persuasion to equip the client's staff and volunteers with the skills they need to seek gifts successfully" (p. 220).

This is the third critical point in understanding the evolution of fund raising at American colleges and universities: Because consulting firms do not solicit gifts, they are dependent on volunteers and staff for the actual solicitation of private support, and their success during the period before fund raising was internalized was largely attributable to solicitations carried out by the trustee-volunteer and the president. The American Association of Fund-Raising Council (AAFRC), which was founded in 1937 as a trade association representing the major fund-raising counseling firms in the nation, states in its Fair Practice Code (AAFRC Trust for Philanthropy, 1987), "Member firms also believe it is the best interest of clients that solicitation of gifts should generally be undertaken by volunteers" (p. 120). As discussed later in chapter 5, this reliance on volunteers by consulting firms, which dominated fund raising until the 1950s, has led to a misinterpretation of the fund-raising function (i.e., the role of the fund raiser is to advise and manage, while actual solicitations are done by volunteers).

Calling it the "evolution of the management of philanthropy," Bintzer (1981) said that "ever-increasing competition for the philanthropic dollar . . . has forced the creation of the skilled, professional, full-time, in-house university staff to cope with these challenges" (p. 217). The fourth, and final critical point, then, is that the primary responsibility for fund raising, particularly the solicitation of gifts, was once held by presidents and/or trustees, but now lies in the hands of the internal fund-raising practitioner.

In summary, fund raising was the primary responsibility of the college president during the colonial period. After the Civil War, members of governing boards took on increased fund-raising responsibility in response to a transfer of managerial power to the president and a movement by business and social leaders to provide an alternative to government control. Between World War I and World War II, commercial fund-raising firms managed and directed gift solicitations by college presidents and trustees. It was only after World War II that fund raising became institutionalized and full-time specialists became primarily responsible for soliciting gifts on behalf of American colleges and universities.

In his 1980 study of 105 private colleges, Coloia (cited in Rowland, 1983) traced this historic transfer of fund-raising responsibilities from the president to the board of trustees and finally to the development officer. Yet, this transfer of fund-raising responsibility, or "evolution in the management of philanthropy," is barely touched on in the fund-raising literature. In fact, chapter 5 on myths and misinterpretation documents how the historical roles of presidents, trustees, and commercial fund-raising firms still dominate the fund-raising literature, resulting in a misinterpretation of the fund-raising function as it exists today.

A serious implication of this evolution—one that has been virtually ignored by fund-raising scholars—is that fund raising has moved out of the hands of senior policymakers and the managers of overall financial resources (i.e., presidents and governing boards) and into the hands of specialized practitioners. These practitioners, as was documented by recent news articles at the beginning of this chapter, frequently research, plan, execute, and evaluate their fund-raising function outside the academic mainstream.

Etzioni (1964/1986) defined such lay administrators as those "who have no training in serving the major goal activities of the organization" (p. 35). He said:

> The strain created by lay administrators in professional organizations leads to goal displacement. When the hierarchy of authority is in inverse relation to the hierarchy of goals and means, there is considerable danger that the goals will be subverted. (p. 35)

Related to Etzioni's point on the danger of goal displacement by lay administrators, Duryea (1973/1986) discussed one of three inadequacies that causes dysfunction within the modern university. He pointed out that the commitment to specialization, both in academics and in administration, has led to a "psychological wedge," and that different attitudes and values have created a "faculty schizophrenia," which "categorizes administrators [such as fund raisers] as minions while expecting them to act as defenders of the academic faith" (pp. 179-180).

Both scholars touch upon the essence of this discussion in that fund raising for colleges and universities has been primarily turned over to lay administrators who—while being outside the academic mainstream—are expected to uphold the goals and freedom of their institution and its faculty. The goal displacement and dysfunction referred to by Etzioni (1964/1986) and Duryea (1973/1986) are evident in recent cases in which the process of soliciting and accepting gifts has resulted in controversy about infringement on institutional autonomy.

Recent Cases of Controversy Related to Fund Raising

In the chapter of his book on accepting gifts, Harvard University President Derek Bok (1982) said that although naming buildings and professorships to recognize donors rarely present a moral problem, "a university must draw the line at some point in seeking to recognize donors" (p. 277). In 1987, even the popular press carried stories about the proposed agreement by Harvard's John F. Kennedy School of Government to proffer the title of officer of the university (a title usually reserved for professors and school administrators) on an oil-rich couple from Texas in exchange for a $500,000 gift ("Harvard title," 1987). In what one report described as a "lame apology [that] did little to spare the school embarrassment," the dean of the Kennedy school—who had granted tentative approval to his fund raisers for the solicitation—is quoted as saying, "I regret that I did not review the draft more carefully" (p. 35).

Although Bok (1982) stated earlier that the issues involved in accepting and recognizing gifts "are encumbered by intangible and symbolic considerations that are often weighted differently by concerned individuals who approach the subject from widely divergent perspectives" (p. 266), his response to the 1987 controversy is emphatic. He said that "The issue is clear cut. It is inappropriate for a donation to the university to be conditioned upon the donor's appointment to a teaching or administrative position" ("Texans delay gift," 1987, p. A26).

Although a somewhat similar situation did not result in controversy, it is enlightening to note that less than 1 month after Bok's ("Texans delay gift," 1987) reaction to the incident at Harvard, Lee Iacocca, chairman of Chrysler Corporation, announced that he plans to return to his alma mater, Lehigh University, upon his retirement from Chrysler to work at the Iacocca Institute for Economic Competitiveness ("Chrysler's Iacocca," 1987). His intentions to assume an institutional position are buried in one of the final paragraphs of a major article in *The Chronicle of Higher Education* on Iacocca's efforts to raise $40 million for Lehigh and his personal contributions of $1 million, plus a $1.5-million matching gift from Chrysler.

In his 1982 book, Bok stated that many areas in the fund-raising process are fuzzy, but that the lines are reasonably clear for gifts that endanger "Justice Frankfurter's four essential freedoms of the university—to determine for itself on academic grounds who may teach, what may be taught, how it shall be taught, and who may be admitted to study" (p. 266).

In September 1987, headlines in educational publications demonstrated that the four academic freedoms, which are closely related to the autonomy of educational institutions, are not immune to the influence of donor relationships. The University of Rochester arranged for a business student to change universities after Eastman Kodak Company, a major corporate donor and supplier of students, complained that because the student worked for a competitor, Fuji Company Ltd., proprietary information would be at risk in the classroom ("U.

of Rochester cancels," 1987). The student was readmitted after faculty members of the business school condemned the action, and Former Treasury Secretary William E. Simon, for whom the business school is named, called the incident "blackmail" and said that the university should have told Kodak to "take a walk" ("U. of Rochester readmits," 1987, p. A34).

More recently, in September 1990 the California State University at San Marcos reversed an earlier decision to accept a $250,000 gift from farmer and rancher Allan O. Kelly for an endowed chair in geology. According to a news item about the reversed decision ("Cal. State U. decides," 1990), Kelly's gift carried the condition that any professor who filled the endowed chair would be required to study Kelly's own geological theories, which, according to the news item, "are rejected by many geologists" (p. A32). The gift was turned down only after its conditions became known in a newspaper article, which prompted faculty complaints that accepting the gift "would compromise the academic freedom of the new university" (p. A32).

Are these recent cases the exception, rather than the norm? Periodic scanning of the "Philanthropy" section of *The Chronicle of Higher Education* and its biweekly sister publication, *The Chronicle of Philanthropy*, leads one to believe that the potentially negative impact of private giving on institutional autonomy increases as gifts increase in size.

The president of Duke University announced in 1987 that Duke might not be able to accept a $20 million gift—the single largest contribution to the institution since James B. Duke's original gift to establish it in 1924—if the donor, businessman Disgne D. Deane, did not agree to change his conditions ("Duke may not accept," 1987). Deane, whose gift would create a research institute on the future of humanity, made his gift with the condition that he be represented on committees that would hire 20 new professors and oversee the operation of the institute. The statement issued by Duke's president said that university officials were "extraordinarily sensitive to the balance needed to protect the institution's autonomy in matters such as faculty appointments while enabling benefactors to support scholarship" (p. 29).

Negotiations for a $70-million gift to the University of Texas Health Science Center at Dallas were interrupted in 1987 when the governor of Texas vetoed a bill that turned out to have been drafted specifically to meet one of the donor's conditions for making the gift ("Negotiations resume," 1987). Because out-of-state students pay four times more for tuition than Texans, and because the donor, H. Ross Perot, wanted the program his gift would create to attract the best students in the country—regardless of residence—the university had a bill introduced that would waive the higher fees. The veto was declared an oversight by the governor's staff, and the bill was approved after a special legislative session. Officials said a $70-million gift would be the largest single contribution from an individual ever received by an institution in the Texas system.

As Texas holds a special claim to "bigness," it was appropriate to learn in 1989 that the largest gift ever received by any institution of higher education in the United States might be forthcoming in that state. A news item in *The Chronicle of Philanthropy* ("Insider," 1989b) reported that Dallas real-estate mogul, Trammell Crow, was preparing to replace Robert Woodruff as the new record holder for the largest charitable gift ever made to higher education. The intended recipient of his reported $108 million gift was the University of Texas at Dallas, which until then had been limited to enrolling students in upper division and graduate study. In July 1989, however, the governor of Texas signed into law a measure enabling the university to admit freshmen and sophomore students. According to the reporter of the news item, "The potential donor apparently requested the change in U.T.D.'s status as a condition of his gift" (p. 6).

In July 1989, 300 hundred faculty and students at the University of Utah medical school signed a petition protesting a plan to change the school's name to honor business entrepreneur James L. Sorenson, who had given $15 million worth of stock. According to an article about the protest ("Petitioners oppose," 1989), "In negotiating the gift, university officials agreed to change the name of the hospital and medical school. . . . [but] Faculty members have argued that they should have been included in any discussions about renaming the medical school" (p. A26). Charging that "the change threatens the reputation of the school because the new name will not be closely identified with the university," the article continued, "Administrators have replied that faculty representation in such decisions is not usual" (p. A26). Less than 2 months after the beginning of the controversy when petition signatures reached 1,500, the University of Utah decided to return the $15-million gift, even though it had a contract with the donor "reached after six years of negotiation" ("$15-million gift," 1989, p. 6).

In summary, recent news items related to the process of soliciting and accepting gifts for colleges and universities document situations in which: (a) fund raisers have offered inappropriate considerations in return for a gift (Harvard); (b) a major donor has announced his or her intentions to assume a position with the recipient institution (Lehigh University); (c) the relationship between an educational institution and a major donor has resulted in a violation of academic freedom (University of Rochester); (d) negotiations over gift conditions have resulted in threats to academic freedom (California State

University at San Marcos), threats to an institution's freedom in making personnel and programming decisions (Duke University), or in changes in the missions of institutions (University of Texas Health Science Center and University of Texas at Dallas); and (e) negotiated terms to recognize major donors have threatened to override faculty and student concerns about damage to institutional reputation (University of Utah).

Although all of these situations illustrate the problem addressed in this book, there remains another issue to discuss in this stage-setting chapter in relation to the effects of soliciting and receiving gifts. Specifically, the usefulness or "utility" of gifts varies greatly and the historical context of fund raising is again important to our understanding of this aspect of fund raising.

Fund Raising in an Era of Limited Means

As described earlier, fund raising for colleges and universities became an internal, organizational function after World War II. During the 1950s and 1960s, institutions of higher education created their first development offices and primary responsibility for fund raising was transferred into the hands of full-time, specialized practitioners. This institutionalization took place during a time that is now referred to as the golden age of higher education—an era of growth, expansion, and unprecedented governmental support (Nielsen, 1985). According to Hall (1987), "The passage of the GI bill in 1944, its renewal in 1952, and the National Defense Education Act in 1958 siphoned massive indirect subsidies into the private nonprofit sector" (p. 18).

Through increasing student tuitions, state appropriations, and federal grants, resources were plentiful enough that colleges and universities could continually add new programs in accordance with ideas and innovations prompted by private gifts restricted in purpose. For example, foundations, according to Nielsen (1985), devoted themselves during these decades to experimentation, expecting the government to assume financial responsibility for new programs that proved promising. As Nielsen said, "With the vastly greater resources available to the public sector in the 1950s, 1960s, and 1970s, and with the nation in a generally expansionist and idealistic mood, this type of foundation contribution to national development reached its apogee" (p. 442).

Individuals and corporations also gave generously during this golden era. According to Hall (1987), "Prosperity of the war and post-war years brought enormous increases in individual and corporate income, which, coupled with high tax rates, stimulated charitable giving" (p. 17). Combining all these factors together, Hall said, "Higher tax rates during World War II and the Korean War, the liberalization of legal doctrines on corporate giving, the refinement of conceptions of corporate social responsibility, and generational factors [growth of assets of foundations] interacted to increase the wealth and influence of the nonprofit sector" (p. 17). Because an educational institution's mission could be broadly defined, most gift purposes, or gift conditions, could fit comfortably within a college's mission. Reflecting on that period, Pray (1981) said, "The practice at most institutions was to add programs without much reexamination of existing programs" (p. 3). As fund-raising revenues increased, "interesting questions about priorities" were raised for the first time, according to Pray, who said that such questions "emerged as a surprise" (p. 3).

Starting in the 1970s, economic and sociopolitical conditions changed, and, according to Hall (1987), "To many the nonprofit independent sector appeared to be in grave danger and by 1973, serious enquiries into its future were underway" (p. 20). Most notable among these inquiries was the Filer Commission. Published by the Department of the Treasury in 1977, the report of the Filer Commission documented the importance of the nonprofit sector, but as Hall pointed out, "it also revealed how little was really known about it—a fact that would become evident with the election of Ronald Reagan in 1980" (p. 20).

What was known, however, was that the new era of the mid-1970s and beyond represented one not of growth, but of limits and austerity for charitable organizations within the nonprofit sector, including higher educational institutions. As Nielsen (1985) stated:

> But now the era of limits and constraints has arrived, and a rethinking and redirection of approaches are necessary. National aspirations have not been abandoned, but the awareness of costs has become acute, an awareness that may become even greater in the future. (p. 442)

Indicative of this current era of limited resources, the findings of a recent survey by the Association of American Universities (AAU) show that nearly 60% of the leading public and private research universities "are consolidating, eliminating, or reducing academic departments" ("Escalating costs," 1989, p. A21). According to the report, "Research universities can no longer be all things to all people, and must build what one institution calls 'selective excellence' in their academic offerings" (p. A21). In light of limited resources, Washington University has announced plans to close its sociology department, Columbia University has decided to eliminate its departments of geography and linguistics, and Johns Hopkins University will shift resources among departments in its school of arts and sciences ("Escalating costs," 1989).

Within this context of economic change, fund raisers today are expected to bring in needed funds to replace tuition lost by declining enrollments and/or declining government allocations.

According to the findings of the AAU survey just cited ("Escalating costs," 1989), "Most universities in the survey reported that they were stepping up fund raising for operational expenses, with many indicating that they were planning or conducting major capital campaigns" (p. A21). Obviously, these stepped-up, fund-raising efforts are expected to generate private gifts in support of institutional goals and current programs, but similar efforts in the past have not necessarily done so.

As discussed in chapter 5 on myths and misinterpretation, most of the dollars given to colleges and universities are restricted in purpose, and often these purposes are not in support of current programming. Dramatic evidence of the financial gap between fund-raising totals and institutional needs is provided by the report on the AAU survey ("Escalating costs," 1989), which stated, "The largest college fund raiser in the country, Stanford University, will carry a deficit of between $2-million to $3-million in 1989-90" (p. A22). It is important to note that Stanford incurred this operating deficit after reaching the midpoint in a $1.1-billion capital campaign—the largest total sought by a university until September 1990 when Columbia University launched a $1.15-billion campaign ("Columbia U. opens," 1990).[1] According to a news item on Stanford ("Give & take," 1989c), two of the three causes of its deficit, which officials had originally projected as high as $14 million, were shortfalls in research funds and unrestricted gifts.

Although most colleges and universities seem to ignore this financial gap between fund-raising totals and institutional needs, as evidenced by the popularity of fund-raising solutions to financial problems, it is clear that each new program that is initiated by gifts restricted in purpose encumbers institutional resources for the future and limits the options of a college or university in allocating future operating funds. Yet, there is evidence in recent issues of the trade and popular publications that fund raisers and their institutions continue to solicit and accept gifts that seem far removed from the central mission of colleges and universities.

---

[1]Other universities conducting or planning capital campaigns in excess of $1.1 billion are Cornell University, $1.25 billion; Yale University, $1.5 billion; and Harvard University, $2 billion.

Recent Cases of Gifts That Raise
Questions of Utility

As described in chapter 1, Ernest Boyer (1989), president of the Carnegie
Foundation for the Advancement of Teaching, questioned whether it was the
donor's or the institution's purpose that was being served when the University
of Southern California (USC) recently accepted a $4-million grant from a local
real-estate developer to establish a center for real-estate development. As
discussed fully in chapter 14 on measuring effectiveness, fund raising is currently
evaluated solely on the basis of dollars raised, with little concern being given to
the purposes of the gifts solicited and received. This form of measurement, it
is argued here, contradicts the current economic era in which colleges and
universities are increasingly turning to fund raising in the expectation that it will
generate revenue needed to support core programs.

It is not difficult to find current examples of major gifts given to colleges
and universities on the condition that they establish new programs, centers, or
schools that appear—at least on the surface—to be virtually unrelated to the
institution's academic core. As related in chapter 1, one such example is the
pledged gift of $10 million from Bill Daniels to establish the separate Institute
for Professional Excellence at the University of Denver to teach business
graduate students "kindness, courtesy, punctuality, cleanliness, proper dress, as
well as academic subjects such as ethics and communications" ("B-schools,"
1989, p. 85).

Robert S. Jepson, Jr., recently pledged $20 million to the University of
Richmond to establish the first school in leadership studies. According to an
article about his gift ("Foundation created," 1989), Jepson said that "selling the
university on the idea of a leadership school was no small task" (p. A22), and
that members of the faculty resisted because they are adverse to change. The
reporter stated, "As with many situations where a donor offers a large sum of
money, suspicions arose about Mr. Jepson's motives and the extent of his
influence on the campus" (p. A22). According to the article, most of the
University of Richmond faculty are taking a wait-and-see attitude, although some
have expressed doubts about whether leadership is an academic discipline (i.e.,
whether it can be taught). The reporter quoted a history professor who said,
"We're going to have something called the Jepson Center for Leadership Studies.
. . . Either it will revive or put to rest those suspicions" (p. A22).

In the same article that reported Daniel's gift to the University of Denver ("B-
schools," 1989), the reporter asked, "Are the B-schools taking on subjects that
really cannot be taught?" (p. 86). In response, a Harvard professor is quoted as

complaining, "Some of these problems they are assigning us are almost insurmountable. They talk of globalization. But you can't teach that with a course" (p. 86). According to the article, "Ethics is a more ticklish pedagogical problem because universities are getting large sums of money to give their students a shot of it" (p. 86). "Harvard," the article continued, "seems almost embarrassed by the $20 million pledged by John Shad, chairman of Drexel Burnham Lambert, to be used to promote ethics and leadership in business" (p. 86).

Although the "embarrassment" may be partly the result of charges of unethical behavior levied at Drexel executives, such as Shad and Michael Milken, during the late 1980s, Harvard's primary cause for embarrassment, according to the article, is that the school still has no idea how to spend all that money on something so far removed from its current offerings.

Concluding this section on the background of the problem, fund raising, as an internal function of colleges and universities, was institutionalized during an era of prosperity and growth when restricted gifts for new programs were solicited and accepted with little, or no, consideration for how the acceptance of such gifts affected current and future resources. Today, in an era of limited growth and "selective excellence," the fund-raising function is looked to as a solution for financial problems caused by declining enrollments and/or government funding. Yet, fund raisers, who are evaluated by the number of dollars they raise, frequently raise major gifts that do not support current programming and that sometimes add to the financial burden of colleges and universities by limiting future allocations of institutional resources.

Not unexpectedly, this aspect of the evolution of the fund-raising function at colleges and universities is related to the earlier discussion on the transfer of fund-raising responsibility to specialist practitioners from college presidents and members of governing boards (i.e., those responsible for policymaking and overall financial decisions for institutions of higher education). As can be readily surmised, presidents and trustees are probably, by virtue of their positions, more cognizant of the needs of an institution and more aware of the financial consequences of accepting a particular gift than are fund raisers who often operate outside the academic mainstream.

For example, fund raisers at the University of Maryland at College Park continue to raise private funds for undergraduate scholarships, financial and merit based, even though their public institution is under state mandate to decrease undergraduate enrollment, tuition is relatively low, undergraduate applications have risen steadily for 10 years, and the senior administrators of the university have identified funds for graduate fellowships as an urgent student-recruitment need.[2] Not only are gifts for alternative purposes lost by the "misdirection" of fund-raising efforts, but the cost of administrating new scholarships (e.g., personnel hours to disseminate information, to evaluate candidates and select a recipient, and to process the funds) encumber future institutional resources for years to come (in perpetuity when such "unneeded" scholarships are endowed).

With these two elements of the fund-raising function's historical evolution at American colleges and universities in mind (i.e., the transfer of primary responsibility for fund raising to full-time, specialized practitioners and the contextual changes in the economic climate of fund raising), chapter 2 concludes by examining characteristics of the current fund-raising function.

CHARACTERISTICS OF THE FUND-RAISING FUNCTION

At the conclusion of Ronald Reagan's term as President of the United States, the new biweekly trade publication, *The Chronicle of Philanthropy*, did a special report on the "profound changes" that took place in the nonprofit sector during the 8 years under the Reagan administration ("Reagan years," 1988). Five of the seven major changes cited in the article were:

- Giving to charitable causes has almost doubled.

- Concentration of wealth in the hands of the "super rich" has led to a variety of innovative fund-raising techniques aimed at the very wealthy, from "ultimate gifts" to "prospect research."

- Competition for donations is increasing as more and more charities are conducting capital campaigns and goals are rising ever higher. More public institutions, from school systems to community colleges to museums, are going after private donations.

- Charities are scrambling to find fund raisers, many of whom can command salaries well into six figures, along with numerous perquisites.

- Philanthropy is in the public eye more than ever before. . . . But scandals have also brought calls for increased regulation. (pp. 1, 19)

Underlying these changes is the drastic cut in federal support for charitable organizations that was implemented by the Reagan Administration. According to Lester Salamon (cited in "Reagan years," 1988), director of the Institute for Policy Studies at the Johns Hopkins University, federal financial support has fallen by about 22.4% from 1980 levels, after adjusting for inflation and

---

[2]As stated earlier at the conclusion of chapter 1, I have worked as a fund-raising specialist and public relations practitioner for more than 16 years and anecdotes drawn from that experience are used to illustrate points throughout this book.

excluding increases in Medicare and Medicaid. The significant decrease in government support has led to a dramatic increase in efforts to raise private gifts during the past decade, which can be described as a fund-raising frenzy. This frenzy is characterized by higher giving totals, larger private gifts, increased capital campaigns, intense competition for fund-raising practitioners, and more calls for regulation.

Leslie Lenkowsky (cited in Reagan years, 1988), president of the Institute for Educational Affairs and a leader of the conservative Philanthropic Roundtable, said that "putting nonprofit groups to the market test of finding private funds has forced many of them either to become better managed and more effective or to go out of business" (p. 19). In contradiction of Lenkowsky's assessment, this chapter contends that financial pressure has forced charitable organizations to place unrealistic demands on fund raising, which has not necessarily led to better management and which may have serious consequences on the future well-being of these organizations, including colleges and universities.

According to the report ("Reagan years," 1988), colleges and schools have weathered the storm fairly well compared to those groups that deal with housing, community development, social services, and employment and job training. For example, half of the 120 agencies that served poor Hispanics in 1980 had gone out of business by 1982 because of government cuts. Similar "death" rates have not occurred in higher education; however, it is debatable whether survival is the only criterion for evaluating the effect of the related pressures of federal cuts and increased need for finding fund-raising dollars on all charitable organizations.

As a nonprofit organization's mission is its reason for being (i.e., unlike business, which primarily exits to earn profits for owners and shareholders, nonprofits exist to carry out their mission), a change in mission or in the means of achieving that mission might be a more revealing indicator of effect. It is conceivable that some charitable organizations, including colleges and universities, are increasingly altering or completely changing their mission in order to attract private gifts.

For example, in 1983 I interviewed for a position as vice president for development and public relations at Salem College in West Virginia—a private, liberal arts institution that primarily served undergraduate students from the Southeastern United States. At that time, a new president, Ronald E. Ohl, had just taken office—his first presidency—and was faced with intense financial pressure to increase private gifts because the small college had virtually no endowment and a declining student enrollment. Located in a relatively rural and economically depressed area and faced with a poor history of fund raising, the college, under the direction of President Ohl, was at that time pursuing a major gift from a donor interested in funding a program in physical wellness, although such a program would be primarily extraneous to its liberal arts mission.

Declining the job because of salary requirements, I was not surprised to read in 1989 that Salem College became the first 4-year college in the United States to merge with a Japanese university, giving partial control of its governing board to representatives of Teikyo University ("Salem College," 1989). As part of the joint-ownership arrangement, Salem, which was described as "struggling to stay afloat," received "millions of dollars for the endowment," and President Ohl announced that the new institution would "focus on international education," with a student body made up of half Japanese and half American students (p. A3).

Less than 1 year after establishing joint ownership of Salem College, Teikyo University of Japan had entered into similar arrangements with three other institutions: C. W. Post, Regis, and Westmar Colleges. Or as summarized in a recent article, Teikyo University "has merged with, bought portions of, or become affiliated with four American institutions" ("'Opportunism,'" 1990, p. A26). Describing the takeover of Westmar College in February 1990, a *Newsweek* article ("After Rockefeller Center," 1990) reported:

> Like many a failing American firm, Westmar College in rural Le Mars, Iowa was barely treading water. Enrollment peaked in 1968; today the school isn't even half full. Last week a white knight rode into town. Bearing a multimillion dollar "gift," Teikyo University of Japan bought into the school and took control of the board of trustees. (p. 71)

The article noted the vulnerability of certain institutions, stating, "For the past year the Japanese and other overseas investors have been negotiating for stakes in American schools. Thus far it's low-profile colleges like Westmar, Regis of Denver, Salem of West Virginia . . . that have felt the urge to merge" (p. 71).

Emphasizing that a "climate of opportunism" pervades these new ventures and threatens their quality and integrity, the co-author of a recent report on American–Japanese educational partnerships said that the "concept of American colleges being bought is repugnant in our culture" ("'Opportunism,'" p. A26).

Higher Gift Totals

According to the Council for Aid to Education (CFAE), private support for higher education grew by more than 75% during the first 5 years of the 1980s, and gifts from private sources in 1985–1986 amounted to 7% of the total $105.4 billion in college and university annual expenditures ("Surge in gifts," 1987). Between 1910, when the U.S. Office of Education first collected such information, and 1987–1988, private gifts and grants to higher education have risen from about $23 million (Haire, 1981) to more than $8 billion, and annual growth during the 1980s averaged nearly 9.5% ("Charitable giving," 1989).   In 1987–1988, foundations gave $1.6 billion to higher education, alumni gave $2 billion, nonalumni individuals gave $1.9 billion, and corporations gave $1.85 billion ("Gifts to colleges off," 1989).

According to a report on the latest CFAE survey ("Gifts to colleges off," 1989), "Private colleges and universities still dominate higher-education fund raising, but more public institutions are increasing their gift-solicitation efforts" (p. A31).   Among the top 20 institutions in fund-raising totals in 1987–1988, 6 are public universities, and 2 of those 6 are ranked in the top 10—the University of Minnesota with approximately $110 million in private support and the University of Wisconsin with more than $89 million.

However, for the first time in 13 years, gifts to colleges and universities declined by 3.5% in 1987–1988.   Indicative of the increasing fund-raising efforts of public institutions, the overall decline actually represented a decline in contributions to private colleges of 7.1% over the year before, whereas gifts to public institutions increased by 3.1% ("Public colleges," 1989).   According to Duronio and Loessin (1989), the portion of private support claimed by public colleges and universities grew from 19% in 1968–1969, to 34% in 1986–1987.

An Era of "Mega and Ultimate Gifts"

As demonstrated by the level of the gifts discussed earlier, these are the times of the *mega gift*, a term popularized by consultant Jerold Panas (1984) to distinguish those gifts of $1 million or more.   According to Arthur Frantzreb, a consultant who has researched and compiled mega-gift statistics, there has been a doubling in the ranks of million-dollar donors to all charitable organizations since 1984:   from 291 in 1984, to 579 in 1986, to 660 in 1987 ("Give & take," 1987; "1988's gifts," 1989).   Although mega gifts fell in 1988 to only 606, Frantzreb's statistics account for 2,136 gifts of $1 million or more between 1984 and 1988 ("1988's gifts," 1989).   Frantzreb also reported that colleges and universities, alone, reported 40 gifts of $5 million to $15 million in 1984, and at least 48 gifts of more than $10 million in 1988, up from 46 in 1987.

The Chronicle of Higher Education periodically prints a listing of those gifts of $20 million or more that have been made to higher education from 1967 to date.   A 1989 issue listed 35 such gifts that ranged from $20 million to $105 million ("Major gifts," 1989).   By November 1990, the list had expanded to 44 such gifts ("Major gifts," 1990).   Of the 44 very large gifts made over the 24 years covered by the list, 34 (77%) had been given in the 6 years from 1985 through 1990, and almost 40% had been made since 1988.

A new term that recently has been introduced to describe such gifts from individuals is *ultimate gifts*, which are defined as "those that an individual can make only once in a lifetime" ("Colleges get more aggressive," 1987, p. 39). According to *The Chronicle of Philanthropy*'s special report on the Reagan years ("Reagan years," 1988), fund-raising efforts during the last decade have focused increasingly on "getting gifts from America's 'super rich'—those individuals who rank in the top 0.5 per cent in wealth and assets" (p. 20). This group, which includes 35,875 Americans who have incomes of over $1 million and 475,000 who have assets of $1 million or more, contributes about 10.3% of all donations, although their importance to higher education is even greater because colleges and universities traditionally attract the majority of gifts from wealthy donors, as discussed in chapter 1. According to the report, the super rich owned 24.4% of American individual wealth in 1986, and the top 10% of all Americans hold nearly 65% of all wealth in the country, as estimated by the Federal Reserve Board.

One of the primary reasons for the rise in mega and ultimate gifts is the increasing number and goals of capital campaigns by colleges and universities.

Increased Capital Campaigns

As documented in chapter 13 on the historical models of fund raising, capital campaigns were developed by fund raisers for the YMCA in the early 1900s (Cutlip, 1965). Periodic, intensive, short "drives" for funds needed for capital projects, such as new buildings, these campaigns have evolved today into intensive, highly structured fund-raising efforts to raise private money for operations, endowment, and capital projects over periods of 5 years or more. They no longer are undertaken periodically, but rather as part of overall fund-raising strategy. As Pray (1981) said, "Today, colleges are engaging in a continuous search for major gifts, usually in what we might call a rolling campaign strategy" (pp. 57-58).

Dittman (1981) explained, "Since the frequency of capital campaigns is accelerating—some leaders believe that one every decade is necessary and justified—and the average length of the campaign is stretching toward five years, the indications are that especially the private colleges will be in a constant state of campaigning" (p. 231). In support of Dittman's prediction, Columbia University launched a $1.15-billion campaign in September 1990, even though it had just completed a capital campaign in 1987 that generated $602 million, "still one of the largest amounts raised by a college or university" ("Columbia U. opens," 1990, p. A34).

Stanford University "redefined the outer limits of fund raising" in 1986 when it announced a $1.1-billion capital campaign ("Reagan years," 1988, p. 22). Currently, at least 145 institutions of higher education are conducting capital campaigns with totals of $15 million or more ("UM enters," 1988). Taken together, these 145 institutions, of which about one third are public, are trying to raise $18 billion, or twice the amount given to all colleges and universities in 1986–1987. Eight universities, all private, are currently in, or planning to launch, capital campaigns in excess of $1 billion: Stanford, University of Pennsylvania, New York University, Boston University, Columbia, Cornell, Yale, and Harvard. Together, these campaigns total $10 billion ("Columbia U. opens," 1990). As summarized by the report on the Reagan years, "Organizations are pursuing fund-raising goals that would have been unimaginable in 1980" (p. 22).

"Everybody is running hard to stay even—that's the gut problem in the economics of higher education today," said Donald Kennedy, president of Stanford, in announcing his university's campaign, which generates $13.5 million in gifts on the average each month, or $1 million every other day ("Fund drives," 1987, p. A75).

Coldren's (1982) findings from her study of capital campaigns for colleges and universities in the 1970s are useful comparative data for emphasizing the increasing number and goals of current campaigns. In her monograph, *The Constant Quest*, Coldren reported that 116 colleges and universities conducted capital campaigns between 1974 and 1979, with an aggregate goal of $8.5 billion, as compared to at least 145 institutions trying to raise between $18 and $28 billion today. The average goal for public institutions in the 1970s was $7 million, whereas the average private institution's goal was $15 million. As compared to current $1-billion campaigns, Coldren said that in the 1970s, 18 private research universities conducted campaigns with goals of $100 million or more.

Public and private institutions differed little in the purposes for which they sought campaign funds (i.e., endowment was the top priority for both, although private institutions sought 16% of their goals for operating income, whereas only 9% of public institutions' goals were for operations). Finally, of 116 campaigns completed in the second half of the 1970s, 12% of the campaigns for public institutions and 21% of the campaigns for private institutions failed to meet their goals. Commenting on the increasing number of capital campaigns, Coldren concluded that peer competition does not adversely affect the success of campaigns.

Kenneth Burke (1985), a fund raiser whose career has been spent with private universities, disagreed with Coldren's conclusion, saying:

> When campaigns were a rarity, an individual could perhaps be expected to commit a substantial gift and not be asked again even in his/her lifetime. As the number of campaigns multiply, donors may be increasingly more reluctant to "give it all" to any particular campaign. (p. 5)

As is discussed in more detail in chapter 8 on the three sources of gifts, the increases in capital campaigns correlate with the rise in mega and ultimate gifts that are needed for lead gifts (i.e., those large, pre-campaign gifts, predominantly from individuals, that set the level for successive gifts). A formal principle of fund-raising campaigns is the "Rule of Thirds," which traditionally has meant that approximately one third of the campaign goal would be raised from 10% or less of the donors (Seymour, 1966). That rule has changed in recent years so that fund-raising experts now predict that less than 1% of the gifts to a campaign will account for one third of the total (e.g., Campbell, 1989). As Coldren (1982) said, the terms *capital campaign* and *major fund drives* could be used inter-changeably.

In fact, a recent study by the American Association of Fund-Raising Counsel (AAFRC) found that in 51 different capital campaigns, ranging in size from $292,000 to $272 million, the top 10 gifts never equaled less than 20% of the total and in some instances amounted to more than 90% (Dalessandro, 1989). As a result, colleges and universities entering capital campaigns have become increasingly dependent on the super rich who can provide the lead gifts necessary to attract other mega gifts and to ensure the success of a campaign, regardless of the actions of thousands of lower level donors who provide the bulk of the number of gifts.

A Comparison of Campaigns Reveals Competitiveness Factor

A local comparison of a private and public university provides insight into the increasing number and the new dynamics of capital campaigns. The Johns Hopkins University is a private institution in Maryland, world-renowned for its medical school. Hopkins traditionally ranks as the top or one of the top two institutions in the country receiving federal research dollars, and it is also traditionally one of the top 10 fund-raising universities in the country, with private gifts and grants accounting for 23% of its budget ("U.S. funds," 1987; "UM enters," 1988). In 1985, approximately 5 years after completing a $100-million campaign, Hopkins launched a new campaign to raise $450 million for endowment and capital purposes. According to a local newspaper article ("UM enters," 1988), "After meeting its five-year, $450 million campaign goal 17 months early, Hopkins has upped the ante and will continue its effort through February 1990" (p. 6G). What the article does not mention is that in 1988, Hopkins announced a projected $4-million deficit in its school of arts and sciences, which eventually led to the resignation of the university's president ("Hopkins delays," 1988).

This anomaly of incurring a deficit while in the middle of a capital campaign is similar, on the surface, to the deficit incurred by Stanford University mentioned earlier in this chapter. As with many capital campaigns, Hopkins was able to reach its overall goal, but the distribution of gifts restricted for special purposes was uneven (i.e., the medical school and other academic units attracted the lion's share of the campaign dollars, leaving the school of arts and sciences underfunded). Hopkins' two-prong answer to the problem was to implement an internal subsidy system—by which the medical school and other wealthy units would financially subsidize arts and sciences programs—and to raise the goal of the campaign so that more private funds could be brought into the institution ("Hopkins delays," 1988).

But there is more to add to the context of this particular capital campaign. Unlike Stanford, which was seeking to appease faculty protests against rising overhead charges billed to research grants, Hopkins' deficit was directly related to the current era of limited growth discussed earlier in this chapter.

Marking the retirement of Steven Muller as president of Johns Hopkins University in June 1990, a local newspaper article ("Hopkins president," 1990) stated, "Dr. Muller built a veritable empire . . . often expanding the Hopkins mission on the strength of a single grant or gift" (p. 1). Muller's advances on behalf of Johns Hopkins, according to his critics, relied on fund raising and ended up costing too much. For example, among the components added by Muller during his 18-year tenure was the Peabody music conservatory, and it is common knowledge in Maryland that this acquisition proved too costly for Hopkins, forcing the university during the 1990 legislative session to exchange assets of the conservatory for public appropriations. The newspaper article on Muller's retirement commented that "some wonder whether his gambling, often with the small fraction of the money Hopkins needed to keep its commitments, risked the university's most precious asset: the core arts and sciences" (p. 4B).

According to a report by Hopkins faculty (cited in "Hopkins president," 1990), the quality of undergraduate and graduate education in the arts and sciences has declined since 1975 and is further threatened by current retrenchment efforts. Faculty members, according to the local newspaper article, say that "[Muller's] vision was limited to areas in which Hopkins had not been involved before," and that it was only at the end of his tenure that "the price of his vision became clear" (p. 4B). As the article concluded:

> For if the university gained a space telescope institute during the Muller years, it also lost the country's most prestigious academic journal on the classics, founded at Hopkins and edited there for 108 years until a deficit in arts and sciences made most of the classics department unaffordable. (p. 4B)

Yet the article marking his retirement ("Hopkins president," 1990) emphasized that Muller, who the governor of Maryland praised as "an extraordinary fund-raiser," had "raised more money for Hopkins than any previous president, beginning with a $100-million campaign a few years after assuming office" and concluding with the current $600-million campaign (p. 4B). Explaining the financial gap between fund raising and institutional needs, Muller insisted that the university had always tried to raise money for the school of arts and sciences, but he said, "The university has been pulled in the direction of where the money is" (p. 4B).

Generalizing from the case of Johns Hopkins, private universities are depending on capital campaigns more than before, are shortening the period between campaigns, and are increasingly raising the goals. In addition, private institutions, such as Johns Hopkins, are finding the current era of limited growth one in which they must struggle to balance the financial gap between raising greater amounts of private dollars and meeting institutional needs that are central to their mission, as opposed to adding new programs.

A number of public institutions, such as the University of Maryland, have recently launched their first capital campaigns ("UM enters," 1988). In October 1988, the 11-campus system of the University of Maryland officially announced its 6-year campaign to raise $200 million for endowment and capital purposes. Maryland, like many public universities in the East, had not started a fund-raising department until the mid-1970s, and private gifts currently account for less than 3% of the university's $1.3-billion budget.

As a result of the large number of private institutions in the State of Maryland, particularly Johns Hopkins University, educational leaders had historically followed a "gentlemen's agreement" that public institutions would concentrate on the public funding arena and that privates would control the private sector. Increased state funding for private institutions and generally low per-capita support from the state prompted the University of Maryland to actively seek private gifts in the mid-1970s. Explaining that many public institutions delayed entering the fund-raising arena until the last two decades, Carbone (1987) said, "As more and more public dollars moved to budgets of independent and church-related colleges and universities, leaders in public higher education mounted appeals for private gifts" (p. 2).

Maryland broke a $10-million fund-raising goal for first time in 1984, and in 1987 it raised $24.6 million, including approximately $6 million in gifts-in-kind (i.e., noncash gifts) ("UM enters," 1988). In comparison, its public peer institutions in the Midwest annually raise considerably more (e.g., as stated earlier, the University of Minnesota raised $110 million and the University of Wisconsin at Madison raised $89 million in 1987–1988), primarily because a strong tradition of private education had not hampered these public institutions from raising private funds early in their history. For example, the University of Minnesota hired fund-raising consultants in the 1920s for its first capital campaign (Cutlip, 1965). According to Curti and Nash (1965), "The tradition of private giving to the University of Michigan was established relatively early in part because of the active efforts of President Angell and others to attract gifts and in part because of the relatively small number of privately supported colleges in the state" (p. 161).

According to the local newspaper article announcing Maryland's first campaign ("UM enters," 1988), "Among public institutions surveyed by the [CFAE], the University of Maryland ranked 25th in fund raising last year, behind many of its peers, including the universities of Minnesota, Wisconsin, Illinois, Michigan and Washington, Ohio State and the University of Virginia" (p. 6G). This "catch-up" position was largely responsible for the University of Maryland's decision to launch its first capital campaign. Financial need was not the primary factor because the same year that the campaign was launched the state legislature had passed long-term legislation that would significantly increase its financial support of public higher education. Rather, the necessity to "raise donor sights" (i.e., to set new levels of private support) was the reason behind the decision to make a quantum leap in fund raising through the use of a campaign.

Also, as is discussed in chapter 14 on measuring the effectiveness of fund raising, many public institutions, such as the University of Maryland, are joining their private counterparts in adopting private support totals as a measure of accountability (i.e., the more money an institution raises, the better it must be in teaching, research, and service and the more deserving it must be of state, federal, and private dollars).

As Rita Bornstein (1989)—who as vice president of development led the University of Miami's recent $517-million campaign—concluded in a report on her study of capital campaigns of $100 million or more:

> Campaigns are, in large part, public relations vehicles. A major campaign can put an institution on the map by increasing its visibility locally and nationally. An

ambitious goal, successfully achieved in less than the stated time frame, strengthens an institution's credibility by signaling that donors have great confidence in the quality of its research and teaching. (p. 17)

According to the University of Maryland's campaign literature, just 10 public universities, including Maryland, account for an aggregate goal of $2.1 billion out of the $18–$28 billion in total goals of the current campaigns referred to earlier. The 10 public universities include a number of first-time campaigns: Ohio State University and Penn State University at $350 million each; Indiana University at $203 million; the Universities of Florida, Maryland, and North Carolina at $200 million; Georgia Institute of Technology at $145 million; and Rutgers, the State University of New Jersey at $100 million (*Minds of Maryland*, 1989).

It should be noted that as of the fall of 1990, Ohio State University and the University of California at Berkeley were vying for the title of largest campaign by a public university, both having raised more than $450 million ("Give & take," 1990).

Concluding this comparison of a private and a public university, it can be generalized that public institutions, particularly those in geographic areas shared by numerous private institutions, are using capital campaigns primarily to catch up with their peer institutions (i.e., to increase levels of private support in a relatively short time). Also many public universities are adopting private support totals as measures of accountability. Such a perspective on fund raising makes dollar totals extremely important to all educational leaders and increases the pressure on institutions to use capital campaigns to raise large amounts of private support.

Private institutions, as was generalized from the case of Johns Hopkins, are entering campaign "modes" more frequently to raise larger amounts of dollars to build endowments and offset operating costs. In this era of limited growth, private colleges and universities are under greater pressure to balance the financial gap between campaign goals and institutional needs. Many of these campaigns of private institutions also are motivated by a competitiveness to raise more money than peer institutions. As Alexander (1990) stated:

> Too often, campaign goals are based on what rival institutions report they have raised, rather than on analysis of an organization's greatest needs and careful evaluation of the giving climate among its donors. A growing number of major research universities, for instance, are rushing to join the "Billion Dollar Campaign Club." (p. 26)

And critics—including some fund raisers— are starting to voice their concern over the growing number of campaigns and the reasons, other than need, behind them. According to a recent article in _The Chronicle of Higher Education_ ("Mount Holyoke," 1989):

> The proliferation of institutions involved in large campaigns, and the pressure on them to join the "$100-million club," as one fund raiser put it, have led to worries that colleges will be seen as greedy. Some say colleges are far too concerned with keeping up with their peers, regardless of what they could legitimately hope to raise. (p. A29)

Addressing members of the Association of Governing Boards of Universities and Colleges at their 1989 annual meeting, Michael Worth (cited in "Give & take," 1989a)—who as vice president of development led George Washington University's recent $75-million campaign—stated, "We're on the verge of losing our credibility" (p. A27). According to Worth, colleges are comparing themselves with other campuses and their mega-million-dollar goals, and are saying, "We have to do as well or better" (p. A27). This "one-upmanship," he said, "has created accounting problems that verge on the unethical"—problems that are discussed in relation to fund-raising ethics in chapter 15 of this book. Worth concluded by echoing Bornstein (1989) that capital campaigns are becoming merely publicity vehicles for colleges.

At a June 1989 symposium sponsored by the Indiana University Center on Philanthropy, scholars and fund raisers took universities and colleges to task for appearing greedy ("Carnegie's gospel," 1989). According to David McCann (cited in "Carnegie's gospel," 1989), director of foundation relations at Cornell University, many institutions and their fund raisers are "conveying the impression of mindless competition about higher and higher financial goals that have no apparent connection to the educational purposes of the institution" (p. 8). In a paper he presented at the 1989 symposium, McCann (whose university launched a $1.25-billion campaign in 1990) questioned whether a university planning a $1-billion campaign could avoid seeming greedy. "The problem," he said, "is that our discourse is all financial" (p. 8). McCann urged colleges and universities to look at fund raising beyond just the narrow focus of giving and getting money and charged planners of fund-raising conferences to pay less attention to techniques and more to larger questions, such as ethics.

Intense Competition for Practitioners

Given the fact that internal fund raising is a new vocation and that institutions of higher education are launching greater numbers of capital campaigns with increasingly greater goals, it is not surprising that fund-raising practitioners are in high demand. Unlike the average salary of $65,100 in 1986, which was reported at the beginning of this chapter, some chief development officers now are reporting salaries of more than $150,000, up from a high of $75,000 in 1983 ("Reagan years," 1988). According to the special report on the Reagan years, "Demand for fund raisers has skyrocketed, and salaries and perquisites have soared along with the demand" (p. 22).

A 1988 membership survey by the National Society of Fund Raising Executives (NSFRE) (1988) stated, "What we have found in the last 36 months is an inflation of salaries which has exceeded the national average, particularly at the upper income levels" (p. 24). According to the NSFRE survey, twice as many fund raisers now make more than $75,000 than did 3 years ago (i.e., 8.4% of the study's respondents make more than $75,000, as compared to only 4% in 1985). However, only 3.4% of the female fund raisers make more than $75,000, as compared with 13.8% of the males. Finally, 4.2% of all fund raisers make more than $90,000. (The last study, conducted in 1985, did not break down salary levels above $75,000.)

As mentioned in chapter 1, membership in the NSFRE has grown from 2,000 in 1979 to 10,000 in 1989, and the greatest proportion of its members, 25.6%, work at educational institutions (NSFRE, 1988). NSFRE estimates that more than half of its members are under age 45.

The Council for Advancement and Support of Education (CASE) lists a membership of 16,000, of which approximately 6,000 are engaged in fund raising for education (Carbone, 1987). Again, approximately half of these educational fund raisers are 40 years old or less, and 55% are either in their first or second year of service in their current positions (Carbone, 1987). Carbone (1987) said, "Given the difficulty in funding positions for new fund raisers, many of the people attracted to these positions are young and sometimes inexperienced workers" (p. 4).

It must be noted here that similar membership growth in other fund-raising associations demonstrates that the competition for practitioners extends beyond higher education. For example, the National Association of Hospital Development (NAHD) has doubled its membership from 1,184 in 1980 to 2,269 in 1988 ("Non-profit hospitals," 1989). A 1988 survey by that association showed that 25% of all hospital development offices were less than 3 years old and 50% were less than 7 years old.

Similar to their counterparts in education, Carbone (1989b) found in his study of fund raisers who belong to one or more of the three major associations, NSFRE, CASE, and NAHD, that "the basic profile of American fund raisers suggests a field characterized by relatively young workers" with "relatively short tenure as full-time fund raisers" (p. 26). Of Carbone's respondents, who represent all categories of charitable organizations, 55% have 5 or fewer years of experience in fund raising.

In addition to being generally young and often inexperienced, fund raisers are acquiring a reputation as transients in higher education. A recent study of 32 job categories at U.S. colleges and universities showed that the "most volatile position" was that of director of annual or planned giving, in which the turnover rate was 58% ("24-pct. turnover rate," 1989). According to that same study, a chief development position had a turnover rate of 30%, as compared to 22% for college presidents. Describing his investigation into charges of "misunderstandings" and "misinterpretation of policy" by members of his fund-raising staff in 1987, the chancellor of the University of California, Berkeley—which launched a $320-million capital campaign that year—was quoted as saying:

> Colleges staff up before capital campaigns, and there is this movable work force—sort of high-level migrant workers—who run from campaign to campaign. They are ready to produce rapidly, but they have more allegiance to doing their job than to their university of the moment. ("Misunderstandings," 1987, p. 20)

Generalizing beyond education, fund-raising consultant Douglass Alexander (1990) stated, "Currently, the average length of stay for chief development officers of [all] nonprofit organizations is approximately two to two-and-one-half years" (p. 26).

In the mid-1980s, the lead paragraph of a trade-publication article ("At $79,300 average salary," 1986) proclaimed, "An explosive growth in colleges' drives for private contributions has led to a critical shortage of top fund raisers" (p. 23). The three-page article continued:

> Advertised job vacancies have soared. Jobs are turning over at a record rate. And the roster of consulting companies specializing in identifying and recruiting top fund-raising talent is growing. Salaries and perquisites for chief fund raisers are skyrocketing. (p. 23)

"The stakes are very, very high," said John Miltner (cited in "At $79,300 average salary," 1986), vice chancellor for university advancement at the University of California at Irvine and 1987 chairman of NSFRE (p. 25). Miltner continued by saying, "You can't have someone heading your development operation who may or may not come through with the millions" (p. 25). John Schwartz (cited in "At $79,300 average salary," 1986), who was president of CAFE in 1986, added, "Today, far too many people are being given major responsibility for programs that they simply are not qualified to direct" (p. 25).

In terms of experience, the highest salaries of chief development officers in 1986 were reported by those who had been in the profession for 16 to 20 years—an average of $73,554 ("At $79,000 average salary," 1986). According to the salary survey, which was conducted by Brakeley Recruiting, the next best-paid group was comprised of fund raisers who had been in the field for 5 years or less. They earned an average of $66,828. "We hypothesize that college presidents and trustees are going outside of academe and recruiting corporate managers to fill their top fund-raising slots," said the study's director and then president of Brakeley Recruiting, Steven Ast (cited in "At $79,300 average salary," 1986, p. 25). "Such a strategy," he added, "can often backfire" (p. 25).

It is clear from the information just given that fund raising is a growing field, and that those administrators responsible for raising private dollars for charitable organizations, particularly colleges and universities, are highly paid, in great demand, move frequently from organization to organization, and often are new to the field of fund raising. Pointing out that short job tenure contributes to faculty mistrust of fund raisers, Trachtman (1987) summarized, "As a result, they are widely thought of as an itinerant fringe of the academic community, with greater loyalty to their profession than to the values of the institution" (p. 12).

Echoing this "separation" from the organizational mainstream, an anonymous fund-raising practitioner with 10 years of experience (cited in Carbone, 1989b) stated, "In general, organizations tend to have unrealistic expectations of their development professionals; tend to see them as [isolates] who should do their work without commitment from and integration with the rest of the organization" (p. 29).

More Calls for Regulation

According to the special report on the Reagan years ("Reagan years," 1988), fund raising has become more visible to the general public during the 1980s, and along with that visibility "have come mounting pressures on charitable organizations to be more accountable" (pp. 22-23). Nine states have adopted a model law drafted by the National Association of Attorneys General that requires charities and fund raisers "to report their fund-raising cost to potential donors and to take other steps to become more accountable to the public" (p. 23).

A recent article in the *NSFRE News* ("Proposed legislation," 1990) reported that 13 states enacted major new legislation governing fund raising in 1989, and that approximately 15 states have pending legislation that would affect fund-raising practice. Common features of the bills, according to the article, are tougher penalties, higher registration fees, and more detailed reporting require-ments. In addition, more than 20 states have proposed or passed laws instituting taxes for charitable organizations that have traditionally enjoyed tax-exempt status

(Lyddon, 1990). Most significant, federal budget negotiators introduced a "floor" on charitable deductions in 1990 as a means of easing the federal deficit ("Tax fallout," 1990).

As stated in the *NSFRE News* article ("Proposed legislation," 1990):

> Policymakers are taking a long, hard look at the activities of charitable organizations these days. Proposed legislation at both the federal and state levels reflects a growing concern about alleged fraudulent or unethical charitable solicitation practices, spurred by media coverage and Congressional hearings on fund-raising abuses. (p. 1)

Some of the situations involving fraudulent and unethical behavior by charitable organizations and their fund-raising practitioners are discussed in chapters 5 and 15. It is sufficient to say here that recent scandals, such as those involving television evangelists Jim and Tammy Bakker, have given rise to public outcry. For example, the Philanthropic Advisory Service of the Council of Better Business Bureaus and the National Charities Information Bureau report that public inquires rose considerably in the late 1980s ("Reagan years," 1988).

In higher education, there have been increasing reports in the media of criminal and unethical behavior related to the acceptance and use of private gifts. For example, in April 1989, the Alabama Ethics Commission found "probable cause" to believe that a fund raiser at Auburn University had violated the state's ethics law and referred the matter to the Alabama Attorney General's office ("Alabama Ethics Commission," 1989).

The commission's investigation was prompted by allegations that Jerry F. Smith, executive director for alumni and development in Auburn's alumni association, had used his position as a state employee for personal financial gain, a felony under Alabama law. Complaints from alumni that Smith had used money from a $50,000 discretionary fund to pay for baby-sitting services, maid service, and family trips helped bring to light the fact that "Smith had also received $30,000 in fees as co-executor of the will of a Georgia woman who left $1.8 million to the Auburn Foundation, the fund-raising arm of the university" (p. A31). As a result of the investigation, Smith resigned his position in May 1989 ("Chief fund raiser resigns," 1989).

The investigation into the fund-raising office at Berkeley referred to earlier in the discussion on the intense competition for practitioners was based on alleged "deviations from personnel policy, and one instance of apparent conflict of interest" ("Misunderstandings," 1987, p. 19). The subjects of the investigation, which focused on outside consulting practices, were two "experienced fund raisers with national reputations," who were hired to head Berkeley's capital campaign (p. 20).

As the result of the chancellor's investigation, one of the fund raisers left Berkeley and shortly thereafter joined Rice University and wrote a book on capital campaigns. As pointed out in the news report:

> The investigation of alleged improprieties in the Berkeley development office was conducted at a time when the regents of the University of California were developing new policies regulating fund-raising activities, largely in response to widely reported abuses at the Santa Barbara campus. ("Misunderstandings," 1987, p. 20)

The abuses referred to at Santa Barbara included the conviction of the former chancellor of that campus for embezzling $174,000 in university funds that included gifts ("Cal. regents," 1989). As Simon (1987) summarized, "With all the criticism comes a barrage of new governmental regulation" (p. 71).

The fact that these examples of questionable practices have appeared in increasing numbers in the media recently should be a reminder that philanthropy, particularly its fund-raising component, is vulnerable to government intervention. As pointed out in the article in *NSFRE News* ("Proposed legislation," 1990), over-regulation of fund-raising activities by state governments could spell disaster for small charitable organizations and would "place heavier administrative burdens (and costs) on larger organizations" (p. 1).

In addition, tax-exempt status is a privilege granted to charitable organizations by federal, state, and local governments—a privilege worth billions of dollars that can be easily rescinded, as demonstrated by current trends. For example, officials of Allegheny County, Pennsylvania filed legal papers in 1990 to remove the exemption from real estate taxes of various facilities at four Pittsburgh-area colleges and universities, including the residence of the University of Pittsburgh's president ("Pa. county," 1990). A county attorney working on a resolution to the problem said that although the colleges were "more conciliatory" during negotiations, before the legal action they had been taking a "divine right" approach to their tax-exempt status (p. A27).

The most important reminder, however, is that the charitable gift deduction, on which fund raising largely is based, is the result of federal laws—a fact that rarely is ignored by legislators. According to an article on the 1990 proposal to limit charitable deductions for taxpayers ("Fate of tax," 1990), "The government loses about $13 billion a year in revenues because of deductions taken for charitable contributions" (p. 31).

It is not surprising, therefore, that in their effort to reduce a federal deficit that is approaching $250 billion lawmakers increasingly gauge public opinion and its support of the charitable deduction. Significantly, after months of intense negotiations, a 3% "floor" on itemized deductions, including charitable deductions, for those taxpayers with incomes above $100,000 went into effect on January 1, 1991 ("3 percent floor," 1990). Although this floor is not expected to lead to major changes in the giving patterns of Americans, tax experts believe the danger lies in the fact that Congress has a history of creating floors on deductions and then raising them (e.g., the medical deduction on federal income tax was gradually increased by Congress over the last 20 years) ("Tax fallout," 1990).

Finally, as William Olcott (cited in "What lies ahead?", 1989), the editor of *Fund Raising Management,* said, "More regulation of fund-raising is coming, clearly; what form it takes is anybody's guess. But no one can say, 'the religious scandals don't affect me.' If they're looking at donations only, they're looking in the wrong place. The real issue is legislation and regulation" (p. 26).

Concluding this discussion, the characteristics of the fund-raising function at charitable organizations today, particularly more calls for regulation, lend strong support to the need for a better understanding of this function. As Bok (1982) said, "Although controversies about gifts have occurred for many decades, little effort has been made to consider the subject with care. As a result, the terrain is unfamiliar" (p. 266).

As is documented in chapter 4, fund raising has not been the focus of much scholarly research. Wallenfeldt (1983) emphasized this fact when he stated:

This area is often neglected in scholarly discussion of the organization and administration of higher education. This neglect means that a highly important influence on institutional programs and services has been overlooked . . .(and) that influence must be recognized because of its major impact on all that happens in colleges and universities. (p. 135)

According to Stanley Katz (cited in "Non-profit sector," 1985), professor of public affairs at Princeton University and a leading historian of philanthropy, it has been only in the late 1970s and 1980s that social scientists and humanists have recognized the importance of charitable organizations in American social development. Much of the reason for the scholarly interest that has emerged, according to John Simon (cited in "Non-profit sector," 1985), professor of law at Yale University and former director of the Program on Non-Profit Organizations (PONPO) at Yale, is a greater awareness in society of the dramatic increase that began about a decade ago in demands made on private philanthropy, public charities, and other nonprofit organizations.

Given the aforementioned, the most persuasive case for studying fund raising may be quite simply that we can no longer afford to tolerate the consequences of our ignorance, nor, for that matter, will our rapidly changing environment permit us to do so.

Summarizing this chapter on the problem that prompted this book, fund raising—as an ongoing set of activities managed by internal specialists—is a new organizational function at American colleges and universities, beginning only 40 years ago. This newness has two important implications for a full understanding of the function as it now exists. Up until World War II, fund-raising activities were the responsibility of first, college presidents, and then trustees, who raised money periodically from private sources as part of their senior roles as policymakers and managers of the institutions' financial resources. Although presidents and trustees are still involved in raising gifts, fund-raising programs today are managed and executed by practitioners who are largely outside the mainstream of academic life with little responsibility for setting policy or managing overall finances. This specialization and separation of the fund-raising function have resulted in a narrow focus whereby fund raising is generally measured by dollars raised rather than by what the function contributes to the overall success of the organization.

Second, fund raising—as a specialized organizational function—developed during an era of expansionism in U.S. higher education when few questions were raised about limiting an institution's academic focus. As a result, restricted gifts that were solicited and received for purposes beyond an institution's traditional programming were rarely viewed as detracting from institutional goals because missions were broadly interpreted and could generally accommodate new programs in response to donor wishes. During this era of expansionism, private support acquired its reputation as "venture capital" (Kramer, 1980), funding that provided the means to academic innovations.

Today, economic factors have led colleges and universities to the conclusion that they can no longer be all things to all people and that they must focus on selective academic goals. These institutions, however, have not reached a congruency between their fund-raising behavior and their limited resources to support selective goals. Major gifts, which are primarily restricted in purpose, are increasingly being solicited and received by institutions of higher education. A number of these gifts are for purposes that appear questionable in relation to selective academic goals.

Finally, the increasing number of major gifts and the increasing amount of fund-raising activity raises the issue of autonomy and the fact that some gifts, by purpose or conditions of the donor, can infringe on the right of an organization to control its own goals and operations. As evidenced in the preceding two chapters and as is documented further throughout this book, the solicitation and acceptance of a gift, particularly major gifts, clearly involves two-way considerations. Donors frequently expect and are given the power to determine—in varying degrees—the goals and the means of pursuing the goals of charitable organizations, including colleges and universities. As Lord (1983) stated, "The fact is that people give in order to *get*. They don't want to feel that they are 'giving away' their money. They want to feel that they are investing it, and getting something in return" (p. 5). In short, fund raising is a new organizational function that solicits and accepts gifts that may not support pre-determined organizational goals and that may, in fact, lead to a loss of organizational autonomy.

Given these conclusions and the important problem they address, the book steps back from its focus on higher education and turns to current perspectives of fund raising for all charitable organizations in order to analyze why this problem remains unresolved. Specifically, the three chapters in Part I provide a critical analysis of definitions, research, and some of the major assumptions on which current perspectives are based.

PART I

CURRENT PERSPECTIVES OF FUND RAISING: CONFUSING DEFINITIONS, SPORADIC RESEARCH, AND MYTHS

Part I examines current explanations of fund raising for all charitable organizations. This section consists of three chapters. Chapter 3 examines current definitions and concludes that a lack of precise definitions, specifically ones that account for differences in types of recipient organizations and types of gifts, have contributed to inappropriate generalizations about philanthropy and confusion about the fund-raising function. Similarly, chapter 4 concludes that research on fund raising is sparse and generally of poor quality; it receives little scholarly attention as a serious subject.

In chapter 5, four major "myths" of fund raising are identified and critically analyzed: (a) the myth of unrestricted gifts, (b) the myth of a broad base of donors, (c) the myth of the volunteer solicitor, and (d) the myth of the invisible fund raiser. In addition, this chapter analyzes the perspectives of fund raising as a sales or marketing function and strongly criticizes such perspectives as inappropriate for an understanding of an organizational behavior dealing with donor motivations that encompass more than the *quid pro quo* of the marketplace.

By critically analyzing definitions related to fund raising, previous research on fund rasing, and some of the major assumptions on which fund-raising principles are based, this section concludes that current perspectives are flawed and rejects them as being inadequate for a full understanding of the organizational behavior of fund raising.

_____Chapter 3

A Critical Analysis of Definitions
Related to Fund Raising

Chapter 3 begins Part I by answering the research question: How do current definitions confuse our understanding of fund raising? After examining definitions about and related to the function, this chapter concludes that a lack of clarity, misinterpretations, and generalizations have created confusion in the literature and have distorted our understanding of the fund-raising function. Building on the earlier discussion of Grunig and Hunt's (1984) definition in chapter 1, this chapter also examines definitions of public relations, which reveals an incongruency between those definitions currently advanced by public relations scholars and those commonly held by fund-raising practitioners.

FROM CHARITY TO PHILANTHROPY

This chapter begins by critically analyzing current definitions about fund raising, including definitions of the function itself, definitions of the process, and definitions of gifts. Through this analysis, an overview is provided of the set of activities known as fund raising, and operational definitions that are critical to later discussions are presented. The second half of this section is devoted to a discussion of the related concepts of charity and philanthropy and to a discussion of varying definitions of public relations.

Fund Raising

There is no consensus on any one definition of fund raising. For the purposes of this book, *fund raising* is defined as the purposive process of soliciting and accepting monetary gifts from individuals, corporations, and foundations by a charitable organization, especially as managed for the organization by fund-raising specialists. Although closely related to sponsored research grants (i.e., those contractual grants primarily from government and corporations that underwrite specific research projects and include overhead costs), fund raising, as used here, does not include this form of financial support. The term *fund raising* is used rather than development because the theory developed in this book applies to all organizations that raise funds and is not limited to educational institutions or other organizations that prefer the term *development*.

As discussed in chapter 1, the fund-raising function is frequently referred to as development in some charitable organizations, particularly at colleges and universities. It should be noted here that fund raisers for nonprofit hospitals also prefer to be called development officers; for example, the professional association to which 80% of these practitioners belong is the National Association for Hospital Development (NAHD) ("Non-profit hospitals," 1989). In addition, fund raisers for arts, culture, and humanities organizations, such as museums, and for human service organizations, such as the United Way, frequently adopt development to describe their function.

Within institutions of higher education, fund raising, alumni relations, public relations, publications, and government relations are frequently structured under the umbrella term of *institutional advancement*, which was conceived and is endorsed by the major professional association of practitioners in these positions, the Council for Advancement and Support of Education (CASE) (Carbone, 1987). According to Rowland (1983), "Institutional advancement . . . is not one activity but a collection of activities designed to cultivate support by increasing constituencies' understanding of institutional goals and missions" (p. iii). In the preface to his earlier book, *Handbook of Institutional Advancement*, Rowland's (1977) definition has a slight, but important difference. He said that rather than "cultivating support" (which emphasizes fund raising), an institutional advancement program is undertaken by an institution to develop understanding and support from all its publics for its educational needs. This subtle difference is important to the purpose of this book in that by recognizing that colleges and universities have needs other than financial ones, a case can be made that fund raising is a specialization of public relations.

Carbone (1986) defined fund raising in educational institutions as "a codeword for a much larger set of concepts, programs and activities associated with . . . translating private resources into the public good" (p. 20). According to Carbone, people who work in fund raising are those who not only raise funds, but also those who "write and edit publications, handle institutional relations, direct alumni and parent programs, manage institutional foundations, or govern and administer or teach in educational institutions" (p. 20). In a later work on fund-raising practitioners, Carbone (1987) again inverted fund raising and institutional advancement by encompassing public relations and other advancement functions under the "umbrella" of fund raising. He said that "the titles these fund raisers hold vary greatly," but that designations such as development, public affairs, and institutional relations are "commonly used to identify fund raisers" (p. 1).

During a personal conversation in January 1989, Carbone admitted that he has a tendency to "forget" about nonfund-raising functions when addressing the field of institutional advancement. He said that public relations practitioners, such as Virginia Carter Smith, the executive vice president of CASE, often remind him that his concentration on fund raising excludes the other functions.

In summary, two of the more prominent educators who have studied fund raising for colleges and universities adopt the concept of institutional advancement in their definitions of fund raising and define all functions incorporated under that term as having the common purpose of cultivating support, with an emphasis on private support (i.e., gifts). Although one educator previously had defined the purpose of institutional advancement more broadly as developing understanding and support, his more recent definition places increased emphasis on the acquisition of gifts as the purpose for all functions. This emphasis on private financial support in accepted definitions creates confusion about the fund-raising function (e.g., is it an organizational function supported by the activities of subfunctions, such as public relations, or is it one element of a broader function?).

Supporting the former viewpoint, the consulting firm of Gonser Gerber Tinker Stuhr (1986) stated, "Public relations should be a functional part of the development department" (p. 2). Saying that public relations needs to be "under the development umbrella," this national public relations and fund-raising consulting firm for colleges and universities defined the preferred organization of the institutional advancement office by stating, "The public relations director should be part of the development team and report to the chief development officer" (p. 2). Yet, Dittman (1981), in his article on the organization of institutional advancement offices, warned, "It is a distinct error to plan only in terms of raising money" (p. 228).

Moving beyond education, Panas (1984) defined fund raising as the "magnificent business of helping others undertake consequential acts of kindness and generosity" (p. 169). It is recalled from chapter 1 that the National Society of Fund Raising Executives (NSFRE) Institute (1986) defined fund raising simply as "the seeking of gifts from various sources as conducted by 501(c)(3) organizations" (p. 40). The significance of the 501(c)(3) designation by the NSFRE Institute is clarified in the discussion on types of nonprofit organizations later in this chapter. For now, it is important to emphasize that the specific focus of the NSFRE Institute's definition, unlike Carbone's (1986) definition for educational fund raising, does not include programs and activities outside of seeking gifts.

Stressing the importance of a basic knowledge of philanthropy, the late Maurice Gurin (1989) said that such knowledge is needed by fund raisers "for guidance in advising and assisting organizations in seeking and accepting gift support" (p. i). Although not necessarily offered as such, Gurin's statement provides a definition of fund raising that is similar to many found in the fund-raising and philanthropy literature (i.e., fund raising is advising and assisting organizations in seeking and accepting gift support). It is critical, therefore, to note that this definition de-emphasizes solicitation, or the asking for gifts, by fund-raising practitioners. The definition is a slanted one in that it defines fund raising as practiced by external fund-raising consultants who, as described in chapter 2, do not solicit gifts.

The definition provided by Gurin is incorporated in his introduction to Gurin and Van Til's (1989) suggested text for a session on philanthropy in fund-raising courses. Although Van Til is an associate professor of urban studies and public policy at Rutgers University, Gurin was a fund-raising consultant, leading one to assume that this slanted definition in Gurin's introduction is largely a result of his external perspective (Independent Sector, 1988; AAFRC Trust for Philanthropy, 1988a). As discussed in chapter 5 on myths and misinterpretation, the perspective of external, fund-raising consultants is embedded in the fund-raising literature, which has supported the perpetuation of myths about the fund-raising function. Gurin's (1989) definition, for example, deals only with the "advising and assisting" components of the fund raiser's role, because fund-raising consultants limit their role to advice and assistance (i.e., they do not solicit gifts on behalf of a charitable organization).

In-house fund raisers, on the other hand, are usually involved in the solicitation of gifts. As executors of fund-raising programs, internal practitioners ask for private money through various mass and interpersonal communications (e.g., annual, lower level gifts are usually solicited through mass mailings written by the fund raiser and donors are generally asked for major gifts during face-to-face meetings that the fund raiser often participates in alone, or as a member of a solicitation team). Yet, a time-worn maxim of fund raising that is provided by another fund-raising consultant and one that is repeated throughout the literature denies the solicitation role of the in-house fund raiser. Howe (1985) defined successful fund raising as "selecting the right person to ask the right person, in the right way, for the right amount, for the right reason, at the right time" (pp. 19-20). Commenting on the mystery of this formula for success, fund-raising consultant and writer Lord (1983) compared it to the old adage that the best way to clean up in the stock market is to "only buy stocks that are going up" (p. 78).

It can be concluded from this discussion that Gurin's (1989) definition of fund raising—and others similar to it—are slanted by the perspective of consultants because it does not incorporate a critical component of the fund-raising function as practiced by in-house practitioners. Such slanted definitions have led to confusion about the fund-raising function (e.g., is fund raising primarily a nonsolicitation function, or is the fund-raising practitioner actively involved in the two-way exchange of considerations, as highlighted in chapter 2?).

Obviously, such definitions are inadequate for the purposes of this book because the subject of analysis is the fund-raising behavior of charitable organizations, and as is documented in chapter 5, that behavior includes the solicitation of both annual and major gifts by internal practitioners. It should be clarified at this point that the definition of fund raising given at the beginning of this chapter incorporates the solicitation of gifts by practitioners (i.e., as managers of a charitable organization's fund-raising process, fund-raising specialists often execute activities themselves, although sometimes they will assign solicitation activities to other staff and/or volunteers).

Unlike definitions of fund raising, there seems to be a widely held consensus on the components of the fund-raising process. As touched on in chapter 1, the generally accepted process of fund raising consists of four steps: research, cultivation, solicitation, and recognition. It will be recalled, for example, that Wood (1989) described major gift solicitation as 25% research, 60% cultivation, 5% solicitation, and 10% recognition. A full discussion of the fund-raising process and agreement among practitioners is given in chapter 11.

Turning now to gifts, this chapter defines charitable contributions on two dimensions: purpose and level. As referred to periodically throughout the preceding pages, gifts may be unrestricted in purpose, or restricted as to their use. A full discussion of this distinction is delayed until chapter 5 on myths and misinterpretation, but it is important to note here that donors are free to restrict the use of their gifts by choosing particular areas to support and/or by placing conditions on the gift. Gifts that have no conditions and are given without stipulation as to their use are unrestricted (i.e., the recipient organization is free to use unrestricted gifts in any way it sees fit). Unrestricted gifts are generally lower level gifts in terms of monetary value, whereas restricted gifts are generally of greater value. In addition, unrestricted gifts are usually generated through "annual giving programs" from a broad base of donors and are, therefore, frequently used synonymously with annual gifts. Restricted gifts are usually generated through "major gifts programs" from a small, selective group of donors and are frequently used synonymously with major gifts.

As introduced earlier in chapter 2, the two primary types of gifts (i.e., annual and major, or capital), can be historically traced to the colonial era. Pray (1981) said that America's early colleges raised capital gifts from a few wealthy benefactors and annual gifts from many donors, including church members, community residents, or friends. Annual gifts have historically been used for current operating expenses of charitable organizations, whereas capital gifts were originally intended for capital projects, such as new buildings.

The definition of capital gifts, however, has been expanded through use to include gifts to endowment (i.e., gifts that are invested to generate income, which is available for spending in perpetuity). According to the National Society of Fund Raising Executives (NSFRE) Institute's (1986) *Glossary of Fund-Raising Terms*, capital gifts are "funds provided for buildings, including construction and equipment, endowment and scholarship" (p. 16). Since 1980, capital gifts have been further redefined as *major* gifts, a term that relates primarily to the size of the gift, not to its use. As a result of inflation and the escalation of levels of giving, as demonstrated in chapter 2, major gifts are currently defined as gifts of $100,000, or more, although just a few years ago $10,000 was considered the floor of major gifts (Winship, 1984). Because of their great monetary value (i.e., their gift level), major gifts are generally restricted in purpose by their donors (Dittman, 1981). This is not to say that major gifts are never given for unrestricted use, only that such instances are infrequent.

In summary, the two dimensions of purpose and level provide a two-way typology of gifts: unrestricted lower level gifts, restricted lower level gifts; unrestricted major gifts, and restricted major gifts. A critical point, however, is that, generally, the majority of gifts to charitable organizations fall into only two of the four categories: unrestricted lower level gifts and restricted major gifts (i.e., lower level gifts given on a regular basis are primarily unrestricted in their use, whereas larger gifts given periodically are primarily restricted as to how they can be used).

This parsimonious typology of gifts on the two dimensions of purpose and level is supported by the fund-raising literature; however, other "types" of gifts, which can be incorporated into the typology just given, are scattered throughout the literature, creating definitional confusion. For example, the term *designated* gifts is frequently used to refer to unrestricted, annual gifts designated for use by a particular subunit of a charitable organization. Although this type of gift is restricted in that it must be allocated to the designated recipient, it is unrestricted in how it is used by that recipient. From the organizational level, however, designated gifts are restricted in nature and are referred to as such in this book.

Another type of gift that frequently appears in the literature is *planned*, or *deferred*, gifts." These gifts are major gifts that may be restricted or unrestricted in purpose, but that are commonly considered distinct because they are not outright gifts (i.e., they are gifts whose benefits are deferred through legal and financial instruments, such as wills and insurance policies, until the death of the donor, or whose benefits are increased through tax-saving vehicles, such as gift annuities and pooled income funds). The NSFRE Institute (1986) defined a planned or deferred gift as "a commitment or gift established during the donor's lifetime, but whose principal benefits usually do not accrue to the charitable recipient until some future time, often after the donor's death" (p. 28).

Dittman (1981) said, "Properly or not, contributions are classified in three ways: 1) annual giving for current operating purposes, 2) capital giving (for convenience these are usually gifts of $10 thousand and more) for buildings, facilities, and endowment, and 3) deferred or planned giving for either annual or capital purposes" (p. 229). Dittman's three classifications of gifts supports the two-dimensional typology defined here in that annual giving generates unrestricted gifts that can be used by the recipient organization as it sees fit to meet any costs incurred in operating the organization, and capital giving— which can be redefined as major giving at a higher monetary value than Dittman's 1981 level—generates gifts restricted in purpose to facilities and endowment. Dittman's third classification can be redefined as major unrestricted or major restricted gifts because Winship (1984) said, "A major gift relates primarily to size, not from whom it comes, for what it will be used, or whether *outright or deferred*" (p. 1; italics added).

Another example from the fund-raising literature demonstrates support for the two-way typology of gifts and also shows how fund raising is plagued by definitional confusion. In his article on prerequisites for successful fund raising, Pickett (1981) gave "four essential means of fund raising: annual giving, capital giving, deferred giving, and prospect research" (p. 12). According to Pickett, annual giving is the continual solicitation of lower level gifts from a broad base of donors for the purpose of meeting annual operating costs. It can be added that its primary solicitation tools are brochures, newsletters, direct mail, phonathons, and special events (i.e., communication techniques that lend themselves to mass audiences). Capital giving and deferred giving, according to Pickett (1981), are the solicitation of large gifts from a small group of donors. It can be added that the solicitation tools generally used in major giving programs are written proposals, letters, phone calls and face-to-face meetings (i.e., interpersonal communication techniques). Unlike capital giving, the prospects for deferred or planned gifts are solely individuals rather than all three sources of gifts (i.e., foundations, corporations, and individuals).

In support of the typology just given, Pickett (1981) redefined capital gifts as major restricted gifts when he said that capital giving "should be expanded from simply including new capital construction to include renovation, endowment, and special projects at significant cost levels" (p. 13). Differentiating between annual and capital, or major, giving, Pickett said (1981), "Giving for annual operations depends on many small gifts, while capital giving relies on fewer but larger gifts" (p. 13). As was pointed out earlier, deferred or planned giving can be incorporated within the two-way typology as unrestricted and restricted major gifts.

Pickett's (1981) use of prospect research, however, does not fit within the typology of gifts because, as mentioned earlier, it is a step in the process of fund raising. Prospect research is commonly viewed by practitioners as the systematic collection of information that may be useful in identifying prospective donors (i.e., those with a higher probability for giving major gifts) and in shaping communication with the prospective donor ("Prospecting for," 1988). By including this set of activities within a description of programs segmented by types of gifts, Pickett adds to the definitional confusion of the fund-raising literature.

From this discussion it can be concluded that gifts to charitable organizations consist essentially of annual gifts or major gifts, which are unrestricted or restricted in purpose, and that the two-dimensional typology captures other types of gifts mentioned in the literature (e.g., planned gifts are unrestricted or restricted major gifts). As the fund-raising literature does not offer concise definitions, this clarification of gifts is important because of the primarily restricted nature of major gifts and the current emphasis on soliciting and accepting such gifts.

For example, Winship (1984) summarized the results of his study, *The Quest for Major Gifts,* by saying, "Whatever lack of uniformity of definition the survey discloses, perhaps the significant thing is that virtually all of the respondent institutions indeed are in the business of seeking major gifts, increasingly and continuously so" (p. 1). Expressing a commonly held view of fund raisers today,

A. H. Edwards (1989), the former vice president for institutional advancement at the University of Maryland, College Park, said:

> Those $25-a-year donors are wonderful . . . . But let's be honest with ourselves. A major gift program can bring in more money in a year than the annual fund can bring in in a decade. And the bigger dollars are more important. (p. 72)

As summarized by Pickett (1981), "Productive fund-raising programs should always be focused on the major givers, and a capital funding effort ensures this focus" (p. 13).

Finally, in his description of the process for raising major gifts, Wood (1989) used a similar dichotomy of gift levels to explain the differences between donors of annual and major gifts. Comparing donor levels within the context of a corporate marketplace, Wood said, "A customer buying a product is much like a direct mail or mass solicitation donor making a gift" (p. 1). In contrast, Wood compared a major donor to a major investor in a corporation, saying that such a person is "not just a casual customer who buys the product, but someone who becomes an insider (partner/owner)" (p. 1).

The difference in the relationships between a charitable organization and these two types of donors (i.e., donors of lower level annual gifts and donors of major gifts) is critical to later discussions on the fund-raising function and organizational autonomy.

Charity and Philanthropy

Carbone (1986), said fund raising means—in ascending order of magnitude—everything associated with solicitation, to development, to institutional advancement, to philanthropy. Fund raising and philanthropy are often used interchangeably in the fund-raising literature. As Gurin (1989) pointed out, there is "an assumption that fund raising can be equated with philanthropy" (p. i).

In addition, the terms *charity* and *philanthropy* are used interchangeably, although numerous scholars have defined these terms differently. For example, the NSFRE Institute (1986) defined charity as "an organization, institution, or advocacy group that seeks philanthropic support" (p. 19), whereas it defined philanthropy as "all voluntary giving, voluntary getting, voluntary service, and voluntary association and initiative" (p. 75). The confusion that has resulted from this lack of clarification has hampered a full understanding of the fund-raising function.

Much like the definition provided by Boulding (1973) at the beginning of chapter 2 (i.e., gifts are the "voluntary, one-way transfer of exchangeables"), Johnson (1973) defined charity as the "'voluntary' transfer of income or goods

. . . from one individual to another or to an intermediary agency" (pp. 84-85). Payton (1988a), who is described as "the leading thinker in U.S. philanthropy today" (Worth, 1989, p. 43), defined philanthropy as "three related activities: voluntary service, voluntary association, and voluntary giving for public purposes" (p. 1). Both of these definitions would seem to fit equally well with charity or philanthropy.

According to *Webster's Seventh New Collegiate Dictionary* (1967), philanthropy is "a philanthropic act or gift or an organization distributing or supported by philanthropic funds" (p. 634). This definition is actually composed of four distinct definitions of philanthropy: (a) philanthropic acts, (b) philanthropic gifts, (c) organizations that distribute philanthropic funds, and (d) organizations that are supported by philanthropic funds. In contradiction of such a broad definition, the entire 30 volumes of the *Encyclopædia Britannica* (1979) contain only slightly more than one column of one page on philanthropy, and that entry is confined to only one type of organization that distributes philanthropic funds. A *philanthropic foundation* is defined as a "legal and social instrument for applying private wealth to public purposes" (Encyclopædia Britannica, 1979, p. 937). This definition underlines the narrow focus of the encyclopedia's entry, which is primarily concerned with the very large foundations created in the early 1900s by the gargantuan fortunes of Carnegie, the Rockefellers and the Fords. Payton (1987) commented on this superficial treatment of philanthropy in the *Encyclopædia Britannica*, saying that as previous editions had devoted significantly more space to it, the small entry was symbolic of a greater disinterest.

Attempting to explain the difference between charity and philanthropy, Cutlip (1965) said that the word, "charity," was replaced by "philanthropy" after World War I. Payton (1987) somewhat agreed with Cutlip, saying, "Philanthropy has succeeded charity as the embracing term, although usage remains very flexible" (p. 22). Payton said, however, that there are two historical dimensions to what he called the philanthropic tradition. The first, charity, is rooted in religion, whereas the second, philanthropy, "comes from classical Greece and has to do with rational, usually large-scale efforts to improve the quality of life in the community" (p. 8). Summarizing, Payton said, "On the one hand, then, the charitable-religious, and on the other, the philanthropic-secular; the impulsive and personal and direct act of mercy contrasted with the reflective, prudent, planned determination to build a better community" (p. 8).

Yet, Frantzreb (cited in Panas, 1984), who is known for his writings on the philosophy of fund raising, said, "The act of philanthropy is a spiritual act—an act of love expressed for one's fellow man" (p. 106). Saying that "philanthropy" comes from two Greek words meaning "love of man," Frantzreb said that people who give away their assets or income buy pride in identification, satisfaction, and accomplishment, and in promise for the future. In what seems on the surface to be a contradiction to his definition of philanthropy as prudent and planned actions to build a better community, Payton (1987), said that "Philanthropy owes its credibility to its altruistic imperative—to remain philanthropic it must by definition give first place to the other rather than to the self" (p. 39).

Boorstin (1963/1983) claimed that in America, private gifts have shifted from charity to philanthropy, or from conscience to community. In line with this definition of private giving, Boorstin declared Benjamin Franklin as the patron saint of American philanthropy because of the great impact he had on organizations in our society.

In their book on fund-raising research, which is discussed in chapter 4, Brittingham and Pezzullo (1990) said that one of the "four notable changes in trends in fund raising" is that "the notion of *charity* has been replaced with *philanthropy*; and theories of donors' behavior have changed accordingly" (p. iii). Elaborating, the authors said, "The emphasis, particularly in fund raising from other than alumni, is on investment or the value of the gift in *noncharitable* terms" (p. 13; italics added).

Weaver (1967/1983), however, stressed that there is a difference between the Judeo-Christian tradition of charity and the Greek and Roman tradition of enhancing the community through gifts (i.e., philanthropy) and that both are still present in our society. Others argue that government has taken over the role of charity in American society, leaving philanthropy to private organizations and individuals. A. R. Hands (cited in O'Connell, 1987), who wrote *Charities and Social Aid in Greece and Rome*, said that in modern times, the role of charity (i.e., direct intervention and assistance of human suffering) falls primarily to government, whereas philanthropy, which he defined as protection or prevention of human misery, is the responsibility of private sources of funding.

Most recently, eight former chapter presidents of NSFRE attempted to define philanthropy at the third National Philanthropy Day luncheon in New York City on November 15, 1988. Their individual definitions ranged from "a secular religion," to "a self-serving, ego-gratifying activity, derived from the survival instinct," to "voluntary service and giving to reform society, alleviate the conditions of the needy, and advance the interests of all classes" ("Philanthropy is," 1988, pp. 1-2). For the purposes of this book, one of the more interesting definitions offered at that event was a "contrarian" view provided by Stephen Wertheimer, who said:

> Philanthropy in America is a special market for the exchange of goods and services within the profit-making free enterprise system. . . . Through philanthropy, the

country determines in large measure the agenda on critical issues of social and
public policy. (p. 2)

According to Gurin (cited in "Philanthropy is," 1988), originator of the program
and author of the definition of fund raising given earlier in this chapter, arriving
at a generally accepted, comprehensive definition of philanthropy is a "near
impossibility" (p. 2).

In summary, definitions of charity and philanthropy have contributed to the
confusion surrounding the fund-raising function. Although some practitioners
and scholars use the two words interchangeably (e.g., Frantzreb, cited in Panas,
1984) others perceive philanthropy as an evolutionary outcome of the earlier
actions known as charity, particularly in democratic societies such as the United
States. Some would argue that charity, as defined by its Judeo-Christian origins
in the Old Testament, is currently practiced more by government than by private
organizations or individuals. Finally, there is little consensus on what actually
constitutes a philanthropic or charitable act (i.e., Is a charitable act based
primarily on altruistic motives, whereas a philanthropic act consists of a greater
degree of self-interest?).

As is discussed shortly, much of this lack of clarity is attributable to the
different types of organizations that are defined as charities by the Internal
Revenue Service (IRS).   Payton (1988b) defined five types of charitable
organizations: religion, education, health, arts, and welfare. He further reduced
these five types to two purposes by saying, "Purposes can be roughly aggregated
into two larger ideas: acts of mercy to relieve suffering, most commonly called
charity . . . and acts of community to enhance the quality of life and to insure
a better future—what is commonly called philanthropy" (p. 1).   Unfortunately,
Payton did not assign his ideas on charity and philanthropy to the five types,
which differ only slightly from the six categories of charitable organizations, as
defined by the American Association of Fund-Raising Counsel (AAFRC) Trust,
which were presented earlier in chapter 1.

To differentiate between charitable organizations and to clarify the role of
altruism in fund raising today, this chapter presents a typology of organizations
for which fund raisers currently solicit and accept gifts. Before doing so,
however, this section turns to public relations and some varying definitions of
that function.

Public Relations

In addition to briefly examining definitions of public relations, the following
discussion provides a historical perspective that helps explain why current

definitions of that function frequently conflict with the views commonly held by fund-raising practitioners and scholars.

As stated in chapter 1, this book uses the definition of public relations formulated by Grunig and first offered in Grunig and Hunt (1984): "Public relations is the management of communication between an organization and its publics" (p. 6). This definition stresses the concept of _managing_ communication programs and the existence of numerous constituencies with which that function must be concerned—two points that are critical to reorienting the fund-raising function to the public relations paradigm.

It will be recalled from chapter 1, that Cutlip (1965) identified _organization_ and _communication_ as the two separate elements important to fund raising, but said that public relations' role is historically one of communication, whereas fund raising is concerned primarily with organizing or managing programs. Pearson (1989), however, said:

> Virtually all definitions of public relations have something in common. Wherever the words public relations are defined or described in current textbooks and journals, two other words or ideas are almost always present with it. These are the ideas of management and of communication. Crable and Vibbert (1986) for instance, call their textbook _Public Relations as Communication Management._ (p. 8)

Pearson (1989) included Grunig and Hunt's (1984) definition within those sharing the two common elements of management and communication, calling it "one of the most parsimonious definitions of public relations" (p. 8). According to Pearson, the emphasis given to management in all of these definitions "underscores the idea that communication activities should be carried out in a thoughtful and planned manner" (p. 9). Supporting this aspect of current definitions, he described the public relations process, which includes research, planning programs, communicating, and evaluation. As discussed in chapter 11 on fund raising as a specialization of public relations, this process of "managing" communication on behalf of an organization is strikingly similar to the fund-raising process mentioned earlier in this chapter.

Pearson (1989) also pointed out that the stress on management in current definitions of public relations "reflects the practitioner's belief that what he or she does contributes to organizational management in the broadest sense, that is, in the articulation of overall organizational philosophy and policies" (p. 10). Given this emphasis on management, it is important to point out, as Pearson did, that "public relations remains quintessentially communication" (p. 10).

Grunig and Hunt (1984) defend their definition as being descriptive, as opposed to a normative definition of what public relations should be. It would be helpful, therefore, to compare their definition to other definitions of public relations. In 1964, Drucker said, "To the general public, public relations means publicity. . . . And the term has thus acquired a rather unfavorable connotation of ballyhoo, press agentry, propaganda, and white washing" (p. 38). After reviewing more than 30 definitions of public relations, the 1987 Symposium report of the Public Relations Society of America's (PRSA) Special Committee on Terminology (Lesly, Budd, Cutlip, Lerbinger, & Pires, 1987) endorsed the following two definitions, which were originally proposed by the 1981 PRSA Task Force on the Stature and Role of Public Relations:

1. Public relations helps an organization and its publics adapt mutually to each other; and

2. Public relations is an organization's efforts to win the cooperation of groups of people. (p.10)

The 1987 Special Committee recommended "that one of these [definitions] be perpetuated through general use" (p. 10).

Obviously all three of these definitions are quite different from each other and from the one offered by Grunig and Hunt (1984). Although the definition offered by Drucker (1964) of public relations as publicity can be viewed as a descriptive definition, it can also be interpreted as a normative theory if publicity is considered the objective of public relations. Those recommended by PRSA (Lesly et al., 1987) are normative in that they define the objectives of what public relations should accomplish (i.e., adapt mutually or win cooperation). Importantly, the differences are largely due to how public relations has been practiced historically. As discussed in chapter 13 on historical models of fund raising, the differences in these three definitions can be explained by Grunig's (1984) four models of public relations (i.e., Drucker's definition, with its emphasis on propaganda, fits Grunig's press agentry model, which is the oldest of the four models, whereas the first of the PRSA definitions, with its emphasis on mutual adaptation, fits Grunig's two-way symmetric model of public relations, which is the newest of the four models). The second PRSA definition, with its emphasis on winning cooperation, falls within the two-way asymmetric model. In summary, differences in defining public relations are attributable to the different ways public relations has been and is still practiced today.

Public relations is an infant scholarly field, according to Grunig and Hunt (1984), although it has been practiced for at least 100 years and some people believe for thousands. It grew from the academic area of mass communication, which was an outgrowth of the behavioral sciences. As Botan and Hazelton (1989) stated, "Public relations can best be understood as a specialized kind of communication" (p. xiii). Researchers have utilized theories from communication, sociology, psychology, economics, and cultural anthropology, among others, to form a new paradigm of public relations that addresses the communication activities of organizations (Grunig, in preparation). This field has only been an active source of inquiry for the last 20 years and, as demonstrated here, is still struggling with the basics of definition.

According to Grunig (in preparation), public relations is often described by other terms, including *business communication* and *public affairs*, "because of the negative connotations of 'public relations'." Regardless of their descriptive titles, however, public relations practitioners "counsel managers, manage communication programs, write and edit, design publications, produce video-tapes, do research, communicate interpersonally, and perform many similar tasks" (Grunig, in preparation).

Many of these public relations activities can be related to fund-raising activities. In fact, the firm of Gonser Gerber Tinker Stuhr (1986) stated, "If public relations is separated from development what happens is that the development department will have to add staff to communicate and this leads to duplication and multiplication of staff" (p. 2).

Echoing Cutlip's (1965) description given earlier and urging that public relations be placed under the organizational umbrella of fund raising, Gonser Gerber Tinker Stuhr (1986) stated: "An effective public relations program is crucial to the success of the development efforts of college and universities. It is the foundation on which are based your college's efforts to obtain understand-ing and support" (p. 1).

This book contends that theoretical and operational links between fund raising and public relations have been ignored in previous research because fund-raising scholars and practitioners have utilized definitions of public relations that differ from those more current definitions that incorporate an element of management. The utilization of these narrower definitions has been supported by the fact that public relations is a relatively new area of scholarly study. In addition, the historical models of public relations, particularly the earliest model of press agentry, have misled fund-raising practitioners and scholars into believing that the purpose of public relations is to serve as a support function for fund raising. As is demonstrated in chapter 11, many public relations practitioners and scholars also view public relations as a support function for fund raising.

Turning now to the organizations that have a fund-raising function for generating revenue through tax-deductible gifts, chapter 3 provides evidence that the failure to differentiate among different types of nonprofit organizations has contributed to misconceptions about donor motivation and confusion about fund raising.

A TYPOLOGY OF NONPROFIT ORGANIZATIONS

The nonprofit, or third sector as described by the philanthropy literature, is the smallest of the three economic sectors (i.e., business, government, and nonprofit). Yet, there are approximately 958,000 nonprofit organizations in the United States, according to 1980–1983 data based on filing of IRS 990 Forms (Independent Sector, 1988). The majority of these nonprofit organizations are charitable organizations, or those tax exempt organizations to which donor contributions are tax deductible. According to Rudney (1987), charitable organizations "account for 93 percent of all nonprofit employment, 91 percent of all nonprofit expenditures, and 94 percent of all nonprofit production" (p. 55).

The nonprofit sector, according to Rudney (1987), employed 7 million full- and part-time workers in 1982, and in 1980, it "purchased goods and services amounting to $142.2 billion" (p. 56). Of those expenditures, charitable organizations accounted for $129 billion, "a sum," according to Rudney, "exceeding the total budget of any nation in the world except the United States, France, West Germany, the United Kingdom, Japan, and probably China and the Soviet Union" (p. 56).

According to Simon (1987), "The sprawling and unruly collection of animals that populate the nonprofit world—from churches to civil rights groups to garden clubs to the National Council on Philanthropy (NCOP)—makes this field hard to grasp and study all at once" (p. 69). For that reason, Simon purposely avoided "all definitional and typological talk" (p. 68) in his study on research on philanthropy. In contrast, this section develops a typology of nonprofit organizations that is helpful in understanding the fund-raising function.

The Complicated Third Sector

Before presenting that typology, however, the section first examines the fund-raising, philanthropy, and public relations literature to demonstrate how the lack of definitions and the generalizations about nonprofit organizations have led to confusion, which has hampered a full understanding of fund raising. Illustrating this confusion, Simon (1987) described the findings of a marketing survey of American households that was recently conducted to find out what people think the differences are between nonprofit and for-profit organizations. According to Simon, 66% of that survey's respondents put Yale University in the for-profit category and 75% did not correctly identify Blue Cross as a nonprofit organization. As Jencks (1987) explained, the beneficiaries of most charitable contributions "are seldom indigent and are often quite affluent" (p. 322).

Summarizing the underlying reason for most of the confusion about charitable organizations, Jencks (1987) stated:

> The diversity of the activities to which Americans contribute poses a terminological problem. Research on giving has recently been dominated by economists, almost all of whom label philanthropic gifts as "charity." Although this term has a pleasing simplicity, it is misleading. To most people—including economists— "charity" conjures up images of the rich helping the poor: medieval lords endowing almshouses, John D. Rockefeller giving away dimes, or the average citizen tossing money in the Salvation Army kettle at Christmas. (p. 322)

Contrary to conventional wisdom, nonprofit organizations are not prohibited by law from making a profit, only from distributing their profit to shareholders and owners (i.e., "the nondistribution constraint;" Hansmann, 1987, p. 27). In fact, many nonprofit organizations operate profit-making programs and frequently accumulate profits each year, as evidenced by their financial accounts and endowments. A reason for the misinterpretation of Yale University as a for-profit organization by the survey respondents mentioned here may be that Yale has an endowment of more than $2 billion, some of which consists of accumulated profits from fund-raising and other programs ("Almanac," 1990).

Also contrary to conventional wisdom, all nonprofit organizations are not charitable organizations (i.e., the two terms should not be used synonymously). Charitable organizations, as is discussed in more detail shortly, are a classification of nonprofit organizations that have been granted 501(c)(3) charitable status by the Bureau of Internal Revenue. Unfortunately, as pointed out by Payton (1987), the use of the term _charity_ by the IRS adds to the confusion between what constitutes charitable and philanthropic acts.

Furthermore, nonprofit organizations that are not designated as charitable organizations by the IRS are still in fact "tax-exempt" organizations because they usually are exempted from paying federal and state income taxes. They are not charitable organizations, however, because money given to them is not deductible from the income taxes _of the provider of the funds._ Rudney (1987) defined the "philanthropic sector" within the nonprofit sector (i.e., charitable organizations) as "privately controlled, tax-exempt organizations to which donor contributions are tax deductible" (p. 55).

Finally, it must be noted that not all nonprofit organizations that have fund-raising functions and even fund-raising practitioners are charitable organizations. For example, political parties raise millions of dollars each year, often with the help of fund-raising specialists, yet gifts to these organizations are not tax deductible.

As can be seen by this discussion, the nonprofit sector is not an uncomplicated arena. Unfortunately, a lack of clarity and too many generalizations about the organizations in this sector have added to the confusion. For example, in his study on government support of nonprofits, Salamon (1987) used the terms *nonprofit, voluntary,* and *charitable* interchangeably to refer to only those 501(c)(3) organizations that are not religious, not grant-making, and are not mutual benefit organizations.

Although Salamon (1987) has good reason to exclude religious organizations from a study on government support because such organizations are excluded from receiving such support by the Constitution, it should be noted that religious organizations are one of the largest segments of 501(c)(3) charitable organizations, whereas mutual benefit organizations, such as labor unions, are not charitable by IRS designation. The confusion over precise terms is further emphasized when Salamon said, "The terms *nonprofit* and *voluntary* are used interchangeably to depict this set of organizations even though many of the organizations covered earn income and much of the work they carry out is conducted by paid professionals" (p. 100).

It should be noted here that Independent Sector (1988), in cooperation with the Foundation Center, is conducting a multi-year research project, *National Taxonomy of Exempt Entities,* to "provide a system for classifying, non-governmental, nonbusiness, tax-exempt organizations, with a focus on IRS section 501(c)(3) philanthropic organizations" (p. xii). According to Independent Sector, "Such a system is critical to developing a common language of definitions. . . . Implementation of this taxonomy will help stimulate research on this sector, and will be a significant step toward more accurate analysis and definition of the voluntary nonprofit sector in the United States" (p. xii). Unfortunately for the purposes of this book, this project will not be completed until after its publication.

As stated earlier, Payton (1987) used religion to differentiate between charity and philanthropy, saying, "The religious tradition—the charitable—is founded on altruism; the secular tradition—the philanthropic—is founded on what Aristotle called prudence and what we would call enlightened self-interest" (p. 27). Yet, Jencks (1987) reported that most money contributed by congregations to local churches goes for services to the same members of those congregations, which Payton would probably agree was more closely related to enlightened self-interest than to motives of altruism. Jencks supported his claim with figures from the Interfaith Research Council, which found, he said, that "local churches typically allocate only 4 percent of their income to 'social welfare' activities and organizations" (p. 322).

Related to Payton's (1987) concept of enlightened self-interest, few Americans would question the charitable status of the United Way or their tax-deductible gifts to that organization, which traditionally uses altruistic slogans, such as "lend a hand." Yet, some portion of most United Way campaigns are allocated to the Boys Scouts of America, a 501(c)(3) charitable organization whose members are primarily the middle-class sons of those very same donors. Similarly, almost all local YMCAs are 501(c)(3) charitable organizations, yet America's increased interest in physical fitness has transformed many of these charities into high-priced health clubs that service a primarily middle class and upper class clientele. This particular contradiction has led to recent attacks by private health clubs on the tax-exempt status of some urban YMCAs, and, in the past 2 years, "local and state courts have placed 'yuppie' Y.M.C.A.'s on the tax rolls in Pittsburgh and Portland, Ore., although the Y is appealing both decisions" ("Private health clubs," 1989, p. 20).

According to an article in *The Chronicle of Philanthropy* ("Responding to criticism," 1989), complaints similar to those levied at YMCAs have been raised about other types of tax-exempt organizations, "but the pressure has been particularly severe on non-profit hospitals, which own billions of dollars in real estate" (p. 20). The article explained that government officials are looking at nonprofit hospitals, which constitute half of the nation's hospitals, "as a huge, untapped source of revenue," and many of these officials argue that "hospitals should provide charity care equal to the value of their exemptions [from sales, property, federal, state, and local taxes]" (p. 20).

Although most people probably identify nonprofit hospitals with medical care for the poor, the IRS currently has no requirements relating charitable activities to hospitals' federal tax-exempt status, which is usually the basis for exemption from all other taxes. A recent study by the U.S. General Accounting Office (GAO) (Nadel, 1990) found that "the link between tax-exempt status and the provision of charitable activities for the poor or underserved is weak for many nonprofit hospitals" (p. i). Illustrating the point made earlier about confusion over nonprofit organizations making a profit, the GAO report stated, "The nonprofit hospitals providing the lowest levels of such care served the fewest Medicaid patients and often had the highest profits" (p. 2). Furthermore, the GAO found that 57% of the nonprofit hospitals it studied provided charitable care valued at less than the value of their tax exemption, which was computed as the amount of tax revenue lost by exempting them from federal and state income taxes, not including lost property and sales taxes (p. 7).

Emphasizing the "blurring" between for-profit and nonprofit organizations, the GAO study (Nadel, 1990) also found that providing medical care to those unable to pay and providing community services, such as health education, "do not distinguish nonprofits from for-profit hospitals" (p. i). The report continued,

"Nonprofit hospitals were just as likely as for-profits to charge a fee for these services and *more likely* to recover the costs of providing them" (p. i; italics added).

According to the article on recent complaints against nonprofit hospitals ("Responding to criticism, 1989), "Elected officials are now starting to pay closer attention to charitable hospitals—and threatening to change existing exemption laws unless the hospitals start doing more to care for the poor" (p. 20). Although few hospitals have lost their tax-exempt status, at least 12 states have attempted to remove charitable status and property tax exemptions from nonprofit hospitals (Nadel, 1990).

In fact, the Select Committee on Aging of the House of Representatives recently introduced a bill, "Hospital Tax-Exempt Status Reform Act of 1990," that threatens to revoke billions of dollars in tax-exempt subsidies. Testifying in support of that bill, the author of the GAO report (Nadel, 1990) stated, "If the Congress wishes to encourage nonprofit hospitals to provide charity care to the poor and underserved and other community services, it should consider revising the criteria for tax exemption" (p. 2).

Clearly, the nonprofit, or third sector is filled with confusion, incorrect generalizations, and contradictions about charitable organizations that make the study of fund raising more difficult. For example, the lead paragraph of an article I recently wrote about the relationship between the fund-raising and public relations function in educational and cultural organizations—which predominately are charities by IRS designation—was rewritten by the editor of the publication in which it appeared so that it incorrectly included "gifts" to political parties (Kelly, 1989b).

The action of that editor, who is a public relations educator, prompts some criticism about definitions of charitable organizations in the public relations literature. Specifically, the lack of precise definitions has led to an underestimation of the number of public relations practitioners who work for nonprofit organizations, thereby, diminishing the importance of these organizations in the study and practice of public relations. For example, Pearson (1989) used demographics from the 1987 membership survey of the International Association of Business Communicators (IABC) to conclude that "most [public relations] practitioners in the U.S. and Canada, about 40 percent, work for corporations" (p. 3). Yet the figures, as cited by Pearson, show that 40% of the IABC members work for corporations, 6.5% work for consulting firms (which, along with corporations, are part of the for-profit sector), and 4% are employed by government, leaving the possibility that the majority of practitioners, or 49.5%, work for nonprofit organizations. Pearson arrived at his misleading conclusion because IABC separates hospitals, educational institutions, and labor unions from "associations or non-profit organizations" (p. 3).

More recently, the *Public Relations Journal*'s 1989 annual salary survey of readers ("PRJ's fourth annual," 1989) created 15 categories of types of organizations for which respondents work as defined by the primary activity of the organization, rather than by the three economic sectors (e.g., industrial/manufacturing, utility, media). As a result, nonprofit associations and foundations are separated from education and from religious and "charitable" organizations, whereas both for-profit and nonprofit organizations whose primary activity is health care are combined.

Although the report ("PRJ's fourth annual," 1989) shows that only 3% of the respondents work for religious or charitable organizations, at least 20% work for nonprofit organizations when percentages are added for those three categories just listed that are obviously composed of nonprofit organizations. This percentage is greater than the survey's "top" organizational category, which places 15% of the respondents as practitioners with consulting firms. In addition to the 20% identified, another 16% of the respondents are questionable as a number of insurance carriers, such as Blue Cross, and half of all hospitals, as noted earlier, are nonprofit. Finally, the survey places 23% of the respondents in a category of "other," which includes scientific organizations that frequently are nonprofit organizations. In conclusion, this 1989 survey shows that 34% of the public relations practitioners work in the for-profit sector, 20% in the nonprofit sector, and 7% in government, although the proportion of nonprofit public relations practitioners may be even greater because 39% of the respondents cannot be easily identified by economic sector.

From these two surveys, we can see that the dominance of corporations and consulting firms in the study of public relations practitioners is not necessarily supported by statistics when organizations are placed within the three economic sectors. In addition, a recent study of the leading public relations textbooks documented that nonprofit organizations are neither well understood by the authors of these texts or given much attention (Kelly, 1990). For example, Crable and Vibbert (1986), whose textbook was mentioned earlier in this chapter, use the term *social/service organizations* to designate "nonprofit, recreational, religious, consumer-based, and conscience groups" (p. 81). Each of the eight textbooks I examined in the study categorized nonprofit organizations differently, yet none mentioned the 501(c)(3) category of charities, as regulated by the IRS. Generally, nonprofit organizations were portrayed as small, poor, and struggling, which forced the authors to treat educational institutions as separate entities. Overall, corporations received a significantly greater amount of space in these texts than nonprofits, and 50% used the for-profit sector exclusively when illustrating key points and principles about the practice of public relations. It is worth noting that the term *philanthropy* was not even listed in the indices of 75% of the textbooks (Kelly, 1990).

As a result of the confusion created by imprecise definitions of nonprofit organizations, public relations practitioners who work for these organizations have not been clearly identified, and the effect the nonprofit mission of their organizations may have on the function of public relations has not been thoroughly explored. Specifically, the relationship between public relations and the financial need of some nonprofit organizations to raise private gifts has largely been ignored by public relations scholars.

Presenting a Typology

Fortunately, Douglas (1983) provided us with a framework to reduce some of the confusion about the differences among nonprofit organizations. This framework is presented in Table 3.1 as a typology of nonprofit organizations. In his book, *Why Charity?*, Douglas (1983) used economic and political theory, which he said are "the disciplines traditionally concerned with the allocation of resources and of roles within society" (p. 18) to find rationale and justification for a third sector.

As clarified throughout this section, there are essentially three sectors of organizations within a democratic society: the public nonprofit sector, or government; the private for-profit sector, or business; and the private nonprofit sector, or what the Filer Commission named the third sector in 1977. According to Douglas:

> We know far less about the Third Sector than we do about the other two. We cannot even say with any precision what proportion of national resources is allocated through its agencies as distinct from the agencies of government and commerce. This lack is itself partly a result of the absence of any adequate theoretical framework. (pp. 12-13)

Douglas said that although "The Filer Commission did not attempt to define the Third Sector. . . the merit of the term 'Third Sector' is that it draws attention to what the organizations constituting it *are not*" (p. 16).

Utilizing legal definitions, we can divide the private nonprofit sector into two broad classifications: noncharities and charities to form the basis for a typology of nonprofit organizations. According to Douglas (1983), the common definition of a *charity* is an organization involved in good works; however, "quite a few institutions that are charities by law would not be recognized as such by lay peo-

Table 3.1
Types of Nonprofit Organizations*

I. **Private for-profit sector** = Market - provides goods and services through *quid pro quo* exchange transactions.

II. **Public nonprofit sector** = Government - provides goods and services considered universally required by all citizens.

III. **Private nonprofit sector** = Third Sector

A. **Noncharities**

1. Benefit for Members Only (e.g., social clubs).
2. Share Collective Good (e.g., trade unions).
3. Affect leglislation (e.g., political action org.).

B. **Charities** - Must benefit an indefinite number of persons.

1. **Pure Public Goods** - goods that have to be made available wihtout charge; impossible to exclude anyone from their use, and they are of such a nature that one person's use does not detract from others' use (e.g., public radio and television).

2. **Positive Externalities** - category of goods that generate significant externalities; each individual's use reduces the resources available for others; people can be excluded; beneficial spillover effects on the rest of society (e.g., colleges and universities).

3. **Eleemosynary**

a. Sympathy - behavior that contributes to one's own utility function; "pleasure at another's pleasure;" beneficiary may be known.

b. Commitment - moral criterion for choice; altruistic choices that do not contribute to one's personal welfare; beneficiary unknown; close to Christian doctrine that charity requires sacrifice (e.g., CARE).

*Derived from Douglas (1983)

ple" (pp. 55-56). The primary distinction between the two major classifications of nonprofit organizations is that the second category is composed of organizations that have been granted a 501(c)(3) designation by the IRS which allows the organizations to accept gifts that can be deducted from federal income tax. The first category, on the other hand, is composed of organizations that are exempted by the IRS from paying federal taxes, but do not qualify for tax deductibility of gifts made to them (e.g., political parties).

According to Section 501(c)(3) of the Internal Revenue Code, to qualify as a charity in the legal sense an organization must be "organized exclusively for religious, charitable, scientific, testing for public safety, literary or educational purposes, or for the prevention of cruelty to children or animals" (Douglas, 1983, p. 55). As Douglas pointed out, "Lawyers haven't been able to define necessary and sufficient conditions for charitable status" (p. 56). Yet, legal definitions are needed because of the great tax advantages enjoyed by charities.

The legal concept of public benefit (i.e., of benefit to the general public) has long been recognized as a necessary (but not always sufficient) condition for an activity to be legally classified as charitable. Using this legal concept, Douglas (1983) identified three categories within the noncharity classification of the private nonprofit sector, which is incorporated in our typology.

First, he distinguished between those organizations whose primary objective is to benefit their members (e.g., social clubs) and those that share the collective good provided by the organization (e.g., trade unions and business and professional associations that cannot exclude nonmembers from gained benefits, such as pay raises or increased prestige). The third category consists of organizations whose primary objective is to affect legislation (e.g., political action organizations).

The legal definition of charities, as outlined in the IRS Code, has an ancient lineage. Douglas (1983) described the index of charitable purposes in the Preamble to the Elizabethan Statue of Charitable Uses of 1601, which includes "maintenance of schools of learning, free schools and scholars in universities" (pp. 57-58). He then grouped the purposes of the Preamble to identify three economic categories within the charity classification, which are also added to the typology of nonprofit organizations.

The first category is composed of organizations that deal with "Pure Public Goods" (i.e., goods which make it impossible to exclude anyone from their use or benefits, and "one person's use of such goods does not detract from anyone else's use") (Douglas, 1983, p. 58). Ancient examples of such goods include bridges, ports and highways, which in democratic societies now fall within the government sector. Modern examples would include public service broadcasting and scientific research.

The second economic category is composed of organizations that deal with "Positive Externalities," which is very similar to the legal concept of public benefit. Douglas (1983) said that the concept of externalities (i.e., "benefits that spill over into society in such a way that the person providing the benefit cannot be fully recompensed by the benefited parties," p. 19) are a key concept in the theory of market failure. Douglas pointed out that market failure through externalities is the traditional argument for both government and nonprofit intervention. For example, because no one can be excluded from the benefits of a strong defense program, government must intervene to make payment compulsory through taxation. According to Douglas, "It is because education is believed to benefit not only the people being educated but also the society as a whole that public education is provided by governments, and private educational institutions are granted special legal and tax privileges" (p. 19).

It is Douglas' (1983) last category within the charity classification, eleemosynary organizations, that most people and many scholars have in mind when they talk about charities, philanthropy and/or nonprofit organizations. Douglas defined this important class of charities as those organizations to which making gifts brings no benefit to its donors (i.e., "those who undertake the activity derive no benefit from it themselves," p. 19). Such activity is the altruistic behavior referred to in so much of the fund-raising literature and that is confused so often with the more general, nonaltruistic giving behavior. An altruistic behavior, as defined by Douglas, would include saving a drowning person at risk to yourself, or sending an anonymous gift to a poor family. According to Douglas, "Self-interest can not explain all human behavior, particularly moral behavior, which Adam Smith described as 'benevolent affections'" (p. 75). Smith's benevolent affections are further dissected by the motivations of imagination and sympathy (i.e., picturing oneself in a undesirable state) and commitment. These two subcategories are added to the typology under eleemosynary organizations.

It is clear from the discussion of Douglas' (1983) work that much of the literature related to giving has failed to distinguish between different types of charities, in an economic and legal sense, and has incorrectly attributed characteristics of giving to eleemosynary organizations to giving to other types of nonprofit organizations. For example, Olson (1965) excluded all philanthropic and religious organizations from his theory of self-interest even though, according to Douglas, "Self-interested behavior even in the economic sense can exist within the nonprofit sector" (p. 72). In a similar manner, Gouldner (1960) excluded acts of philanthropy from his norm of reciprocity although, as discussed later in this book, reciprocity is rarely absent from giving behavior to charitable organizations.

Calabresi (1975) even distinguished at least four varieties of altruism that in different ways may be viewed as "a commodity which has value in our individual preference functions" (p. 36). These valued commodities vary from the pleasure one person may get from another's well-being to the generalized pleasure people get from the knowledge that they live in a society of mutual charity and trust.

With these definitions and typology in mind, this book focuses its attention on those nonprofit organizations that are classified as charitable organizations by the IRS. In so doing, it deals with all three types of charitable organizations (i.e., public goods, positive externalities, and eleemosynary), although its in-depth analysis on colleges and universities is, by definition, an analysis of charitable organizations with positive externalities. It should be noted here that, on close examination, the majority of charitable organizations would probably fall within the category of positive externalities. For example, churches, as stated earlier, benefit their members (i.e., gifts are used primarily to pay for such member services as the maintenance of the church, the salary of a minister, and operations). Yet, the benefits generated by gifts spill over into society (e.g., the existence of the church benefits society by upholding high moral standards). Gifts to cultural organizations, such as an opera company, may benefit the donor by upgrading the quality of the productions, but society also benefits from such gifts by the preservation and propagation of culture for the benefit of future generations. Indeed, under the typology presented here, it is a difficult task to identify eleemosynary organizations, which is contrary to the conventional wisdom of fund raising.

Supporting the conclusion of this section that eleemosynary organizations are a small portion of charitable organizations, Jencks (1987) basically agreed with the estimation that "less than a tenth of philanthropic giving is charitable in this sense" (p. 322). He said, "Whatever the actual fraction, it seems best to use the term 'philanthropy' to describe gifts in general, and to reserve the word 'charity' for those gifts that are specifically aimed at the poor or the needy" (p. 322). Jencks pointed out that gifts to meet charitable needs constitute a small portion of philanthropic gifts. He explained, for example, that gifts to hospitals are "seldom earmarked for people who could not otherwise afford to use the hospital" (p. 322), and that gifts to colleges and universities are primarily intended to upgrade the institution as a whole. "Only a small fraction of all gifts to colleges and universities goes for scholarships to help poor students," he said (p. 322).

By focusing on organizations with positive externalities, it is important to remember that in the market sector, individuals enter into exchange relationships to advance their own interests. According to Douglas (1983), "We say that a choice is 'rational' in terms of market economics when in any transaction the *quid* received is equal to or greater than the *quo* forgone in terms of the individual's self-interest" (p. 23). In the third, or philanthropic sector, as Douglas pointed out, the laws governing charitable organizations do not demand the total absence of any *quid* in exchange relationships, only that the benefits "must not be fully captured by the *quid pro quo* but must spill over into society at large" (p. 62). This point is critical to later discussions, particularly those in chapter 5 on fund raising as a marketing function.

In conclusion, it is clear from the previous discussion, that the failure to differentiate charitable organizations by legal and political concepts has contributed to the confusion about the fund-raising function and misconceptions about donor motivation. By concisely defining charitable organizations as public goods, positive externalities, and eleemosynary, this book enhances the definition of fund raising given at the beginning of this chapter to include the fact that fund raising is the purposive solicitation and acceptance of gifts that may be, but most often are not, made for altruistic reasons.

Summarizing chapter 3, a lack of clarity, misinterpretations, and generalizations have created confusion in the literature and have distorted our understanding of the fund-raising function. For example, two of the more prominent educators who have studied fund raising for colleges and universities define all institutional advancement functions as having the common purpose of cultivating support, with an emphasis on generating gifts. Definitions of fund raising, such as the one offered by Gurin (1989), are slanted by the perspective of consultants because they do not incorporate the solicitation component of the fund-raising function as practiced by internal practitioners. Different types of gifts are not well-defined in the fund-raising literature, although gifts to charitable organizations consist essentially of lower level gifts and major gifts, which are unrestricted or restricted in purpose. A two-dimensional typology, based on level and purpose, is presented to capture and clarify the primary types of gifts related to fund raising.

Although some practitioners and scholars use charity and philanthropy interchangeably, others perceive philanthropy as an evolutionary outcome of the earlier actions known as charity, and some argue that charity is currently practiced more by government than by private organizations or individuals. There is little consensus on what actually constitutes a philanthropic or charitable act. Theoretical and operational links between fund raising and public relations have been ignored in previous research because fund-raising scholars and practitioners have utilized definitions of public relations that differ from those definitions currently being advanced by public relations scholars.

Finally, the failure to differentiate charitable organizations by legal and political concepts has contributed to the confusion about the fund-raising function and misconceptions about donor motivation. By concisely defining charitable organizations as public goods, positive externalities, and eleemosynary, this book clarifies the fact that gifts may be, but most often are not, made for altruistic reasons.

This chapter concludes that charity best describes fund-raising and donor behavior for those organizations that are primarily eleemosynary, and that philanthropy best describes fund-raising and donor behavior for those organizations whose goods and services are defined as positive externalities or public goods (e.g., universities, churches, and public television). Therefore, in response to the question raised earlier in this chapter, it can be stated here that a charitable act is based primarily on altruistic motives, whereas a philanthropic act includes a greater degree of self-interest.

Adding to the confusion created by imprecise definitions of fund raising, charity, philanthropy, and charitable organizations, Gardner (1983) called philanthropy "the invisible sector" (p. xi). He said, "There are libraries full of research and writings on the business sector and on government. In contrast, the body of writings on the nonprofit sector is modest indeed" (p. xi). Concluding chapter 3, the book turns its attention to Gardner's "body of writings" to document the inadequate attention that fund raising has received as a serious subject of scholarly study.

Chapter 4

An Analysis of the Body of Knowledge: A Need for Research

This chapter answers the research question: Why has previous research failed to provide a full understanding of fund raising? Within this chapter, four sections examine: (a) gaps in the research on philanthropy, (b) weakness of the research on educational fund raising, (c) the absence of fund raising as a topic in communication and public relations research, and (d) the practitioners' need for research. The chapter concludes that research on fund raising is sparse and generally of poor quality and that it receives little scholarly attention as a serious subject of study.

GAPS IN THE RESEARCH ON PHILANTHROPY

As stated in chapter 1, there has been increased scholarly activity in the area of philanthropy since the early 1980s. Economists, sociologists, political scientists, and historians, among others, have begun to define a domain of philanthropy; however, the growing literature on philanthropy has virtually ignored the fund-raising behavior of organizations.

According to Curti (1965), a 1956 conference on the history of American philanthropy first called attention to the need for scholarly investigation of "the impact of philanthropy on American institutions and values" (p. xi). The conference report listed 14 broad topics that needed study, including "education . . . and fund raising." Curti also said, "Except for the more or less incidental treatment of fund raising in the invaluable studies of F. Emerson Andrews and in two or three monographic treatments of particular agencies . . . the bibliography in the Princeton Conference report indicated that no one of the fourteen areas had been as much neglected as the history of fund raising" (p. xi).

In 1965, Cutlip's book, *Fund Raising in the United States: Its Role in America's Philanthropy*, became the first detailed and scholarly investigation on the evolution of fund raising that "has had a profound effect on American philanthropy, on the institutions it supports, and on the increasingly broad segment of the public involved in the getting and giving of funds" (p. vii). According to Cutlip, "The public relations and fund-raising professionals, versed in the ways of mobilizing effort and exerting pressure, are, in part, a reflection of this spectacular growth and, in part, contributing agents" (p. viii).

It could be assumed, from the early call for research just documented and the scholarly response that resulted in the mid-1960s, that Cutlip's (1965)[1] seminal work would have led to a rich research tradition on fund raising and to further exploration of the relationship between fund raising and public relations. Such an assumption would be false.

According to Layton (1987), Cutlip's 1965 book remains "the only comprehensive history of American fund-raising" (p. 173). The annotation of Cutlip's book is also the only time public relations is mentioned in Layton's entire 308-page bibliography, *Philanthropy and Voluntarism: An Annotated Bibliography*. Published as part of a new joint program of the American Association of Fund-Raising Counsel's (AAFRC) Trust for Philanthropy and the Association of American Colleges (AAC), this first comprehensive bibliography on philanthropy references 1,614 publications, of which only 9 books and 11 articles—or slightly more than 1%—deal with fund raising.

In comparison, 148 books and articles (9.2%) deal with religion (Layton, 1987). In response to a perceived need to address the lack of research on this subject, Independent Sector's 1989 research conference focused for the first time on religious philanthropy. At that March 1989 meeting, Peter Dobkin Hall, of the Yale Program on Nonprofit Organizations (PONPO), lamented the low percentage of publications with a religious focus ("Link to religion," 1989). Confusing Layton's bibliography with research projects identified by Independent Sector, a reporter covering the 1989 research conference said, "And only 2 per cent of nearly 2,200 books listed in *Philanthropy and Voluntarism: An Annotated Bibliography*, by Daphne Niobe Layton, dealt with religion, according to an analysis by Mr. Hall" (p. 9). Regardless of the confusion between the two

---

[1]Cutlip's (1965) book was reprinted in 1990 with a new preface by the author and an introduction by John J. Schwartz. Aside from these two additions, the book remains unchanged.

sources, Hall's strong reaction to a 2% share of the literature for studies on religious philanthropy emphasizes the sparse attention being paid to the role of fund raising, which receives even less attention in the study of philanthropy.

By way of further comparison, Layton's bibliography contains 110 articles and books on philanthropy in other countries and cultures. The perceived lack of research on comparative philanthropy has led recently to increased funding for this area.

For example, the Center for the Study of Philanthropy at the Graduate School and University Center of City University of New York (CUNY) advertised research grants of up to $1,500 throughout the winter of 1989 to scholars engaged in research on philanthropic issues "outside the United States," (e.g., "Center for the study," 1989). In addition, the Johns Hopkins University has incorporated an International Fellows Program in Philanthropy into its Institute for Policy Studies.

Layton (1987) pointed out that many of the same gaps in the literature that were originally cited by Curti in 1957—and repeated in his foreword to Cutlip's book (Curti, 1965)—remain after more than 30 years. According to Layton, the literature on foundations, voluntary associations, and relief and social welfare "account for almost half the citations" (p. xv) in her bibliography (e.g., there are 267 articles and books on foundation).

As the editor of the first comprehensive bibliography on philanthropy and voluntarism, who is not "rooted in some aspect of it," Layton said she is in a good position to "assess its strengths and weaknesses" (p. xv). In pointing out three primary areas in which far more scholarship is needed (i.e., "worrisome gaps") Layton included fund raising as an area most in need of additional scholarly attention. She explained that "While there is an enormous practical literature on fund-raising, there is almost nothing which examines the phenomenon of 'getting' with the same depth and comprehension that the phenomenon of giving has received" (p. xv).

Panas (1984), a leading fund-raising consultant, confirmed the dominance of practical literature in fund raising by saying, "Almost all [books] deal with the mechanics of fund raising, the 'nuts and bolts' of organizing a development office or structuring a campaign" (p. 8). Carbone (1986) said that fund raising has an enormous body of lore and experience, but limited theoretical knowledge.

Of particular importance to this book's later examination of the effect of fund raising on organizational autonomy, is Layton's (1987) following statement: "Within this realm, the impact of fund-raising and competing for resources on the performance of nonprofit organizations merits particular attention" (p. xv). In his monograph on an agenda for fund-raising research, Carbone (1986) raised similar questions about the need for research on the effect of fund raising on organizational autonomy, asking:

> How are institutional priorities and procedures affected by philanthropy? What occurs when an institution first initiates a fund raising effort? When a small institution receives a single major gift, what happens? How does a major gift impact other fund-raising efforts? (p. 29)

Throughout her book, Layton (1987) highlighted, through annotations, "244 works of scholarly quality or other exceptional value in illuminating aspects of giving, volunteering, and associated topics" (p. xii). Only two works on the topic of fund raising were selected for annotation: Cutlip's 1965 history of American fund raising, and a 1978 article on how federated campaigns, such as United Way charities, raise and allocate funds. Four of the 20 fund-raising entries were published previous to 1970.

From a disciplinary perspective, Layton (1987) argued that scholarship on philanthropy is dominated by history, and that those studies "reveal a marked bias toward the nineteenth century" (p. xv). She believes that economics and sociology are relatively well represented in the literature, but feels that new disciplinary approaches are "badly needed" (i.e., more scholarship is needed on fund raising from other perspectives, including philosophy, politics, and anthropology). Although Layton does not specifically call for the application of a public relations framework to the study of fund raising, her strong arguments in favor of more research in this area from a variety of perspectives supports the need for this book.

Independent Sector's (1988) most recent annual compilation of research projects on philanthropy, voluntary action, and not-for-profit activity, *Research in Progress: 1986-87*, references 916 projects in progress as of that time period, of which only 35, or less than 4% are on fund raising. An examination of the titles and descriptions of these 35 projects reveals that 17 (49%) are administrative in purpose (e.g., Conrad's project, "How to Solicit Big Gifts," p. 184). In addition, 3 of the 35 entries are designed to produce reference works for researching prospective donors (e.g., the Taft Group's project, "Fundraiser's Guide to Private Fortunes," pp. 190-191). Of the remaining 15 projects listed under fund raising, two studies are by Carbone on a fund-raising research agenda (1986) and on fund raisers in academe (1987), which are cited throughout this book, and five are studies by Duronio and Loessin on measuring the effectiveness of fund raising, the results of which are examined in this book's later chapter on fund-raising effectiveness (e.g., Duronio & Loessin, 1989).

The remaining eight entries (Independent Sector, 1988), or 23% of the fund-raising research projects in 1986–1987, include such diverse projects as a 3-

year-old study by the Council for Advancement and Support of Education (CASE) on fund-raising expenditures that was not completed until 1990 ("It costs," 1990), and an annual survey of the results of fund-raising programs by the Fund-Raising Institute. Only six of the projects, or 17%, are being conducted by educators as identified by faculty titles and personal knowledge (e.g., although Robert Carbone is identified as director of the Clearinghouse for Research on Fund Raising, he is a professor in the College of Education at the University of Maryland; therefore, his two projects are included in those being conducted by educators, as opposed to practitioners and organizational administrators).

From 1983 to 1988, *Research in Progress* has referenced 2,717 research projects and only 80 (3%) have been on fund raising (Independent Sector, 1988). In comparison, 95 projects have been conducted during that same time period on corporate philanthropy, 76 on foundations, and 62 on individual giving. In other words, 9% of the research studies over the 5-year period were on "giving" behavior and only 2% were on "getting" behavior. As Payton summarized (1987), "The perspective of asking is less often examined than the perspective of giving" (p. 41). It appears, however, that research interest in fund raising is growing somewhat faster than interest in the giving of private funds. For example, there were 23 more fund-raising projects in 1986–1987 than there were in 1985–1986, an increase of 192%, whereas projects on corporate, foundation, and individual giving increased by 36, representing only a 75% increase over 1985–1986.

According to the latest edition of *Research in Progress* (Independent Sector, 1988), the most concentrated research interest for special industry studies is overwhelmingly on education, with 47 projects focusing on educational organizations, whereas the next largest "industry" is health organizations, on which 29 projects are being conducted. Over the 5-year period during which Independent Sector has compiled such information, 193 (33%) of the 585 special industry studies have dealt with education and instruction. Payton (1987) partly explained this concentration of research interest when he said, as stated in chapter 1, "If philanthropy permeates American life as a whole, it is even more evident in higher education" (p. 9). There is, according to Payton, evidence of philanthropy on every American campus.

Not only is fund raising underrepresented in the philanthropy literature, but until recently nonprofit organizations and philanthropy have been ignored as serious subjects for scholarly research. As mentioned in chapter 2, Katz (1987), who in addition to being a professor at Princeton is also president of the American Council of Learned Societies and chairman of Independent Sector's research committee, believes that it has only been in the past decade that social scientists and humanists have recognized the importance of nonprofit and charitable organizations. He said, "Academic centers for the study of philanthropy began to emerge in the early 1970s with the opening of the Rockefeller Archives Center in Pocantico Hills, New York, and the Program on Non-Profit Organizations at Yale" (p. x).

Since 1985, 13 philanthropy-research centers have been established ("Insider, 1989a), including Duke University's Center for the Study of Philanthropy and Voluntarism, the one mentioned earlier in this chapter at the CUNY Graduate Center, and the newest center—the Center on Philanthropy, directed by Robert Payton—which was established at Indiana University in 1988. Independent Sector reports that there are 20 academic centers and other programs in operation to study philanthropy and the management of nonprofit organizations, as of February 1989 ("Research centers," 1989).

The Yale Program, PONPO, is one of the oldest and largest of these 20 centers, first initiated by John D. Rockefeller, III in the late 1970s. According to Brian O'Connell (1987), president of Independent Sector, "During that time it has developed the first sustained comprehensive research effort on the sector" (p. 103). The recently published book, *The Nonprofit Sector: A Research Handbook* (Powell, 1987), covers past and current work undertaken at PONPO. According to a testimonial on the book's cover by Katz, "This book is likely to be the bible of researchers on the non-profit sector for the next decade. It is a superb, comprehensive, and thoughtful piece of work." Yet, in the entire 24 chapters, covering 463 pages, there are no studies dealing specifically with the function of fund raising, and, in fact, the term *fund raiser* does not appear in the book's index. As Payton (1987) confirmed, "Those who serve as agents of benefactors and as agents of recipients, for example, claim a very small part in the literature of philanthropy" (p. 40).

As of this writing, there is no general academic publication on philanthropy. John Simon (1987), the originator with Rockefeller of PONPO, said that the entire area of nonprofit organizations "has been largely ignored by the world of academic research" (p. 68). He summarizes the limited research on nonprofit organizations and the role of philanthropy by various academic disciplines when he said:

> If you look through standard texts on economics that are assigned to college or high school students, you will find almost no reference to this voluntary part of our economy. Political scientists . . . have paid little systematic attention to the role that nonprofit organizations other than political parties play in the political process. Turning to American historians, we find that they have written no accounts of the voluntary sector as comprehensive and ambitious as the histories that

American scholars have produced about *British* charities. . . . Psychology scholars have produced a literature that contains a good deal of work on person-to-person altruism and helping behavior but say very little about what makes me or you give to charitable organizations. . . . The sociologists tend . . . to develop general theories about organizational life . . . without focusing on the special qualities that characterize the world of voluntary institutions. . . . Legal scholarship, again with a few exceptions, has paid very little attention to the third sector. (pp. 68-69)

Simon gave a partial explanation for this sparse research tradition when he stated:

Finally, it must be said that this subject of study has not been perceived as "mainstream"—as a broad central avenue to career advancement in academe. Hence, graduate students do not typically choose non-profit institutions as subjects for their books, and junior faculty members do not work in this area as a way of publishing their way up the academic ladder. (p. 69)

Confirming Simon's (1987) evaluation of the lack of research on the third sector, Jencks (1987) added:

In fact, sociologists have hardly studied philanthropic giving at all, and psychologists, although interested in many other forms of altruism, have not studied people who give away their money in real-life situations. As a result, we do not know much about the non-economic determinants of philanthropic giving. (p. 326)

Summarizing this section, research on the third sector (i.e., nonprofit organizations and philanthropy) has been largely ignored until recently by scholars in the various academic disciplines because of its perception as an unproductive path to academic advancement. Added to that absence of research, fund raising—an important function within the third sector—has been ignored, or limited, as a research subject historically and within the current and growing body of literature on philanthropy.

Although Simon (1987) provided some insight into the reasons why the third sector has been ignored by scholars, neither he nor others attempt to explain the lack of research on fund raising as documented here. It is a hypothesis of this book—one that is more fully addressed in the later chapter on presuppositions—that the lack of research on fund raising can be partially attributed to worldviews held by lay people, practitioners, and scholars that fund raising is not a subject that should be studied (i.e., it is not a neutral object that can be scientifically observed).

In addition, many find fund raising distasteful and not worthy of serious study. Payton (1987) illustrated such a mindset when he explained that the mechanics of raising money, or the "ordinary business calculation associated with the high aspiration of marshalling funds to help starving children" (p. 133) is of little interest to most people. Payton stated:

A lot of people don't want to be bothered with the fund-raising, don't like it, find it distasteful, and don't want to be involved with it at all. They want to limit themselves to a "concern for the problem." (p. 133)

WEAKNESS OF THE RESEARCH ON EDUCATIONAL FUND RAISING

This section examines historical and current research on educational fund raising and concludes that the relatively few studies in this area are primarily administrative in purpose with very few introspective studies or basic studies that lead to theory building.

According to Carbone (1987), "There is an extensive literature on professors, deans, and presidents, but relatively little has been written about staff members of academic institutions who devote their time and energies to fund raising" (p. 1). These fund raisers are worthy of study, according to Carbone, because the fiscal health of American colleges and universities has, in recent years, depended increasingly on their effectiveness.

As explained in chapter 3 on definitions, *institutional advancement* is the umbrella term endorsed by CASE to describe all five of the functional areas served by this educational association: institutional relations (or public relations), educational fund raising (or development), alumni relations, government relations, and publications. As CASE is the leading professional association for fund raisers and public relations practitioners working in U. S. educational organizations, its compendium of doctoral dissertations provides an excellent overview of the research conducted on educational fund raising.

A review of CASE's *Research in Institutional Advancement: A Selected, Annotated Compendium of Doctoral Dissertations* (Rowland, 1983) and its *Addendum* (Rowland, 1986) reveals that graduate research on institutional advancement is of irregular quality, with little evidence of an interrelationship between the six functional areas or of any systematic building of knowledge. Although a number of the studies within the university relations functional area are grounded in communication theories, there is generally an absence of theoretical frameworks for most of the studies. As Rowland (1983) admitted in his introduction, "The systematic study of institutional advancement, employing social science and management-based research methodologies, is of comparatively recent origin" (p. iii).

The studies on educational fund raising in CASE's compendium and addendum of doctoral dissertations (Rowland, 1983, 1986) are largely administrative (e.g., Pickett's 1977 study on the organizational characteristics of effective fund raising). There are few, if any, studies on basic research or theory building.

Those studies that do appear to have a theoretical base rely heavily on organizational models developed by educators or on attitude theories. As is discussed shortly, the numerous examples of the latter, which frequently seem unrelated to each other, give the impression that the research on educational fund raising is obsessed with motivations and attitudes of donors (e.g., Allen's [cited in Rowland, 1983] 1981 comparative study of alumni attitudes toward Black church-related colleges in Texas).

As directly related to the focus of this book on organizational autonomy and the later use of public relations theory as an analytical tool for identifying models of fund raising, the CASE compendium and addendum (Rowland, 1983, 1986) include no attempts to identify models of fund raising other than the "ideal" or "effective" model, nor do any of the doctoral studies utilize communication or public relations theory to explain fund raising. In addition, studies that deal with autonomy are found predominantly in the functional area of government relations. Although four studies in educational fund raising do examine the relationship between foundations and educational institutions, only two of them are concerned with influence and none raise the concept of institutional autonomy.

Rowland (1983) pointed out that, historically, dissertations on institutional advancement have been done primarily by students in departments of higher education and schools of communication. There is little evidence of students in other academic disciplines exploring this area of study. A review of Rowland's compendium, and its 1986 addendum, reveals that students in departments of communication largely have restricted their dissertation efforts to the functional area of institutional or public relations, with few, if any, studies directed at fund raising. Students in departments of education, on the other hand, have conducted studies in all five functional areas.

According to Carbone (1986), "Up to now . . . research on fund raising has been sporadic, scatter-gun, and often pedestrian" (pp. 22-23). He argued that much of the research on fund raising has been done by practitioners and that "it seems evident that serious research on fund raising should _not_ be conducted by practicing fund raisers or those in related institutional advancement areas" (p. 23).

In support of this view, Carbone (1986) said that few fund raisers have the time to do substantive research, and that even those practitioner/graduate students who complete a thesis or dissertation do so not as part of on-going research interests, but as a credential for a promotion or a new job. In such instances, completed research work is put aside for career interests, resulting in little publication of the findings or any systematic building of the knowledge.

As summarized by Jacobson (1986), a basic problem in fund-raising research is the "lack of coordination of research activities, resulting in redundancy, findings of marginal quality, [and] uneven standards of dissemination" (p. 37). Blakely (1985) said, "Instead of providing continuity in advancement research, the trend appears to be toward isolated, one-shot investigations" (p. 64). More than likely, the phenomenon of a research tradition dominated by part-time scholars who are juggling degree requirements and a full-time job is largely responsible for the repetition of study after study on donor motivations and attitudes, without the accumulation of evidence that would support more substantial research.

As early as 1953, Andrews warned, "We can seldom know all the complex factors that move another person to action, and he himself, with every attempt at honesty, may be quite mistaken" (p. 2). His warning about the complexity of donor motivations resulted from a study commissioned by the Russell Sage Foundation and conducted by the National Opinion Research Center in the early 1950s. Involving extensive interviews concerning attitudes toward giving, the study's major finding, according to Andrews, was that "motivation was affected by so many variables that there seemed little possibility of statistical validity" (p. 3).

Today, donor motivation continues to be a mystery—one that has captivated the attention of fund-raising scholars almost to the exclusion of other equally, or even worthier, research problems and topics. The search to identify cross-situational attitudes and beliefs that underlie donor behavior—the alchemy of fund raising—has fascinated researchers for decades and is partially responsible for the slow accumulation of a scholarly body of knowledge. According to Burke (1988), who is the author of one of the more recent dissertations on educational fund raising, "One of the first systematic attempts to discover the motivating force for alumni giving was a study done by Carter and Lyle which sampled the alumni of Stanford" (pp. 12-13). Carter and Lyle's (cited in Burke, 1988) 1962 study, according to Burke, showed "no stable relationship between alumni attitudes and giving" (p. 13), and, in fact, these early researchers of alumni motivations reported that both alumni donors and nondonors had a very positive image of Stanford.

Yet, the purpose of Burke's (1988) doctoral study 26 years later was to examine the relationship between alumni attitudes and giving, or in his words, "to determine what relationship exists between perception of institutional image and giving by alumni" (p. 7). Limiting his study to alumni of Johns Hopkins University, Burke found little evidence of any significant relationship between alumni perception of 15 institutional characteristics and alumni giving performance. For example, he reported, "There were no apparent differences in the distribution of large donors and non-donors who were highly negative on any trait" (p. 113).

I conducted a study in 1979 on predicting alumni giving at the University of Maryland by measuring 45 variables, including attitude variables, that might discriminate the alumni donor from the nondonor. Among other literature, I drew from an even earlier doctoral study by MacIsaac (1970), who studied donors at Cornell College, Drake University, and Iowa State University to determine donor attitudes that would be of significance to fund raisers at these institutions. Using the statistical technique of discriminant analysis, which was later used in Burke's (1988) study, my 1979 study yielded 15 variables that accounted for 87% of the difference between alumni donors and nondonors. Of the 15 variables identified, only two were indicators of attitudes held by alumni and both of them characterized nondonors rather than donors (Kelly, 1979). Neither my study nor the earlier study by MacIsaac is mentioned in Burke's 1988 work.

Still today, the search for the "magic buttons" of fund raising continues to be the most popular problem in current research. Just at one institution—the University of Maryland at College Park—the recent doctoral dissertation by Burke (1988) and another doctoral study in progress are designed to identify the motivations behind the philanthropic behavior of donors. As Burke stated: "Generally, in previous research, the principal relationship investigated was alumni attitudes compared to alumni giving. . . . The results of the studies are conflicting, suggesting the need for further research and refinement of the methodology" (p. 12). Echoing Jacobson (1986), this book contends that Burke's study is indicative of the general state of research on educational fund raising (i.e., fund-raising research is dominated by studies on donor attitudes and motivations that are flawed by redundancy, findings of marginal quality, and an absence of cumulative knowledge). Or, as Paton (cited in Carbone, 1986) said, "Some of the reported research does not contribute to a cumulative improvement of knowledge and understanding about development performance so much as it produces an accumulating store of potentially relevant but diffuse findings and bit and pieces of information" (p. 21).

As a basis for his 1988 study, Burke reviewed nine studies on alumni attitudes and giving that spanned a 20-year period from 1962 to 1981. At least four of those studies conclude that there is little, or no, direct relationship between alumni attitudes and alumni giving: Allen, 1981; Carlson, 1978; Carter and Lyle, 1962; and Hall, 1967 (all cited in Burke, 1988). The other five studies, according to Burke, "suggest that a positive image may be . . . a necessary precursor for giving" (p.12): Caruthers, 1972; Gardiner, 1975; McKee, 1975; McKinney, 1978; and Spaeth and Greeley, 1970 (all cited in Burke, 1988). Altogether, these nine studies provide little basis for yet another study on cross-situational attitudes of prospective donors.

Burke (1988) pointed out another limitation to much of the research on fund raising—a limitation he repeated in his study: "Virtually all studies in this area have been conducted with an alumni population from a single institution" (p. 12).

Silberg (1987) is interviewing 10 to 15 donors of $1 million or more to the University of Maryland to determine what motivates alumni and nonalumni individuals to donate large gifts and how they decide which educational institution gets their gifts.

In her 96-page prospectus, *Factors Associated With the Philanthropic Behavior of Major Donors: A Proposal for a Research Study*, Silberg (1987) cited little of the literature used by Burke (1988) and few of the previous studies on motivations of donors to colleges and universities. Indeed, she overlooked a study on her own topic by Hunter (1968), a CASE member who interviewed 30 donors who had each made a gift of $1 million or more to colleges and universities.

Hunter, as reported by Young (1981), found five common motivations for giving through self-reporting on motivating factors by major donors: "(1) 'self-generated convictions' as to the institution's merits; (2) objectives and plans of the institution; (3) efficiency of the institution; (4) competence of the institution's leadership; and (5) tax advantages" (p. 75). Interestingly, Silberg cited the work by Young as a reference, but made no mention of Hunter's study.

Silberg (1987) did include in her literature review, however, preliminary work by Schervish, a Boston College sociologist who is studying philanthropy among millionaires, and White's (1986) study of the charitable behaviors of Americans. According to Silberg, White's study is based on a survey of 1,100 adults, 18 years of age and over, and focuses on "charitable giving patterns, preferences and peculiarities of Americans" (p. 37). Silberg acknowledged that the conclusion of White's study is "that an array of factors combine to motivate an individual to make a contribution" (p. 37), including income level, life experience, age, religious involvement, and marital status.

Like many students of educational fund raising, Burke (1988) and Silberg (1987) earned or are earning their degrees in higher education planning, policy, and administration. They both are also full-time practitioners who conducted their fund-raising research as part-time scholars. Interestingly, Carbone (1987), who criticized the research work of such part-time scholars, is the advisor for both of these studies. As pointed out by Rowland (1983), education is one of the two academic disciplines responsible for the majority of dissertations on institutional advancement. The fact that students of education must usually go outside their academic discipline for a theoretical framework on which to base their studies on donor attitudes and motivations (i.e., sociology, psychology, and communication) may be a contributing factor to the lack of a cumulative and systematic body of research on the fund-raising process.

Defending his view that serious research on fund raising should not be conducted by practitioners, Carbone (1986) pointed out that "many fund raisers who complete graduate study do so in fields where methods are inappropriate or where methodological requirements are extremely modest" (p. 23). As Carbone's (1987) study of fund raisers shows that 26 (53%) of the 49 doctoral degree holders in his sample hold degrees in education, it may be that schools and colleges of education are, in part, responsible for the less than rigorous research that has been produced in fund raising and the other areas of institutional advancement. At the very least, it points out the need for disciplinary approaches to fund raising other than education.

Brittingham and Pezzullo (1990) support this discussion in their book, *The Campus Green: Fund Raising in Higher Education*, which summarizes the research in educational fund raising. As these authors stated, "Studies of institutional effectiveness . . . and analyses of donors' behavior have dominated research in fund raising for the last 20 years" (p. iii). Explaining the search for "magic buttons," or researchers' preoccupation with administrative studies focused on attitudes and beliefs that underlie donor behavior, Brittingham and Pezzullo said, "Investigators of fund raising in higher education have naturally been drawn to studies of donors' behavior, just as practitioners have longed for a simple list of characteristics that could help them identify likely donors from longer lists. The cumulative results of these studies have been somewhat disappointing, given their relatively high numbers" (p. 90).

Brittingham and Pezzullo (1990) said scientific research on educational fund raising is limited, fragmented, and of marginal quality. It is weakened, they stated, by a "widespread lack of follow-up on initial or exploratory studies that might strengthen and extend or correct the initial efforts" (p. vi). Like Carbone (1986), Brittingham and Pezzullo attributed much of the weakness of the literature to practitioner/graduate students, who produce most of the dissertations on fund raising, but who do not pursue subsequent research on the topic. They noted that few practitioners who complete these dissertations seek careers as scholars, and said that "the topic of *fund raising* is more likely based on the student's employment in the field of development rather than on an organized research program" (p. 86). Finally, Brittingham and Pezzullo stated, "Most dissertations appear to emanate in higher education administration programs" (p. 85).

As Brittingham and Pezzullo (1990) have produced the latest source of information on the state of research in educational fund raising, it is useful here to compare some of their findings with the concepts used in this book. As recalled from the chapter on definitions, Brittingham and Pezzullo said that theories of donor behavior have changed in accordance with the shift from charity to philanthropy. According to these authors, an increased understanding of what motivates donors to give was the basis for the shift, and theories of fund raising reflect this new knowledge. After completing their review of the research, they stated, "The more promising models of individuals' behavior as donors depart from models of pure altruism in favor of exchange models, which attempt to explain donors' motives based on receipt of 'goods'—perquisites, tokens, or honors—in exchange for the gift, and a repeated disequilibrium that follows, leaving the donor with a need to respond to recognition and acknowledgment with yet more gifts" (p. iv).

Significantly, Brittingham and Pezzullo (1990) separate individuals from foundations and corporations when referring to models of donor behavior, which is not the approach used in this book; however, they do support this book's movement away from altruism as an explanation for giving behavior. Indeed, these authors' discussion of the application of exchange theory is useful to developing a new approach to fund raising. For example, they attempted to explain the difference between marketing and philanthropy by stating the following:

> Economic models of the exchanges of gifts differ from exchanges in the market-place in several ways, the most obvious being that in market exchanges, money (or goods) is exchanged for goods or services and a sense of balance and complete-ness is achieved; that is, the transaction is completed. (pp. 34-35)

As discussed in chapter 2, the legal definition of gifts is that their full benefit is not captured in the exchange process, but spill over into society; therefore, Brittingham and Pezzullo provide some support for later arguments against the appropriateness of a sales or marketing perspective of fund raising. Unfortunate-ly, these scholars actually take what is defined here as a marketing perspective when they completed their distinction between a market transaction and a gift by explaining, "In exchanges of gifts, a gift upsets the balance and the recipient is beholden to the giver, calling for another exchange in which the donor and recipient change places" (p. 35).

In their interpretation of the use of exchange theory in fund raising, Britting-ham and Pezzullo (1990) overemphasized the direct benefits accrued by donors in the gift–recipient relationship, saying that when a charitable organization responds to a gift "with its return gifts of recognition and its announced perquisites and invitations to briefings and dedications, honorary degrees, and even the donor's name on a building . . . donors are cultivated to even higher levels of giving and receive even higher levels of gifts in exchange" (p. 35).

Regardless of these scholars explanation, it is difficult to discern a difference between market transactions and gift exchanges in such an interpretation of exchange theory. As fully discussed in chapter 6, benefits are critical to managing environmental interdependencies with donors, and gift exchanges do involve direct as well as indirect benefits, including economic ones. However, this book takes a different approach than the one advanced by Brittingham and Pezzullo (1990). It argues that an accurate assessment of philanthropy from all three sources of gifts is a balance between idealism and self-interest. Or, expressed another way, the concept of contributing to the public good is a necessary (by legal definition), but not always a sufficient condition of a giving behavior to charitable organizations that are classified by our typology in chapter 3 as those dealing with positive externalities, or public goods. Philanthropy, therefore, lies at where the self-interests of donor and charitable organization meet, with the necessary condition that the benefits generated by the gift exchange are not entirely captured by the actors involved, but spill over into society.

Expanding on the quote given in the chapter on definitions, Payton (1987) emphasized that "to remain philanthropic [philanthropy] must by definition give first place to the other rather than to the self. It is not that self-interest does not often yield altruistic benefits; what matters is that acts guided primarily by self-interest are called something else. They are not philanthropic in intent" (p. 39). Agreeing with Payton, this book contends that there are two conditions that define gifts to non-eleemosynary organizations—conditions that must be incorporated into any theory of fund raising. First, gifts must be charitable in purpose in that they serve the public interest (i.e., contribute to the public good), and second, gifts must serve the self-interests of either the donor or the recipient, or both. By de-emphasizing the first condition, gift giving and getting move toward market transactions, and the closer they do so, the more likely that the autonomy of charitable organizations will be lost through external control by donors or through increased government intervention, which is discussed fully in chapter 5.

The confusion on exchange theory created by Brittingham and Pezzullo (1990) is due to the fact that they use their book, which is described as "a comprehensive summary of what research has been done on fund raising" (p. xix), to elaborate on their own conjectures about its application to fund raising. In actuality, they provide little scholarly evidence in support of their propositions, citing less than a handful of studies on educational fund raising that utilize exchange theory. Unexplainably, they do not cite the one study in their references of approximately 200 articles, papers, books, and dissertations that includes the term *exchange* in its title.

The point must be made here that few studies of fund raising have actually utilized exchange theories. Rather, most fund-raising studies on donor motivations and behavior have dealt with attitudes, beliefs, and demographics, as documented in Brittingham's and Pezzullo's (1990) review of the research.

For example, unlike the sparse evidence they provide on studies using exchange theory, the authors present a multipage table on variables that are predictors or nonpredictors of alumni donations—a table that draws from 14 different studies, including my master's study (Kelly, 1979), which was discussed earlier. As an aside, my 200-page thesis provided evidence that belonging to a religious group was a predictor of a *nongiving* behavior for alumni, but a mistake in my 2-page abstract prompted Brittingham and Pezzullo to list my study in support of the commonly accepted axiom that religion is a predictor of giving; thus, foolish mistakes and simplified literature searches perpetuate flaws in our understanding of fund raising.

Be that as it may, Brittingham and Pezzullo (1990) highlighted the concept of exchange theory in relation to fund raising, but provide little evidence of its use in more than a few scholarly works. However, they do raise important research problems through their discussions. For example, in addition to the consequences of their emphasis on direct and escalating benefits, they stated that through gift exchanges "a donor gets a sense of influencing educational policy" (p. 14).

Leaving exchange theory, they later asked, "To what extent do large gifts, frequent gifts, or timely donations that accomplish a specific purpose create special obligations for an institution toward the donor? What are the nature and the degree of the obligation? When should a gift be refused?" (p. 56). Such unanswered problems raise the issue of autonomy, as addressed in this book.

Similar to their treatment of exchange theory—but in a less significant and indirect manner—Brittingham and Pezzullo introduced the concept of autonomy in response to their last question. Although they do not use the term anywhere in their book or relate exchange theory to their discussion, they do give "reasons," or situations in which, a college or university should turn down a gift. These reasons are directly related to the theory of donor relations developed in these chapters.

According to Brittingham and Pezzullo (1990):

> Institutions may decide to refuse gifts for at least four reasons: (1) The source of funds may influence or appear to influence the institution's objectivity or freedom; (2) the source of money may be so 'tainted' that the gift is unacceptable; (3) the restrictions on the gift (in direct or indirect costs) may be unacceptable to the institution; or (4) the institution may become unacceptably dependent on a single donor. (p. 68)

As in the case of exchange theory, the authors provide "thin" evidence to support their four reasons (i.e., they use only one citation for each reason and none are studies on fund raising).

In relation to protecting an institution's freedom and accepting tainted gifts (their first two reasons), Brittingham and Pezzullo cited Bok (1982), who is also used as a source for this book. They supported their third reason on costly gift restrictions with one practitioner's article from CASE *Currents*. The evidence they provide for the fourth reason of dependency are the news articles about Kodak's demands on the University of Rochester's business school in 1987, which are also used as one source for this book's discussion on autonomy. In short, these scholars again raise important problems about fund raising that are addressed in this book, and by their inability to cite scholarly studies, they demonstrate the weakness of current research in addressing those problems.

Finally, Brittingham and Pezzullo (1990) supported the development of a theory of donor relations when they said, "The practice of fund raising is thinly informed by research that can lead to greater effectiveness, help institutions understand the role fund raising plays in higher education, or illuminate the dilemmas it presents to practitioners and institutional leaders" (p. 1).

THE ABSENCE OF FUND RAISING AS A TOPIC IN COMMUNICATION AND PUBLIC RELATIONS RESEARCH

Turning to the literature on communication and public relations, a title search of the leading communication research journals, such as *Journalism Quarterly, Public Opinion Quarterly, Public Relations Review*, and *Public Relations Research and Education*, finds few studies on fund raising (e.g., Ferguson, Doner, & Carson, 1986), although fund "giving," as Layton (1987) called it, is increasingly mentioned as a program of corporate public relations. In addition, a review of *Journalism Abstracts* up to 1989 indicates that little graduate work is being done on fund raising in the communication field, although the Supreme Court has defined fund raising as a constitutionally protected form of free speech ("Postal inspectors," 1989). Published by the Association for Education in

Journalism and Mass Communication (AEJMC), a recent edition of *Journalism Abstracts* (Fowler, 1989) includes 374 abstracts of dissertations and theses accepted for graduate degrees from July 1, 1987 to August 31, 1988. Of these research theses, only a study of volunteer blood donors is indexed under the term *fund raising*, whereas a dissertation on the value of applying management information systems to corporate arts programs is the only other study related to *philanthropy* (a term not used for indexing the journalism abstracts).

In his review of public relations research from 1975 to 1985, Pavlik (1987) made no mention of studies dealing with fund raising, and, in fact, the term *fund raising* is not mentioned once in the entire book. An earlier survey of public relations research by Grunig and Hickson (1976) also did not cite any studies on fund raising. It should be noted that both studies on public relations research found that a small, but growing percentage of this new field's literature actually deals with theory building (i.e., 2% up to 1976 and 34% up to 1987).

The Body of Knowledge Task Force of the PRSA Research Committee (1988) confirms the absence of fund raising as a viable subject of study in public relations and communication, but also provides an important theoretical link for shifting the public relations paradigm to include a theory of donor relations. Consisting of "twenty leading public relations educators and practitioners," the task force worked for more than a year "to define the subject matter of public relations and codify the body of knowledge" (p. 3). Organized under six major headings, the task force's report consists of more than 750 citations, of which only 9, or slightly more than 1%, can be identified as publications about fund raising. For example, under the subheading of education within the major heading of "Contexts for Professional Practice" are Bronzan's (cited in Body of Knowledge, 1988) 1976 book on fund raising for athletic programs and Rowland's (1977) *Handbook of Institutional Advancement.*

More importantly for the purpose of this book, the Body of Knowledge Task Force (1988) clearly intends that fund raising should be defined as a component of public relations when it incorporates the subheading, "Fund-Raising," as the seventh element and function of the professional practice of public relations, along with media relations, community relations, financial and investor relations, internal relations, public affairs, and marketing, marketing support and consumer relations.

The "newness" of defining fund raising as a function, or specialization, of public relations is revealed by the fact that only 6 citations are identified for the fund-raising subheading, whereas internal relations contains 29 citations. Four of the six books cited by the Body of Knowledge Task Force are used in this book, including Dannelley's (1986) guide to literature on fund raising and public relations.

Dannelley's book, *Fund Raising and Public Relations: A Critical Guide to Literature and Resources*, was hailed by Jacobson (1987) as a welcome sign "that diverse sources are beginning to codify and improve a growing body of knowledge about philanthropy, fund raising, and public relations" (p. 61). One of the first books since Cutlip's (1965) seminal work to deal with fund raising and public relations as functional partners, Dannelley's guide was expected to draw close parallels between the two practices. The fact that it was written and compiled by a public relations educator like Cutlip, who had developed an interest in fund raising, generated expectations that overlaps in the profession, the process, and the practice of the two fields would be revealed. Although Dannelley perpetuates, in the words of Jacobson, "the time-proven premise that public relations and fund raising are inextricably bound" (p. 62), he failed to discover any theoretical congruency between the two. Instead, the guide to 170 books and 100 articles in magazines, journals, and other periodicals published between 1975 and 1985 dwells on the "usefulness" of shared techniques and information between the two practices.

Although Dannelley's (1986) book contributes to the purpose of this book by providing the first integrated bibliography on fund raising and public relations, it is basically a superficial treatment of the subject, revealing little knowledge of the history or practice of fund raising. For example, Dannelley incorrectly placed the beginning of modern fund raising in the 1920s when a fund-raising friend, whom he included in the book's acknowledgments, organized the advisory board system for the Salvation Army; thus, ignoring the fund-raising activities of the colonial days, the post-Civil War era of the great philanthropists, the YMCA school of fund raising, and the multimillion-dollar campaigns of the Red Cross during World War I (Cutlip, 1965). More importantly, he began his work with the false assumption that as "the mysterious arts of fund raising and public relations . . . are backed up by a distinctive and respectable body of knowledge, these practices are becoming full-fledged professions" (p. 4).

In addition, only a handful of the approximately 270 articles and publications referenced by Dannelley (1986) have a direct bearing on the relationship between the two functions. At least one third of the listings are how-to booklets or brochures issued by private organizations or government agencies (e.g., there are six booklets by Conrad Teitell's consulting firm on planned giving devices, such as charitable remainder unitrusts, and at least three manuals and guides to the use of computers in nonprofit organizations). Another approximate one third of the annotated works are qualified with the phrase, "Though not on public relations [or fund raising]." The remaining approximate one third of the references frequently contain erroneous or misleading information. For example, he referred to Brakeley's 1980 book (cited in Dannelley, 1986) as "a comprehensive and practical handbook for the entire spectrum of eleemosynary institutions, from major universities to the local Girl Scout troop" (p. 33), although, as explained in chapter 3 of this book, it is misleading to define either universities or the Girl Scouts as eleemosynary charitable organizations. Another example of erroneous or misleading information is provided by Dannelley's abstract of Nielsen's (1985) book, *The Golden Donors*, in which he said that Nielsen recommended sweeping reforms in "corporate foundations," although Nielsen's book is about the major, independent foundations, such as Ford and Rockefeller, and not about corporate foundations.

It would appear that Dannelley (1986) used undergraduate students to help research and write the book and that he failed to provide appropriate editing that would ensure accuracy. For example, in his abstract of Grunig and Hunt's (1984) *Managing Public Relations*, Dannelley inaccurately credited me with the statistical technique of discriminant analysis, saying, "They offer pertinent advice on identifying active donors and offer the term, ascribed to Kathleen Kelly, 'discriminant analysis'" (p. 56).

Regardless of the guide's flaws, Dannelley (1986) contributed to the need for this critical book by emphasizing the fact that no other scholar has attempted to place fund raising within the public relations paradigm, even though the two fields have co-existed in close proximity for years. Through his bibliography on the recent literature of public relations and fund raising, Dannelley provided valuable clues from a variety of scholars, practitioners, and educators that support the purpose of this book (e.g., his assertion that Grunig and Hunt's, 1984, description of public relations as an applied social science "could be applied as well to fund raising and development," p. 56).

In addition, in his abstract of Hillan and Natale's 1977 book about government grants, Dannelley (1986) said:

> While the book is not specifically about public relations, the described management-level applications read not unlike the RACE formula for developing problem-solving public relations programs: research, action, communication, and evaluation. People versed in executive-level public relations will perceive a strong resemblance between the work being done in public relations and the work suggested in this book. (p. 63)

Summarizing this section, there is an absence of fund raising as a viable subject of scholarly research in public relations and communication. This absence has been documented historically and by the most recent dissertations and theses in these fields. However, some recent attempts have been made to bring fund raising into the public relations paradigm, most notably the report by the Body of Knowledge Task Force of the PRSA Research Committee (1988) that includes fund raising as an element and function of public relations. These recent efforts, while lacking in substance, provide a rationale for approaching fund raising from a public relations perspective.

PRACTITIONERS' NEED FOR RESEARCH

Leading practitioners like Robert Payton, former vice chancellor for development and planning at Washington University in St. Louis and president of the Exxon Education Foundation from 1977 to 1987, have called for more research in the field of philanthropy. Payton (1988c), a former college president who, as stated earlier, currently serves as director of the Center on Philanthropy at Indiana University in Indianapolis, said:

> Philanthropy is a non-subject in American higher education. It is a blind spot. We in the profession have simply failed to make it a field of intellectual inquiry with an accepted place in American colleges and universities. Although some encouraging things are going on . . . we have not yet begun, as a society, to think and talk carefully and critically about this enormous sector. (p. 4)

Carbone's (1986) *Agenda for Research on Fund Raising*, which was mentioned earlier, grew out of a June 1985 seminar on the need for research that was attended by 36 institutional advancement officers, scholars, consultants, foundation directors, and association executives. Discussions resulted in the suggestion of four broad categories of needed studies: "Reviews of existing research, studies that deal with philanthropy and the philanthropic environment, studies about fund raisers and their professional activities, and studies concerned with the management of fund raising" (p. 26). In addition, participants concluded that the long-range goal of fund-raising researchers should be to increase the theoretical component of the field. According to Carbone, "General theories are not available for the guidance of fund raising practitioners" (p. 22). Practitioners are, he said, badly in need of "predictive generalizations" to guide in problem solving, rather than using intuition or "narrow generalizations derived from practice" (p. 22).

James Fisher (1985), president emeritus of CASE, described educational fund raising as an "anomaly" in higher education—an anomaly that has remained unresolved by previous research. Fisher said:

> We must remember that today, in most cases, we are an anomaly in academe. We are accepted at the academic conference table largely out of a pressing need for us

rather than out of appreciation for what we are and what we do as professionals. The key will be for us to remain at that table after 1995. (p. 12)

As stated in chapter 1, Laudan (1977) said that anomalies hold a special place in theory building and the establishment of research domains. According to Laudan, if an anomaly cannot be explained by current theories, then new or competing theories will be looked to for explanation. Given this viewpoint from the philosophy of science, it is logical that scholars interested in fund raising look to other domains under which fund raising may be explained.

The major challenge currently facing researchers interested in fund raising is summarized by Jacobson (1986) in an appendix to Carbone's (1986) monograph on the research agenda for fund raising: "We need to develop a conceptual framework of theory and research that is powerful enough to critically examine the process of fund raising and develop a body of knowledge that is transferable and scientifically based" (p. 38).

This book is designed to critically examine fund raising and to develop a conceptual framework of theory and research by shifting the public relations paradigm to encompass fund raising. According to Kuhn (1962), a paradigm is defined by a community of scholars with common literature and common education and initiation. As can be concluded from the analysis of research in this chapter, there is little evidence of a scholarly body of knowledge that can support fund raising as a separate paradigm of study. In addition, fund raising has not been included in the emerging domain of philanthropy, as stated in chapter 1 and documented in this chapter. Finally, fund raising can be viewed as an anomaly since research on it has concentrated on administrative problems and has failed to resolve the important problems facing practitioners, such as those raised by Fisher (1985) above and those problems embedded in the four questions that began chapter 1.

Summarizing this chapter, research on the third sector (i.e., nonprofit organizations and philanthropy) has been largely ignored until recently by scholars in the various academic disciplines. Added to that absence of research, fund raising—an important function within the third sector—has been ignored, or limited, as a research subject historically and within the current and growing body of literature on philanthropy. The relatively few studies on educational fund raising have been primarily administrative in purpose with very few introspective studies or basic studies that lead to theory building.

There is an absence of fund raising as a viable subject of scholarly research in public relations and communication. This absence has been documented historically and by the most recent dissertations and theses in these fields. However, some recent attempts have been made to bring fund raising into the public relations paradigm, most notably the report by the Body of Knowledge Task Force of the PRSA Research Committee (1988). Finally, there is a great need for research on fund raising that can be used by practitioners to solve problems and guide their behavior. This need is clearly demonstrated by the perception of fund raising as an anomaly in higher education.

Concluding chapter 4, the book now turns to a critical analysis of fund-raising principles that uncovers some flawed assumptions on which these current principles are based.

Myths and Misinterpretation of the Fund-Raising Function

This chapter answers the following research question: What underlying assumptions of current fund-raising principles are invalid? Four major "myths" are identified and critically analyzed: (a) the myth of unrestricted gifts, (b) the myth of a broad base of donors, (c) the myth of the volunteer solicitor, and (d) the myth of the invisible fund raiser. In addition, this chapter analyzes the perspectives of fund raising as a sales or marketing function and strongly criticizes such perspectives as inappropriate for an understanding of an organizational behavior dealing with donor motivations that encompass more than the *quid pro quo* of the marketplace. The chapter concludes that such perspectives, based on a business mentality, are likely to lead to loss of organizational autonomy by relinquishing control to donors or by bringing about increased government regulations, including changes in the tax-exempt status of charitable organizations and the tax deductibility of gifts to them.

FOUR MAJOR MYTHS OF FUND RAISING

As discussed in chapter 2, the fund-raising function at colleges and universities has undergone numerous changes since its beginning in the colonial era, resulting today in a set of ongoing activities managed by lay administrators. This evolution has contributed to a misunderstanding of the fund-raising function. Specifically, current fund-raising principles are based on assumptions formulated in earlier eras that bear little relationship to the function as practiced today. This section critically analyzes four major myths of fund raising to demonstrate the inadequacy of current explanations.

The Myth of Unrestricted Gifts

A generally accepted principle of fund raising is that private support provides the means to independence for charitable organizations, or as Kramer (1980) described it, private support is the "venture capital" of higher education. An underlying assumption of this principle is that the majority of gifts to all charitable organizations are primarily unrestricted in purpose (i.e., gifts may be used to pursue self-determined goals). This assumption is grounded in the post-Civil War era when private, or independent, colleges and universities—which relied on private support for operating costs—were distinguished as being more autonomous than their public counterparts. Government funding was viewed as restrictive in nature, interfering with the institution's right to set and pursue its own goals.

In contrast, gifts were viewed as providing more flexible funding, allowing independent institutions to avoid the restrictive hand of the government. As Gardner (1983) said, "At the heart of the problem is the familiar conflict between the government's need for accountability and the [charitable organization's] need for independence" (p. xii).

Ironically, the distinction between public and private institutions of higher education was blurred before the Civil War. Rudolph (1962) pointed out that many of today's prestigious private institutions owed their existence in the early days to public financial support, only making a virtue of being "private" when that aid was no longer available. For example, American's oldest college, Harvard, was never totally a "private" school, although gifts surpassed public aid and tuition as a source of income (Curti & Nash, 1965). Even after the Civil War, a number of states provided public funds for private colleges. In 1896, for example, Johns Hopkins University was given a $50,000-a-year appropriation for 2 years from the Maryland legislature (Curti & Nash, 1965). As is discussed in chapter 10, the distinction between public and private institutions of higher education is blurred once more today.

Be that as it may, private colleges have historically promoted their independent status as a means to attracting private gifts. Cutlip (1965) quoted the president of Ripon College, who asserted in a fund-raising appeal from the early 1950s, "The small independent colleges stand virtually alone as bulwarks of independence in its true meaning" (p. 518). Commenting on this assertion, Cutlip said, "This statement is often mocked by the small college president going, hat in hand, to the corporate giver who sometimes attaches strings to his gift, either stated or subtly implied" (p. 518).

Contrasting the underlying assumption of the restrictive nature of public funds with the unrestricted nature of private funds, Kramer (1980) said:

> Traditionally, the principle of private benefaction has been that funds are given to support purposes that academics themselves are to interpret and specify in their day-to-day entrepreneurial and protective activities. The principle of public benefaction now seems to be that the funds themselves are the instrument of the public purpose; that is, they are intended as levers of control. (p. 16)

A current principle of fund raising, therefore, assumes that private funds have historically created "autonomous" charitable organizations (e.g., gifts established "independent" colleges) and gifts now serve to protect the autonomy of charitable organizations, particularly colleges and universities. A description of the founding of Stanford University, which is provided in chapter 8, exposes the flaws of this principle in relation to the historical role of private support, and three case studies of charitable organizations from Powell and Friedkin (1987), provided in chapter 9, demonstrate the fallacy of the principle in relation to the modern role of private support. For the purposes of this chapter, however, it is important to demonstrate that the principle's underlying assumption (i.e., that the majority of gifts to all charitable organizations are primarily unrestricted in purpose) is basically false.

The myth of unrestricted support is perpetuated by scholars such as Kramer (1980), who argued that private gifts enable colleges and universities to set their own priorities, to "adapt, take risks and give operational expression to autonomously developed ideas about what they should strive to accomplish" (pp. 4-5).

Saying that private support is as valuable to public institutions as it is to private colleges and universities, Kramer claimed that gifts enable public institutions to take risks and that without them, such institutions would degenerate into little more than public utilities, "unable to make the creative contribution that the people of the states expect of them" (p. 5).

Yet, the assumption that most private support is unrestricted in nature has little basis in the history of fund raising. For example, Curti and Nash (1965) described a few of the large, unrestricted gifts made by individuals to Harvard in the early 1900s, concluding, "By and large, however, such unrestricted giving was long the exception rather than the rule" (p. 192). Curti and Nash explained that "In their own giving as individuals, alumni generally preferred to specify a particular purpose, though now and then gifts were made without strings." Moving to the mid-1900s, Curti and Nash said:

Necessary as gifts and bequests from individual alumni and friends were in enabling colleges and universities to meet rising costs, admit more students, expand plant, and improve programs, they left much to be desired from the point of view of any institution. For one thing, most of the individual gifts were for special purposes rather than for general endowment, so necessary to increase faculty salaries, to take care of contingencies, and to meet needs related to changing situations. (p. 200)

Curti and Nash (1965) cited a writer from 1887 who reported that the criticism of educational philanthropy he heard most frequently concerned the predominance of special and restricted giving at the expense of general endowment. Finally, a 1954 survey by the Council for Aid to Education (CFAE) found that "colleges most wanted unrestricted grants so they could carry on their own programs, using funds as they saw fit without influence from the corporations" (Curti & Nash, 1965, p. 254). Regardless of academe's desires, less than 36% of all corporate gifts to higher education in 1956 were unrestricted, and student scholarships were the Number 1 funding priority of corporations, whereas colleges and universities ranked scholarships as fourth on their list of funding needs (Curti & Nash, 1965).

In short, what colleges and universities want in private support and what they have historically gotten are two different things; yet the myth of unrestricted giving has continued to this day. For example, the winning study of the 1989 John Grenzebach Outstanding Published Scholarship Award for Research on philanthropy for education is based on the underlying assumption that private support is primarily unrestricted in nature. According to the winning authors, "Unlike appropriations and allocations from government and income from many other sources, voluntary support for colleges and universities takes on relatively unrestricted spending forms" (Leslie & Ramey, 1988, p. 115). Saying that "much voluntary support may be expended almost without constraint," the authors concluded, "Voluntary support is becoming the *only* source of real discretionary money and in many cases is assuming a critical role in balancing institutional budgets" (pp. 115-116).

Yet, widely available statistics on private giving to colleges and universities prove otherwise. The Council for Aid to Education (CFAE) produces an annual report, *Voluntary Support of Education*, that will serve to disprove the myth of unrestricted gifts. Each year, CFAE surveys American colleges and universities on their fund-raising results. The respondents to this survey have averaged 1,200 of the approximately 3,000 institutions in the United States. Although the respondents represent only about one third of all colleges and universities, their fund-raising results account for approximately 85% of the annual total given to higher education each year, as estimated by CFAE. For example, the estimated total of voluntary support to higher education for 1986–1987 was $8.5 billion, of which $7.3 billion was claimed by the 1,174 institutions that reported to the CFAE survey that year. It would be difficult, therefore, to argue that the reporting institutions were not representative of all colleges and universities that engaged in fund raising.

The annual CFAE report includes six categories of purposes of support: unrestricted and restricted use for current operations, unrestricted and restricted use for endowment, capital, and loan funds. The latter two categories are generally defined as gifts for restricted purposes in that they are primarily given for specific building projects or student loan programs. In addition, gifts to loan funds in 1987–1988 totalled only $24.7 million, or 0.4% of the total gifts to higher education (CFAE, 1989).

With this explanation of gift purposes in mind, a comparison of the first four categories in 1987–1988 and 1986–1987 sheds light on the relatively small proportion of private support that is currently given to colleges and universities for unrestricted use. As summarized in Table 5.1, 420 public institutions and 722 private institutions participated in the CFAE survey of 1987–1988, for a total respondent pool of 1,142 colleges and universities. These institutions reported total gifts of approximately $7 billion, of which $1.1 billion was given for unrestricted use for current operations and $0.4 billion was given for unrestricted endowment. Unrestricted giving, therefore, totalled $1.5 billion of the total $7 billion raised, or only 21% of all gifts.

The statistics are even more revealing when broken down by public and private institutions. Private institutions reported total gifts of $4.5 billion in 1987–1988, of which only $1.2 billion were unrestricted for current operations and endowment, which means that unrestricted gifts accounted for only 27% of all private support to private colleges and universities. Public institutions raise a dramatically smaller proportion of unrestricted gifts. Of the $2.56 billion in private support reported, only $0.26 billion was unrestricted, or slightly more than 10% of all private support to public institutions.

This low proportion of unrestricted giving to higher education in the 1989 report is not a spurious incident. In 1986–1987, total private support to the CFAE respondent institutions was $7.3 billion, of which $1.4 billion was given for unrestricted use for current operations and endowment. In other words, only 19% of all private support to colleges and universities in 1986–1987 was for unrestricted purposes (CFAE, 1988).

With such figures available, it is difficult to understand how scholars continue to perpetuate the myth of unrestricted gifts (i.e., that private giving provides flexible funds and that spending is not generally prescribed). The perpetuation of this myth has led to a misinterpretation of the fund-raising function that ig-

Table 5.1
Unrestricited Gifts to U.S. Colleges and Universities 1987-1988

Public Institutions (N = 420):

Total Private Support	-	$2,555,293,000
Unrestricted Current Operations	189,324,000	
Unrestricted Endowment	67,199,000	
Total for Unrestricted Purposes	-	$ 256,523,000
Unrestricted Purposes as Percentage		
of Total Private Support	-	**10.0%**

Private Institutions (N = 722):

Total Private Support	-	$4,485,992,000
Unrestricted Current Operations	925,668,000	
Unrestricted Endowment	279,270,000	
Total for Unrestricted Purposes	-	$1,204,938,000
Unrestricted Purposes as Percentage		
of total Private Support	-	**26.9%**

Public and Private Institutions (N = 1,142):

Total Private Support for		
All Colleges and Universities	-	$7,041,284,000
Unrestricted Current Operations	1,114,992,000	
Unrestricted Endowment	346,469,000	
Total for Unrestricted Purposes	-	$1,461,461,000
Unrestricted Purposes as Percentage		
of Total Private Support	-	**20.8%**

Source: *Voluntary Support of Education 1987-1988,* published by the Council for Aid to Education (1989)

nores its "true" effect on organizational autonomy (i.e., if gifts are unrestricted in their use, autonomy is enhanced because gifts provide the means to pursue self-determined goals, but if gifts are restricted in purpose, autonomy may be lost because the wishes of the donors may be incongruent with self-determined goals). Kramer (1980) illustrated the misinterpretation of the current situation in fund raising when he said, "Some donors give money on terms that are seriously restrictive, although this is the exception rather than the rule" (p. 47). As documented earlier by examples from current news items in chapter 2, this book contends that such situations happen frequently enough to be a concern and to dispel the myth of unrestricted gifts. Like other scholars, Kramer (1980) did not acknowledge the cost and loss of autonomy related to restricted gifts for operations or endowments that are given for purposes not covered in institutional budgets. Demonstrating a philosophy of fund raising that is incongruent with today's era of limited resources, as discussed shortly, Kramer said:

When an endowment imposes a new mission on an institution, it will often be a quite acceptable one, increasing the balance and scope of the institution's programs. Moreover, large donors are likely to have rather conservative ideas of academic excellence for the long term that are not too hard to reconcile with those of institutions. (p. 19)

As fully quoted in chapter 15 on presuppositions, Flexner (cited in Cutlip, 1965) refuted such a viewpoint as he chastised colleges and universities in 1930 for accepting gifts that were in reality institutional liabilities. This point is illustrated by an example drawn from the University of Maryland, which in 1983 accepted a gift of personal computers from IBM valued at approximately $6 million. That gift has today cost the university millions of dollars in institutional funds to fulfill the purposes of the grant. Fortunately, the "computerization" of the campus was a university priority when the gift was accepted, but the magnitude of resources needed to carry out and maintain the "gift" was not anticipated so that discretionary funds that were previously earmarked for improving academic standards were tied up for 3 years in support of the computer project.

As Curti and Nash (1965) summarized, "A college can refuse the donation, accept it and the conditions under which it is given, or take the philanthropist's money but not his ideas" (p. 20). It is the contention of this book that the first option given by Curti and Nash limits institutional autonomy because it diminishes the charitable organization's means to pursue its goals. The second option, as explained more fully in later chapters, is conditioned on some loss of autonomy with a potential for great loss. The third option, which may be chosen more frequently than generally acknowledged, is considered unethical and socially irresponsible. Curti and Nash provided an early example of Harvard selecting the third and unethical option when they described the conditions of the gift establishing the Hollis Professorship—the first endowed professorship in the United States—and the actions of the board and the administration in ignoring those conditions. Defending his arguments about the unrestricted nature of gifts, Kramer (1980) partially agreed with the options given here, but provided what is later explained as an asymmetrical view of fund raising when he said:

Donors (if still living) can usually be persuaded to see that flexibility will be needed in the use of a fund that they wish future generations to be grateful for. . . . An institution can usually afford to reject an entirely inappropriate private gift because the accountability the donor seeks to impose applies only to that gift. The gift will usually not be of such a size or needed so desperately that rejection threatens the survival of the institution. (pp. 19-20)

Kramer, like other scholars, did not differentiate between major gifts and lower level, annual gifts as defined in chapter 3. He, therefore, did not deal with the significant number of instances in the literature in which donors have historically imposed conditions that were accepted along with major gifts. For example, in 1881, Joseph Wharton proposed to found the first U.S. business school at the University of Pennsylvania. According to Curti and Nash (1965), "The hundred thousand dollars Wharton offered to fulfill his proposal tempted the trustees into immediate acceptance" (p. 74). Wharton, who later gave the university an additional $500,000, had definite ideas about what should be taught in the business curriculum, specifically, the necessity of a protective tariff for American industry. Far from keeping his desires hidden from the accommodating trustees, "his original 1881 letter included a section under the heading 'General Tendency of Instruction,' in which he demanded that Wharton students be taught those principles in opposition to free trade" (Curti & Nash, 1965, p. 75). Curti and Nash reported that his conditions were satisfactorily carried out and said, "He found it remarkable that American manufacturers continued philanthropic support of [colleges that taught opposition to protectionism]" (p. 75).

Although Curti and Nash (1965) did not include Wharton as one of their three examples of philanthropists who in the past encroached on institutional freedom, they did point out that Wharton's conditions were not in the best interest of the recipient organization. "Such a request," they said, "ignored the fact that an institution of higher education was not the personal possession of the man who financed it" (p. 263). Curti and Nash concluded, "The optimum relationship seems over the years to have been one in which the donor gave little but his money" (p. 263). This conclusion can be closely related to Kramer's asymmetrical option of persuading donors to provide flexibility in their gifts as stated earlier.

Kramer (1980) also seems to lend some support to Curti and Nash's (1965) third option of accepting the gift, but not the conditions. Admitting that not all gifts are made with flexible forms of accountability to the donor, Kramer said, "Nonetheless, accountability for private gifts tends to be to broad goals which are, or can be interpreted to be, the performance-oriented goals of the institution itself as it autonomously shapes its own future" (p. 21). Setting aside the issue of "interpreting" donor conditions, Kramer assumed here and earlier in the discussion that the goals of an academic institution are broad enough to encompass the purposes of most restricted gifts. This assumption can be viewed as a corollary myth to unrestricted gifts (i.e., gifts that are not unrestricted in purpose act as such since they support expansive institutional goals). As discussed in chapter 2, charitable organizations, including colleges and universities, currently operate in an era of limited resources that requires selective goals and objectives. Unlike the golden age of the 1950s and 1960s—when fund raising was first internalized—colleges and universities cannot afford to broaden institutional goals in order to assume the purposes and meet the conditions of any and all gifts offered.

Proclaiming that "fund-raising dollars . . . can have a disproportionate impact in shaping [the] programs" of colleges and universities, Dunn (1986) fell victim to the corollary myth of restricted gifts when he said, "President and deans aggressively seek gifts for . . . curricular projects _critical to the institution's development_" (p. 1; italics added).   Like other scholars who have no direct experience with fund raising, Dunn assumed that colleges and universities solicit and accept restricted gifts only in support of academic programs or projects that have been predetermined to be of value in meeting institutional goals.   How, then, would Dunn explain the acceptance of some of the major, restricted gifts mentioned earlier in this book, such as the $4-million gift to the University of Southern California to establish a center for real-estate development, or the $10-million pledge to the business school at the University of Denver to establish a separate institute to teach students kindness, courtesy, punctuality, cleanliness, and proper dress, or the $20-million gift to the University of Richmond to establish a school of leadership?

Although the purposes of these gifts may conceivably be of some value to the recipient organizations, it is extremely doubtful that anyone would define them as "critical to the institution's development."   Dunn, it should be added, is the vice-president for planning at Tufts University and a leading researcher in the area of measuring the effectiveness of fund raising.

It must be pointed out here that many restricted private gifts from corporations, foundations, and individuals are made for purposes that coincide with the stated priorities of the institution.   Indeed, trade publications frequently run articles about success stories of colleges that sought and received funding for special-project campaigns, building campaigns, or scholarship drives.   It is the contention of this book, however, that such successes should not lull institutions of higher education, or other charitable organizations, into the acceptance of the myth of unrestricted gifts, or its corollary, the myth of restricted gifts. Paraphrasing Kramer (1980)—who was addressing the issue of state-government funding—undoubtedly, many academics, lulled by the coincidence of their purposes with those of private donors and by the permissiveness of private accountability, are inclined to think that formal and implied conditions on gifts do not matter much. Consequently, in the future they will be unprepared for an assertion of accountability and a greater insistence for external control by private donors, who have become more sophisticated and demanding in their major giving activities.

The Myth of a Broad Base of Donors

Related to the myth of unrestricted gifts is the myth of a broad base of donors. This myth is based on the false assumption that private support consists primarily of numerous and equal gifts from multiple donors. Much of the philanthropy literature characterizes donors, particularly individuals, as a faceless mass that has little influence on a charitable organization. For example, Kramer (1980) said:

> The main developments in philanthropic support for higher education in this century have, if anything, increased the distance between the sources of funds and academic initiative and decision making. . . . The growing importance of alumni-giving programs has meant that less rides on the decision of the average donor. . . academic leadership . . . can rely on the fact that the biases of individual alumni will often be in opposite directions, tending to cancel each other out. (pp. 13-14)

Ignoring completely the potential impact of mega or ultimate gifts, as described in chapter 2, Kramer (1980) said, "In this century the important types of philanthropic assistance have thus become more numerous and therefore individually less likely to obtain dominance over academic decision making" (p. 14). Perpetuating this myth, O'Connell (1983) said, "Only in the United States are the gifts of the wealthy simply the peak of a pyramid with a very, very broad base—a base of modest contributions made by millions of individuals" (p. xii). To support his statement, O'Connell pointed out that in 1982, individuals gave 90% of all gifts to charitable organizations and that half of those individuals had incomes of $25,000 or less.

The reason that both Kramer (1980) and O'Connell (1983) can make these statements is that they fail to distinguish between levels of gifts and different types of charitable organizations (i.e., they assume that gift amounts are equal and are distributed equally among all charitable organizations). Dealing with the latter point first, most of the philanthropy literature is based on generalizations about aggregate totals without differentiating gifts to different types of charitable organizations. For example, O'Connell's argument about philanthropy's broad base of modest gifts by individual donors who earn $25,000 or less is weakened when it is pointed out that almost 50% of all gift dollars go to religious organizations (AAFRC Trust for Philanthropy, 1989c), which traditionally attract lower income donors (Jencks, 1987). Although no such breakdown is readily available, it can be hypothesized that a report on giving to all charitable organizations except religious organizations would not fully support O'Connell's statement.

As discussed in more detail in chapter 8 on the three sources of gifts, aggregate totals have created what appears to be a U-shaped relationship between income and giving, "with the rich and the poor making more effort than those in the middle" (Jencks, 1987, p. 323). Arguing that private giving takes two forms—"paying your dues" and "giving away your surplus"—Jencks (1987) explained that broad-based giving consists primarily of lower level gifts to certain types of charitable organizations (e.g., churches and national health organizations, such as the Heart Fund and the Cancer Society), whereas larger gifts from wealthy donors go to other types of charities, such as universities and hospitals. According to Jencks, "The percentage of income given to some organizations clearly falls as income rises, whereas the percentage given to other organizations clearly rises as income rises" (p. 325). He concluded, therefore, that the U-shaped distribution of IRS data is a by-product of aggregating the two different types of giving that are made to distinct types of organizations (i.e., combining heterogeneous categories from symphonies and art museums to the United Way produces an inaccurate picture of American philanthropy).

The myth of a broad base of donors to all charitable organizations has disguised the fact that some gifts have a greater value to organizations than others. This unequal value is best illustrated by the giving patterns of current capital campaigns. For example, the University of Miami reported that 61,000 donors had made gifts to its capital campaign, which had raised $483 million by July 31, 1989 ("Energetic Board Chairman," 1989). Yet, the university—which has since completed the campaign—also reported that gifts from only 76 of those donors accounted for $239 million of the total dollars raised. In other words, 0.1% of all donors to the University of Miami's capital campaign had provided 50% of the total gift dollars. In fact, only two gifts, a charitable lead trust valued at $20 million and a $27.5-million gift from another donor, accounted for 10% of the campaign total. Clearly, the gifts from these top donors have more value to the university than any of the other 60,924 gifts, and it can be assumed that their importance is not lost on the donors or the university.

As outlined in chapter 2 and discussed more completely in chapter 9 on sources of gifts, the success of capital campaigns depends on major gifts that provide the bulk of the money raised. Current fund-raising formulas predict that less than 1% of the gifts to a campaign will account for one third of the total (e.g., Campbell, 1989). If such few gifts can make the difference between success and failure, why do charitable organizations continue to spend time and money on raising lower level gifts from multiple donors? Or, if 76 donors can give $239 million, why does the University of Miami employ a fund-raising staff of almost 100 people to raise gifts from 61,000 donors ("Energetic board chairman," 1989)?

Curti and Nash (1965) provided an answer that reveals the historical basis for the myth of a broad base of donors. According to these scholars of philanthropy, giving to colleges and universities up until the 1920s consisted primarily of large gifts from nonalumni individuals (i.e., those "friends" of higher education, like Andrew Carnegie, who believed that the first of seven priorities for philanthropy was to found a university or, alternatively, to support an existing one [Carnegie, 1889/1983]). Curti and Nash pointed out that critics decried this dependence on private gifts and the predominance of restricted purposes for which they were made. "It was all these criticisms," according to the authors, "that spurred the movement to emphasize the importance of a mass base of unrestricted giving" (p. 167). Curti and Nash continued, "The most obvious sources to supplement or supplant large individual gifts from friends of colleges and universities were alumni, foundations, and corporations" (p. 167).

As discussed in chapter 6 on systems theory, this conscious move to expand sources of private funding can be viewed as a strategy to weaken environmental dependencies that threaten organizational autonomy. In other words, a historical dependence on major, restricted gifts from a few donors led colleges and universities to solicit gifts from a broad pool of alumni, corporations, foundations, and friends in order to preserve the power of the academy to determine its own goals and the means of pursuing them. Such a strategy, of course, is only successful if it reflects reality (i.e., if dependencies are diffused over a broad number of alternative sources).

As described in the later chapter on the historical models of fund raising, the end of World War I brought the intensive, broad-based drive of the YMCA school of fund raising to charitable organizations, including America's colleges and universities (Cutlip, 1965). This model, which depended on armies of volunteers and thousands of lower level donors, dramatically changed the patterns of philanthropy. Cutlip (1965) summarized this movement to a broad base of donors up to the mid-1960s when he stated:

> Philanthropy, in America's first three centuries, was carried along on a small scale, largely financed by the wealthy few in response to personal begging appeals. . . . There were few organized drives, in the modern sense, before 1900. World War I and the decade that followed provided the seedbed for the growth of today's fund raising and *today's people's philanthropy.* (p. 3; italics added)

As we begin the last decade of the 1900s, reality has changed. Although colleges and universities, as well as other charitable organizations, continue to espouse Cutlip's (1965) theory of a people's philanthropy, the increasing number of capital campaigns and the mega and ultimate gifts that they depend on have once again placed such institutions into a dependency relationship with a few external sources of private funds. As can be seen from earlier chapters and the example of the University of Miami, the current fund-raising behavior of colleges and universities does not support the myth of a broad base of donors. Although gifts are solicited from numerous sources, these charitable organizations are increasingly dependent on a smaller and smaller percentage of those gifts.

Summarizing the first half of this section, two current principles of fund raising are based on the flawed assumptions that gifts are basically unrestricted in nature and are provided from a broad base of philanthropic sources. Historically, major gifts have usually been restricted as to their purpose, and current giving statistics demonstrate that approximately 80% of all current gift dollars to American colleges and universities are restricted. Although some scholars perpetuate the myth of the flexibility of private gifts by claiming that restricted gifts rarely deviate from the stated goals of a charitable organization, current and historical evidence proves otherwise. An earlier dependency on a few sources of private support prompted colleges and universities to expand their donor base after World War I, giving rise to the myth of a broad base of donors. Today, an increasing emphasis on capital campaigns and major gifts has eroded that base so that fund raisers for charitable organizations, particularly institutions of higher education, tend to look to fewer donors to provide greater amounts of private funds.

The Myth of the Volunteer Solicitor

The combination of changes in the fund-raising function, as described in chapter 2, with the historical role of commercial fund-raising firms has led to other myths and contributed to an incomplete explanation of fund raising. A generalization that has led to the misinterpretation of fund raising is that both internal and external fund raisers perform the same function for a charitable organization, including colleges and universities. In most cases, this generalization is false. Basically, the field of fund raising is dominated by consulting firms rather than firms that execute programs, and the staffs of fund-raising consulting firms do not solicit gifts. In-house fund raisers, on the other hand, do solicit gifts, and they are increasingly doing so with less participation by other administrators or volunteers.

As is recalled from earlier chapters, fund raising for charitable organizations was primarily a function of external consultants between World War I and World War II. It was only in the early 1950s that fund raising became an internal function managed by lay administrators. This evolution has largely been ignored in the fund-raising literature, which has led to a number of false assumptions about the function of fund raising. Specifically, much of the practitioner literature that provides the basis for current explanations of fund raising has been written by fund-raising consultants who have a limited perspective on the function. As is shown shortly, the false assumptions they have embedded in the literature have led to a slanted definition of fund raising, a myth about the role of the volunteer, and a corollary myth of the invisible fund raiser. Most importantly, the generalization that both internal and external fund raisers perform the same function—a generalization that has previously been unchallenged—has hidden the impact that fund raising has on institutional autonomy.

It should be noted at this point that Lord (1983), Panas (1984), Pray (1981), Broce (1986), and Seymour (1966) primarily are used in this book to represent the fund-raising literature. This selection is justified in that the books by these practitioner-authors represent five of the six books recently recommended by the Council for Advancement and Support of Education (CASE) as training resources for educational fund-raising practitioners ("Continuing education," 1989). All six books, including Gurin's (cited in "Continuing education," 1989) *Confessions of a Fund Raiser*—which is not used—were written by fund-raising consultants, although two of the consultants previously worked as internal fund raisers at colleges and universities.

Unlike other fields, such as accounting, architecture, and public relations, commercial firms in fund raising primarily serve in a counselor's role, rarely executing programs on behalf of client organizations. A comparison with the field of public relations helps describe this unique character of fund-raising consulting firms.

First, it must be qualified that there are, indeed, commercial firms that execute fund-raising programs. Fund-raising firms that specialize in planned giving, for example, often provide "hands-on" service in preparing legal documents and in one-on-one meetings with prospective donors. In addition, firms that provide communication services, such as direct mail specialists, can be retained to execute fund-raising programs. Such firms are technical specialists that deal with parts of a fund-raising operation, but never with the operation as a whole. Therefore, when referring to fund-raising firms, we are generally speaking of those that consult on campaigns and overall development efforts (e.g., Lord, 1983). Such firms comprise the majority of the commercial fund-raising arena.

There is, however, a growing segment of commercial fund-raising firms that do externally execute general solicitation programs from beginning to end. Referred to here as *solicitation firms* for clarification purposes, these private companies stand outside the mainstream of fund raising as it is referred to in most of the literature (e.g., no solicitation firm is a member of the American Association of Fund Raising Counsel [AAFRC]). Solicitation firms concentrate almost exclusively on mass solicitations, which generate relatively small, unrestricted gifts (although the total dollars raised can be significant). Primarily, these firms specialize in one of three fund-raising techniques: direct mail, phonathons, or benefits.

Solicitation firms are rarely used by colleges and universities, but are hired by other types of charities, including social service, health, and separately incorporated 501(c)(3) organizations of fraternal groups. These solicitation firms, as discussed here and also in the later chapter on presuppositions, have been the primary target of investigations on fund-raising fraud and unethical conduct.

In particular, the high proportion of funds raised for charity that is kept by some of these firms to pay for operating costs has resulted in increased government intervention. For example, Illinois' attorney general recently charged a solicitation firm in Houston, Texas—Telesystems Marketing Inc.—with fraud after discovering that $2.4 million of the $2.5 million it had raised in 1988 for the National Children's Cancer Society had gone to cover administrative costs. ("Ill. charges cancer group," 1989).

In Minnesota, a report by the attorney general found that only 33% of the money raised by all solicitation firms in that state during 1987 and 1988 had gone to charities. According to an article on the report ("Minn. charities," 1989), another Houston-based company, Telestar Marketing Inc., kept more than 97% of the money it raised from a campaign for a local Kiwanis Club. The article stated, "Special-event fund raisers such as Telestar have been the target of particular criticism by state regulators, who say the companies often use deceptive or misleading tactics to persuade donors to purchase tickets to circuses, concerts, and other events" (p. 21).

Cutlip (1965) said that the traditionally poor reputation of commercial fund raising, represented today by solicitation firms, helped convince the majority of early fund-raising companies to stay away from the actual solicitation of gifts. Also, as noted in chapter 2, consulting, or nonsolicitation firms, are exempt from registering or posting bond in many states. For example, the State of California requires solicitation firms to register and pay a $2,000 fee annually, whereas there are no such laws governing fund-raising consulting firms ("State laws governing," 1990).

Be that as it may, there are commercial firms in both public relations and fund raising that primarily execute programs, although the public relations firms are more prevalent and more accepted in their field. For example, if an organization decides to use an outside firm to generate publicity for a new product, it can hire a public relations firm that specializes in media relations to write promotional copy and use its expertise to ask for and obtain free space and airtime from the mass media. In fund raising, if an organization decides to use an outside firm to generate lower level gifts from a broad base of donors, it can hire a solicitation firm that specializes in phonathons to write promotional scripts and use its expertise to ask for and obtain funds from the donor public. In either case, the organization could hire in-house practitioners to deliver the same service.

In addition to firms that primarily execute programs, there are commercial consulting firms in both public relations and fund raising that primarily provide counsel, or advice, to client organizations on a fixed fee basis. Consultants in both fields provide a full range of services up to the execution of a program, including research, planning, and evaluation. Although in-house practitioners could theoretically deliver the same services, outside consulting firms are valued for their objectivity and supposedly higher level of expertise. According to Lord (1983), "Counsel's autonomy can make it easier for them to say what needs to be said, and to insist on doing things right" (p. 106).

It is at the point of offering comprehensive services (i.e., counselling and execution) that fund raising differs from the commercial organizations of public relations. The majority of public relations firms today, particularly the larger firms, offer themselves to organizations as external consultants who also provide program execution, but fund-raising firms do not. As described by the AAFRC (1989a) in its glossary, "Fund-raising counsel, as defined by the Model Charitable Solicitation Act, does not solicit or retain custody of contributions" (p. 10). Generally, organizations without public relations staff can purchase staff time and services from external firms to consult with management and execute programs. Organizations without fund-raising staff, on the other hand, cannot turn to external fund-raising firms for the same dual service. Rather, charitable organizations that wish to tap the objectivity and expertise of fund-raising consulting firms are required to have internal paid staff, or a cadre of volunteers, to execute the resulting programs.

In a rare attempt in the literature to distinguish between the different "types" of fund raisers, Lane, Levis, and New (1989) identified five categories that support this discussion: fund-raising counsel, fund-raising directors, boards and other volunteers, paid solicitors, and technical-assistance advisors. Emphasizing the difference between counselors and internal fund raisers, these researchers stated, "As a staff member, [an internal fund raiser] may solicit funds . . . [whereas] a counsel is not a staff member of the organization being served and does not solicit funds" (p. 11). Lane et al. said that unlike board members and other volunteers who "are important raisers of funds in any organization," paid solicitors (i.e., commercial solicitation firms) require a fee or commission to "directly appeal for funds" (p. 11). Finally, they define a technical-assistance advisor as one who, although he or she has special expertise, "is not considered to be a fund raiser" (p. 11).

As stated in chapter 3, the operational difference between the function of in-house fund raising and the more limited function of fund raising as practiced (and propagated in the literature) by outside consultants has resulted in slanted definitions of the fund-raising function (e.g., the definition offered by the late author and consultant Gurin, 1989, that fund raising is "advising and assisting organizations in seeking and accepting gift support," p. i). In addition to slanting accepted definitions, the unique difference between the external and internal functions of fund raising has helped create what is referred to in this book as the myth of the volunteer and its corollary, the myth of the invisible fund raiser. Fund-raising consultant Lord (1983) dedicated his book, _The Raising of Money: Thirty-Five Essentials Every Trustee Should Know_, to the volunteer, who he described as "the heart and soul of philanthropy" (p. v). Fund-raising consulting firms, as commercial ventures, have developed and propagated a widely accepted principle for fund-raising success: Fund raisers—both internal and external—are directors behind the scenes, whereas volunteers are the actual fund raisers (i.e., the solicitors of gifts). This principle is expressed in operational terms by Lord, who said, "It's a simple equation. When the professional's fund-raising knowledge and management skills are combined with the volunteer's influence, the result is success" (p. 101).

Under this principle, the fund-raising function is dependent on volunteers to personally solicit the gift (i.e., the volunteer is traditionally involved in the most critical aspect of fund raising, closing the gift). Wilkerson and Schuette (1981) said that "conventional wisdom assumes the volunteer to be central to the solicitation process" (p. 30). According to fund-raising consultants Phillips and Richter (1989), "The very fact that volunteers are instrumental and responsible for 'closing' gifts had been the underlying strength of our nation's philanthropic spirit" (p. 33). The authors used the past tense in their statement because in early 1989 the National Society of Fund Raising Executives (NSFRE) removed its fixed-fee requirement from its code of ethics, which has generated a great deal of discussion about commission-based pay for fund raisers and seriously challenged the myth of the volunteer.

Faced with the possibility of having their consulting fees tied directly to solicitation results, consultants are arguing that commissions would destroy the volunteer's role because it would be too risky to stake their entire commission on the work of good-intentioned, but unpredictable, inefficient, unpaid volunteers. Commissions, according to Phillips and Richter (1989), would lead to bypassing volunteers when it came to closing gifts, which would minimize the commonly accepted importance of volunteers in the fund-raising process. This would destroy the future of cost-effective philanthropy because more internal fund raisers would have to be hired. Although not included among the authors' predicted consequences, commission payment might also force fund-raising consultants to change their practice of nonsolicitation (i.e., without unpaid volunteer solicitors or enough internal fund-raising practitioners, firms might have to provide staff that would actually solicit gifts on behalf of the client organization).

As discussed in chapter 13 on the historical models of fund raising, the volunteer solicitor is a concept that has evolved with the development of different models of fund raising practiced by fund-raising consulting firms. For example, a pyramid structure of volunteers has historically been a mainstay of the press agentry model, the earliest fund-raising model. According to Cutlip (1965), the fund-raising model advanced by the Ward-Pierce-YMCA school and practiced by many of the early fund-raising firms (the press agentry model) was built on the concept of getting large numbers of people to ask even larger numbers of people to give. Because the early versions of the press agentry model emphasized an army of faceless volunteers, the public spotlight was focused on the fund-raising consultant, who was largely credited with the success of campaigns. Of course, campaign failures were also laid at the doorstep of fund-raising firms practicing this model, and failing to make a campaign goal must have had a chilling effect on recruiting new business. As Lord (1983) said, "The best firms are known for making the goal. After all, *their* reputations—and their survival as businesses—depend on it" (p. 105).

It is not surprising, then, that in the later versions of the press agentry model, fund-raising firms chose to place the fund raiser behind a curtain of volunteer leadership, such as the one provided by Franklin D. Roosevelt's visible, but perfunctory role as chairman of the campaign for the Cathedral of St. John the Divine in the late 1920s (Cutlip, 1965). The concept of volunteer leadership further evolved into its modern form under the two-way asymmetric model of fund raising and its leading historical figure, John Price Jones. According to Cutlip (1965), the fund-raising campaign for the National Cathedral in Washington, DC in the late 1920s was managed and directed by Jones' firm under "the nominal leadership" of chief volunteers General John J. Pershing and Senator George Wharton Pepper, who "provided a prestigious front for the Jones-directed campaign" (p. 285). Jones found what Cutlip referred to as a "front" an effective way to increase the altruistic image of a campaign by down-playing the commercial function of his fund-raising firm. He refined the psychological technique of placing prestigious volunteers in "starring roles" and of delegating the fund raiser to behind-the-scene direction. Cutlip quoted Jones, who said:

I have always sought to work quietly. My work is that of stage director, laying out the work for the other person and staying out of the spotlight. It has been our aim to get the work done and not fight for the credit. (pp. 285-286)

In addition to the good business sense of down-playing commercialism in what was largely considered to be a philanthropic endeavor, Cutlip (1965) related a tale from Jones' papers that shows he had also learned a difficult lesson earlier in his career about the need for commercial fund raisers to remain "invisible." According to Cutlip:

Jones had ruefully learned a few years earlier not to claim all the credit in a fund drive. After the Johns Hopkins campaign [1924–1926] the Jones firm put out a pamphlet taking credit for having "raised" the Johns Hopkins sums. This brought a blistering attack from Abraham Flexner [of Rockefeller's General Education Board which had over the years given millions of dollars to Johns Hopkins]. Thereafter Jones, in public utterances, was careful to claim only that he had "assisted" in raising the money. (p. 286)

It is a contention of this book that the profit-motive incentive of commercial fund-raising firms—particularly their need to maintain a low profile in achieving "institutional success" in fund-raising drives—historically accounts for the accepted role assigned to the fund raiser in today's philanthropic process—that of the necessary, but "invisible" player.

The Myth of the Invisible Fund Raiser

A corollary to the myth of the volunteer, the invisible fund raiser is a commonly accepted component of the principle of fund-raising success advanced by consultants. A retired director of development for Dartmouth College (cited in Pray, 1981) advised:

Development is a great way to earn a living and fulfill a sense of working for something larger and more important than yourself. But you had better be sure your ego is in good shape because you will need to have a _passion for anonymity._ (pp. 374-375; italics added)

According to Phillips and Richter (1989), "It is a widely accepted fund-raising axiom that professional development officers must do 90 per cent of the work involved in soliciting gifts, and in return receive 10 per cent of the credit for resulting success" (p. 33). In other words, volunteers commonly receive 90% of the recognition and credit, at the expense of fund raisers, in order to compensate them for their unpaid service and, according to the myth, because they perform the most critical 10% of the solicitation effort (i.e., closing the gift). Payton (1987) summarized the conventional wisdom on the invisible fund raiser when he said, "Most of the actual *asking* for money is not done by the fund-raisers themselves, of course. It is their task instead to stimulate and organize others to do so" (p. 41). This myth has hidden the impact fund raisers have on organizational autonomy because their activities are viewed as outside the negotiation process involved in soliciting a gift.

As is demonstrated later in the chapters on systems theory and autonomy, the act of soliciting private gifts is, by its nature, an act that involves managing a resource dependency with an external group or individual. The negotiations involved in managing resource dependencies result in the enhancement or loss of the recipient organization's autonomy. Contrary to the myth of the invisible fund raiser, today's in-house practitioner takes an active role in soliciting gifts, but the impact of that role on organizational autonomy is ignored in current explanations of fund raising.

Managing the fund-raising program, not soliciting gifts, is the primary function of the fund raiser, according to the principle advocated by consulting firms. Or as Lord (1983) said, "The development officer, in most cases, should not be expected to personally solicit contributions or recruit volunteers" (p. 101). The fund raiser, according to the principle, is not to do, but to see that things get done by others—a description of the fund-raising function that closely emulates that of the consultant's. In fact, Lord admitted that his criteria of a "good development officer" is greatly influenced by his external perspective. He said, "This job description has been modeled for us, to a great extent, by the development officers who *are* in business—the outside fund-raising consultants" (p. 104).

Today, many fund-raising consultants, who are also prolific writers in the fund-raising literature, are chastising charitable organizations and internal fund raisers for diminishing the role of the volunteer in the fund-raising process. Fund raisers, they say, have adopted an inappropriate role of soliciting gifts (i.e., a growing number of internal fund raisers have replaced the mythical volunteer in asking for money). Yet, in his survey of 68 educational institutions that are members of CASE, Winship (1984) found little evidence to support this charge. He said:

> Voluntarism has been charged in some quarters as diminishing. . . . The survey suggests otherwise. There may be a reordering of the respective roles, with professional staff moving more prominently into front-line positions, but there is no general sense of less voluntarism. (p. 5)

Winship generalized his findings to say that major gifts (i.e., those gifts of $100,000 or more) are obtained for educational institutions by the three principal soliciting groups in roughly the following percentages: collectively, volunteers account for 39%, presidents account for 38%, and development officers, or senior fund raisers, obtain 23% of the major gifts. Commenting on the relatively high percentage of major gifts raised by fund-raising practitioners, he said, "That should not be surprising, yet it carries a message to those who feel that senior development officers should be manager and orchestrators, but not solicitors" (p. 1)

It must be interjected here that compensating unpaid volunteers by giving them the credit for successful gifts and the fact that fund raisers are dependent to a high degree on board members and trustees (the primary group of volunteers) and on presidents for their jobs may affect the assignment of gifts to the three categories just mentioned (i.e., fund raisers may actually be responsible for an even higher percentage of major gifts, but prefer to share the credit with their superiors and loyal volunteers). Describing a dress rehearsal for internal fund raisers who were preparing to make a request for a major gift, a recent article on the University of Pennsylvania's $1-billion capital campaign ("Major domo," 1990) pointed out that "Many people often work with a donor on a gift, and Penn staff members try whenever possible to give public credit to volunteers for bringing in gifts" (p. 20). Although volunteers seem to command much of the credit in the literature, many fund-raising practitioners believe that no single person is responsible for a major gift. For example, Cornell University prides itself on involving over 100 trustees, faculty, staff, and other friends in playing a key role in cultivating and soliciting major gifts (Winship, 1984).

Winship provided comments from his respondents regarding the role of volunteers vis-à-vis internal fund raisers. These comments are insightful in their emphasis on the existence of staff solicitations and also on the presence of guilt at not following the principle for fund-raising success largely advanced by fund-raising consultants. For example, representatives of private coeducational colleges included a fund raiser from Pepperdine University who said, "We have not done as well involving volunteers as we should" (p. 28). Yet Pepperdine can hardly be evaluated as unsuccessful in solicitations of major gifts because in 1988, just one of the gifts it received was a $6-million gift from the Arnold and Mabel Beckman Foundation for a program in managing technology. Another fund raiser at Louisiana College said, "Very few gifts come just from volunteer solicitation but rather from a combination of volunteers and staff" (p. 28), and another from Amherst said, "We intentionally put a staff person, or professional with a volunteer whenever and wherever possible and that is because prospective contributors now ask tough questions" (p. 29). Representing private universities, a fund raiser at Baylor University commented, "A few volunteers are successful when working with development staff" (p. 29), and one at Duke University said, "There have not been many volunteers asked to assist" (p. 30). Representing public universities, a fund raiser at Ball State University estimated that before 1980 about 80% of major gifts were the result of the solicitations made by an individual foundation board president, but since then, said the fund raiser, "probably 80% come from staff solicitations" (p. 30). A fund raiser at Indiana University said, "Volunteers have been helpful in initial evaluations and preliminary contacts but not active solicitors" (p. 30). As documented in chapter 2, the University of Minnesota is one of the most successful public universities at raising private dollars; yet a Minnesota fund raiser said, "Volunteers have not been doing substantial work here." He or she later commented, "It cannot be overemphasized that we are oriented to staff solicitation of major gifts" (p. 37).

Perhaps the consensus of the respondents is best expressed by a fund raiser at a professional school who said (cited in Winship, 1984), "Often the solicitation is not by a volunteer but would not have been successful without the volunteer" (p. 31). In other words, volunteers do play an important role in working with fund-raising practitioners to open doors to prospective donors and in other aspects of the research, cultivation, solicitation, and recognition stages. But the recent evidence supports the contention of this book that the critical role of the volunteer in soliciting gifts is a myth based in an era before the fund-raising function was internalized and perpetuated by fund-raising firms that limit their services to a nonsolicitation role. By discrediting this myth, fund raising can be examined from a new perspective—one that incorporates the concept of organizational autonomy. This reexamination is urgently needed in light of the increased level of major giving to colleges and universities, as outlined in chapter 2, and the potential threat to institutional autonomy that results from lay administrators soliciting and accepting such gifts.

Supporting the argument presented here, Pray (1981) stated:

> There would appear to be a weakening of the belief in the hitherto unquestioned maxim that a volunteer should almost always be used in preference to a staff person in any role involving public notice or contact with another volunteer or major donor. Most of us are no strangers to the advice that the development officer should almost never, expect in very special cases, take a public leadership position. This was always to be the role of the president, a trustee, or a key volunteer. (p. 179)

Today, according to Pray, "More and more chief development and advancement officers have proved themselves capable of assuming prominent posts in development strategy . . . working directly with trustees, making themselves highly visible in public meetings, and *partnering* appropriate staff, volunteers, or other colleagues in . . . negotiations with important foundations, corporations and individual donors" (p. 179). Unlike the conclusion of this book, however, Pray believed that the traditional roles of the volunteer solicitor and the invisible fund raiser resulted from a lack of competence of early practitioners. Without acknowledging the role of fund-raising consultants, such as himself, Pray said, "Indeed, we begin to suspect that the folklore of what is appropriate behavior grew out of a lack of ability of the earlier development people to play this more important role, more than it did out of the reality of the situation" (p. 180).

The "problem" of diminishing volunteer participation was a major element in a speech on creating the right environment for the giving of major gifts by Robert L. Thompson, chairman and CEO of Ketchum, Inc., at a recent CASE conference. Thompson (1989) admonished fund raisers that if their educational institutions wished to raise major gifts, then networks of volunteer solicitors would have to be reestablished. At the same conference a few hours later, Carbone (1989a), who conducted one of the rare introspective studies on fund raising in 1987, said that volunteers were an anomaly in the professionalism of the practice. Specifically, Carbone questioned how fund raising could ever be considered a profession because the literature professed that the fund-raising function is dependent on volunteers, which means that lay persons are proficient in what is supposed to be the specialized knowledge of professionals.

The response of this book to both speeches is that the role of the volunteer in American fund raising has largely been a myth historically perpetuated by consulting firms to de-emphasize the commercial aspect of their role in the fund-raising process and to provide a buffer between their financial success and the success of their fund-raising campaigns. Underlying both of these reasons is the dominant perspective on fund raising that has been provided by consulting firms (i.e., fund raising is a consulting function, not a solicitation function). This book takes a different viewpoint: that the "business" of fund raising (i.e., the survival of fund-raising firms as businesses) has, historically, had an undue influence on the explanation of fund raising, which has resulted in flawed assumptions and incomplete explanations of the function.

Finally, a few words must be added about the role of the president in the fund-raising process. As explained in chapter 2, presidents were the primary fund raisers of American colleges and universities up until the Civil War (Rudolph, 1962). As documented in Winship's (1984) study, presidents are still actively involved in fund raising; however, much of the fund-raising literature incorrectly refers to presidents as the chief fund raisers for their institutions. Such an assumption contributes to the myth of the invisible fund raiser (i.e., the role of lay practitioners is not critical in the process of fund raising because the chief executive officers of colleges and universities—as well as other charitable organizations—play a more important role). Pray (1981) emphasized the fallacy of such an assumption when he pointed out that presidents are the chief fund raisers in the same way that they are the chief administrators of all functions undertaken by colleges and universities. Pray concluded by saying, "The president falls short of this leadership role, however, if he or she attempts also to function as the chief operating officer in any of the divisions of the university" (p. 189). In addition, Cramer (cited in Pray, 1981) said, "While it is probably true that only the president can represent the institution before some constituencies, I do not believe that this is true as often as some egotistical presidents and some retiring development officers might believe" (p. 358).

FUND RAISING AS A SALES OR MARKETING FUNCTION

In light of the influence historically exerted by commercial firms on the definitions and roles of fund raising, it is not surprising that the function, itself, has been primarily explained in terms of the more traditional functions of business (i.e., sales and marketing). In fact, Lord (1983) saw little difference between philanthropy and business, explaining, "People buy from companies, invest in them and work for them because they feel that the enterprise can satisfy their human needs and desires, and because they believe in the *people* who represent the enterprise" (p. 77). He added that enabling a donor to "develop a *sense of ownership*" is the "basic *quid pro quo* in the business of development" (p. 31).

Much of the fund-raising literature deals with fund raising as a sales function. For example, selling gift opportunities is a reoccurring theme in Panas' (1984) book on how to raise mega gifts. In his tenet for success #40, Panas urged fund raisers to sell "the sizzle," and in Tenet #43 he said, "First sell the institution, then interpret how the program can be of everlasting benefit to the community, or to the world, or to mankind" (p. 190). After stating in Tenet #44 that major donors wish to give to "a cause of consequential proportions," Panas suggested:

> Even a new roof or the replacement of a boiler should be transformed into a selling point of significance. . . . Odds of getting a mega gift are far better if the new roof can be shown to be a reordering of social and human services. The new roof is the steak; serving mankind is the sizzle. (p. 191)

Although Panas urged fund raisers to sell the institution and the "sizzle," he warned them in Tenet #14, "Do not sell the needs of the institution" (p. 177). Need, according to Panas and other fund raisers, is not a motivating force in giving. Finally, while explaining Tenet #16, Panas said, "Help the prospect sell your program. Watch for the signals. Get the prospect as close to the program as possible. The best auto salesman gets you into the driver's seat" (p. 178).

In the opinion piece cited earlier about the impact of commission fees on the myth of the volunteer, Phillips and Richter (1989) used a sales approach to explain how commissions will upset the traditionally accepted division of labor in the fund-raising process. They asked, "What salesperson would be willing to stake an entire commission on a sale that required him or her to identify the prospect, cultivate the prospect's interest, prepare the marketing materials, develop the strategy for a 'sales approach,' and then forfeit participation in the final 'close'?" (p. 33).

Freeman (1987) also defined the fund-raising function as sales when he said:

> Make no mistake, the success of the career of the fund raiser is directly related to the volume and magnitude of the gifts. To succeed is to sell the institution and its needs to the prospective donor and to obtain whatever that prospect is capable of and willing to give. (p. 74)

A number of consultants argue against the sales approach to fund raising, including Lord (1983), who said, "When we ask for money. . . . We are counsellors, not salesmen" (p. 76). Apparently not satisfied with the explanations offered by sales or counselling, Lord adopted a marketing perspective, saying:

> The marketing approach is far more appropriate to the _people business_ of fund raising. It's also more effective. This approach focuses on providing satisfaction and fulfillment for the donor, rather than getting the donor to take what the institution has to offer. (p. 77)

Quoting Drucker, Lord said, "The aim of marketing is to make selling superfluous . . . to understand the customer so well that the product or service fits him and sells itself" (p. 77). According to his 1983 book, Lord's earlier book, _Philanthropy and Marketing_, "is widely recognized as the first and best work on the application of marketing principles to fund raising" (p. 119).

Contrary to his salesman approach outlined earlier, Panas (1984) agreed with Lord (1983), saying, "Successful fundraising is simply effective marketing. And effective marketing is helping others to meet their needs while accomplishing yours" (p. 176).

Both Panas (1984) and Lord (1983) criticize a sales approach to fund raising. Lord said, "Unfortunately, many institutions still think of fund raising as a 'hard sell.' They train a 'sales force' and put them in the field with sales objectives, quotas and sales promotion literature" (p. 77). Describing the sales approach to fund raising as "aggressive, manipulative selling," Lord warned that prospects for major gifts resist such approaches. Panas agreed, saying, "People resent overbearing solicitors who push to make the sale" (p. 192). Describing the reaction of major donors to this approach, Panas said, "They resist pressure and find it acutely repugnant. The most effective solicitor listens—and then moves directly to make the potential donor's dream one in the same with that of the institution" (p. 192). Completing a circle back to sales, Panas concluded his 65 tenets of success by saying, "But every salesperson knows that finally, inevitably—you must ask for the order. This is the greatest commandment of all" (p. 198).

There is evidence that marketing has received fairly wide acceptance as an appropriate approach to fund raising. For example, Silberg (1987) adopted a marketing perspective for her study of factors associated with the philanthropic behavior of major donors. According to Silberg, this approach is appropriate because "charity is concerned with an exchange function" (p. 8). As both Silberg (1987) and Burke (1988) use Kotler's perspective on nonprofit marketing to explain fund raising, it would be helpful here to interject a definition of marketing management from that scholar. According to Kotler (1972), "Marketing management is the analysis, planning, implementation, and control of programs designed to bring about desired exchanges with target audiences for the purpose of personal or mutual gain" (p. 13). As stressed by Kotler, marketing is centered around exchange relationships that result in personal or mutual gain. It can be postulated that fund-raising scholars have found this approach to be appropriate because of the element of exchange (i.e., it offers a fuller explanation of the two-way donor–recipient relationship than the altruistic approach of one-way distribution of private goods for public benefit as defined by Boulding, 1973, at the beginning of chapter 2). As pointed out in chapter 4, this book also assumes that gift-giving is an exchange relationship, but rejects the marketing approach because of its inappropriateness for explaining fund raising, which is discussed in more detail shortly.

The acceptability of the marketing perspective also can be seen by the growing interest in applying marketing techniques to fund-raising problems, both in research and in practice. Payton (1981) said, "Marketing and advertising practices are generally accepted as development tools" (p. 284). In his agenda for research on fund raising, Carbone (1986) called for more scholarly research on the application of market research techniques to different problems of fund raising. The 1989 winner of the American Association of Museums' annual competition for fund-raising materials, the John Michael Kohler Arts Center in Sheboygan, Wisconsin, attributed its successful fund-raising campaign in 1988 to a market research study ("An appeal," 1989). With the help of an advertising executive who serves on its board of trustees, the arts center conducted a marketing analysis that resulted in the identification of three different types of donors and their reasons for giving: user-based donors, who give because they use the facility; community-based donors, who give because of a sense of responsibility to area institutions; and status-based donors, who give because of the prestige it affords. According to the article on the winning campaign ("An appeal," 1989), "The analysis helped the arts center make a more effective pitch" (p. 15).

As discussed in chapter 4, Brittingham and Pezzullo (1990) use a marketing perspective to explain the value of exchange theory to fund raising research. For example, they stated, "Developing models of donor behavior . . . is essential to the successful marketing of fund-raising efforts" (p. 35). The popularity of applying a marketing perspective to all the communication activities of charitable organizations, including fund raising, was documented in _The Chronicle of Philanthropy_ in a recent opinion piece by Leet (1989), who said, "In the coming decade, the byword of wiser nonprofit organizations will not be 'communications' but 'marketing'" (p. 36).

Steinberg (1987) said that the market structure paradigm is invaluable for understanding the function and performance of nonprofit organizations. He found little difference between the market sector and charitable organizations, stating, "Advertising is in many ways analogous to fund-raising, foundations play the role of the stock market in providing initial equity capital, and sales of goods and services are important sources of revenue for both types of organizations" (p. 134). As described later in chapter 13, Steinberg used a model of advertising to create a fund-raising model through which donors exchange gifts for factual fund-raising literature. Concluding that the method used by charitable organizations to obtain resources is similar to that of sales in for-profit firms, Steinberg said, "Fund-raising programs are expenditures by the nonprofit firm to produce donative payments in the same sense that expenditures on marketing result in sales in for-profit firms" (p. 122).

Steinberg (1987) said that just as buyers make explicit trades to obtain goods or services in return for money, donors make implicit trades when they make gifts that result in direct and indirect benefits. Some of the examples of direct benefits given by Steinberg are a front-row seat at the opera, public recognition as a good citizen, and job advancement. He added that a lower crime rate is an example of an indirect benefit. If donors are motivated to give by the direct benefits they will receive, Steinberg concluded, "a donation is not different from a purchase" (p. 121).

This book argues that there are three major reasons why it is inappropriate to approach fund raising from a marketing perspective. Before discussing those reasons, however, it is necessary to provide a second definition of marketing by Kotler (1982) from his book, *Marketing for Nonprofit Organizations.* Offering a definition modified for nonprofits, Kotler stated:

> Marketing is the analysis, planning, implementation, and control of carefully formulated programs designed to bring about voluntary exchanges of values with target markets for the purpose of achieving organizational objectives. It relies heavily on designing the organization's offering in terms of the target markets' needs and desires, and on using effective pricing, communication, and distribution to inform, motivate, and service the markets. (p. 5)

Differences are apparent when comparing this definition with the one given earlier by Kotler (1972) (i.e., "Marketing management is the analysis, planning, implementation, and control of programs designed to bring about desired exchanges with target audiences for the purpose of personal or mutual gain," p. 13). Most obvious is Kotler's (1982) emphasis on voluntary exchanges of values, as opposed to desired exchanges, and the changed purpose of such exchanges from personal or mutual gain to achieving organizational objectives. It should also be noted that Kotler referred to fund raising as "donor marketing" in his 1982 book, which clearly indicates that he intended for fund raising to be explained by his definition of nonprofit marketing. Regardless of this scholar's efforts to encompass charitable organizations and their fund-raising function within the marketing perspective, this book argues that such a perspective is flawed and uses Kotler's definitions of marketing to help expose those flaws.

First, marketing is concerned with consumer publics, but the consumers of a charitable organization's products and services often are not donors, nor are its donors always consumers. It is recalled, for example, that the market research study for the Wisconsin arts center discussed earlier identified three different "types" of donors, of which only one consisted of consumers, or users. Pointing out elements in Kotler's (1982) definition, S. Dunn (1986) said Kotler's use of the term *target markets* emphasized the "product orientation" of marketing. Discussing the definition further, Dunn added, "The marketer offers benefits to the *consumer* so that she as well as the marketer will benefit from whatever activity takes place" (p. 111; italics added). As Grunig and Grunig (1988) stated, "At the theoretical/management level, the marketing function is concerned with products and services and customer publics" (p. 5).

The consumer markets for many charitable organizations are fee-paying customers, such as prospective students, sick patients, or opera fans, who frequently are not donors. For other charitable organizations, consumer markets consist of nonpaying clients, such as homeless persons, pregnant teenagers, and victims of AIDS, who rarely are donors. Few, if any, fund raisers would define donors as their organization's consumers (i.e., buyers and users identified by the charitable organization's mission), although—as discussed throughout this book—donors may benefit from a charitable organization's products and services through the gift-exchange relationship.

The second major reason why it is inappropriate to approach fund raising from a marketing perspective is because the marketer's defined role is to generate sales by changing an organization's products and services, whereas the acknowledged role of the fund raiser is to support a charitable organization's offerings by generating gifts.

It is recalled that in his definition of nonprofit marketing, Kotler (1982) said that marketing "relies heavily on designing the organization's offering in terms of the target markets' needs and desires" (p. 5). In other words, organizations depend on the marketing function to identify needs and desires of target markets and to then shape the organizations' products and services so as to better meet those needs and desires. Taking a marketing perspective of fund raising, therefore, would assume that fund raisers are responsible for influencing a charitable organization's offerings so that it will be more likely to satisfy the needs and desires of donors.

Rather than raising gifts in support of the mission of a charitable organization, a fund raiser utilizing a marketing perspective would strive to modify the organization's mission in order to raise the greatest amount of gifts possible. As Grunig and Grunig (1988) stated, "The major purpose of marketing is to make money for an organization by increasing the slope of the demand curve" (p. 5). Carried to an extreme, this would mean that a school of education—an academic discipline that traditionally does not attract a large amount of private support—would introduce business courses into its curriculum because donors, particularly corporations, have demonstrated a "desire" to exchange gifts with schools of business. More realistically, such a perspective of fund raising would encourage a liberal arts college to offer professional programs, such as business, thereby generating more private support, but also significantly changing the mission of the college.

As Brittingham and Pezzullo (1990) said, "The literature on fund raising makes much of the point that fund raisers should _not_ set their institution's priorities for fund raising; they should raise money for institutional priorities" (p. 57; italics added). This argument has particular bearing on the case for protecting and enhancing the autonomy of charitable organizations through the fund-raising process, as presented in this book.

Third, and most significant, a marketing perspective is inappropriate for fund raising because in market exchanges the quid pro quo is fully captured, whereas in gift exchanges some of the benefits spill over into society. It must be remembered that the market sector is primarily explained by economists in terms of rational decisions of self-interest.

That is to say, individuals enter into exchange relations in the marketplace to advance their own interests, or in Kotler's, 1972, definition, "for the purpose of personal or mutual gain"). According to Douglas (1983), "We say that a choice is 'rational' in terms of market economics when in any transaction the *quid* received is equal to or greater than the *quo* forgone in terms of the individual's self-interest" (p. 23).

An intention to exchange money for benefits of equal or greater value for oneself is, by legal definition, a nongiving behavior. As discussed in earlier chapters, the laws governing charitable organizations do not demand the total absence of any *quid* in exchange relationships involving tax-deductible gifts, but they do demand that the benefits "must not be fully captured by the *quid pro quo* but must spill over into society at large" (Douglas, 1983, p. 62). In other words, a market transaction consists of a direct exchange between what is forgone and what is gained, whereas a gift does not.

It is also recalled from the discussion in chapter 4 on Brittingham and Pezzullo's (1990) use of exchange theory that there are two conditions that define gifts made to noneleemosynary organizations, which should be incorporated into any theory of fund raising: Gifts must be charitable in purpose in that they contribute to the public good, and they must serve the self-interests of either the donor or the recipient, or both. The absence of the first condition defines a market exchange; the absence of the second condition defines an altruistic act (i.e., a voluntary, one-way transfer of exchangeables to an eleemosynary organization).

Illustrating this concept, Anne Alexander (1988), vice president of the AT&T Foundation, said, "A corporation gives money to a university so the university can use it to, ultimately, further the corporation's philanthropic goals—in its own self-interest and that of society at large" (p. 13).

It is the necessary condition of contributing to society at large, or to the public good, that distinguishes gift giving and getting from market transactions. For example, when purchasing a car, buyers seek economic and social benefits for their self-interest from that particular purchase—benefits that they believe are equal to or greater than the cost of the car.

When making a gift, however, donors seek benefits for the public good (as interpreted by them), although they may gain economic and sociopolitical benefits for themselves, and, indeed, those benefits may be factors in the decision to make a gift. The point is that gifts are not market exchanges because the benefits resulting from the exchange are not fully captured by the actors involved).[1]

This point is most clearly illustrated by the presence of economic benefits in gift exchanges. For example, IRS regulations demand that the fair market value of any tangible, direct benefits provided to a donor, such as tickets to athletic events, free dinners, or plaques, must be deducted from the gift before it is deducted from taxable income. If the total value of the benefits equals the monetary value of the gift, the contribution is disallowed for deduction. In other words, whether the benefits derived from making a gift are economic, social, or political, if they are equal to or exceed the value of the gift, the exchange is not philanthropic. As quoted earlier in this discussion, Steinberg (1987) said that when donors are motivated to give by the direct benefits they will receive, such as a seat at the opera, public recognition, and job advancement, "a donation is not different from a purchase" (121).

Although this book agrees with Steinberg's conclusion, it does not agree with his application of the market structure paradigm to fund raising. Such an application places an overemphasis on direct benefits accrued by donors through gift exchanges, thereby subverting the necessary condition of the public good. It is recalled from chapter 4 that Brittingham and Pezzullo's (1990) application of exchange theory to fund raising resulted in the same overemphasis, which was defined as a marketing perspective. This perspective, as demonstrated at the conclusion of this chapter, leads to increased government regulation. In other words, the tax-exempt status of charitable organizations and the deductibility of gifts can only be protected "if the gifts are charitable in purpose _and_ serve the public interest" (Levy & Oviatt, 1989, p. 133; italics added).

In preparation for the discussion in chapter 6 on systems theory, it is necessary once again to stress that benefits are a fundamental concept in managing interdependencies with donors through the fund-raising function. However, it must be remembered that the economic and sociopolitical benefits exchanged in these relationships never fully capture the totality of benefits generated by the gift.

In summary, there are three reasons why it is inappropriate to approach fund raising from a marketing perspective: (a) marketing is concerned with consumer publics, but donors and consumers are not synonymous; (b) the marketer's defined role is to generate sales by changing an organization's products and

---

[1]Although it could be argued that society benefits from replacing an old car with a new one because of reduced pollution, such benefits are not a necessary condition of the purchase decision, but can be viewed as a byproduct of a decision based on utilitarian value.

services, but the acknowledged role of the fund raiser is to support a charitable organization's offerings by generating gifts; and (c) in market exchanges the *quid pro quo* is fully captured, but in gift exchanges some of the benefits spill over into society.

To supplement these reasons, this section turns to the discipline of economics to document that even scholars in that field have recognized the need to go beyond market explanations of philanthropy (i.e., to reject sales and marketing as explanations for fund-giving and fund raising). To incorporate philanthropy within the self-interest, or utility maximization model—which has been successful in the study of both economics and politics—Bolnick (1975) turned to the behavioral sciences to provide a model of philanthropic decision making. He explained that "a satisfactory understanding of philanthropic activity requires a broadening of economic behavioral models to include social and psychological motivations" (pp. 220-221).

According to Bolnick's model, the probability of an individual choosing to follow a behavioral norm prescribing a gift is dependent on the stochastic function of four independent variables: indirect social pressures from identification with reference groups, direct social pressures as perceived by the individual, the economic utility for the individual of making the contribution, and the cost of making it. Expressed as a parsimonious equation, Bolnick's model is as follows:

$$Pr(B) = F(I,D,E,C)$$

Pr = Probability operator (not determinant solution)
B   = Behavioral norm prescribing a contribution
F   = Stochastic function of four independent variables
I   = Indirect social pressures from identification with reference groups
D   = Direct social pressures perceived
E   = Economic utility of B for the individual
C   = Cost (objective) of doing B

Rather than assuming that individuals make gift decisions by only weighing the cost of doing so against the return (economic utility) in the neo-classic model of the market, Bolnick's model explains that an individual will make his or her choice by weighing social gratifications and costs, as well as the economic utility and cost of his or her action (i.e., based on a satisfactory level of net rewards).

It is not the purpose of this book to defend or advance Bolnick's (1975) model; rather, it is introduced here to emphasize the need to incorporate factors outside of economics in any approach to fund raising. The following discussion, then, demonstrates how such a model is useful for rejecting current perspectives of fund raising as a sales or marketing function and for advancing a new approach to fund raising.

First, as already stated, Bolnick's model demonstrates the incomplete explanations offered by the generally accepted sales or marketing approach to fund raising (i.e., by association, the need for an expanded economic model to explain gift decision-making negates the appropriateness of using an approach to fund raising that is based on the more narrow self-interest model).

Second, Bolnick's (1975) model is valuable for the simple fact that it does not disallow some _quid_ for the _quo_ given. As demonstrated most clearly with corporate donors, who have a self-proclaimed giving motivation of "enlightened self-interest"—which is discussed in the later chapter on the three sources of gifts—gift–recipient relationships frequently include economic benefits for donors. For example, giving money to underwrite undergraduate scholarships for accounting majors is a popular gift for large accounting firms because it gives them leverage in hiring the scholarship recipients after graduation, thereby saving the money they would spend recruiting employees from a shrinking pool of candidates and sometimes saving money they would spend in salary wars with other bidders. In short, Bolnick's model supports the theory of donor relations developed in this book, which assumes the presence of possible economic benefit to the donor. As is described shortly, the presence of self-interest in giving behaviors—as well as factors related to institutional autonomy—prescribe some level of negotiations in the solicitation and acceptance of gifts. As McKean (1975) said, pursuing self-interest or maximizing utility does not mean selfishness, but "the purposeful behavior to achieve _whatever_ yields preferredness" (p. 29).

Third, the social costs of giving and of not giving are reflected in Bolnick's (1975) model. Fund raisers have long acknowledged the effective use of volunteers in providing peer pressure on prospective donors to obtain gifts; indeed, much of the enduring strength of the myth of the volunteer has been based on their ability to influence peer behavior. Boulding (cited in Bolnick, 1975) claimed that in our large, heterogeneous society, "it is almost always necessary to reinforce philanthropy with coercion" (p. 210). The use of volunteers in applying peer pressure acknowledges the existence of a perceived "cost" to the donor in not making a gift (e.g., loss of respect, disharmony for not following primary group norms, shame, guilt, etc). As Bolnick explained, "We have seen how individuals can seek gratification not only from economic transactions, but from social interaction as well. In fact, 'social man' might rationally accept economic costs in order to maintain gratifying, consonant social relationships" (p. 220).

Finally, Bolnick's (1975) model is useful because it approaches fund giving as a complicated social and economic decision, which illuminates the presence of both pragmatic and moral imperatives in the decision to make a gift. Economists tell us that people are basically bifurcated; that is to say, they express pragmatic decisions when acting in the market, but they express their interpretation of moral imperatives when dealing with social policies, and sometimes the latter is not consistent with economic self-interest. For example, senior citizens may vote to raise their own taxes in support of day care centers because they believe a society should take care of its young children.

Following this line of thought, it can be hypothesized that when acting in the philanthropic arena—the third sector, as opposed to the government and market sectors—people express decisions that are a combination of their two sides. For example, people may give away part of their income in support of abortion because they believe a society should not bring unwanted children into the world. Bolnick's model takes into account the two sides of humans and supports this book's hypothesis that in the philanthropic arena people express *both* pragmatic decisions and their interpretation of moral imperatives (i.e., a decision to make a gift is based on the utilitarian value of the exchange as perceived by the donor, a sense of responsibility to serve the greater public good, and an interpretation of what constitutes the public interest).

Therefore, corporations, foundations, or individuals making gifts to charitable organizations classified by our typology in chapter 3 as those dealing with positive externalities or public goods are seeking benefits for themselves—such as an educated employee pool, gratitude, or political power—and benefits for the public good, with the strength of the variables changing in each situation. As Bolnick said, "Man need not be 'bifurcated' to act in his own traditionally defined self-interest in some instances, and in the public interest in others; in both cases the same underlying motivations may be at work, with only the strength of certain variables being altered" (p. 221).

Summarizing this chapter on myths and misconceptions, there are a number of flawed assumptions underlying current principles of fund raising. Although scholars and practitioners propagate the view that gifts provide flexible funding, major gifts have historically been restricted as to their purpose, and current giving statistics document that approximately 80% of all gift dollars to American colleges and universities are restricted. Although charitable organizations, including colleges and universities, expanded their donor base after World War I in response to criticism about dependencies on a small number of donors, the current emphasis on capital campaigns and major gifts has led to increased dependencies on those few donors who are capable of making mega or ultimate gifts. The myth of unrestricted gifts and the myth of a broad base of donors have hidden the fact that an increased focus on donors of major gifts can affect the autonomy of charitable organizations.

The myth of the volunteer solicitor and its corollary, the myth of the invisible fund raiser, are primarily attributable to the historical evolution of the fund-raising function and to the self-interests of commercial fund-raising firms that do not solicit money as part of their consulting service. In contrast to current principles that assume volunteers are critical to the solicitation of gifts and that the role of fund-raising practitioners is to manage the process behind the scenes, evidence shows that internal fund raisers do solicit major gifts today. The acceptance of these myths has hidden the fact that lay administrators, rather than chief policymakers, are currently responsible for managing and executing the solicitation and acceptance of gifts that may or may not support organizational goals.

In addition, current perspectives of fund raising as a sales or marketing function are inappropriate for an understanding of this organizational behavior. Such business-oriented explanations are flawed by the assumption that the act of giving to a charitable organization is analogous to a market exchange (e.g., donor motivations can be explained as desires to exchange gifts for benefits of equal or greater value). Even economists have recognized the need to go beyond market explanations of philanthropy to incorporate economic and sociopolitical benefits within gift decisions. An economist's model that includes variables such as social gratifications and costs, as well as economic utility and cost, demonstrates the inappropriateness of using a sales or marketing approach to fund raising.

Through the same model, this book also rejects explanations of fund raising as a function that deals primarily with altruistic behavior by donors, and it concludes that donor–recipient relationships include the presence of possible economic and sociopolitical benefits for the donor. In addition, people express both pragmatic decisions and their interpretation of moral imperatives in the philanthropic arena; therefore, donors making gifts to noneleemosynary organizations are seeking benefits for the public good, as well as benefits for themselves, with the strength of certain variables changing in each situation.

Finally, it is argued here that continued adherence to the current principles and perspectives of fund raising analyzed in this chapter may lead to loss of autonomy by organizations relinquishing control to donors or by prompting increased government regulations, including changes in the tax-exempt status of charitable organizations and the tax-deductibility of gifts to them. For example, it was pointed out in the earlier discussion on fund raising as a marketing function that such a perspective can lead charitable organizations to change their mission, trading some of their autonomy in exchange for gifts. Based on a marketing perspective, goods and services produced by the charitable organization will grow out of needs and desires of donors rather than out of the organization's mission. In other words, donors—through the fund-raising function—will assume a high degree of control over what the charitable organization does, creating organizational objectives outside the central mission. Such situations involving colleges and universities were described in chapter 2.

In relation to loss of autonomy through regulation, the vulnerability of charitable organizations to government intervention also was well documented in chapters 2 and 3. The point here is that trends toward increasing government regulation are linked to the current principles and perspectives of fund raising. For example, the U.S. General Accounting Office's report on hospitals and tax-exemption (Nadel, 1990) discussed earlier in chapter 3 said that the business mentality of some nonprofit hospitals provided a strong argument for revoking their tax-exempt status. The report stated, "It was not uncommon for nonprofit hospitals' strategic goals to resemble those of for-profit institutions. For example, both focus on increasing market share, rather than targeting underserved populations" (p. 1). Although fund raising is not mentioned in the report, it can be assumed that the fund-raising activities of these nonprofit hospitals did not include raising private gifts for indigent care (i.e., fund raising did not support the mission of a hospital classified by the IRS as a charitable organization). It can also be assumed that, based on a marketing or sales perspective, fund raisers for such nonprofit hospitals concentrated on gifts that had little to do with taking care of "underserved populations." As pointed out by Jencks (1987) in chapter 3, gifts to hospitals are "seldom earmarked for people who could not otherwise afford to use the hospital" (p. 322). In other words, the fund-raising behavior of these charitable organizations (i.e., nonprofit hospitals) concentrated on target markets and shaped the services of those organizations to meet the unmet needs of donors, not of indigent patients who the hospitals may soon be legislated to serve under their mission as "charitable."

Promoting planned gifts as tax shelters also can be linked to a sales or marketing perspective of fund raising. When Congress raised capital-gains tax rates in 1986, gifts of appreciated property became an attractive financial-planning option. As a result, the promotion of planned gifts primarily as tax shelters became more common. Although most of the criticism has been directed at financial professionals who charge commissions or finders fees, fund raisers commonly use tax advantages as a "sales point" in their solicitations. Fund-raising consultant Robert Sharpe (1989) predicted that this current emphasis by fund raisers on the tax-shelter aspects of planned gifts will raise the ire of legislators and bring about detrimental changes in the federal tax laws. As Sharpe said, "If you act like a tax shelter, Congress will eventually treat you like one, and the prevailing mood in a revenue-starved Congress is not a kind one toward tax shelters" (p. 40).

According to Sharpe (1989), this would not be the first time that a marketing mentality toward planned gifts has led to increased regulation. As fund-raising offices were staffed by full-time practitioners in the 1960s, he said, many "began to believe that *how* a gift was made could be as attractive as *why* it was made" (p. 40). As a result, Congress responded to what it perceived as abuses of the charitable deduction with sweeping legislation in 1969. According to Sharpe, "Lawmakers intended to make certain that a legitimate gift element existed and that 'profitable' charitable gifts which could be *marketed* as just another tax shelter were not possible" (p. 40; italics added).

Rebuking those who promote planned gifts primarily as tax shelters, an informal group of planned-giving officers from 15 colleges and universities issued a statement in 1989, which said, "We are appalled by recent promotions which appear to be 'selling' charitable gift arrangements as tax shelters or commercial transactions . . . without any appreciation of the true nature of a charitable contribution" ("Fund raisers assail," 1989, p. 1). In short, the solicitation of planned gifts, with emphasis on the tax advantages of such gifts, is indicative of the current business-oriented mentality of fund raising, although such a mentality is embedded in many other fund-raising activities, which also have prompted attention from government regulators.

The IRS recently stepped up its surveillance of benefits related to gifts, warning charitable organizations and their fund raisers that they are responsible, to some extent, for informing donors of the portion of gifts that can be deducted from federal income tax. As related to the earlier discussion on benefits accrued by donors, fund raisers increasingly have relied on gift incentives or premiums, such as membership dinners and special access to research findings, to "market" lower level, annual gifts and major, restricted gifts. For example, William Olcott (1990), the editor of *Fund Raising Management*, recently commended a charitable organization that works with emotionally handicapped people in Trenton, New Jersey for its "unique way of saying thank you to its corporate donors—it offers them seminars on employee training and motivation" (p. 8).

According to Olcott:

Payback to corporations is designed to match their contributions. There are four classes of membership . . . each level receives a benefit package. For example, an associate member [for $750] gets two corporate half-day workshops for 25 employees, a quarterly newsletter, a recognition certificate and invitations to receptions and special events. (p. 8)

Such a marketing, or *quid pro quo*, approach to raising gifts has not gone unnoticed by the IRS. According to an article in *Giving USA Update* (AAFRC, 1988b), "Premiums, recognition items and awards tied to philanthropic donations came under increased scrutiny by the Internal Revenue Service (IRS) in 1988, and fund raisers were warned to inform donors that only the amount of the gifts *in excess* of the value of any premiums is tax deductible" (p. 3; italics added).

Perhaps most indicative of the potential loss of autonomy inherent in the current sales and marketing perspectives of fund raising is the fact that in the summer of 1989, high-ranking officials of the U.S. Postal Service and the Federal Trade Commission (FTC) suggested that Congress expand the authority of the FTC to all nonprofits, including charitable organizations ("Colleges are nervous," 1989). The proposed legislation was prompted by a Congressional hearing in July 1989 on deceptive fund-raising practices. Significantly, the hearing occurred as the Justice Department was investigating whether some colleges were violating federal antitrust laws in the way they set tuition and award financial aid, and as the U.S. Post Office was preparing to levy fines and penalties against numerous charitable organizations for using nonprofit postal rates to mail material on profit-making activities, such as selling insurance policies to alumni ("Colleges are nervous," 1989).

Keeping in mind the trends discussed in chapters 2 and 3 toward increased state regulation of fund-raising activities, challenges to the tax-exempt status of charitable organizations at the local, state, and federal levels, and limits on the charitable deduction for federal taxpayers, it is clear that fund raising has affected the autonomy of charitable organizations by inviting government intervention.

Indeed, examples of how current perspectives of fund raising are leading to increased government regulation have not yet been exhausted, and more are provided in later chapters of this book. For example, a full discussion on the commercialization of fund raising through the relatively new phenomenon of cause-related marketing is reserved for chapter 12 on the management of corporate contributions.

It is important here, however, to refer to an opinion piece, written shortly before his death, by Maurice Gurin (1990), who pointed out that charity leaders and fund raisers have embraced cause-related marketing, which links the promotion of corporate products with philanthropic causes. Condemning charitable organizations who are increasingly entering these marketing arrangements, Gurin said:

Their volunteer leaders and fund raisers are apparently not interested that such funds represent business income, probably most often unrelated-business income, which is subject to taxation. That could become a major problem if Congress begins to take a closer look at the amount that charitable organizations earn from cooperative ventures, and decides that too many of these groups are earning too much money from them. (p. 37)

Turning from lost autonomy through government regulation to lost autonomy through donor control, Gurin said, "They do not seem to be worried that by meeting the requirements of commercial arrangements they might have to modify their program objectives, thus compromising their integrity" (p. 37).

Summarizing the entire discussion of this section, Gurin (1990) said, "Over the past decade, philanthropy has become more and more commercialized. It's high time that leaders in the voluntary sector call a halt to, if not try to reverse, this dangerous trend that threatens to alienate donors and undermine the integrity of philanthropy" (p. 36).

Situations in which government intervention and major donors threaten the autonomy of charitable organizations—as outlined here and in other chapters of this book—provide strong evidence that continued adherence to commonly accepted principles and perspectives of fund raising are inappropriate and dangerous. In light of the evidence presented, current perspectives of fund raising are rejected, and this book turns its attention to developing a new perspective. In Part II, fund raising is approached from a macrolevel, utilizing systems theory and the concept of organizational autonomy to provide a theoretical foundation on which to build a new theory of donor relations.

PART II

SYSTEMS THEORY AND AUTONOMY: APPROACHING FUND RAISING FROM A MACROPERSPECTIVE

By discrediting current principles and perspectives, the stage is set for approaching fund raising from a new perspective—one that is based on systems theory and the concept of autonomy. Beginning Part II, chapter 6 turns to systems theory for a theoretical foundation on which to build a theory of donor relations, concluding that the relationships between donors and recipient organizations, are best understood as an interdependency of groups and organizations within an environment. Chapter 7 builds on the issue of autonomy within the context of environmental interdependencies by focusing on higher education for an in-depth analysis of the concept of institutional autonomy and the effect of fund raising on American colleges and universities.

Chapter 8 then analyzes the three primary sources of private support to answer the research question: In relation to institutional autonomy, how do foundations, corporations, and individuals differ in their potential to infringe on a charitable organization's power to determine its goals and the means of pursuing those goals? Generalizing beyond colleges and universities, chapter 9 analyzes three classic studies to document cases of charitable organizations that have changed their mission and goals primarily because of their dependency on external, philanthropic funding sources.

Chapter 6

Systems Theory: Charitable Organizations and Their Environments

This chapter approaches fund raising through the framework of systems theory. Drawing from the literature on organizational behavior and the sociology of organizations, it focuses on the resource dependence perspective of Pfeffer and Salancik (1978), Gouldner's (1960) norm of reciprocity, Blau's (1986) theory of social and power exchange, and Mintzberg's (1983) power theory to provide a theoretical explanation for the relationships between charitable organizations and the donors in their environment. The chapter concludes that contrary to conventional wisdom, these relationships are best understood not as benevolent, business, or pseudo relations, but as interdependencies of groups and organizations within an environment.

These fund-raising interdependencies constitute an ongoing exchange process that requires management and negotiation by the charitable organization, especially by those practitioners who manage its fund-raising programs. The concept of autonomy is a central issue in the exchange process in that the power of an organization to determine and pursue its own goals is affected by how successful an organization is at managing its interdependencies. Although absolute autonomy is impossible, organizations in all three economic sectors of our society (i.e., business, government, and nonprofit) strive to maintain autonomy by dominating or cooperating with groups or other organizations within their environments. Finally, charitable organizations in the nonprofit sector face a double-edged sword in relation to interdependencies with donors in their environment: In order to enhance their autonomy, they must seek external funding to support their institutional goals, but in so doing, they risk losing autonomy by accepting gifts that may limit their power to determine goals and the means of pursuing them.

Grunig's (e.g., 1976, in preparation) theory of public relations, which is grounded in systems theory, is introduced in the last section of this chapter. A central premise of Grunig's theory is that autonomy is the most abstract and general goal of organizations and that the primary purpose of public relations is to enhance and protect organizational autonomy by effectively managing communications between an organization and the various publics in its environment. It is argued that this theory is of particular value in explaining the relationship between the autonomy of charitable organizations and managing external relations, including those with donor publics.

A RESOURCE DEPENDENCE PERSPECTIVE

Starting with theories such as the theory of contingency (Lawrence & Lorsch, 1967), contemporary literature on organizations is grounded in the open-systems theory as defined by Katz and Kahn (1978). The early contingency theory subsumed both the classical and human relations theories of organizations and built on even earlier work by Burns and Stalker (1961) to include the role of environmental forces, such as market demand, on the structure and behavior of an organization.

According to Katz and Kahn (1978), the open-systems theory draws heavily from three major research traditions: (a) Marxism, which approaches organizations as subunits in a "superstructure," or social system; (b) structural functionalism, which contributes to the concept of the boundary role; and (c) general systems theory, which approaches organizations as living organisms that can die. Katz and Kahn contend that organizations are dependent on their environments for survival and success and that environmental influences (i.e., forces that interpenetrate organizational boundaries) help shape the structure and behavior of organizations. According to Robbins (1987), open-systems theory defines organizational environment as general and specific, the latter being composed of those groups and individuals that are affected by the organization and/or that can affect the organization (i.e., those publics "directly relevant to the organization in achieving its goals," p. 143). Whereas the general environment encompasses conditions that may impact the organization potentially, Robbins said that the specific environment "is the part of the environment with which management will be concerned because it is made up of those critical constituencies that can positively or negatively influence the organization's effectiveness" (p. 143). "It is," according to Robbins, "unique to each organization and it changes with conditions" (p. 143). As described more fully in chapter 10 on the fund raiser in a boundary role, Robbins emphasized that there is a boundary that separates an open system from its environment.

According to Pfeffer and Salancik (1978), interdependence is a consequence of open systems. The resource dependence theory of these scholars advances the perspective that organizations are controlled by their relationships to external sources of necessary resources. The amount of control (i.e., the degree of autonomy that is given up by the recipient organization in order to obtain the resource) is negotiable. According to Pfeffer and Salancik, "Organizations are other-directed, involved in a constant struggle for autonomy and discretion, confronted with constraint and external control" (p. 257). These scholars defined organizational effectiveness as how well the organization has satisfied "the demands of those in its environment from whom it requires support for its continued existence" (p. 60). As discussed in the later chapter on measuring fund-raising effectiveness, it is useful to think of the concepts of corporate social responsibility and institutional accountability in terms of effectiveness as defined by Pfeffer and Salancik.

Pfeffer and Salancik (1978) described the relationship between an organization and its environment as a quasi-marketplace, in which representatives of the focal organization are continually negotiating and allocating organizational control with members of critical publics on whom the focal organization depends for its survival and success. The vulnerability of the organization, according to these scholars, is determined by its degree of dependency on a resource and the external sources of this resource (i.e., the greater the dependency, the higher the potential for loss of autonomy). Pfeffer and Salancik illustrated their point by referring to a study conducted by Salancik on defense contractors and their compliance to federal policies on affirmative action. The results of this study showed that heavy dependence on the Department of Defense for revenue had a highly positive relationship to compliance with affirmative action policies, whereas dependence of the Defense Department on a contractor for a crucial part (e.g., being sole source for a part needed by the Defense Department) had a negative relationship to affirmative action compliance. They concluded by saying, "It is exactly such influences on behavior, resulting from the organization's transactions or exchanges with external organizations, that are what is meant when we say that organizational behavior is constrained and shaped by the demands and pressures of organizations and groups in its environment" (p. 59).

Pfeffer and Salancik (1978) listed 10 conditions that determine an organization's vulnerability to external control, including importance of a particular resource and lack of alternate sources for that resource. The scholars said that problems also arise in situations of resource dependence when the organization ignores or misreads the importance of an external dependency relationship and the potency of each external group to affect the organization's continued survival and success. "This is especially likely," they said, "when the focal organization itself enters a new field of activity" (p. 79). As described in earlier chapters, internalized fund raising is a relatively new function for charitable organizations, including colleges and universities (e.g., Pray, 1981). It is conceivable, therefore, that fund raising by such organizations increases the likelihood that relationships with external sources of gifts may lead to external compliance because the importance and potency of interdependencies with donors may be ignored or misread. Pfeffer and Salancik said, "Compliance is a loss of discretion, a constraint, and an admission of limited autonomy" (p. 94).

Pfeffer and Salancik (1978) described four strategies for organizations to use to avoid external control, which can be related to charitable organizations involved in fund raising: (a) building an inventory (e.g., building endowments to avoid dependence on annual lower level donors of unrestricted gifts or on major donors of restricted gifts); (b) defining terms of the exchange relationship (e.g., establishing fund-raising policies that standardize procedures and define unacceptable gift conditions); (c) developing substitutable exchanges (the most effective strategy) (e.g., developing a broad base of lower level and major donors); and (d) diversifying and building alternative financial sources (e.g., seeking a balance between user fees, public funding, and gifts).

As discussed in the preceding chapter on myths and misconceptions, American colleges and universities expanded their base of donors after World War I in response to critics who claimed that these important institutions were dependent on the major gifts of a small number of wealthy donors (Curti & Nash, 1965). By soliciting and accepting gifts from large numbers of alumni, friends, corporations, and foundations, colleges and universities weakened their donor dependence by developing substitutable exchanges and by diversifying sources of private support. According to Pfeffer and Salancik (1978), "Organizations with many small suppliers are potentially less controlled than ones with a few major suppliers" (p. 271). These scholars added that diversification does not reduce demands from external sources of resources—in fact, it creates the potential for more—but diversification does reduce the focal organization's need to respond to any given demand. In relation to this discussion of Pfeffer and Salancik's resource dependence perspective, the move by colleges and universities to expand sources of private gifts after World War I can be described as a strategy used by institutions of higher education to protect their autonomy.

Diversification of funding sources from the public and private sectors is a common theme in the literature of higher education. Unfortunately—as discussed earlier in the chapter on myths—arguments in favor of funding diversification have frequently supported the false assumption that private funds provide flexibility and autonomy, as opposed to public funds, which are highly constrained (e.g., Kramer, 1980). Discussing voluntary support in the 1980s in a book published by the American Council on Education, Haire (1981) stated:

> Many private gifts are, of course, restricted for particular uses, but they do not impose undesirable and unwelcome restrictions on admissions, hiring, or curricula. Because each gift, bequest, or grant is typically small in relation to any institutional budget, it cannot be accompanied by burdensome regulations that impose donor-conceived standards on the operations of the academy. (p. 140)

Haire's viewpoint of private gifts is discredited by the examples provided in chapter 2 of major gifts that have imposed unwelcome restrictions and donor-conceived standards on colleges and universities. In addition, his beliefs do not take into account the recent rise in mega and ultimate gifts and the significance of these gifts to capital campaign goals, as described in chapters 2 and 5. The resource dependence perspective, on the other hand, explains fund-raising situations, such as those presented in chapter 2, as instances in which the organizational behavior of colleges and universities has been constrained and shaped by a dependency relationship with donors in their specific environment. Noting that past history of successful influence encourages more attempts, Pfeffer and Salancik (1978) stated, "Organizational autonomy may be lost progressively as behaviors and decisions are increasingly constrained" (p. 95).

An irony of the resource dependence perspective, as pointed out by Pfeffer and Salancik (1978), is that because of its external dependencies, an organization often seeks to stabilize the exchange relationships that threaten its autonomy. This is particularly true for charitable organizations that need external financial resources to independently pursue their goals, but risk loss of autonomy when seeking those resources. Pfeffer and Salancik discussed two methods that organizations use to stabilize resource relationships: (a) joint endeavors (e.g., industrial-university partnerships, such as the Whitehead Institute at the Massachusetts Institute of Technology); and (b) _cooptation_, which Pfeffer and Salancik defined as "managing the environment by appointing significant external representatives to positions in the organization" (p. 161) (e.g., appointing donors to boards of trustees and related foundation boards). Although both of these methods stabilize the funding relationship between recipient organization and donor, they also formalize external control (i.e., joint endeavors and cooptation, by their nature, forfeit some degree of organizational autonomy).

For example, commenting on the industrial-university partnerships currently being established to boost technology transfer in the United States, an official with the American Physical Society said, "We're going to start shoving our universities into more applied and even more developmental work" ("More partnerships," 1989, p. A22). The official said that such partnerships could lead many academic researchers to forgo basic studies, which would also pose a threat to graduate training.

The method of cooptation to stabilize funding relationships with external donors is widely practiced by charitable organizations and their fund-raising practitioners. Paul Franz (1981), who was vice president of development at Lehigh University for more than 30 years and who is considered a leading fund-raising practitioner, recommended following the fund-raising adage that "you should place your top donors on the . . . governing board" (p. 163). He said, "A well-constituted board must have a good potential to raise funds, and this means that at least half of the members should have the capability to give and to solicit major gifts" (p. 163). A widely accepted axiom regarding the role of the trustee in fund raising is "give, get, or get off." A recent article in the *Wall Street Journal* ("Prestigious positions," 1988) reported, "The American Society for the Prevention of Cruelty to Animals in New York requires new trustees to sign a statement agreeing to make a 'substantial' donation, to 'actively' engage in fund raising and to devote at least two hours a month to ASPCA activities" (p. 31).

Finally, in his study of boards of university-related foundations for public institutions, Worth (cited in Rowland, 1983) found that most board members are selected "either for their potential as donors or as fund raisers" (p. 56). He said that although it is rare for foundation boards to be directly involved in decisions on institutional policy, they "often influence university operation through the allocation of unrestricted gifts and the determination of fund-raising goals and purposes" (p. 56).

In support of the effectiveness of cooptation for stabilizing external resource dependencies, Pfeffer and Salancik (1978) referred to a study Pfeffer conducted on the membership of hospital boards of directors. The study showed that those nonprofit hospitals that were most successful (i.e., documented growth in size and budget) were those that had boards composed of members selected for their fund-raising potential and ability. On the other hand, government-owned hospitals were more successful if they had directors oriented to hospital administration.

Although Mintzberg (1983) said that positions on some boards represent status rather than a serious say in decision making, he added that the price of cooptation often can be real power. Pfeffer and Salancik (1978) said that there are costs "which organizations are willing to bear . . . for the benefits of predictable and certain exchanges" (p. 183).

Although many of them receive government funding and are profit making, charitable organizations are dependent to different degrees on tax-deductible contributions from external constituencies. Muelder (1978), for example, said, "Economically speaking, higher education is dependent and even parasitic as an institution. Its sources of income are gifts, taxes and tuition" (p. 16).

According to Powell and Friedkin (1987), "Precisely because nonprofit organizations depend on external sources for support, they may find it necessary to bend and shift with the prevailing political and economic winds" (p. 180). Powell and Friedkin said there are three generic explanations for change in all types of organizations, one of which is the resource dependence perspective that "emphasizes the tendency of organizations to alter their structures and goals in order to obtain the resources needed to survive" (p. 182). According to these scholars:

> The core of resource-dependence theory is the view that organizations will (and should) respond to the demands of those groups in the environment that control critical resources. Because organizations are not internally self-sufficient, they require resources from the environment; hence, they become dependent upon those elements that provide the most needed forms of support. The managerial task, according to this approach, is to respond to environmental demands and constraints and attempt to mitigate these influences. (p. 182)

Powell and Friedkin (1987) used the resource dependence perspective to analyze the relationship between donors and the programming staff who were involved in producing the public television series, "Dance in America." This analysis of a public benefit charity, as defined by the typology of nonprofit organizations presented earlier in chapter 3, illustrates how dependency on fewer donors facilitates external control of a charitable organization. According to the scholars, "As long as resources were abundant, the staff was able to manage the divergent demands of the different funders either by playing them off against one another or by attending to them sequentially" (p. 182). However, the scholars said that "when resources shrunk and only a few funding sources provided the bulk of the money, the staff lost its room to maneuver and the funders gained much greater say in program content" (p. 182).

A critical variable of external control, according to Pfeffer and Salancik (1978), "is the extent to which the organization represents a resource or potential tool to be used by others" (p. 273). As stated in chapter 1, colleges and universities enjoy a higher level of autonomy than other types of organizations largely because of their special value to society (e.g., transmitters of culture and knowledge). Describing the increasing dependence of economic and political organizations on institutions of higher education, Muelder (1978) said:

> The term *multiversity* expresses the plural service roles that higher education plays in the nation. Hardly an activity in contemporary culture does not look to the university for leadership and guidance in proliferating specializations . . . higher education has tended to change in response to prestige and pressure. (p. 2)

As Pfeffer and Salancik (1978) pointed out, "The more useful the resources of an organization are to others, the more demands the organization will face" (p. 273). Obviously then, colleges and universities are of particular interest to groups and organizations in their environment because of the resources they hold (e.g., knowledge, trained manpower, scientific innovation, prestige, and even athletics). Agreeing with this conclusion, Mintzberg (1983) said that "hospitals and universities are perceived as vital ones to society, and so attract the attention of external influencers" (p. 405). It can be assumed, therefore, that this external interest in charitable organizations, such as universities and hospitals, likely is manifested in private gifts to these institutions.

Summarizing this section, open systems create interdependencies between organizations and other groups and organizations in their environment. The resource dependence perspective holds that organizations are shaped and constrained by their relationships with external sources of needed resources. Because of their dependence on external sources, organizations are involved in a constant struggle for autonomy.

Charitable organizations, which are dependent on external sources for financial support, are particularly susceptible to external control. Gifts constitute one form of financial support for such organizations, and relationships with the donors who provide this revenue (i.e., foundations, corporations, and individuals) represent external resource dependencies that may infringe on the charitable organization's power to determine and pursue its own goals. Control lost or gained through negotiations with these resource providers is largely determined by the vulnerability of the recipient organization, which, in turn, is determined by the extent to which an organization has come to depend on certain types of exchanges. If a charitable organization, such as a college, does not have a sufficient endowment, it is vulnerable to external control by donors, as illustrated in chapter 2 by the case of Salem College and its takeover by a Japanese university. A charitable organization is vulnerable if it does not control the rules of exchange, as illustrated also in chapter 2 by the case in which fund raisers at Harvard's Kennedy school agreed to exchange the title of officer of the university for a $500,000 gift. A charitable organization is vulnerable if it does not have alternative sources of private gifts and diversification of funding sources, as illustrated in chapter 2 by the dismissal of a student by the University of Rochester's school of business in response to a demand by the Kodak corporation, on which the school is dependent for students and private support.

Finally, charitable organizations strive to stabilize external dependencies on donors through joint ventures, such as industrial-university partnerships, and through cooptation, such as placing major donors on governing boards. Although such strategies do reduce the environmental uncertainty related to the need to continually raise private gifts, they also abdicate some degree of organizational control to external sources of gifts. In addition, such strategies may increase the vulnerability of a charitable organization by encouraging dependence on gift exchanges involving joint partners or coopted donors.

For example, when I assumed the vice presidency of development and public relations at Mount Vernon College in 1982, this small, private, women's college in Washington, DC was approximately $2 million in debt. Contributing to this deficit was the fact that for generations, the college had depended on its relationship with Marjorie Merriweather Post, heiress of the Post Cereal fortune, an alumna, major donor, and trustee of the college. According to fellow administrators, this dependency was so strong that for years before her death Ms. Post would schedule an annual visit to the president to learn the amount of deficit incurred by the college that year, at which time she would write a personal check to cover the deficit.

Convinced that Ms. Post's role as a trustee would prompt her to provide a major bequest on her death, Mount Vernon continued to operate in the red, failed to build an adequate endowment, and rarely solicited gifts from other alumnae or friends. It is not surprising, then, that when Ms. Post died and Mount Vernon College received only $100,000 and 10 Cadillac limousines, the college was unprepared to adjust to its new financial circumstances; therefore, in 1982, much of my efforts as vice president were spent trying to convince other wealthy alumnae, who had never been solicited by their alma mater, that the college needed their private support.

From this discussion, we can see that charitable organizations can become dependent on external sources of gifts and that such dependencies can lead to loss of control. Yet, systems theory concerns itself with *interdependencies* (i.e., mutual dependence of groups and organizations in an environment). To better understand the dependencies of sources of gifts *on* charitable organizations, this chapter now turns to a discussion of the norm of reciprocity.

THE NORM OF RECIPROCITY

In our complex and specialized society, interdependencies between organizations and groups in an environment are managed through an exchange process that involves economic, political, and social resources. Basically, charitable organizations are dependent on external sources for private funding, and these sources are dependent on the recipient organizations for some form of reciprocity. The exchange process is an ongoing one that requires management and negotiation in order to achieve some degree of equilibrium between what is gained for the organization and what is lost in the exchange.

The renowned organizational sociologist, Alvin W. Gouldner (1960), wrote a seminal article on interdependency relationships, the *Norm of Reciprocity*, in which he said that this norm has "no less a role [than] maintaining the stability of social systems" (p. 172). According to Gouldner, "The general norm simply requires that one return some [unspecified] benefits to benefactors" (p. 171). It assumes that "a social unit or group is more likely to contribute to another which provides it with benefits than to one which does not" (p. 164). The norm of reciprocity builds on open-systems theory and the resource dependence perspective to add theoretical depth to the later discussion of institutional autonomy and external sources of private gifts.

Using Gouldner's (1960) terms, it can be stated that an explanation of the stability of the relationship between a charitable organization and its donors requires investigation of mutually contingent benefits rendered and of the manner in which this mutual contingency is sustained. According to Gouldner, "The latter, in turn, requires utilization of two different theoretical traditions and general orientations, one stressing the significance of power differences and the other emphasizing the degree of mutual dependence of the . . . parties involved" (p. 164). In other words, the ongoing process of soliciting and accepting gifts from donors for a charitable organization depends on: (a) the benefits which a donor in turn receives from a charitable organization; (b) the power which the charitable organization possesses relative to its donor; and (c) the alternative sources of money and philanthropic gratifications accessible to each, beyond those provided by the other.

It is important to note the presence of the term *philanthropic gratification* in the third condition just given, which is defined here as gratification derived from benefits and the satisfaction of contributing to the public good. A necessary condition of a gift, it is recalled from earlier discussions, is that it be charitable in purpose by contributing to the public good. As emphasized in this chapter, interdependencies are managed through an exchange process that involves economic, political, and social resources. Relationships between donors and those charitable organizations classified as having positive externalities and public good are based on exchanges of various combinations of these resources. However, it must be repeated that these exchanges never fully capture the benefits of gifts because, by legal definition, some benefits spill over into society.

In other words, although the theory of donor relations developed in this book incorporates systems theory and assumes the presence of benefits to the donor in a gift exchange, it does not support direct benefits that equal or exceed the value of the gift. Such benefits are indicative of a marketing transaction (i.e., the *quid pro quo* of the marketplace), as opposed to a donor–recipient relationship, as discussed chapter 5.

In support of this critical point, Gouldner (1960) excluded charity from his norm of reciprocity because of the absence of self-interest in situations dealing exclusively with altruistic behavior. It is only because we have distinguished eleemosynary organizations, which are best described as charities, from those organizations having positive externalities and public good that we are able to apply the norm of reciprocity to gift exchanges. It is necessary to keep in mind, therefore, that unless otherwise noted, this chapter focuses on noneleemosynary organizations and assumes a condition of charitable purpose in gifts made to them.

Gouldner (1960) raised the issue of autonomy involved in a donor–relationship, saying, "The problem can also be approached in terms of the functional autonomy of two units relative to each other" (p. 164). For example, a college may have many alternative sources for the funding that it normally receives from a donor (i.e., it may be able to replace a gift by gifts from other donors, by increasing enrollment, by increasing tuition, by asking for increased government support, etc.). The donor, however, may be dependent on the college's gratifications (e.g., peer approval, pride of affiliation, recognition, prestigious position, etc.) and have no, or comparatively few, alternatives. Of course, the reverse is also probable, as demonstrated in chapter 2.

Fund raisers are frequently the "front line" for their charitable organizations when offering appropriate expressions of appreciation and recognition to donors. As pointed out in earlier chapters, the reciprocal expressions or benefits traditionally used by fund raisers range from plaques, to names on schools, to positions of influence within the organization. In a nontheoretical and unstudied way, fund raisers realize that the appropriate recognition can be a decision factor in the closure of a gift. Recall, for example, that it took the University of Utah 6 years to negotiate a $15-million gift that included naming its medical school after the donor and that when faculty protested the name change, the University felt obligated to return the gift ("$15-million gift," 1989).

Saying that the norm of reciprocity holds that "those whom you have helped have an obligation to help you," Gouldner (1960) explained, "The conclusion is clear: if you want to be helped by others you must help them; hence it is not only proper but also expedient to conform with the specific status rights of others and with the general norm" (p. 173).

At one extreme of the norm of reciprocity, the benefits exchanged are equal; at the other extreme, one party may give nothing in return for the benefits it has received. Much more common, however, is the intermediary case in which one party gives something more or less than that received. It must be emphasized that the noneconomic value of the benefits involved in a reciprocal relationship can only be assigned by the perception of the receiver (i.e., a benefit, such as a recognition dinner, might be viewed by some donors as too much of a reward and by others as too little). Gouldner (1960) described the benefit value of being too much or too little as a continuum bounded on both ends by exploitation.

It can be hypothesized that charitable organizations have established an equilibrium in some donor relations (i.e., both donor and recipient organization perceive that the benefits they exchange are equal). For example, donors of unrestricted lower level gifts may perceive even a preprinted thank-you card to be of a value equal to their gift. It is possible, however, that in the case of some gifts a third party would not make the same value judgement as the actors in the exchange situation. For example, although administrators at the University of Utah and the donor perceived equal value in the exchange of $15 million for naming Utah's medical school, the faculty of that school obviously did not judge the $15-million gift to be adequate compensation for what they perceived to be a loss of reputation resulting from the name change.

It is further hypothesized that some charitable organizations seem to give nothing in return for the gifts they receive. As noted earlier, Gouldner (1960) explained that among the special mechanisms that compensate for a breakdown in reciprocity are culturally shared prescriptions of one-sided or unconditional generosity, such as the feudal notion of *noblesse oblige*. It is possible that some donors, who continue to provide what economists or other social scientists would describe as significant financial support to a charitable organization, do so with no expectation for reward. They, for example, may make gifts anonymously and spurn any efforts by the organization to reciprocate through donor-recognition gifts, special events, or even special communications. An organization may have a number of such donors, and if there is a tradition of giving behavior and family wealth, it is possible that the fund-raising function may base its activities on a philosophy of noblesse oblige.

Third, it is hypothesized that the fund-raising function of most charitable organizations involve donor relationships in which one party gives something more or less than that received. For example, a college may view a gift of $1,000 as a low to moderate gift and through its gift-club structure provide, in return, a personalized form letter and two extra issues of the alumni magazine, whereas the donor valued his or her gift higher and expected much greater recognition, such as an invitation to the president's home. On the other hand, it is also possible that donors provide gifts of relatively little value to a college (e.g., scholarships for employees' children who are already enrolled at the college) and the fund-raising function exchanges such gifts with what would seem to be unsuitably high rewards, such as hosting a recognition event in the donor's honor, or giving preferential treatment in admission). The case cited by Olcott (1990) in chapter 5 likely would fall into this category because the benefits provided by the New Jersey social service agency to corporate donors seem unsuitably high (i.e., reciprocating for a gift of $750 with two workshops on employee training, a quarterly newsletter, a recognition certificate, and invitations to receptions and special events appears to be an unbalanced exchange).

Following Gouldner's (1960) lead, it is hypothesized that the majority of donor relations falls in the third, or intermediary, category that lies between equal value and unconditional generosity and that most of the imbalance in benefit exchanges are in the mid-range of the continuum bounded on both ends by exploitation, either of the donor or of the charitable organization by the other party. Arguing for the need to research such extremes, Gouldner said, "Contrary to the dictionary definition . . . exploitation can be employed simply to refer to certain transactions involving an exchange of things of unequal value" (p. 166). Gouldner pointed out that the study of exploitation (e.g., the sociological study of incest) helps develop mechanisms that serve to prevent and control such situations. In this light, it may be stated that although this book hypothesizes that most of the imbalance in benefit exchanges with donors falls in the mid-range of Gouldner's continuum, one of its results—as presented in chapter 16—is to develop propositions from the new theory of donor relations to guide the behavior of fund-raising practitioners and to help them avoid situations of exploitation. In other words, this critical analysis of the fund-raising function and its effect on organizational autonomy will lead to solutions for controlling exploitation of charitable organizations and of their donors, even though the probability of such may be rare.

Much of the literature on fund raising has been based on the sociological concept of role systems in which rights and duties are always complementary (e.g., the presupposition of noblesse oblige assumes the right of charitable organizations to be the recipients of contributions). The fallacy of this concept, according to Gouldner (1960) is that "complementarily connotes that one's rights are another's obligations, and vice versa" (p. 169). He illustrated his point by saying that a man may be obligated to tell the truth, even to a known liar, but it would be foolish to assume that the liar has a right to be told the truth. Gouldner said, "Reciprocity, however, connotes that each party has rights and duties" (p. 169). Supporting an assessment that complementary role systems are not appropriate for the study of fund raising, Lord (1983) stated, "Institutions are not entitled to charity. The days of hand-wringing and arm-twisting are drawing to a close. Institutions must earn and attract *investment*" (p. 5). In other words, although donors may feel obligated to make gifts (i.e., contribute to the public good), it would be wrong to assume that charitable organizations have a right to receive private gifts. Rather, the study of fund raising should be approached through the concept of reciprocity, which assumes only that both the recipient organization and the donor have rights and duties that may not be complementary.

In utilizing the norm of reciprocity in the study of fund raising, it is important to remember that reciprocity is universal, but not unconditional (i.e., the obligations imposed on charitable organizations vary greatly and are contingent on the gifts conferred by donors). "Unlike specific status duties," explained Gouldner (1960), "and like other general norms, this norm does not require highly specific and uniform performances from people whose behavior it regulates. . . . Instead, the concrete demands it makes change substantially from situation to situation and vary with the benefits which one party receives from another" (p. 175).

Gouldner said that among the four variables that determine the degree of obligation for a benefit is the intensity of the recipient's need. From this variable, it can be surmised that the obligations imposed by the norm of reciprocity likely will vary with the institutional wealth of a charitable organization. In other words, it can be hypothesized that a charitable organization with relatively few resources, such as a nonselective, liberal arts college with little or no endowment, would be more likely to perceive a large obligation (and reciprocate accordingly) when given a $1-million gift than would an institution of great wealth, such as Yale University, which has an endowment of $2.3 billion ("Almanac," 1990). "Given significant power differences," stated Gouldner, "egoistic motivations may seek to get benefits without returning them. . . . The situation is then ripe for the breakdown of reciprocity and for the development of system-disrupting exploitation" (p. 174).

On the other hand, Gouldner (1960) pointed out that "the norm may lead individuals to establish relations only or primarily with those who can reciprocate, thus inducing neglect of the needs of those unable to do so" (p. 178). This helps explain, for example, why some charitable organizations have a low success rate for attracting major gifts, and why an imbalance in private support will probably always exist. For example, the 183 doctoral institutions in the Council for Aid to Education's (CFAE) 1987–1988 survey—which represent about 6% of all American colleges and universities—accounted for approximately 66%, or two-thirds of gift dollars to higher education in 1987–1988 ("Gifts to colleges off," 1989). By comparison, the 150 community colleges in the CFAE survey accounted for only $68 million, or less than 1% of the total contributions. In addition, Rudney (1987) reported, "Less than one percent of all educational institutions account for 70 percent of the total assets of all educational philanthropic organizations, including 53 percent of the physical assets and 77 percent of the financial assets" (p. 62). Admitting that this inequality of private support also exists among different academic departments within a college or university, Bok (1982) stated:

> Business schools will be better endowed than schools of education, while medical research will expand more rapidly than philosophy departments. Such influences are troubling, but they are inevitable and often quite understandable as well. . . . In any event, universities have little choice in the matter. (pp. 267-268)

The norm of reciprocity, according to Gouldner (1960), safeguards powerful people against the temptations of their own status. Gouldner explained that power is lost and gained in many forms (e.g., if a party has to ask for a reciprocal gift, his or her power is diffused by the very act of asking). It can be assumed that this safeguard helps prevent a greater degree of organizational autonomy lost through the fund-raising process. It also, however, places even greater responsibility on the fund-raising practitioner who is often the key actor in the exchange of benefits with donors.

It would be wrong to make the assumption that the exchange of benefits involved in soliciting and accepting private gifts commonly involves abdicating a high degree of organizational autonomy. It is likely, as stated earlier, that the cases of exploitation reported in chapter 2 are uncommon. Gouldner (1960) explained that when life runs smoothly "the obligations binding members are not explicitly recognized" (p. 176). He said, "It is only when the relationship breaks down that the underlying obligations are brought to light" (p. 176). The extent of exploitation within reciprocal relationships between donors and charitable organizations, therefore, can only be determined through research or through incidents of dysfunction of the social system that are brought to our attention through the media.

Gouldner (1960) admitted, however, that because the norm of reciprocity imposes obligations, a number of issues may arise, such as whether the benefits to the donor are appropriate or sufficient in view of the absence of common yardsticks (i.e., which giving and returning may be compared?). This is a critical point in an analysis of fund raising. For example, if—as pointed out in chapter 2—Lee Iacocca can give $1 million to Lehigh University as part of a $40-million campaign he is chairing and announce to the national press that he plans to retire from Chrysler to the Iacocca Institute for Economic Competitiveness at Lehigh ("Chrysler's Iacocca," 1987), isn't it conceivable that a $5-million donor at another institution might also expect an organizational position in return for his or her gift?

Summarizing this section, Gouldner's (1960) norm of reciprocity permeates all social interaction, requiring that an organization or person return some benefits to benefactors. Charitable organizations are dependent on external sources for private funding, and these sources are dependent on the recipient organizations for some unspecified benefits that differ from situation to situation and from organization to organization. Reciprocity may take the form of thank-you cards, plaques, named buildings, appointments to internal boards, prestige by affiliation, free football tickets, or a degree of control in the organization, among others.

The noneconomic value of gifts and reciprocal benefits are determined by the perception of the actors involved in the exchange process, and the most common situation is one in which one party gives something more or less than that received. When imbalances are extreme, we say that exploitation of either the donor or the charitable organization has taken place. Exploitation can include a loss of control by the charitable organization when there is an imbalance of power and when the degree of dependency on the donor is great. One of the four variables that determine the obligation owed to donors is the intensity of the recipient's need at the time the benefit is bestowed. Therefore, if a charitable organization in great need of funding receives a relatively large gift from a donor, that organization may reciprocate by exchanging organizational control for the gift. On the other hand, donors usually enter into exchange relationships with those recipients that can provide the benefits *they* desire (e.g., admiration of peer group, trained manpower, or ingratiating behavior). As a result of the latter issue, private gifts are not distributed equally (e.g., major gifts are rarely given to small, unknown organizations even if their need is great—such as feeding starving children—but are instead generally made to the most prestigious organizations, such as doctoral universities, museums, and hospitals).

Finally, the negotiations involved in such interdependencies, including forms of reciprocity, are critical to the amount of control a charitable organization abdicates in the gift exchange process. Because many exchangeables are not objectively valued, fund-raising practitioners may offer inappropriate benefits in order to attract gifts that may not be valued as equivalent by third parties, such as faculty members. For example, at one university, a New Jersey real-estate developer was offered an honorary degree by fund raisers during negotiations for a $20-million gift for renovating athletic facilities. Although a faculty committee on honors and awards is responsible for determining and selecting deserving recipients of honorary degrees, the fund raisers made the offer without clearing the prospective donor's name with the committee. The donor has now been awarded the degree without making the proposed gift, and the fund raisers are hoping that such an honor will generate $1 million or $2 million after-the-fact. As Brittingham and Pezzullo (1990) stated, "The relationship between donor and institution may be seen as a gift relationship for public and ceremonial purposes, but it also has elements of a contractual or business-type relationship, particularly in private negotiations before the actual donation" (p. 62).

Robert Cialdini (1987), a professor of psychology at Arizona State University, urged educational fund raisers to use Gouldner's (1960) norm of reciprocity, which he referred to as a "principle of personal influence" (p. 49), in their efforts to raise gifts. Somewhat in agreement with the efforts of the fund raisers just described, he said, "Actively generate a series of benefits so that benefits will flow in return" (p. 49). Obviously, benefits conferred by fund-raising practitioners on behalf of a charitable organization should be of concern to those interested in a charitable organization's survival and success.

THEORY OF SOCIAL AND POWER EXCHANGE

Blau (1986) expanded on Gouldner's (1960) norm of reciprocity with his theory on social exchange, which deals with "voluntary actions of individuals that are motivated by the returns they are expected to bring and typically do in fact bring from others" (p. 91). In contrast to Gouldner, Blau believes that social exchange precedes the norm of reciprocity, which he said "merely reinforces and stabilizes tendencies inherent in the character of social exchange itself" (p. 92).

According to Blau (1986), the concept of social exchange is not derived from psychological principles that govern the motives of individuals, but is purely social in nature. "The objective of exchange theory," he said, "is to explain social life in terms of exchange principles by analyzing the reciprocal processes composing exchange, not to explain why individuals participate in certain exchange relations in terms of the *motives* and the underlying psychological principles" (p. ix; italics added). Explaining why the exchange theory does not deal with motivations, Blau stated:

> A person for whom another has done a service is expected to express his gratitude and return a service. . . . The emergent properties [relationships between elements in a structure] of social exchange consequent to this interdependence cannot be accounted for by the psychological processes that motivate the behavior of the partners. (p. 4)

It is recalled from chapter 3 that much of the research on fund raising has focused on donor characteristics, motivations, and attitudes (e.g., Burke, 1988). Although described by Brittingham and Pezzullo (1990) as the most promising of those dealing with donor behavior, there have been few studies that have been conducted on the interdependent relationships, or social exchanges, between charitable organizations and their donors. Apparently, this is not unique to the subject of fund raising. According to Blau (1986), social relations often are simply treated as characteristics of individuals, whereas, he said, "The concept of social exchange directs attention to the emergent properties in interpersonal relations and social interaction" (p. 4).

However, Blau (1986) would not necessarily support this book's use of social and power exchange theory in its efforts to explain donor relations. Throughout his discussion of social exchange and philanthropy, Blau implied that there are three types of giving, which he said have different degrees of social exchange involved in them. First, Blau circumscribed the concept of exchange by setting two limits on the range of social conduct it encompasses: When an individual gives money because another holds a gun to his head, it is coercion; and when an individual gives money because his conscience demands that he support the underprivileged, it is pure philanthropy with the only reward being internal approval of the superego. This first type of giving, which Blau referred to as "pure philanthropy," involves no social exchange and conforms with internalized standards.

The second type of giving, which Blau referred to as "organized philanthropy," involves indirect social exchange (i.e., a substitute for direct-exchange transactions) and conforms to social pressures. Defining this type of giving, Blau stated:

> Men make charitable donations, not to earn the gratitude of the recipients, whom they never see, but to earn the approval of their peers who participate in the philanthropic campaign. Donations are exchanged for social approval, though the recipients of the donations and the suppliers of the approval are not identical. (p. 92)

In support of this second type of giving, Blau (1986) repeated the 1954 findings of someone he defined as an expert on the subject of philanthropy, saying:

> One student of the subject has emphasized that charitable contributions are largely motivated by the specific rewards they produce for businessmen in the form of furthering their careers in the business world and of maintaining good public relations for the corporations they represent. (p. 260)

It is critical to note that Blau cited a philanthropy expert who focused only on businessmen and that the citation was more than 30 years old when Blau revised his book. Obviously, this is a limited description of philanthropy because there are donors who are not businessmen and there are benefits other than those cited. Although there are social and economic variables in a giving behavior, as demonstrated in chapter 5 by Bolnick's (1975) model of philanthropic decision making, the weight of the variables differ in each situation.

Finally, Blau (1986) identified a third type of giving that he defined as a social exchange (i.e., it is not giving to conform with internalized standards, or giving to conform to social pressures). He said, "A social exchange is involved if an individual gives money to a poor man because he wants to receive the poor man's expressions of gratitude and deference and if he ceases to give to beggars who withhold such expressions" (p. 91). In support of his differentiation between pure philanthropy involving no social exchange and gift giving that is a social exchange, Blau quoted von Mises (cited in Blau, 1986), who stated:

> Making one-sided presents without the aim of being rewarded by any conduct on the part of the receiver or of a third person is autistic exchange. The donor acquires the satisfaction which the better condition of the receiver gives to him. The receiver gets the present as a God-sent gift. *But if presents are given in order to influence some people's conduct, they are no longer one-sided, but a variety of interpersonal exchange between the donor and the man whose conduct they are designed to influence* (p. 91; italics added)

Contrary to Blau's (1986) three types of giving, it is the contention of this book that there are only two types. As concluded at the end of the discussion of the different types of nonprofit organizations in chapter 3, Blau's pure philanthropy is applicable only to a very small proportion of what is commonly described as charitable acts (i.e., gifts made out of pure altruistic motives to an unknown recipient through charitable organizations that Douglas, 1983, defined as eleemosynary). Blau's second type of giving, organized philanthropy, is disputed here as a narrow description of giving, which disregards donors other than businessmen and the variances in reasons for giving. This book contends that all philanthropic acts other than those described as charitable acts can best be understood as exchanges between donors and recipients directly or through charitable organizations that are noneleemosynary. Such acts, as assumed by the theory of social exchange, are designed to influence the behavior of the recipient.

Blau (1986) broadly defined power as referring "to all kinds of influence between persons or groups, including those exercised in exchange transactions, where one induces others to accede to his wishes by rewarding them for doing so" (p. 115). According to Blau, power is inherently asymmetrical, and he said, "Its source is one-sided dependence" (p. 118). In order to specify the conditions that produce an imbalance of power in exchange transactions, Blau reformulated a schema developed by Emerson for examining power-dependence relations and their consequences. The following is another version of the reformulated schema that has been simplified and adapted to specify the conditions that produce an imbalance of power in exchange transactions between a charitable organization and donors.

A charitable organization that needs private gifts can:

1. supply a donor with a service that the person wants badly to induce him or her to offer his or her gift in return;
2. obtain the needed gift elsewhere;
3. can coerce the donor to furnish the gift;
4. learn to resign itself to do without gifts; or
5. comply with the donor's wishes. (Assumes the organization is not willing or able to choose alternatives 1–4; leads to domination over it.)

In addition to specifying the conditions that produce an imbalance of power, Blau (1986) said the schema "can be employed to indicate the conditions of social independence" (p. 119). In other words, the first four alternatives enable charitable organizations to maintain social independence and to avoid the fifth alternative of compliance or loss of autonomy. According to Blau, the first condition of strategic resources promotes independence (i.e, a charitable organization that has enough of the right resources to use as effective inducements for donors is protected against dependency on a single donor). From this condition, it can be concluded that the fund-raising function at a prestigious and wealthy institution, such as Stanford University, has a lower probability of losing autonomy to powerful donors because of the resources it has to induce private contributions (e.g., prestige of affiliation).

Alternative sources from which needed gifts can be obtained, the second condition, fosters independence of charitable organizations (i.e., a charitable organization that has a broad base of donors who annually contribute private support and who are prospects for major grants to a variety of purposes is protected against becoming dependent on any one donor). We can conclude from this condition that a charitable organization with a large and broad donor base has a lower probability of losing autonomy to powerful donors because it has alternative donors from whom it can obtain a needed gift. As Blau (1986) emphasized, "Generally, the greater the difference between the benefits an individual supplies to others and those they can obtain elsewhere, the greater is his power over them likely to be" (p. 120). It also should be noted that this condition is identical to one of Pfeffer and Salancik's (1978) four strategies for avoiding external control and to one of Gouldner's (1960) three conditions of the exchange process (i.e., developing substitutable exchanges and possessing alternative sources for necessary resources). ·

The ability to use coercive force to compel donors to make gifts is the third condition that produces an imbalance of power in exchange transactions between a charitable organization and a donor. "Superior coercive power," according to Blau (1986), "makes people relatively independent of others inasmuch as power includes the ability to prevent others from interfering with one's conduct" (p. 120). Although the use of force may, on the surface, seem limited in the fund-raising process by definition (i.e., a gift implies voluntary action), the presence of coercion can be identified in various aspects of modern fund raising. As quoted in chapter 5, for example, Boulding (cited in Bolnick, 1975) claimed that in our heterogeneous society, "it is almost always necessary to reinforce philanthropy with coercion" (p. 210). Volunteers apply peer pressure, and, as described in chapter 13, solicitations, such as card-calling dinners used by the United Jewish Appeal, have been described as "a type of blackmail" (Whitaker, 1974, p. 43).

In addition, power through membership in coalitions is commonly used by charitable organizations to solicit and accept private support. For example, most private colleges, particularly small institutions, belong to regional independent college funds, such as the Maryland Independent College Fund. These coalitions solicit businesses annually and divide the proceeds among institutional members.

Solicitations are generally based on the implied threat that unless businesses support their regional independent college fund, they will be solicited individually by tens of private colleges each year and be forced to use up even more resources to satisfy competing demands. As Blau (1986) said, "Since there is strength in numbers, independence can be won through forming coalitions capable of enforcing demands" (p. 120).

The power of a coalition, with its implicit threat of individual solicitation, also is used effectively for raising money for the United Way Charities (i.e., giving once saves businesses the burden of being solicited hundreds of times by charitable organizations in their community). Businesses, in turn, have been accused of using coercion to solicit gifts from employees that constitute the majority of the company's contribution to the United Way. This condition of coercion is illustrated by a recent law suit in which an employee sued the Cleveland Electric Illuminating Company, saying he was fired from his engineering job for "failure to cooperate with the company's policy of giving to United Way" ("Lawsuit charges," 1989, p. 5). Describing the company's fund-raising practices as "extortion," the employee said, "United Way was a good cause, but the way the company was arrogantly dictating to people to give was for the wrong reasons" (p. 5). The manager of public information for the company—one of United Way's largest corporate givers in Cleveland—said that "the company has a very strong commitment to United Way," and that it has established a "fair-share giving level" for employees that is based on their salaries (p. 5). In response, the vice-president of marketing at United Way Services in Cleveland is quoted as saying, "I have seen coercion coming from the middle where there is a manager who is over-zealous because he thinks management at the top wants to meet goals" (p. 11).

Coercion can also be identified in challenge grants from foundations, corporations, and individuals, in that such gifts are contingent on others giving first. As noted in chapter 13, Payton (1987) said, "Charity needs coercion—or at times seduction, or manipulation, or threat—to come into being" (p. 41).

The absence of need for private gifts is the fourth condition of imbalance of power, or of independence. Again, this condition is similar to Pfeffer and Salancik's (1978) fourth strategy of alternative sources of funding. A difference, however, is that although a diversification of funding that includes private support may help a charitable organization avoid external control, it is unlikely that many such organizations could afford to meet Blau's condition of resigning itself to do without gifts because such a decision might entail dependency on other funding sources, such as government, or a change in status to for-profit. A community college (i.e., a 2-year, public college), for example, may be heavily financed by both state and local government; therefore, it may not perceive a need for soliciting and accepting private gifts. In such a case, the probability for loss of autonomy to donors will be extremely low, but the institution may suffer loss of freedom through its dependency on government funding sources.

Carbone (1987) reported that the fund-raising function at most public community colleges is "oriented toward seeking federal grants rather than gifts from private sources" (p. 6). It is estimated that only 200 of the approximately 1,200 community colleges in the United States currently have active fund-raising programs ("Community colleges," 1989). From such information, it can be concluded that the majority of 2-year, public colleges have a relatively low probability for dependence on a private donor.

In addition to government funding, a college's need for private gifts can be alleviated by sources of revenue, such as high tuition fees that cover close to 100% of the operating costs, or high revenue from auxiliary services, or high enrollments. However, as Blau stated, "Needs do not remain constant" (p. 120) and as government and other funding shifts, probability for dependence relationships can also change.

Finally, it can be concluded that if the first four conditions are not met by a charitable organization, the fifth condition of power imbalance will exist (i.e., if a charitable organization does not have inducement resources, a broad donor base, the power to use coercion, or diversification of funding sources to meet its needs, then that organization will have a higher probability of loss of institutional autonomy).

As does Gouldner (1960), Blau (1986) sees the norm of reciprocity as an equalizing force, in that "individuals who receive needed benefits from others are obligated, less the supply of benefits cease, to reciprocate in some form, whether through expressions of gratitude, approval, material rewards, services, or compliance" (p. 336). In this statement, Blau provides us with a hierarchy of benefits that an organization uses to reciprocate: (a) gratitude, (b) approval, (c) material rewards, (d) services, and (e) compliance. By applying these ascending categories of benefits to the fund-raising process, it is clear that how a charitable organization chooses to reciprocate for gifts is related to loss of autonomy by degree (i.e., sending letters of gratitude to donors has less impact on organizational autonomy than providing preferential admissions for children and friends). As indicated by his fifth category of benefits (i.e., compliance), Blau demonstrated that reciprocity can impose situations of imbalance. He said, "If persons are obligated to accede to another's wishes because he renders essential services to them for which they cannot otherwise compensate him, their compliance reciprocates for the unilateral services they obtain and in this sense restores balance, but it also creates an imbalance of powers" (p. 336).

There may be many who would tend to demand that charitable organizations limit social exchanges with donors to Blau's (1986) first category of reciprocal benefits (i.e., gratitude), or to expressions of approval and respect, without offering other benefits for making gifts. Although they may seem innocuous, benefits within these first two categories, however, can also include elements of external control. For example, a common way for charitable organizations to express gratitude and approval for major gifts is to name buildings and programs after the donors of the gifts. Defending this practice, Harvard's president, Derek Bok (1982), said it does not represent an affirmation of a donor's character, but only a way of acknowledging the source of the donation. He admitted, however, that although "the naming of a program or a building is not a certificate of good character, it does invest the benefactor with a certain respectability" (p. 276). Discussing this practice in relation to accepting gifts from donors who have engaged in immoral behavior or earned their fortunes in reprehensible ways, Bok (1982) countered by saying, "To name a building for a donor, or for one of his relatives, is not the same as awarding an honorary degree; its meaning is much more ambiguous" (p. 276). Yet, Bok admitted that few universities would accept a Hitler Collection of Judaica or a Capone Institute of Criminology because such names would devalue the academic enterprise. As demonstrated by the University of Utah situation mentioned earlier in this chapter, even naming buildings and programs for respectable donors can be perceived as damaging to an institution's reputation, or bearing a "cost" to a charitable organization. The value of such benefits, therefore, should not be underestimated in the exchange process.

In addition, Blau warned:

> Respect often does not remain an adequate compensation for contributions that entail costs in time and effort to the one who makes them. . . . Those who benefit from such instrumental help, therefore, become obligated to reciprocate in some other way, and deferring to the wishes of the group member who supplies the help is typically the only thing the others can do to repay him. (p. 127)

Blau (1986) also said, "As people become accustomed to a certain level of social gratification, which they may have initially considered extraordinary, they come to take it for granted and to expect at least that much gratification from their associates in the future" (p. 144). These statements represent a dilemma for charitable organizations, who follow the commonly held axiom that the best prospects for major gifts are those who have given before. It is recalled from chapter 5, for example, that Brittingham and Pezzullo (1990) claimed that exchange models explain donor motives based on receipt of "goods" in exchange for a gift and a "repeated disequilibrium" that leaves the donor with a need to respond with yet more gifts. In this way, they said, "donors are cultivated to even higher levels of giving and receive even high levels of gifts in exchange. The cycle ratchets ever higher" (p. 35).

Clearly, the fund-raising function often requires exchange benefits beyond gratitude, respect, and social association. These benefits of material rewards and services may include providing free tickets to athletic events, sponsoring workshops or seminars, purchasing goods or services from donors' companies, or offering preferential treatment in admissions. As argued in chapter 5, an overemphasis on direct benefits, particularly those of economic value to the donor, move the fund-raising function closer to a marketing perspective, which, in turn, can lead to loss of autonomy from donors or from government intervention. For example, an emphasis on recognition gifts and premiums has led to increased surveillance by the Internal Revenue Service (IRS), which may lead to further regulation regarding the charitable gift deduction.

Finally, as Blau (1986) pointed out, "The satisfactions human beings experience in their social associations depend on the expectations they bring to them as well as on the actual benefits they receive in them" (p. 142). These expectations, according to Blau, are formed not only by past self-experiences, but also by learning what benefits others have obtained in comparable situations. As noted earlier in this chapter, announcements of unusual benefits to donors who have contributed major gifts to an institution, such as the announcement made by Lee Iacocca about his retirement position at a center named for him, serve to set a potentially dangerous precedent for the fund-raising function at charitable organizations.

Summarizing this section, Blau's (1986) theory approaches exchange behaviors as social relationships, not on the basis of the psychological motivations of the actors, which often do not take into account inherent properties of the relationship that the actors bring to the exchange. This theory suggests that previous fund-raising studies, which focus on characteristics, attitudes, and motivations of donors, are limited in their explanation of the fund-raising process. It should be repeated here that relating exchange theory to philanthropy is not an idea new to this book. Lowenberg (1975), for example, said, "The quid pro quo of the exchange relationship is an integral part of the social interaction in the fundraising arena. Reciprocity, a basic process of social interaction, is also the norm in fundraising" (p. 8).

Although not a new theoretical link, there are few fund-raising studies utilizing exchange theory and little evidence of it being used for more than assigning motivations to donors (i.e., there has been little, or no, use of exchange theory to explain the behavior of charitable organizations in a donor—recipient relationship). For example, Silberg (1987) said that exchange theory is important because "it is a major theme running through almost all of the motives given for philanthropic activities" (p. 34). She continued by saying, "For instance, when people give because they have a need to help others, the exchange that they receive is the fulfillment of that need. The same is true for those giving because of power, prestige, appreciation, or for membership in a particular social group" (p. 34).

In contrast to previous studies that focus on donor motivations, this book utilizes exchange theory to understand fund raising as a process in which a charitable organization seeks to exchange social, economic, and political benefits it possesses for private funds from donors. In the social relationships that result, the power of each relative to the other affects the outcome.

Blau (1986) provided five conditions that lead to an imbalance of power in a social exchange such as that involved in fund raising. A charitable organization may have: (a) strategic resources to induce a donor, (b) alternative sources for the gift, (c) the power to coerce the donor, (d) the ability to get along without the gift, or (e) no alternative but to comply with the donor's wishes. These conditions can also be viewed as a charitable organization's power to protect and enhance its autonomy in the fund-raising process (i.e., if a charitable organization does not have, or chooses not to use, inducements, a broad base of donors, force, or the determination to get along without the gift, its only alternative is compliance).

Blau (1986) also provided a hierarchy of reciprocal benefits that a charitable organization can use in a social exchange involving gifts from donors: gratitude, approval, services, material rewards, and compliance. These benefits, in turn, provide categories of the inducement resources that constitute Blau's first condition of power imbalance (i.e., when a donor makes a gift, a charitable organization may reciprocate through expressions of gratitude, such as a thank-you letter; expressions of approval, such as naming a building for the donor; services, such as loaning works of art; material rewards, such as awarding vendor contracts; or compliance, such as allowing the donor to select the recipients of the scholarship he or she has funded). Although the first two categories of benefits may be preferred by the charitable organization, Blau said that respect, which is synonymous with the second category, is often perceived as insufficient in an exchange relationship and that the provider of goods or services also tends to expect increased benefits over time. In addition, expectations for benefits are affected by those conferred on others.

Although Blau (1986) distinguished between giving that involves no social exchange (the donor receives no benefit except self-satisfaction), giving that involves indirect social exchange (the donor receives benefits from his or her peers, not from the gift recipient), and giving that involves social exchange (the donor receives benefits from the recipient), this book dismisses the second type of giving as incomplete and inaccurate. It adopts the other two types, concluding that there are two distinct types of giving: (a) charity to unknown recipients through eleemosynary charitable organizations that provide no benefits in exchange, and (b) philanthropy to recipients directly or through organizations that provide public good and positive externalities, which involve social exchange (i.e., reciprocal benefits are provided by the individual recipient and/or the recipient organization). Based on the description given earlier in chapter 3, the former type represents a very small proportion of fund raising as it is practiced today by charitable organizations.

The section concludes that fund raising predominantly involves a social exchange relationship between a charitable organization and a donor, in which the power of each relative to the other determines the outcome of the exchange. If a charitable organization does not have or choose to use resources for inducement, alternative sources of gifts, force, or the ability to get along without the gift, it will give up some of its autonomy in exchange for the gift. Therefore, organizations that have strategic resources that can induce a donor (i.e., a donor desires the charitable organization's gratitude, approval, services, or material rewards) will have a lower probability of compliance than those that do not have or choose not to use such resources. Often a charitable organization, through its fund-raising function, must provide benefits beyond gratitude and approval in order to induce continued gifts from a donor. Such benefits may eventually include compliance.

MINTZBERG'S POWER THEORY

Building on Blau's (1986) discussion of power in social exchanges, this chapter now turns to Mintzberg's (1983) theory of power to provide insight into the degree of autonomy lost or gained through social exchanges involved in fund raising. In his book, *Power in and Around the Organization*, Mintzberg (1983) raised the question, "For whom does the organization exist?" and answered it by saying, "For anyone who can gain the power to determine its actions" (p. 243). Underlying Mintzberg's power theory is the premise that organizational behavior is a power game in which various players (influencers) seek to control the organization's decisions and actions. As Mintzberg noted, influencers often are called *stakeholders*, and he defined internal and external coalitions of stakeholders that can control organizations.

Mintzberg's (1983) power theory is particularly valuable to this discussion of the interdependent relationship between a charitable organization and its donors for two reasons: (a) it emphasizes the critical importance of negotiations in the process, and (b) it provides a "conceptual horseshoe" that demonstrates eight possible means of controlling an organization. According to Mintzberg, all organizations have four primary goals, including "control of the organization's environment to ensure an adequate degree of independence [especially from external influences]" (p. 247). He said that the question of how much power organizations really need "to control their own affairs is a matter of opinion" (p. 274). This matter of opinion of what is an adequate degree of independence, according to Mintzberg, accounts for two different ways organizations pursue their goal of control: (a) pursuing it to a point where the organization has enough room to maneuver in order to pursue other goals, or (b) being "so obsessed with dominating forces in its environment that the quest for autonomy looks more like lust for power" (p. 274). As is discussed shortly in the section on Grunig's (e.g., 1976, in preparation) theory of public relations, an organization can chose to handle its environmental interdependencies through cooperation or domination.

Regarding the former, Mintzberg (1983) said, "Organizations seek to avoid being controlled [but] ironically, to gain some control over activities of another organization, the focal organization must surrender some of its own autonomy" (p. 261). Cooperation, according to Mintzberg, "means giving up one kind of power to gain another" (p. 183). In other words, although an organization strives to preserve its autonomy, interdependencies with groups and organizations in its environment will necessitate some loss of autonomy (i.e., in order to raise gifts from external donors, charitable organizations will abdicate some degree of their independence). The degree of autonomy lost or gained through the fund raising process will be determined through the process of negotiations with donors. As Mintzberg said, "When an organization doesn't or can't control, its second choice is to negotiate" (p. 183).

Through the process of negotiations, therefore, the fund-raising function can affect the degree of organizational control lost or maintained in relationships with donors. As is discussed in chapter 10 on the fund raiser in a boundary role, the degree of autonomy lost and gained is greatly influenced by those at the focal point of exchange (i.e., the actors who participate at the point where external forces and the organization meet).

According to Mintzberg (1983), the basic problem underlying attempts to control an organization is that organizational staff want autonomy, but various constituencies have their own expectations of the organization's behavior. Mintzberg said, "The setting for the confrontation is simple: The Internal Coalition seeks autonomy while the External Coalition seeks control" (p. 409). Therefore, we can say that conflicts arise between charitable organizations and their donors because of that public's expectations of the economic, social, and political responsibilities of charitable organizations. As illustrated by colleges and universities, the basic problem is that the professionals employed by these institutions want autonomy, but donors who contribute to the institutions do so with the intention of affecting the institutions' behavior in fulfillment of certain expectations.

Or as Curti and Nash (1965) explained in chapter 5, the professional staff of colleges and universities consider the best donors to be those who only give of their money, not of their ideas. Mintzberg (1983) said that if charitable organizations were controlled by those on whom it had an impact, there would be no issue of who should control it.

In relation to this point, Mintzberg presented a "conceptual horseshoe" that demonstrates eight possible "means" of controlling an organization. From left to right, the means start out as what can be viewed as liberal positions and become more conservative as the horseshoe doubles back, so that by configuration, the extreme views at both ends are closest together. The eight means of control, or positions on the horseshoe, are:

1. nationalize it (i.e., proponents argue for governmental control of the organization);
2. democratize it (i.e., proponents argue for representation on the organization's board of directors and participation in decision making);
3. regulate it (i.e., proponents argue that the government should impose formal constraints on organizations, but not as severe as those resulting from nationalization);
4. pressure it (i.e., proponents believe that applying external pressure encourages behavioral changes of organizations);
5. trust it, which is at the top of the horseshoe (i.e., proponents believe that organizations act responsibly, balancing the economic and social goals of many constituencies);
6. ignore it (i.e., proponents argue that organizational mission necessitates behaving in a responsible manner);

7. induce it (i.e., proponents advocate "paying it to be good," in
    support of constituency goals); and
8. restore it (i.e., those proponents at the extreme right advocate
    giving control of organizations back to its rightful owners).

In the case of for-profit organizations, a corporation's various publics, or
stakeholders, are likely to adopt the four left-hand positions, or means of control,
that favor social goals on Mintzberg's (1983) conceptual horseshoe: nationalize
it, democratize it, regulate it, or pressure it. The corporation, on the other hand,
is more likely to favor the three right-hand positions that favor economic goals:
ignore it, induce it, or restore it. "Trust it," in the middle, represents a balance
between the two philosophies.

In the case of charitable organizations and their donor publics, however, the
first two and the last two positions on both sides of Mintzberg's (1983)
horseshoe are *not* conflicting means of control. It is unlikely, for example, that
either donors or charitable organizations would advocate control through the two
extreme positions on the horseshoe of "nationalize it" or "restore it." The very
concept of voluntary giving is an alternative to public funding, and charitable
organizations, by definition, do not have rightful owners as do for-profit
organizations (i.e., shareholders). It should be mentioned, however, that,
historically, the missions of many charitable organizations have been assumed by
government. For example, during World War I, ambulances and medical care
for U.S. soldiers were the responsibility of charitable organizations, but by World
War II this responsibility was assumed by the federal government (Cutlip, 1965).
As pointed out in chapter 3, many scholars say that government has now
assumed the former role of charity, leaving only philanthropy to the private
sector. Therefore, when demands are great enough and services are deemed to
be of great interest by the general public, charitable organizations can be
"nationalized" in the sense that their missions are assumed by the government.
Such a movement, however, is usually supported by both the charitable
organization and its donors.

Similarly, the second position on the left-hand side, "democratize it," and the
second-to-the-last position on the right-hand side, "induce it," are not conflicting
positions between a charitable organization and its donors. As pointed out
earlier in this chapter, charitable organizations have traditionally used representation on governing or related foundation boards as a means to stabilize funding
relationships and as a benefit given in exchange for gifts. Donors have accepted
such positions as rewards for their gifts and as a means of affecting decision
making by the charitable organization. In other words, charitable organizations

generally accept economic inducements as a legitimate means of controlling their behavior, whereas donors who want a voice in decision making are provided such positions through cooptation because of the financial resources they provide.

The remaining three positions, or means of control, on Mintzberg's (1983) horseshoe are, however, conflicting ones. Donors are more likely to adopt the other left-hand positions of "regulate it," or "pressure it," whereas the charitable organization is more likely to favor the remaining right-hand position of "ignore it." As with for-profit organizations, "trust it"—at the top of the horseshoe—remains a position of balance between the two philosophies and represents the status quo. Explaining such conflicts, Blau (1986) said, "On an abstract theoretical level, opposition can be conceptualized in terms of the conflict between autonomy and interdependence of substructures in a macrostructure" (p. 302).

As stated earlier, professional staff of charitable organizations desire autonomy in carrying out the mission of the organization (i.e., they prefer that donors give of their money, but not of their ideas). They essentially believe that they know what is best for the organization's success and survival and that donors should give money but then ignore the recipient of their gifts.

Donors, on the other hand, may adopt the position that charitable organizations should be regulated to ensure that they meet expectations of donors. As pointed out in earlier chapters, there recently have been increased calls for regulation of fund raising. For example, at a hearing on deceptive fund-raising practices held in July 1989, officials of the U.S. Postal Service and the Federal Trade Commission (FTC) suggested that Congress expand the authority of the FTC to all nonprofit entities ("Colleges are nervous," 1989).

A key concern among donors and government officials is the percentage of gifts that actually go to the purpose for which the gift was solicited, as opposed to the percentage that is used to cover administrative and fund-raising costs. Although charitable organizations, including colleges and universities, prefer that donors "ignore it," increasing reports of abuse and the reluctance of charitable organizations to voluntarily provide fund-raising costs have moved numerous donors into a "regulate it" position of control on Mintzberg's (1983) horseshoe.

In addition, some donors have adopted the position of "pressure it," by which they believe they can affect the behavior of charitable organizations through means of pressure. As stated earlier, there are numerous, and often competing, expectations of charitable organizations, particularly colleges and universities. Because they provide financial resources to such organizations, donors often feel a need and a right to express their particular expectations by pressuring the recipients of their gifts. For example, individuals who provide major gifts to a school of business often apply pressure to that school to behave in a manner congruent with the individual's expectations (e.g., teaching business students ethics, as described in chapter 2). Again, the charitable organization would find such a position in conflict with its preferred position of "ignore it," as demonstrated by the priority it gives to unrestricted gifts that do not constrain how private funds are to be used (e.g., Kramer, 1980).

Through their role as negotiators, fund-raising practitioners can help resolve such conflicts between charitable organizations and their donors. In her study of activist groups and corporations, L. Grunig (1986) found that "the activist stance tended to go from 'pressure it' or 'regulate it' to 'trust it' at the first sign of the organization's being willing to negotiate" (p. 45). As discussed in more detail in the chapter on fund-raising models, practitioners of the two-way symmetric model seek to understand and to cooperate with their external donor publics knowing that some organizational autonomy must be conceded in donor relations. As L. Grunig said, "After all, if real communication is to occur, there has to be the possibility of mutual influence" (p. 59). On the other hand, practitioners of the other three fund-raising models try to dominate their environment, much as Mintzberg (1983) described at the beginning of this section. It is argued later in this book that the former model is more ethical and socially responsible and will help charitable organizations save autonomy and money in the long run.

Finally, it is interesting to note that Mintzberg (1983) is against corporate giving. In the final chapter of his book, titled "A Personal View," he said that although few people believe a corporation should solve social problems, "many . . . believe it should donate to charity" (p. 650). He continued by stating, "I am increasingly convinced it should not. . . . Who are corporate managers to decide on the allocation of funds to quasi public universities? Corporate values cannot help but get mixed up in noncorporate issues" (p. 650).

Summarizing this section, some organizational autonomy is lost by the very existence of donor relationships, and negotiations between charitable organizations and their donors determine to a large degree how much is exchanged for gifts. As Mintzberg (1983) said, if an organization can not control, it must negotiate. As fund-raising practitioners are often the actors in the charitable organization's social exchange relationships with donors, fund raisers have to learn the vital skills of negotiation.

In addition, fund raisers must be able to negotiate the conflicting positions of charitable organizations and donors, as represented on Mintzberg's (1983) conceptual horseshoe of means of control. Unlike for-profit organizations, four of the positions are not conflicting for charitable organizations and their donor publics; however, three positions are: The charitable organization prefers that donors "ignore it," whereas donors often take the positions of "regulate it," or "pressure it." Underlying these conflicting positions is the professional staff's desire for autonomy and the expectations donors hold of the charitable organization's behavior. Increased calls for regulation of fund raising emphasize the need for charitable organizations and those practitioners who manage its fund-raising function to recognize the importance of negotiations in donor relations for the purpose of preserving and enhancing autonomy.

With the critical role of negotiations and the fund-raising practitioner in mind, this chapter concludes by briefly discussing Grunig's (e.g., 1976, in preparation) theory of public relations.

GRUNIG'S THEORY OF PUBLIC RELATIONS

Although Grunig's (e.g., 1976) public relations theory is examined in greater detail later in the book, it is introduced here to establish its value in explaining the relationship between managing environmental interdependencies and organizational autonomy. Grunig's theory of public relations is rooted in systems theory and is based on the central concept that autonomy is the fundamental goal of an organization because the successful attainment of all goals is dependent on some degree of autonomy. In point of fact, the public relations theories developed over the last 16 years by James E. Grunig, professor at the University of Maryland, figure prominently in this book, as does the current research he is conducting with a team of colleagues under a 6-year grant from the International Association of Business Communicators (IABC) Foundation.[1] The IABC project promises to be a seminal research study in public relations and organizational communication, and many of the findings of the extensive literature review already completed by the team of researchers (Grunig, in preparation) are directly applicable to developing a theory of donor relations.

According to Grunig (in preparation), public relations plays a key role in managing, through domination or cooperation, the interrelationships an organization has with the various publics in its environment. Through his efforts to explain and predict the public relations behaviors of organizations, Grunig (1984; Grunig & Hunt, 1984) has developed four models of public relations that explain

---

[1]These colleagues include David Dozier of San Diego State University, William Ehling of Syracuse University, Larissa A. Grunig of the University of Maryland, Jon White of the Cranfield School of Management in the United Kingdom, and Fred Repper, retired vice president of public relations for Gulf States Utilities of Beaumont, Texas.

how an organization manages its environmental interrelationships. These four models, which are discussed in greater detail in chapter 13, are press agentry, which is a one-way flow of communication for the purpose of publicity; public information, which is a one-way flow of communication for the purpose of information dissemination; two-way asymmetric, which utilizes scientific research to persuade; and two-way symmetric, which uses scientific research to reach mutual understanding. The first three models help an organization adapt to its environment by dominating it. The two-way symmetric model, on the other hand, helps an organization manage its interdependencies by cooperation (i.e., creating a dialogue with publics and maintaining a balance between account-ability and autonomy through negotiations). As discussed in chapters 13 and 15, Grunig (e.g., in preparation) recommends the two-way symmetric model of public relations for socially responsible organizations and hypothesizes that this model is the most effective of the four in minimizing organizational loss of autonomy and in maximizing opportunities for enhancing autonomy.

Grunig (in preparation), therefore, has defined the contribution of public relations as what it *saves* an organization by helping to maintain autonomy from external forces such as government regulation or activist pressures. Grunig (cited in "Computer chat," 1987) stated:

> We believe the major goal of an organization is autonomy from its environment, freedom to pursue its goals without interference. . . . Moving down one level of abstraction, we believe that organizations are interdependent with publics . . . that limit autonomy. If an organization can manage that interdependence, it sacrifices some of its autonomy but it reduces the risk of losing even more autonomy. (p. 30)

It should be noted here that the concept of managing interrelationships is not a new idea to public relations. In 1952, Edward Bernays, who frequently is referred to as the father of public relations, wrote:

> Improving public relations for an individual or an institution is not a matter of using this or that tool or technique to bring about the desired effect. The total person or institution needs to be brought into a better relationship or adjustment with the environment upon which he or it depends. (p. vii)

In addition, there are currently other scholars who approach public relations as an organizational function responsible for environmental relationships. For example, Baskin and Aronoff (1988) defined public relations as "the central subsystem through which management responds to and attempts to influence an organization's environment" (p. 19).

Be that as it may, Grunig's (e.g., in preparation) theory is of particular value in approaching fund raising as the management of interdependencies between charitable organizations and their donor publics. In addition to tying public relations to the concept of organizational autonomy, Grunig provided a segmentation of an organization's publics that relates fund raising to environmental interdependencies. Grunig and Hunt (1984) used Esman's four types of linkages that are critical to the survival of an organization (i.e., enabling, functional, normative, and diffused) to explain why organizations have public relations programs, or specializations. These programs are targeted for specific groups or publics, such as government, employees, and investors, and are referred to as government relations, employee, or internal, relations, and investor relations. Charitable organizations, according to Grunig and Hunt (1984), have a particularly important linkage to donors:

> Nonprofit organizations maintain their functional linkages with the users of their services. . . . But many must also maintain a critical enabling linkage with sources of funds if they are to survive. Among the organizations that must raise funds are colleges and universities. (p. 361)

In other words, donors, including individuals, corporations, and foundations, are important groups and organizations in the specific environment of those nonprofit organizations classified by the IRS as charities. Donors are an "enabling" public in that they are a public that controls the resources that *enable* charitable organizations to exist. A public relations program, or specialization, targeted at this enabling public would be referred to as *donor relations*. In short, donors are an enabling public whose resources are needed by the charitable organization to survive and succeed and whose relationship to the organization must be managed to maintain and enhance autonomy.

In summary, Grunig (e.g., 1984; Grunig et al., 1986) has developed a theory of public relations rooted in systems theory that defines the contribution of public relations as how well it manages interdependencies between an organization and its various publics. This theory holds that organizations sacrifice some of their autonomy by managing interdependence with groups and organizations in their environment, but by doing so they reduce the risk of losing even more autonomy. Grunig identified four models of public relations, three of which help organizations adapt to their environment by domination, whereas the two-way symmetric model helps organizations adapt by cooperation. The latter model uses negotiation to enhance and protect organizational autonomy.

Grunig and Hunt (1984) pointed out that organizations historically have structured their public relations programs to communicate with those strategic publics in their environment that affect or are effected by the organization's behavior. An organization's need to communicate with publics such as employees and stockholders has resulted in public relations programs of employee relations and investor relations. Four linkages between an organization and its environment help define strategic publics: enabling, functional, normative, and diffused. Using these concepts, donors can be defined as an enabling public that provide necessary resources for charitable organizations, much like shareholders provide revenue for corporations. Fund raising, therefore, can be viewed as managing interdependencies between a charitable organization and its donor public. This function helps a charitable organization adapt to its environment by dominating it or by cooperation. Through negotiations, the fund-raising function can help the organization save autonomy and decrease the risk of abdicating control of the organization to donors. As stated earlier in this chapter, Powell and Friedkin (1987) said that the managerial task is to respond to external demands and "attempt to mitigate these influences" (p. 182).

In conclusion, systems theory explains the relationship between charitable organizations and donors as environmental interdependencies, in contrast to conventional wisdom, which views these relationships as benevolent, business, or pseudo relations. These fund-raising interdependencies constitute an ongoing exchange process that requires management and negotiation by the charitable organization so that it can protect and enhance its autonomy.

The resource dependence perspective holds that organizations are shaped and constrained by their relationships with external sources of needed resources. Gifts constitute one form of financial support for such organizations, and relationships with the donors who provide this revenue (i.e., foundations, corporations, and individuals) represent dependencies on external resources that may infringe on the charitable organization's power to determine and pursue its own goals. Control lost or gained through negotiations with these resource providers is largely determined by the vulnerability of the recipient organization, which, in turn, is determined by the extent to which an organization has come to depend on certain types of exchanges. Charitable organizations strive to stabilize external dependencies on donors through joint ventures and cooptation, but these strategies require that some degree of organizational control be forfeited.

The norm of reciprocity requires that a charitable organization return some benefits to its donors. Although charitable organizations are dependent on external sources for private funding, these sources are dependent on the recipient organizations for some unspecified benefits that differ from situation to situation and from organization to organization. The noneconomic value of gifts and reciprocal benefits are determined by the perception of the actors involved in the exchange process, and the most common situation is one in which one party gives something more or less than that received. The negotiations involved in such gift exchanges are critical to the amount of control a charitable organization abdicates in the process.

As an exchange relationship, fund raising can be viewed as a process in which a charitable organization seeks to exchange social, economic, and political benefits it possesses for private funds from donors, and the power of each relative to the other affects the outcome. The theory of social and power exchange provides five conditions that lead to an imbalance of power in fund raising. A charitable organization may have:

1. strategic resources to induce a donor;
2. alternative sources for the gift;
3. the power to coerce the donor;
4. the ability to get along without the gift; or
5. no alternative but to comply with the donor's wishes.

This theory also provides a hierarchy of reciprocal benefits that a charitable organization can use in a social exchange involving gifts from donors: gratitude, approval, services, material rewards, and compliance.

Based on exchange theory, this chapter concludes that there are two distinct types of giving: (a) charity to unknown recipients through eleemosynary charitable organizations that provide no benefits in exchange; and (b) philanthropy involving social exchange to recipients directly or through organizations that provide public goods and positive externalities.

Some organizational autonomy is lost by the very existence of donor relationships, and negotiations between charitable organizations and their donors determine to a large degree how much is exchanged for gifts. As Mintzberg (1983) said, if an organization can not control, it must negotiate. As fund raisers are often the actors in social-exchange relationships with donors, these practitioners have to learn the vital skills of negotiation. Increased calls for regulation of fund raising emphasize the need for charitable organizations to recognize the importance of negotiations in donor relations for the purpose of preserving and enhancing autonomy.

Grunig's (e.g., in preparation) theory of public relations defines the contribution of public relations as how well it manages interdependencies between an organization and its various publics. This theory holds that organizations sacrifice some of their autonomy by managing interdependence with groups and organizations in their environment, but by doing so, they reduce the risk of losing even more autonomy. Organizations have historically structured their public relations programs to communicate with those strategic publics in their environment that affect or are effected by the organization's behavior. Four linkages between an organization and its environment help define strategic publics: enabling, functional, normative, and diffused. Using these concepts, donors, can be defined as an enabling public that provide necessary resources for charitable organizations. Through negotiations, the fund-raising function can help the organization save autonomy and decrease the risk of abdicating control of the organization to donors.

Thus, the fundamental goal of charitable organizations is autonomy from their environments, which include interdependent relationships with donors that limit autonomy. By managing these interdependencies through their fund-raising function, charitable organizations sacrifice some of their autonomy, but reduce the risk of losing even more. If interdependencies with donors are not managed or are ignored (i.e., donor relations are not recognized as potential sources of external control) fund raising may lead to a greater loss of organizational autonomy. The next chapter in this book, therefore, focuses on the institutional autonomy of colleges and universities and discusses how external funding sources can affect the power of these charitable organizations to set and pursue their own goals.

Institutional Autonomy

This chapter builds on the issue of autonomy within the context of environmental interdependencies by analyzing the relationship between the educational concept of "institutional autonomy" and private support. Assuming that the fund-raising function in colleges and universities shares similarities with the function in other charitable organizations, this chapter draws from the literature of higher education to document that resource dependency relationships with donors can and do infringe on institutional autonomy.

The chapter concludes that in order to be effective, charitable organizations must maintain a relatively high degree of autonomy so that they might determine and pursue their own goals. Fund raising, therefore, contributes to organizational effectiveness by soliciting gifts that enhance autonomy (e.g., gifts that are made in support of internally determined goals), and by negotiating the conditions of gifts that threaten to infringe on organizational autonomy. An analogy is drawn in the final section between the relationship of donors and charitable organizations and the autonomy lost by research universities through their external funding relationship with the federal government.

PRELIMINARY DEFINITIONS OF INSTITUTIONAL AUTONOMY

As stated earlier in chapter 1, the selection of higher education for in-depth analysis of the fund-raising function is justified on five bases:

1. its ranking as one of the top categories receiving the most gift dollars;
2. its documented status as a preferred recipient of gifts from wealthy individuals;
3. its employment of the greatest proportion of fund raisers;
4. its rich literature on institutional autonomy; and
5. because the effects of private support are readily evident in institutions of higher education.

Addressing the last basis, Curti and Nash (1965) stated, "Today, for better and for worse, our colleges and universities bear the marks left by philanthropy to an extent that is rare among American institutions" (p. v).

It was documented in chapter 1 that education receives the largest share of gift dollars second only to religion (AAFRC Trust, 1989c), and that higher education receives approximately 87% of the total given to education ("Gifts to colleges off," 1989). In addition, colleges and universities receive the majority of major gifts along with hospitals (Jencks, 1987). Historically, according to Hall (1987), "Big business and private wealth underwrote the growth of universities, libraries, hospitals, professional organizations, and private clubs" (p. 9), whereas those nonprofit organizations, such as labor unions, looked out for the interests of the middle and lower classes. As also documented in chapter 1, education employs the greatest proportion of practitioners belonging to fund-raising associations (Carbone, 1989b).

Because of higher education's inherent value to a democratic society (e.g., transmitting culture and values), American colleges and universities enjoy an autonomy of special status—one that is considered of a higher level than that of for-profit organizations and other nonprofits (e.g., Carnegie Committee, 1982; Duryea, 1973/1986). Institutional autonomy and the related concept of academic freedom, therefore, have received a great deal of attention by education scholars, particularly those in the area of governance. Largely, however, the subject of analysis has been the relationships between government and educational institutions (e.g., Dressel, 1980). Relatively little work has been done on how relationships with donors affect institutional autonomy. Be that as it may, the literature of higher education provides a rich resource for analyzing fund raising and its effect on organizational autonomy.

Before turning to the historical background of institutional autonomy and governance, this chapter discusses some preliminary definitions of autonomy and its related concept of academic freedom. Altbach and Berdahl (1981) divided the concept of institutional autonomy into two parts: college autonomy of a *substantive* nature is defined as the power of a college or university to determine its own goals and programs, and college autonomy of a *procedural* nature is the power of an institution to determine the means by which its goals and programs will be pursued. This distinction is relevant to a discussion of fund raising and institutional autonomy. As Lee (1968) stated, "The common goals of higher education may be almost infinite, but the local *means to pursue them are always finite*, and the nation may be better served if each institution pursues only those goals which are suitable to its requirements, needs, and abilities" (p. 15; italics added).

Whereas academic freedom is defined by Altbach and Berdahl (1981) as an *individual* protection, they said, "Autonomy constitutes *corporate* concepts relating to the legal entity, whether it be a single campus or a multi-campus system" (p. 3). In an earlier work, Berdahl (1971) described another important difference between academic freedom and institutional autonomy: The first is universal and absolute and the other is of necessity parochial and relative. Berdahl said that "autonomy is related to academic freedom in that the latter is more likely to flourish in an autonomous institution" (p. 8). Although related, however, they are not synonymous.

Dressel (1980) defined autonomy in higher education as "the ability of a university or college . . . to govern itself without outside controls" (p. 1). Dressel said, "Brief reflection upon this definition leads immediately to the conclusion that autonomy in the sense of complete independence would be possible only if an institution were financially independent" He added, "It is evident that no institution can receive support from public or private sources and maintain complete autonomy" (p. 1).

Dressel approached autonomy with the assumption that absolute autonomy is neither possible or desirable for educational institutions. Society extends autonomy to a college or university because it believes that in certain areas or facing certain problems that institution has knowledge, insight, competence, and social values that permit it to make wiser and better-based judgments or actions than others who are less well-informed and educated. He said, "The ultimate justification for autonomy is that society benefits from the extension of autonomy to the university, but judgments as to the exercise of autonomy vary because of underlying values involving differences in interpretation, priorities, and decision making" (p. 92).

Pointing out that there was never a period in which universities were completely autonomous, Dressel (1980) said, "The fundamental point here is that universities were not founded solely or even primarily for students, faculty, or trustees, but for the benefit of society at large" (p. viii). He criticized those who advocate complete autonomy for colleges and universities (i.e., those who wish the performance and impact of a university be taken on faith), saying, "There is no such thing as complete institutional autonomy; it is always limited by the needs and interests of those served" (p. 2).

Echoing Mintzberg's (1983) and Grunig's (cited in "Computer chat," 1987) statements given earlier on the degree of autonomy needed by organizations, Dressel said, "Any discussion of autonomy must focus on the nature and extent of autonomy required for effective operation of the institution, on the institution's fulfillment of its responsibilities to society, and on the capability, responsibility, and sensitivity with which that autonomy is exercised" (p. x). Dressel described the dilemma of the double-edged sword faced by colleges and universities in their fund raising behavior when he said, "Without adequate funding, there is no autonomy, because there is no freedom to consider alternatives, to experiment and innovate, or to improve existing programs and develop new ones" (p. 18). As autonomy is limited by the needs and interests of public and private sources of funding, Dressel stated:

> Survival is ultimately the supreme value. Institutions do what they must do to acquire support. The critical question, then, becomes one of the extent and nature of the limitations which can be imposed on the autonomy of an institution without eroding its effectiveness. (p. 2)

Dressel (1980) disagreed somewhat with Berdahl's (1971) conclusion that academic freedom is absolute, whereas autonomy is parochial and relative. He said that as "a privilege extended to competent and responsible scholars" (p. 4), academic freedom varies with time and circumstances, as does autonomy. To illustrate his point, he said that, historically, many private colleges have been autonomous, but have not extended academic freedom to their faculty or permitted a high degree of individual autonomy. When Dressel referred to such situations, he was obviously relating autonomous institutions to a lack of government control and not to control by donors, as demonstrated when he said, "The president, board, and donors have tightly dominated such institutions" (p. 4). Taking a broader viewpoint, this book holds that colleges and universities "dominated" by trustees and donors, as well as those highly controlled by public sources of funds, do not enjoy a high degree of autonomy and, therefore, are more susceptible to loss of academic freedom.

According to Dressel (1980), substantive autonomy involves those rights of an institution that are "primary, sanctioned, or antecedent, such as life, liberty, property, and reputation" (p. 5). This explanation is valuable in that it expands on Altbach and Berdahl's (1981) definition of substantive autonomy to provide further insight into how environmental interdependencies with donors can affect the substantive autonomy of colleges and universities. For example, the case described in chapter 2 and referred to in chapter 6 about the University of Utah's medical school can now be understood as a threat to substantive autonomy because the reason that the faculty and others protested naming their institution for the donor of a $15-million gift was that such an exchange would damage the *reputation* of the school (i.e., substantive autonomy involves primary and sanctioned rights, such as reputation). Dressel warned, however, that the extension of substantive autonomy to an organization implies responsibility and accountability. He said, "The use and the results of autonomy are subject to review, and those who misuse it are answerable to those who extend it" (p. 5).

Procedural autonomy, according to Dressel (1980), pertains to the exercise of substantive autonomy (i.e., the means by which an institution's goals and programs will be pursued). Again expanding on Altbach and Berdahl (1981), Dressel said, "Procedural autonomy has to do with those decisions, operations, or policies characterizing the way in which an institution uses its resources" (p. 7). From this definition, we can see that gifts restricted in purpose (e.g., the gift described in chapter 2 that created the Jepson School for Leadership at the University of Richmond) infringe on the procedural autonomy of educational institutions by their very nature (i.e., procedural autonomy is diminished when donors make gifts to charitable organizations because these gifts dictate how the organization uses those resources). Yet, Dressel pointed out that all gifts, to some degree, infringe on procedural autonomy because the acceptance of restricted or unrestricted funding requires accountability to the funding source. He said, "When state or federal governments, private foundations, or individual donors give dollars to an institution, they may reasonably require that a report be made on the uses and impact of those funds" (p. 7).

Although Dressel (1980) admitted that the distinction between substantive and procedural autonomy is useful, he emphasized that substance and process are interrelated. He stated:

> Intervention affecting procedural autonomy can be irritating; intervention into substantive autonomy can be vicious and destructive. Ultimately, however, ruthless intervention into procedural autonomy and external control of processes result either in control of substance or complete destruction of substance. (p. 9)

In transition to the following section on the historical background of institutional autonomy, Dressel (1980) reiterated that the degree of organizational autonomy is not fixed, but varies through relationships with environmental groups and organizations (i.e., autonomy is lost or enhanced through managed interdependencies). Underlining the systems theory approach of the previous chapter, Dressel said that although autonomy may be vested by constitutional recognition or assigned by law, it may also be "acquired by persuasiveness, through recognition of personal expertise, by influence over the opinions or actions of others, by threat or favor . . . and by use of power in matters or areas directly or only marginally related to the field in which autonomy is sought" (p. 11).

HISTORICAL BACKGROUND OF INSTITUTIONAL AUTONOMY AND GOVERNANCE

According to Duryea (1973/1986), the concept of institutional autonomy has its origin in 15th- and 16th-century England where the concept of corporate autonomy was first conceived. English universities were granted legal corporate autonomy, and the concept transferred to America. In 1701, Yale University formalized the corporate entity tradition that American higher education would follow when its charter was granted as a legal corporation under the governance of a board composed of external members. Although the new states often regarded the first colleges as their own, the relationship was legally clarified in the landmark 1819 Dartmouth College case, which recognized the college's charter as a contract that had to be upheld by state officials, as well as by institutional directors (Duryea, 1973/1986). A major argument used by Daniel Webster, who represented Dartmouth before the Supreme Court in that case, was that colleges needed their independence in order to attract private gifts. If independence were lost, declared Webster, "Benefactors will have no certainty of effecting [sic] the object of their bounty" (Carnegie Committee, 1982, p. 9).

In 1869, the first public university was established in Georgia approximately 150 years after the founding of Harvard (Moos, 1981). Through charters and legislation, state officials and legislatures followed the governance model of private institutions and basically granted public colleges corporate status under boards of external governors (Duryea, 1973/1986). This parallel development of corporate status in both the private and public sectors of higher education has been the basis for the concept of institutional autonomy. Duryea added, however, that Americans modified the corporate autonomy concept inherited from England and incorporated a responsiveness to societal needs, thus establishing the dualism of autonomy versus accountability in American colleges and universities.

Lee (1968) pointed out that although the concept of the research university was transferred from Germany, resulting in the establishment of such universities as Johns Hopkins, the adoption of a public service function set apart the

American university from its British or German forefathers. Lee said that when the Morrill Act established the land-grant institutions in 1862 for

> the purpose of developing and applying intellectually based expertise to an expanding agricultural and industrial economy. . . . The academy's sudden diversion into practical fields represented the grafting of distinctively native limbs on the imported German tree—applied research was coupled with its "pure" counterpart, and the function of public service, of responsiveness to social needs, was added to the functions of teaching and inquiry. (p. 4)

By the 20th century, American universities were committed to a threefold mission of instruction, research, and public service, which frequently have seemed incompatible by various constituencies. According to Lee (1968), "The notion that colleges and universities have a duty to perform public service has changed the whole relationship between the university and society in the United States" (p. 8).

The literature of higher education governance (e.g., Carnegie Committee, 1982; Duryea, 1973/1986) emphasizes that institutional autonomy of higher educational institutions has evolved beyond the concept of corporate autonomy. It has taken on a special and higher status because of its critical mission, such as being the primary vehicle for transferring Western culture.

This special status, which is similar to the "higher" autonomy held by the mass media in the United States (i.e., freedom of the press) has, in effect, elevated the right to autonomy by institutions of higher education over that claimed by other organizations, including for-profit corporations and other types of nonprofit organizations.

In its 1982 book, *Control of the Campus: A Report on the Governance of Higher Education*, the Carnegie Committee for the Improvement of Teaching emphasized the special autonomous status traditionally enjoyed by the academy. The authors pointed out, however, that throughout their histories colleges and universities have had to negotiate autonomy with the most powerful forces in society (e.g., various religious organizations and state and federal government).

Baldridge, Curtis, Ecker, and Riley (1977/1986) said that one of the characteristics that set colleges and universities apart from other complex organizations is environmental vulnerability. Establishing a continuum of autonomy from "independent" on one end and "captured" at the other, these scholars of higher education governance placed colleges and universities in the middle between free-market business firms at the "independent" end and public school districts at the "captured" end. According to the authors, strong external pressure can result in the faculty and administrators losing some control over the curriculum, the goals, and the daily operation of the institution.

Altbach and Berdahl (1981) said that the issue of institutional autonomy is one of balance (i.e., external forces and degree of autonomy must continually be monitored and adjusted). McConnell (1981) agreed that autonomy is not a clear-cut issue, but one that must be kept in balance.

The concept of institutional autonomy must also incorporate the concept of professional autonomy (i.e., decentralization of control) that has developed in higher education, particularly at research universities. It is this autonomy that is most closely related to academic freedom, that is, "the freedom of the scholar in his/her teaching and research to pursue a scholarly interest wherever it seems to lead and without fear of termination of employment for having offended some political, religious, or social orthodoxy" (Altbach & Berdahl, 1981, p.3). Albert (1985/1986) outlined the professional autonomy in research universities that grew out of the professional and structural segmentation of departments after 1900. The power over academic matters was delegated to homogeneous subunits who, according to Albert, gained a high degree of internal autonomy, but also started a dependency on external forces, such as federally sponsored research grants and professional accreditation.

Pfeffer and Salancik (1978) emphasized that autonomous subunits help an organization cope with competing demands from its environment and used universities as an example of how structural differentiation can help an organization simultaneously satisfy multiple constituencies. These scholars said, "The organization can thus make small accommodations to interest groups without redirecting the activities of the entire organization" (p. 274). The departmentalization of research universities, therefore, would appear to be a strategy by which external demands are absorbed by the departments, making the total institution less vulnerable to resource dependencies, including those with donors. As Albert (1985/1986) pointed out, however, these semi-autonomous subunits are, themselves, prone to dependencies on external forces.

There has been a recent movement toward decentralized fund raising at research universities that would indicate that new dependencies are developing between academic departments and donors. According to McCarty and Young (1981), "Colleges or schools within universities become matched with their environments by technical and exchange interdependencies of innumerable kinds" (p. 278). In her study of fund raising at research universities, M. Hall (1989) found that approximately twice as many universities had fund raisers for their business and engineering schools than institutions that did not, and that the majority of these fund-raising positions were less than 6 years old. Hackman (1985/1986) found through her study of power in the allocation of resources within colleges and universities that internal power accrues to those departments that are successful in bringing in resources. Similarly, in a 1974 study of academic units at the University of Illinois, Pfeffer and Salancik (1978) found that the best predictor of departmental power was the proportion of outside grant and contract money the department brought to the university.

These studies provide evidence of the movement toward departmental fund raising and some of the reasons for this movement. It must be pointed out, however, that bringing fund raising closer to the academic "core" of the university (i.e., academic departments) raises concerns about the potential effect of fund raising on professional autonomy, as well as on academic freedom. In fact, Dressel (1980) claimed that academic departments are the primary justification for institutional autonomy (i.e., there must be a high degree of autonomy for colleges and universities in order to *buffer* the academic unit from external control).

In other words, although decentralized fund raising may help the university protect its overall autonomy by coping with competing demands from its environment, such departmental efforts may also lead to infringement of the more highly valued concept of academic freedom, as well as a loss of departmental autonomy.

It may also be hypothesized that if an institution of higher education loses a high degree of departmental autonomy to external donors, the total institution will eventually suffer by losing control over its power to set and pursue its own goals. As the Carnegie Committee (1982) stated, "Control of the academic core is the one function that we may not lose without losing everything" (p. 203). This line of thought is explored further in the final section on the relationship between research universities and the federal government.

As is recalled from chapter 6, Pfeffer and Salancik (1978) said that the critical variable in determining external interest in an organization is its perceived usefulness (i.e., can its resources be used as tools to meet the objectives of other groups and organizations?). If we define the mission of higher education in the sense of a research university (i.e., a tripartite mission to teach, to advance knowledge, and to serve), we can better understand the deep and diverse interest in institutions of higher education and the multiple efforts that are made to control it.

Duryea (1981) stated:

American higher education during the course of this century has steadily become a critical resource for an increasingly sophisticated and complex culture. It mans the portals to careers in a wide variety of occupations and professions, provides expertise to government and industry as well as other societal entities, and generates knowledge essential for a wide swath of affairs, ranging from personal and social health to the maintenance of the economic system to space exploration. (p. 30)

According to Gould (1968), "In a world of change, [colleges and universities] are the single greatest instrument of change, 'the vehicle of social change and advance'" (p. 229).

It is this inherent value to society and to all competing external groups that provides the rationale for maintaining substantial amounts of autonomy for colleges and universities.

Corson (1968) provided five reasons why American society increasingly turns to its universities for help with problems: Universities have "unique institutional strengths, a substantial monopoly of human talent, a discipline of objectivity, a commitment to the search for new knowledge, and values" (p. 84). It is the possession of these unique qualities, according to Corson, that makes it inevitable that our knowledge-based society, with its increased specialization, will turn to universities with increased frequency. He explained, "For the solution of new problems, in both public policy and individual enterprise, the society seeks the specialized talent that can create new knowledge or apply it to new problems" (pp. 87-88).

As opposed to the traditional ivy-covered walls of academe, Corson (1968) said that the growing interdependency of our society has created a new organization that he calls "the wall-less university" (p. 88). This open structure is defended by Re (1968), who said, "Because universities claim almost a monopoly on talent and intellectual power, society is justified in demanding that higher education contribute in proportion to this professed ability" (p. 93). But the danger of such relationships is pointed out by Stoke (cited in Corson, 1968) when he said, "The more nearly society is operated on the basis of knowledge carefully gathered and impersonally applied, the more nearly the processes of higher education and of social action coincide, and the more nearly the processes of public administration and of legislation become those of the academic community" (p. 86).

Underlining the difference of what he saw as a new system of organization based on interdependence, Corson (1968) said, "The American society now avidly and hungrily seeks talent for the solution of many more problems than those of [past eras]. . . . That need poses for the university vastly greater demands than it has confronted to date" (p. 88). Corson raised two key questions when he asked, "Can the institution accept such responsibilities and maintain its autonomy? Where is the money coming from?" (p. 89). As outlined previously, the resource dependence perspective of Pfeffer and Salancik (1978) would describe institutions of higher education as organizations on which there are constant external attempts to control because they are highly valued by so many groups and organizations in our society.

A number of educational scholars have commented on the growing external pressures to which America's institutions of higher education have been subjected in recent years. Gould (1968) stated:

It is unnecessary for me to catalog the internal and external relationships of the university—relationships with . . . government agencies, with foundations, with potential or actual donors, with alumni, with the community. What *is* necessary is that we stand up to the realization that every one of these constituencies has *its own* goals for higher education, goals which may not necessarily be those of the university itself. And then it is equally necessary for us to ask ourselves *whose* goals are the ones we are working toward, ours or theirs? Who is making the basic determinations, and for what reason? And are these determinations the appropriate ones? (p. 222)

In the foreword to the book commemorating the 50th anniversary of the American Council on Education (ACE), *Whose Goals for American Higher Education?*, ACE President Logan Wilson (1968) wrote:

Our campuses are no longer enclaves set almost entirely apart from the surrounding society. . . . The large and heterogeneous population to be served has diverse notions about goals, and every constituency has its own views about priorities. . . . It is no wonder that institutions of higher education are moving from autonomy toward heteronomy. This is an understandable response to the new and growing demands for their services, and in a sense these pressures are a collective compliment to higher education's increased importance in a rapidly changing society. (p. viii)

The editors of the same book, Dobbins and Lee (1968), said:

The problem involves not merely competing visions of true purpose, but also competing preferences regarding priorities, means, and forms of governance by which aspirations are considered, articulated, and adopted. With so many underlying disagreements among the constituencies of higher education, there is need for an attempt to understand the dissonances and consonances among them. (p. xi)

It is clear from the historical background on institutional autonomy and from the discussion of systems theory in the last chapter of this book, that there is a tension between external sources of private support and the concept of institutional autonomy.

According to Wolfenden (1968), former chairman of the now-defunct University Grants Committee in Great Britain, a relationship of tension between a funding source and universities is not necessarily a situation that calls for alarm or distress. He said, "Tension, I am told by my physicist friends, is a necessary condition of movement and action" (p. 206). Wolfenden warned, however, that if the funding source insists on "calling the tune because it pays the piper," or if universities claim the right to ignore the society that supports them because of absolute autonomy, "there will inevitably be not just tension but friction; and friction, my same physicist friends tell me, is apt to generate heat, and in certain conditions, explosion" (p. 206).

AUTONOMY AND GIFTS: TENSION, FRICTION, OR EXPLOSION

The impact of private support on institutional autonomy in higher education is summarized by Harcleroad (1981), who stated:

> Private constituencies . . . can and do have significant impact on institutional autonomy and academic freedom. Much of this impact is positive, supportive, and welcome. However, those that provide funds can affect institutional trends and direction by determining what types of academic program or research efforts to support. . . . Acceptance of grants moves institutions in the direction dictated by fund sources, and faculties are well advised to consider this possibility as the "crunch" of the 1980s and 1990s become greater in more and more institutions. (p. 217)

The positive impact of private support on institutional autonomy is well recorded in educational history. For example, American colleges in the 17th and 18th centuries were primarily under the authoritarian control of organized religion through the power of church-appointed governing boards. According to Lee (1968), "It was not unusual for trustees to shape the curriculum, prescribe the work of the classroom, write the rules of behavior for students, hire and discharge faculty, and conduct final oral examinations" (p. 3). But when the early colleges faced the problems of financial instability between 1800 and 1860, they turned away from the church to individuals for support. (It should be noted that Lee incorrectly attributed alumni giving with this movement away from dependence on the church, but as documented in chapter 5, wealthy individuals were the primary source of private support until after World War I.) Be that as it may, by the beginning of the Civil War "secular philanthropy [had] loosened sectarian control over the intellect" (Lee, 1968, p.3). More examples of the positive impact gifts have had on American higher education are presented shortly, as well as in the next chapter on sources of private support and autonomy.

On the negative side, however, how strongly can we argue that institutions of higher education and their faculty still hold control of the academy? Lee (1968) responded to this question by stating:

> Coherence within the campus is disrupted by centrifugal forces which cause institutions to lose control over activities within their own walls. The decision of whether to build first a student union, a library, a classroom, or a science building is determined more by the availability of Federal loans than by internal needs. Universities apply for, accept, and house research grants without adequately checking

whether the research supports and enhances the purposes of the university or whether it diverts energies, space, time, and effort from more important institutional endeavors. In the academic game of grantsmanship, universities, by seeking the same prizes and badges of prestige, conform to values which have been determined by external forces. (p. 15)

Discussing the impact of private external forces on higher education, Harcleroad (1981) said, "All except those established very recently have been modified over the years and changed greatly in response to pressures from external forces. . . . Those in existence today are the survivors, the institutions that adapted to the needs of their constituencies" (p. 199).

Although the tension between accountability to external constituencies and institutional autonomy is still heatedly argued in most American institutions, British universities seem to be more advanced in recognizing that autonomy cannot be complete or absolute. British scholar Venables (1978) said:

Absolute autonomy is of course impossible: a network of relationships [government and other external constituencies] . . . determine how the needs of society and individual citizens should be met. . . . There can be no formal set of answers, only an ever-changing balance of interests within which the maximum degrees of freedom must be strenuously maintained. (p. 305)

Discussing the importance of accountability and its relationship to autonomy, Nason (1981) said:

The defense of the freedom of the university, which means in some sense its autonomy, however, must not blind us to its other function, namely, to insure the continuity and stability of society. As devices for transmitting values, attitudes, behavior patterns, educational institutions will inevitably reflect, sometimes enthusiastically and sometimes reluctantly, the nature of the society that supports and uses them. As the society changes, so will the institutions. (pp. 256-257)

How can American institutions of higher education serve both masters (i.e., defend their freedom while reflecting society)? Although it may be more comfortable to defend the right of the academy to set its own path, how do we explain those situations when external funding sources have "forced" our educational institutions to change for the better? Although it is difficult to defend value judgments on what is "better" in context of a college or university's societal role, many historical changes in these institutions were a result of donor insistence and a number of those changes would, by today's standards, be judged changes that were for the better.

For example, Reginald Wilson (1989), ACE's senior scholar and former director of its Office of Minority Concerns, said that the Julius Rosenwald Foundation used its philanthropic dollars to force institutions of higher education into hiring Black faculty members in the 1940s. Julius Rosenwald, the founder of Sears, Roebuck and Co., was a major contributor to the YMCA and YWCA, as well as to colleges and universities. A historical figure frequently cited in the literature on philanthropy, Rosenwald is probably best known for his 1929 attack against gifts in perpetuity (i.e., gifts used to create endowments from which only the income is used to fund specific purposes and/or programs in perpetuity) (O'Connell, 1983).

Emulating its founder's social activism, specifically a concern about education for Blacks, the Rosenwald Foundation formed a Race Relations Fund in the early 1940s and found that in 1942 there were only two "Negroes" on the faculties of U.S. "White" colleges and universities and that both were in nonteaching positions (Wilson, 1989). Based on this information, the Fund sent letters to the presidents of some 500 universities and colleges, urging them to hire Black faculty members and attaching the names of approximately 200 Black candidates with PhDs and 300 with master's degrees. Only 25% of the presidents replied, and of those responses, the majority were pessimistic about hiring Black faculty members at their institutions.

These dismal results, according to Wilson (1989), led the Fund to initiate a grants program that offered subsidized salaries for Black faculty members hired by White colleges and universities. Wilson said that the dollar power of the grants program was responsible for a dramatic increase in the hiring of Black faculty, including an eminent Black scholar in sociology at the University of Chicago (i.e., a number of colleges and universities changed their institutional behavior in order to take advantage of the money offered by the Rosenwald Foundation). From the perspective of the theory of power and social exchange discussed in the preceding chapter, we can conclude that during the 1940s, some predominately White institutions in the United States found the exchange of dollars for Black scholars to be acceptable. Of course, others did not; and Wilson said that it was not until they were "dragged kicking and screaming into compliance by the federal government" almost 25 years later that American colleges and universities accepted, at least in principle, the tenet of equal opportunity for Black faculty members. As discussed in chapter 10, Grunig's (Grunig & Grunig, 1989) theory holds that conflict with external publics can be good for the very reason that it can stimulate change. He argued, however, that organizations still must manage such conflicts in order to preserve as much autonomy as possible.

As described in chapter 8 on sources of private support and autonomy, gifts have historically been responsible for other positive changes (e.g., opening the doors of higher education to women and lowering religious and ethnic barriers). It is hypothesized that even the strongest proponents of absolute autonomy would defend such "positive" intrusions on institutional autonomy as justifiable. This is, perhaps, the heart of the tension between accountability to society and institutional autonomy. In addition, Mintzberg's (1983) conceptual horseshoe should be recalled from chapter 6, which emphasizes that organizational staff want absolute autonomy, but external forces seek control of the organization.

The controversy, according to Altbach and Berdahl (1981), "involves interdependence and conflict of external constituencies and universities, with what each owes the other and what each owes to values which are inherent in its own distinctive nature and which are not harmonious with the values of the other" (p. 305). They suggested that constituencies (e.g., donors) act to either influence or control universities and colleges, and that decisions will have to be made in each case whether the relations in question are in rough balance or whether they need adjustment either toward more autonomy or more accountability.

But as McConnell (1981) pointed out, "Accountability is still further complicated by a question of what special interests should be served and what should be put aside" (pp. 39-40). He added, "Only when an institution's goals are defined, the groups to be served are identified, and the relevant programs of teaching, research, and public service are determined can an institution's effectiveness be estimated."

In an article about higher education's reaction to the critical book, *ProfScam* ("AAUP president," 1989), Ohio State Rep. Michael A. Fox, ranking Republican on the House Education Committee, asked:

> In a world where there are more demands for accountability at every level of government, what's so different about higher education that we should allow it to be exempt from those measures? This is where I part company with the higher-education community, which has guarded their [*sic*] independence and autonomy saying, "Give us the money and leave us alone." Those who insist on clinging to those notions will be rolled over. (p. A19)

In summary, private support has had both positive and negative impact on the autonomy of colleges and universities. The positive impact has ranged from secular gifts helping to diffuse religion's authoritarian control of educational institutions in the mid-1800s to the hiring of Black faculty members in the 1940s. On the negative side, private funds have moved colleges and universities in the direction dictated by fund sources, and these institutions have been criticized for conforming to values determined by donors. The tension between accountability to external constituencies and institutional autonomy is not an easy one to resolve in that the freedom of the university must be weighed against the university's responsibility to reflect the society that supports and uses it. Relations with external constituencies, such as donors, must be continually adjusted so that a balance is maintained between autonomy and accountability. As Brittingham and Pezzullo (1990) said, "Each request for support for a particular purpose is a statement about what the institution would like to become (or remain). . . . And each accepted gift, with all of its stipulations and restrictions, is a statement about what the institution is willing to become" (p. 57).

Before turning to the next chapter on the three primary sources of private giving and their impact on autonomy, it is useful to examine the funding relationship between the public sector—the federal government—and American colleges and universities, specifically public and private research universities who are the recipients of billions of dollars in federally sponsored research.

AUTONOMY AND THE FEDERAL GOVERNMENT

Unlike the interdependent relationship between colleges and donors, the funding relationship between research universities and federally sponsored research has received a great deal of critical attention in the higher education literature, and analogies between the two will help provide a new perspective of fund raising. According to Spencer (1968):

> During World War II, the government found that it had to intensify, many times over, the amount of research it supported. It needed answers to specific questions, most of them in science and engineering. Naturally, it went for the answers to society's chief repositories of wisdom and talent—the universities. For reasons of patriotism or esteem or money or what have you, the universities proved eminently receptive to the call. This process of demand and response has multiplied and remultiplied since World War II. (p. 56)

Spencer and other critics maintain that the federal government has come to dominate the university's research time and facilities. "As the demands of the beast have grown, the universities have fed it, apparently with more and more willingness," said Spencer (p. 56). In 1965, congressional hearings on teaching and research, "Conflicts between the Federal Research Programs and the Nation's Goals for Higher Education," were conducted, primarily due to the allegations that some 85% of all research conducted in universities at that time was sponsored by the government and that "government-sponsored research was impairing the teaching capacities of the university" (p. 56).

Although teaching was an issue for congressmen, many faculty, particularly those in the social sciences who received less than 6% of the $5.3 billion in sponsored research, objected to the government's calling the tune in research direction. "Over-all," said Spencer (1968), "the critics charge that the government has run roughshod over education in order to achieve its goals in development and research" (p. 57).

Addressing all forms of federal funding in the 1960s, including research funding, Hobba (1976) stated:

Congress discovered that a few dollars invested at the margin of higher education would pay tremendous benefits in the accomplishment of national objectives. By concentrating its resources at the margin in categorical programs, the Federal Government was able to direct the expenditure of approximately a third of the nation's higher education budget by underwriting a sixth of the costs. (p. 92)

Perkins (1966) said that the issue of federal research dollars and institutional autonomy is limited to a very few educational institutions, basically the 200 universities that place strong emphasis on research as part of their mission. Perkins claimed these institutions have taken on the status of "intellectual holding company," and pointed out that in 1962, only 10% of the then 2,000 accredited colleges and universities received 97% of all government research funds. This reduction of focus (i.e., concentrating on the small percentage of the population most actively involved in an external funding relationship) is an issue that arises in later discussions about institutional relations with donors. Primarily, few scholars have focused their attention on the very small percentage of institutions and external funding sources that account for the majority of dollars produced by college–donor relationships. Such a focus provides strong evidence for reinterpreting the function of fund raising at American colleges and universities.

In the meantime, it is also important to remember that in the government–university relationship, there is little if any evidence of applied coercion to get a research project under way. As Spencer stated (1968):

The universities can say "no" whenever they want. Obviously, they ought to have done so more often. I question the judgement of many universities for . . . diverting resources excessively from the teaching function, for giving the dignity of their name to enterprises that at best have a doubtful place in the university community. (p. 60)

Albert (1985/1986) discussed a 1980 magazine article by Sen. Daniel Moynihan, outlining the negative consequences of federally sponsored research and bemoaning the growth of federal influence on the academic mission. Moynihan specifically berated university presidents from the 1957–1972 era for failing to ensure that a portion of the federal money was made available for unrestricted use. "It was at least possible for the universities to have negotiated a distinctive relationship between themselves and the national government. . . . That this was not done involved a profound failure of leadership" (cited in Albert, 1985/1986, p. 96).

Albert (1985/1986) ridiculed Moynihan's ignorance of the organizational context of modern American universities that would have brought university presidents into direct confrontation with their faculties if such action had been taken. As is recalled from the earlier section on the historical background of institutional autonomy, an academic revolution took place at the turn of the century, when authority in academic matters was transferred from the president to the faculty. According to Albert, increasing professionalism of the faculty, particularly those at the 100 major research campuses in the United States, led to the departmentalism of higher education and an organizational structure that Pfeffer and Salancik (1978) and Weick (1976/1986) described as "loosely coupled systems." It should be noted that Albert reduced the educational segment known as research universities down to 100 from Perkins' (1966) 200. This book adopts Albert's grouping for use later in this discussion because it is the one most commonly used to rank research dollars and is considered by most educational scholars to be America's elite institutions. In addition, the 3% of the some 3,000 American colleges and universities included in this grouping of 100 are generally the same institutions that appear in top rankings for private support. Albert emphasized the importance of this small, but critical group, saying, "The research universities include some 10,000 departments that are arrayed rather symmetrically in about 100 disciplinary communities on about 100 major research campuses and tied together in an interdependent national system" (p. 90).

It is primarily these 100 research universities that have achieved a high degree of professionalism with semi-autonomous departments that Cohen and March (cited in Baldridge et al., 1977/1986) referred to as "organized anarchy." In this type of institution, each individual is seen as making autonomous decisions: Teachers decide if, when, and what to teach; students decide if, when, and what to learn; legislators and donors decide if, when, and what to support. There is not coordination, control, or explicit superordinate goals. Decisions are a consequence of the system but intended by no one and controlled by no one. According to Albert (1985/1986):

> The shift to departmentalism was accelerated by the entry of the federal government as a major source of funds allocated directly to individual researchers and handled by their departments. The various departments became more independent of the internal administration and more dependent on the support of external constituencies. (pp. 86-87)

Albert developed a matrix showing external support agencies and their direct relationship to the university's central administration and its departments. He summarized these relationships by saying, "Although the institution is allotted a share of funding in the form of indirect costs, the central university administration is typically bypassed or plays only a minor role in a process that cumulatively defines the priorities, the staffing, and the research mission of the institution (by summation)" (p. 89). As mentioned earlier in the section on the historical background of institutional autonomy, this decentralization of federal funding relationships is analogous to a current trend in fund raising, particularly at American research and comprehensive universities where fund raising is being conducted by components, or academic units.

Spencer (1968) recommended that universities, as a community, set some new rules regarding the acceptance of government funds for research projects. Although, he did not raise the issue of academic freedom involved in imposing limitations on research funding, Spencer did address institutional autonomy by saying:

> If universities have accepted limitations on their freedom of action in the controversial area of recruiting football players, then it should not be impossible for them to reach agreement on a similar discipline for building research structures. The objective is the same in both cases: the preservation of the integrity of the university as a social institution. (p. 60)

Although Albert (1985/1986) stopped short of recommending such radical changes in the research infrastructure, he did raise serious questions about the "cost" external federal funding has had on the autonomy of research universities (i.e., their power to determine goals and the means of reaching those goals). He described the growth period of the 1950s and 1960s as a time when the increasingly decentralized universities adapted to change by "adding new academic units under the stimulus of readily available federal research funds and the growth in student enrollments" (p. 84). Supporting the issue raised in chapter 2 of the changing context of fund raising, Albert continued, stating:

> Proposals to add units were often based on the availability of new sources of external funding and did not call on existing units to give up their claims on resources. But what about starting new programs and departments now in this day of declining enrollments, horizontal budgets, and finite resources. Aren't we still paying for those new programs of the 60s in annual salaries and physical maintenance? (p. 84)

Clark Kerr (1972), president emeritus of the University of California, took a much stronger stance than Albert on the negative impact federal research dollars have had on the institutional autonomy of colleges and universities. In his book on the _multiversity_, a term Kerr used to describe the totally different organization that resulted from the influx of federal research money after World War II, Kerr blamed the influence—in Mintzberg's (1983) terminology, "power"—of vast amounts of federal grants for the current weakness of major research universities to control their own affairs. These universities, said Kerr, have fallen prey to "imbalances" that are a natural result of external influence. He pointed to the dominance of research over teaching, science over humanities, graduate studies over undergraduate concerns, and the existence of multitudes of "unfaculty," who work on campuses for federally sponsored projects with no other service required to the university as examples of the effects of external funding.

Although other cases could be made for these effects, most academics would agree that the infusion of federal research dollars in the middle of this century have helped "shape" the organizational structure, resource allocation, physical plant, and personnel of major research universities.

Commenting on Kerr's term (which he used prior to his 1972 book), Perkins (1966) discussed some of the strains that "emerged in and are a result of 'multiversity' situations with multivaried functions" (p. 37). Perkins pointed out that in 1962–1963, only 33% of the $0.5-billion budget for the University of California at Los Angeles (UCLA), a major recipient of federal research grants, went for items related to teaching.

Lehecka (1968) warned educators that changes brought about by external funding sources are not likely to be the result of any conspiracy, but rather the result of unpreparedness by the recipient. The deluding nature of resource dependency relationships is revealed when Lehecka stated:

> Clark Kerr has said that no one created or planned the multiversity. It just happened. A university should not become a "happening." If it cannot plan or control its own development, how can it help a city or a nation plan its future? (p. 98)

Kerr and Gade (1981) provided evidence that federal research dollars are still a threat to institutional autonomy. According to these education scholars, a "hot issue" throughout the late 1970s and into the 1980s was the pressure from the federal government on universities to produce more applied research—research that can quickly be translated into solutions to current problems. This pressure is perhaps even more intense today as federal and state governments increasingly look to universities for help in economic development efforts (e.g., transferring technology to the marketplace). Kerr and Gade say:

> Within the universities . . . there has been a shift away from basic and towards applied research. Basic research spending in universities and colleges increased 20 percent in constant dollars during the decade of the 1970s; applied research spending increased 74 percent. (p. 118)

Of academic research and development expenditures by colleges and universities in 1968, only 19% were spent on applied research; in 1978, that proportion had risen to 26% (Kerr & Gade, 1981). The authors warned that the temptation to shift more funds into applied areas in hopes of a quick "payoff" should be weighed against "the ultimate payoff to society of pursuing scientific research in directions dictated by the nature of the disciplines themselves" (p. 119).

Kerr and Gade (1981) also raised the issue of the distribution of federal research funds, which was discussed earlier. Specifically, they emphasized that the general idea of disbursing billions of dollars in research funds to the some 3,000 institutions of higher education in the United States is a myth that minimizes the high degree of dependency a few select institutions have on these funds. Kerr and Gade (1981) said, "In 1978, the 100 leading universities, in terms of receipt of federal funds for research and development, received over 80 percent of all such funds, a proportion that held steady during the 1970s" (p. 119). In 1986, that proportion had increased to 85%, that is, only 3% of the approximately 3,000 U.S. colleges and universities received approximately 85% of federal research grants, which in 1986 accounted for $5.5 billion of the $6.5 billion awarded ("U.S. funds," 1987).

According to Kerr and Gade, "This pattern results from decisions made during World War II, and followed since, that research funds should go to institutions that have the best scientists and the greatest possibility of extending the frontiers of scientific investigation" (p. 119).

The National Science Foundation figures reported in *The Chronicle of Higher Education* ("U.S. funds," 1987) show that Johns Hopkins University was the leader in attracting federal funds in 1985–1986, receiving $445.7 million in research funds that year and a total amount of federal funding of $465.5 million. The next highest institution was the Massachusetts Institute of Technology, which received $188 million in sponsored research and development and $212.4 million in total federal funds. The top three universities in total federal obligations for fiscal 1986 (i.e., federal funds set aside for payment to institutions) were *private* universities: Hopkins, MIT, and Stanford University. Total federal obligations totaled $11.6 billion in 1985–1986, of which the top 100 universities received $7.3 billion, or 63% of the total.

Kerr and Gade (1981) pointed out that universities that administer these grants have frequently found themselves involved in clashes with the external source of their billions of dollars in research funding (i.e., agencies of the federal government) over management practices, including the accounting procedures being used. In addition, the scholars said there has been increasing federal regulation of the actual content of research (e.g., federal guidelines prohibiting certain kinds of experiments in genetic engineering) that may foreshadow even more serious intrusion into academic freedom. "The government–university partnership in scientific research," summarized Kerr and Gade (1981), "appears to be a permanent one, but no longer one in which the federal partner supplies the funds and the university partner takes them, no strings attached" (p. 119). They concluded, "New rules for the partnership will need to be negotiated" (p. 119).

As Spencer (1968), Albert (1986/1987), Kerr and Gade (1981), and others make clear, receiving funding—in this case federal research and development grants—can have long-term costs in both dollars and constraints on autonomy for institutions of higher education, particularly for those 100 public and private research universities that receive most of the dollars. Echoing Spencer, Hall (1988) pointed out that universities and their faculties have not been coerced into their partnership with the government and dispelled any notions of a conspiracy theory being responsible for loss of autonomy. He said:

> Although the federal government began to be a significant factor in the funding of research during and after World War II, its funding activities, funneled through such agencies as the National Science Foundation, the National Institutes of Health, and, by the 1960s, the endowments for the arts and the humanities, were more influenced by priorities set in the universities (the most important of which remained private institutions) and in the academic professions (which were organized as private nonprofit entities) than by politics. (p. 64)

It wasn't until the Nixon presidential years, according to Hall (1988) that "the National Science Foundation and the Institutes of Health began determining their research and grant-giving priorities along political lines, underwriting research activities (such as 'a war on cancer') that could be counted on to yield political and public relations benefits" (p. 65). As stated by Spencer (1968) earlier, the universities, in their growing dependency on external research dollars from the federal government, willingly feed the demands of the beast.

Lehecka (1968) supported an underlying premise of this book—the premise of the current era in higher education being one of limited resources, as discussed in chapter 2—when he said:

> A university cannot say "Yes" to every request that comes its way, however worthy the purposes. Rather, it must consider what resources it has available (and these are always finite) and then establish priorities for their use. It must weigh the consequences of any added function it assumes. (p. 98)

Concluding this section, resource dependency relationships with external sources of dollars, such as the relationship between research universities and the federal government, have an inherent potential for loss of autonomy by the recipient organization—a loss that may be minimized only through negotiations. At the same time, the earlier issue of accountability always must be weighted when discussing autonomy. Leaving aside for a moment the funding of research, Kramer (1980) charged that much of the federal government's intrusion in the 1960s and 1970s into the affairs of the academy was done in the name of social legislation and fiscal responsibility. He harshly criticized the government for using public funds as levers for controlling institutional behavior, such as integration and affirmative action, and compared this devious behavior to the more admirable behavior of the private source of funding who gives with no thought of using the gift as an instrument for personal purpose. Unlike the case that can be made against the federal government for intruding on institutional autonomy through research dollars, it is difficult to agree with Kramer's viewpoint when it comes to social purposes (e.g., the degree of autonomy lost can be perceived as a worthwhile price to pay for gaining some degree of racial equality in colleges and universities).

As was demonstrated in the earlier description of the Rosenwald Foundation's efforts to force colleges to hire Black faculty, the same quandary is readily apparent in the area of private support. An imperative need to be socially responsible (i.e., to be accountable to society) can sometimes outweigh the academy's special privilege of institutional autonomy.

Albert (1985/1986) provided a transition from federal research funding to private sources of support when he said, "Inadequacies of federal funding and retrenchment imposed by state governments have moved virtually every university to a search for added support from industrial corporations" (p. 103).

Before the book turns its attention to the three primary sources of private support—including corporate donors—and their effect on institutional autonomy, this chapter concludes with a summary of its main points. The concept of institutional autonomy can be defined as *substantive* in nature (i.e., the power of a college or university to determine its own goals and programs) and *procedural* (i.e., the power of an institution to determine the means by which its goals and programs will be pursued). Whereas autonomy is a corporate concept that is of necessity parochial and relative, academic freedom is an individual protection that is universal and absolute. Absolute autonomy is neither possible nor desirable for colleges and universities because all public and private funding involves some loss, and society extends autonomy to these institutions because it believes that society benefits from such action (i.e., colleges and universities are accountable to society). Therefore, discussion of autonomy must focus on the nature and extent of autonomy required for effective operation of the institution and on the institution's fulfillment of its responsibilities to society.

Fund raising presents a double-edged sword for colleges and universities: Without adequate funding, there is no autonomy because there is no freedom to consider programming alternatives, but the needs and interests of donors also limit autonomy. The critical question is one of the extent and nature of the limitations that can be imposed on the autonomy of an institution without eroding its effectiveness. Therefore, this chapter concludes that interdependencies with donors must be managed to avoid the risk of a great loss of autonomy.

The concept of institutional autonomy has its origin in 15th- and 16th-century England where the concept of corporate autonomy was first conceived, but Americans incorporated a responsiveness to societal needs, thus establishing the dualism of autonomy versus accountability. Because of their usefulness to other groups and organizations, colleges and universities have had to negotiate autonomy throughout their histories with the most powerful forces in society (e.g., religious organizations and state and federal government). Following Altbach and Berdahl (1981), this chapter concludes that the issue of institutional autonomy is one of constant balancing, in which interdependencies must be continually monitored and adjusted; they cannot be left to happenstance.

Finally, the selective distribution of federal grants and their documented effect on the institutional autonomy of major research universities provides new insight on external resource dependency. The influx of federal research money to universities after World War II resulted in "multiversities," in which external influence has established dominance of research over teaching, of science over humanities, of graduate studies over undergraduate concerns, and the existence of multitudes of "unfaculty," who work on campuses for federally sponsored projects with no other service required to the university. In short, external funding has created an imbalance and has weakened such research universities to the point where they generally do not control a large portion of their own affairs.

Salamon (1987) claimed that the effects of federal research funding has shocked educators and scholars because they refused to perceive the potential loss of autonomy while it was happening. He said this general reaction results from the lack of "an analysis that takes account of the true history of government–nonprofit relationships and that comes to terms with the current shape of government–nonprofit ties" (p. 108).

This book is designed to prevent a similar situation in the private funding area by analyzing the history and shape of donor–recipient relationships. In support of this objective, the book now turns to an examination of the three sources of gifts and their documented impact on institutional autonomy.

Chapter 8

Autonomy and the
Three Sources of Gifts

Staying with a focus on higher education, this chapter analyzes the three primary sources of private support to answer the research question: In relation to institutional autonomy, how do foundations, corporations, and individuals differ in their potential to infringe on a charitable organization's power to determine its own goals and the means of pursuing those goals?

Historical and current evidence is provided that—contrary to conventional wisdom—funding relationships with all three sources share an inherent potential for loss of institutional autonomy. As pointed out in chapter 5, the myth of a broad base of donors is based on the false assumption that private support consists primarily of numerous and equal gifts from multiple donors. An important conclusion of this chapter is that major gifts—whether from foundations, corporations, or individuals—have the potential, on an individual basis, to infringe on institutional autonomy. This conclusion refutes the literature that characterizes donors, particularly individuals, as a faceless mass that because of their diversity can not affect autonomy (e.g., Kramer, 1980).

According to Salamon (1987), "Government has become the single most important source of income for most types of nonprofit agencies, outdistancing private charity by roughly two to one" (p. 99). Citing a study by Rudney, Salamon said that "private nonprofit organizations (exclusive of churches, which are not eligible for government support) received a larger share of their income from government as of 1974 than they did from all sources of private giving combined—corporate, foundation, and individual" (p. 101).

Why then are private gifts so important to charitable organizations, particularly to those colleges and universities that are aggressively pursuing private funds, as described in chapter 2? Gifts to higher education have grown roughly by more than 300% in the 1980s, and funds from private sources now amount to about 7% of the total $105.4 billion in the annual expenditures of colleges and universities ("Surge in gifts," 1987). Commenting on the percentage of higher educational expenditures accounted for by gifts, John Haire (1981), president of the Council for Aid to Education (CFAE), said, "While this proportion is less impressive than the 50 percent that reflects the importance of governmental support, it is a vital element in institutional revenues and represents the margin that is so critical to the independence and vitality of all higher education" (pp. 139-140).

Dunn (1986) believes that private giving exerts a disproportionate effect in the shaping of institutional programs, saying that although private giving ranks only fourth or fifth as a source of revenues for colleges and universities, its growth has outpaced both inflation and institutional expenditures. As discussed in chapter 5, Kramer (1980) called private gifts "the venture capital of higher education." He pointed to their flexibility in use and to the lack of restrictions, regulations, and procedures so commonly tied to government funding.

In support of Kramer's (1980) assessment, Useem (1987) cited studies that document a general lack of accounting and evaluation in the area of corporate philanthropy. He concluded, "This suggests that the simple act of associating with the recipient is often more important to a company than how the recipient applies the gift" (p. 354).

Ylvisaker (1987) said that until the 1969 Tax Reform Act, foundations had little interest in evaluating grantees' performance. And although few, if any, scholars have examined the issue of accountability to individual donors, there is a general assumption throughout the practitioner literature that individual gifts rarely require more than thanking and perfunctory reporting. But as Salamon (1987) pointed out:

> The notion that the nonprofit sector is independent, after all, can be misleading. Financially, the sector is almost inevitably dependent—on private sources of funds if not public ones. And historically, private funds have often come with strings every bit as onerous and threatening to agency independence as any government has devised. (p. 114)

Salamon described a few of the ways that private funding sources have pressured charitable organizations to alter their goals, concluding, "These sources frequently have their own priorities and concerns that may or may not accord with the priorities of voluntary agencies" (p. 114).

FOUNDATION DONORS AND AUTONOMY

As one of the three sources of private funds, foundations historically have received the greatest attention from scholars in the fields of philanthropy and higher education and the greatest amount of criticism for their infringement on institutional autonomy. According to Curti and Nash (1965), "Since foundations generally place conditions on their grants in order to promote specific ends that frequently depart from traditional practice, they have received more critical examination than other sources of philanthropic support" (p. 235). The authors pointed out, however, that few have objected except those institutions that did not get money during the decade from 1955 to 1965 when foundations were "the most lucrative source of voluntary aid for higher education" (p. 235).

Harcleroad (1981) said that the approximately 5,000 foundations with assets of $1 million or more "provide significant help to higher education institutions, and by their choice of the areas they will finance they entice supposedly autonomous colleges to do things they might not do otherwise" (p. 202). "Institutional change," he pointed out, "continues to be a prime goal of foundations as it has been for most of the past century" (p. 202).

According to Ylvisaker (1987), there are 23,600 active U.S. foundations, which are profiled in the introduction to the 1985 edition of the *Foundation Directory*. "The combined assets of the 23,600 foundations," according to Ylvisaker, "are $64.5 billion, or about half of the total assets [$125 billion, estimated by *Forbes* in 1984] of America's 400 wealthiest individuals" (p. 360). He reported that foundation annual grants of $4.8 billion in 1980 were 3.7% of the estimated total operating expenditures ($131 billion) of all charitable organizations and roughly 0.5% of the federal government's budget ($1 trillion).

Parallel to the selective distribution pattern of the small percentage of colleges and universities that receive the majority of gift dollars and federal research funds—as discussed in chapters 5 and 7—a relatively small number of foundations dominate the philanthropic scene. Only 4,402, or 19%, of the 23,600 foundations in 1985 had assets over $1 million or annual giving over $100,000; yet, they accounted for 97% of total foundation assets, 85% of total grants and all paid staff. Just 15 foundations, such as Ford, J. Paul Getty, MacArthur, and Kellogg, had assets of $500 million or more and accounted for 28.2% of total foundation assets and 13.6% of total grants (Ylvisaker, 1987).

There is little doubt that the major foundations (i.e., those with assets of $250 million or more) are in very influential positions due to their wealth. Much of this wealth and influence has been directed at American colleges and universities. According to Ylvisaker (1987), "Colleges and universities have long been the

major instruments and beneficiaries of foundation giving, though their share of
total funding has abruptly declined in recent years" (p. 370). Ylvisaker provided
tables from an unpublished study by Shepard that creates a longitudinal data base
covering the giving of the nation's 47 largest, noncorporate, private foundations
from 1955 to 1979. These tables show that in 1965, colleges and universities
received 57.7% of the total dollars granted by foundations, but only 38.6% in
1979. Of course, these grants were not distributed equally among America's
some 3,000 institutions. For example, community colleges, which constitute the
largest segment of higher education, received 0.4% of the total dollars granted
by foundations in 1965 (nothing before) and 0.3% in 1979 (Ylvisaker, 1987).

To provide more current (but not comparable) data, Ylvisaker used the
Foundation Center Grants Index of 400+ Foundations to develop tables on the
giving of the 100 largest foundations. He found that private colleges and
universities received 23.1% of the total dollars given by the top 100 foundations
in 1982, but only 18.3% in 1984. Public colleges and universities received 8.5%
in 1982 and 9.6% in 1984. Finally, community colleges remained low priorities
for foundations as indicated by the fact that they received only 0.3% of the
dollars given by the largest 100 foundations in 1982 and 0.5% in 1984
(Ylvisaker, 1987).

Money, Selectivity, Concentrated
Influence, and Leverage

Although they are relatively small, Ylvisaker (1987) said, "Foundations are still
generally credited with—and often resented for—playing a disproportionate
influential role in the private and public sectors of American society" (p. 360).
The influence of these few foundations, according to Ylvisaker, derives primarily
from their vast sums of money, from their selectivity, from their ability to
concentrate on or change the behavior of recipient organizations, and from the
leverage they can apply. Referring to the first source of influence, Ylvisaker
stated:

> Tiny though they are against the larger canvas of American society, foundations
> have managed to exert a significant influence (not always benign) on the nation's
> private and public affairs. Partly, but only partly, this is due to the simple fact of
> their having what everyone in society would like a piece of: money and the power
> that goes with it. (pp. 371-372)

But Ylvisaker claimed there are substantial reasons why foundations have become
influential other than money. "These reasons go directly to the generic role and
art of philanthropy; its ability to choose, concentrate, and leverage," he said (p.
372).

Keeping in mind Altbach and Berdahl's (1981) definitions of substantive and procedural autonomy, it is enlightening to examine what Ylvisaker (1987) said is the key issue in the effect foundation donors can have on the autonomy of charitable organizations. He explained that among the ways foundations can exert a significant and sometimes determining influence on charitable organizations is to "expand and influence the choice not only of goals but also of the means of implementing them" (p. 373). In addition, according to Ylvisaker, "Foundations can—and necessarily do—maximize their influence by being selective. . . . [and] by selecting points of leverage that convert small inputs into the greater energy needed to redirect larger forces" (p. 373).

The primary source of foundation influence (i.e., money) is closely related to the fact that under the Tax Reform Act of 1969, foundations are required by law to distribute a percentage of their assets each year. As Ylvisaker (1987) pointed out, the total assets of all foundations are less than the total assets of the 400 wealthiest individuals in America; however, those individuals are not required by law to distribute their wealth, as are foundations.

Related to the second source of influence, selectivity, foundations are—as are all donors—free to select the recipients of their money. It should be noted here that terms such as *benevolence, charity, generosity,* and so forth, are not used in this chapter when describing the giving of private money to colleges and universities as their use might convey the false impression that institutions of higher education are eleemosynary charities, rather than charities with positive externalities, as defined by Douglas (1983). Ylvisaker (1987) provided a 1983 ranking of the top 25 organizational recipients of grant dollars from foundations with assets of $100 million or more, which shows that 13 of the top 25 were institutions of higher education. All 13 of these institutions are members of the top 100 research universities discussed in chapter 7 on the relationship between research universities and the federal government (e.g., Johns Hopkins, Harvard, Yale, University of Michigan, and the University of California).

Solely through their selectivity, foundations can dramatically impact not only the autonomy of the recipient institutions, but also many of the institutions that are not selected as recipients. For example, in 1910, a trustee of John D. Rockefeller's General Education Board, Dr. Abraham Flexner, issued a report calling for the closing of all but 31 of the existing 155 medical schools in the United States. Citing the "deplorable conditions" in medical education, the foundation launched a series of grants that would build Johns Hopkins into a model medical school and improve medical education at a select group of other colleges and universities, if they agreed to certain conditions (e.g., doctors at recipient institutions had to agree to give up their private practice for full-time teaching). After two decades and $78 million, America's medical schools were greatly improved and greatly reduced (Curti & Nash, 1965).

According to Curti and Nash (1965), the Carnegie Foundation for the Advancement of Teaching used pension funds in the early 1900s to standardize admissions, to define essential elements of a "true" college, and to greatly reduce the number of denominational colleges. Established with a gift of $10 million from Andrew Carnegie to support pensions for college professors, the foundation used membership in the pension fund as a reward for those institutions that conformed to certain standards (e.g., if professors were to receive pensions, their college had to have at least six professors and admit only those students who had completed 4 years of secondary education. Curti and Nash reported, "In an effort to eliminate church control of colleges the foundation had been chartered with the stipulation that no pensions would be given to the faculties of institutions under sectarian control" (p. 220). Hundreds of colleges dropped their religious affiliations in order to qualify.

The first Congressional committee to investigate foundations, the Walsh Commission of 1915, expressed a deep concern about colleges changing their sectarian charters in order to qualify for the Carnegie pension fund money. Emphasizing how such action clearly demonstrates that foundations threaten institutional autonomy, the commission stated, "It would seem conclusive that if an institution will willingly abandon its religious affiliations through influence of these foundations, it will even more easily conform to their will any other part of its organization and teaching" (cited in Whitaker, 1974, p. 101).

According to Curti and Nash (1965), both the Carnegie Foundation for the Advancement of Teaching and Rockefeller's General Education Board "were aware that they could frequently influence institutions, even without giving them benefits directly, by the lure of philanthropy and the example of others" (p. 221).

In relation to Ylvisaker's (1987) third source of influence, foundations have traditionally considered themselves "change agents." Their ability to change the goals of recipient institutions and/or the means to pursue those goals (i.e., Altbach and Berdahl's, 1981, definition of substantive and procedural institutional autonomy) is frequently viewed as their *raison d'etre*. As is recalled from the beginning of this section, Harcleroad (1981) said that institutional change is the prime goal of foundations. Haire (1981) said, "Foundation giving is generally unconventional, which means that innovative and experimental projects will continue to command an important share of foundation interest . . . general operating support of an unrestricted nature is becoming a rarity in the foundation community" (p. 142). Addressing this focus on funding "innovative projects," the co-director of a charitable organization in the area of international development said, "Sometimes the project in question is truly innovative, but a new project to manage may be just what an organization needs least" ("If charities," 1989, p. 36).

Related to the earlier discussion on the myth of unrestricted support in chapter 5, a recent article ("Some foundations," 1989) stated:

> Throughout the history of organized philanthropy, many foundations have firmly held that their money should be spent only on new, experimental programs, or "project support." At the same time, non-profit groups have countered that they first must receive "operating support" to cover their most basic needs, such as staff salaries and telephone service. The debate has often ended in a stalemate. (p. 4)

Reporting on a June 1989 conference on the debate between operating and project support, the aforementioned article ("Some foundations," 1989) said that between 87.4% and 83.3% of all foundation dollars to charitable organizations between 1985 and 1987 were restricted as to their use. It is important to note that this low percentage of unrestricted support from foundations, according to this article, came directly after the $70 billion decline in support by the federal government in the first half of the 1980s, during the same time that mergers and corporate restructuring threatened corporate giving programs and pressured corporate donors to "finance projects with tangible results, rather than merely subsidizing operations," and when individual donors "often preferred to make high-visibility gifts, such as endowing a gallery, rather than contributing to less-glamorous causes such as utility bills" (pp. 4-6).

Complaints about the high percentage of restricted gifts traditionally made by foundations in their role as change agents prompted one foundation director at the June 1989 meeting to question whether such gifts "weren't setting the priorities for non-profit organizations" ("Some foundations," 1989, p. 6). Another foundation trustee is quoted as saying:

> Too often project grants cost an institution rather than support it. The grant seldom covers all the costs involved. The institution must spend its own money to complete the foundation-funded program. Its own money is better spent, I submit, to pay the rent and the telephone bill. (p. 6)

Finally, grant seekers argued at the June 1989 conference that the restricted nature of most foundation gifts merely encouraged deceptive grant proposals. One fund raiser was quoted as saying, "You create a situation in which we have to bend the truth or out-and-out lie to stay alive" (p. 6).

Summarizing this discussion on restricted giving, foundations historically have restricted the majority of their gifts to all charitable organizations, including colleges and universities. Because institutional change has been and continues to be their prime goal, foundations provide little flexible funding to help charitable organizations set and pursue their own goals. Rather, foundations, because of their restricted giving patterns, have been charged with setting the priorities of charitable organizations, costing them institutional funds in order to complete foundation projects, and forcing charitable organizations to manipulate and deceive donors in order to survive.

Yarmolinsky (1961/1983) operationalized the theory of social and power exchange discussed in chapter 6 in relation to foundation donors when he explained:

> There is a process of exchange here which enables foundations to bring home to the universities ideas about planning for research projects, curriculum planning, organization of activities . . . which have already made real contributions to the planning process, and even to the substantive organization of the university world. (p. 349)

Yarmolinsky (1961/1983) used Galbraith's theory of countervailing power to underline how foundations serve as a "useful" societal force in their relationships with colleges and universities. Claiming that unlike wealthy individuals, who may not have much say in programs they give to, Yarmolinsky said that when a university president, faculty member or fund raiser enters the foundation door:

> Very likely he will have to make some changes in [the program], not as a result of compulsion, but simply as a result of the process of exchange of ideas with the foundation people, who are not prepared to buy someone else's idea without being able to contribute a little bit of their own. After all, the justification for the existence of a staff in a foundation implies that *not all of the ideas will come from the donee*. (p. 349; italics added)

Yarmolinsky is obviously proud of the manner in which foundations have helped to shape funded programs, although he said, "The universities, until recently, would have denied it vigorously" (p. 349).

According to Curti and Nash (1965), "From the standpoint of the shaping of American higher education, foundation philanthropy's principal importance has been helping to make the college or university a center for research and advanced study" (p. 236). Yet, these scholars of educational philanthropy described foundation control over research as "a subject of much concern to academicians," and "an unpalatable situation" (p. 236). In a microanalogy to the double-edged sword dilemma of charitable organizations discussed earlier in this book, they stated:

> Here, clearly, was a tragic dilemma for the serious scholar. While he might appreciate the necessity of complete freedom to pursue the subject of *his* choice, he nonetheless realized that without money to provide that most essential element in

scholarship—free time—his chances of making a contribution to knowledge were slim indeed. (p. 236)

Boorstin (1963/1983) pointed to this relationship between scholarly research and foundation funding as one of two problems in philanthropy today. He related how ironic it is for professors to find themselves appealing for funds from foundation officials who left university life precisely because as former faculty members they were unable to produce research that satisfied these very same professors. Boorstin said, "The fact that we in academic life know what kind of project will appeal or will not appeal to the foundations is one of the worst things that can be said about them" (p. 140). He concluded that foundations are freezing agents, not catalysts for change.

Leveraging—Ylvisaker's (1987) fourth and final source of foundation influence—is used frequently by foundations to increase the impact of their gift and to ensure that their funds are not tied up in dependency relationships with recipient organizations. The most common forms of leveraging are matching, or challenge, grants by which foundations pledge an amount of money only if an equal or greater amount is raised from other sources. The Kresge Foundation, for example, is one of only two major foundations that uses nearly all its funds for capital grants (i.e., money for construction and renovation of buildings). A grant from Kresge requires that the first three-quarters of the project cost be raised from other funding sources. According to Nielsen (1985), "The matching-fund requirement, given the prestige of Kresge grants, enables a recipient organization to leverage the money and obtain additional resources that in most cases it otherwise could not" (p. 282). Nielsen does not mention that all too often matching requirements force colleges and universities to use institutional funds or unrestricted gifts targeted for other purposes to meet the capital match. In other words, the means to pursuing a goal are often dictated by foundation leveraging.

Nielsen (1985) raised a fifth source of foundation influence that Ylvisaker neglected: strategic placement in an interlocking network of corporate and government leaders. Describing the 36 major foundations (i.e., those with assets of $250 million or more), Nielsen stated:

Because they are closely associated with rich donor families and prominent corporate and other leaders, they lie at or near the center of gravity of the American establishment. Their position in the intricate web of personal and institutional influence gives them a power that less strategically located institutions do not have. (p. 7)

Just one of many examples of such a network is provided by Whitaker (1974) when he related, "On one memorable occasion when the Rockefeller Foundation—which has a rule that a trustee must absent himself from the discussion of applications in which he has an interest—came to consider an application from the Council on Foreign Relations, every single trustee present consequently had to leave the room" (p. 100). Such relationships illustrate how interdependencies with one source of gifts can affect relations with other sources; thereby, strengthening the dependency of the recipient organization on its focal funding source.

A Historical and Critical Perspective

According to Ylvisaker (1987), "Foundations were first given legal definition in the English Statute of Charitable Uses in 1601. . . . But it was not until the turn of the twentieth century that they became of substantial size and prominence, and not until after World War II that their numbers and scale of activity caused them to be seriously considered as an important social institution" (p. 374). As discussed in chapter 2 and as is also demonstrated later in the section on individual donors, many of the characteristics of the current fund-raising era are relatively recent phenomena (e.g., three out of four of America's larger foundations did not exist prior to 1950; Ylvisaker, 1987). Commenting on this new era of philanthropy, Ylvisaker said:

> It has taken Americans—and, for that matter, grant makers themselves—some time to get a sense of what modern philanthropy is all about. It both is and is not the personal kind of charity that lingers on in the stereotype of the fortunate giving to the unfortunate. . . . But other concepts have flowed into the philanthropic mix and have given foundations some different and sometimes clashing colorations. (p. 374)

Drawing from Ylvisaker (1987), Nielsen (1985), and Curti and Nash (1965), an evolution of American foundations and their philosophies of giving can be sketched. Andrew Carnegie turned from the altruistic tradition of charity to a rhetoric of the responsibility of wealth to improve society, creating his foundations to focus on the factors that produced society's ills, not the unfortunate, themselves. Rockefeller, who employed the first grant maker in order to better organize his gift giving, built his foundations on a belief in partnerships between philanthropy and science to deal with root causes of social ills. Acknowledging the contributions of Carnegie and Rockefeller, Nielsen (1985) said that in all foundation efforts today "the scientific or professional approach . . . rather than old-fashioned charity is dominant" (p. 419).

Finally, in 1950, planning for the Ford Foundation "started with those concepts and went a step beyond—explicitly designating 'public affairs' as a major involvement of that soon to be dominant foundation" (Ylvisaker, 1987, p. 375).

According to Ylvisaker, "The foundation movement was ready for takeoff by 1950; lift was provided by a federal and state tax structure that made foundations an attractive shelter for the great personal and corporate affluence of the postwar period" (p. 375).

In relation to the Ford Foundation, Curti and Nash (1965) described how foundations took a step further away from charity with the establishment of this largest of all American foundations. They said, "Disinterested benevolence did not figure as a primary motive when Henry Ford and his son Edsel established their philanthropic agency on January 15, 1936" (p. 228). According to these scholars, the new estate taxes introduced by the Roosevelt administration and the fact that the Fords did not want to sell stock to outsiders and lose control of the Ford Motor Company created a problem that was solved by a foundation. Curti and Nash said, "A philanthropic foundation would be established to which both Henry and his son, Edsel, could bequeath their common-stock holdings and thereby avoid payment of estate taxes" (p. 229). After the deaths of Edsel in 1943 and his father in 1947, the Ford Foundation acquired about 90% of the Ford Motor Company stock with an estimated value of more than $2 billion.

It was after 1950 that foundations became what Ylvisaker (1987) called "a conspicuous factor in public affairs." And it was after their venture into the public affairs arena that foundations came under almost continuous attack by legislators and the media. "The fact was that foundations had grown beyond public understanding," said Ylvisaker (p. 375). In 1969, Congress began a series of hearings, primarily prompted by charges of subversion. Although Congress passed the Tax Reform Act of 1969, Ylvisaker said that as a result of the hearings the government "accepted foundations as legitimate and useful instruments of a democratic society" (p. 375).

According to Ylvisaker, a valid perception of foundations and their role today can be derived from the dual needs of our democratic society: to miniaturize and to maximize choice. "The larger the society has become, the more predictably and compulsively Americans have created a plethora of devices enabling them to gain some leverage on the system without having to go through the wearying process of winning total control or consensus" he said (p. 376). In addition, Ylvisaker said that the role of foundations is to exist as a "private counterpart to the legislative process, a freestanding alternative that allows for independent considerations of the public interest and private allocations of resources for public needs" (p. 376).

Acting as "private legislatures," foundations, according to Ylvisaker (1987), are increasingly controlled by government rules and regulations (e.g., foundations are forbidden to lobby, must adhere to reporting and disclosure standards, and are prohibited from self-dealing, even though the directors of for-profit corporations are required only to avoid the perception of self-dealing). In addition, the IRS mandates that foundations pay out 5% of the market value of their assets in grants to charitable organizations each year (AAFRC Trust, 1989c). The regulation of this segment of the philanthropic sector can be viewed as a precedent by those who are concerned about increased regulation of fund raising, as discussed in chapters 2, 3, and 5.

As noted earlier, foundations historically have been criticized for their intrusion on institutional autonomy. Whitaker (1974) voiced a frequent complaint about foundations' assault on substantive autonomy when he said:

> In response to an application, foundations have been known to impose conditions which a university only accepts reluctantly in order to obtain the grant, or so as not to alienate future potential support from the donor. Whole new departments have been created as "foundation bait." The entire pattern of what some universities are doing is being determined by the appeal a particular field, or even an academic individual, has for foundations or corporate patrons. (p. 216)

Whitaker also provided an example of how foundations have affected procedural autonomy by tying up institutional funds that a college or university may need to pursue its determined goals when he said:

> Yet, although the foundations' grants often have a beneficially innovative impact . . . for the university they can become—financially—Trojan horses. After the foundation has "primed the pump" of new commitments and moved on, the pumps remain as continuing—and inflating—liabilities. One $34,000 grant from a foundation cost a university close to $500,000 in the ensuing twelve years. (p. 218)

It is recalled from chapter 7 that by investing at the margin of higher education during the 1960s the federal government gained control of institutional budgets by re-directing other funds to the support of federal goals. As developed throughout this book, major restricted gifts from foundations, corporations, and individuals frequently have the same effect (i.e., internal resources are reallocated to support the purposes of private gifts because the full costs rarely are covered by the donor).

In defense of foundation donors and their impact on institutional autonomy, Whitaker (1974) pointed out that universities, like foundations, are not ends in themselves (i.e., they must also serve society). He said, "Foundation projects provide links with the outside world—and ones which universities are after all entirely free to accept or reject" (p. 219). The first point in Whitaker's statement is a critical one that was raised in chapter 7, specifically in the section on the historic origins of the concept of institutional autonomy. American colleges and universities have accepted a public service role, as well as the more traditional roles of teaching and research. They must continually demonstrate their accountability to society—particularly their public service contribution—and foundations provide a means to do so. Also in chapter 7, an example was given of positive intrusions on institutional autonomy. The fact that it was a foundation that helped "induce" colleges and universities to hire Black professors demonstrates how foundations can help colleges and universities be more accountable (i.e., by serving as a link to the larger society, foundations can help ensure that educational institutions are in harmony with societal values).

The second point made by Whitaker (1974) is also critical: Institutions of higher education that are threatened by potential loss of autonomy can simply not seek foundation funding. As reiterated previously, however, those institutions that do not seek private support will diminish their ability to determine and carry out their goals as a result of constraints on resources, thereby, reducing their own autonomy.

Supporting the concept of environmental interdependencies as an explanation for donor relations, Whitaker also pointed out that foundations have a reciprocal dependence on universities. Foundations recruit a majority of their executives from universities; they depend on universities for projects and programs to carry out their foundation objectives; they rely on university research departments for their research needs; and they use university faculty as program assessors. In particular, it should be noted that the dependency on universities for research should not be minimized. According to an article in _The New York Times_ (cited in The Barton Gillet Letter, 1989), "Most of the $1.6 billion given by American foundations in 1988 was earmarked for research" (p. 2).

As institutions of higher education are dependent to some degree on foundation funding and as foundations, in turn, are dependent on these institutions for research, personnel, and operations, it can be concluded that relationships with foundation donors can best be explained as environmental interdependencies grounded in systems theory as presented in chapter 6.

Marxist scholars, as well as other observers of the foundation world, argue that foundations act to preserve the present, general structure of society. Foundations, they say, are by nature conservative and lack innovativeness; they function primarily as "an indirect tool of the ruling class" (Whitaker, 1974, p. 222). At the very least, according to a former editor with Twentieth Century Fund, "The status quo is clearly made more bearable as its various cracks and fissures are plastered over, while thousands cheer" (Whitaker, 1974, p. 221). A central premise held by Arnove (1980) is that foundations like Carnegie, Rockefeller, and Ford have a corrosive influence on a democratic society. He said that these foundations "represent relatively unregulated and unaccountable concentrations of power and wealth which buy talent, promote causes, and, in effect, establish an agenda of what merits society's attention" (p. 1).

Certainly the subject of interlocking trusteeships seems to support such criticism. According to Whitaker (1974), studies have documented historically at least informal networks of foundation trustees. For example, Lindeman (cited in Whitaker, 1974) found that of all the foundation trustees who had graduated from college, 36% had gone to only three institutions—Harvard, Yale or Princeton—and Domhoff (cited in Whitaker, 1974) reported in his book, *Who Rules America?*, that just over half the trustees of the 13 largest foundations attended one of these same three universities. Whitaker said that at one foundation the trustees average 5.6 positions apiece on other foundation boards and cited Walter Annenberg, who was at that time an officer or trustee of nine foundations, as an example. Whitaker (1974) concluded:

> It is impossible to ignore the overall conclusion that, despite certain admirable individual exceptions, foundation trustees constitute a wholly unrepresentative influence, and one which supports the established traditions of the power elite; and furthermore that, since they tend to fill vacancies with others similar to themselves, this bias towards the status quo is self-regenerating. (p. 90)

As was pointed out in the discussion on federal research funding, conspiracy theories are an unsatisfactory explanation of interdependent relationships between institutions of higher education and external funding sources. However, in the book, *Philanthropy and Cultural Imperialism: The Foundations at Home and Abroad*, Colwell (1980) wrote:

> A very experienced foundation person noted in an interview that there has been an unspoken agreement among the foundations which support social research not to turn the spotlight of social analysis on themselves as actors in American society. For example, there is evidence that Floyd Hunter and C. Wright Mills never received substantial foundation support after their major studies of what they considered the power structure in the United States. (p. 433)

On a personal note, economist Julian Simon, a colleague at the University of Maryland, told me about seeing a letter from an official at a major foundation, which warned another researcher that if he insisted on listening to the views of Simon he would not get any money from that foundation. Simon said that Theodore Schultz, Nobel laureate in economics, has written and spoken extensively about the fact that economists have allowed themselves to be manipulated by the foundations.

The evidence, as presented here, would suggest that foundations are not villains, or part of a conspiracy, but are instead a powerful source of funds that interact with colleges and universities through a relationship of environmental interdependency. Foundations, in their role as change agents, do present threats to institutional autonomy; however, foundations, as conservative funding sources, also tend to enter funding relationships with those institutions that are least likely to become dependent on them (i.e., recipients receiving the greatest amount of foundation dollars are those same universities that also receive the greatest amount of private support and federal research grants). Continuing on the latter point, the pattern of selective distribution of all gifts correlates with the distribution of foundation grants (i.e., 79% of the foundation dollars given to public institutions in CFAE's 1987–1988 survey and 62% of those given to private institutions went to the 183 doctoral universities [16% of the institutions reporting] that also received 67% of all private support; "Gifts to colleges off," 1989).

These figures would suggest that foundations, like the federal government, tend to funnel their resources to a very small portion of the higher education population and that because of their alternative sources of private support and the reciprocal dependency between them and foundations, these universities are not likely to relinquish a high degree of autonomy in exchange for the gifts. This point is further strengthened by Rudney's (1987) statistics given in chapter 7 that the largest educational institutions, which represent less than 1% of all such institutions, account for 70% of the total assets of all colleges and universities. In contrast to this unequal economic distribution in education, large health organizations hold only 28% of all health assets. Or as Whitaker (1974) said about the funding relationship between foundations and higher education, "From being charity for the poor, it has become an elite subsidizing elites" (p. 217).

Summarizing the section on foundation donors, foundations historically have been the subject of criticism for their influence in American higher education. In addition to the vast sums of money they are required to give away, foundations are able to influence charitable organizations because of their selectivity, their role as change agents, and their leverage. Their selectivity influences those colleges and universities that receive foundation funding and also affects nonrecipient institutions, as documented by the closing of medical schools through the grants of Rockefeller's General Education Board in the early 1900s. Foundations primarily see their role as change agents who fund innovative programming with restricted, noncontinuous grants—a role that often leads colleges and universities in unanticipated directions with financial liabilities during and after the grants are expended. Using leverage, foundations increase the impact of their grants by coercing colleges and universities into raising funds from other donors or into using institutional resources in support of foundation objectives.

As a source of private funds, foundations are a relatively small group that funnel the majority of their education dollars to a small group of universities (e.g., 68% of all foundation dollars reported in CAFE's 1987–1988 survey were received by 183 doctoral universities, or only 16% of the participating institutions). This selective distribution has been clouded by the fact that foundations, like the other two sources of gifts, report their giving in aggregate totals (i.e., although foundation grants represent only 3.7% of total operating budgets of *all* charitable organizations, not all charitable organizations receive foundation grants, but rather colleges and universities are major recipients, and, as documented here, the majority of those dollars go to a small percentage of educational institutions).

Foundations are basically conservative, and although they are criticized for their power to change the behavior of colleges and universities, they are also criticized for their efforts to maintain the status quo. For such critics, the role of change agent is seen as one that represents the foundation's interpretation of the means to protect current society. A point that is often overlooked is that foundations are dependent on universities for hiring staff, carrying out programming objectives, for research, and for program assessment. In addition, foundations can be perceived as being dependent on all charitable organizations because of the fact that they are required by law to distribute 5% of the market value of their assets each year.

This section concludes, therefore, that the motivations of foundation donors can best be understood as neither benevolent nor villainous, but in the context of environmental interdependencies that provide a broad range of economic, social, and political reasons for giving. Within this context, the exchange process involved in soliciting and receiving a gift from a foundation necessitates some loss of institutional autonomy. A second conclusion, therefore, is that major gifts from foundations can, individually, affect the substantive and procedural autonomy of colleges and universities.

CORPORATE DONORS AND AUTONOMY

As pointed out in the preceding chapter on institutional autonomy, the Carnegie Committee (1982) reported that colleges and universities historically have had to negotiate with powerful external forces to maintain and protect their autonomy. While severely criticizing professional or specialized accrediting agencies as the current worst offenders of reducing autonomy, the committee described a second "villain" on the horizon: the benevolent corporation. The report stated that the greatest threat to autonomy in the future will come from the corporate sector as educational institutions continue to take on corporate priorities and leave themselves vulnerable to outside influences.

The Carnegie Committee (1982) claimed that businessmen long have had influence in the educational world by serving on governing boards and by exerting their influence as wealthy benefactors. Useem (1987) confirmed this charge when he reported, "A 1978 survey of the presidents and chairmen of more than 500 large American corporations found that . . . two-thirds sit on the governing board of a university" (p. 341). "Increasingly," the authors of the Carnegie report said, "academic decisions are being shaped by decisions in the [corporate] board room" (p. 23).

The Carnegie Committee (1982) raised a second point about corporate relations that is significant for this book. Preoccupation on the part of the academy with the priorities of business, it said, may mean that the larger social mandates, which have earned higher education its favored status in American society, will be compromised. Increasingly, university presidents are taking on state economic development priories by accompanying gubernatorial delegations to woo corporations; start-up incubators are being "nested" on campuses; and in-dustrial–university institutes, or joint ventures as described by Pfeffer and Salancik (1978), are multiplying. In short, the priorities of business can be perceived as replacing top priorities of American higher education.

More generally, Payton warned (1987):

> The interaction of voluntary, not-for-profit, private-sector, public-interest organiza-tions and institutions with government and business can lead to a confusion of roles. Any of the three sectors can be compromised by borrowing too many of the core values of the other. Some overlap is necessary as well as desirable; too much leads to an essential compromise of purpose and method. (p. 40)

Useem (1987) said that philanthropy is not a major factor for corporate donors and they, in turn, are not major factors in funding charitable organizations (i.e., as a whole, companies give less than 1% of pre-tax income, and major charitable organizations seldom receive more than 10% of their income from corporate gifts). Indeed, it is important to remember that contributions from individuals for the past decade have averaged double the corporate rate, about 1.9% of personal income, as compared to the 1% of corporate income (Useem, 1987). Yet, Useem said that corporate contributions are "an important element in strategic planning by the business and nonprofit sectors alike" (p. 340).

Extremely similar to foundations, of which 19%, or 4,402, provide 85% of all grants, only 7.5% of America's 2.2 million companies, or 154,000 businesses, provide gifts of $500 or more a year (Useem, 1987). It is recalled that 96, or 0.4% of all foundations, account for half of all foundation assets and 35.8% of all foundation grants reported in the 1985 *Foundation Directory* (Ylvisaker, 1987). Of the nation's 1,127 corporations whose assets exceeded $0.5 billion in 1977, only 900 of them, or 0.1% of the businesses that make a gift of $500 or more, give 50% of all corporate grants (Useem, 1987). As Useem stated, "It should be noted, too, that virtually all corporate giving is by the nation's major firms" (p. 340). In short, relatively few foundations and corporations make most of the foundation and corporate gifts to charitable organizations. In his introduction to the book featuring the statistics just quoted, Powell (1987) said:

> Useem and Ylvisaker discern important patterns in corporate and foundation giving. In both cases, a small number of organizations dominates grant giving. The authors suggest ways in which the pluralism of the voluntary sector may be harmed by this dominance as well as ways in which this degree of influence affords special opportunities. (p. xiii)

According to Useem (1987), "Education is the leading beneficiary of corporate dollars, receiving more than two-fifths, or 40.7 percent" (p. 342). According to the Council for Aid to Education (CFAE) (cited in "Gifts to colleges off," 1989), in 1987–1988, corporations gave $1.85 billion in gifts to higher education, an increase of only 2% from the year before. "Continuing a trend, private institutions received 6 percent less support from companies last year, public colleges 8 percent more," stated an article on the CFAE report ("Gifts to colleges off," 1989, p. A30).

Similar to foundations, distribution of these corporate gifts is far from equal. The 1987–1988 CFAE figures, for example, show that the 183 doctoral universities, which—it is recalled—represent only 6% of all colleges and universities, but receive 68% of all foundation dollars, were also the recipients of 77% of all corporate gift dollars ("Gifts to colleges off," 1989). According to Useem (1987), "Companies prefer recipients that are prestigious, large, and located near headquarters or plants with large staffs" (p. 342). In a study of the 30 to 40 premier educational and cultural organizations and major corporations in Minneapolis and St. Paul, Galaskiewicz and Rauschenbach (cited in Useem, 1987) found that the size and prestige of the charitable organizations are strong predictors of the number of firms giving to each and the amount contributed.

Enlightened Self-Interest and Social Responsibility

Strikingly different from foundation and individual donors, corporate donors have *proclaimed* philanthropic motivations of "enlightened self-interest." Basically, corporations seek to enhance their position in the marketplace through their philanthropic actions. To justify to shareholders the giving away of profits, corporate contribution committees and chief executive officers try to match their corporate needs to the funding opportunities presented by charitable organizations. For example, local utility companies will usually support volunteer fire departments in areas where they have facilities, and high-technology corporations will support engineering scholarships to attract future employees.

Before changes in banking regulations, Useem (1987) pointed out that commercial banks limited their corporate contributions to their own community, saying, "Commercial banks are not permitted to engage in interstate banking, and their prosperity depends strongly on the condition of the local economy" (p. 349). Similarly, utilities, which are geographically bound, invest heavily (generally more than other types of corporations) in local charitable organizations because they can not relocate if the economy or quality of life decreases. Finally, a recent news article reported that a group of life and health insurance companies is financing a new $16.2-million-grants program to support AIDS-education projects and to increase services to people with the disease ("Life- and health-insurance," 1989). Concerned about the growing number of AIDS claims, which cost the industry an estimated $779 million in 1986–1987 alone, a spokesperson said, "The AIDS issue is not only a corporate public-involvement priority but essentially a bottom-line business concern for the life- and health-insurance industry" (p. 7).

It is important to stress this combination of a "bottom-line business concern," with a "public-involvement priority." As discussed earlier, particularly in chapter 5 on the marketing perspective of fund raising, philanthropic decisions are neither solely altruistic or solely pragmatic. Rather, the theory of donor relations developed in this book holds that philanthropic goals derive from the donor's own self-interest and his or her interpretation of what is in the public interest. Although corporations—as is true of all types of donors—may seek pragmatic benefits from making a gift, the benefits of the gift are never fully captured in the donor–recipient exchange (i.e., some benefit spills over into society). If all the benefits are captured, however, the exchange becomes a market transaction, not a philanthropic exchange. Therefore, the term _enlightened self-interest_ emphasizes both the social and pragmatic variables present in corporate philanthropy.

Calling corporate philanthropy "an oxymoron," Hayden Smith (1988), a senior vice president of CFAE, stated, "Corporate giving is not altruistic" (p. 7). Continuing, he said, "Unlike private foundations, corporations do not exist to give money away to charitable enterprises; rather, their purpose is to produce and sell goods and services at a profit for their stockholders" (p. 7). Explaining that attitudes toward the relationships between business and other sectors have changed dramatically since the late 1950s, Smith said, "Of special interest here has been the emergence of two concepts: enlightened self-interest and corporate social responsibility" (p. 8).

In support of the concept of corporate social responsibility, Levy and Oviatt (1989) said that a 1986 study by Yankelovick, Skelly, and White found that two thirds of America's chief executive officers justified corporate giving in terms of "helping the needy, doing what is 'ethically correct,' and improving communities in which employees live and the company does business" (p. 130). As quoted in chapter 5, Anne Alexander (1988), vice president for education programs for the AT&T Foundation, explained enlightened self-interest by saying, "In a philanthropic partnership, a corporation gives money to a university so the university can use it to, ultimately, further the corporation's philanthropic goals—in its own self-interest and that of society at large" (p. 13).

It is appropriate at this point to note that corporate foundations should not be confused with *private*, or *independent*, foundations, such as those discussed in the previous section. Corporate foundations, like the AT&T Foundation, essentially were established by corporations before 1969 because of tax advantages and in order to provide a leveling influence between corporate profits and grants. The tax advantages have essentially disappeared, and corporate foundations—as opposed to *independent* foundations—frequently are controlled by managers and directors of the affiliated corporation.

The concept of enlightened self-interest is widely acknowledged by fund raisers, and corporations are solicited on such a basis (i.e., solicitations to corporations emphasize what the donor will derive from giving money more so than do solicitations of other private-gift sources). As a newsletter from the fund-raising firm of Barnes & Roche, Inc. (1989), advised, "By identifying the quid pro quo, development officers can, for example, find new and deeper 'pockets' by getting a corporation to sponsor a program, arranging for the loan of a corporate executive, or swapping corporate market research for access to a market" (p. 1). Emphasizing an exchange basis for corporate giving, the newsletter said, "You need to reach a point where you can say to your corporate contact, 'How can we help each other?' rather than saying, 'What can you do for me?'" (p. 2). Finally, the Barnes & Roche newsletter, which focuses on strategies for increasing corporate support, stated, "Perhaps you should remind the bank that your organization has done all the giving and has not been on the receiving end" (p. 3).

In researching this book, a colleague, who is vice president of development and alumni affairs at a private university, urged me to exclude corporations from a critical analysis of fund raising because gifts from this source do not represent "true" philanthropy. In somewhat agreement, a vice president of Mobil Oil Corporation said, "The exigencies of a much more competitive market are causing business executives to create a new cost-benefit of corporate giving" ("Corporate gifts," 1987, p. A27). Acknowledging that some view this concept as "pseudo-philanthropy," the Mobil Oil vice president responded, "I'm not even sure altruism is relevant" (A27).

Yet, Peter Goldberg (cited in "Corporate gifts," 1987), then vice president for public responsibility at Primerica Corporation, criticized such a view of corporate giving as a "blurring of philanthropy and marketing" (p. A.27). More recently, Goldberg (cited in "Jimmy Carter," 1989), who lost his job with Primerica because of a corporate merger, said that he is fearful that mergers and acquisitions, coupled with a new bottom-line-orientation of managers and changing shareholder values, are "creating a corporate culture that holds philanthropy incompatible with business" (p. 8). A. Alexander (1988), however, pointed her finger at recipient organizations and criticized university administrators who "use the same language to describe contractual relationships, economic development projects, and charitable contributions" (p. 13). Differentiating between industrial partnerships and corporate philanthropy, Alexander said, "A campus–corporate business partnership tends to be a trade. . . .[whereas] we want *value*, as distinct from a return, for the philanthropic dollars spent—value for the commonwealth" (pp. 13-14).

Alexander (1988) emphasized the fact that most corporate gifts are restricted in purpose when she said, "To make an impact with our gifts, we in business must focus our support where we think it will have the most effect on the specific social problems *we* want to address" (p. 13; italics added). She continued by saying, "In other words, our motive is not simply to help an institution; it's to help the institution help society" (p. 14). As discussed in chapter 12, Alexander's employer—the AT&T Foundation—takes an enlightened approach to philanthropy that is often incongruent with the philanthropic behavior of other corporations. For example, a recent news article ("Company may pull," 1989) reported that Magnavox Control Systems, which gives about $50,000 per year in contributions to community organizations in Whitley County, Indiana, has threatened to stop all charitable contributions because county commissioners derailed plans to improve a road running by one of its area businesses. The company announced its intentions, according to a spokesperson, in order to "make a point about the need for community cooperation," (p. 6). According to another recent article ("Corporate-gift plan," 1989), requests by New Jersey Bell Telephone Company and General Dynamics have resulted in the Federal Election

Commission ruling that companies "can promise to make donations to a charity as a way of encouraging their employees to donate to the companies' political-action committees" (pp. 24-25).

As Goldberg (1989) said, "The marriages of corporate social responsibility to corporate definitions of self-interest seem fragile and tenuous, vulnerable to changing perceptions in corporate America of what constitutes self-interest, and how best to pursue it" (p. 23).

After arguing that corporations provide little of the funding for charitable organizations (e.g., corporate contributions in 1982–1983 represented only 1.3% of the total expenditures of all colleges and universities), Useem (1987) admitted that *most* charitable organizations receive no business gifts and a few receive much. Although he acknowledged that such an unequal distribution means that corporate donors are more influential at some charitable organizations, he said, "Managers of the favored institutions assert that business largesse erodes neither programming autonomy nor administrative independence" (p. 353). He cited a study of the Metropolitan Opera of New York, whose general manager "flatly denies any external influence by the opera's benefactors" (p. 353). Supporting the earlier chapter on systems theory, particularly Pfeffer and Salancik's (1978) strategies for avoiding external control and Blau's (1986) conditions of power imbalances in exchange relations, Useem added, "Yet the condition permitting the Metropolitan Opera to retain such fierce independence—numerous generous contributors—is not enjoyed by most nonprofit organizations" (p. 354). He concluded, "Thus, nonprofit organizations highly dependent on the gift of a small set of large corporate contributors are least able to resist the benefactors' preferences" (p. 355).

Useem (1987) provided examples of a number of cases in which corporate donors have limited the autonomy of the recipient organization. For example, DiMaggio's (cited in Useem, 1987) study showed how corporate art sponsors, interested in improving their image, have influenced resource-starved museums to focus on blockbuster exhibitions that draw mass publics and publicity, regardless of the preference of the museum. Useem pointed to subtle, but noticeable changes in the programs of universities caused by self-swayed administrators who "entice business interest" and seek corporate gifts by focusing attention and resources on science and engineering curriculum and applied research, rather than on humanities programs and basic research. Useem echoed accusations by a number of so-called alternate charities when he said, "Managers of social service organizations may quietly discourage programs, such as community organizing or abortion counseling, that could embarrass or anger company contributions" (p. 355).

Similar to foundations and the federal government, corporations have an interdependency relationship with America's major research universities (i.e., they are dependent on universities for research results that can be applied to the marketplace, for future employees, for continuing education programs, and for corporate-university partnerships in research and development efforts). H. Smith (1988) said that the specific rationale on which businesses justify their investment in higher education is based on the fact that they rely on these institutions for: (a) newly trained employees, (b) basic research that fosters new products, (c) public services that benefit the communities in which corporations are located, and (d) general contributions to the health of the economy and society. He concluded by saying, "All these dependencies are, in varying degrees, explicit elements in the philosophies, policies, plans, and programs of corporate contributions" (p. 9). It can be added that these "dependencies" are also the pragmatic and social benefits sought by the corporation in a donor–recipient exchange with colleges and universities.

Emphasizing Gouldner's (1960) concept of reciprocal benefits, Rozell (1987) said, "Corporations have played a major role in supporting higher eduction and advanced research—enterprises that bring returns to the business community in terms of a larger pool of trained individuals, as well as significant developments in technology and business practices" (p. 95).

A Historical and Critical Perspective

Karl (1982/1983) summarized the history of philanthropy of corporations in America, saying that disputes rest on two extreme views: the corporation as a socially responsible system, and "the belief that powerful corporations can endanger the public's right to govern" (p. 378). He said that whichever perspective is taken, corporate giving is based on the idea that corporations should be able to influence public policy directly through the power to decide how their contributions are spent.

Corporate giving is a relatively new phenomenon. Individuals have the longest history of private giving in America, as described in earlier chapters of this book. Foundations basically began with the formation of the Rockefeller and Carnegie foundations at the beginning of the 19th century and entered an era of influence in public affairs during the 1950s with the formation of the Ford Foundation (Ylvisaker, 1987). But corporations were prohibited from making charitable contributions until the Tax Code was amended in 1936, and only in 1953 was a corporate gift to a general university budget ruled by the courts to be acceptable as an act of a good citizen (Cutlip, 1965). When the court overturned the direct-benefit precedent under which the 1953 suit had been brought (i.e., until 1953, only gifts that resulted in a direct benefit to the corporation could be deducted), it redefined benefit in terms of the survival of the corporation in a free enterprise system.

According to H. Smith (1988), "By the end of World War II, it became apparent that the long-term welfare of corporations and their stockholders required . . . that corporations might need to sacrifice some of their short-term profits to serve their ultimate self-interest" (p. 8). More recently, Smith said, the concept of corporate social responsibility emerged, holding that "its not merely *permissible* for corporations to become involved in social concerns in the name of self-interest; it's the corporations' *duty* to help solve social problems and advance the nation's welfare by making money, facilities, and employee time available to the charitable community" (p. 8).

Karl (1982/1983) said, "It is not going to be any easier for corporations to define what is socially responsible than it is for individuals" (p. 383). Touching on the issue of power imbalances in gift exchanges, he said, "Philanthropic behavior is separated from political action by a very thin line. . . . It is a hard lesson, but money, even generously and sweetly given, is still power" (p. 383). Karl's only advice to corporate donors was to follow the path of the foundations by funding narrow programs that limit the spirit of free inquiry, but help a donor avoid charges of influence.

Although the management of corporate philanthropy is examined further in the chapter on corporate public relations, Haire (1981) summarized the concept when he said:

> Business firms now seek out, with full-time personnel . . . new opportunities for the effective application of their contribution dollars in all areas of philanthropy . . . [Charitable organizations] can provide the contributor . . . with opportunities to make intangible investments of a philanthropic character that yield demonstrable long-run returns to the donor comparable to the tangible investments of a conventional profit-oriented character. (p. 145)

But even corporate leaders are sometimes surprised at the "returns" offered companies by college fund raisers who seem more anxious to raise dollar goals than to support their institution's goals through corporate gifts. Horton (1981), who at the time was director of university relations for IBM, described a situation in which colleges and universities offered to change their institutional priorities in exchange for gifts, saying:

> In recent years some educational institutions, in their eagerness to be seen as deserving of corporate support, have created programs to fit the mold of what they think the companies would most like to support—chairs of free enterprise, for example. . . . they represent something not likely to be at the very top of a college's funding needs. . . . The business firm's representative should want his or

her company's investment in a college to be central to the institution's purpose, not peripheral to it. (p. 149)

In response to the issue raised by Horton (1981) of colleges creating programs to fit the mold of what they think companies would most like to support, it is recalled from the last section that Boorstin (1963/1983) lamented the fact that research is shaped by faculty members who know what projects will or will not appeal to foundations. Such evidence from the literature allows this section to conclude that major gifts from corporations and foundations can not only infringe on institutional autonomy individually, but also collectively (i.e., a perception of what will appeal generally to corporate and foundation donors can cause a charitable organization to change its behavior in a way that is incongruent with self-determined goals and objectives).

Scholars, such as Baumol (1975), argue against the social responsibility role for business, saying that the primary job of business is to make money for its stockholders. According to Baumol, a role of social responsibility for corporations is not only unachievable, but also undesirable from the viewpoint of charitable organizations. Explaining his reasoning on the latter point, he stated:

> Corporate management holds in its hands enormous financial resources. Voluntarism suggests, or rather demands, that management use these resources to influence the social and political course of events. . . . [T]he power of interference with our lives and the lives of others . . . is surely intolerable. The threat to effective democracy should be clear enough. (pp. 46-47)

Criticizing such reasoning, Rozell (1987) said, "It borders on paranoid-like fear of the motivations of business leaders, assuming that self-interested behavior and the public good are necessarily in conflict" (p. 96). Rozell said that this "radical approach," as well as the "free market approach," "refuses to even consider that a mutually beneficial relationship can exist between donor and recipient of corporate funding" (p. 95). He used the views of economist Milton Friedman to represent the "free market approach" to corporate giving. Friedman, like Baumol (1975), contended that all corporations should get out of the business of philanthropy, but for reasons quite different. According to Rozell, Friedman condemned corporate philanthropy for three reasons: (a) he denied the existence of the whole notion of social responsibility; (b) he believes that the principal responsibility of the corporate executive is not charity, but to make as much money as possible; and (c) he believes that the corporate executive has no right to spend other people's money (i.e., funds that rightfully belong to stockholders). As directly related to the subject of analysis in this chapter, Friedman (cited in Rozell, 1987) said, "There is no justification for permitting deductions for [corporate] contributions to charitable and educational institutions" (p. 93).

Olasky (1987) agreed with the free market approach, saying that extreme social responsibility places the corporation in a position of trying to do something that cannot be economically done and that corporations "do not have a right to do morally" (p. 151). According to Olasky, the cynicism of corporate "philanthropy" has been highly apparent during this decade, but rarely revealed in the literature. He quoted an anonymous corporate contributions officer on the manipulative uses of corporate contributions, saying:

> There are some naive people who actually think that our contributions are contributions. They're not. They're public admissions of our fears—fear of a politician, fear of an executive at some other company, fear of the public interest groups. (p. 125)

Harold Simmons, a Texas businessman who in December 1988 pledged $41 million to the University of Texas Southwestern Medical Center and who has acquired his wealth by earning a remarkable 95% average annual return on his business investments in the past 15 years, believes philanthropy is an activity to be undertaken by individuals rather than corporations. Simmons ("An ambitious Texas," 1989) said:

> I don't know that the corporation has the right to give its money away. It belongs to the stockholders. Pay a dividend to them and let them give it away is what I'd say to do. A corporation should be greedy. A corporation is not an altruistic organization. (p. 6)

Simmons, who is referred to as one of the leading practitioners of the hostile takeover, has successfully acquired 50 companies during his career, including the *Fortune*-500 corporation, N. L. Industries Inc., which had its giving program eliminated upon acquisition.

Finally, Rozell (1987) said there is a third approach to corporate giving, the "neoconservative approach," which generally holds that corporate leaders must begin to discriminate with regard to whom their philanthropic activities support. Rozell used the views of William E. Simon and David Packard to represent this approach, both of whom are considered leading businessmen and philanthropists (e.g., it is recalled from chapter 2 that the business school at the University of Rochester is named after Simon; also, Packard gave $70 million to Stanford University in 1986 and has established one of the largest private foundations). According to Rozell, these businessmen "contend that the business community should support only those groups, universities, scholars, and research organizations that advance a free-market economic system" (p. 96). He said that this approach is based on three premises: (a) that strong leftist, anti-business bias exists within academic establishment; (b) because academe is dominated by leftist intellectuals, corporations must exercise care in deciding whom to support; and

(c) "philanthropy can no longer be based on generosity or altruism" (p. 96). Illustrating this approach, Packard (cited in Rozell, 1987) stated:

Hostile groups of scholars are, to a large degree, responsible for the anti-business bias of many of our young people today. And I do not believe it is in the corporate interest to support them—which is what we do to a greater or lesser degree with unrestricted funds. (p. 96)

Criticizing such views, Rozell (1987) said, "This approach to corporate philanthropy poses a significant threat to the academic community where independent research and freedom of inquiry are highly valued" (p. 91). Rejecting all three approaches to giving (i.e., radical, free market, and neoconservative), he provided three principles as a beginning of an alternative theory:

1. There is a relationship between corporate philanthropy and public policy.
2. It is not realistic to expect that corporate donors be totally disinterested with regard to how funds are spent by recipients.
3. The donor should have a clearly articulated policy for giving.

As demonstrated shortly, Rozell's principles are compatible with the conclusions of this section. Basically, corporate giving to colleges and universities, particularly in support of research, can influence ideas, opinions, and public policy, which supports this section's conclusion that institutions of higher education need to manage relationships with corporate donors for the purpose of preserving as much autonomy as possible, thereby, protecting academic freedom. Colleges and universities must recognize that donors of major gifts, including corporate donors, are not disinterested parties who are unlikely to restrict the use of their gifts, which supports this section's conclusion that major gifts are rarely unrestricted and that such gifts can affect institutional autonomy to a high degree unless interdependencies with major donors are managed effectively. As Rozell said, "Involvement does not necessarily mean interference" (p. 104).

Finally, clearly articulated policies for both donors and recipient organizations help define terms of exchange relationships between donors and charitable organizations, which, as recalled, is one of Pfeffer and Salancik's (1978) strategies for avoiding external control. Illustrating the necessity of this principle outside of higher education, the Corporation for Public Broadcasting adopted a policy statement in 1988 "aimed at preventing politicians and donors from influencing the kinds of programs that public radio and television stations can broadcast" ("Public broadcasting," 1988, p. A3).

A corporation's overall concept of social responsibility, according to Useem (1987), is the leading variable determining the level and the purposes of corporate giving. However, he said, "If a firm's managers feel that making gifts will benefit employee morale, promote product sales, enhance the company's reputation, or reduce government interference, they are likely to do so; but if they see no *payback* for the company, they are far less likely to make contributions" (p. 348). Reviewing the correlation between corporate social responsibility, reputation, and profitability, Useem (1987) concluded that any direct benefits for a corporation's profitability are long-term, or related to public relations. According to Preston (1981), the results of the "scattered empirical studies" that have dealt with social performance of corporations and profit, or effectiveness, indicators have been mixed. Based on these studies and on his survey of the literature, Preston concluded "that there is practically no evidence of any strong association among socially relevant behaviors, whether desirable or undesirable, and any of the usual indicators of economic success" (p. 9).

O'Connell (1987), however, provided evidence "on the positive relationship between corporate public responsibility, including corporate giving, and financial performance" (p. 229). O'Connell cited James Burke, chairman of Johnson and Johnson, who used the findings from a survey of companies that had received the Advertising Council's Public Service Award to conclude, "Those companies that organize their business around the broad concept of public service over the long run provide superior performance for their stockholders" (cited in O'Connell, 1987, p. 229). After researching those 15 award-wining corporations that had existed for 30 years, had a written set of principles about public service, and had evidence of the principles being practiced for at least a generation, Burke (cited in O'Connell, 1987) stated:

> These companies showed an annual 11 percent growth in profits compounded over 30 years! That happens to be better than three times the growth of the Gross National Product . . . which grew at 3.1 percent annually during the same period. If anyone had invested $30,000 in a composite of the Dow Jones 30 years ago, it would be worth $134,000 today. If you had invested . . . $2,000 in each of these companies instead . . . your $30,000 would be worth over $1,000,000! (pp. 229-230)

Useem (1987) said that the greatest value of gifts is their ability to help enhance corporate autonomy by improving public image—or public standing—and the business climate. He pointed to studies of the direct impact of corporate giving that show how contributions usually improve a firm's public standing. He said, "One national survey, for instance, revealed that the public is aware that firms vary in social responsiveness—and that the public's perceptions correlate with the actual level of company contributions" (p. 354). An improved public image, as Useem pointed out, may have no immediate payback for a firm, but it does improve a company's position when dealing with matters of interest to the general public, such as union negotiations, plant closings, or tax legislation. Although this book would argue that Useem's use of the term *public image* is inappropriate because of its generally accepted connotation of artificiality, it agrees with his conclusion that contributions improve a corporation's standing in the community, which, in turn, enhances autonomy by giving the corporation more freedom in dealing with issues of public concern.

As demonstrated in the chapter on corporate public relations, Useem's (1987) arguments that contributions can help enhance corporate autonomy are advocated and expanded by Levy and Oviatt (1989). For example, Levy and Oviatt said that corporate philanthropy is an effective means for communicating with activist groups that threaten the corporation with government intervention. For now, it is important to stress that Useem's arguments support the conclusion of this section that the relationship between a charitable organization and a corporate donor is best explained as an environmental interdependency through which both organizations strive to protect and enhance their autonomy.

Regarding the value of corporate contributions in improving the business climate, Useem (1987) explained how the activist period of the 1970s made the business sector more aware of the need to improve the climate in which it operates (i.e., to enhance a political and social environment supportive of the capitalistic system). Corporate contributions, he said, help improve a climate conducive to business, and he reported that, not coincidentally, corporate philanthropy more than doubled during the latter part of 1970s from $1.2 billion in 1975 to $2.4 billion in 1979, outstripping all other forms of private giving (p. 354). As Burke (cited in O'Connell, 1987) concluded after his research on the 15 socially responsible companies that had dramatically increased their shareholder value, "If we make sure our enterprises are managed in terms of their obligations to society . . . that is also the best way to defend this democratic, capitalistic system that means so much to all of us" (p. 230).

Not surprisingly, corporate donors, like foundation donors, are criticized for making gifts to preserve the status quo. Preston (1981) said, "Although very little is known about the detailed distribution of corporate contributions, it seems obvious that they are overwhelmingly devoted to the preservation of the status quo" (p. 13). In support of Useem's (1987) concept that corporate philanthropy enhances autonomy through improved public standing and business climate, Preston stated:

> But the continuing growth of corporate socio-political activity is not really explainable by a concern with "survival" in this sense, but rather by a strong interest in the maintenance of the existing social and political system into the indefinite

future. Thus, management practice in these areas has less to do with the profit-orientation of the firm . . . than with the setting and process within which profit-oriented behavior takes place. (p. 11)

Finally, Preston supported this book in its approach to donor relationships as environmental interdependencies by saying that both contributions and political activity by corporations "arise from essentially the same conditions—large, continuing and complex relationships between the organizations and its host environment—and are carried out for comparable purposes. . . . the preservation of the basic social-political status quo" (p. 10).

Summarizing this section, corporate donors operate at the nexus where social responsibility and enlightened self-interest meet. Like foundations, corporations are dependent on institutions of higher education, particularly research universities (i.e, corporations are dependent on universities for employees, research, and services to the communities in which they operate). In addition, corporations support colleges and universities because of education's general contributions to the health of the economy and society.

Unlike foundations, however, corporations make gifts generally, not because they are required to by law, but because doing so supports their proclaimed "enlightened self-interest," and their role as a socially responsible corporation. That is to say, corporations make gifts not only to act in the interest of the public, but also to acquire needed resources, such as technical knowledge and skilled labor, and to increase their autonomy by improving their public standing and the business climate in which they operate. Like foundations, corporations generally prefer to support projects and specific programs (i.e., their gifts are usually restricted in purpose). Following the conclusion from the preceding section that major gifts from foundations can, individually, affect the substantive and procedural autonomy of colleges and universities, this section concludes that major gifts from both foundations and corporations can, individually, affect institutional autonomy. In addition, examples from the literature of colleges creating programs to fit the mold of what they think companies would most like to support and of faculty members shaping research to appeal to foundations leads to the conclusion that major gifts from corporations and foundations can not only infringe on institutional autonomy individually, but also collectively (i.e., a perception of what will appeal generally to corporate and foundation donors can cause a charitable organization to change its behavior in a way that is incongruent with self-determined goals and objectives).

Like foundations, corporate donors are a relatively small group (i.e., although there are many organizations in the foundation and corporate worlds, only a few account for the majority of gift dollars). Like foundations, corporations claim to be a small player in the philanthropic arena, an argument they support by using aggregate totals that average their contributions over all charitable organizations, when—in fact—there are relatively few recipients of corporate gifts. And like foundations, corporations funnel the majority of their education dollars to a small group of research universities. Whereas higher education received the majority of all foundation dollars before 1970, today, higher education is the leading recipient of all corporation dollars.

Like foundations, corporations are basically conservative and have been criticized for using gifts to preserve the status quo. Indeed, it can be concluded at this point in the chapter that, generally, all sources of major gifts are, by nature, conservative (i.e., major donors support the existing societal structure from which they acquired the wealth they give away). Also like foundations, corporations have been criticized for their influence in American higher education; indeed, many argue against the entire concept of social responsibility for corporations, including the giving away of profits to colleges and universities.

Unlike the benevolent corporation as a villain in the Carnegie Committee's (1982) report, this section concludes that the motivations of corporate donors are neither benevolent nor villainous, but that, like foundations, their motivations can best be understood in the context of environmental interdependencies. As such, the relationship between a charitable organization and a corporate donor is one that involves an exchange process through which both organizations strive to protect and enhance their autonomy. Agreeing with Rozell's (1987) three principles, it can be concluded that major gifts can negatively affect institutional autonomy to a high degree unless interdependencies with major donors are managed effectively; that clearly articulated policies for both donors and recipient organizations help define terms of exchange relationships, which reduces the risk of external control; and that institutions of higher education need to manage relationships with corporate donors for the purpose of preserving as much autonomy as possible, thereby, protecting academic freedom.

Finally, this section agrees with Payton (1987) that colleges and universities can be compromised by borrowing too many of the core values of the business sector, but also agrees with Rozell (1987) that mutually beneficial relationships can exist between donor and recipients of corporate funding.

INDIVIDUAL DONORS AND AUTONOMY

Living individuals are the primary donors to higher education, as they are to all U.S. charities ("Gifts to colleges off," 1989). Alumni and other individuals provide about half of all private contributions to colleges and universities. In

1987–1988, individuals gave $3.9 billion, or 48.8%, of the $8.1 billion in private funds to higher education. As mentioned earlier, 1987–1988 was the first year in more than a decade that private contributions to colleges and universities declined, and the primary reason for the decline was a decrease in gifts from individuals (i.e., alumni gifts to all institutions declined 13% and gifts from nonalumni dropped 6.7%).

Like foundations and corporations, educational gifts made by individuals are not distributed equally. Whereas 77% of corporate dollars and 68% of foundation dollars went to the 183 research universities in CFAE's 1987–1988 survey of gifts, 62% of the individual dollars also went to those same institutions. It can, therefore, be stated at this point that the majority of gift dollars to higher education from all three sources of private support is funnelled to a very small percentage of institutions (i.e., those research universities that represent only 6% of the approximately 3,000 U.S. colleges and universities.

Finally, it must be emphasized that individuals provided the vast bulk of the $104.4 billion given to all U.S. charities in 1988—an estimated $86.7 billion, plus $6.8 billion in bequests, for a total of almost 90% of all gifts ("Charitable giving," 1989).

Given the importance of their role in American philanthropy and in private support for higher education, it is surprising that little has been written about individual donors in the scholarly literature of philanthropy or higher education. Unlike foundations and corporations, individuals have rarely been criticized for influencing the recipients of their gifts; rather, they are commonly viewed as benevolent, disinterested sources of financial support. For example, in the opinion piece referred to earlier about foundations restricting their support to "innovative" projects ("If charities," 1989), the co-director of an international development agency said, "Individual donors, the 'little people' who sacrifice to contribute $25 or $100 to charities they believe in, make a statement of faith in the capability of the groups they support to carry out worthwhile programs" (p. 36).

It can only be assumed that individual donors have not merited much attention because of generalizations about their many numbers and common impact (i.e., each gift has equal value). It is a contention of this book that this lack of scholarly interest is at least partly the result of the misconception that individual donors are a faceless mass, too diverse to constitute an external source of funding that may influence or control a charitable organization. For example, in their award-winning study on fund raising discussed in chapter 5, Leslie and Ramey (1988) emphasized the short shrift given to individual donors when they said, "Support by individuals thus entails the independent decisions of large numbers of donors, and the links between an institution and any individual are in general of limited importance" (p. 122).

In addition, this book holds that studies on the motivations of individual donors to higher education, which constitute much of the scholarly literature as discussed in chapter 4, have been based on asymmetrical assumptions about fund raising (i.e., they assume that the value of research on motivations for giving is to help institutions influence future donors while giving little thought to how such motivations can influence colleges and universities). These asymmetrical assumptions (which are discussed in chapter 15), combined with a preoccupation with administrative research, have led to an array of doctoral studies on individual donor motivation that is generally of poor quality, that has failed to build a cohesive body of knowledge, and that ignores the interdependency between charitable organizations and their individual donors.

There is one very recent and significant exception to this assessment of the literature on individuals and philanthropy: Teresa Odendahl's (1990) book, *Charity Begins at Home: Generosity and Self-Interest Among the Philanthropic Elite.* Although it does not deal directly with fund raising, Odendahl's book contributes to this discussion in that it incorporates the concept of loss of autonomy through donor–recipient relationships with individuals. In her book, Odendahl argued that the charitable tax deduction has created a system that perpetuates the upper classes of American society and enables wealthy individuals to control charitable organizations. Means of this elite control, she said, ranged from selectivity (i.e., choosing which organization gets the gift) to serving on boards, making policy, and hiring chief executive officers or presidents.

Approaching philanthropy from an anthropological and a feminist perspective, Odendahl used statistical data and interviewed 140 individuals who are multimillionaires and 170 advisers to the wealthy. Contrary to Panas (1984), who similarly drew from interviews with individual donors of $1 million and whose findings are outlined shortly, Odendahl found a subculture of philanthropy, controlled by the rich and benefiting the rich. Saying that reaction to her findings has been hostile, Odendahl (cited in "Philanthropy promotes," 1990) said, "I wanted to shed some light on the assumption that philanthropy is all good news. Of course [the wealthy donors] want it to be viewed in a good light" (p. A30).

Odendahl's (1990) book documents the fact that individual donors, like corporate and foundation donors, are criticized for making gifts to preserve the status quo. According to Odendahl, wealthy individuals make gifts to gain social acceptance and to gain influence over public policy and civic affairs, which helps them to maintain their social positions. She concluded that American philanthropy is a vehicle by which the elite perpetuate upper class wealth, life styles, elite institutions, and influence over social policy. As pointed out earlier, it can be concluded that, generally, all sources of major gifts—foundations, corporations, and individuals—are, by nature, conservative (i.e., major donors support the existing societal structure from which they acquired the wealth they give away).

In comparison to scholarly works, a great deal has been written about individual donors in the practitioner literature. As discussed in chapter 4, much of our fund-raising knowledge is based on anecdotal evidence. Books, such as Panas' (1984) *Mega Gifts: Who Gives Them, Who Gets Them,* concentrate on the mysterious, generous, and often religious and psychological factors commonly associated with gifts from individuals. Among Panas' findings are that people who give away large sums of money will be loved, will be joyful, will increase their income in direct proportion to their giving, and will probably live longer. Panas asked the fund-raiser reader, "Why don't we do a more effective job of selling the joy?" (p. 166).

In a description of his working project, *Major Academic Donations: A Form of Social Exchange,* Hale (cited in Independent Sector, 1988) reported that he is applying the theory of social exchange to individual donors of major gifts, who, he said, are "motivated by intrinsic and extrinsic benefits" (p. 14). According to Hale, "Descriptions of major donor behavior are often attributed to altruism based on donor accounts. However, donors also give for reasons of self-interest, which is often hidden in public accounts" (p. 14).

Although Panas' (1984) reciprocal benefits acquired by individual donors may contribute to dependency on charitable organizations, Hale's (cited in Independent Sector, 1988) explanation provides a broader approach to the exchangeables available in such relationships. Recalling Blau's (1986) hierarchy of benefits presented in chapter 6 (i.e., gratitude, acceptance, material rewards, services, and compliance) and Gouldner's (1960) contention that the norm of reciprocity changes from situation to situation, it can be stated that individual donors of major gifts are dependent on colleges and universities for benefits that range from having a school named after them, to enhanced prestige by affiliation, to positions of influence within the organization. Such dependencies do not negate feelings of joy that are reported through anecdotal evidence in the practitioner literature, but do encompass other social, economic, and political benefits.

As demonstrated in chapter 5, this book contends that much of the anecdotal material presented in practitioner literature consists of myths and misconceptions that have led to false assumptions about the function of fund raising. Furthermore, misconceptions about donors, including the motivations of individual donors, have hidden the negative impact that gifts can have on institutional autonomy. For example, O'Connell's (1983, 1987) books, like so many others on philanthropy, are filled with optimistic, admirable tales of good works, or as O'Connell said (1987), "good examples of gifts that [have] made a difference" (p. vii). Unfortunately, O'Connell's self-proclaimed intentions to make American citizens more aware and appreciative of the positive contributions of philanthropy and nonprofit organizations—intentions that are reasonable in light of his role as president of Independent Sector, which represents all U.S. charities—often result in presenting case studies of philanthropy that ignore or omit negative factual information that could lead to a more complete understanding of fund raising. One such case is on the founding of Stanford University, which is presented here to document the validity of applying the concept of institutional autonomy to fund raising—particularly fund raising in relation to individual donors of major gifts.

The Founding of Stanford University

O'Connell (1987) has nothing but high praise and laudatory remarks for Leland and Jane Stanford's efforts to establish Stanford University in 1885. O'Connell related how the founding of the University was prompted by the death of the Stanfords' only child and quotes a sentimental passage from the history of the now-prestigious institution:

> Governor Stanford who had remained at Leland's bedside continuously, fell into a troubled sleep the morning the boy died. When he awakened he turned to his wife and said, "The children of California shall be our children." These words were the real beginnings of Stanford University. (p. 31)

O'Connell (1987) pointed out that the university was founded on the highest ideals and notes that Charles Eliot, president of Harvard, encouraged the Stanfords to not only contribute land and buildings for the new institution, but also to give an endowment of at least $5 million. O'Connell quoted Leland Stanford's response, which we assume comes from the same institutional history as the quote just given: "'Well, Jane, we could manage that, couldn't we?'" (p. 32). Except for a remark about the fact that Stanford University admitted women from its beginning, O'Connell drew the curtain on this philanthropic case by saying, "The rest of the story is well known" (p. 32).

In their 1965 book, *Philanthropy in the Shaping of American Higher Education*, Curti and Nash highlight facts about "the rest of the story" that provide not only negative implications of philanthropy as it relates to autonomy and academic freedom, but also a more complete picture of the relationship between the Stanfords and "their" university. Completing the partial quote given in chapter 7, Curti and Nash (1965) stated:

> Gifts and bequests made possible an expansion of higher education as the nation grew. . . . Yet philanthropy sometimes proved to be a liability to its recipient. Today, for better and for worse, our colleges and universities bear the marks left by philanthropy to an extent that is rare among American institutions. (p. v)

Leland and Jane Stanford are among the three cases used by Curti and Nash (1965) to discuss encroachment of institutional autonomy and academic freedom by founders. According to the authors, "When a philanthropist sought to intervene personally with the object of his benefactions, as was the case with Jonas Clark, the Leland Stanfords, and Henry Durant, the freedom that higher education demands for greatness was seriously compromised" (p. 263). Curti and Nash pointed out that institutional histories usually "hesitate to discuss the limitations as well as the advantages of accepting large donations" (p. 320). "The line between creative giving and coercion is thin," they said (p. 263).

Early reports of the Stanford's intentions to found a university included the fact that it would be endowed with the total family estate, estimated to be $20 million, which in 1885 was an incredible amount of money. Although the Stanfords were hailed by most for their unbelievable generosity, Curti and Nash (1965) tell us, "Stanford's numerous enemies spared no invective in denouncing him for egotistically enshrining the memory of his son in an institution that California, in view of the slender enrollment at the struggling state university, did not need" (p. 118). In addition, many criticized the size of the Stanfords' generosity, saying that the railroad magnate was pouring "ill-gotten" treasure into his son's educational monument.

According to Curti and Nash (1965), "The new California institution only appeared to be the richest educational enterprise in the world" (p. 118). When it finally opened in 1891, it had no endowment, only a fledgling campus and some land. Leland Stanford had decided to keep his money and manage it for the benefit of his institution. Curti and Nash explained, "Aware that bequests often failed to be managed in a way to realize the donor's intention and convinced that he could best handle his own fortune, Stanford merely assured David Starr Jordan, whom he had chosen as president, that he could have all he needed" (p. 119).

When Leland died just 2 years after Stanford opened, his wife was his sole heir and, according to the charter of the University, she was given complete control of the institution. Financial troubles quickly followed. The university had no funds for operating until Leland's will was probated, and it looked like the estate was $8 million in debt. Faculty were forced to take pay cuts and frequently did not receive pay at all, even though the court allowed Jane to pay them as personal servants out of the $10,000-a-month she received for living expenses. In 1894, the federal government filed a contingent claim for $15 million against the estate, which Jane successfully fought before the Supreme Court. Problems with her husband's former railroad partners finally motivated Jane to give her Southern Pacific properties to the university in 1899, but the income was not nearly enough to pay for operations. In addition, as Curti and Nash (1965) pointed out, "Since the impression still prevailed that the university was incomparably rich, gifts from new donors were slow in coming" (p. 119). It wasn't until the 1940s when the value of California land skyrocketed that Stanford University reached some form of financial security.

Financial freedom, however, was not the major tension between Jane Stanford and the university she and her husband founded. Curti and Nash (1965) related a number of incidences of infringement of academic freedom at Stanford University during its early days. For example, when a political scientist on the Stanford faculty offended Mrs. Stanford, a devout Christian, by his remarks on religion during an address in 1898, he was quickly fired. According to Curti and Nash, "Although President David Starr Jordan tried to persuade 'the mother of the University' that Powers should be kept because of his value to the institution, he bowed to her imperious will" (p. 132).

A few years earlier, Jane had forbid members of the Stanford faculty from participating in any political activities after a professor of economics and sociology had publicly support William Jennings Bryan in the campaign of 1896. When this same professor, Edward A. Ross, publicly defended socialist Eugene V. Debs, Jane wrote President Jordan, saying:

> When I take up a newspaper. . . and read the utterances of Professor Ross . . . and realize that a professor of the Leland Stanford Junior University, who should prize the opportunities given him . . . thus steps aside, and out of his sphere, to associate himself with the political demagogues of this city, exciting their evil passions . . . and literally plays into the hands of the lowest and vilest elements of socialism, it brings tears to my eyes. I must confess I am weary of Professor Ross, and I think he ought not be retained at Stanford University. (Curti & Nash, 1965, p. 132)

In accordance with the university's charter, Mrs. Stanford could act in place of the trustees and exercise complete power, even though President Jordan was vested with the power to hire and fire faculty. Although Jordan knew that this infringement of the valued principle of academic freedom would lower Stanford's prestige among all scholars, he was unable to protect his faculty from their powerful patron. Ross was dismissed, as was another professor who protested against the violation, and still others resigned in protest. According to Curti and Nash (1965), "Jordan, lacking the strength to defend academic freedom against the bias and strong will of Mrs. Stanford, rationalized his position on the ground that the institution might face financial ruin if she was defied" (p. 133).

In summary, it can be stated that the founding of Stanford University illustrates how an institution of higher education, dependent on one individual donor and lacking alternative sources of funding, is forced to forfeit virtually all of its autonomy, which, in turn, leads to infringement on academic freedom.

Mega Donors Past and Present

Such external control of an educational institution by an individual, as demonstrated by the Stanford case, may be considered by some to be a remnant of the past. Indeed, at the beginning of the 20th century the industrial revolution had resulted in an excess of capital in the hands of a few individuals who used their fortunes to found universities. The $35 million John D. Rockefeller gave to build the University of Chicago would be worth more than $500 million today, which, according to O'Connell (1987), "makes it the largest gift ever provided to education" (p. 33). It should be remembered that education has been a primary beneficiary of the relatively recent philanthropy based on the Greek tradition (i.e., helping individuals through building better communities). In his 1989 essay, renamed "The Gospel of Wealth," Andrew Carnegie (1889/1983) identified and elaborated on the seven "best uses to which a millionaire can devote the surplus of which he should regard himself as only the trustee" (p. 106). The first and best use of excess capital was the founding of a university.

Literally scores of wealthy individuals took his advice, either before the fact or shortly after. The names of university founders read like the who's who in educational institutions today and also document the positive aspects of the relationship between higher education and individual donors of major gifts. According to Curti and Nash (1965), John Harvard, Elihu Yale, and other individual donors laid their hand prints on higher education in the colonies by establishing America's first colleges. People like Stephen Van Rensselaer at Rensselaer Polytechnic Institute and Ario Pardee at Lehigh University turned the focus of education toward the practical arts. Through their financial means, Matthew Vassar, Henry Wells, and Mary Lyons opened higher education to women. John D. Rockefeller greatly affected the availability of higher education for black students through gifts made by his General Education Board, and it was Joseph Wharton and Edward Tuck who by their philanthropy focused higher education's attention on the need to train young people for the world of business.

Curti (1958/1983) provided an inventory of these names and the positive impact their role as founders had on higher educations when he stated:

> Private initiative also got under way much needed vocational [technical] training, as the names of Rensselaer, Cooper, Pratt, Drexel and Carnegie, to name only a few, suggest. And philanthropists also made possible the establishment of the first professional schools of mines, business and journalism. . . . Higher education for women owes a great deal to such philanthropists as Cornell, Curant, Vassar, Goucher and Sophia Smith. The Stanfords, the Vanderbilts, the Candlers and the Dukes helped build a university tradition on the West Coast and in the South. The Carnegie Foundation and the Rockefeller foundations revolutionized medical education and research. (pp. 171-172)

Although there are few opportunities today to found universities, the potential to forfeit high degrees of institutional autonomy to individual donors still exists. Contrary to conventional wisdom, the hundreds or thousands of individuals who contribute to any one charitable organization are not equal in their ability to influence the organization. As described in chapter 2, this is the era of mega gifts (i.e., gifts of $1 million or more). Such gifts have become so common in higher educational fund raising that their occurrence generally attracts only a brief mention in the trade publications and virtually no notice in the lay press. Instead, public attention has focused on ultimate gifts, multi-million-dollar gifts that often are proclaimed by the recipient institution as the largest in their histories. As also pointed out in chapter 2, ultimate gifts appear regularly in higher education's major trade publications, documenting the growing number of wealthy individuals who follow in the tradition of America's earliest philanthropists. It is recalled that there has been a doubling in the numbers of million-dollar donors from 291 in 1984 to 606 in 1988 ("Give & take," 1987; "1988's gifts," 1989). These same articles also report that colleges and universities, alone, reported 40 gifts of $5 million to $15 million in 1984, and at least 48 gifts of more than $10 million in 1988, up from 46 in 1987.

As also mentioned in chapter 2, _The Chronicle of Higher Education_ periodically prints a listing of those gifts of $20 million or more that have been made to higher education from 1967 to date. A 1990 issue lists 44 such gifts that range from $20 million to $105 million. What was not mentioned earlier, however, is the fact that all but 4 of the 44 gifts were made by individuals, and the remaining 4 were from "family foundations" (i.e., foundations controlled by the founders or their families). For example, two of the foundation gifts were from the Arnold and Mabel Beckman Foundation, which O'Connell (1987) described as a two-person operation consisting of Mr. Beckman and his secretary. No major foundations or corporations have made gifts big enough to qualify for the ranking. Of the 44 gifts made over the last 24 years, 77% had been given in the 6 years from 1985 through 1990, and almost 40% had been made since 1988 ("Major gifts," 1990).

The largest gift, as it has been for more than a decade, is Robert W. Woodruff's gift of $105 million to Emory University in 1979. Comparing Woodruff's gift to Rockefeller's total gifts to the University of Chicago, O'Connell (1987) said, "In constant dollars, Robert Woodruff's gift of $100 million [*sic*] to Emory University probably stands as the largest" (p. 33). Although not mentioned in *The Chronicle of Higher Education*'s November 1990 listing ("Major gifts," 1990), Nielsen (1990) said that C. B. Pennington recently gave $125 million to Louisiana State University, which would qualify him as the donor of the largest gift to higher education to date.

One of the recent $20-million donors, Robert Jepson, discussed his goals as a donor at the 1989 CASE National Conference ("A foundation," 1989). As is recalled from chapter 2, Jepson pledged $20 million to the University of Richmond to establish the first school in leadership studies, prompting faculty members to question Jepson's motives and the extent of his influence. Describing his giving as "individual philanthropy," Jepson said, "It's the gift of us" (p. A22).

Jepson, whose family foundation gives away more than $1.5 million each year, said he is primarily interested in small to moderate-sized, private colleges because that is where the donations can have the greatest effect.

Factors Explaining Mega Gifts

There are at least three significant factors that explain the increased mega or ultimate gifts made by individuals to higher education: inflation, the fact that colleges and universities are the preferred recipients of gifts from wealthy individuals, and the increasing number and size of capital campaigns. The first factor, although significant is quite obvious: inflation (i.e., larger gifts are being made now because money is worth less than it was 20 years ago).

The second factor is related to the fact that there are now more individuals with excess capital than before. According to Nielsen (1985), "The industrialization and immense development of the American economy in the 120 years since the Civil War have produced a few million millionaires (as of 1980 it is estimated that some 700,000 were alive and prospering), several hundred centimillionaires, and a dozen or two billionaires" (p. 3). As stated earlier in this chapter, Ylvisaker (1988) said that the assets of the 400 wealthiest Americans is greater than the total assets combined of all 23,000 foundations in the United States.

Although their size is relatively small in relation to the total population, wealthy individuals are particularly important to an analysis of private giving to higher education. According to a study by Feldstein (cited in Jencks, 1987), "In 1962, those with incomes over $50,000 constituted only 0.1 percent of all American families, but they accounted for almost half of all the money given to both hospitals and educational institutions" (p. 321). Similarly, Brossman (1981) cited a 1976 study by the American Council on Education (ACE) showing that 70% of the gift dollars received by colleges and universities come from fewer than 0.5% of all donors.

Jencks (1987) proposed an untested theory on individual donor motivations—one that removes generalizations about individual donors and recipient organizations—that helps this book explain the difference between funding relationships with donors of mega gifts and lower level donors. By examining the IRS's figures for charitable deductions claimed by taxpayers who itemized in 1981, Jencks documented a U-shaped curve in giving by Americans. For example, the mean charitable deduction as a percentage of adjusted gross income (AGI) is higher for those individuals in the lower income categories than for those in the mid-level categories. At the other end of the spectrum, the mean charitable deduction as a percentage of adjusted gross income rises as income rises. For example, those individuals with an AGI of $100,000 to $499,999 in 1981 had a mean charitable deduction of $6,560, or 4.1% of AGI, but those in the next highest category, $500,000 or more, had a mean charitable deduction of $90,880, or 8.9% of AGI. Jencks (1987) concluded, "The relationship between income and philanthropic effort thus appears to be U-shaped, with the rich and the poor making more effort than those in the middle" (p. 323).

Jencks (1987) documented the longevity of this U-shaped relationship by reporting that IRS figures show that in 1963, 1970, and 1981 mean charitable deductions as a percentage of adjusted gross income decrease as incomes increase until a "tipping point" of twice the median family income is reached and then they rise. For example, the median family income in 1981 was $22,000 and it was twice that much when deductions as a percent of AGI starts to rise again.

Jencks (1987) said that although no one has tried to explain the U-shaped relationship, "My own very tentative explanation is that philanthropy takes two distinct forms which I will call 'paying your dues' and 'giving away your surplus'" (p. 324). According to Jencks, the U-shaped distribution revealed in the IRS statistics is a by-product of pooling these two kinds of philanthropy.

"Paying your dues," according to Jencks (1987), is best illustrated by individual gifts to local churches. He said, "In deciding how much to give, all members feel a desire to do their fair share" (p. 324). The perception of fair share, however, has a leveling influence on gifts in proportion to income (i.e., donors are motivated to give something, but not in direct correlation to their ability to give). In addition to churches, Jencks said that gifts to organizations such as the United Way are also a form of "paying your dues," and like donations to local churches, they claim a declining fraction of income as income rises. He elaborated:

> I suspect that the same is true of gifts to organizations like the Heart Fund and the Cancer Society that solicit door to door. Once asked, many people feel obliged to give "something" but look for the minimum respectable gift (their "dues"). (p. 325)

If gifts to local churches exemplify a "paying your dues" motivation, Jencks (1987) said that gifts to major universities best illustrate the second and completely different category of individual gifts: "giving away surplus." According to Jencks, surplus is determined by each individual in relation to his or her material wants and the lifestyle of peers. Although many individuals who could be classified as wealthy have essentially unlimited material wants and would not perceive any surplus to give away to charity, there are also many who do decide that they have money left over to give. To support his dichotomy of individual giving, Jencks pointed out that nonalumni, who have no formal reason to "pay their dues" to a university are responsible for almost half the money given to colleges and universities. He said, "I know of no hard data on these donors, but impressionistic evidence suggests that they are usually very rich and that they usually give to major universities" (p. 325). It should be noted that Jencks cited no source for his estimate that nonalumni are responsible for almost half the money given to colleges and universities, but this estimate is obviously incorrect as alumni *and* nonalumni, together, only account for almost half of the gifts to higher education, and in 1987–1988 nonalumni individuals only gave $1.9 billion of the total $8.2 billion given to higher education ("Gifts to colleges off," 1989). Even with his incorrect estimate, however, Jencks' point is still valid (i.e., a significant portion of gifts to colleges and universities come from nonalumni).

Jencks (1987) hypothesized that gifts based on the motivation of "giving away surplus" are also related to hospitals and arts organizations. As the two different categories of gifts seem closely related to different types of charitable organizations, Jencks argued that disaggregating these organizations in statistics on philanthropy would remove the U-shaped relationship to income. For example, poor people seldom give money to colleges and universities so that mean gifts in proportion to AGI would rise as income rises in statistics based solely on giving to higher education. To support his argument, Jencks referred to a study by Feldstein that found that as their income rose, people gave a rising fraction of their income to hospitals and educational institutions, and he said that there is no reason to predict a change in that pattern. On the other hand, statistics on giving to churches would show a definite decline in the percentage of income given as income rose.

Jencks' (1987) conclusions on the different types of charitable organizations and his untested theory relate well to the discussion in chapter 3 on the three types of charitable organizations drawn from Douglas (1983) (i.e., pure public goods, positive externalities, and eleemosynary). Specifically, this book, as does Jencks, calls for a disaggregation of charities, as generalized by the IRS as 501(c)(3) organizations, so that donor relationships and the function of fund raising can be examined in a new perspective. In short, Jencks' untested theory supports the conclusion first presented in chapter 3 and expanded in chapter 6 that a failure to differentiate charitable organizations has led to inappropriate generalizations about donor motivations. It was concluded in those chapters that charity refers to gifts made for altruistic reasons to unknown recipients directly or through eleemosynary organizations and that philanthropy refers to gifts made through social exchanges with organizations with public benefit and positive externalities. As it relates to this section, a failure to differentiate charities with positive externalities, such as colleges and universities, from eleemosynary charities, such as CARE, has led to flawed assumptions in previous studies about individual giving to higher education. Finally, Jencks (1987) admitted, "We know very little about the way in which individual giving affects the recipients" (p. 336).

Jencks (1987) fell into his own trap of generalization when he reported that individuals' propensity to give has declined in recent decades (i.e., he generalizes among all types of charitable organizations and all income groups). In 1954, Jencks (1987) reported, Americans gave 2.15% of personal income to charity. Economists have used that statistic as a standard of propensity to give by assigning it a value of 100. In comparison, individuals in 1982 gave only 1.88% of personal income, scoring only 61 on the scale measuring propensity to give. In response, said Jencks, charities have turned to government subsidies and user fees as alternative sources of funding. Rudney (1987) confirmed Jencks' conclusions by citing 1980 figures showing that charitable organizations, excluding religious organizations, received only 22% of their support from gifts, whereas government grants and sales accounted for 35% and user fees accounted for 36%. (The remaining 7% was provided by investment income.)

From these statistics, Jencks (1987) concluded, "Given the immense growth in government support for the nonprofit sector over the past generation, and the nonprofits' increasing capacity to impose user charges, the need for private gifts has surely declined" (p. 338). Yet, the increasing number of capital campaigns, particularly those by colleges and universities, would seem to contradict this conclusion.

The third factor underlying the increase in mega and ultimate giving by individuals is the increase in the number and size of capital campaigns. Although discussed in chapters 2 and 5, this factor is reintroduced here to provide greater insight on individual donors.

As Pray (1981) said, "Today, colleges are engaging in a "continuous search for major gifts, usually in what we might call a rolling campaign strategy" (pp. 57-58). It is recalled from chapter 2 that Stanford University "redefined the outer limits of fund raising" when it announced a $1.1-billion capital campaign in 1986 ("Reagan Years," 1988, p. 22). Currently at least 145 institutions of higher education are conducting capital campaigns with goals of $15 million or more ("UM enters," 1988). Taken together, these 145 institutions, of which about one third are public, are trying to raise $18 billion, or twice the amount given to *all* colleges and universities in 1986-1987. As summarized by the report on the Reagan years, "Organizations are pursuing fund-raising goals that would have been unimaginable in 1980" (p. 22).

As discussed in chapter 2, capital campaigns are one of the three factors responsible for the increasing number of mega and ultimate gifts from individual donors because individual donors play a critical role in these fund-raising drives. Throughout the history of campaigns, fund raisers have repeatedly found that a very few people account for a large portion of the funds raised. This consistent observation has resulted in a formal principle of fund raising, the "Rule of Thirds" (Seymour, 1966). Traditionally, fund raisers knew from experience that approximately one third of the campaign goal would be raised from 10% or less of the donors. These donors—overwhelmingly individuals, rather than corporations or foundations—could make or break a campaign's success. As a result, campaigns were structured around "lead gifts," or those very large gifts that would constitute one third of the goal. Lead gifts were solicited during the pre-campaign period, before a formal announcement was made, for the simple reason that if the one third rule was not adhered to, it was highly probable that the campaign would not succeed and should be called off before it was officially launched.

Although the Rule of Thirds still underlies the structure of current campaigns, there has been a dramatic decrease in the number of donors who are responsible for the majority of a campaign's dollar totals. Some fund-raising experts now predict that less than 1% of the gifts to a campaign will account for one third of the total. As Donald Campbell (1989), a fund-raising consultant and former campaign director at a number of colleges and universities, explained:

[The Rule of Thirds] says you should expect one-third of your campaign goal from the top 10 donors, the next third from the next 100 donors, and the remaining third from all others. However, as competition for philanthropic dollars has increased, institutions have found that they need to secure more money from fewer people. Consequently, a more realistic formula these days says you should expect 10 percent of your goal from the first gift; perhaps 25 to 30 percent from the next 10; and 25 to 30 percent from the next 100; and another 25 to 30 percent from all other donors. (p. 26)

In other words, Campbell and others predict that only 11 donors (most of whom would probably be individuals) will provide 40% of a campaign's total and only 111 gifts will constitute 70% of the goal. As was described in chapter 5, the University of Miami reported that 76 of the 61,000 donors to its capital campaign accounted for $239 million, or 50%, of the total dollars raised ("Energetic board," 1989).

According to David Dalessandro (1989), assistant vice president for development at Carnegie Mellon University and campaign director for that university's 5-year $200 million campaign:

The American Association of Fund-Raising Counsel has gathered statistics for 51 campaigns ranging in size from $292,000 to $272 million. In these campaigns the top 10 gifts never equaled less than 20 percent of the total and in some instances amounted to more than 90 percent. (p. 19)

Needless to say, when colleges and universities decide to launch a capital campaign their primary concern and concentration are on those very few individuals who are capable of making mega or ultimate gifts of $1 million or more. These institutions, therefore, have become increasingly dependent on a small pool of individuals who can provide the lead gifts necessary to attract other major gifts and to ensure the success of a campaign, regardless of the actions of thousands of lower level donors who provide the bulk of the *number* of gifts. Such dependency places individuals in a powerful position when negotiating mega and ultimate gifts with colleges and universities.

It is a conclusion of this section that, contrary to the generalizations found in most of the literature, individual donors are not a massive public too diverse to exert influence on a college or university. Rather, the discussion of mega and ultimate gifts and capital campaigns supports the conclusion that institutional autonomy can be affected by individual donors of major gifts (e.g., those individuals who can provide strategically important lead gifts to a college's proposed capital campaign). According to Jencks (1987), "The importance of individual contributions to an organization depends on its alternative sources of income" (p. 336). Therefore, like foundations and corporations, individuals capable of providing major funding have the potential to seriously infringe on the institutional autonomy of colleges and universities. The extent of autonomy lost will depend largely on the institution's ability to effectively manage the interdependency relationships with these three sources of gifts.

In summary, living individuals are the primary donors to higher education, as they are to all U.S. charities. Like foundations and corporations, educational gifts made by individuals are not distributed equally (e.g., 62% of the gift dollars given by individuals to colleges and universities in the 1987–1988 CFAE survey went to only 183 research universities). Unlike foundations and corporations, individuals generally have not been criticized for influencing the recipients of their gifts; rather, they are commonly viewed as benevolent, disinterested sources of financial support. The founding of Stanford University, however, illustrates how an institution of higher education, dependent on one individual donor and lacking alternative sources of funding, is forced to forfeit virtually all of its autonomy, which, in turn, leads to infringement on academic freedom.

This section concludes, therefore, that like foundations and corporations, individual donors are neither benevolent nor villainous, but can best be understood as groups in the environment of an institution of higher education with whom they are interdependent. Unlike foundations and corporations, however, the dependencies of individual donors of major gifts *on* colleges and universities cannot be generalized, but differ from situation to situation (i.e., reciprocal benefits in dependency relationships with individuals cover a broad range of economic, social, and political needs).

Contrary to conventional wisdom, the hundreds or thousands of individuals who contribute to any one charitable organization are not equal in their ability to influence the organization; rather those individuals who can provide mega or ultimate gifts are extremely powerful in their exchange relationships with recipient organizations. There are three factors that explain the increased mega or ultimate gifts made by individuals to higher education: inflation, the fact that colleges and universities are the preferred recipients of gifts from wealthy individuals, and the increasing number and size of capital campaigns.

Higher education traditionally attracts gifts from the small percentage of American individuals who control a great deal of the wealth (i.e., poor people rarely give to colleges and universities). One conclusion of this section is that a failure to differentiate charities with positive externalities, such as colleges and universities, from eleemosynary charities, such as CARE, has led to flawed assumptions in previous studies about individual giving to higher education. The increasing number and size of capital campaigns by colleges and universities have made these institutions more dependent on a small pool of individuals who can provide the lead gifts necessary to ensure the success of a campaign, regardless of the actions of thousands of lower level donors who provide the bulk of the *number* of gifts.

It is a conclusion of this section that, contrary to the generalizations found in most of the literature, individual donors are not a massive public too diverse to exert influence on a college or university; rather, the increasing number of mega and ultimate gifts and capital campaigns supports the conclusion that institutional autonomy can be affected, individually, by individual donors of major gifts.

Concluding this chapter, the analyses of the three sources of private support and autonomy provide evidence that major gifts from foundations, corporations, and individuals have in the past and can in the future limit college substantive autonomy—the power to determine its goals—and procedural autonomy—the power to choose the means of pursuing those goals. Whereas major gifts from all three sources of private support can limit institutional autonomy individually, evidence was provided that major gifts from foundations and corporations can also infringe on autonomy collectively (i.e., a perception of what will appeal generally to corporate and foundation donors can cause a charitable organization to change its behavior in a way that is incongruent with self-determined goals and objectives).

In addition, this chapter concludes that rather than being dissimilar, the three sources of private support have much in common. Although there are many such organizations, relatively few foundations and corporations make most of the gifts to charitable organizations. In relation to colleges or universities, relatively few foundations, corporations, and individuals provide most gift dollars. The majority of gift dollars to higher education from all three sources of private support is directed to a very small percentage of institutions (i.e., major research universities).

Finally, this chapter concludes that motivations of corporate, foundation, and individual donors can best be understood as neither benevolent nor villainous, but rather within the context of environmental interdependencies. Whereas foundations and corporations are dependent on colleges and universities largely for employees and research, individuals seek reciprocal benefits that range from gratitude to compliance. In addition to seeking benefits in their own self interest, all three sources of gifts seek benefits for the public good, as described in chapter 5.

In order to generalize beyond colleges and universities, chapter 9 turns to three case studies of different types of charitable organizations. These case studies, selected from secondary sources, document famous cases of charitable organizations that have changed their goals because of their dependency on external, philanthropic funding sources. They provide new insight into the dynamics of fund raising (i.e., the inherent danger of losing autonomy while seeking external dollars that would enhance the autonomy of the recipient organization).

Chapter 9

Three Cases Studies on Autonomy

This final chapter of Part II answers the research question: What evidence can be found to substantiate the hypothesis that all gift sources can cause all types of charitable organizations to change their goals? This chapter analyzes three classic studies, selected from Powell and Friedkin's (1987) work on organizational change in nonprofit organizations, that document cases of charitable organizations that have changed their goals primarily because of their dependency on external sources of private support.

From these cases, the scholars concluded that, contrary to conventional wisdom, charitable organizations may be more subject to external pressures that induce them to change than for-profit organizations, although it is a widely held belief that charitable organizations deviate little from their professed mission. Indeed, Payton (1989), who has worked in all three economic sectors (i.e., business, government, and nonprofit) said that "flexibility and responsiveness are more characteristic" (p. 65) of charitable organizations than organizations in the other two sectors.

At the conclusion of this chapter, the book draws together some of the important findings and conclusions of the four chapters compromising Part II. Basically, systems theory and the concept of organizational autonomy provide a new way of approaching fund raising (i.e., fund raising is the management of environmental funding relationships that contributes to organizational effectiveness by enhancing and protecting autonomy).

THREE CASE STUDIES

According to Powell and Friedkin (1987), "When ethnography is done well, the richness of detail presented in an individual case can take our understanding well beyond the simple structures of the causal arguments developed by the author" (p. 183). The case studies discussed by Powell and Friedkin, therefore, are used in this book to support a new perspective of fund raising although none of the three studies were intended to do so by the original scholars.

The following case studies are 3 of 10 originally selected by Powell and Friedkin (1987) to document their critical work on organizational change in nonprofit organizations. The authors advance the thesis that although conventional wisdom tells us that for-profit organizations have much more freedom in pursuing their ultimate goal (i.e., earning profits for their shareholders) than do nonprofits, there actually is not much difference between business and charitable organizations when it comes to organizational change processes. According to Powell and Friedkin, "Few would dispute a firm's mandate to change its activities in pursuit of financial gain, but many people would question a nonprofit's deviation from its professed mission" (p. 180). The authors believe that "nonprofits may be both more subject to pressures that induce them to change and more capable of responsive change than our standard accounts would have us believe" (p. 180). The primary reasons for Powell and Friedkin's critical attack on conventional wisdom supports the new perspective of fund raising taken by this book (i.e., relationships with private sources of funds are environmental interdependencies that must be managed by charitable organizations in order to avoid external control). They stated:

> Moreover, precisely because non-profit organizations depend on external sources for support, they may find it necessary to bend and shift with the prevailing political and economic winds. In addition, large nonprofit organizations frequently have multiple stakeholders—that is, a variety of constituencies making demands upon them. Responding to these demands often requires considerable flexibility. (p. 180)

Powell and Friedkin (1987) said the case studies they use from the literature on organizational change were selected because those studies are regarded as classics in the field (i.e., they provide enduring contributions to research on organizations), or because they are recent examples of case studies that share common elements (e.g., an attention for detail, "a concern with the informal features of an organization, its soft underbelly consisting of a tangled web of relationships, dependencies, conflicts, politics, and values," p. 183). According to Powell and Friedkin, "The common theme running through these studies is how organizational goals are changed—weakened or subverted—or successfully maintained in the face of altered external conditions and changing internal pressures" (p. 183).

Case 1: Social Service Organizations for the Blind[1]

In his 1976 analysis of social service organizations for the blind, Scott (cited in Powell & Friedkin, 1987) found that the stated goals of the agencies were to enhance the welfare of the blind; however, he also found that factors other than client need more strongly influence the agencies' service delivery. Powell and Friedkin (1987) said that organizational persistence and the *perceived* interests of individual donors "were the major forces that Scott identified as responsible for goal displacement" (p. 183).

At their beginning approximately 100 years ago, social service organizations developed programs and services targeted for children and healthy adults—the needy population at the time. Today, most blind people are female, elderly, and only partially blind, yet the majority of services still are directed at children and employable adults. Scott concluded that the institutionalization of early programs was partly responsible for the discrepancy between stated goals to serve the needy and modern programs that ignored most of them. But Scott also concluded that a second, and perhaps more powerful force in this discrepancy, was the relationship between the charitable organizations and their donors. Powell and Friedkin (1987) stated:

> Fund-raising concerns, however, also explain the lack of attention paid to the majority of the blind population. Blind children evoke more sympathy from funders than do the elderly blind, and programs to employ blind adults appeal to widely shared values of personal independence. Whether accurate or not, agency administrators perceive that programs for the young, educable, and employable will enjoy better funding than those for the elderly. (p. 183)

The motivations of giving money out of sympathy and a desire to help people to help themselves that social service administrators attribute to prospective donors are well documented in the fund-raising literature (e.g., Seymour, 1966). The first, of course, is a cornerstone of the conventional wisdom on charitable giving, which has its roots in the Judeo-Christian philosophy as discussed in the earlier chapter on definitions. It is also, according to our typology developed from Douglas (1983), a motivation related to eleemosynary charities.

Andrew Carnegie, in his 1889 article later renamed "The Gospel of Wealth," was perhaps one of the first, or at least the most famous donor to advance the

---

[1]The discussion of all three case studies is drawn from Powell and Friedkin (1987).

philanthropic philosophy of helping others to help themselves. According to Carnegie (1889/1983), the Greek tradition of philanthropy (i.e., helping others by improving the community) was "better" than the Christian tradition of sympathy. Carnegie believed and often stated that rich people helping beggars did more harm than good. He wrote, "In bestowing charity, the main consideration should be to help those who will help themselves" (p. 105).

Scott's (cited in Power & Friedkin, 1987) findings about the fund-raising concerns of agency administrators point out the importance of the concept of *perceptions* of donor motivations and their impact on organizational autonomy. It is recalled from chapter 8 that such organizational perceptions were also responsible for colleges and universities changing their priorities to meet the perceived wishes of corporate donors and for faculty shaping their research to appeal to foundation donors. Other case studies have and will demonstrate in this book that influence of actual donors can lead to displacement of goals, but Scott's case study demonstrates that a reliance on perceptions of perspective donors can have an equally powerful effect on the autonomy of charitable organizations.

In addition, whereas the examples of the effects of perceptions cited earlier involved corporate and foundation donors, Scott's study concerns itself with individuals. Scott did not study the motivations of individual donors, but only the perceptions of motivations for giving that social service administrators attributed, collectively, to all perspective donors. It can be concluded, therefore, that individual donors, as well as corporate and foundation donors, have the potential to affect organizational autonomy collectively, as well as individually (i.e., by perceptions of what appeals to individual donors, charitable organizations may change their behavior in order to attract future gifts from individuals).

If a charitable organization lacks formative research on donor motivations, it will usually rely instead on unscientific assumptions developed by administrators, particularly fund raisers. These assumptions, or perceptions—whether accurate or not—can be as powerful as actual donor motivations in their ability to affect the way an organization carries out its fund-raising function, as well as its power to determine its goals and the means to achieving them (i.e., its substantive and procedural autonomy).

Scott's study shows that the influence of fund raising on the service delivery of social service organizations for the blind is detrimental to both the majority of blind people whom these agencies are ostensibly intended to serve and to the small minority of the blind population that is the beneficiary of the private gifts. Obviously, by developing their programming around the groups who are "fundable," social service organizations for the blind are not meeting the service needs of the majority of blind Americans today (i.e., the female, elderly, and partially blind). On the other hand, the emphasis on programs for the young and employable have forced social service agencies to vigorously, and often unethically, compete for the small number of "marketable" blind people who can participate in the programs and who, in turn, can be used by the agencies to attract more private gifts.

According to Powell and Friedkin (1987), "Rather than fostering independence, the agencies guard their 'desirable' blind and increase their clients' dependence by providing housing, employment, and recreation" (p. 183). This, the authors concluded, completes the process of goal displacement because the welfare of even those who are helped is diminished, not enhanced.

Scott's (cited in Powell & Friedkin, 1987) case study provides an opportunity to reintroduce the concept of fund-raising models. Although a full discussion of the four models of fund raising is delayed until chapter 13, it is helpful to outline some major characteristics of the press agentry model, as identified in this book, in order to fully understand the implications of Scott's case study. Like the subject of analysis in Scott's study, charitable organizations practicing the press agentry model are highly likely to target their fund-raising appeals to donor motivations of sympathy.

Appeals targeted to the donor motivation of helping others to help themselves are also frequently found in those charities practicing this model. As with the motivations of sympathy and helping others to help themselves, a lack of research and a reliance on perceptions of donor motivations are characteristics of the press agentry model of fund raising.

Based on the appeals targeted to sympathy and helping others to help themselves, the lack of research to confirm or deny perceived donor motivations, the absence of truth in fund-raising strategies, and the apparent one-way communication between the organizations and their donor publics, it is hypothesized that the social service organizations studied by Scott primarily practiced the press agentry model of fund raising. The purpose of this model is to propagandize a cause through one-way communication that is dependent on emotion and is not necessarily based on the truth. Little, if any, research is used in this model, and it is estimated that it is currently practiced by 50% of all charitable organizations, primarily national health and social service agencies and religious organizations.

Although Powell and Friedkin (1987) focused on the organizational changes brought about by fund raising rather than on the function itself, their presentation of Scott's case study documents how the press agentry model can help displace organizational goals, resulting in a loss of substantive autonomy.

The illustration of the press agentry model provided by Scott's analysis allows another concept to be briefly introduced in this chapter, that of social responsibility of *recipient* organizations. Basically, different models of fund raising can have negative and positive effects not only on organizational autonomy, but also on society. In the case of Scott's (cited in Powell & Friedkin, 1987) social service organizations for the blind, the press agentry model led to loss of autonomy and also caused the organizations to act in a socially irresponsible manner (i.e., their programs were detrimental to both the blind majority and the "fundable" blind who were encouraged to become dependent on agency programs). This concept is fully covered in chapter 15 on presuppositions of fund raising.

Case 2: Mobilization for Youth

Helfgot (cited in Powell & Friedkin, 1987) analyzed the history of Mobilization for Youth (MFY), a social welfare agency concerned with juvenile delinquency in New York City. His case study is particularly useful because his analysis includes the 4-year planning stage of the organization, its beginning in 1962, and its first 10 years of operation. Because of its long-term approach, it demonstrates how goals of a charitable organization can be changed, even in the very beginning, by the explicit and implicit demands of private funding sources. "In general," said Powell and Friedkin (1987), "MFY's history is a story of organizational change generated by a dependency on external sources for resources" (p. 183).

Stimulated by the federal government's "war on poverty," the first proposal to found the organization and provide funding was based on a traditional service delivery model to combat juvenile delinquency, which was initially rejected by its three primary funding sources: the National Institute of Mental Health, the President's Committee on Juvenile Delinquency and Youth Crime, and the Ford Foundation.

All three funders, however, suggested changes or held out demands that would make the proposal and the project more attractive to them. According to Powell and Friedkin (1987), "The final proposal bore little resemblance to the original idea conceived by the Lower East Side settlement houses. Instead, it was heavily influenced by the interests and demands of organizations outside of the community that MFY would serve" (p. 184).

Although the primary funding sources, including the Ford Foundation, were first interested in the project because of their attraction to new theories on how delinquency was a product of community factors, not individual inadequacies, MFY's operating programs soon emphasized cultural inferiority. Helfgot (cited in Powell & Friedkin, 1987) argued that this emphasis, although inconsistent with MFY's initial rationale, was consistent with the objectives of the elite funding organizations.

The external funders, according to Helfgot's findings, were not really interested in fundamental reform, but in greater social control—a social control made possible by the power of their money and one that would be enforced by the community itself. "For most of the period of Helfgot's research, the powerful sponsors maintained control over MFY's programs and philosophy," said Powell and Friedkin (1987, p. 184).

In the late 1960s, MFY went through a period of militancy, once again emphasizing a structural approach to combating delinquency (e.g., participating in rent strikes, civil rights demonstrations, and voter registration drives). These actions, according to Helfgot, provoked a public attack on the charity, "including charges of communist infiltration, misappropriation of funds, and precipitation of riots" (cited in Powell & Friedkin, 1987, p. 184).

Although cleared of all charges, the crisis forced the agency to permanently withdraw from a focus on structural changes in society, and it became one consisting of professionals trying to help disadvantage youth adjust to existing circumstances.

Finally, the multi-year commitments from the three primary funding organizations ended, leaving MFY to face a financial crisis. Trading the last of its original goals for long-term funding, MFY successfully sought to become a designated Manpower Research Center under the U.S. Department of Labor.

The object of analysis for Helfgot's case study is a charity with positive externalities (i.e., one whose beneficial spillover affects the rest of society beyond the intended recipients; Douglas, 1983) as compared with Scott's (cited in Powell & Friedkin, 1987) study of eleemosynary charities. Also in comparison to Scott, Helfgot was able to document explicit demands made by external funding agencies, including a foundation, that changed the goals of the recipient organization in its formative years (i.e., the differences between the initial proposal that was rejected and the funded proposal). His study, like Scott's, provides a dramatic example of how external funding sources can control the operations of charitable organizations, even to the point of complete displacement of goals.

Helfgot's study also reinforces the earlier conclusions of chapter 8 that major gifts from all three sources have the potential, individually, to severely limit the autonomy of recipient organizations.

Case 3: The California Institute of the Arts

Continuing this issue of the power of major gifts to affect organizational autonomy individually, Adler's (cited in Powell & Friedkin, 1987) study of the California Institute of the Arts demonstrates how one major individual donor (including his friends and family) can externally control an institution of higher education in modern times. Scott's study, it should be emphasized, dealt with numerous individual donors—both major and lower level donors—and Helfgot's case study dealt with the federal government and the powerful Ford Foundation. The dependence on one donor in this case study supports the contention of systems theorists, such as Pfeffer and Salancik (1978), Gouldner (1960), and Blau (1986), that a lack of diversified and numerous sources for a needed resource can lead to external control and compliance of an organization (i.e., severely limit its autonomy).

In addition, Adler (cited in Powell & Friedkin, 1987) found in Cal Arts a case study on Mintzberg's (1983) response to the question: For whom does the organization exist? Mintzberg, it is recalled from the earlier chapter on systems theory, responded to this question by stating that an organization exists for any one of the multiple stakeholders who have the power to affect its decisions. The most primary decisions, of course, relate to the organization's power to determine its goals and the means of pursuing them.

Adler's case study focused on the dilemma faced by an educational institution when the ideological opinions of the faculty conflict with those of the trustees and the force of financial power determines the outcome (i.e., he who pays the piper calls the tune).

Describing the rapid changes in institutional goals brought about by ideological and financial pressures, Powell and Friedkin (1987) stated:

> The California Institute of the Arts was founded as an avant-garde art scene, a utopian community for artists of all media to experiment and create, unhindered by market pressures and lay opinion. . . . Within two years of its establishment, Cal Arts was largely transformed into a more conventional and conservative private art school. Within five years, public statements of philosophy espoused a new, more professional direction and utopian proclamations were increasingly out of favor. As numerous institute members said, "the dream had died." (p. 189)

One man, Walt Disney, was responsible for the founding of Cal Arts, and it was the trustees' commitment to fulfilling his "dream" that brought them into conflict with the faculty. After setting aside millions of dollars for establishing the Institute, Disney died shortly before final plans were approved. Well before construction was completed, lavish plans and cost overruns had used up all of Disney's gift. According to Powell and Friedkin (1987), "This increased the school's already strong dependence on the Disney family and created a perpetual atmosphere of insecurity and crisis" (p. 190).

In addition to financial problems, Adler (cited in Powell & Friedkin, 1987) pointed out that Cal Arts was founded on a premise that contained a fundamental contradiction: creating an institution for an avant-garde culture that inherently disapproved of its own institutionalization. In addition, the Disney legacy, as translated by the trustees, was one of elaborate public spectacles, whereas the artist-faculty members attracted to Cal Arts had little concern for public consumption of their work. Powell and Friedkin reported (1987):

> In Cal Arts' early days its members reveled in the "joke" they had pulled on the conservative funders who had committed apparently unlimited monies for a radical and spectacularly equipped artists' playground. It soon became apparent, however, that the "joke" was on the artists, as the trustees began to exercise their considerable control. (p. 189)

The dependence on Disney's family and the remainder of his wealth led to a "stacking" of the board of trustees. Rather than selecting trustees who might have brought new sources of private funding with them (e.g., wealthy trustees who might have been interested in funding programs in support of the original goals of the institution), board members were selected on the basis of their personal and financial ties to the Disney family. From the perspective provided by Pfeffer and Salancik (1978), the institute sought to stabilize its funding dependency on the Disney family by cooptation. As concluded in chapter 6, although forms of cooptation, such as board membership, reduce environmental uncertainty, they can also lead to greater dependence on particular sources of private funding.

In the case of Cal Arts, the trustees' ability to raise and maintain a sufficient endowment—which is a strategy to avoid external control, described by Pfeffer and Salancik (1978) as building an inventory—was diminished in order to maintain ties to the independent wealth of the Disney family. In moves that further ensured that the institute would not enhance its autonomy, administrators nominated board members who were sympathetic to their academic disciplines, rather than those who could help raise private funds. According to Powell and Friedkin (1987), "As financial pressures increased, the utopian character of the institute dissipated and values originally scorned became the keys to survival" (p. 190).

The values soon forced upon and/or adopted by the Institute's faculty included a move toward professionalism, which was perceived as a source of power for dealing with the trustees. In addition, fund-raising efforts, particularly those geared toward propagating the Disney "dream," demanded a more traditional curriculum.   As Powell and Friedkin (1987) explained, "Control of the purse strings soon translated into control over educational policy, as those arts most useful in fund-raising, such as classical music and dance and conventional theater, grew in favor with the trustees, and less marketable arts were severely cut back or eliminated" (p. 190).

As is recalled, Berdahl (1971) said that although institutional autonomy and academic freedom are not synonymous, they are closely related.   And Dressel (1980) said, "The fact, however, is that if a university budget is so rigidly specified that there can be no flexibility in definition or performance of academic tasks, academic freedom is so constrained that it is virtually nonexistent" (p. 22). From these explanations, we can conclude that budget cuts made by the Cal Arts trustees constituted infringement on academic freedom in the area of determining curriculum, or what should be taught.   The loss of autonomy brought about by dependency on an external funding source led not only to this example of infringement on academic freedom, but also extended to the area of who should teach.   According to Powell and Friedkin (1987), the board of trustees demonstrated the extent of its control when it refused to hire the philosopher Herbert Marcuse for a position in the Institutes's School of Critical Studies even though he had been approved by the faculty.

Concluding this analysis of three case studies, the causal arguments abstracted from these cases provides evidence of the powerful effects fund raising can have on institutional autonomy, regardless of funding source or type of charity. Although some of the arguments were more implicit than explicit in the original studies, they help demonstrate how autonomy provides a new perspective of fund raising—a perspective that dispels much of the conventional wisdom and generalities currently used to explain that function.

CONCLUSIONS OF PART II

At this point, it is helpful to draw together some of the findings and conclusions of the four chapters in Part II. Approaching the relationships between charitable organizations and the donors in their environment, chapter 6 concluded that contrary to conventional wisdom, these relationships are best understood not as benevolent, business, or pseudo relations, but as interdependencies of groups and organizations within an environment.   These fund-raising interdependencies constitute an ongoing exchange process that requires management and negotiation by the charitable organization, especially by those practitioners who manage its fund-raising function.   The concept of autonomy is a central issue in the exchange process in that the power of a charitable organization to determine and pursue its own goals is affected by how successful that organization is at managing its interdependencies. Although absolute autonomy is impossible, all charitable organizations, as well as organizations in the other two sectors, strive to maintain autonomy by dominating or cooperating with groups or other organizations within their environments. Finally, charitable organizations in the nonprofit sector face a double-edged sword in relation to interdependencies with donors in their environment: In order to enhance their autonomy, they must seek external funding to support their institutional goals, but in so doing, they risk losing autonomy by accepting gifts that may limit their power to determine goals and the means of pursuing them.

Open systems create interdependencies between organizations and other groups and organizations in their environment. The resource dependence perspective holds that organizations are shaped and constrained by their relationships with external sources of needed resources. Because of their dependence on external sources, organizations are involved in a constant struggle for autonomy.

Charitable organizations, which are dependent on external sources for financial support, are particularly susceptible to external control. Gifts constitute one form of financial support for such organizations, and relationships with the donors who provide this revenue (i.e., foundations, corporations, and individuals) represent external resource dependencies that may infringe on the charitable organization's power to determine and pursue its own goals. Control lost or gained through negotiations with these resource providers is largely determined by the vulnerability of the recipient organization, which, in turn, is determined by the extent to which an organization has come to depend on certain types of exchanges. A charitable organization, such as a college, is vulnerable to external control if it does not have a sufficient endowment, if it does not control the rules of exchange, and if it does not have alternative sources of private gifts and diversification of funding sources.

Finally, charitable organizations strive to stabilize external dependencies on donors through joint ventures, such as industrial–university partnerships, and through cooptation, such as placing major donors on governing boards. Although such strategies do reduce the environmental uncertainty related to the need to continually raise private gifts, they also abdicate some degree of organizational control to external sources of gifts. In addition, such strategies may increase the vulnerability of a charitable organization by encouraging dependence on gift exchanges involving joint partners or coopted donors.

In our complex and specialized society, interdependencies between organizations and groups in an environment are managed through an exchange process that involves economic, political, and social resources. The exchange process is an ongoing one that requires management and negotiation in order to achieve some degree of equilibrium between what is gained for the organization and what is lost in the exchange.

The norm of reciprocity permeates all social interaction, requiring that an organization or person return some benefits to benefactors. Charitable organizations are dependent on external sources for private funding, and these sources are dependent on the recipient organizations for some unspecified benefits that differ from situation to situation and from organization to organization. Reciprocity may take the form of thank-you cards, plaques, named buildings, appointments to internal boards, prestige by affiliation, free football tickets, or a degree of control in the organization, among others.

The value of noneconomic gifts and reciprocal benefits are determined by the perception of the actors involved in the exchange process, and the most common situation is one in which one party gives something more or less than that received. When imbalances are extreme, we say that exploitation of either the donor or the charitable organization has taken place. Exploitation can include a loss of control by the charitable organization when there is an imbalance of power and when the degree of dependency on the donor is great. One of the four variables that determine the obligation owed to donors is the intensity of the recipient's need at the time the benefit is bestowed. Therefore, if a charitable organization in great need of funding receives a relatively large gift from a donor, that organization may reciprocate by exchanging organizational control for the gift. On the other hand, donors usually enter into exchange relationships with those recipients that can provide the benefits *they* desire (e.g., admiration of peer group, trained manpower, or ingratiating behavior). As a result of the latter issue, major gifts are not distributed equally, but are instead generally made to the most prestigious organizations, such as research universities, museums, and hospitals.

Finally, the negotiations involved in such interdependencies, including forms of reciprocity, are critical to the amount of control a charitable organization abdicates in the gift-exchange process. Because most exchangeables are not objectively valued, fund-raising practitioners may offer inappropriate forms of recognition in order to attract gifts that may not be valued as equivalent by third parties, such as faculty members.

Blau's (1986) theory approaches exchange behaviors as social relationships, not on the basis of the psychological motivations of the actors, which often do not take into account inherent properties of the relationship that the actors bring to the exchange. As an exchange relationship, fund raising can be viewed as a process in which a charitable organization seeks to exchange social, economic, and political benefits it possesses for private funds from donors, and the power of each relative to the other affects the outcome. Blau provided five conditions that lead to an imbalance of power in a social exchange, which can also be viewed as a charitable organization's power to protect and enhance its autonomy in the fund-raising process (i.e., if a charitable organization does not have, or chooses not to use, inducements, a broad base of donors, force, or the determination to get along without the gift, its only alternative is compliance).

Blau (1986) also provided an hierarchy of reciprocal benefits that a charitable organization can use in a social exchange involving gifts from donors: gratitude, approval, services, material rewards, and compliance. These benefits, in turn, provide categories of the inducement resources that constitute Blau's first condition of power imbalance. Although the first two categories of benefits may be preferred by the charitable organization, Blau said that respect, which is synonymous with the second category, is often perceived as insufficient in an exchange relationship and that the provider of goods or services also tends to expect increased benefits over time. In addition, expectations for benefits are affected by those conferred on others.

Although Blau (1986) distinguished between giving that involves no social exchange (the donor receives no benefit except self-satisfaction), giving that involves indirect social exchange (the donor receives benefits from his or her peers, not from the gift recipient), and giving that involves social exchange (the donor receives benefits from the recipient), this book dismisses the second type of giving as incomplete and inaccurate. It adopts the other two types, concluding that there are two distinct types of giving: (a) charity to unknown recipients through eleemosynary charitable organizations that provide no benefits in exchange, and (b) philanthropy to recipients directly or through organizations with public good and positive externalities that involve social exchange (i.e., reciprocal benefits are provided by the individual recipient and/or the recipient organization). By definition, the former type represents a very small proportion of fund raising as it is practiced today by charitable organizations.

The book concludes that fund raising predominantly involves a social exchange relationship between a charitable organization and a donor, in which the power of each relative to the other determines the outcome of the exchange. If a charitable organization does not have or does not choose to use inducement resources, alternative sources of gifts, force, or the ability to get along without the gift, it will give up some of its autonomy in exchange for the gift. Therefore, organizations that have strategic resources that can induce a donor (i.e., a donor desires the charitable organization's gratitude, approval, services, or material rewards) will have a lower probability of compliance than those that do not have or choose not to use such resources.

Some organizational autonomy is lost by the very existence of donor relationships, and negotiations between charitable organizations and their donors determine to a large degree how much is exchanged for gifts. As Mintzberg (1983) said, if an organization cannot control, it must negotiate. As fund-raising practitioners are often the actors in the charitable organization's social exchange relationships with donors, fund raisers have to learn the vital skills of negotiation. In addition, fund raisers must be able to negotiate the conflicting positions of charitable organizations and donors, as represented on Mintzberg's (1983) conceptual horseshoe of means of control. Unlike for-profit organizations, four of the positions are not conflicting for charitable organizations and their donor publics; however, three positions are: The charitable organization prefers that donors "ignore it," whereas donors often take the positions of "regulate it," or "pressure it." Underlying these conflicting positions is the professional staff's desire for autonomy and the expectations donors hold of the charitable organization's behavior. Increased calls for regulation of fund raising emphasize the need for charitable organizations and those practitioners who manage its fund-raising function to recognize the importance of negotiations in donor relations for the purpose of preserving and enhancing autonomy.

Grunig (e.g., 1984, in preparation) has developed a theory of public relations grounded in systems theory that defines the contribution of public relations as how well it manages interdependencies between an organization and its various publics. This theory holds that organizations sacrifice some of their autonomy by managing interdependence with groups and organizations in their environment, but by doing so, they reduce the risk of losing even more autonomy. Grunig identified four models of public relations, three of which help organizations adapt to their environment by domination, whereas the two-way symmetric model helps organizations adapt by cooperation. The latter model uses negotiation to enhance and protect organizational autonomy.

Organizations have historically structured their public relations programs to communicate with those strategic publics in their environment that affect or are effected by the organization's behavior. The organization's need to communicate with publics such as employees and stockholders has resulted in public relations programs of employee relations and investor relations. Four linkages between an organization and its environment help define strategic publics: enabling, functional, normative, and diffused. Using these concepts, donors can be defined as an enabling public that provides necessary resources for charitable organizations, much like stockholders provide revenue for corporations. Fund raising, therefore, can be viewed as managing interdependencies between a charitable organization and its donor publics. This function helps a charitable organization adapt to its environment by dominating it or by cooperation. Through negotiations, the fund-raising function can help the organization save autonomy and decrease the risk of abdicating control of the organization to donors.

The concept of institutional autonomy can be defined as _substantive_ in nature (i.e., the power of a college or university to determine its own goals and programs) and _procedural_ (i.e., the power of an institution to determine the means by which its goals and programs will be pursued). Whereas autonomy is a corporate concept that is of necessity parochial and relative, academic freedom is an individual protection that is universal and absolute. Absolute autonomy is neither possible or desirable for colleges and universities because all public and private funding involves some loss, and society extends autonomy to these institutions because it believes that society benefits from such action (i.e., colleges and universities are accountable to society). Therefore, discussion of autonomy must focus on the nature and extent of autonomy required for effective operation of the institution and on the institution's fulfillment of its responsibilities to society.

As stated earlier, fund raising presents a double-edged sword for colleges and universities. The critical question is one of the extent and nature of the limitations which can be imposed on the autonomy of an institution without eroding its effectiveness. Therefore, the book concludes that interdependencies with donors must be managed to avoid the risk of a great loss of autonomy.

Institutional autonomy has its origin in 15th- and 16th-century England where the concept of corporate autonomy was first conceived, but Americans incorporated a responsiveness to societal needs, thus establishing the dualism of autonomy versus accountability. Because of their usefulness to other groups and organizations, colleges and universities have had to negotiate autonomy throughout their histories with the most powerful forces in society (e.g., religious organizations and state and federal government). The selective distribution of federal grants and their documented effect on the institutional autonomy of major research universities provides new insight on external resource dependency. The influx of federal research money to universities after World War II resulted in "multiversities," in which external influence has established dominance of research over teaching, of science over humanities, of graduate studies over undergraduate concerns, and the existence of multitudes of "unfaculty," who work on campuses for federally sponsored projects with no other service required to the university. In short, external funding has created an imbalance and has weakened such research universities to the point where they generally do not control a large portion of their own affairs. Following Altbach and Berdahl (1981), this book concludes that the issue of institutional autonomy is one of constant balancing, in which interdependencies must be continually monitored and adjusted; they cannot be left to happenstance.

Examining historical and current evidence on the three primary sources of private gifts (i.e., foundations, corporations, and individuals), the book concludes that, contrary to conventional wisdom, funding relationships with all three sources share an inherent potential for loss of institutional autonomy. A related and important conclusion is that major gifts from all three sources have the potential, on an individual basis, to infringe on institutional autonomy. This conclusion refutes the literature that characterizes donors, particularly individuals, as a faceless mass that because of their diversity cannot affect autonomy.

Foundations historically have been the subject of criticism for their influence in American higher education. In addition to the vast sums of money they are *required* to give away, foundations are able to influence charitable organizations because of their selectivity, their role as change agents, and their leverage. Their selectivity influences those colleges and universities that receive foundation funding and also affects nonrecipient institutions, as documented by the closing of medical schools through the grants of Rockefeller's General Education Board in the early 1900s. Foundations primarily see their role as change agents who fund innovative programming with restricted, non-continuous grants—a role that often leads colleges and universities in unanticipated directions with financial liabilities during and after the grants are expended. Using leverage, foundations increase the impact of their grants by coercing colleges and universities into raising funds from other donors or into using institutional resources in support of foundation objectives.

As a source of private funds, foundations are a relatively small group that funnel the majority of their education dollars to a small group of universities (e.g., 68% of all foundation dollars reported in CAFE's 1987–1988 survey were received by 183 doctoral universities, or only 16% of the participating institutions). This selective distribution has been clouded by the fact that foundations, like the other two sources of gifts, report their giving in aggregate totals (i.e., although foundation grants represent only 3.7% of total operating budgets of *all* charitable organizations, not all charitable organizations receive foundation grants, but rather colleges and universities are major recipients, and, as documented here, the majority of those dollars go to a small percentage of educational institutions).

Foundations are basically conservative, and although they are criticized for their power to change the behavior of colleges and universities, they are also criticized for their efforts to maintain the status quo. For such critics, the role of change agent is seen as one that represents the foundation's interpretation of the means to protect current society. A point that is often overlooked is that foundations are dependent on universities for hiring staff, carrying out programming objectives, for research, and for program assessment. In addition, foundations can be perceived as being dependent on all charitable organizations resulting from the fact that they are required by law to distribute 5% of the market value of their assets each year.

It can be concluded, therefore, that the motivations of foundation donors can best be understood as neither benevolent nor villainous, but in the context of environmental interdependencies that provide a broad range of economic, social, and political reasons for giving. Within this context, the exchange process involved in soliciting and receiving a gift from a foundation necessitates some loss of institutional autonomy. A second conclusion, therefore, is that major gifts from foundations can, individually, affect the substantive and procedural autonomy of colleges and universities.

Corporate donors operate at the nexus where social responsibility and enlightened self-interest meet. Like foundations, corporations are dependent on institutions of higher education, particularly research universities (i.e, corporations are dependent on universities for employees, research, services to the communities in which they operate, and education's general contributions to the health of the economy and society). Unlike foundations, however, corporations make gifts generally, not because they are required to by law, but because doing so supports their proclaimed "enlightened self-interest," and their role as a socially responsible corporation. That is to say, corporations make gifts both to acquire needed resources, such as technical knowledge and skilled labor, and to increase their autonomy by improving their public standing and the business climate in which they operate. Like foundations, corporations generally prefer to support projects and specific programs (i.e., their gifts are usually restricted in purpose). Following the conclusion that major gifts from foundations can, individually, affect the substantive and procedural autonomy of colleges and universities, this book concludes that major gifts from both foundations and corporations can, individually, affect institutional autonomy. In addition, examples from the literature of colleges creating programs to fit the mold of what they think companies would most like to support and of faculty members shaping research to appeal to foundations leads to the conclusion that gifts from corporations and foundations cannot only infringe on institutional autonomy individually, but also collectively.

Like foundations, corporate donors are a relatively small group (i.e., although there are many organizations in the foundation and corporate worlds, only a few account for the majority of gift dollars). Also like foundations, corporations claim to be a small player in the philanthropic arena, which they support by using aggregate totals that average their contributions over all charitable organizations, when—in fact—there are relatively few recipients of corporate gifts. And like foundations, corporations funnel the majority of their education dollars to a small group of research universities. Whereas higher education received the majority of all foundation dollars before 1970, in the 1990s higher education is the leading recipient of all corporation dollars.

Like foundations, corporations are basically conservative and have been criticized for using gifts to preserve the status quo. Indeed, it can be concluded that, generally, all sources of major gifts are, by nature, conservative (i.e., major donors support the existing societal structure from which they acquired the wealth they give away). Also like foundations, corporations have been criticized for their influence in American higher education. Many argue against the entire concept of social responsibility for corporations, including the giving away of profits to colleges and universities.

Unlike the benevolent corporation as a villain in the Carnegie Committee's (1982) report, this book concludes that the motivations of corporate donors are neither benevolent nor villainous, but that, like foundations, their motivations can best be understood in the context of environmental interdependencies. As such, the relationship between a charitable organization and a corporate donor is one that involves an exchange process through which both organizations strive to protect and enhance their autonomy. Agreeing with Rozell's (1987) three principles, it is concluded that major gifts can negatively affect institutional autonomy to a high degree unless interdependencies with major donors are managed effectively; that clearly articulated policies for both donors and recipient organizations help define terms of exchange relationships, which reduces the risk of external control; and that institutions of higher education need to manage relationships with corporate donors for the purpose of preserving as much autonomy as possible, thereby, protecting academic freedom.

Living individuals are the primary donors to higher education, as they are to all U.S. charities. Like foundations and corporations, educational gifts made by individuals are not distributed equally (i.e., the majority of gift dollars individuals give to colleges and universities go to a small percentage of research univer- sities). Unlike foundations and corporations, individuals generally have not been criticized for influencing the recipients of their gifts; rather, they are commonly viewed as benevolent, disinterested sources of financial support. The founding of Stanford University, however, illustrates how an institution of higher education, dependent on one individual donor and lacking alternative sources of funding, is forced to forfeit virtually all of its autonomy, which, in turn, leads to infringement on academic freedom.

Therefore, like foundations and corporations, individual donors are neither benevolent nor villainous, but also can best be understood as groups in the environment of an institution of higher education with whom they are interdependent. Unlike foundations and corporations, however, the dependencies of individual donors of major gifts _on_ colleges and universities cannot be generalized, but differ from situation to situation (i.e., reciprocal benefits in dependency relationships with individuals cover a broad range of economic, social, and political needs).

Contrary to conventional wisdom, the hundreds or thousands of individuals who contribute to any one charitable organization are not equal in their ability to influence the organization; rather those individuals who can provide mega or ultimate gifts are extremely powerful in their exchange relationships with recipient organizations. There are three factors that explain the increased mega or ultimate gifts made by individuals to higher education: inflation, the fact that colleges and universities are the preferred recipients of gifts from wealthy individuals, and the increasing number and size of capital campaigns. Higher education traditionally attracts gifts from the small percentage of American individuals who control a great deal of the wealth. A conclusion of the book, therefore, is that a failure to differentiate charities with positive externalities, such as colleges and universities, from eleemosynary charities, such as CARE, has led to flawed assumptions in previous studies about individual giving to higher education.

The increasing number and size of capital campaigns by colleges and universities have made these institutions more dependent on a small pool of individuals who can provide the lead gifts necessary to ensure the success of a campaign, regardless of the actions of thousands of lower level donors who provide the bulk of the _number_ of gifts. The increasing number of mega and ultimate gifts and capital campaigns supports the conclusion that institutional autonomy can be affected, individually, by individual donors of major gifts.

Finally, an analysis of three case studies provides evidence of the powerful effects fund raising can have on institutional autonomy, regardless of funding source or type of charity. At this point, three major conclusions of the book can be stated:

1. _All_ sources of donors—foundations, corporations, and individuals—have potential for infringing on the autonomy of charitable organizations through their gifts;

2. *All* types of charitable organizations—even those eleemosynary charities most closely related to altruistic gifts, as demonstrated by the case study of social service organizations—are vulnerable to losing autonomy during the process of raising private gifts; and

3. *All* gifts (i.e., major gifts, individually and collectively, and lower level gifts, collectively, as demonstrated by the chapter on gift sources and by the case study of social service organizations) have potential to affect organizational autonomy negatively.

These findings and conclusions, based on systems theory and the concept of organizational autonomy, provide a strong argument for shifting the public relations paradigm and reorienting fund raising to that scholarly field. The book moves, then, to Part III and the task of reorienting fund raising to public relations.

PART III

SHIFTING THE PUBLIC RELATIONS PARADIGM: APPROACHING FUND RAISING FROM A DIFFERENT PERSPECTIVE

In Part III, the function of fund raising is approached from a public relations perspective, specifically the public relations theory developed by Grunig (e.g., 1976, 1989b, in preparation; Grunig & Grunig, 1989; Grunig & Hunt, 1984). This section of the book addresses the research question: Given that current perspectives are inadequate for a full understanding of the fund-raising behavior of charitable organizations, what other body of knowledge can provide a theoretical framework? Composed of three chapters, Part III opens with chapter 10, which examines the fund raiser in a boundary role of a charitable organization. Chapter 11 compares the functions of fund raising and public relations, arguing that fund raising is a specialization of public relations. Finally, chapter 12 presents an organizational precedent from the for-profit sector, which has placed corporate philanthropy within the public relations function.

The Fund Raiser in a Boundary Role

Following the conclusion of the preceding section that relationships between a charitable organization and its donors can best be understood as environmental interdependencies, this chapter focuses on the fund-raising practitioner in a boundary role between an organization and its environment. This chapter responds to the research question: Within the context of systems theory and autonomy, how can fund raising be reinterpreted on a macrolevel as a public relations function (i.e., as a negotiator of organizational autonomy with strategic donor publics)? This chapter concludes that, contrary to conventional wisdom, the primary purpose of fund raising is not to raise money, but—as for public relations—to enhance and protect organizational autonomy by effectively managing communications between a charitable organization and the donor publics in its environment. Focusing once again on higher education, a second section provides a brief examination of the differences between public and private institutions engaged in fund raising. Chapter 10 concludes that, based on systems theory, 4-year public and nonselective private colleges may be more vulnerable to infringements on autonomy by private donors than other types of institutions.

THE FUND RAISER: A PROTECTOR OF AUTONOMY?

One of the strategies an organization uses to reduce its dependence on the environment, according to Robbins (1987), is to create boundary roles. He described boundary roles as those at the nexus of interaction between an organization and its environment.   Adams (cited in Robbins, 1987) said, "Boundary roles are the linkage or mechanisms that organizations create to relieve the threats of uncertainty posed by dependence" (p. 158). Public relations is among the examples of boundary role functions given by Robbins, who said that organizations read their environment and identify those elements that can influence their success or failure through such positions.

Grunig and Hunt (1984) described the boundary role of public relations as serving the organization with "one foot in the organization and one outside" (p. 9) (i.e., public relations serves on the boundary between an organization and the strategic groups and organizations in its environment).   Grunig and Hunt said, "As boundary personnel, public relations practitioners support other organizational subsystems by helping them communicate across the boundaries of the organization to external publics" (p. 9).   In addition to interpreting the organization to its publics, however, public relations practitioners also interpret the publics to the organization's managers.   Although the former half of the role is generally more familiar (i.e., communicating organizational messages to various audiences), public relations practitioners also engage in techniques such as environmental scanning in order to inform the managers of their organization about issues and publics within the environment that may affect the organization's ability to succeed and survive.

Describing the boundary role position of corporate public relations practitioners, Levy and Oviatt (1989) stated, "PR is by its nature Janus-faced. It serves best when its perceptive vision is trained simultaneously inwardly on the corporation and outwardly on the world" (p. 136). In Organ's (cited in Robbins, 1987) terminology, practitioners in boundary roles handle input acquisition and disposal of output transactions, filter inputs and outputs, search and collect information, represent the organization to the environment, and protect and buffer the organization. Organ said:

> It is through the reports of boundary agents that other organization members acquire their knowledge, perceptions, and evaluations of organization environments. It is through the vigilance of boundary agents that the organization is able to monitor and screen important happenings in the environment. (p. 158)

It should be noted here that not all public relations scholars agree with the concept of the public relations practitioner in an organizational boundary role. Olasky (1987) argued:

> Boundary-spanning hubris has left [public relations practitioners] still removed from the public, but often not part of business either. In the middle ground they have been unsuccessful as spokesman for anyone, but have merely sown confusion about the purpose of corporations. (p. 149)

Regardless of such criticism, public relations as a boundary role of organizations is a central concept in Grunig's public relations theory, which—as discussed in chapter 6—is rooted in systems theory. Grunig and Grunig (1989) explained that "public relations departments deal with the 'public affairs' of an organization—the interdependencies that organizations have with other systems in their external and internal environments" (p. 28). These "other systems" are the organizations and groups in a focal organization's environment referred to in the earlier discussion of systems theory, and we redefine organizations and groups here as publics. According to Grunig and Hunt (1984), these "systems may be other organizations, such as a government agency that regulates a business firm, or they may be 'publics,' groups of people with common interests who are not always organized into a formal organization" (p. 140). A generally accepted concept in public relations is that the mass, or general, public is made up of specific groups with whom an organization needs to communicate. Grunig and Hunt stated, "A 'general public' is a logical impossibility. Publics are always specific; they always have some common problem. Thus, they cannot be general" (p. 138).

Defining these common problems that form publics, Grunig and Hunt (1984) said they are the "consequences that an organization and its publics have on one another" (p. 138). These scholars explained that if an organization and the organizations and publics in its environment did not have consequences on each other, there would be no basis for open-systems theory. They said, "Without consequences, systems would not interpenetrate, and organizations could limit themselves to a closed-system approach to management" (p. 139). As opposed to closed-systems, Grunig and Hunt said, "Organizations are linked to other systems through consequences—either when the organization has consequences on another system, or when another system has consequences on the organization" (p. 140). Explaining that interpenetrating systems may do something that creates conflict with the organization, Grunig and Hunt said, "Determining how consequences link an organization to other systems in its environment, therefore, represents the most central question that public relations practitioners must face" (p. 139)

As described in chapter 6, Grunig and Hunt (1984) used Esman's four types of linkages that are critical to the survival of an organization to explain why organizations have traditionally created certain public relations programs, or specializations. Explaining that they are "the most frequent linkages organizations have with other systems," Grunig and Hunt said, "These linkages identify likely groups of publics that have mutual consequences with the organization" (p. 139).

These linkages to strategic publics or organizations are:

1. enabling linkages to those publics, such as stockholders, who provide the authority and control the resources that enable an organization to exist;
2. functional linkages to those internal and external publics, such as employees and customers, who provide inputs and take outputs and who are critical to an organization's ability to function;
3. normative linkages to those organizations that face similar problems or share similar views with the focal organization; and
4. diffused linkages to publics, such as community activists, who may form around single issues resulting from the consequences of the organization's behavior on them.

Grunig and Hunt (1984) said the concept of linkages is useful for determining "the interpenetrating systems most likely to upset an organization's equilibrium" (p. 140). These scholars explained that organizations and publics that interpenetrate the boundary of a focal organization may create conflict and that each time an interpenetrating system upsets the equilibrium, the organization tries to restore it. They stated, "To resolve the conflict, the organization generally will have to negotiate and compromise with the interpenetrating system, and frequently change its behavior" (p. 139). Pointing out that organizational theorists hold that organizations make contact with linked organizations and publics through boundary personnel, Grunig and Hunt emphasized that public relations programs primarily serve as linkages with publics.

It is the contention of this book that fund raisers, like public relations practitioners, serve in a boundary role for their charitable organizations. Some examples of organizations and publics that are linked through consequences to a charitable organization as described by Grunig and Hunt (1984) are the trustees on its board who are an enabling public, users of its services who are a functional public of an output nature, charitable organizations with similar missions who are a normative public, and protesters who represent a diffused public.

Based on Grunig and Hunt's concept of linkages to interpenetrating systems in an organization's environment, as presented here and in chapter 6, this book holds that donor relations describes the management of communication between a charitable organization and its donor publics, much the same way that investor relations describes the public relations programs that are targeted to investors of publicly owned, for-profit organizations. As such organizations are to varying degrees dependent on sources of private support that *enable* them to exist, fund raisers manage the linkage to donors in their charitable organization's environment in order to relieve threats of uncertainty about the ongoing flow of gifts.

There is some evidence in the fund-raising literature that supports this approach to the fund raiser as an interpreter of the organization in a boundary role, who manages relationships through a process of social exchange. Describing the fund raiser as a strong right arm to the academic dean and the president in academic planning, Cramer (cited in Pray, 1981) said, "As the chief external 'interpreter' of the institution, the development officer has a great deal to contribute to this area" (p. 352). Pray (1981) described fund raising as a boundary role when he said, "To be a part of the line of contact between the institution and the better impulses of humanity outside is a privilege we share with relatively few others" (p. 403). Describing fund raising within the context of social and power exchange theory, Pray stated:

> It is part of a complicated and subtle process of brokerage and exchange of value. If the values are not present for exchange, the institution will not long survive, no matter how good the techniques; and if they are, those who assist in the exchange will help guarantee its survival without compromising quality. (p. 401)

Finally, Brittingham and Pezzullo (1990) said, "Decisions that institutions make about what private support to pursue or accept help define their mission and *boundaries*" (p. 83; italics added). Emphasizing that gifts can influence colleges and universities in significant ways, these scholars said that fund raisers help redefine the relationships between institutions and external donors by the kinds of gifts they solicit and the way they solicit them.

Although numerous members of a charitable organization may be involved in fund-raising activities (e.g., the chief executive officer), it is the specialist who manages the organization's fund-raising function who is expected to ensure a continuing income of contributions (i.e., fund raisers reduce the environmental uncertainty of private support). In addition, this discussion points out that boundary roles protect and buffer an organization from its environmental dependencies. Describing the philanthropic arena of donors and fund raisers, Payton (1987) said, "To practice philanthropy is to engage in a constant struggle with the claims of self-interest" (p. 277). Thus, the practitioners who manage fund-raising programs on behalf of charitable organizations can be properly described as serving in a boundary role through which they reduce environmental uncertainly of private support by managing interdependencies with donors and by buffering the organization against claims of self-interest.

This boundary role is critical to understanding the fund-raising practitioner's pivotal position in determining the amount of organizational autonomy lost or gained through the solicitation and acceptance of gifts. As Dressel (1980) said, "Inevitably, there will be times at which those involved in the continuing interaction and negotiation between the university and the public or its agencies will differ as to the measure of institutional autonomy that should be awarded the university and as to the nature, character, and source of appropriate constraints which may be placed upon the institution or its faculties" (p. ix).

Following this train of thought that the degree of autonomy lost or gained through an exchange process such as fund raising is determined by "those involved in the continuing interaction and negotiation," it is helpful at this point to summarize some of the characteristics of fund-raising practitioners discussed in earlier chapters of this book. It is recalled, for example, that fund raising, as an internalized function managed by practitioners, is relatively new in charitable organizations, particularly institutions of higher education and nonprofit hospitals. A serious implication of fund raising evolving from a responsibility of chief executive officers and trustees to specialists is that this revenue-generating function moved out of the control of senior policymakers and the managers of overall financial resources in the early 1950s and into the hands of lay administrators. In addition, the economic climate for charitable organizations has changed dramatically since fund raising first became internalized (i.e., fund raising became an organizational function during an era of growth, expansion, and unprecedented governmental support for charitable organizations, but today these same organizations are operating in the post-Reagan era of reduced governmental support and limited resources).

It is also recalled from chapter 2 that fund raisers are generally young and often new to their vocation, with more than half of the fund-raising practitioners belonging to the National Society of Fund Raising Executives and to the Council for Advancement and Support of Education being under 45 years old. As Carbone (1987) said, "Given the difficulty in funding positions for new fund raisers, many of the people attracted to these positions are young and sometimes inexperienced workers" (p. 4). In addition to their youth and sometimes lack of experience, fund raisers are acquiring a reputation as transients, with directors of annual or planned giving having a turnover rate of 58% and chief development officers changing jobs at a rate of 30% in colleges and universities ("24-pct. turnover," 1989). The chancellor of the University of California, Berkeley described fund raisers as "high-level migrant workers. . . . [who] have more allegiance to doing their job than to their university of the moment" ("'Misunderstandings,'" 1987, p. 20).

Commanding salaries often in six figures, these fund raisers are intensely sought, but as Schwartz (cited in "At $79,300 average salary," 1986) stated,

"Today, far too many people are being given major responsibility for programs that they simply are not qualified to direct" (p. 25). In short, fund raising is a growing field, and those administrators responsible for raising private dollars for charitable organizations are highly paid, in great demand, change jobs frequently, are young, and often are new to the field of fund raising. These characteristics and the concept of fund raising as a boundary role discussed earlier raises questions about the fund-raising practitioner's ability to protect and enhance organizational autonomy in the social exchange process involving the solicitation and acceptance of private funds. Or as Payton (1987) said, "The emergence of new 'professionals' in the roles of *almoner* and mendicant raises new questions about how philanthropic policy is formulated, and whose values it reflects" (p. 42).

Focusing on colleges and universities, a common theme in the fund-raising literature is that fund-raising practitioners are isolated from the academic core; that they neither appreciate nor understand the academic values of these complex institutions. Pray (1981) said, "Some development officers are unable to identify intellectually or socially with senior faculty" (p. 142). Emphasizing the need for fund raisers to be a part of the "central fabric of the institution," Johnson (cited in Pray, 1981) said, "The more a development officer can be like a member of the faculty and have the empathy, sensitivity, and understanding to establish strong rapport with deans and other academic officers, the more likely it is that he or she will function effectively" (p. 352). Reflecting on the fact that a phenomenal 84% of the respondents in his study of fund raisers in academe had served less than six years in their current position, Carbone (1987) asserted that such high career mobility does not bode well for institutions of higher education and that the acceptance or rejection of prevailing academic values has an impact on this less-than-desirable turnover rate.

Sensing the potential danger of lay administrators who have little identification with the overall mission of the institution, some fund-raising practitioners and scholars believe that an internalization of prevailing values is badly needed. Carbone (1987), for example, recommended that fund raisers involve themselves more in campus life and "soak up more of the academic values" (p. 18). Advancing the idea that fund raisers need terminal degrees to serve effectively as officers of colleges and universities, Frick (1981), who has a PhD, said that these specialists must become educators who have a substantial knowledge of higher education apart from their vocational expertise and who also teach. Concurring, Pray (1981) said, "One way, of course, is to continue education, become knowledgeable in some field of scholarship at a level of competence equal at least to the minimum expected of an instructor . . . and be able to discuss intelligently with faculty the problems of the institution in a manner demonstrating a real grasp of the complexities and problems of education" (p. 142). Pray concluded by saying, "It is not just a nice thing to do—it is an essential" (p. 142).

Describing the essential qualities of the development officer, Payton (1981) stated, "The university exists for teaching and research, and it needs money to pursue those ends. Fund raising is not an end in itself; other priorities come first" (p. 282). As discussed in chapter 2, Etzioni (1964/1986) defined lay administrators, such as fund raisers, as those "who have no training in serving the major goal activities of the organization" (p. 35). He said that the strain created by these specialists in professional organizations leads to displacement of goals. As is discussed in chapter 14, the success of fund raising is currently measured by the amount of money raised. In other words, those serving in boundary roles between their charitable organization and its donor publics manage their programs not by what gifts contribute to the organization's primary goals, but by dollar totals. The means, therefore, are more likely to displace the intended ends.

"Balancing institutional pressures toward improving the bottom line in fund raising with issues of matching fund raising with institutional priorities" (p. 73), according to Brittingham and Pezzullo (1990), is one of the major dilemmas facing fund raisers. Finally, Payton (1981) said, "Those who best understand how to advance the economic purposes of the university and to *protect its academic integrity* while doing so will emerge as the true development officers of the future" (p. 284; italics added).

From this discussion, we can conclude that there is a clear and present danger that exists in current situations in which the fund raiser as a boundary role manager interacts and negotiates with donor publics to determine the constraints placed on a charitable organization by the solicitation and acceptance of gifts. In Grunig and Hunt's (1984) terms, donors represent an interpenetrating system that may create conflict for charitable organizations, but the managers of the organization's linkage to this enabling public generally operate (or are forced to operate) in a manner that ignores the consequences that the behavior of donors can have on the charitable organization and its primary goals. In addition, current perspectives of fund raising do not openly acknowledge that charitable organizations must negotiate and compromise with the interpenetrating system and, as a result, must frequently change their behavior in response to conflicts created by donors. Grunig (in preparation) stated:

> Conflict occurs when publics move in a different direction from that of the organization, resulting in friction or collisions. Conflict could also occur when a

potentially supportive public has not been motivated to move with the organization and, in a sense, "drags its feet" when it could accelerate the movement of the organization toward achieving its goals.

It should be noted at this point that Grunig's (Grunig & Grunig, 1989) theory does not assume that conflict is necessarily bad for an organization. As described in the earlier chapter on institutional autonomy, charitable organizations, such as colleges and universities, are accountable to the society they serve. When there has been conflict in the past between the behavior of such organizations and the behavior expected by external sources of gifts, donors have frequently used their gifts to bring about change within such institutions. As Grunig and Grunig said, "Conflict, therefore, can be good for an organization because it stimulates change" (p. 58). However, Grunig's theory holds that organizations still must manage such conflicts in order to preserve as much autonomy as possible, and recommends a symmetrical approach to conflict management, which is discussed later in Part IV.

Given the concept of the boundary role practiced by fund raisers, this book follows Grunig's (in preparation) theory and advances a new approach to fund raising as donor relations. Pray (1981) also perceived a need to approach fund raising from a different perspective. He said, "We may now need an expanded conceptual framework within which to develop the larger parameters of programs now required" (p. 389). Unfortunately, Pray recommended combining administrative affairs, or the business function of charitable organizations, with fund raising, saying, "Synergistic gains can be realized by relating financial and business management with fund raising in a unified systems approach that employs new kinds of management organization and operations" (p. 390). This book contends that such a "Total Resource Advancement" approach to fund raising would further blur the lines between philanthropic relationships and market exchanges, which could, in turn, result in loss of the charitable deduction for gifts on federal income taxes and the tax-exempt status of charitable organizations. Instead of a "business approach," this book turns to the public relations paradigm for a new perspective of fund raising.

Grunig (in preparation) said that "managed interdependence is the major characteristic of successful organizations." Organizations, he said, are effective when they attain their goals. "However," Grunig stated, "goals must be appropriate for the organization's environment, or strategic publics within that environment will constrain the autonomy of the organization to meet its goals." Describing them as stakeholders, Grunig said that strategic publics are those "that threaten or enhance the autonomy of the organization to pursue its goals." He defined excellent public relations departments as those that manage communication with these strategic publics. These statements, drawn from a theory of public relations, summarize the traditional tension between the dual concepts of the autonomy and accountability of charitable organizations, particularly colleges and universities (i.e., the autonomy to pursue internally defined goals leads to effectiveness, but goals that are incongruent with those of strategic publics will lead to environmental constraints).

It is necessary here to briefly discuss Grunig's theory of publics (e.g., 1976, 1989b, 1989c; Grunig & Hunt, 1984). According to Grunig (1989c), publics are formed around issues, as opposed to market segments for which products are created. Historically, publics have been confused with markets and audiences, and public relations practitioners have primarily utilized demographics and cross-situational attitudes to identify publics. Grunig (Grunig & Hunt, 1984) used sociologist Herbert Blumer's and philosopher John Dewey's definitions of publics as those forming around issues to build a situational theory of publics. According to Grunig and Hunt, "Dewey's and Blumer's definitions of publics . . . suggest that publics consist of individuals who detect the same problems and plan similar behaviors to deal with those problems" (p. 144). As Grunig (1989b) summarized:

> The situational theory of publics begins with the assumption that publics form around specific situations or issues produced by the consequences that organizations have on people outside the organization. The theory explains when and how people communicate about these situations and what effect communications about the situations might have. (p. 5)

Grunig's (1989b, 1989c; Grunig & Hunt, 1984) basic theory utilized three independent variables: problem recognition, constraints, and level of involvement. The extent to which a person sees a problem in an issue or situation and the level of constraints he or she perceives in his or her ability to do something about the problem produces a four-cell matrix of communication behaviors: problem facing (i.e., high problem recognition and low constraints), constrained, fatalistic, and routine. These behaviors, when related to level of involvement, produce eight publics and their probability of communicating (e.g., low involvement, low problem recognition, and high constraints would identify a public that would only process information and would be an unlikely receiver for communication). In early research, Grunig used the eight combinations to define nonpublics, latent publics, aware publics, and active publics who are or are not likely to communicate about a particular issue or situation. In recent research, Grunig used canonical correlation to identify those publics with a high probability of active communication behavior on a set of situational issues included in each study. In summary, although linkages help identify types of stakeholders for an organization, Grunig's theory of publics helps identify which of those stakeholders differ in the extent to which they become active in doing something about a consequence of an organization.

As demonstrated in the preceding chapters, donors generally are considered to be strategic publics of most charitable organizations, and it is argued here that communication with this public should be managed by the public relations department that aspires to excellence. Grunig's (in preparation) normative theory of how a public relations department *should* manage communication specifies that in order to practice public relations strategically, an organization "develops programs to communicate with the publics, both external and internal, that provide the greatest threats to and opportunities for the organization." Yet, as also demonstrated in earlier chapters, communication with donor publics is rarely the responsibility of public relations departments in charitable organizations. For example, it is recalled that the consulting firm of Gonser Gerber Tinker Stuhr (1986) advised, "Public relations should be a functional part of the development department," and recommended that the "public relations director should be part of the development team and report to the chief development officer" (p. 2).

Such advice on organizational structure, which is inverse to Grunig's (in preparation) theory, has been followed at many charitable organizations (i.e, in many charitable organizations, public relations is a subfunction of fund raising; Kelly, 1989b). In addition, Grunig (as is true of other scholars) rarely refers to donors when discussing the strategic management of public relations. Yet, Grunig recommended an "integrated" public relations department that is responsible for communicating with all strategic publics that may limit or enhance organizational autonomy, saying that such an operational system is characteristic of effective organizations. Grunig said, "Only in an integrated department is it possible for public relations to be managed strategically." Saying that public relations functions should not be subordinated under other departments, Grunig advised, "Develop dynamic horizontal structures within the department, to make it possible to reassign people and resources to new programs as new strategic publics are identified and other publics cease to be strategic."

The horizontal structure recommended by Grunig (in preparation) provides a second important argument for redefining fund raising as a public relations specialization of donor relations. As Grunig pointed out, strategic publics are not a constant; at times some publics are more important to an organization than others and vice versa (i.e., strategic publics change with their ability to affect organizational autonomy). As Grunig said, "Organizations plan public relations programs strategically, therefore, when they identify the publics that are most likely to limit or enhance their autonomy and design communication programs that help the organization manage its interdependence with these strategic publics." The identification of strategic publics is the second step in a five-step process outlined by Grunig for the strategic management of public relations, which is discussed more fully in chapter 11. Keeping in mind that publics form around issues, the first two steps in Grunig's process are for public relations managers to identify issues that are important to the organization, and then to segment those publics that respond differently to those issues.

It is important here to emphasize that environments are not objective reality for the managers of organizations; instead, Grunig (in preparation) said that "managers choose, subjectively, to observe only parts of their environment." Grunig continued by saying, "The parts they choose to observe are products of their mindset and organizational culture." Also, Grunig and Grunig (1989) stated the following:

> As Kuhn (1979) points out, the organization only can respond to the parts of the environment of which it is aware. Public relations departments, therefore, contribute to organizational success through systematic monitoring of relevant external constituencies, those that can affect or are affected by the organization. (p. 29)

Summarizing this point, the specific environment of organizations (Robbins, 1987), including charitable organizations, is a product of managerial choice and the effectiveness of public relations departments in bringing strategic publics to the attention of those managers.

It must also be emphasized that public relations, as defined by Grunig (Grunig & Hunt, 1984), assumes responsibility for all the publics in an organization's specific environment. Explaining that marketing departments use communication to develop and dispose of products, Grunig and Grunig (1989) said, "Whereas marketing communicators deal only with the consumer public, public relations practitioners deal with all other publics that affect or are affected by an organization" (p. 28). Although Grunig's differentiation between marketing and public relations works well in explaining the public relations behavior of for-profit organizations, it blurs somewhat when applied to charitable organizations. For example, although prospective students can be defined as the consumer public of colleges and universities and can be appropriately assigned to the marketing function handled by the admissions office (i.e., admissions communicators deal only with the consumer public), once students enroll they become members of an important internal public that generally is assigned to the public relations department. A similar situation occurs with other types of charitable organizations, such as churches, which recruit users of their services who then become members, who—in turn—represent a strategic internal public. This would not be the case, however, for other types of charitable organizations, such as nonprofit hospitals. Therefore, we can conclude that the marketing function in charitable organizations deals with the consumers and/or the _prospective_ consumers of those organizations' products and services, whereas the public relations function is concerned with all other environmental publics, including, in some cases, current consumers.

Also unlike for-profit organizations, charitable organizations generally have a fund-raising function that deals only with their donor publics, whereas public relations practitioners deal with all other publics that affect or are affected by the charitable organization (e.g., legislators, nondonor alumni, community residents, and employees). As stated earlier in this chapter, many charitable organizations have subsumed the public relations function under fund raising. A study of members of the Public Relations Society of America (PRSA) who work for educational and cultural organizations found that in 40% of the organizations the fund-raising function was dominant over the public relations function; in 42% the two functions were perceived as equal; and in only 19% of the organizations fund raising was subordinate to public relations (Kelly, 1989b).

Given the discussion about Grunig's (in preparation) advice to develop dynamic horizontal structures for public relations departments, we can conclude that the first two types of structures in the PRSA study can lead to a lack of attention to strategic publics that may constrain or enhance the autonomy of charitable organizations. In other words, if fund raising is _not_ integrated into the public relations function of a charitable organization, a concentration of attention and resources on donor publics may cause the managers of that organization to ignore other key publics that form around an issue and create conflict. In the PRSA study (Kelly, 1989a), a director of public relations for a California college of design pointed out that "there are publics that the fund raisers neglect and I need to make that my priority" (p. 35). Unfortunately, that same respondent predicted that in the future, public relations departments will be expanded "to support the fund-raising department," (p. 35).

Focusing on higher education, there is an apparent danger in the current trend to hire fund raisers to head the institutional advancement function at colleges and universities (i.e., fund raisers generally concentrate on donor publics without the training to recognize and establish relationships with other strategic publics that are crucial to the success and even survival of their organizations). In illustration, less than 1 year before nationally known, basketball star Len Bias died of a drug overdose in June 1986, a fund raiser replaced Patrick J. Hunt, a public relations practitioner skilled in media relations and strategic management, as the head of institutional advancement for the University of Maryland at College Park. Although private support had become increasingly important to Maryland, the national front-page crisis dramatically proved that relationships with other publics could be just as, if not more, important to the success of that institution.

According to one source, the Bias tragedy was on the front page of *The Washington Post* and/or its sports section longer than the Watergate scandal. The 5,000 employees of the university received all their information from the mass media, and the first time any of Maryland's 37,000 students had an opportunity to communicate with the chief executive officer of the campus was on Ted Koppel's "Nightline," during which students vented their anger, confusion, and frustration on national television—further damaging the reputation of the university and its managers. The consensus of many public relations professionals who followed the crisis was that a hard-working public information staff was no substitute for a senior public relations manager when it came to crisis situations.

On a more general note, higher education witnessed students becoming activist groups that threatened the very survival of many institutions in the late 1960s. Given increased reports today of racial violence on campus, skyrocketing tuition, and an "uncaring" environment for undergraduate students at research universities, it is likely that students are once again a strategic public for many colleges and universities. Yet, it is hypothesized here that few of those institutions that have an institutional advancement function headed by a fund raiser, or those that have separate departments for fund raising and public relations, have identified students as a strategic public and have created communication programs to maintain relationships with this potentially antagonistic public.

Supporting this argument, Brittingham and Pezzullo (1990) said that many colleges and universities today may be reluctant to deal openly with student problems, such as "racial and ethnic intolerance," because they fear that even acknowledging that such problems exit on their campuses will bring a withdrawal of alumni support. According to these scholars, "Institutions might feel subtle or overt pressure in the name of donor relations to mute their discussion of difficult issues" (p. 68). In other words, when fund raising is not under public relations, the public relations function is unable to circumvent a focus on donors that prevents charitable organizations from responding to other strategic publics as they emerge. If ignored, such nondonor publics may seriously affect the organizations' success, perhaps at a greater cost than decreased alumni support.

On a lighter, but illuminating note, a public relations colleague at a public university in the Northeast recently described an experience with his new vice president for institutional advancement, who is a fund raiser. The public relations practitioner arranged to have the vice president seated next to the chairman of the state's senate budget committee—which oversees the university's annual budget—at an important dinner with university representatives, key legislators, and major donors. At the conclusion of the dinner, the fund-raising manager warned his public relations employee that at future events, he wanted to be seated next to "someone who was important."

It is recalled that public relations, as a boundary role, contributes to organizational effectiveness by monitoring the environment and bringing emerging issues and strategic publics to the attention of the organization's managers. Fund raising, as a subsuming or separate function of public relations, interferes with this critical role by de-emphasizing or ignoring environmental interdependencies other than those with donors, which leaves a charitable organization vulnerable to external control. As Grunig (in preparation) stated, "If organizations choose the most appropriate public relations strategy for communication with strategic publics, then that strategy will *help the organization to manage critical environmental interdependencies* and make the organization more effective."

In summary, public relations is a boundary role that helps an organization manage environmental interdependencies, thereby, reducing environmental uncertainty and buffering the organization from demands of interpenetrating systems. If interpenetrating systems move in directions other than that of the focal organization, conflict occurs and negotiation and compromise must take place. Such conflict may cause the organization to change; however, even if the change is positive, the organization still must manage the conflict to reduce the risk of losing a high degree of autonomy.

Like public relations, fund raising is a boundary role of charitable organizations, responsible for helping these organizations manage their interdependencies with donor publics. As such, fund-raising practitioners are responsible for the continuing interaction and negotiation with donors that determine the degree of autonomy lost or gained through the solicitation and acceptance of gifts. Given the fact that fund raisers are lay administrators who are highly paid, in great demand, change jobs frequently, are generally young, and are often inexperienced, there is some doubt as to their ability to protect the central mission of a charitable organization through the fund-raising process. As discussed in chapters 5 and 6, these charitable organizations and their fund-raising practitioners rarely view the solicitation and acceptance of gifts as environmental interdependencies with all their related implications. In short, fund raising as currently practiced can increase the vulnerability of a charitable organization to external control.

In addition, fund raising contributes to the vulnerability of charitable organizations because it causes such organizations to de-emphasize or ignore strategic publics other than donors that may threaten or enhance the organization's autonomy. Grunig's (e.g, 1988, 1989b, in preparation; Grunig & Grunig, 1989; Grunig & Hunt, 1984) theory holds that public relations helps an organization manage environmental interdependencies with all its publics, whereas marketing is concerned only with consumer publics. Public relations contributes to organizational effectiveness by identifying strategic publics in the organization's environment that affect or are affected by the behavior of the organization as it relates to strategic issues. Grunig said that excellent public relations departments (i.e., those that will help organizations achieve their goals) are structured horizontally so that an organization can reallocate staff and resources as strategic publics change. Fund raising, with its one-dimensional focus on donor publics, supports managers in subjectively choosing an environment that may exclude strategic publics that have the power to infringe on organizational autonomy. Those charitable organizations that have subsumed public relations under fund raising, or have created separate departments for the two functions, have added further to their vulnerability by emphasizing donor publics over other strategic publics even in situations in which such an emphasis is inappropriate and dangerous.

In relation to both points, Pfeffer and Salancik (1978) warned that when an organization does not recognize or ignores environmental interdependencies, the organization is vulnerable to external control (i.e., charitable organizations that do not recognize fund raising as an interdependency with donors or that ignore other environmental interdependencies, such as relationships with community residents, in favor of donor relations risk losing high degrees of their autonomy). Therefore, this section concludes that, on a macrolevel, fund raising can and should be explained as a part of the public relations function of charitable organizations and that such a perspective helps to protect and enhance the autonomy of these organizations.

This section further concludes that, contrary to conventional wisdom, the primary purpose of fund raising is not to raise money, but—as a part of public relations—to enhance and protect organizational autonomy by effectively managing communications between a charitable organization and the donor publics in its environment.

The following chapter on fund raising as a specialization of public relations adds to the arguments presented here. Before continuing, however, chapter 10 concludes with a brief examination of differences related to the fund-raising function at public and private institutions of higher education.

FUND RAISING AT PUBLIC AND PRIVATE INSTITUTIONS

It may be argued that the recognition of fund raising as a boundary role that helps charitable organizations manage donor interdependencies varies among such organizations, including colleges and universities. Tolbert (1985/1986) used the resource dependence perspective of Pfeffer and Salancik (1978) to study organizational behavior differences in the fund-raising function at public and private universities. The central concept of her study was the institutionalization of fund raising and government relations (i.e., how socially accepted and defined these functions are within the organization). She stated, "A central premise of this approach is that dependence relationships can, over time, become socially defined as appropriate and legitimate" (p. 328).

According to Blau (1986), institutionalization (i.e., establishing formal procedures that preserve and rigidify patterns of social conduct and relations) perpetuates the legitimate order and the social values that sustain an organization through time. Therefore, the institutionalization of the fund-raising function can be viewed as a protection against loss of autonomy because relations with donors are less affected by individual practitioners when there is a high degree of institutionalization. In addition, the institutionalization of this internal function would indicate that fund raising is recognized as a boundary role that helps a charitable organization manage interdependencies with donors.

Applying a theory of organizational behavior to fund raising at public universities, Hedgepeth (1989) said that public universities are "mature" organizations, but that "the fund-raising organizations themselves are in the 'infant' or 'emerging' stages" (p. 16). Stating that "mature organizations resist new ways of behaving," Hedgepeth said that public universities "often see fundraising as an element outside normal operations, and often see new behavior, styles and values as intrusive or even hostile" (pp. 16, 18). "As a result," he said, "the institutional ownership necessary for resolving conflict and agreeing on action needs is often sadly lacking" (p. 18). In other words, it can be hypothesized that public universities do not recognize fund raising as a boundary role and that ownership of the fund-raising function in relation to managing environmental interdependencies is lacking. This, in turn, would lead to greater vulnerability in relation to external control.

According to Tolbert (1985/1986), the resource dependence approach holds that administrative structure (i.e., the number of fund-raising practitioners at different types of colleges and universities) reflects efforts to ensure a stable flow of resources and to manage problems and uncertainties associated with exchange transactions. Tolbert said that in the institutionalization approach advanced by

Zucker (cited in Tolbert, 1985/1986) the environment is conceptualized in terms of understandings and expectations of appropriate organizational form and behavior that are shared by members of society. Pressure is brought to bear when organizational behavior is perceived as deviating from the normative understandings. When behavior is out of balance with norms, institutional legitimacy and survival may be threatened.

Tolbert said that in dependency relations that are not institutionalized, the number of administrative offices and positions associated with the management of the relations is likely to grow in relation to the magnitude of the dependency. She said, "Thus, the institutionalization of dependency relations determines whether or not increasing dependence will directly affect the proliferation of formal administrative offices within organizations" (p. 329). Noting that approximately 10% of the income of private institutions comes from gifts, whereas only 2% of the income of public institutions is derived from gifts, Tolbert hypothesized that fund raising is institutionalized at private colleges and universities and governmental relations at their public counterparts.

Using national data that included sources of revenues and administrative offices and positions, Tolbert drew a sample of all institutions classified by the Carnegie Commission as either "doctoral" or as "comprehensive" universities, which were stratified by public and private control. Based on the two dependent variables, number of public-funding offices and number of private-funding offices, Tolbert found that dependence on government appropriations for private universities was significantly related to differentiation, and dependence on private support was a strong predictor of differentiation for public universities. Therefore, she concluded, "As expected, dependence on public or private sources of funding predicts the proliferation of administrative offices only when the dependencies are not aligned with traditional patterns" (p. 337).

Tolbert's (1985/1986) findings provide evidence that fund raising is not institutionalized at public doctoral and comprehensive universities, whereas it is at private universities. These findings suggest that public institutions may be less likely to recognize the boundary role played by fund raising, and, thereby, be more susceptible to infringements on autonomy by donors.

However, Tolbert's study contains a number of questionable indicators that raise doubts about the validity of her conclusions. For example, indicators for institutionalization of fund raising included the position of director of admissions in offices managing private funding, but did not include decentralized, component fund raisers, such as those discussed in chapter 6. The three positions Tolbert measured to determine the institutionalization of public funding were chief planning officer, director of information, and director of institutional research, but not vice presidents or directors of government affairs. In addition, the dependency on public funding was measured as the proportion of total revenues accounted for by government appropriations, grants, and contracts, whereas the dependency on gifts was measured as the proportion accounted for by contributions and *self-generated funds, including tuition, fees, and endowment income.* Yet the author shows in a comparative chart of revenue percentage that in the latest year available, 1973–1974, federal government grants and contracts accounted for *an equal percentage* of revenue for both public and private universities, and that for the private institutions, government grants represented a *higher* percentage of total revenues (i.e., dependency as measured by Tolbert) than private gifts (11% vs. 9.5%).

As a result of these flaws, this book does not accept Tolbert's (1985/1986) conclusions in whole, but turns now to a brief examination of the funding differences between private and public institutions of higher education. This review provides insight into the vulnerability of different types of colleges and universities that are dependent on external sources of gifts.

It is recalled that Pfeffer and Salancik's (1978) resource dependence perspective explains that the charitable organizations most vulnerable to donor interdependencies are those that do not or can not adopt four strategies to avoid external control: (a) building an inventory of the resource (i.e., an endowment); (b) possessing formal and informal norms that prescribe the behavior of the exchange process; (c) creating alternative sources for the resource (i.e., a broad base of donors); and (d) diversifying funding (e.g., user fees, government funding, and gifts).

Kerr and Gade (1981) explained that tuition and fees at private colleges and universities have provided about 50% of their total income for the past 50 years and private gifts have remained steady at about 15% of income, but funds generated by endowments have drastically fallen "from almost one-third of private institutional income in 1930 to less than 10 percent in the late 1970s" (pp. 122-123). Based on the discussion in chapter 5, it can be assumed that the remaining 25% of total income for "private" institutions comes from government sources.

Those private colleges that traditionally attract small enrollments cannot raise tuition and fees high enough to replace lost income from endowments without suffering a disabling loss in enrollment. Efforts to increase annual private giving do not seem to be a promising solution either, given the 50-year plateau of gifts accounting for 15% of income. Finally, although private institutions can manage their endowment to provide maximum return, the very nature of an endowment (i.e., the income from which is to be used in perpetuity) coupled with lack of control over the economy demands that a conservative approach be taken to management of an endowment.

Efforts to replace the loss of endowment income, therefore, would seem to lead to two alternative sources of funding. The first is to seek increased government funding, which carries a relatively high potential for loss of autonomy. According to Kerr and Gade (1981), the increased public financing that private colleges and universities have already received, along with the dramatic growth in enrollment of the public sector, has led to a corresponding public concern with coordinating and planning for higher education, which has resulted in more intrusion by government. Kerr and Gade reported, "In 1980, only one state lacked a mechanism for coordination of all higher education within the state, including the private sector; forty years earlier, only one state had such a mechanism" (p. 120).

The second alternative to replace loss of endowment income is to increase fund-raising efforts in the area of major endowed gifts (i.e., focusing on the cultivation and solicitation of those foundations, corporations, and individuals capable of providing endowed gifts of $100,000 or more). Such a strategy, it can be presumed, has led many private colleges into capital campaigns in order to build their endowments.

These capital campaigns, as discussed in chapters 2, 5, and 8, are dependent on a small percentage of donors. It is exactly this type of situation (i.e., not enough endowment income, a dependence on major donors, an absence of viable alternative sources of resources, and an urgent financial need) that is described by Pfeffer and Salancik (1978) as characteristics of vulnerability that can lead to loss of organizational control.

In other words, private 2- and 4-year colleges with small student enrollments and small endowments are positioned poorly to protect institutional autonomy as it relates to sources of private support. Their need for major gifts creates an imbalance in power between the institution and those few foundations, corporations, and individuals that have the resources to provide large dollar amounts and also want to be affiliated with the institution.

As a result of the cost squeeze that is being experienced by many private institutions, it can be concluded that private colleges and universities will increasingly turn to major donors for needed resources and/or to government. Either situation may, in turn, lead to external control by funding sources. As Kerr and Gade (1981) predicted, "The private research, comprehensive, and highly selective liberal arts colleges appear highly resilient, but, while they are less vulnerable than the 2-year institutions and the less selective liberal arts colleges, they, too, will encounter difficulties" (p. 122).

As described earlier, public and private research universities, which represent less than 6% of all institutions of higher education, receive about two thirds of all gift dollars ("Gifts to colleges off," 1989). It also is recalled that these same institutions receive the majority of federal research funds. It can be concluded, therefore, that such institutions (i.e., those educational institutions that have the most complex missions and that usually are among the largest of institutions) are less vulnerable than other colleges and universities in interdependent relationships with donors. Mintzberg (1983) said, "It is the big university that can best confront the big government that finances it" (p. 277). It may also be said that it is the big university that can best confront major donors who help finance it. According to Pfeffer and Salancik (1978), "Organizations that are large have more power and leverage over their environments. They are more able to resist immediate pressures for change, and, moreover, have more time in which to recognize external threats and adapt to meet them" (p. 139).

As described in chapter 14, researchers who have attempted to measure the effectiveness of fund raising consistently have found that institutional wealth and size are related to what they define as fund-raising success. It is the conclusion of this book that systems theory helps explain this phenomenon, but that such studies should change their one-dimensional focus of measuring dollar amounts to incorporate measurements on the degree of autonomy enhanced or lost through the fund-raising process.

Concluding this brief examination of one subcategory of charitable organizations, it can be stated that private institutions of higher education are generally more vulnerable to external control through interdependencies with donors than are public institutions, but that large and wealthy public and private research universities are least vulnerable. It can be added here that public colleges facing financial constraints similar to those faced by nonselective, 2- and 4-year private institutions may also be vulnerable to donor control. As pointed out in chapter 6, however, extremely few community colleges (2-year public institutions) have active fund-raising programs, but rather are dependent on government funding. Therefore, 4-year public colleges and 2- and 4-year nonselective, private colleges may be the most vulnerable to compliance in the solicitation and acceptance of gifts.

In support of these conclusions, it is recalled from chapter 2 that the four institutions taken over by Teikyo University of Japan in 1989 and 1990 were 4-year nonselective, private colleges. There also appears to be some empirical evidence. As discussed in chapter 14, two studies of colleges and universities, Dunn and Hutten (1985) and Dunn, Terkla, and Secakusuma (1989), measured "support leverage," or the percentage represented by gifts in an institution's

Educational and General (E&G) budget, as an indicator of fund-raising success. This independent variable is relevant because it actually measures the importance of donors in comparison to other sources of financial support, which would indicate a degree of dependency on donors. Both studies found that the smaller the institution, the more dependent it is on donors. As Dunn et al. (1989) said, "It appears that the fewer students an institution has, the lower its endowment, the more modest its budget, and the more scarce its alumni, the higher its fund-raising leverage is likely to be" (p. 55).

These conclusions, it should be added, do not refute Tolbert's (1985/1986) findings because her sample was drawn from public and private doctoral and comprehensive universities and did not include 2- and 4-year colleges. In other words, resource dependencies with donors exist to varying degrees at all colleges and universities, but strategies to avoid external control are not equally available to these institutions; rather, some institutions, such as 4-year public colleges and 2- and 4-year nonselective, private colleges may be more vulnerable. In addition, the relative newness of the fund-raising function at some of these institutions adds to their vulnerability because that function may not be completely institutionalized (i.e., fund raising is not commonly recognized as a boundary role that helps a charitable organization manage interdependencies through interaction and negotiation). As Pfeffer and Salancik (1978) explained, an organization that enters a new field of activity is likely to ignore or misread the importance of an external dependency relationship and the potency of the related external group to affect the organization's continued survival and success.

In conclusion, fund raising is a boundary role of charitable organizations, responsible for helping these organizations manage their interdependencies with donor publics. As such, fund-raising practitioners are responsible for the continuing interaction and negotiation with donors that determine the degree of autonomy lost or gained through the solicitation and acceptance of gifts. On a macrolevel, fund raising can be explained as part of the public relations function of charitable organizations, a perspective that helps protect and enhance the autonomy of these organizations. This chapter further concludes that, contrary to conventional wisdom, the primary purpose of fund raising is not to raise money, but—as a part of public relations—to enhance and protect organizational autonomy by effectively managing communication between a charitable organization and the donor publics in its environment. Finally, after examining variation in the recognition of fund raising as a boundary role within public and private universities, this chapter concludes that private institutions of higher education are generally more vulnerable than are public institutions, but that large and wealthy public and private research universities are least vulnerable.

In support of its argument that a public relations approach to fund raising can helps a charitable organization manage interdependencies with donors for greater effectiveness, the book now turns to chapter 11 and an analysis of fund raising as a specialization of public relations from meso- and microlevels.

Chapter 11

Fund Raising as a Specialization of Public Relations

Continuing the examination of fund raising from a public relations perspective, this chapter argues that fund raising is a specialization, or branch, of public relations. Specifically, this chapter answers two research questions: How can fund raising be reinterpreted on a mesolevel, or departmental level, and on a microlevel as a public relations function. After comparing the functions of public relations and fund raising, this chapter concludes that theoretical links between the two functions have been ignored in previous research because public relations scholars have not understood the fund-raising function and those studying fund raising have limited the definition of public relations to techniques and publicity. It is also concluded here that fund raising, as an organizational function, traditionally has been separated from public relations because of the historical models of both functions (i.e., in earlier years, public relations was primarily a publicity function and fund raising was primarily a function that organized armies of volunteer solicitors). Finally, chapter 11 concludes that, based on the processes, objectives, and techniques they share, fund raising can be redefined as a specialization of public relations, which this book calls donor relations.

There have been few attempts either by scholars or practitioners to place fund raising within the public relations paradigm. As pointed out in the earlier chapter on the need for research, a title search of the leading communication research journals, such as *Journalism Quarterly*, *Public Opinion Quarterly*, *Public Relations Review*, and *Public Relations Research and Education*, found few studies on fund raising, although "fund giving," as Layton (1987, p. xv) called it, is mentioned as a program of corporate public relations. In addition, *Journalism Abstracts* up to 1988 cites very few examples of graduate work on fund raising, although journalism has historically been the academic "home" of public relations. For example, only 1 of the 374 theses abstracted in the 1988 *Journalism Abstracts* (Fowler, 1989) deals with philanthropy, although it is not indexed under philanthropy, but under news management systems, public relations, and arts news (Temple, cited in Fowler, 1989). In addition, this study adds little to the body of knowledge on fund raising because it focuses on managing corporate philanthropy to the arts and on testing the hypothesis that corporate managers will be more inclined to support giving programs if such programs are administered by public relations practitioners using sophisticated management tools, such as management information systems.

A notable exception to this absence of interest in fund raising are Grunig and Hunt (1984), who mention corporate contributions in their discussion of community relations and who include approximately four pages on fund raising in their chapter on "Promotion, Fund Raising, and Public Communication Campaigns." Unfortunately, the public relations scholars begin that chapter by describing fund raising and the other two categories as often being "the most mindless of PR programs" (p. 356). Grunig and Hunt also incorrectly stated that most charitable organizations place the fund-raising function within the public relations department, although the only source they cited as a basis for this conclusion was one article in the *Public Relations Journal* that described the successful integration of public relations, marketing, and fund raising at one nonprofit hospital. In contrast, a recent national survey of members of the Public Relations Society of America (PRSA) who work for educational and cultural organizations provides evidence that the public relations function is kept separate from or is subsumed by the fund-raising function in the majority of charitable organizations (Kelly, 1989a).

As discussed in chapter 2, a growing number of charitable organizations during the 1980s recognized the impact that donors have on their survival and success and established or expanded fund-raising departments to manage the communication between them and this special public. Structurally, however, the fund-raising department often has been set apart from or placed over the public relations function (Kelly, 1989a). Although fund raising is generally recognized to have some relationship to the public relations function, neither has embraced the other as its own. Fund-raising practitioners, who are largely misinformed about the newer definitions of public relations, perceive it as solely a publicity or publications function and assign it to a supportive role that somehow helps make their job easier or harder. Public relations practitioners, who are often viewed as technicians rather than managers of communications, are expected to get news releases printed in newspapers, draw crowds to special events, and produce award-winning brochures. As Dannelley (1986) said, "Fund-raising books tend to speak only in terms of publicity in connection with funding efforts" (p. 137). Yet, often development officers who find an environment that is unresponsive or even hostile to their fund-raising efforts will turn to public relations officers and order them to fix or improve the image of the organization so that more money can be raised (Kelly, 1988).

This perception of public relations, which commonly is held by fund-raising practitioners, is illustrated by the statements on the supportive role of public relations provided by Gonser Gerber Tinker Stuhr (1986) in the preceding chapters. For example, this national consulting firm for colleges and universities describes public relations as a collection of techniques and a publicity function that is crucial to the success of fund-raising programs. The firm's viewpoint of public relations is described in its 1986 publication, "The Role of Public Relations in a Comprehensive Development Program," in which it said that communicating the right image, as well as "skills in doing layouts, meeting publication deadlines and keeping a brisk output of news releases" (p. 4) are important elements of an effective public relations program.

Public relations practitioners, on the other hand, have spurned fund raising as something outside their functional area. To them, fund raising is mysterious (i.e., it generates millions of dollars through seemingly invisible techniques). It is demeaning (i.e., fund raisers beg for money, which lowers the prestige of the organization). And it is somewhat shady (i.e., the only things fund-raising practitioners seem to care about is raising a dollar and selling themselves to the next highest bidder). Discussing her findings on the insertion of fund-raising material in university periodicals that generally are edited by public relations practitioners, Shoemaker (1989) reported:

> Some periodical editors don't mind having an insert devoted to fund-raising material because that usually means they don't have to use their own pages to report on the same matters. . . . Other editors, however, would rather keep campaign reports, honor rolls, and gift requests from ever invading any part of their editorial domain. They argue that such a pairing makes it look like the institution's main reason for communicating to alumni is to raise money. (pp. 47-48)

During a visit to Stanford University in the summer of 1990, fund raisers complained to me that announcements and articles about gifts to the $1.1-billion campaign they were conducting rarely were included in Stanford's faculty-staff newsletter. When I raised this issue with a member of the editorial staff, she told me that too much emphasis on fund raising damaged the credibility of the publication with its internal audience and that gifts of even $5 million were not newsworthy. Stanford, like a number of universities conducting capital campaigns, has created a special communication department within the Office of Development, consisting of 16 practitioners. Related to earlier discussions in this book about the number of fund raising practitioners employed by institutions of higher education, I was told during my visit that Stanford had approximately 600 employees working in the various areas of institutional advancement, including 200 fund raisers.

A narrow and prejudicial perception of fund-raising practitioners is illustrated by the behavior of PRSA and its 15,000 members who generally distance themselves from practitioners engaged in fund raising. According to PRSA's (1989) *Eligibility Guidelines* for membership, fund raising is one of several work areas that, over the years, "have been found to be somewhat difficult to assess" (p. 10). The guidelines state, "Directors of development for colleges, universities or alumni associations usually qualify for membership *provided that their functions are broader than contacting for funds and involve developing goodwill and communicating with the university's publics*" (p. 11; italics added). It is difficult to understand how educational fund raisers could raise gifts without "developing goodwill and communicating with the university's publics" (p. 11). In fact, most fund raisers—aside from those commercial solicitation firms discussed in chapter 5—emphasize that solicitation is only one step in the fund-raising process, as discussed in more detail shortly.

In addition, PRSA's (1989) guidelines for membership indicate that this professional society advances a supportive role for public relations in the fund-raising process. The guidelines state, "Fund raisers who are principally concerned with developing a climate of public understanding and publicizing the fund campaign are more apt to be eligible than those who develop lists of contributors, make solicitation calls and manage teams of fund-drive workers" (p. 11).

A study of PRSA members who work for educational and cultural organizations, which was referred to earlier, found that the majority of public relations practitioners believe an equal, cooperative, but separate relationship with fund raising is the ideal (Kelly, 1989b). Of the 184 respondents in the study, 106 (58%) reported responsibilities solely in the public relations function, with no responsibility for fund raising. Frequent comments from these practitioners included the following: "I have nothing to do with fund raising. Fund raising is completely separate. We have a separate, but cooperative relationship" (Kelly, 1989a, p. 25). Reporting equality with a separate fund-raising foundation for his association, one public relations practitioner said, "Our public relations functions have such a profound effect on the organization and education as a whole that it shouldn't be diluted with the fund-raising responsibility" (pp. 4-5). A director of information services for an East Coast school district stated:

> The two must work together, but there is a clear dichotomy which needs to be maintained. PR must keep its hands clean of fund raising. The people a public relations person deals with must know he is not involved in fund raising; they must know that the PR person is not out to get money. (p. 31)

Of those responding to the PRSA study (Kelly, 1989a), 57 (31%) reported dual responsibilities in public relations and fund raising, although their role in fund raising was primarily a support function focused on public relations techniques, such as publications, press releases, and special events. A Los Angeles museum fund raiser referred to public relations, from which he had just changed functions, as "support staff." A public relations practitioner said, "The public relations people handle whatever needs to be promoted or written about in publications in order to assist development" (p. 35)

Based on a factor of whether the public relations function is dominant over or subordinate to the fund-raising function, the PRSA study (Kelly, 1989b), as stated in chapter 10, found that public relations is dominant in only 19% of the educational and cultural organizations represented in the sample, whereas it is subordinate to fund raising in 40% of the organizations and equal to it in 42%. The findings of this exploratory study provide evidence that the function of fund raising is rarely recognized as a specialization of public relations and that in most charitable organizations fund raising is a separate function from or is dominant over public relations. Defining her position as "public relations first, and then some fund raising," an executive assistant to the president of a Northwestern university summarized:

> There is great concern among PR people that they'll be gobbled up by the fund raising. The bottom line is money in PR, so fund raising directs the activities. . . . You can have public relations without fund raising, but you can't have fund raising without PR. (p. 5)

A small minority of the sample in the PRSA study (Kelly, 1989a) provided comments that support the concept of fund raising as a specialization of public relations. Responding to a question on the future relationship between public relations and fund raising, a public information/public affairs officer for a Kentucky public school district—which uses "existing staff" rather than fund raisers for soliciting and accepting gifts—said, "Fund raising is becoming a subset of public relations" (p. 33).

A public relations specialist for a Southern technical school that does fund raising "when the need arises" said, "Fund raising is one aspect of the PR spectrum" (pp. 33-34). When asked about the future, the same practitioner replied, "Public relations will continue to be general and fund raising one of its specifics" (p. 34).

An accredited public relations practitioner (i.e., someone who has passed the PRSA accreditation examination), who is also the executive director of development for a well-known Southern university, said, "All people business; all relationships. [My] position is a specialization of public relations, much like marketing is" (p. 34).

A study of the leading textbooks used in teaching public relations revealed that fund raising is neither well understood by public relations educators, or given much attention (Kelly, 1990). In spite of the fact that all of the textbooks mentioned fund raising, most gave the subject only a nod in passing, while still managing to create confusion about its relationship to public relations. For example, Cutlip, Center, and Broom (1989) gave two very different views. In the beginning of their book, the authors stated, "Fund-raising and membership drives occur within the context of an overall program designed to influence an organization's relationships with various publics; therefore they are part of the larger organizational function—public relations" (p. 16). Yet, toward the end of their book, the authors reversed themselves, saying:

> At this point we need to clarify that generally the public relations function is not always directly responsible for the fund-raising campaign. It is the public relations task to provide a favorable climate for the fund raiser, usually a specialist. The two functions must work in close cooperation, but as a general rule it is best not to combine the functions, whether in a university or in the Alliance for the Arts. (pp. 519-520)

An explanation for these "two voices" is likely attributable to the recent addition of Broom as one of the authors, and that he perceives fund raising as a part of public relations, whereas Cutlip has traditionally ascribed to a separate-but-equal view, as described shortly.

Finally, although Grunig and Hunt (1984) included fund raising as part of public relations and also referred to fund raisers as "specialists" in their textbook, they make little effort to advance a case that fund raising is a specialization of public relations. They do, however, provide valuable theoretical linkages that allow this book to outline how fund raising can be considered a specialization of the public relations function on meso- and microlevels.

REINTERPRETING FUND RAISING ON A MESOLEVEL

Citing a 1960 psychological study conducted by the American College Public Relations Association (ACPRA), Pray (1981) said that fund raisers and public relations practitioners represent two distinct styles or functions: the fund-raising specialist who "views his job as meeting certain specified dollar goals within a certain period of time"; and the specialist in image building who "views his task as that of acquainting the larger community with the 'image' of the university in order to develop a broader base of financial support *as well as for other reasons*" (p. 4).

In his history of fund raising in the United States, Cutlip (1965), who is an internationally known public relations educator, identified organization and communication as the two separate elements important to fund raising, but said that the role of public relations is traditionally one of communication, whereas fund raising is concerned primarily with organizing or managing programs. Yet, as discussed in the earlier chapter on definitions, Pearson (1989) argued that virtually all current definitions of public relations, including Grunig and Hunt's (1984), have two elements in common: management and communication.

Although a full discussion of the historical models of public relations and fund raising is delayed until chapter 13, it is important to point out here that the oldest model of public relations is the press agentry model, which uses one-way communication with complete truth not essential for its purpose of propaganda (Grunig & Hunt, 1984). The oldest model of fund raising, as mentioned in chapters 5 and 9, is also the press agentry model, which uses one-way communication with complete truth not essential to propagandize a cause. The leading historical figures associated with the press agentry model of fund raising are Pierce, Ward, and the YMCA school of fund raisers who operational-ized short, intense, highly structured campaigns to raise millions of dollars from a broad base of small donors through armies of volunteers (Cutlip, 1965). In short, the oldest model of public relations envisions public relations as a publicity function unrelated to management, and the oldest model of fund raising envisions fund raising as a management function that uses public relations for publicizing its structured campaign.

Although Cutlip (1965) provided most of the evidence in support of the historical models of fund raising identified in chapter 13, he failed to recognize them as distinct models and, like other public relations scholars, based his explanation of the relationship between public relations and fund raising on the oldest model of fund raising. On the other hand, fund-raising scholars and practitioners generally have based their explanations of this relationship on the oldest model of public relations (i.e., press agentry). The historical models, therefore, have contributed to a traditional separation of fund raising and public relations as organizational functions (i.e., early models envisioned public relations as a publicity function and fund raising as an organization or management function).

As Cutlip pointed out, many of the fund-raising firms that emerged in the first half of this century started as both fund-raising and public relations for-profit companies. Today, those firms either have split the functions between two separate organizations (e.g., the fund-raising consulting firm of Ketchum, Inc. and Ketchum Public Relations), or have dropped the public relations function (e.g., Brakeley, John Price Jones). A few of the newer fund-raising firms (e.g., Gonser Gerber Tinker Stuhr) have incorporated public relations into their services, but, as demonstrated earlier, that function has primarily been limited to a role in support of fund raising. Few, if any, of the major public relations consulting firms offer fund-raising services.

In his description of the post-World War II beginnings of the John Price Jones firm, Cutlip revealed his commonly shared "separate-but-equal" view on the relationship between public relations and fund raising. He pointed out that although the founder John Price Jones conceived his company as a fund-raising and public relations firm, the firm's senior vice president, Robert F. Duncan, insisted that these two were separate fields. Cutlip (1965) evaluated the two philosophies and disagreed with the conclusion of this chapter when he said, "The test of time validated [Duncan's] position. Today fund raising and public relations, in terms of business organization, are distinctly separate professions, though the two functions are inextricably intertwined in the art of raising money" (p. 178).

According to conventional wisdom, the reason for this division of labor in the consulting field is that public relations is a support function for fund raising, but a primary function when it comes to publics other than donors and consumers. In 1988, Harold Burson, chairman of the board of Burson-Marsteller—one of the two largest public relations firms in the world—wrote in personal correspondence:

> The relationship of fund raising and public relations is a subject of substantial interest to me. My own view of the relationship is, I fear, somewhat counter to yours. I regard public relations as a support function to the development effort overall just as I feel public relations supports a marketing program.

This book contends that a lack of understanding about fund raising and narrow definitions of public relations, as well as the historical models of both functions, have misled scholars and practitioners into believing that fund raising is a separate or superior function as compared to public relations.

As described in chapter 10, Grunig and Hunt (1984) used Esman's four types of linkages that are critical to the survival of an organization (i.e., enabling, functional, normative, and diffused) to explain the traditional organization of public relations programs that are targeted for specific publics. Building on Grunig and Hunt's application, chapter 10 redefined fund raising as donor relations, in much the same way that investor relations describes the public relations programs of for-profit organizations that are aimed at investors (i.e., a public that provides authority and controls the resources that _enable_ these organizations to survive and succeed).

In support of the redefinition of fund raising as donor relations, a number of fund raisers currently use the analogy of corporate investors to describe donors and the fund-raising process. In his chapter on creating authentic involvement, Lord (1983), for example, stated, "One could argue that the donor should have as much to say about the future of the institution as the stockholder does about the future of the company. As investors, both are entitled to influence the setting of policy" (p. 31). Lord said that enabling the donor to "develop a _sense of ownership_" is the "_basic quid pro quo_ in the business of development" (p. 31). Emphasizing fund raising as a process of social exchange between a charitable organization and its donor publics and the potential for external control in this exchange, Lord stated, "When we recruit investors, we must give them a share of ownership. It's the process of exchange; we owe them. As many businessman is fond of saying, "There's no free lunch"—not from government, and not from philanthropy, either" (p. 31).

It is recalled from chapter 3 that Wood (1989) compared a major donor to a major investor in a corporation, saying that such a person is "not just a casual customer who buys the product, but someone who becomes an insider (partner/ owner)" (p. 1). He said, "Major donors are major investors in our organizations and deserve to be treated like major stockholders" (p. 1). Panas (1984) also used this analogy. For example, when advancing his hypothesis that giving begets financial return to the donor, Panas asked, "How can we let people know that there is a direct return on their _investment_ to charity?" (p. 157; italics added).

Aside from the textbooks discussed earlier, few public relations authors have included fund raising within their discussion of public relations as an organizational function. In fact, Bill Cantor and Chester Burger (1989)—veteran public relations counselors and owners of one of the largest public relations executive search firms—replaced the chapter on fund raising in the second edition of their popular book, *Experts in Action: Inside Public Relations*, with one on corporate philanthropy. Cantor and Burger's book is described by Robert Dilenschneider (1989), president and chief executive officer of Hill and Knowlton—the second of the two largest public relations firms in the world—as "a comprehensive guide to the theory and practice of public relations" (p. 3). The replacement of the chapter on fund raising can be viewed as a step backward in encompassing fund raising within the paradigm of public relations and emphasizes the lack of practitioner support for the conclusions of this book.

Even in the first edition of Cantor and Burger's (1984) book, the chapter on fund raising does not define the function as a specialization, or component, of public relations. Rather, a leading fund-raising practitioner and president of the World Rehabilitation Fund emphasized the "symbiotic relationship" between the two and that they are "inseparable" (Rusk, 1984, p. 262). Rusk, who displays a lack of understanding about public relations and its growing body of knowledge, found "a striking parallel between the effective use of direct mail in fund raising and the effective use of public relations in shaping public opinion" (p. 262). Unlike fund raising, which he said deals solely with the communication objective of action, Rusk said, "In the case of public relations, the final objective might merely be the swaying of public opinion" (p. 265). Although Rusk acknowledged that public relations programs may have behavior objectives for their target audience, such as "contacting a legislator, writing a letter, attending a meeting or purchasing a product" (p. 265), he saw no reason to assume that public relations and fund raising share more than a symbiosis.

As discussed earlier, higher education scholars approach fund raising and public relations as subfunctions of *institutional advancement*, a term that has been advanced by the Council for Advancement and Support of Education (CASE) to describe the various responsibilities of its total membership and to define a unifying profession. Carbone (1987) said that the organizational function of institutional advancement encompasses "a wide variety of related activities—fund raising, alumni programs, public relations and publications, grantsmanship, government relations, and in some cases student recruitment and admissions" (p. 1). It is important to note that, using Grunig and Hunt's (1984) concept of linkages, Carbone's description of institutional advancement—a description that is widely accepted in the literature and in practice—can be redefined as the function of public relations that has been organized by some of the identifiable publics important to the survival and success of colleges and universities. The exceptions to this redefinition are publications, which most public relations scholars would consider a communication medium that crosses all publics and specializations, and grantsmanship, which can be considered a communication technique. Carbone supported the case for defining donors as an enabling public of charitable organizations when he said, "The raison d'etre for these institutional advancement experts is easily stated: Increasing the fiscal assets of institutions through programs that build understanding and monetary support of graduates, parents, friends, community members, public officials, foundations, corporations, and society in general" (p. 1).

According to Grunig (in preparation), public relations departments are managed strategically and add to organizational effectiveness when, following a five-step process, practitioners:

1. identify issues important to their organization;
2. segment publics that respond differentially to those issues;
3. identify objectives for communication programs designed to help manage the organization's interdependence with its strategic publics;
4. use objectives to plan communication programs; and
5. evaluate the effects of those programs (i.e., did they achieve the objectives set for them and as a result contribute to organizational effectiveness?).

It is recalled from the preceding chapter that Grunig's (1989b) situational theory of publics assumes that publics form around specific issues produced by the consequences that organizations have on people outside the organization. And whereas linkages, as reviewed earlier, help identify types of stakeholders for an organization, Grunig's theory of publics helps identify which of those stakeholders differ in the extent to which they become active in doing something about an organizational consequence. At this point, it is helpful to discuss how Grunig's theory and the first two steps of the strategic process just given relate to the way fund raising currently is managed.

There is general agreement in the fund-raising literature that donor research is important to the success of raising private funds. Pickett (1981), it is recalled from chapter 3, called research one of the four essential means of fund raising, saying, "Every fund-raising program at a college or university should have professional staff assigned to prospect research to produce more and better information on potential donors" (p. 13). Pickett also said that fund raisers should do everything possible to exploit the environmental position of a charitable organization, such as a college, through research.

As recommended by most scholars and practiced by some practitioners, research generally is used in fund raising to identify potential donors of major gifts and to gather information that is helpful in matching donor interest to organizational need (i.e., research helps fund raisers decide what they will ask a major donor to support). According to Ray (1981), "To be successful, [the fund-raising program] must have the ability to identify possible major donors and to collect and organize information on which to base effective work by staff and volunteers" (p. 81).

Prospect identification essentially is a continuous system of gathering names of prospects and evaluating them on their ability to make a major gift. Some of the sources used by fund raisers to identify prospects and evaluate gift potential are admissions records of students that list parents' occupation and titles, proxy statements and probate records, alumni questionnaires, news clippings, ad hoc committees of peer individuals, annual foundation reports, and lists of donors to similar organizations. As Ray warned, however:

> Do not select the Rockefellers, the Mellons, Bob Hope, and the Ford Foundation just because they have a lot of money. There must be some connecting thread, relationship, *consanguinity of interest in programs*, or a real possibility of developing some link before listing and research begin. (p. 83; italics added)

It is this relationship or "link" to the charitable organization that helps fund raisers identify those enabling publics who have a higher probability of giving than other prospects with equal amounts of discretionary income or assets. And it is on those few major-donor prospects who are linked to the charitable organization that fund raisers concentrate. As Ray (1981) stated, "Usually an institutional prospect research system will limit its efforts, in the interest of cost effectiveness, to those individuals and organizations with an adjudged potential to make capital gifts of an agreed-upon minimum amount—say $10 thousand or $15 thousand for the small institution and limited objective to $100 thousand or even higher for the major university" (p. 82).

As just described, the second element of fund-raising research, as advocated by much of the literature, is matching the interest of potential donors to the purpose of a proposed major gift. As Ray advised, "Accumulate data on attitudes, prejudices, and interests for consideration in the strategy of cultivation, solicitation, and reward" (p. 84). In other words, the interest of major-donor prospects greatly influences what they are asked to support (i.e., fund raisers frequently shape their solicitations around donor interests). For example, once a need is identified by a charitable organization, the fund raiser is advised to review the prospective major donors linked to his or her organization and then choose those prospects who have a probability of sharing an interest in the identified need. Just as the public relations practitioner seeks to identify those publics concerned with a particular issue important to his or her organization, the fund raiser asks which individuals, corporations, and foundations have a mutual interest in the funding need.

If a university, for example, decides that it needs to attract a top scholar to its journalism school, the fund raiser should conduct research on private funding sources that are able to endow a chair and that are likely to agree with the need for a journalism chair (Kelly, 1988). Such sources may be newspaper companies, wealthy journalism alumni, and foundations that give high priority to journalism education.

Throughout the fund-raising process, the fund raiser is advised to match institutional needs with major donor needs or desires. If a prospective donor wants to endow a journalism chair, but wants it to be restricted to broadcast news, the fund-raising practitioner must negotiate the terms of the gift based on his or her organization's needs. In other words, if the situation just described occurs and there is a growing number of students and a shortage of faculty in that academic area, the university may decide to modify its funding need to match the wishes of the donor. Unfortunately, the university, through its fund raiser, may decide to accept such a gift even if no such need exists, as illustrated in chapter 2.

Strategic steps in fund raising, therefore, are to identify those donor publics who are capable of making major gifts; who are likely to do so because of their "link" to the charitable organization; and who share a common interest in the purpose of the requested gift. The concept of "matching donor interest" is a common one in the fund-raising literature, and from the discussion here, it can be linked to Grunig's (in preparation) first two steps of strategic public relations management.

In other words, the fund-raising literature recommends that fund-raising practitioners identify issues important to their organization and then segment donor publics that respond differentially to those issues. This perception of fund raising largely replaces the emphasis on persuasion in the solicitation and acceptance of gifts with the concept of environmental interdependencies discussed earlier. As Aldous Huxley (cited in Lord, 1983) said, "It's not very difficult to persuade people to do what they already long to do" (p. 42).

The book now turns to the section on reinterpreting fund raising on a microlevel to discuss the last three steps of Grunig's (in preparation) five-step process of strategic public relations management.

REINTERPRETING FUND RAISING ON A MICROLEVEL

Approaching fund raising on a microlevel, this section analyzes the processes, objectives, programs, and techniques shared by fund raising and public relations. As pointed out in chapter 3, there seems to be general agreement in the fund-raising literature on the process involved in soliciting and accepting gifts (i.e, the generally accepted process of fund raising consists of four steps: research, cultivation, solicitation, and recognition). It is recalled, for example, that Wood (1989) described major gift solicitation as 25% research, 60% cultivation, 5% solicitation, and 10% recognition. Wood also renamed these steps as "the four R's" of obtaining large gifts: research, romance, request, and recognition. Explaining his use of the term *romance*, Wood said, "Asking someone who has a lot of money—but no relationship with your organization—to make a major gift is like asking an attractive stranger to marry you just because you think they're eligible" (p. 1).

Discussing each of the four steps in sequential order, Wood first addressed the importance of research in prospect identification, calling this step "'the homework' of information-gathering" (p. 1). As just pointed out, Wood assigned 60% of the major gift solicitation to romance, or cultivation, saying, "We all know the research and ask must take place, but success is also determined by the romance period to educate and cultivate the prospect into being motivated to give" (p. 1). Focusing on the request step, Wood emphasized the importance of written communication in the fund-raising process by saying that every solicitation for a major gift "should be made both verbally and in writing," and that major donors deserve a "customized proposal for a specific size gift" (p. 6). An important aspect of the request step identified by Wood is negotiation, which is a critical point in this book's earlier discussion of the fund raiser as a negotiator of organizational autonomy lost or gained through the fund-raising process. Wood simply stated, "The request must often include negotiation" (p. 6).

Finally, Wood (1989) discussed the fourth stage, which he called recognition, and emphasized its importance in the fund-raising process by repeating a generally accepted fund-raising axiom that satisfied donors are the best prospects for future gifts. He also explained that there are many forms of recognition available to fund raisers, including naming buildings, presenting plaques, and sending mementos. Saying that human nature requires that gifts be recognized, he said, "The difference is how and at what level, ranging from flagrant egotism to anonymous piety" (p. 6). Wood concluded by saying, "There is no magic or mystery to the process" (p. 6).

Dittman (1981) said that the development program is built on five sequential activities: "interpretation, communication, involvement, solicitation, and recognition" (p. 227). In comparison to the four steps of the fund-raising process just given, Dittman's sequential activities can be seen as highly congruent because interpretation can be redefined as research, and communication and involvement can be combined under the cultivation step. In conclusion, then, there is general agreement that the fund-raising process is composed of activities and tasks related to research, cultivation, solicitation, and recognition.

It should be noted, however, that some practitioners would argue that stewardship should be added as a fifth and essential step in the fund-raising process. Based on his analogy of donors as shareholders, Lord (1983) said, "Good stewardship means protecting and managing the donor's investment—so that it produces the best possible return" (p. 91). Hopkinson (1989) took an even broader view of stewardship, saying, "Sometimes referred to as donor relations, stewardship covers the entire relationship between a donor and the institution" (p. 55).

Hampton (1989) said that stewardship consists of three parts: expressions of thanks, donor reports on the use of the gift, and developing strategies for further solicitations. Both Hopkinson and Hampton advocated the establishment of a systematic and institutionalized stewardship function within the development department.

As a point of clarification, the common usage of the term _donor relations_ to describe stewardship programs, as just demonstrated by Hopkinson, should not be confused with the theory of donor relations developed in this book. Although divisions or programs for donor relations are related to the theory, they are not synonymous (i.e., such current programs are support functions of fund raising, whereas the theory of donor relations encompasses the entire function). Although Hopkinson's asserts that donor relations covers the entire relationship between a donor and a charitable organization, in point of fact, programs currently referred to as donor relations have been established to take on the responsibilities of communication and stewardship because fund raisers are too busy raising new gifts to spend time on maintaining interdependent relationships with current donors, as described shortly. Therefore, although such programs are related to the theory of donor relations developed in this book, they are not completely compatible with the theory.

Similarly, the major-gifts program at Cornell University is related to the theory of donor relations. Describing the stewardship of major gifts as "the practice of 'nurturing fund raising,'" Cornell's director of capital projects, David Dunlop (cited in Hampton, 1989), said that such stewardship "helps you reap a continual harvest of funds and good will and still meet short-term campaign or annual fund goals" (p. 59).

Bearing a closer relationship to the theory, Cutlip, Center, and Broom (1985) also use the term *donor relations* in their public relations textbook. According to these public relations educators, there are many staff functions dealing with an organization's relationships with publics as part of the larger public relations function. They added, "Some of the other names commonly used include consumer relations or consumer affairs, government affairs, or government relations, constituent relations, community relations, member relations, *donor relations*, investor relations, employee communication, and media relations—to list but a few" (pp. 16-17; italics added).

As pointed out earlier, however, these authors presented two viewpoints: one toward the beginning of the book, which defined fund raising as a specialization of public relations, as demonstrated here, and the other toward the end of the book, which matched Cutlip's view of fund raising as being a separate function from public relations. Although these public relations educators create confusion with their "mixed" views, Cutlip, Center, and Broom (1985) do add to the theory of donor relations developed in this book by providing a small, but significant indication of the appropriateness of shifting the public relations paradigm to incorporate fund raising.

Returning to the topic of stewardship, Hopkinson (1989) argued for a distinct stewardship function because fund raisers don't have enough time for stewardship and "sometimes don't accord attending to old gifts the same high priority as developing new gifts" (p. 55). In addition, Hopkinson said, "Deans and faculty can play an important role here in fulfilling the stewardship function, but it's not ultimately their responsibility" (p. 55). In other words, the specialists who manage the fund-raising programs for charitable organizations often ignore stewardship responsibilities because of pressure to bring in new gifts, and the recipients who benefit from gifts—at least indirectly—are not responsible for thanking donors, reporting on the use of the gift, or devising strategies for future solicitations of previous donors. As Hopkinson said, "Development officers usually work under pressure and tight deadlines to bring in new gifts and meet annual or capital campaign goals" (p. 55). Yet, this same practitioner-author claims that, fundamentally, "stewardship is the total range of responsibilities an institution undertakes when it accepts a contribution" (p. 55).

Be that as it may, stewardship generally is defined by the fund-raising literature as reporting to donors on the use of their gifts and is collapsed into the recognition step of the fund-raising process. As Horton (1981) said, "The idea of stewardship is often in our minds, of course. . . . Perhaps it will suffice to say we do what we can in this area, knowing that if time allowed we could always do much, much more" (p. 267).

A commonly accepted description of the public relations management process is the RACE formula (cited in Grunig & Hunt, 1984). This decision model advocates a four-step process of research, action, communication, and evaluation. In comparison with the process of fund raising just described, the RACE formula bears striking similarities. For example, the action and communication steps generally are interpreted as planning and executing communication programs, which correlate to the cultivation and solicitation stages of the fund-raising process. Unlike public relations, however, a formal evaluation step currently is not included in the fund-raising process because it is generally accepted that the only way to measure fund-raising success is by measuring dollar counts. As discussed fully in chapter 14, fund raising is commonly evaluated by the number of dollars raised, sometimes divided by the costs of fund raising. It is argued here that such a narrow focus on evaluation is inappropriate for measuring the effectiveness of fund raising, particularly because only 5% of the fund-raising process, according to Wood (1989), involves solicitation (i.e., asking for gifts).

After a review of various decision models that have been applied to public relations, Grunig and Hunt (1984) provided a "behavioral molecule that is well-grounded in systems theory and that brings all of these decision models together into a single and powerful theory" (p. 104). The behavioral molecule consists of six segments that are described as sequential, but that often occur simultaneously: detect, construct, define, select, confirm, behave, and detect, and so on. Grunig and Hunt demonstrated how fund raisers follow the same steps of developing and executing a program as do public relations practitioners. Utilizing the first edition of Broce's (1986) book, _Fund Raising: The Guide to Raising Money From Private Sources_, Grunig and Hunt identified segments of the behavioral molecule in Broce's description of the fund-raising process.

As advocated by Broce (1986), fund raisers should establish organizational objectives and use those objectives to determine what kind of fund-raising programs are needed. Grunig and Hunt (1984) identified this as the detect and construct segments of the behavioral molecule (i.e., fund-raising managers identify an organizational problem, define it, chose an objective that suggests what it will take to solve the problem and formulate alternative solutions). Identifying and researching donor prospects, who Grunig and Hunt defined as active publics, also take place in the construct segment. Cultivation of prospective donors, which includes visiting prospects, holding special events, and sending out publications, is part of the behave segment (i.e., practitioners execute the program by doing something). In this case, the behave segment deals with a communication objective different than affecting a giving behavior in donors (i.e., cultivation programs are designed to obtain objectives other than giving as the fund-raising manager has determined which donor prospects are not yet ready for solicitation). As Grunig and Hunt pointed out, cultivation is "also part of the select and confirm segments—to determine the best method of solicitation" (p. 363).

Writing a case statement or a proposal is also in the construct segment (i.e., a document is written that addresses the problem and shows why the organization needs funds and why donor prospects should contribute). Solicitation, the actual asking of prospects to give money, is identified by Grunig and Hunt (1984) as the behave segment (i.e., the fund-raising programs that have a giving behavior as an objective and that deal with those active donor-publics who are identified by the manager to be ready for solicitation are executed). Grunig and Hunt said that although most of the fund-raising literature stresses the importance of research, the actual research conducted by fund-raising practitioners is limited. Formative research in the construct segment of the behavioral molecule consists primarily of prospect research on the ability and propensity of giving for major donors from corporate, foundation, and individual sources. Evaluative research in the second detect segment, as mentioned earlier, consists primarily of comparing growth in dollar totals. This comparison of the behavioral molecule and the earlier RACE formula with the fund raising process provides evidence that the process of fund raising is similar to that used in public relations.

Contrary to conventional wisdom, this book contends that fund raising is essentially a *communication* function and provides evidence in this section by comparing the fund-raising process discussed earlier with the five communication objectives of public relations. According to Grunig and Hunt (1984), there are five objectives for public relations programming that are based on the components of the entire communication process: (a) communication, (b) retention of message, (c) belief in a cognition, (d) formation or change in attitude, and (e) affecting behavior. These objectives state what effects communication will have on an organization's publics, which may be cognitive, attitudinal, or behavioral. As listed earlier, Grunig (in preparation) said that public relations is managed strategically when practitioners identify objectives for communication programs that help an organization manage its environmental interdependencies; use those objectives to plan communication programs; and evaluate the effects of those programs by measuring achievement of the objectives set for them.

Many public relations scholars, including Grunig (e.g., Grunig & Hunt, 1984), stress that public relations objectives should support organizational goals, including financial goals, and that by helping the organization communicate with its strategic publics, public relations contributes to organizational success. Public relations, therefore, can help an organization gain awareness, understanding, belief, favorable attitudes, and behavior—the five objectives of public relations—with members of its strategic publics through the management of communication. Grunig and Hunt (1984) warned, however, "that each effect is less and less likely to occur as you move from communication to behavior" (p. 133). These public relations scholars advised, "So be realistic about objectives. Most frequently, your objective will be communication, accuracy, or understanding. . . . Save attitudes and behavior for PR problems where those objectives are absolutely necessary: such as fundraising, promotion, or lobbying" (p. 133).

Grunig (in preparation) argued that "communication programs seldom change behavior in the short term, although they may do so over a longer period." He said that by choosing short-term, cognitive effects (i.e., changes in the way people think about and understand issues) practitioners can maximize the chances for long-term behavioral changes. He continued by saying, "The less excellent programs, in contrast, will expect direct and powerful effects on the behavior of vaguely defined publics in the short term." According to Grunig, communication programs change behavior in the short term only under the following specific conditions: the behavior to be changed must be a simple one; the program must be aimed at a well segmented public, executed flawlessly, and supplemented by interpersonal support among members of the segmented public.

From the discussion here, we can conclude that fund raising is one of those public relations specializations that requires—at some point—a communication objective of affecting behavior in the short term. Yet, fund raising, like other public relations specializations, can maximize long-term behavioral changes by selecting short-term cognitive effects for the majority of its programs. Grunig's (e.g., in preparation; Grunig & Hunt, 1984) theory of communication objectives is supported by current fund-raising practices and axioms. For example, fund-raising practitioners acknowledge that changing behavior in the short term is often an unrealistic objective. Lord (1983) said, "It's very difficult to turn a nongiver into a giver" (p. 85). Rather, fund raisers concentrate their attention on those few prospects who, according to Lord, have the financial capability of giving, the rationale for giving to a particular program, *and* a history of giving to the same or other organizations. As Lord said, "Experience shows that the best prospects for the immediate future are those who have given in the past" (p. 49). Expanding on that principle, Panas (1984) said that there is no evidence that million-dollar donors "make a gift in that range without any prior experience of giving or history in the institution itself" (p. 52). He provided what he defined as one of the major axioms of fund raising when he stated: "Those who give to you, those who will be making the largest gifts . . . are those who have given to you in the past. So valid is this rule, you can actually take it to the bank!" (p. 53).

In support of achieving long-term behavioral changes, another commonly accepted fund-raising axiom is that it takes an average of 3 years to obtain a major gift (e.g., Seymour, 1966). As Lord (1983) said, "If time is *not* provided, the development process will degenerate into a series of 'shakedowns'—in which the easy money is taken, and the building of relationships neglected" (p. 104). In addition, fund-raising authors, such as Lord, recognize the need to always replenish the pool of perspective contributors. Lord advised fund raisers to concentrate efforts on the few who will do the most and then broaden the pool to "the 'grassroots' donors who will someday become your new top ten" (p. 49). Most of the fund-raising literature acknowledges the importance of cultivation programs that lead up to solicitation. If designed to meet short-term cognitive objectives, cultivation programs can maximize the probability of long-term behavioral effects. Unfortunately, many fund raisers—and public relations practitioners—establish attitudinal effects as the objectives of such programs.

The argument that fund raising does more than just raise money (i.e., it also has an objective of educating its publics) has historically hampered efforts to produce standardized measures of cost-efficiency in fund raising. Not surprisingly, all solicitations do not meet an objective of giving behavior. Fund raisers often justify such "failures" by pointing out that other communication objectives are likely to have been reached in communicating with the prospective donor (e.g., although a donor did not give, he or she now knows more about the needs of the organization). Reviewing this issue in his history of fund raising, Cutlip (1965) concluded by saying, "Then as now the professional insisted that a fund-raising campaign is educational as well as remunerative and part of the costs are properly chargeable to education and public relations" (p. 221).

Finally, the specific conditions outlined by Grunig (in preparation) for achieving short-term behavioral effects is closely followed in the solicitation step of fund raising (i.e., donors, particularly major donors, are well segmented, as described in the previous section; the behavior change sought is a simple one in that donor prospects are often previous donors to the same organization and are asked to make a gift in support of a specific project; the solicitation step is well executed, often scripted down to speaking points for each member of the solicitation team; and the solicitation frequently includes interpersonal support from a volunteer who is also a member of the segmented donor public).

Illustrating the latter point, Franz (1981) described the solicitation of a major gift by a team that included a trustee-volunteer, stating:

The prospect was impressed and perhaps flattered by the stature of his visitors. It was difficult for him to say "no" when confronted by an individual who undoubtedly was his peer. . . . The prospect was aware that the trustee was fully capable himself of making a gift in the magnitude of the one he was soliciting. The prospect was aware that the trustee had a long record of generous giving and that he believed in the university he represented. (p. 161)

It should be noted at this point that not all public relations scholars or practitioners agree with Grunig's (e.g., in preparation) emphasis on short-term cognitive effects for public relations programs. Stating that the future of public relations lies in affecting human behavior, an editorial in the trade publication, *PR Week* ("Behavioral science," 1988), stated, "The end must be to influence behavior, to persuade people to take action, whether that action involves buying more of a certain product, or supporting a certain piece of legislation, or holding on to certain shares in a takeover battle" (p. 6). The president and chief executive officer of Burson-Marsteller, James Dowling (1988), explained this new "bottom-line mentality" by stating the following:

Management doesn't want to hear about employee communications; they want to hear about how that contributes to employee productivity. They don't want to talk about annual and quarterly reports; they want to know whether their financial communications will enhance the value of the company shares or protect them from a hostile takeover. They don't want to hear about product publicity per se, they want to know about products moving off shelves or out of dealer showrooms. They don't want to talk about government relations as a means of getting invited to a state dinner, they want to talk about ballots in boxes or regulations and legislation passed, amended, or defeated. (p. 10)

In other words, some public relations practitioners would argue that all public relations programs should be designed and evaluated for a communication objective of affecting behavior. Although this book does not agree with this viewpoint, it does support the case for redefining fund raising as a specialization of public relations (i.e., the behavioral objectives of fund-raising programs are congruent with the behavioral objectives of public relations programs).

A proponent of this behavioral viewpoint, Patrick Jackson (cited in "To get clout," 1988) said, "Behavior is really the only thing that matters in public relations" (p. 24). Saying that most college public relations offices are one-way publicity units, Jackson added, "After all, it's wonderful if everybody loves Siwash University, but I don't care how many people love it unless that love is reflected in behavior—in enrollment, in support, in donations" (p. 24). Jackson has voiced his agreement with the major conclusion of this book in personal conversations, stating his belief that fund raising is a program, or specialization, of public relations. In fact, Jackson (cited in "To get clout," 1988) used fund raising as a model for reorienting public relations to behavioral objectives. He recommended a two-part system for the public relations function that is based on well-segmented publics targeted for communication through in-house, or controlled media, and reinforced through peer group interaction. Commenting on the two-part system, Jackson stated:

> We already do this in fund raising, where we start out with mailings and maybe some publicity about our campaign. Then what happens? Bam! We arrange for someone to call potential donors up, to go see them. That is the same model we need for dealing with issues, recruitment, and so on. (p. 27)

As stated previously, this book does not support the viewpoint that public relations should be oriented solely toward behavioral objectives. In fact, an examination of the fund-raising process demonstrates how fund raising can be understood as a specialization of public relations using Grunig's (e.g., in preparation) theory of objectives.

Fund raisers generally claim that, in comparison to public relations, solicitation is unique to their function. Yet, as described earlier, a solicitation activity designed to generate gifts (e.g., solicit a major gift through interpersonal communications or an unrestricted lower level, or annual, gift through a mass medium, such as direct mail) is a communication activity with the communication objective of affecting behavior. Nor are fund-raising programs primarily concerned with behavior objectives. Wood (1989), for example, described the major gift process as 5% solicitation. In other words, only 5% of the major-gift process is designed to affect donor behavior on a short-term basis, whereas the remaining 95% can be related to the other four communication objectives and to the public relations activity of researching strategic publics.

Following research, cultivation is the second step in the fund-raising process, and as Wood (1989) said, it constitutes 60% of the activities related to raising major gifts. According to Lord (1983), the best way to cultivate relationships with donors is by involving them in the management of the organization, but he added, "Another method of cultivation includes all those activities that come under the heading of public relations" (p. 38). Included within such activities, Lord said, are news coverage in the print and broadcast media, editorials, public service advertising, a speakers' bureau, and benefits and special events. Focusing on special events, Geier (1981) described the important role regional programs play in the cultivation stage of fund raising and how public relations directors can contribute to the success of such events. While outlining its "contributions," Geier actually placed the entire activity—except the list of invitees—in the domain of public relations. He said, for example, that the public relations director's counsel is important in the selection of the right speaker and the right subject, in the choice of location for meetings, the accommodations of a meeting room, and all aspects of planning the event.

Rather than arguing that fund raising is a specialization of public relations, it is more difficult when discussing the cultivation step of fund raising to argue that it is not. As Ray (1981) summarized, "The development, alumni, publications, and public relations offices are constantly concerned with the process of cultivating the goodwill, friendship, and support of all constituencies" (p. 85).

As discussed previously, the final step of the fund-raising process after research, cultivation, and solicitation is recognition. Hampton (1989) outlined some of the activities related to this step: writing personal thank-you letters, "selecting tasteful 'trinkets and beads'" (p. 59), planning dedication ceremonies, memorial masses, and scholarship receptions, and producing donor publications, such as newsletters, gift reports, and calendars. As with the cultivation step, these activities are strongly related to the public relations function. In fact, the earlier discussion on the importance of stewardship in the fund-raising process provides a case for redefining most of that process as a function of public relations. For example, Bucknell University set up a separate division for "donor relations" in 1988, which "includes publications and proposal writing along with the usual special events and gift acknowledgments" (Hampton, 1989, p. 59). Because proposal writing is a communication activity used in the solicitation step, publications and special events are communication activities used in the cultivation step, and gift acknowledgments are communication activities used in the recognition step, one reaction to the establishment of such an office of donor relations might be to question what activities are left for fund raisers as distinct practitioners. In support of this question, Hopkinson (1989) stated, "In many cases, especially those involving major gifts, stewardship includes maintaining and cultivating a long-term personal relationship with donors, who, after all, are an institution's best prospects for future gifts" (p. 55).

Turning now to techniques and the similarities between those used by fund-raising and public relations practitioners, Grunig and Hunt (1984) stated, "Each of the [communication] objectives may be chosen for a public relations program, such as press or community relations, or for a public relations technique, such as a press release or an open house" (p. 133). In other words, although a press release might be an appropriate technique for creating awareness, public relations scholars generally agree that it would be ineffective when behavior is the objective. From special events to speeches, public relations practitioners are advised to select the most appropriate techniques to achieve the desired objective of their programs. As the degree of difficulty in attaining objectives increases, the techniques selected move from mass to interpersonal communication.

According to Howe (1985), fund raisers—whether they are practitioners or volunteers—should apply the theory of communication effects to their solicitation efforts. He said, "Some professionals concerned with public relations and fund raising use a 'ladder of communication effectiveness'" (p. 19). Howe presented a graph of communication techniques ascending in their effectiveness of transmitting messages—from handout, advertisement, news item and brochure, up to small group discussion and one-to-one conversation. He concluded by stating the following:

> The message is clear: when soliciting an important contribution, do it in person. Use the highest rung on the ladder possible within your budget and manpower capabilities. Don't be lulled into thinking that a general written appeal can do the job of a personal note. Don't expect a phone call to be as effective as a visit. (p. 19)

As advocated by Howe (1985), the selection of communication techniques is based on the same principle for fund raising and public relations. For example, although annual giving (i.e., programs that generate unrestricted lower level gifts) is primarily built on mass communication techniques, such as direct mail, major gift solicitation requires the same interpersonal communications that the public relations manager is advised to use in legislative relations or in dealing with activist publics. According to Geier (1981):

> As a general rule, the techniques of communication as applied to fund raising bring into play the mass media for reaching the last committed audience—those persons who have the least knowledge of and commitment to the institution. . . . For audiences whose knowledge of the institution and commitment to it are greater, communication techniques change from mass distribution of information to messages specifically designed and directed to smaller and smaller audiences. Finally, the most committed, the prime prospect, is best dealt with on a personal, one-to-one basis. (p. 207)

In their book, *Managing Public Relations*, Grunig and Hunt (1984) listed some of the public relations techniques used by fund raisers:

> Media relations techniques to announce and promote a campaign.
>
> Letter writing and direct mail solicitation of prospects.
>
> Writing of proposals to foundations or corporations.
>
> Intensive campaigns that feature such techniques as media promotion, staged events, telethons, and celebrity support.
>
> Provision of ongoing information to donors or prospective donors through magazines, newsletters, or annual reports.
>
> Speeches to donor groups.
>
> Interpersonal contacts with key prospects. (p. 363)

These communication techniques demonstrate little difference between the fund-raising and public relations functions. Some fund-raising practitioners, particularly those who view public relations as a publicity function, might criticize Grunig and Hunt's listing for wrongfully assigning interpersonal contacts as a technique to public relations. However, public relations practitioners, particularly those who serve in a management function, would defend the importance of interpersonal techniques to their field. For example, interpersonal contacts are recommended for corporations when dealing with activist groups, and they have been proven valuable in community relations programs. In media relations, practitioners use interpersonal contacts to affect the behavior of reporters and assignment editors (e.g., getting a reporter to cover a particular event). Pearson (1989) said, "Indeed, a good media relations program is itself founded on respectful interpersonal relationships between source and reporter" (p. 407).

The expansion of public relations beyond media relations has emphasized the function's use of interpersonal as well as mass communication. As Pearson (1989) argued:

> Mass media channels and media relations programs will always be important components of public relations practice. But it needs to be remembered that the close association of PR and journalism is also an historical phenomena. . . . And media relations has been joined by government relations, community relations, employee relations, investor relations, customer relations and stockholder relations, to name a few of the main areas of practice. (p. 406)

Summarizing this chapter, public relations is a management _and_ communication function, which utilizes interpersonal and mass communication techniques. The argument is made that fund raising, on a meso- and a microlevel, is a specialization, or branch, of public relations. This argument is based on the traditional organization of the public relations function by segmentation of an organization's publics as discussed in chapter 10, on an examination of the five communication objectives, and on a comparison of the common processes, programs, and techniques shared by fund raising and public relations.

There have been few attempts either by scholars or practitioners to place fund raising within the public relations paradigm. After reviewing literature on the organizational level of these two functions, this chapter concludes that theoretical links between the two functions have been ignored because of misunderstandings of the fund-raising function and limited definitions of public relations. In addition, this chapter concludes that fund raising, as an organizational function, has traditionally been separated from public relations because of the historical models of both functions. The findings of an exploratory study of PRSA members who work for educational and cultural organizations provides evidence that the function of fund raising is rarely recognized as a specialization of public relations and that in most charitable organizations fund raising is a separate function from or is dominant over public relations (Kelly, 1989a).

On the mesolevel, the fund-raising concept of "matching donor interest" can be linked to Grunig's (in preparation) first two steps of strategic public relations management. In other words, the fund-raising literature recommends that fund-raising practitioners identify issues important to their organization and then segment donor publics that respond differentially to those issues. On the microlevel, the generally accepted process of fund raising consists of four steps: research, cultivation, solicitation, and recognition. Using the RACE formula (cited in Grunig & Hunt, 1984), which advocates a four-step process of research, action, communication, and evaluation, and Grunig and Hunt's behavioral molecule, the chapter concludes that the process of fund raising is similar to that used in public relations.

Using Grunig's (in preparation; Grunig & Hunt, 1984) five communication objectives of public relations, this chapter concludes that fund raising is a public relations specialization that requires—at some point—a communication objective of affecting behavior in the short term, but it can also maximize long-term behavioral changes by selecting short-term cognitive effects for the majority of its programs. The application of this theory of communication objectives to fund raising is supported by current fund-raising practices and axioms, which strengthens the premise of this book that fund raising is basically a communication function.

Finally, the techniques used by fund raising provide little, if any, differentiation between the fund-raising and public relations functions, and the selection of techniques is based on the same communication objectives for fund raising as it is for public relations (e.g., whereas annual giving is primarily built on mass communication techniques, major gift solicitation requires the same interpersonal communications that the public relations manager is advised to use in legislative relations or in dealing with activist publics).

Although there have been few attempts to include fund raising, or "gift getting," within the public relations paradigm, there is a related precedent in the for-profit sector where some public relations practitioners recently have integrated "gift giving" within their departments. The book turns now to that related precedent to further strengthen its argument that fund raising is a specialization of public relations.

Chapter 12

Corporate Public Relations: A Precedent

This chapter presents an analogy of public relations practitioners within corporations who have recognized the value of integrating the philanthropic activities of their organizations into their public relations programs. This analogy is presented in response to the question: Given the fact that little attempt has been made to place fund raising within the public relations paradigm, what evidence can be found to substantiate the hypothesis that fund raising can contribute more to organizational effectiveness as a subfunction of public relations than as a separate function?

Chapter 12 reviews the concept of corporate contributions and recent efforts to tie "gift giving" to corporate programs with public relations and marketing objectives. Criticism of these trends reveals that the issue of autonomy is a central one to the "giving and getting" of corporate gifts. This chapter concludes that charitable organizations, like corporations, can reap economic and sociopolitical benefits by incorporating fund raising within the public relations department. A related conclusion is that raising money for the sake of raising money is short-sighted and costly—just as giving away contributions in isolation of other corporate objectives leads to ineffective philanthropy. Finally, this chapter concludes that incorporating fund raising into the public relations function of charitable organizations increases effectiveness by helping those organizations manage threats to their autonomy and by mobilizing support for them.

Levy and Oviatt (1989), public relations managers at AT&T, demonstrated how contributions—or philanthropy from the perspective of the provider of gifts—

adds to the effectiveness of corporations when integrated within the public relations function. As mentioned in chapter 11, the second edition of Cantor and Burger's (1989) book replaced the chapter on fund raising with a chapter on "Corporate Philanthropy," which was written by Reynold Levy, corporate vice president and founding president of the AT&T Foundation, and Frank Oviatt, Jr., AT&T director of public relations. These public relations practitioners argued that corporate contributions belong within the public relations function, saying, "For the corporation, philanthropy is a business pursuit to be managed. . . . It is also a function that can and should be integral to intelligent public relations management" (p. 137). The authors recognized that their approach to philanthropy is a new and largely unusual one, stating:

> Rare is the PR officer who understands the third sector. . . . There is little sense of what a serious relationship between for-profit and not-for-profit institutions mean. . . . Indeed, the importance of corporate philanthropy as an indispensable element of public relations management may even go unrecognized. (p. 127)

Levy and Oviatt (1989) acknowledged that corporations have complex motivations for giving, but, in agreement with the conclusions reached in chapter 8, these public relations practitioners said that the motivations of individuals and private foundations are also complex. To Levy and Oviatt, corporate philanthropy means balancing idealism and self-interest, which is argued here to be an accurate assessment of philanthropy from all three sources—an assessment that underlines the importance of negotiations in the fund-raising process. Saying that philanthropy lies at where the interests of benefactor and beneficiary intersect, Levy and Oviatt argued that the overlapping interests of charitable organizations and the various functions of corporations (e.g., "marketing and sales, recruiting and personnel, public affairs, and community relations to name just a few," p. 137) are "mind-boggling" (p. 137). They said that none of the corporate functions just listed can be successful acting in isolation from the others, but that the relationship between a corporation and charitable organizations "needs to be managed overall by a party respected . . . for its objective judgement, impartial thinking, communication, and *negotiating skills*" (p. 137; italics added). The authors concluded, "None is so qualified as professional public relations to have primary responsibility for these interfaces through corporate philanthropy" (p. 137).

According to Levy and Oviatt (1989), the idealism of corporate philanthropy is demonstrated by a 1986 study by Yankelovick, Skelly, and White, which found that two thirds of America's chief executive officers justified corporate giving in terms of "helping the needy, doing what is 'ethically correct,' and improving communities in which employees live and the company does business" (p. 130). These idealistic motivations are referred to by the authors as "traditional" reasons for corporate giving. A fifth traditional reason, they said, is to limit the scope of government (i.e., the more services provided by charitable organizations, the less government is required).

Addressing the overall concept responsible for these idealistic motivations, Levy and Oviatt support the commonly accepted, yet controversial argument discussed in chapter 8 that philanthropy is integral to the activities of a socially responsible corporation—an argument that Baumol (1975), Olasky (1987), and others refute. However, Levy and Oviatt believe that corporate philanthropy should not be justified on such admirable motivations alone, and they provide compelling arguments as to how contributions can be *managed* by public relations practitioners to yield economic and sociopolitical benefits for the corporation. For example, the authors pointed out that the economic power of the nonprofit sector, which includes more than 800,000 organizations that spend more than $200 billion annually, is a strong reason for utilizing corporate gifts to stimulate and sustain relationships. In other words, corporate donors frequently are also contractual vendors to their recipient organizations.

This economic reason for utilizing corporate contributions to stimulate and sustain relationships has significance for the management of fund raising. The simple fact is that it is difficult for a charitable organization to raise corporate gifts if it ignores the profit motives of corporations. On the other hand, the mixing of philanthropic and market relationships is not without problems.

For example, I recently managed the solicitation of a grant of $1.5 million to endow a faculty chair from a competitor of AT&T. As a three-way partnership between the University of Maryland, its business school, and the corporate partner, a telecommunications center, funded by institutional monies, was to be established around the endowed chair (i.e., allocations of internal funds are often used as a demonstration of institutional commitment to the purpose of the gift and as leverage to attract private gifts and vice versa). Less than 1 month after the $1.5-million proposal was presented to the corporation, a $32.8-million telecommunications contract for the university—on which the corporate prospect had bid—was awarded to AT&T. Although the lost contract never entered into formal discussions on the proposed grant, corporate officers let it be known that the solicitation, which was based on an industrial-university "partnership," had been damaged by awarding a profit-making project to a competitor. Five months after the contract was awarded, the chairman of the corporation formally turned down the fund-raising proposal, citing economic difficulties faced by his company.

In contrast, shortly after AT&T was awarded the contract for the new telecommunications system by the University of Maryland, that corporation made the first payment on a $1-million grant, which had developed from a multi-year research project with a faculty member in the psychology department. This example points out that a charitable organization's business relationships can and do impact on the management of the fund-raising function. In this instance, the timing of the request for a gift from AT&T's corporate competitor demanded the impossible: that the corporation losing the contract would ignore its self-interest and act on altruistic motives alone. In AT&T's case, the decision to make a gift, which must be emphasized grew out of a long-term relationship, was strengthened by the presence of economic benefits in the relationship. As was pointed out by Gouldner (1960) in chapter 6, "A social unit or group is more likely to contribute to another which provides it with benefits than one which does not" (p. 164).

This is not to assume, however, that there should be a perfect correlation between a gift and direct, economic benefit for the donor. As discussed in earlier chapters, self-interest, including direct benefits, is secondary to the public interest in gift exchanges.

Levy and Oviatt (1989), for example, emphasized that the tax-deductibility of their company's contributions can only be protected "if the gifts are charitable in purpose and serve the public interest" (p. 133). In other words, gifts from corporate vendors grow out of relationships that are established for long-term benefits, which may include economic benefits at some point. Gifts do not have a causal relationship with direct benefits, as interpreted by Brittingham and Pezzullo (1990) in chapter 4.

Setting aside ethical and legal issues, it also would not be in the university's self-interest to award a $32.8-million contract in exchange for a $1.5-million gift (that was restricted for a specific purpose) if the donor's bid on the contract was significantly higher than bids from other companies—which was the case in the example just given. It must be remembered that in a market transaction, the university, as well as other charitable organizations—who, contrary to conventional wisdom, are concerned with profits—seek economic benefits (*quid*) that are equal to or exceed the *quo* foregone in that transaction.

Rather than viewing gifts as a direct result of a business contract, a charitable organization should utilize established relationships with corporate vendors to segment a prospect pool for researching, cultivating, and soliciting private gifts. In short, the profit motivation of corporate donors cannot be isolated from fund raising, nor should the economic power of charitable organizations be ignored in the process of raising gifts.

Furthermore, it can be argued that managing fund raising within the public relations function would help ensure that donor–recipient relationships with corporate vendors are dealt with in a socially responsible manner. Following the lead of Levy and Oviatt (1989), the public relations function would provide the necessary broader perspective that can protect donor relations from being reduced to transactions of self-interest (i.e., as part of its responsibility for managing relations with _all_ publics, the public relations function would diffuse a narrow focus on donors and examine such relationships as they affect members of other publics, such as nondonor companies and legislators).

Economic power is just one of the four "nontraditional" reasons Levy and Oviatt (1989) gave for utilizing corporate gifts to stimulate and sustain relationships with charitable organizations. The other three reasons were: power of public respect, access to activist groups, and increased power for the public relations department. Levy and Oviatt argued, for example, that the "power of public respect" (p. 131) commanded by many charitable organizations and their leaders can be of great value to a corporate donor. They pointed out that opinion surveys concerning public trust consistently rank university leadership far higher than business leaders. Theories based on affinity would support the benefits gained by corporations when affiliated with charitable organizations and their leaders who hold high public trust. Because of their public relations orientation, Levy and Oviatt are among the few who recognize that relationships with charitable organizations frequently provide strong communication channels to and cultivation opportunities for "a set of highly influential shapers of public opinion" (p. 131).

As with all of Levy and Oviatt's (1989) economic and sociopolitical reasons for incorporating philanthropy within the public relations function, a case can be made for generalizing this argument to the "getting" of gifts. Just as funding relationships with charitable organizations help corporations communicate with and cultivate opinion leaders, so too does fund raising provide communication channels and cultivation opportunities for charitable organizations to influence corporate leaders, and through them, government officials. For example, the University of Maryland's College of Engineering was successful in obtaining a $5 million enhancement grant from the state legislature in 1983 largely because of the testimony offered by corporate leaders whose companies were major donors to the engineering school. Working together, the then director of university relations, Patrick Hunt (who was referred to earlier in chapter 10), and the dean of engineering arranged to have businessmen like the president of the local Westinghouse division—the state's largest private employer—testify in support of the enhancement bill. As employers _and_ major donors, these business leaders spoke with credibility and conviction about their interest in increasing the quality of engineering education in Maryland.

Nor are such communication channels and cultivation opportunities limited to corporations. Donor relationships with alumni also can be utilized by colleges and universities to influence opinion leaders. In a recent presentation titled, "The Influence of Alumni on the Legislative Process," Vaughan (1988) expressed his indignation at what he perceived to be short-sighted, fund-raising goals that circumvent the full benefits of alumni relations. He said that fund raising has taken a dominant role in today's institutional advancement efforts, which has blinded colleges and universities to issues and publics that are important to their survival and success. He said, "We've let that all important quest for a few development dollars cloud our vision" (p. 27). As an example, Vaughan pointed out that public institutions such as his (i.e., the University of Texas) receive significantly more money from state appropriations than they do from private gifts; yet, alumni of such institutions usually are asked to only give money without being asked to get involved in the legislative process. Calling alumni "permanent stockholders of the university," Vaughan recommended that they should be used as "card carrying lobbyists" for their colleges and universities (p. 13).

Vaughan (1988) contended that American institutions of higher education are facing a crisis of accountability, saying, "Universities are not perceived as productive, innovative suppliers of trained minds, but I suggest as burgeoning bureaucracies which every year come back to legislators for greater budgets" (p. 10). Echoing the argument presented in chapter 10 that fund raising isolated from public relations can result in charitable organizations ignoring key publics other than donors, Vaughan stated:

> We're worried about raising peanuts instead of getting alumni meaningfully involved in the institution. . . . I'm not against fund raising. . . . It's important, it's just not the most important. What we're talking about here is the most important. If we don't get public confidence for our institutions, what do you have left? (p. 27)

Levy and Oviatt's (1989) relatively new approach to corporate contributions also allowed them to point out an often overlooked, but important argument for establishing and maintaining a well-managed program of philanthropy within the public relations department: It provides access to activist groups for the purpose of engaging in meaningful dialogue. As the authors pointed out, all social movements—from historical ones such as child labor laws to the more modern issues of environmental and consumer protection, equality of economic and educational opportunity, advocacy for the handicapped and the aged, and neighborhood empowerment—have originated in the nonprofit sector. The authors tie this facet of our democratic society to the opportunities provided by corporate contributions when they stated:

> The corporation, then, has a choice. It can deal with such historic movements generated by these groups *after* they have crystallized. . . . Or it can interact with these organizations and their issues before they become forces to be reckoned with on their own terms. The PR officer who takes an active approach, viewing these entities as potential partners, consultants, and allies, finds new meaning in philanthropy. It is an open door for access, one route by which this constituency can be reached and meaningfully engaged. (p. 131)

As discussed later in the chapter on fund-raising models, the description of public relations behavior just given would be defined as the two-way symmetric model of public relations—a model that Grunig (in preparation) advocated as a socially responsible one, as well as one that is pragmatically more effective than the other three models. In other words, when the purpose of public relations is to achieve mutual understanding between an organization and its publics, philanthropy can be a means to establishing dialogue that facilitates such understanding. As is discussed shortly, however, some corporations and their corporate foundations recently have been criticized for donating funds to activist groups as a means for "buying them off," rather than for establishing a two-way flow of communication.

From the perspective of gift getting, philanthropy also provides access to constituencies forming around an issue whose actions may be damaging to a charitable organization. For example, high-technology companies may perceive their local university as being unresponsive to their applied research needs (i.e., university faculty are perceived as being more interested in basic research than in applying knowledge to new technologies). Rather than ignoring this issue and the public forming around it, fund raising can help the university interact with members of this public and address the issue of their concern before they become a force to be reckoned with on their own terms. If ignored, managers of such companies might take their complaints to state government, which might lead to task forces, reports, and new regulations (i.e., a loss of autonomy). On the other hand, the fund-raising function, managed by public relations, can help the university engage in meaningful dialogue with such a public through the funding of applied research grants for faculty.

In such a case, the donors would restrict their gifts to the purpose of applied research, and faculty who were interested in receiving grant funding (e.g., as an alternative to summer teaching) would conduct appropriate research that would produce the desired results. As mentioned earlier in this book, such industrial-university partnerships are already quite common; the difference, however, is that fund raising, as managed by the public relations office, would take an active approach to seeking out such partnerships, not solely for the dollars raised, but for the purpose of establishing a dialogue with a potentially antagonistic public. In other words, fund raising in such an instance would help a charitable organization enhance its autonomy by seeking out sources of external funding and protect its autonomy by seeking gifts that resolve emerging conflicts between the organization and its strategic publics. The value of such gifts to a charitable organization surpasses the face value of the gift, for as Grunig (in preparation) said, "The major purpose of public relations is to *save* money for the organization by managing threats to its autonomy and mobilizing support for it." The negotiations involved in this exchange process, of course, would be critical to a satisfactory outcome for both parties, as recommended under the two-way symmetric model of fund raising, which is discussed in chapter 13.

As a point of clarification, however, it must be noted here that the two-way symmetric model of fund raising—as described in the example just given—bears some resemblance to the marketing perspective of fund raising, which was rejected in chapter 5. It is recalled that one of the reasons a marketing perspective is inappropriate is because the marketer's defined role is to generate sales by changing an organization's products and services, whereas the acknowledged role of the fund raiser is to support a charitable organization's offerings by generating gifts. In that both the two-way symmetric model and the marketing perspective of fund raising respond to needs and desires of donor publics, the two are, indeed, similar. However, the significant difference is that fund raising as a marketing function shapes an organization's products and services in order to generate gifts, whereas the two-way symmetric model of fund raising responds to needs of strategic donor publics in order to enhance and protect autonomy, thereby saving the charitable organization money.

As stated in chapter 5, "The major purpose of marketing is to make money for an organization by increasing the slope of the demand curve" (Grunig & Grunig, 1988, p. 5). The primary purpose of fund raising—as approached from a public relations perspective—is not to make money, but to help a charitable organization effectively manage environmental interdependencies with donors.

It should also be noted that the example of how the two-way symmetric model "shaped" a university's offerings to satisfy the needs of a strategic public was not only consistent with the research mission of a university, but also satisfied what we can assume to be a need of the institution. In other words, by generating funding for applied research grants, the model satisfied the needs of the high-technology companies and provided financial support for faculty who desired supplemental income for such work. Carried to an extreme, a fund raiser approaching the same situation from a marketing perspective would ignore the needs of the strategic public if the level of funding was lower than alternative prospects, or would direct all research efforts toward applied rather than basic purposes if the demand was high.

In summary, the two-way symmetric model enhances and protects a charitable organization's autonomy by helping it be more accountable to those publics that are critical to survival and success, whereas the marketing perspective of fund raising strives to raise the greatest amount of gifts possible at the expense of both autonomy and accountability.

The fourth and final nontraditional reason that Levy and Oviatt (1989) gave for managing corporate contributions within the public relations function was the increase in status with senior management that these responsibilities bring to the function. Levy and Oviatt said, "We further see philanthropy as another factor that helps bring PR people to the decision table and into the confidence of top management" (p. 137). Grunig and Grunig (1989) stated the following:

> When public relations managers have power in the dominant coalition, they can influence organizational ideology and the choice of publics in the environment for which strategic public relations programs are planned. At that point, public relations practitioners can fulfill a communication counseling and management role—and truly practice the profession defined for them in public relations textbooks but seldom fulfilled in the real world. (p. 60)

Philanthropy, according to Levy and Oviatt (1989), "offers a path into the CEO's office and confidence that may be without parallel among the avenues normally available to a PR officer" (p. 131). Because philanthropy traditionally operates at the highest management levels of corporations, the chief executive finds him or herself personally involved in fund-raising efforts with a network of peers, among whom she or he wants to be accepted. As Levy and Oviatt stated, "Whoever can professionally handle such matters on behalf of the CEO wins his or her gratitude, respect—and time" (p. 132).

It can be generalized that this reasoning holds true not only for the public relations manager of for-profit organizations that provide philanthropic resources, but also for those who help senior management acquire such resources for a charitable organization. Grunig (in preparation) said that public relations managers "gain power when they have knowledge and skills that help organizations manage crucial environmental interdependencies—such as skills in financial relations when stockholders are a key interdependency or skills in government relations when government is a key public." Following Grunig, it can be concluded that public relations managers of charitable organizations gain power when they have knowledge and skills in fund raising when donors are a key interdependency.

If we assume that salary is to some extent a reward for perceived value in managing crucial interdependencies, then a comparison of salaries offers some evidence that charitable organizations currently perceive a greater value in fund raising than in public relations. Although other factors affect salary differences between public relations and fund-raising practitioners (e.g., the current unbalance of supply and demand in the fund-raising field), it is revealing to note that one third of the respondents in the PRSA study of educational and cultural organizations stated that fund raisers make $10,000 to $40,000 more a year than public relations practitioners (Kelly, 1989b). Many of the PRSA respondents believed that this salary difference was justified because of the difference in demand for the two functions. One consultant, who described her function as 50% marketing, 25% fund raising, and 25% public relations, said, "There are few good fund raisers and when you find one, you are willing to pay for it [sic]; whereas, there are a lot of public relations people" (Kelly, 1989a, p. 4).

In higher education, a recent salary study of academic administrators showed that chief public relations officers at all U.S. colleges and universities make an average of $16,450 a year *less* than chief development officers, and that those chief administrators who manage both the public relations *and* fund-raising functions earn an average of $22,460 more than the public relations officers ("Administrators' pay," 1989).

Finally, Levy and Oviatt (1989) supported the theory of donor relations developed in this book by saying, "A corporate public relations officer has as much reason to understand, stay informed about, and be concerned with the third sector as with the fourth estate, the employee body, the electorate and their chosen representatives, neighbors living near company facilities, and customers, wherever they may be" (pp. 136-137). In other words, these public relations practitioners advocate a reorganization of the public relations function to include donor relations, as well as the more traditional programs of media relations, employee relations, government relations, community relations, and consumer relations. Anticipating resistance by public relations practitioners to incorporating philanthropy into their function, Levy and Oviatt warned, "Yield to others or regard this function as a cloying 'necessary evil' and PR inflicts damage on its own professional standing. Worse, it deprives the company it purports to serve of the value such relationships afford" (p. 137).

This warning is equally applicable to those public relations practitioners who work for charitable organizations, who—as described in chapter 11—believe that the ideal relationship between public relations and fund raising is a separate, but equal one. By yielding the responsibility for donor relations to specialized fund raisers or by regarding fund raising as a distasteful and mysterious activity, these public relations practitioners are damaging their own power within such organizations, as documented in chapter 11 by the number of public relations departments reporting to the fund-raising function. As pointed out by Grunig (in preparation), organizational power comes to those who can help an organization manage a key interdependency, and if donors are considered such, fund raisers will continue to gain power at the expense of the public relations function that distances itself from donors. More importantly, by denying responsibility for donor relations, public relations practitioners reduce the effectiveness and increase the vulnerability of their charitable organizations because they are not in a position to influence the choice of publics in the environment for which strategic public relations programs are planned. As illustrated in chapter 10, when donor relations is not approached as one of many important linkages to the environment, the charitable organization may be damaged by conflicts with other key publics—conflicts that can lead to extreme costs and loss of autonomy.

Unfortunately, the views of Levy and Oviatt (1989) represent a new approach for corporate philanthropy—one that is just starting to receive notice by public relations scholars and practitioners. Only a small number of corporations hold similar views. According to an article in *pr reporter* ("Strategic giving," 1987), Arco, Procter & Gamble, and Dayton Hudson are three corporations that practice "strategic giving," which the president of the Arco Foundation described as investing in the future of the company. Recommending that corporate contributions be viewed as part of the entire public affairs and corporate process, the article stated, "It's essential management understand that the benefit of contributions affects the entire company, e.g. quality of future employees, community support, etc." (p. 2).

Today, many major corporations in the United States continue to operate their philanthropic activities through separate corporate foundations that are not headed by public relations practitioners, or through organizational departments other than public relations. In a number of cases, corporate contributions are utilized to support the objectives of individual departments (e.g., employee recruitment or product development) without the centralized management recommended by Levy and Oviatt (1989).

At the 1989 conference of the Mid-Atlantic District of the Council for Advancement and Support of Education (CASE), corporate contribution officers representing Pfiser Corporation, GTE Corporation, and General Motors told an audience of educational fund raisers that by the year 2000, almost all "gifts" they administer would have to demonstrate a direct impact on their corporations' "bottom line" ("Corporate philanthropy," 1989). The examples of such fundable projects within education included college scholarships to attract engineers and technicians, secondary school grants to reverse the diminishing pool of skilled labor, and research in fields related to corporate product lines. Other than a continued need for programs that would match gifts made by employees and provide grants to geographic areas of production (i.e., elements of employee relations and community relations), there was little mention of philanthropic objectives in support of social responsibility (i.e., Levy & Oviatt's traditional reasons for establishing relationships with charitable organizations), or for objectives related to Levy and Oviatt's nontraditional reasons.

As is recalled from the beginning of this discussion, Levy and Oviatt (1989) recommended that philanthropy be managed overall by the public relations function because separate corporate functions, such as marketing, cannot achieve in isolation the success that is possible through the integration of corporate contributions. Although these practitioners made no apologies for gifts given in support of corporate objectives, they argued that such gifts are *not* market transactions, but part of a socially responsible and effective approach to philanthropy.

They said, for example, that the best philanthropic programs are those that are characterized "by well-defined criteria and priorities that relate closely to company objectives and business plans" (p. 132). Yet, they emphasized that their approach to philanthropy is not a market exchange one that might characterize isolated giving in support of departmental objectives, stating:

> No grant is ever based on quid pro quos, or to realize immediate, short-term company benefits. Rather, philanthropy should be approached as a long-term investment that stimulates and reinforces the overall relationship with nonprofit institutions. (p. 133)

Levy and Oviatt presented an approach to philanthropy similar to the theory of donor relations developed in this book when they stated the following:

> By integrating our involvement with the third sector, we believe we win dividends most responsibly and consistently—in recruitment, in the market-place, in access to research, in our strong association with community service, and in fostering a reputation for excellence. (p. 133)

In other words, philanthropy—whether approached from the giving or getting of gifts—can increase the effectiveness of an organization, on the basis of both social responsibility and pragmatic objectives, when it is integrated within the public relations function. Therefore, this book recommends that fund raising for charitable organizations be integrated within the public relations function and that a two-way symmetric model of fund raising be adopted, which is discussed in more detail in later chapters.

In addition to the supporting evidence just provided, Levy and Oviatt gave one more substantial reason for integrating the philanthropic function within a public relations department that seeks the benefits of long-term relationships and not short-term, quasi-market results—a reason that is rarely acknowledged by most corporate donors. As these practitioners said, "Positioning the company as a thoughtful contributor to key nonprofit institutions is not only what works best, but what is legally required" (p. 133). As referred to earlier, they wisely pointed out that the tax-exempt status of their company's foundation and the deductibility of company contributions to the foundation can only be protected "if the gifts are charitable in purpose and serve the public interest" (p. 133). As discussed in chapter 5 and as elaborated on in the final chapter of this book, the closer gift giving and getting move toward market transactions, the more likely that public opinion will turn against charitable organizations and that government will move to rescind the special tax benefits conferred on these organizations. As Ylvisaker (1987) stated, "But inexorably, those who practice modern philanthropy and those who are affected by it have come to realize that this process of private considering and giving for the public interest is itself a matter of the public interest" (p. 376). And Payton (1987) added:

> Philanthropy owes its credibility to its altruistic imperative—to remain philanthropic it must by definition give first place to the other rather than to the self. It is not that self-interest does not often yield altruistic benefits; what matters is that acts guided primarily by self-interest are called something else. They are not philanthropic in intent. (p. 39)

In other words, fund raising—if not managed as philanthropic exchanges with donor publics—may prompt regulatory changes that could threaten the very existence of charitable organizations in the United States.

As discussed earlier, much of corporate philanthropy is moving in directions that unfortunately might prompt such regulatory action. The fact that some practitioners and scholars call corporate philanthropy an oxymoron underlines the danger of such trends. Perhaps one of the most visible indicators of a "market mentality" in gift giving and getting is the trend toward "cause-related marketing" in corporate philanthropy. This trend demonstrates how a nonintegrated approach to corporate contributions, as well as a nonintegrated approach to fund raising, can significantly alter the philanthropic relationship between charitable organizations and corporate donors and endanger the tax advantages enjoyed by both. Ironically, the trend toward cause-related marketing is being used today to justify the integration of corporate contributions within the public relations function.

In his research report on the public relations body of knowledge (which has no relationship to the study discussed in chapter 4 by the PRSA Task Force, 1988), Walker (1988) said that the combination of marketing with philanthropy from the corporate donor's perspective helps to define the parameters of public relations knowledge. In defense of this inclusion of philanthropy within the public relations domain, Walker cited several articles from recent issues of *pr reporter* and *purview* and excerpted the following quote from *purview* about cause-related marketing: "Marketing and public relations professionals are increasingly linking corporate contributions to marketing. . . . Following the model of American Express which tied corporate contributions to marketing efforts, more companies are searching for ways to benefit from philanthropy" (p. 63).

In the Fall of 1983, the American Express Company ran a national advertising campaign that promised to donate a penny to the refurbishing of the Statue of Liberty for each use of its charge card and $1 for new cards issued (Dannelley, 1986). At the conclusion of the campaign, card usage had increased 28%, the number of new card holders had risen by more than 45%, the company's card business had had its best fourth quarter ever, and American Express presented checks totaling $1.7 million to the Statue of Liberty–Ellis Island Foundation. The company's then marketing executive, Jerry Welsh (cited in Dannelley, 1986), who is largely credited with starting the trend in cause-related marketing, was quoted in 1984 as saying, "The wave of the future isn't checkbook philanthropy. It's a marriage of corporate marketing and social responsibility" (p. 129).

According to Shell (1989), cause-related marketing has moved away from sports-oriented and more traditional charitable sponsorships to support for human rights and social problems (e.g., Johnson & Johnson, makers of feminine hygiene products, is combating domestic violence by funding shelters for battered women). Such corporate philanthropy, Shell said results "in the best of all promotional worlds: higher visibility, a unique image niche resulting from association with worthy projects and stronger ties to the community" (p. 8). Corporate managers involved in cause-related marketing maintain that their participation is motivated primarily by their belief in social responsibility and that the causes they select to support reflect their corporate values.

However, former American Express executive Welsh (cited in Shell, 1989) said that such managers "must not lose sight of the fact that a cause-related promotion is, ultimately, 'just a marketing tool'" (p. 13). Welsh said that in order to be successful, corporations have to be sure that the cause is compelling to the target market that has been pinpointed as the corporation's primary consumers. "It has to be specific and meet your marketing needs," he said (p.

13). Comparing it to promotional or advertising campaigns, Shell (1989) said, "Cause-related marketing's ability to secure an exclusive niche that helps increase a company's visibility is making it increasingly attractive to companies that can afford the costs" (p. 13).

Regardless of any self-proclaimed motivations of altruism, cause-related marketing is designed to yield direct, short-term benefits to corporations in the form of increased sales. As related to public relations, cause-related marketing is product promotion (i.e., programs are designed to affect the buying behavior of the corporation's consumer public).

It is argued here that such direct benefits generated from marketplace exchanges can be detrimental in the long run to charitable organizations and to the corporations who deduct their gifts to such organizations. As Payton (1987) said, "Philanthropy is often compromised by its use of marketplace techniques" (p. 38).

It is further argued that corporate philanthropy is not as successful when used primarily in support of the objectives of one organizational function, such as marketing, as it is when managed for the overall effectiveness of the corporation, as recommended by Levy and Oviatt (1989). For example, by focusing their philanthropy primarily on consumer publics, corporations will miss out on the benefits that might be gained through philanthropic relations with other strategic publics, such as activists or influential opinion leaders.

In addition, public relations departments that limit their involvement in corporate philanthropy to efforts in support of marketing objectives will not gain the same degree of organizational power referred to by Levy and Oviatt, nor will they contribute as much as they could to the effectiveness of their corporations (i.e., their concentration on helping the corporation *make* money will displace their primary purpose of helping the corporation *save* money by effectively managing environmental interdependencies).

Independent Sector recently surveyed 17 companies and 13 charitable organizations that had engaged in cause-related marketing. According to an item about the survey in CASE *Currents* ("Making the case," 1989), "The companies reported that such marketing created a 'win-win' situation for them, the cause, and the consumer" (p. 14). Several of the charitable organizations, however, reported that the increase in funds raised was lower than what they had expected. "Problems occur," according to the *Currents* item, "mostly in recognizing the differences between businesses and nonprofits" (p. 14).

Discussing industrial-university partnerships and the fact that corporate support for research often has strings attached, the president of the Association of American Universities (cited in "'In' box," 1987) stated:

If a lion and a lamb are going to lie down together, they'd better have a good idea about their intrinsic differences. Otherwise, when they wake up for breakfast, they're likely to find that one will be the breakfast. (p. A15)

Or, as Payton (1987) is quoted in chapter 8:

The interaction of voluntary, not-for-profit, private-sector, public-interest organizations and institutions with government and business can lead to a confusion of roles. Any of the three sectors can be compromised by borrowing too many of the core values of the other. (p. 40)

In other words, increased and widespread use of cause-related marketing may lead to the "commercialization" of philanthropy, which, in turn, may damage the tax-deduction of gifts and the tax-exemption of charitable organizations. For example, a Maryland drugstore chain recently started a sales promotion program that will donate 5% of the company's gross receipts to local charities ("Drugstore chain," 1989). Requiring charitable organizations to register with the company in order to qualify for contributions, Fantle's drugstores launched its program with advertisements that stated, "If you're worried about the environment, hunger, child abuse, cancer, poverty, AIDS, and homelessness, now you can do something about it. Go Shopping" (p. 14).

Fantle's management predicts that the boost in sales provided by the contributions program will far outweigh the costs to the company ("Drugstore chain," 1989). The managers have a good basis for their prediction because their program is modeled after a similar one conducted by a supermarket chain in Richmond, Virginia that contributes twice the percentage of sales to charity, and still that chain's marketing and communications coordinator said, "If we didn't think that we were coming out with more benefits than costs, we wouldn't continue it" (p. 14).

As emphasized in earlier discussions, Douglas (1983) said the laws governing charitable organizations demand that the benefits in a gift exchange relationship "must not be fully captured by the *quid pro quo* but must spill over into society at large" (p. 62). On the basis of this legal definition, cause-related marketing as described here cannot be defined as philanthropy because the benefits to the donor actually exceed the costs.

As is recalled from chapter 5, Gurin (1990) condemned cause-related marketing for commercializing philanthropy in a recent opinion piece, "Joint Fund-Raising Ventures With Business Are Making Philanthropy Too Commercial." Gurin said that such ventures will result in charitable organizations modifying their program objectives and increased government regulation (i.e., losses of high degrees of autonomy). Concerned with the profound effect this trend may have on the very existence of charitable organizations, Gurin said,

"The services philanthropy provides to society are far more important to business than is the help some charities can provide to corporations seeking to bolster their short-term profits" (p. 37).

It is useful here to point out a few other indications that the giving of gifts is more appropriate for the public relations function rather than the marketing function of corporations. Discussing new approaches to building consensus through community relations, Lowengard (1989) said that corporate affairs officers see community relations as "inextricably linked with the business of corporate philanthropy" (p. 24). According to Lowengard, these practitioners turn naturally to solving the social problems of the community through gift giving programs when referring to community relations (e.g., educational outreach programs, job training and urban unemployment, and child care). Lowengard said there are two branches of community relations: one that is marketing driven, "in which the primary thrust of the effort is to draw attention to the product" (p. 25), and one that she credited to John Hussey, executive vice president of Hill & Knowlton. Quoting Hussey, Lowengard said that the second type of community relations is developed and practiced in order "to gain community support and maintain the freedom to operate among publics that might not easily understand or appreciate the benefits of the products being manufactured" (p. 25). Hussey's version of community relations, as practiced by corporate public relations officers who link philanthropy with such programs, correlates with Useem's (1987) argument discussed in chapter 8 that corporations make contributions to preserve their autonomy (i.e., in times of crisis, such as a plant closing, corporations are granted more flexibility by community residents if they have increased their public standing through corporate contributions).

The former president of the General Electric Foundation, Paul Ostergard (cited in "GE bucks crowd," 1988), seems to support the concept of incorporating philanthropy within the public relations function. Addressing contributions officers from U.S. corporations at a Conference Board workshop in February 1988, Ostergard detailed a new direction for the GE Foundation, saying, "Policy innovations include targeting grants to local areas to better serve General Electric's various 'relations interests,' which include public and community relations, employee and customer relations, and government affairs" (p. 2).

In the introduction to his book, Dannelley (1986) reprinted an article from the October 1984 issue of *PR Journal*, which presented a panel discussion on the role of public relations in the giving of gifts by corporations. The opinions of the "leading authorities on philanthropy," who made up the panel, were mixed in that a few advocated management of corporate contributions by the public relations function, whereas others recommended a close, but separate approach.

For example, John Schwartz (cited in Dannelley, 1986), who was then the executive vice president of the National Council on Fund Raising, said that public relations practitioners are becoming more educated and involved in philanthropy, but added, "Still, unless the public relations person also heads the giving program, practitioners are not the decision makers on grants" (p. 15). Schwartz said that public relations practitioners can be helpful in corporate contributions "without necessarily having the same outlook as the corporate giving officer" (p. 15). On the other hand, James Joseph (cited in Dannelley, 1986), president of the Council on Foundations, said that corporations should "combine into one unit all entities serving their publics" (p. 15). He continued by stating:

> Public relations ought to interact with government relations; together they should interact with community relations; and the three should coordinate with the corporate-contributions staff. All four entities ought to report to someone who has total responsibility for the corporate publics—perhaps the vice president for public relations. (p. 15)

Saying that he formerly headed such a unit in 1972 at Cummins Engine Co., Joseph (cited in Dannelley, 1986) reported, "The integrated approach to the responsibilities of the corporation gave management a far greater impact than it would have had if those entities were allowed to operate individually and in isolation" (p. 16).

Turning now to activist publics, corporations, as mentioned earlier in this chapter, have been criticized for using contributions to "buy off" activist groups that threaten their autonomy. For example, the Playboy Foundation, which gives about 65% of its grant money to women's organizations, has been charged by some groups as trying to silence protests against *Playboy* magazine ("'Reparations,'" 1989). Describing the situation of a self-avowed feminist nun, who was offered support from the Playboy Foundation when funding for shelters for homeless and ex-convict women was denied by her church, the article just cited said, "It was a dilemma that many other non-profit organizations . . . had been forced to confront at one time or another over the years: whether to take grants from a publisher that had become synonymous with busty nudes, and bunny suits" (p. 4). Accepting the offer of help, the nun is quoted as saying, "If women and children are hungry, we're not going to put a dollar bill under a microscope" (p. 4).

In contrast, critics of *Playboy* question the company's motives in making women's organizations a priority of its foundation, and one of them—a legal scholar and anti-pornography activist—believes *Playboy* is trying to "buy" the women's movement, saying that "organized opposition to pornography will be impossible as long as women's groups are economically beholden to *Playboy*" (p. 6).

Another critic ("'Reparations,'" 1989), whose battered-women's shelter will not accept *Playboy* funds, said, "If they give to women's groups, it eases their conscience and dilutes our ability to say what they're doing is wrong" (p. 6). Officials of women's organizations that accept *Playboy* money argue that corporate America has a long history of financing programs to fight social problems that they are accused of helping to cause. As the article stated, "Oil companies support environmental programs, tobacco companies support athletic events, and *Playboy* supports women's work" (p. 7).

Indeed, this assessment seems an accurate one. According to a recent article ("A new tobacco," 1989), there is a correlation between the fact that "smoking-related diseases kill proportionally more blacks than whites" and that minority organizations, such as the National Association for the Advancement of Colored People and the National Urban League, "receive generous contributions from the tobacco industry" (p. 20). Saying that Black organizations deny that they have been co-opted by their tobacco donors, the article quoted the chief fund raiser of the Urban League as saying, "The Urban League was founded on a partnership with business and black America. I frankly don't believe you can spend your time kicking or nibbling the ankles of people who you expect to be in partnership with" (p. 20). In response, a letter-to-the-editor from the vice president of Philip Morris U.S.A. (Kochevar, 1989) said that the article unfairly implied that "America's black leadership is for sale" (pp. 19-20).

Similarly, the alcohol industry has been criticized for its gift giving to charitable organizations that seek to influence public opinion and public policy on drunk driving and other issues. According to another recent article ("Drunk-driving foes," 1989), there are "extensive financial links between alcohol interests and several key groups" (p. 13), such as Students Against Drunk Driving (SADD). Pointing out that Anheuser-Busch gave $850,000 to SADD, or almost half of all gifts received by that group from 1983 through 1988, the article stated, "The group's independence, [critics] charge, has been seriously compromised by its heavy reliance on contributions from Anheuser-Busch Inc., the nation's largest brewing company" (p. 12). Some charitable organizations that support stricter regulation of alcohol, such as Remove Intoxicated Drivers (RID), refuse to accept gifts from industry representatives, and the president of RID explained the reasoning behind such behavior by saying, "You should not take money from an industry where, if your goals are met, you are going to deprive it of half its income" (p. 1). Also criticizing the acceptance of industry gifts, a lobbyist for the National Council on Alcoholism, which severed its financial ties to the alcohol industry in 1982, stated, "It's a 30-pieces-of-silver mentality. They buy you out for a mess of pottage" (p. 12).

Discussing the influence of industry gifts, the article ("Drunk-driving foes," 1989) pointed out that several charitable organizations that receive substantial contributions from alcohol-beverage makers have rejected or declined to take a stand on recent proposals by the Surgeon General to combat drunk driving. According to the article, "While alcohol-company officials deny exercising that kind of control, they say their policy is to avoid giving money to organizations that support 'extremist' measures" (p. 13). Defending the philanthropic activities of alcohol companies as part of their efforts to be good corporate citizens, an industry spokesman said, "We believe we are fulfilling our objective to be a part of the solution to the problem of alcohol abuse" (p. 12).

Responding to the article, a letter-to-the-editor by a certified fund-raising executive (i.e., one who has passed NSFRE's certification exam) of one of the charitable organizations that receives gifts from alcohol companies (Pidgeon, 1989) said that such donors do not infringe on autonomy because "they have consistently honored our council's policy that all gifts must be unrestricted in nature" (p. 29). Emphasizing the viewpoint of corporate giving as reparation for creating the problem in the first place, the same executive said, "Restriction advocates seem to forget that the alcoholic-beverage industry not only should, but has an obligation to, fund educational efforts to reduce abuse and alcoholism" (p. 29).

Finally, environmental charities seem to be moving toward a donor relationship with corporations in general, some of whom have been charged with environmentally harmful business practices. According to an article on the subject ("Many environmental groups," 1989), "While some continue to reject corporate donations on principle, others now detect no taint" (p. 4). For example, the corporate fund raiser for the National Audubon Society is quoted as saying, "Certainly in the past, there was a lot more feeling that you can't take corporate money because you are compromised, you are selling out" (p. 4). Although "corporate donations have lost the stigma they once had" (p. 4), the article pointed out that the search for corporate dollars by environmental organizations largely has been prompted by the growing competition for private gifts. The National Audubon fund raiser, for example, reported that his organization received only about $150,000 in corporate gifts in 1986, but expected to get nearly $1 million in such gifts in 1989, and said, "In general in the non-profit world, every day it gets more competitive for every dollar" (p. 4).

Unlike the examples related to specific industries given earlier, the case of corporate gifts to environmental organizations illustrates how such giving can facilitate two-way communication. According to the president of the Conservation Fund (cited in "Many environmental groups," 1989), "The trend has been from hostility, which came out of the Earth Day movement, to realizing that we have to work together and to find areas of common interest" (p. 4). Saying that his charitable organization continues to seek common ground where corporate and environmental interests converge, this president stated, "It's a very exciting time for cooperation rather than confrontation" (p. 4). Describing an associates program that charges corporate members $10,000 each, the director of the National Wildlife Federation (cited in "Many environmental groups," 1989) said that this group "tries to look at issues that are not already polarized or in court" (p. 5). She added that although her organization may take a different position on some issues from that of the companies represented in the associates program, "there are plenty of areas where we find a meeting of the minds" (p. 5). Addressing the fact that corporations and their charitable recipients may take different sides of an environmental issue, such as the preservation of the Alaskan wilderness, the National Audubon fund raiser cited earlier said, "Sometimes there are big policy areas that cause friction" (p. 5). However, in agreement with a selected "dialogue" approach, he added, "My point of view is that we can agree to disagree on certain issues, but that should not preclude companies and environmental groups from working together" (p. 5).

It must be pointed out, however, that some environmental organizations still view corporate giving as a means to influencing policy. The Citizens' Clearinghouse for Hazardous Waste refuses all corporate contributions because, as its executive director (cited in "Many environmental groups," 1989) said, "Corporate money usually comes with strings, or the appearance of strings" (p. 6). She continued by saying:

> Most of the people we work with are local community groups, which usually are in a position opposing the very companies that are offering lots of money. It's a moral issue. How can you say you're promoting the public's health and, on the other hand, take money from the very companies that are damaging it. (p. 6)

It should also be added that, like the alcohol industry, the companies most interested in showing support for the environment are those whose business practices are most affected by environmental regulation and that these companies rarely support the most litigious environmental groups. Instead, they direct their support to charitable organizations working on conservation, preservation of wildlife, public education, and other topics that arouse little controversy. According to its coordinator of corporate contributions (cited in "Many environmental groups," 1989), for example, Chevron U.S.A. "is concerned that

[it] not fund environmental groups that may be lobbying on the other side of issues like offshore drilling" (p. 6). Chevron's coordinator said, "We wouldn't support activities that are in opposition to our business interests" (p. 6).

This discussion of corporate giving to activist groups emphasizes that the issue of autonomy is a central one to the "giving and getting" of gifts. As demonstrated, charitable organizations can limit their autonomy to pursue goals when their goals are in conflict with those of the corporate donors from whom they have solicited and accepted gifts. Corporations, on the other hand, may use contributions to externally control activist groups and, thereby, avoid litigation and confrontation (i.e., seek to enhance their autonomy through gifts). It is argued here that such forms of gift giving and getting are neither socially responsible nor effective. It is further argued that "checkbook" philanthropy, rather than the long-term relationships recommended earlier by Levy and Oviatt (1989), will create unrealistic demands and conflict between corporations and activist groups.

Pires (1989) supported these arguments in her article, "Working With Activist Groups." Defining activists as "the people, outside the circle of elected and appointed officials, who set the nation's political agenda," she said, "Your company *must* reach out and work long and hard at forming relationships with activist groups before it can hope to gain their support" (p. 32).

She addressed the issue of corporate philanthropy when she advised the following:

> Search for cooperative activities that will allow your people and theirs to *work* together, to get to know one another. Only this interaction, over time, breaks down the stereotypes and builds trust. The annual, anonymous corporate check just won't do it. (p. 32)

Saying that an unrestricted grant is the most greatly appreciated thing a corporation can do for an activist group, Pires warned, "But understand, as you send the check, that it *guarantees* nothing. Consumer and public interest groups are not for sale" (p. 32).

Pires (1989) also warned corporations, "If you use them, mislead them, patronize them, or in any other way attempt to 'cash in' on the relationship, they'll remember when the next issue arises" (p. 31). Finally, Pires' article is directed at public relations practitioners, who, she said, can help corporations establish and maintain relationships with activist groups by playing "the role of the 'insider/outsider'" (i.e., their boundary role) (p. 31). As pointed out earlier by the president of the Conservation Fund, cooperation rather than confrontation is the basis for building donor relations.

Arguing against socially responsible behavior as an approach to dealing with activist groups, Olasky (1987) supported his position by describing the results of a 1984 grant of $125,000 that Honeywell, Inc. made to underwrite a four-part series of seminars on arms spending. According to Olasky, the major defense contractor had long been a target of peace activists, and "the seminars were an overture to the activists and were well-received" (p. 125) because to the activists it was proof that Honeywell's top executives were being responsive to their demands. Olasky pointed out, however, that the activists' campaign intensified once the series concluded. Rather than supporting his position, Olasky's illustration emphasizes the ineffectiveness of using corporate contributions for short-term results and without the benefit of long-term relationships. It also demonstrates the need for the management of corporate philanthropy by those who are responsible for environmental relationships (i.e., public relations practitioners).

However, Olasky (1987) also refuted the role of public relations in corporate philanthropy. Such interference, he believes, leads to corporations being managed in the public interest, rather than in the interest of stockholders and employees. Olasky saw corporate contributions as a "big brass ring" (p. 149) that public relations practitioners are trying to grab. He described a "new public relations ideology," which he claimed endorses that "a substantial chunk of corporate profits must be contributed to various causes designated as worthy" (p. 149).

Summarizing this chapter, a few corporate public relations practitioners are finding philanthropy a natural area for their expertise. These innovators provide evidence that the giving of money, appropriately managed, can significantly contribute to corporate goals of social responsibility, as well as to more pragmatic goals related to economic and sociopolitical benefits. In addition, these practitioners demonstrate that public relations can utilize donor relationships to help corporations enhance and protect autonomy. Gifts to activist groups, in particular, can provide a means to avoid confrontation and litigation; however, philanthropy is most effective—and most socially responsible—in such situations when it is used as one route by which activists can be reached and meaningfully engaged in dialogue.

In contrast to those public relations practitioners who are managing philanthropy in support of overall corporate goals, practitioners who use cause-related marketing as a "philanthropic" vehicle for boosting sales are reducing corporate effectiveness by focusing contributions only in support of marketing objectives. By so doing, such practitioners ignore the benefits their corporations could gain through donor relationships with strategic publics other than consumers. It is argued in this chapter that such a short-sighted focus of philanthropy can increase the vulnerability of corporations in relation to their autonomy (e.g., activists that are ignored when it comes to corporate contributions are more apt to demand regulations that may limit corporate autonomy and cost the corporation money). In addition, widespread use of cause-related marketing—and its acceptance by charitable organizations—may prompt attacks on the tax-exempt status of charitable organizations and the tax deduction of gifts made to them.

It is the conclusion of this chapter that fund raising—the other side of the philanthropic coin—should also be incorporated into the pubic relations function in order to maximize its contribution to organizational effectiveness. The analogy of corporate philanthropy provides strong evidence that donor relationships, managed by public relations practitioners, can enhance the autonomy of charitable organizations by raising gifts in support of overall goals and protect autonomy from donors who seek to control such organizations.

Given the evidence presented here, the question arises: If fund raising is placed within the public relations paradigm, how do the theories of that paradigm help explain the fund-raising behavior of charitable organizations? For answers to this research question, the book turns to Part IV, in which public relations theories are used as analytical tools to complete the building of a theory of donor relations.

PART IV

USING PUBLIC RELATIONS THEORIES AS ANALYTICAL TOOLS FOR EXPLAINING FUND RAISING

After theoretically grounding fund raising within the paradigm of public relations, the book turns to current theories from that paradigm to provide a new way of explaining the fund-raising behavior of charitable organizations. Part IV consists of three chapters that use public relations theories to identify models of fund raising, to analyze the measurement of fund-raising effectiveness, and to examine presuppositions about the fund-raising function.

In chapter 13, Grunig's (1984; Grunig & Hunt, 1984) theory of public relations models is used to identify four historical models of fund raising, and evidence from the fund-raising and philanthropy literature is presented to demonstrate their continued use today by different organizations. In chapter 14, the concept of strategic public relations management is used to critique the current principles and practices of measuring fund-raising effectiveness by dollars raised, and a normative theory on how fund-raising effectiveness *should* be measured in relation to its effect on autonomy is presented. In chapter 15, Grunig's (1989a; Grunig & White, in preparation) presuppositions about public relations are used to draw analogies that help explain why worldviews about the role of fund raising in society have led to a misinterpretation of the function and to unrealistic demands that threaten organizational autonomy.

Chapter 13

Four Models of Fund Raising

This chapter answers the research question: *How* do charitable organizations practice fund raising in different ways? Although researchers have attempted to define "ideal" models of fund raising (e.g., Gabrielsen, Webb, cited in Rowland, 1983) and characteristics of "effective" models (e.g., Loessin & Duronio, 1989; Pickett, 1977), this chapter represents the first time that theoretical models have been developed to explain how fund raising is practiced differently in different charitable organizations.

Based on its earlier conclusion that fund raising is a specialization, or a branch, of public relations, this chapter applies Grunig's (1976, 1984; Grunig & Hunt, 1984) theory of public relations models to fund raising to identify models of the fund-raising behavior of charitable organizations. The first section uses Grunig's theory as an analytical tool to examine the history of fund raising in the United States and concludes that, historically, there have been four models of fund raising: press agentry, public information, two-way asymmetric, and two-way symmetric. The second section answers the research question: Given the four models of fund raising identified historically, what evidence can be found to substantiate the hypothesis that these four models continue to be used by charitable organizations today? Chapter 13 concludes that all four of the historical models of fund raising are still in practice today and hypothesizes that 50% of all charitable organizations predominately practice the press agentry model, 15% practice the public information model, 30% practice the two-way asymmetric model, and only 5% practice the newest model, the two-way symmetric. It is argued in this chapter that the last model, which is more socially responsible and pragmatically more effective than the three older models, will remain under-utilized and largely unknown until fund raising finds an academic home in public relations departments with full-time scholar-teachers.

THE HISTORICAL MODELS OF FUND RAISING

Grunig's Four Models of Public Relations

Four models of public relations behavior have been developed by Grunig (1976, 1984; Grunig & Hunt, 1984). First using the concepts of synchronic and diachronic communication in 1976, Grunig introduced four models in 1984 that result from the combinations of direction (one-way vs. two-way) and balance of intended effect (asymmetrical vs. symmetrical). In their seminal textbook, *Managing Public Relations*, Grunig and Hunt (1984) discussed the four models of public relations behavior that describe the "different ways public relations has been practiced throughout history and at present" (p. 13). The four models are: the press agentry/publicity model, the public information model, the two-way asymmetric model, and the two-way symmetric model. According to the authors, "The models help us to understand different stages in the history of public relations, because public relations seems to have passed through stages that resemble the four models" (p. 14). Using the analogy of adults who remain in one of the stages of childhood, Grunig and Hunt explained the presence today of all four models by stating, "Similarly, many public relations practitioners or departments today practice one of the earlier models of public relations, and have not developed fully into using a more advanced model" (p. 14).

The term *models* is used to emphasize the abstraction of the four types of public relations that have evolved through history. Grunig and Hunt (1984) explained by stating the following:

> In scientific usage, a model is a representation of reality. The human mind can never grasp all of reality in total, but it can isolate and grasp parts of that reality. It then uses those parts of reality to construct ideas. Those ideas model reality, although they also simplify it by not including all of reality. (p. 21)

The authors pointed out that by observing the most important components of public relations behavior, models can be constructed that facilitate understanding of both the history of public relations and how it is practiced today. They warned, however, that models are simplifications, and they stated, "Simplifications are always false in part, because they always leave something out. Not everything any single public relations person does will fit any of the models perfectly" (p. 21)

Table 13.1, "Characteristics of Four Models of Public Relations," is reproduced here from Grunig and Hunt (1984) with modifications in the percentage of organizations practicing the models today. These modifications have resulted from the findings of recent research by Grunig and his students (e.g., Fabiszak, Lauzen, and Pollack, cited in Grunig & Grunig, 1989). In addition, approximate years during which the individual models evolved have been added to the original table.

Table 13.1
Characteristics of Four Models of Public Relations*

| | Models | | | |
Characteristics	Press Agentry/ Publicity	Public Information	Two-Way Asymmetric	Two Way Symmetric
Dates	1850–1900	1900–1920	1920–1960	1960–
Purpose	Progaganda	Dissemination of information	Scientific persuasion	Mutual understanding
Nature of communication	One-way; truth not essential	One-way; truth important	Two-way; unbalanced effects	Two-way; balanced effects
Communication model	Source → Rec.	Source → Rec.	Source → Rec. ← Feedback	Group → Group ←
Nature of research	Little; "counting house"	Little; readability, readership	Formative; evaluative of attitudes	Formative; evaluative of understanding
Leading historical figures	P.T. Barnum	Ivy L. Lee	Edward Bernays	Bernays, educators, professional leaders
Where practiced today	Sports, theater, product promotion	Government, nonprofit associations, business	Competitive business; agencies	Regulated business; agencies
Estimated percentage of organizations practicing today	50%	15%	20%	15%

*Reproduced with modifications from Grunig and Hunt (1984)

As mentioned earlier in this book, the oldest model and the one most commonly practiced today is the press agentry/publicity model.[1] Starting with P. T. Barnum in the 1830s, press agents and public relations practitioners have sought to get the name of their organizations or clients before the general public, usually through the mass media. The purpose of this model (i.e., the function it provides for its organization) is propaganda. Grunig and Hunt (1984) said, "Practitioners spread the faith of the organization involved, often through incomplete, distorted, or half-true information" (p. 21).

The second model, which can be attributed to Ivy Lee's work at the beginning of this century, is the public information model. This model places the public relations function in the role of in-house journalist with a primary purpose of disseminating factual information to the various publics interested in the organization. The public information model, commonly found in government agencies and what Grunig and Hunt (1984) referred to as "nonprofit agencies" (p. 26), relies on press releases and controlled media (i.e., in-house publications) to disseminate information on the organization.

The third model, which the father of public relations, Edward L. Bernays, is credited with starting in the 1920s, is the two-way asymmetric model whose purpose is scientific persuasion. Bernays and others recognized that research on its publics could help an organization meet overall objectives (i.e., by learning more about target audiences, messages could be shaped that would change attitudes and affect behavior). Although similar in purpose to the press agentry model, the two-way asymmetric model uses social science theory and research on attitudes and behavior to help organizations sell products, create a desired image, and persuade publics to accept the company line.

The fourth model, which has emerged since the 1960s through the work of various educators, is the two-way symmetric model. This model uses research not only to shape messages, but also to position the organization in harmony with its important publics. According to Grunig and Hunt (1984), practitioners of this model "serve as mediators between organizations and their publics," with a goal of mutual understanding (p. 22). As noted in chapter 6, some of Bernays work contained symmetrical concepts, although he predominantly practiced the two-way asymmetric model of public relations.

It is recalled from chapter 10 that the public relations function, in its boundary role, interprets the organization to its various publics and, in turn, interprets the publics to the organization. In the two-way asymmetric model, this interpretation

---

[1]Originally called the press agentry/publicity model, Grunig has dropped the latter half of the name and now refers to this model simply as the press agentry model (Grunig & Grunig, 1988).

is used primarily for persuasion—defined by Grunig and Hunt (1984) as "communicating only those characteristics of an organization that the public will accept" (p. 22).

In the two-way symmetric model, interpretation by the public relations function may also be used to change the attitudes or behavior of the organization's management if it is out of balance with the attitudes, knowledge, and behavior of certain publics. Grunig and Grunig (1989) explained by saying, "'Two-way symmetrical' public relations departments use bargaining, negotiating, and conflict-resolution strategies to bring symbiotic changes in the ideas, attitudes, and behaviors of both the organization and its publics" (p. 31).

This book contends that fund raising, as a specialization of public relations, can be explained by Grunig's (1976, 1984; Grunig & Hunt, 1984) four models. It is important to repeat, however, that models are simplifications and that not everything any single fund raiser does will fit any of the four models perfectly.

There are few advocates who would attempt to explain fund raising within the paradigm of public relations. As emphasized earlier in the book, a relatively small number of scholars have examined the relationship between the two organizational functions of public relations and fund raising, and only a few have provided evidence of more than a symbiotic relationship, although they have made no attempts to demonstrate a stronger connection between the two. One of the most revealing works, in relation to Grunig's (1976, 1984; Grunig & Hunt, 1984) four models of public relations, is Cutlip's (1965) book, *Fund Raising in the United States*. As hailed by Grunig and Hunt, Cutlip was the first educator to conceptualize a symmetric model of public relations. In the first of six editions of the successful textbook, *Effective Public Relations*, which he wrote with Allen Center (Cutlip & Center, 1952), he defined the purpose of public relations as bringing an institution and its publics "into harmonious adjustment" (p. 5).

When Cutlip (1965) found that the "significant story of fund raising had never been fully and factually set down in one volume" (p. vii), he abandoned his original intentions to write a monograph on the role of public relations in philanthropy and instead wrote his book on the history of U.S. fund raising. This seminal work takes a public relations perspective of how fund raising has been practiced since colonial days and up until the early 1960s. It must be emphasized here that Cutlip's (1965) book, as noted in chapter 4, was reprinted in 1990, but adds little information on the history of fund raising from the early 1960s to the present. As described by Layton (1987), Cutlip's 1965 book remains "the only comprehensive history of American fundraising" (p. 173), and as such, is used extensively in this chapter.

Cutlip began the preface of his book by explaining that his professional interest in public relations and its impact on American society had led him to the conclusion that "public relations has been a substantial force in the rise of philanthropic giving to its present unprecedented heights" (p. vii). Indeed, Cutlip referred to American fund raising as the "organized public relations-oriented fund raising" which has had a highly beneficial impact on our society (p. vii).

As discussed in chapter 11, Cutlip (1965) holds a separate-but-equal view on the relationship between public relations and fund raising, saying that although they are intertwined in the art of raising money, they are "distinctly separate professions" (p. 178). Regardless of his views, Cutlip introduced evidence very early in his book in support of the application of Grunig's (e.g., Grunig & Hunt, 1984) models of public relations to fund raising. Recognizing different historical stages of fund raising, for example, he said, "The evolution of fund raising in the United States from the individual 'begging missions' of the nation's early centuries into today's multibillion-dollar height is a typically American story" (p. vii).

Early Fund-Raising-Like Activities

As with public relations, fund-raising-like activities are as old as civilization itself. As Panas (1984) stated, "Philanthropy is as old as time. It traces its ancestry to the city-state of Athens, and seven centuries before that to the Egyptian Pharaohs who established 'bequests' to support religious rites" (p. 12). According to Cutlip (1965), "Organized philanthropy supported by systematic fund raising is a twentieth-century development in the United States" (p. 3). He said that in the first three centuries of America's history, philanthropy was "carried along on a small scale, largely financed by the wealthy few in response to personal begging appeals" (p. 3). Yet, as Cutlip outlined the fund-raising behavior of charitable organizations before 1900, supportive evidence is provided that important components of that behavior can be explained by Grunig's (e.g., Grunig & Hunt, 1984) first two models of public relations (i.e., the models make sense out of the many diverse communication activities that Cutlip called fund raising in the United States before 1900).

For example, Cutlip (1965) said, "There were few organized drives, in the modern sense, before 1900" (p. 3). Yet, he recognized that the contemporary models of fund raising evolved out of earlier fund-raising behavior when he stated:

> Nevertheless, America's modern high-pressure, fund-raising drive has its roots deep in the nation's history. As the skills and techniques of fund raising have advanced

. . . so has her philanthropy progressed, from the "begging mission" and lottery of the colonial period to the highly organized, concentrative $10 billion a year enterprise of our times. (p. 3)

Because the first systematic effort to raise private gifts in the United States was for Harvard in 1641, the oldest model of fund raising—the press agentry model—traces its roots to the fund-raising-like activities of America's early colleges and universities. Starting with the colonial period of 1745–1775, Cutlip stated, "Appeals to the general public by means of subscription lists and lotteries brought the infant colleges some funds. Occasional bequests brought in a bit more" (p. 5). Cutlip described a series of four lotteries used by Harvard from 1775 to 1806 to attract money for general purposes and buildings. He concluded, "It is not surprising that these hard-pressed colleges turned to the dubious device of the lottery. . . ." (p. 5), and he declared them a wasteful and costly fund-raising method, saying, "Not only did sponsoring lotteries tarnish the good name of the college, but it received only 2.3 per cent of the money the public gambled for 'the chance of enriching themselves'" (p. 5).

The use of lotteries, subscriptions, and even begging continue today. Although we define these early efforts as fund-raising-like activities, they have been adopted by the more well-defined models, so that today we see them used particularly by those charitable organizations practicing the press agentry and public information models. For example, a modern version of lotteries is still used by some commercial solicitation firms, which has generated a great deal of criticism from legislators and fund-raising practitioners.

The Beginnings of the Press Agentry Model of Fund Raising

Charitable organizations seeking private gifts in the 1800s added special events, or entertainment, to their techniques for attracting funds. The use of entertainment and lotteries, announced through the mass media of that period, parallels the press-agentry techniques of public relations as practiced by historical figures such as P. T. Barnum. According to Grunig and Hunt (1984), Phineas T. Barnum, consummate showman and founder of the Barnum & Bailey Circus, utilized dubious press-agentry techniques to attract members of the general public to his shows (i.e., he created largely fabricated stories to motivate people to buy tickets). Barnum's famous statement, "There's a sucker born every minute" (cited in Grunig & Hunt, 1984, p. 29) underlines not only the philosophy of the forefathers of public relations, but also those of fund raising.

In the press agentry model of fund raising, charitable organizations in early American history sought to affect philanthropic behavior, as opposed to market behavior, by publicizing and staging events, such as charity balls, fairs, auctions, debating contests, and theatrical productions. For example, Cutlip (1965) said, "Church collections, bazaars and benefits, collections of foodstuffs, and direct newspaper appeals for cash were used" by Irish relief committees in the United States during the late 1840s to respond to the Irish famine (p. 10). Cutlip added, "This effort was powered by vast amounts of emotion-laded publicity, featuring graphic accounts of starvation in Ireland" (p. 11).

Indeed, efforts publicizing the philanthropic cause, through newspapers and special events, were the way funds were generated. It can be concluded from these early examples, therefore, that the purpose of the press agentry model of fund raising was to propagandize the cause through messages that were dependent on emotion.

As can be seen from Table 13.2, the earlier table on Grunig's (Grunig & Hunt, 1984) four models of public relations has been adapted to describe the four models of fund raising, including the oldest model, press agentry. It should be noted that little of the descriptive information for the models has been changed from Grunig's public relations models. For example, as previously stated, the purpose of the press agentry model is to propagandize a cause. The table further shows that the nature of communication for the press agentry model is one-way, with truth not being an essential factor, and communication being dependent on emotions.

Little research is conducted by practitioners of the press agentry model, and fund-raising results are evaluated by dollar totals and the number of donors. The leading historical figures associated with this model are Charles Sumner Ward, Lyman Pierce, and their YMCA associates, who are discussed shortly. It is estimated that 50% of all charitable organizations practice the press agentry model, particularly national health and social service agencies, as well as most religious organizations. Discussion of the characteristics of each of the other three fund-raising models is delayed until historical evidence is introduced in support of those models.

Although it would not be refined until molded and directed at mass audiences by the YMCA fund raisers in the first years of the 20th century, the press agentry model of fund raising emerged during the Civil War as a process to sell government bonds. And, similar to public relations, it was a notorious historical figure much like Barnum who led the way.

Jay Cooke, the well-known financier, headed up the Union's war-bond drive during the War Between the States and demonstrated that with pressure and emotion, the press agentry model could be tremendously successful at raising dollars. As Cutlip (1965) stated:

But it was the Civil War (1861–1865) that produced an *early model* of the twentieth-century American high-pressure organized fund drive. Its initiator was the fabled financier Jay Cooke. Parrington calls Cooke the first modern American, "to understand the psychology of mass salesmanship." (p. 11; italics added)

Table 13.2
Characteristics of Four Models of Fund Raising*

	Models			
Characteristics	*Press Agentry/ Publicity*	*Public Information*	*Two-Way Asymmetric*	*Two Way Symmetric*
Dates	1820–1920	1904–1920	1920–1980	1980–
Purpose	To propagandize a cause	To disseminate needs	To scientificially persuade giving	To reach mutual understanding
Nature of communication	One-way; truth not essential; dependent on emotions	One-way; truth important; dependent on "enlightenment"	Two-way; unbalanced effects; dependent on strategic positioning	Two-way; balanced effects; dependent on congruency
Communication model	Source → Rec.	Source → Rec.	Source → Rec. ← Feedback	Group → Group ←
Nature of research	Little; evaluative of $ and doors	Little; mailing list, prospect research; evaluative of donors	Formative; evaluative of $	Formative; evaluative of enhancement & protection of autonomy
Leading historical figures	Ward-Pierce-Y school	Bishop Lawrence/ Ivy L. Lee	John Price Jones	Few educators & professional leaders
Where practiced today	Natl. health & social service agencies, religious org.	Cultural org., public colleges, conservation/ wildlife	Private ed., hosp/medical ctrs., public universities, consultants	Some universities, some consultants
Estimated percentage of organizations practicing today	50%	15%	30%	5%

*Adapted from Grunig and Hunt (1984)

According to Cutlip (1965), Cooke, to a great extent, was responsible for financing the "Union cause" through the sale of government bonds to the public "on a hitherto unprecedented scale" (p. 11). Cutlip said, "He pulled out all the emotional stops to 'sell patriotism' to the North with thorough organization and effective publicity" (p. 11). It is important at this point to note that the "success" of both the press agentry model and the two-way asymmetric model are exemplified in this chapter by illustrations drawn from war-time eras (i.e., large fund-raising totals are inextricably linked to the involvement and emotions brought on by national war). Commenting on the success of emotional appeals, Cutlip said, "Tugs at the heartstrings were then, are now, and perhaps always will be an almost surefire method of getting people to open their purse strings" (p. 21).

It should also be noted here that Cutlip's history ends before the current era of fund raising as an internalized function; therefore, Cutlip primarily focused on the fund-raising efforts of senior managers, trustees, and other volunteers, and commercial fund-raising firms.

Cutlip quoted Parrington's description of Cooke's press agentry methods, which will sound extremely familiar to those knowledgeable about the press agentry model of public relations, stating, "He subsidized the press with a lavish hand, not only the metropolitan dailies but the obscurest country weeklies. He employed an army of hack writers to prepare syndicate matter and he scattered paying copy broadcast" (p. 11). Critical of this early model, Cutlip described Cooke's methods as "exploitation of patriotic appeals" (p. 12) and pointed out that while Cooke was raising funds to support the war through the widespread sale of government bonds, he also managed to bring a nice profit to Jay Cooke & Company.

From Jay Cooke earning a profit for his company while raising funds for the war, it was only a small step to the commission-paid fund raisers who appeared in American philanthropy shortly before the turn of the century. These solicitors, who worked under financial arrangements similar to the contingency fees of modern lawyers, were extensively used by charitable organizations from 1898 to 1918. According to Cutlip, "The commission-paid solicitor disappeared from the philanthropic scene after World War I, with the emergence of the modern professional fund raiser and the Community Chest" (p. 16). Yet, the abuses perpetrated over barely two decades by these commission-paid fund raisers a century ago still plague contemporary fund raisers. For example, in 1889, the president of the Denver Society—the first financial federation of charities in the United States—addressed the inherent danger in hiring fund raisers who worked for a percentage of the private gifts collected, stating:

In their extremity [organizations affiliated with the Society] were persuaded to engage professional solicitors who retained the larger amount of the sums collected, giving the remainder to the institutions. This caused much unfavorable comment and met the disapproval of the Charity Organization Society. (cited in Cutlip, 1965, p. 15)

As is recalled from chapter 5 on the myths and misinterpretation of fund raising, today—100 years after the Denver Society condemned fund raisers who worked on a percentage fee—identical practices by some commercial solicitation firms have brought a barrage of government investigation and regulation. As Cutlip (1965) pointed out, "The stories of cheating by the first paid charity solicitors may well account for the donor's persistent resentment at giving part of his dollars to any paid fund raiser and the public's mistaken notions about today's ethical fund raiser who works for a fixed fee, not on a percentage basis" (p. 16).

In public relations, the derogatory term frequently applied to practitioners is *flacks*, which according to Grunig and Hunt (1984), is a description of "publicists who shoot all their weapons at the press in the hope that some of the flak will hit home" (p. 30). Its historical roots are found in the press agentry origins of public relations.

Similarly, a derogatory term that is often applied to fund-raising practitioners is *hucksters*, which has also evolved from the press agentry model. For example, during a speech at the 1990 CASE conference, G. David Gearhart (cited in "Lax rules," 1990), senior vice president for development and university relations at Pennsylvania State University, said that loose standards for counting gifts made to capital campaigns are fueling public perceptions that fund raisers are "hucksters."

Americans still used events and entertainment in 1878–1880 to raise relief funds for the Irish Famine, although Jay Cooke's "exploitation of patriotism" through the mass media had proven extremely successful at raising funds without special events. According to Cutlip (1965), "Benefits, bazaars, charity socials, and appeals through the press were the old reliables of nineteenth-century fund raising" (p. 21).

But apparently one early fund raiser who learned some of the lessons taught by Cooke was Clara Barton, who founded the American Association of the Red Cross in the late 1800s. Cutlip stated, "From the start Clara Barton recognized the value of publicity and knew how to get it. In her little band of organizers were three able newspapermen of the time" (p. 20). Starting with the first mission of the Red Cross, which took place even before the new organization's charter had been received, Barton effectively utilized the mass media to raise

private contributions of cash and gifts-in-kind (i.e., noncash donative goods).
Cutlip reported:

> When the disaster struck, Clara Barton took the simple step of wiring the Associated
> Press and a few leading newspapers that the Red Cross would accept and distribute
> contributions. This powerful yet succinct message to the AP brought a national
> flood of gifts: "Everything is needed; everything is welcome." (p. 20)

Before continuing with discussion of the historical tracing of the press agentry
model of fund raising, this section turns to the beginnings of the second fund-
raising model, which also has its roots in the mid-1800s.

Beginnings of the Public Information
Model of Fund Raising

As Grunig and Hunt (1984) explained, the public relations models did not
supersede each other by chronological years, but rather public relations evolved
through stages toward maturity. The emergence of a new model did not mean
the demise of a previous stage, which explains why all four models are still in
practice today. This staged progression is evident in the history of fund raising
as well.

As early as 1853, the first signs of the public information model of fund
raising appeared in New York City. Unlike others of his era, Charles Loring
Brace believed that private gifts could be raised efficiently and with greater
morality by disseminating truthful and accurate information. According to
O'Connell (1987), Brace started out to assist boys selling newspapers on the
streets, but he gradually broadened his efforts until he formed "one of New
York's most important agencies, the Children's Aid Society" (p. 74). According
to Cutlip (1965), "Brace was among the first of our social welfare pioneers to
rebel against the then common cheap exploitation of human emotions" (p. 21).
Brace, who in 1880 recalled the reasoning behind his adoption of what is defined
in this book as the public information model, stated:

> I was determined to put this [raising money] on a sound and rational a basis as
> possible. It seemed to me, that, if the facts were well known in regard to the great
> suffering and poverty among the children of New York, and the principles of our
> operation were well understood, we could more safely depend on this *enlightened*
> public opinion and sympathy than on any sudden "sensation" or gush of feeling.
> Our Board fully concurred in these views, and we resolutely eschewed all "raffles"
> and pathetic exhibitions of abandoned children, and "pedestrian" or other exhibitions
> offered us for the benefit of humanity, and never even enjoyed the perfectly
> legitimate benefit of a "fair." (cited in Cutlip, 1965, pp. 21-22; italics added)

As Cutlip pointed out, "Brace was among the first of the fund raisers to
realize that only an informed public support will prove to be a long-term support

and that, conversely, emotional support though easily aroused can, and usually does, quickly vanish" (p. 22). As summarized in Table 13.2, the purpose of the public information model of fund raising is to disseminate needs information. Whereas the press agentry model is dependent on emotions, the public information model relies on "enlightenment" (i.e., the model is dependent on a rational, intelligent, and compassionate donor public). The nature of communication is one-way, and in contrast to the press agentry model, truth is important. Little research is conducted by practitioners using this model aside from research on prospective donors and on mailing lists. Fund-raising results are evaluated primarily by the number of donors who contribute (i.e., the organization strives for a broad base of donors), although total dollars raised is considered important.

Relying on the mass media and organized religion (i.e., the press and the pulpit) to disseminate his fund-raising messages, Brace generated gifts through the modern public relations techniques of speech giving and story placements. Brace described his "media relations program" by saying, "I made it a point, from the beginning, to keep our movements, and the evils we sought to cure, continually before the public in the columns of the daily journals" (cited in Cutlip, 1965, p. 22).

Just as the work of the muckrakers helped bring about the public information model of public relations in the first years of the 20th century, the social problems they worked to expose helped advance the new model of public information for fund raising. According to Grunig and Hunt (1984), "Established institutions needed a new kind of public relations to respond to the publicity war against them, something more than the whitewash of press agentry or the silence of the public-be-damned approach" (p. 31). In the same vein, Cutlip (1965) said, "The increasing needs of the poor, the handicapped, and the victims of technological change, resulting from America's head-long jump into the twentieth century as a major industrial nation of urban dwellers, could no longer be financed by nineteenth-century methods" (p. 23). Describing the need for a new kind of fund raising, Cutlip stated:

> There was increasing disenchantment with the benefit or bazaar as a means of raising funds on the part of both the money givers and the money raisers. The latter increasingly realized that in using such benefits a large part of the funds raised were consumed by the enterprise that produced them, and the net income seldom matched the toil and effort. Charity socials and entertainments became so common as to cause grumbling and irritation among the well-to-do who supported such enterprises. (p. 23)

As the public information model took form, however, fund raisers for the Young Mens Christian Association refined the press agentry model and brought its full effect onto the fund-raising scene.

The Press Agentry Model Refined by the YMCA School of Fund Raisers

According to Cutlip (1965), "The whirlwind, intensive campaign to raise large sums of money in a short period of time by bombarding the public with surefire appeals and by recruiting scores of volunteers to solicit many times their number had its origins in the Young Men's Christian Association" (p. 38). Saying that the "campaign method" produced larger sums than any known means of fund raising, Cutlip stated:

> This campaign method had its genesis in the Young Men's Christian Association, just before America turned the calendar to a new and quite different twentieth century. The innovators were Charles Sumner Ward and Lyman L. Pierce, two young imaginative and ambitious Y.M.C.A. secretaries. (p. 26)

First developed to raise money for YMCA buildings, the YMCA campaign method was soon used to build hospitals, churches, colleges, civic centers, and other capital projects in the United States. In other words, the capital campaign as described earlier in this book is a descendent of the YMCA fund-raising method, which is defined in this chapter as the press agentry model of fund raising.

The first dramatic evidence of the "Y school" and its use of the press agentry model of fund raising was provided in 1905 by YMCA efforts in Washington, DC. Within just 10 years, the Y fund raisers increased the YMCA's assets in Washington from $35 million—which had been accumulated over a 55-year history—to $60 million, or a 271% increase in one-fifth the time. Although its efforts in Washington, DC attracted the greatest attention, a YMCA campaign in Seattle had raised $12,000 in just 48 hours as early as 1888.

Its characteristics were easily recognizable: a short-time period, an army of volunteers, a competitive atmosphere, gimmicks—such as a clock—to apply time and money pressures on the volunteers and the prospective donors, and a great deal of emotion. According to Cutlip (1965), Ward's strategy for getting funds donated to public causes "lay in organized and keen work concentrated into a small period of time" (p. 41). Ward, himself, called his way of practicing fund raising the "intensive method" (cited in Cutlip, 1965, p. 82). However, Ward also candidly explained the philosophy behind his method when he said, "To get the agony over with quickly was the main idea which prompted this movement" (cited in Cutlip, 1965, p. 41).

Similar to the press agentry model of public relations, truth was not always essential, which is somewhat ironic as the "fathers" of this fund-raising model were secretaries of the Young Mens Christian Association until they opened their commercial fund-raising firm after World War I. According to Cutlip, both Ward and Pierce were "deeply religious and strongly motivated by [their] christian beliefs" (p. 43). Even when joining the commercial sector as profitable fund-raising consultants, Ward and Pierce "were impelled by a missionary zeal, regarded their work as 'Christian stewardship,' and said so on many occasions" (p. 43). Yet, their intensive, high-pressured methods of fund raising were viewed by some as contradictory to their beliefs. For example, when Pierce took his campaign method of fund raising to Australia and New Zealand in 1906 to finance YMCA buildings in those countries, Cutlip said, "This American high-pressure system brought criticism as well as results" (p. 49). According to Cutlip, a September 16, 1907 issue of the Christchurch *Truth* ran a story about Pierce under the headline, "Slick up to Date 'Christianity'" (p. 49), which stated:

> A pushful American arrived here on Saturday to shove off a movement which he calculates and reckons will extract 15,000 pounds from the pockets of Christchurch people. It has been done in the magic name of "Christianity" in Wellington and Dunedin, and this city will now be told to go and do likewise. (p. 49)

Cutlip said that John Price Jones, the historical father of the two-way asymmetric model of fund raising who is discussed shortly, "frequently, in private, would derogatorily refer to the Ward-Pierce 'YMCA School' of fund raisers as 'the Christers'" (p. 43).

According to Cutlip, "In the 1905–1915 decade Ward and those using his tightly organized methods succeeded in raising some $60 million in capital funds for the [YMCA]" (p. 82). In addition, the new federations of charitable organizations forming during that same time period adopted the press agentry model as practiced by the Y fund raisers. As Cutlip said, "Fund raising for the new federations accelerated the spread of the 'whirlwind' money-raising campaign, as the Ward–Pierce technique was coming to be called" (p. 75). Headed by publicists, who were frequently referred to as good propagandists, the federations concentrated on getting their names before the public through the mass media. Cutlip explained by saying, "The federation idea had brought the need for the intensive fund-raising campaign which in turn had necessitated intensive publicity" (p. 81).

Saying that there was "understandable concern about the publicist's exploitation of the fear motive," Cutlip stated, "Yet something as new, as flamboyant, and as tainted with overtones of 'press agentry' . . . would naturally draw the fire of many conservative businessmen and publicity-shy social workers" (p. 81). Criticizing this method, Bogen (cited in Cutlip, 1965) wrote in 1917, "This, naturally, carries publicity to an extreme and may, unless judiciously presented, do harm, injuring the very elements whom the Charities are to serve" (p. 80).

According to Cutlip, "Ward was a strong believer in a saturation publicity drive to build a favorable opinion climate for the competing teams of solicitors [in his fund-raising campaigns]" (p. 82). Taking leave from the YMCA in 1911, Ward took on his first hospital fund campaign and hired former newspaperman, Frederick Courtenay Barber to operate the publicity function. Reminiscent of P. T. Barnum, Barber is described by Cutlip as a "flamboyant showman," who was "a hard drinker," and a contrast in personality with the solemn, religious, teetotalers, such as Ward and Pierce (p. 80). Specializing in hospital campaigns, Barber established the first commercial fund-raising firm just 2 years later in 1913, combining "his flair for showmanship with the lessons Ward had taught him" (p. 83).

Cutlip (1965) quoted Arnaud C. Marts, co-founder of Marts & Lundy—one of the largest contemporary fund-raising firms—who described Barber by stating:

> Mr. Barber was a spectacular personality who organized community campaigns with all the fanfare and spectacle of a circus. He put on a great show and charged substantial fees, and I suspect in many cases operated on a percentage basis. A friend . . . has told me of the parade which Barber organized as a part of his campaign publicity. At the head of the parade, in a beautiful phaeton, with high stepping horses, rode Barber himself, in a frock coat and a high silk hat. The contrast between the Barber type of circus and the Lyman Pierce and Charles Ward type of behind the scenes campaign is very striking. (p. 83)

Although Barber is described in Cutlip's (1965) book as a man with "very few principles," who gave fund raising "a bad name," his fund-raising efforts cannot be easily distanced from those of Ward and Pierce (i.e., all practiced the press agentry model of fund raising). For example, describing Ward's campaign for the London YMCA, Cutlip stated, "Conservative Britons did not readily respond to Ward's methods of publicity and pressure. Some London newspapers referred to Ward as the 'Yankee Wizard'" (p. 84). In addition, Ward launched a campaign to raise $4 million in 2 weeks for the YMCA and the YWCA in Greater New York, which Cutlip described as a "whirlwind assault on New York's pocketbook" (p. 85). Finally, Cutlip said that Ward was not only raising money, but also was "teaching persons of means the often *painful lesson* of their obligation to support charitable causes and conditioning the public to the *high-pressure fund drive* which today is commonplace in our society" (p. 87; italics added). In short, Ward and other members of the YMCA school of fund raising, including Pierce and Barber, created pressure on donors to give through the use of saturation publicity. As Cutlip stated, "Ward's systematic organization of solicitation that brought the strongest possible pressure on those catalogued as able to give was bound to outrage many. But the system brought in the cash to meet campaign goals!" (p. 87).

As the power of the press agentry model is so thoroughly demonstrated and documented within the framework of World War I, the continued discussion of its characteristics is delayed until after the historical father of the public information model is introduced.

The Public Information Model Refined by Bishop Lawrence

At the same time that Ward and Pierce were launching their short-term, intensive campaign method in Washington, DC, Cutlip (1965) said, "Another pioneer fund raiser was setting out to raise a really big sum, $2.5 million by *an entirely different approach*" (p. 50; italics added). Bishop William Lawrence's approach to fund raising, which was the refinement of the public information model discussed earlier in relation to Brace in the 1850s, reflected—to a great extent—his New England distaste of public display, which repelled him from the high-pressured drives developed by Ward and Pierce. Cutlip quoted Lawrence as saying:

> I dislike the word "campaign" in this connection almost as much as I abhor "appeal." "Campaign" suggests force or pressure, methods whereby people are dragooned to give. "Appeal" suggests a call upon the sympathies and emotions of people, melting them to give. Both methods are weak and liable to bring reaction. (p. 51)

In 1904, Lawrence became president of the Harvard Alumni Association and was immediately drafted by President Charles Eliot, who is discussed later in this chapter, to organize a campaign to raise $2.5 million for faculty salaries in the liberal arts. Describing in his memoirs the underlying philosophy of his approach to fund raising—which is defined here as the public information model—Lawrence stated:

> We were agreed as to certain principles. The friends of the University were to be given an *opportunity* to strengthen the College by the increase of the salaries of the teachers. . . . There was to be no crowding or jamming for subscriptions. It were better not to complete the full amount. As a matter of fact, the total gift fell short only about one hundred thousand dollars. We could doubtless have gotten the whole by pressure, but it was worth the amount to close with the good will and confidence of the alumni. (cited in Cutlip, 1965, p. 52; italics added)

As can be seen from the description just cited, Lawrence's approach to fund raising was quite different than that of Ward and Pierce, who, as Cutlip said, "exulted in their dramatic, last-minute push to meet a goal deadline by a fixed date and hour" (p. 52). Cutlip's use of adjectives and verbs, in fact, is indicative of the two very different models as practiced by the Ward-Pierce-Y school and by Bishop Lawrence. In comparison to the description of Ward and Pierce's methods, for example, Cutlip described Lawrence's work as a trustee of Wellesley College by saying, "Some months before the fire, a *quiet* drive to raise $1 million for an endowment had been started" (p. 93; italics added). Curti and Nash (1965) described Lawrence's fund-raising efforts on behalf of Harvard as a "campaign that was carried through with *minimum* organization and publicity" (p. 201; italics added).

The Harvard campaign of 1904–1905 netted approximately $2.4 million, and significantly, the money raised was not for buildings as it was for the campaigns of the YMCAs. Bishop Lawrence acknowledged that in addition to raising a large amount of money, he had had to overcome the popular sentiment at the beginning of the 20th century that people would give to buildings that they could see, but could not be expected to give large amounts for intangible purposes, such as faculty salaries.

After raising almost $2 million for Wellesley College approximately 10 years later, Bishop Lawrence launched the largest campaign up to that date when he organized a drive in 1916 to raise over $5 million for the Church Pension Fund Campaign, a national effort to support the clergy of the Episcopal Church and their families. Although Cutlip (1965) distinguished somewhat between the two different approaches to fund raising (i.e., the two earliest models), he stressed their commonality in relation to public relations by saying, "Like Ward and Pierce, Bishop Lawrence realized that a fund drive must be built upon a platform of public opinion conditioned by persuasive publicity" (p. 96). This book disputes Cutlip's commonality and supports its position by pointing out that Ivy Lee, the father of the public information model of public relations, helped Bishop Lawrence refine his new model of fund raising (i.e, the public information model).

Convinced that publicity "was the great problem" in his Church Pension Fund Campaign, Lawrence consulted his friend Edward W. Bok, a successful magazine editor for the Curtis Publishing Company (Cutlip, 1965, p. 96). Bok's advice, according to Lawrence's memoirs, was to "depict, describe your pathetic cases," because, he said, "People give when their sympathies are touched" (cited in Cutlip, 1965, p. 96). "Elated by this guidance from a distinguished editor, Lawrence returned to New York," according to Cutlip, "and invited Ivy Lee to his office for a conference" (p. 96). Lee, who had reopened his public relations firm while retaining John D. Rockefeller, Jr. as his principal client, rejected Bok's advice, telling Lawrence that repeated cries for appeals had made it impossible to depict an old parson or his widow and orphan in such a way as to move people to contribute. As related by Cutlip, Lee told Lawrence:

> The sympathies of the American people are bruised and raw with the cr[ies]. . . . Moreover, in the long run emotional appeals lose their force. The American people, intelligent, just, and generous to a cause that appeals to them want facts and figures. (pp. 96-97)

Lee's advice on fund raising was congruent with the publicity policy he had developed of "the public be informed" (Grunig & Hunt, 1984, p. 33). That is to say, people will give, not because of emotional appeals or an intense, pressured campaign, but because they have all the facts and figures they need to reach the rational decision to give. The public information model of fund raising, therefore, relies heavily on what Grunig and Hunt referred to as the "Domino Theory" (i.e., increased communication will lead to increased awareness, which in turn will lead to positive attitudes and, finally, to positive behavior). This theory of powerful communication effects over a short term has been disproved by scholarly research and replaced with theories of cognitive effects, as demonstrated by Grunig's (in preparation) theory of communication objectives discussed in chapter 11.

Together, Ivy Lee and Bishop Lawrence developed the public information model of fund raising that would be applied to the $5-million Church Pension Fund. "And a campaign of publicity based on facts more than on emotion is what these two shrewd students of public behavior agreed upon in conferences over the next week," stated Cutlip (1965, p. 97). At the close of Bishop Lawrence's fund-raising career almost 25 years later, his biographer concluded that Lawrence—like Ivy Lee—had built his success on a high regard for his audience's ability to use information to reach rational and right decisions. Cutlip quoted Lawrence's biographer, saying:

> Here is found the real keynote of Bishop Lawrence's success as a money raiser. To be sure, he spent untold hours in securing the right publicity, in the arranging of lists, in the writing of letters in his own hand. But fundamental was his faith in the *sense of responsibility* of the average man and woman. (p. 268; italics added)

This discussion supports the conclusion of this section that the nature of communication for the public information model, as refined by Lawrence and Lee in the early 1900s, was one-way and, in contrast to the emotionally dependent model of press agentry, it was dependent on a rational, intelligent, and compassionate public (i.e., it was dependent on enlightenment).

"As one would expect of one so expert in promoting large philanthropic gifts, Lawrence possessed a shrewd sense of publicity and paid much attention to the press," stated Cutlip (1965, p. 97). Describing the activities of what students of public relations would recognize as a journalist-in-residence, a characteristic of the public information model of public relations, Cutlip said that Bishop

Lawrence took advantage of slow news days during which to place stories; he added a local angle by having each bishop make an announcement in his own diocese; he pulled together nationwide, simultaneous publicity; he saturated New York City by deluging the newspapers with facts on the problem of retirement, in general; and by simply adding the name of his organization to the release, he linked his cause to a broader issue of concern on the media's agenda (i.e., provision for all elderly citizens) which helped ensure headline coverage.

According to Cutlip (1965), "As the publicity poured out, 'thousands of rivulets of assessments began to pour into the Church Pension Fund'" (p. 98). In less than 10 days after the formal announcement to the press on March 1, 1916, more than $1 million in pledges had been received, and journalist-in-residence Lawrence had the news announced to the media through a publicity release sent from the library of J. P. Morgan, a credible news source on finances. One year later, on March 1—the campaign's deadline—Bishop Lawrence announced that pledges and cash received by the Fund had passed the $6-million mark, well beyond the original goal of $5,064,000. According to Cutlip, "The flood of contributions continued and by September, 1917, the total reached $8,750,000—making philanthropic history. . . . Bishop Lawrence had established himself, on the eve of World War I, as America's champion fund raiser" (p. 99).

The Power of the Press Agentry Model in Time of War

If the public information model of fund raising had set a new record in total money raised, it was shortly and soundly broken by the power of the press agentry model that Ward and Pierce brought to the Red Cross during World War I. Just 4 months after the official close of the Church Pension Fund, the Red Cross raised *$114 million in 8 days*.

Under its self-imposed charge to "Bind up the wounds of a bleeding world," Cutlip (1965) said that the American Red Cross War Council was created by President Wilson at the beginning of the war to combine all relief efforts and concentrate them in the hands of a single organization. Chairman Henry F. Davison, a partner in the firm of J. P. Morgan, hired "the champion money-raiser" Ward, who, with Pierce, served for the duration of the war on loan from the YMCA. Davison also persuaded Ivy Lee to become his personal assistant in charge of public relations. In fact, it is quite likely that Lee was the one who created the charge to "Bind up the wounds, etc." because he helped shaped Chairman Davison's acceptance speech in which the slogan was first issued and then institutionalized.

President Wilson proclaimed the week of June 18–25, 1917 as National Red Cross Week, which, according to Cutlip (1965), "was one of the first intensive uses of the 'week' idea in publicity" (p. 116). The drive opened with the observance of Red Cross Sunday on June 17 in the nation's churches. Cutlip described this fund-raising phenomenon by stating:

> Pulpit, press, and people responded in the fervor of war-born emotions and before the eight-day drive was done a total of $114,023,640.23 had been collected, an oversubscription of 14 per cent. History had been made as the American people saw what large sums could be attained through the intensive fund-raising campaign hitherto used only at the community level for charity or a civic or church building. (p. 116)

As Cutlip noted, "The total collected represented more than one dollar for every man, woman, and child in the United States" (p. 119).

Much of Lee's work at the Red Cross showed his mastery of the public information model. For example, Cutlip (1965) quoted him as writing, "We shall give to the newspapers some kind of story practically every morning and every afternoon" (p. 127). However, it is apparent from the correspondence Cutlip cited between Lee and Davison, that the father of public information adopted a press-agentry approach to public relations for much of his work on behalf of the American Red Cross War Council. For example, in August 1918, Lee urged Davison to make a trip to Europe to inspect the Red Cross work there so that Lee could then stage a tour to 13 cities upon Davison's return, which would conveniently coincide with the Christmas membership drive. Writing to Davison, Lee said, "We would have a great hip-hip-hurrah time and have the population of the United States enrolled as Red Cross members" (cited in Cutlip, 1965, p. 127).

"Yet," according to Cutlip (1965), "Lee himself thought the Red Cross intensive publicity program represented only a wartime need" (p. 129). Cutlip quoted Lee's departing advice to the Publicity Department staff at the conclusion of the war, stating:

> The time has come when we ought to consider . . . the steady demobilization of the Publicity Department. . . there is no necessity to devote either the time or the money to a continued and active stimulation of the work of the Red Cross; that we ought to let the interest grow out of our work, instead of having a great organization that would merely stimulate that activity. (p. 129)

Cutlip called Lee's advice shortsighted and lacking in perception, but credits him for "[bringing] in the money" through his "prodigious, professional public relations campaign for the Red Cross in wartime" (p. 129). Ironically, Cutlip concluded that what appears to be Ivy Lee's temporary adoption of the press agentry model of fund raising led the way to the future use of the model. "His publicity patterns would be copied in future fund-raising efforts," he said (p. 129).

As World War I lasted only 19 months, it is truly amazing that, in total, the Ward-directed campaigns during the war raised more than $690 million. This figure, provided by Cutlip (1965), is even more impressive when one realizes that at the same time Americans also gave $13.9 billion through five drives for Liberty Loans. Although the results are impressive, it must be stressed that the press agentry model, as practiced by Ward, Pierce, and Lee during World War I, rested on a foundation of pressure, competition, emotion, and even coercion. Describing the first Red Cross campaign of the war, Cutlip stated:

> A quota was set for each city, town, and hamlet to give it a goal to reach. . . . City was matched against city in the fund-raising competition—an old technique of Ward's. . . . All media vied to *promote the cause* of the Red Cross and thus prove their patriotism. As the Kansas City *Star* thundered, "Kansas City must have no slackers." (p. 117; italics added)

Similarly, Cutlip described the second Red Cross campaign by quoting an official, who said, "The psychosis of war affected the drive even more than the campaign a year earlier, and there was sometimes a hysterical note in the newspapers' repeated demands that there must be no failure in backing the war effort and no 'slackers' in the Red Cross drive" (p. 132).

According to Grunig and Hunt (1984), the Creel Committee on Public Information (CPI) during World War I gave rise to the two-way asymmetric model of public relations, evolving beyond Ivy Lee's public information model that was instrumental before the war. The CPI used tools of the public information model, but it achieved great success during World War I because it made use, "without knowing it, of psychological principles of mass persuasion" (p. 38). Describing the two-way asymmetrical approach of the CPI, these public relations scholars said, "Essentially, what they and other propagandists did was to construct messages that appeal to what people believe and want to hear" (p. 38). Grunig and Hunt said that the Creel Committee gave birth both to the idea "that mass persuasion was possible and that it could have its base in social science," and to a new generation of public relations practitioners "who left the committee after the war to go into practice for themselves" (p. 38). Similarly, the American Red Cross War Council also produced a new generation of fund-raising consultants, who started their firms with a new idea about mass persuasion of donor publics.

According to Cutlip (1965), "In the hindsight of history it appears obvious that the nation's newly discovered philanthropic potential—so dramatically uncovered in World War I—would be exploited to meet the dammed up needs of colleges, hospitals, preparatory schools, libraries, and the mushrooming social agencies" (p. 157).

Cutlip continued by saying, "The YMCA campaign techniques which had been so spectacularly successful in raising more than a half billion dollars in national fund drives were bound to be utilized by organizations desperately needing big sums of gift money" (p. 157). Upon the close of the war effort, Ward and Pierce were convinced by some of the more junior fund raisers they had trained to open a commercial fund-raising firm. Carrying over their intensive, high pressured campaigns, the Ward-Pierce-Y school of fund raisers turned their missionary zeal to raising money for charitable organizations—and also for themselves.

Although the press agentry model generated millions of philanthropic dollars—just as the public relations model was responsible for millions of dollars in sales through free media publicity—there is evidence of its failures and frequent ethical abuses. Scattered throughout the middle of his book, Cutlip provided examples of a number of campaigns conducted after World War I under the Ward-Pierce-Y method that failed to reach their goals: The 1919 Red Cross fund for $25 million "failed dismally and set off a wave of bitter criticism," even though the same techniques were used that had been so successful during the war (pp. 209-210); the first attempt at federated fund raising for colleges under Lyman Pierce at the end of 1919 raised less than $3.5 million of the $5-million goal for nine private colleges in Wisconsin (pp. 255-257); the quota approach used by Tamblyn & Brown in its 1923 drive for Mt. Holyoke failed to reach the $3-million goal (p. 263); and in perhaps the most impressive and controversial failure of the 1920s, a campaign managed by Tamblyn & Brown for the Cathedral of St. John the Divine in New York City was finally ended after 6 months even though it was $5 million short of its $15-million goal (pp. 271-282).

The latter example of a failed campaign also provides an illustration of the behavior of the historical practitioner of the press agentry model that frequently bordered on the unethical. In January 1925, Episcopal Bishop William T. Manning set out to raise $15 million in 65 days to complete the construction of the Cathedral of St. John the Divine in New York. According to Cutlip (1965), "The Tamblyn & Brown campaign for the cathedral followed the standard Ward-Pierce pattern" (p. 277). Elmer Davis, who later headed the World War II Office of War Information (OWI) and who was a critic of Bishop Manning, called the quotas and other techniques used by Tamblyn & Brown, "organized nagging" (Cutlip, p. 277).

The slogan of the cathedral campaign was, "A House of Prayer for All People," which Cutlip described as "a hypocritical fund-raising device and nothing more" (p. 272). Although the campaign needed the philanthropic dollars of Jews, Baptists, and other non-Episcopalians, Bishop Manning and his fund raisers had no intention of allowing members of other religions to participate in the sacrament of communion or to conduct religious services from the sanctuary of the completed cathedral. When John D. Rockefeller, Jr., a Baptist, gave $500,000 to the campaign with a "plea" that "the 'large outside friendly interest should be represented on the Cathedral's Board of Trustees by a small number of laymen of sister churches,'" Bishop Manning accepted the check, but turned down the request to put non-Episcopalians on the cathedral's board (Cutlip, 1965, p. 275). In the public dispute that followed, which included letters in the media, Manning expressed his belief that the clause attached to the campaign's largest gift "makes no condition to its acceptance and imposes no obligation" (cited in Cutlip, 1965, p. 276). Criticizing Manning's philosophy toward accepting the gift from Rockefeller, but not its condition, journalist Davis wrote, "If the merchandiser had been any but a Bishop, offering holy wares, this would have seemed perilously like misrepresentation of the quality of the goods" (cited in Cutlip, 1965, p. 277).

A campaign to complete a second "giant, Gothic Episcopal cathedral"—the National Cathedral—was conducted during the same time in Washington, DC. Noting the publicity coup that the Washington Cathedral fund raisers had scored by "obtaining" the bodies of Admiral George Dewey and President Woodrow Wilson to place in cathedral crypts, Cutlip said that a freshman employee of Tamblyn & Brown wrote an internal memorandum suggesting that the remains of the then-alive, ex-President William Howard Taft be considered for his firm's client, the Cathedral of St. John the Divine in New York. Cutlip stated, "No wonder *Time* was moved to comment that these professional fund raisers 'have had to be patient, elusive and resourceful, with the corporate manners of an undertaker and the understanding of a Freud'" (p. 282).

John Price Jones and the Two-Way Asymmetric Model of Fund Raising

Although the work of the Creel Committee was to establish a new public relations model that relied on scientific knowledge to help efforts to persuade, the two-way asymmetric model of fund raising did not emerge from the similar work of the Red Cross during World War I, but from the work of John Price Jones and the agency he started at the close of the war. As Cutlip (1965) stated:

Jones came from the world of journalism to bring *a new approach* and new intensity to the art of getting people to give money. He developed a lucrative fund-raising business quite independent of the influence and ideas of the Ward-Pierce-Y school. (p. 170; italics added)

Like Bernays, who Grunig and Hunt (1984) described as "the most celebrated of the third generation of public relations practitioners" (i.e., those who practiced the two-way asymmetric model) (p. 41), Jones used research to "sell" the philanthropic needs of his organizational clients, netting them $746.63 million over his 31 years of work as a fund-raising consultant. Discussing Bernays, Grunig and Hunt stated:

> Like other practitioners of the two-way asymmetric model, he most often practiced this role by finding out what the public liked about the organization and then highlighting that aspect . . . or by determining what values and attitudes publics had and then describing the organization in a way that conformed to these values and attitudes. Bernays called these strategies the "crystallizing of public opinion" and the "engineering of consent." (p. 40)

According to Cutlip (1965), "Jones brought great advances to the art of fund raising. . . . He had a genius that enabled him to harness the newly discovered power of publicity to the efficient business methods he admired, and thus to create a wholly *new approach to fund raising*" (p. 183; italics added). Cutlip described Jones' two-way asymmetric model of practicing fund raising, stating:

> Jones's fetish for research, for careful record keeping, and for thorough planning made the methodical Charles S. Ward appear slovenly and haphazard by comparison. Jones brought to fund raising a deep appreciation for the value of research and planning, an increased emphasis on public relations, and in his penchant for paper work he codified the principles and procedures of fund raising. The London *Economist* has called him "the most famous of the expert fund-raisers." (p. 170)

In relation to Jones' "fetish for research," it is important to note that, as in the two-way asymmetric model of public relations, research is used in the asymmetric model of fund raising to shape messages that are attractive to donor publics. For example, Cutlip quoted one of the recommendations made by a Jones executive at the end of the depression, saying, "Greater care must be taken insofar as the larger givers are concerned to determine interests and attitudes so as to make the most effective appeal along the *avenue of least resistance*" (p. 318; italics added).

Jones, who graduated from Harvard in 1902, was a newspaper reporter for almost 15 years, including stints on *The Washington Post*, the New York *Globe*, the *Press*, and the *Sun*. Upon joining an advertising agency in 1917, he was loaned by his firm to work on the Liberty Loan drives in New York City, during which time he learned the principles of fund raising from Guy Emerson, who had been trained in the "art" of fund raising by Bishop William Lawrence during the Episcopal Church Pension Fund campaign. After the Armistice, Emerson, who had also graduated from Harvard, recommended Jones for a temporary fund-raising position at their mutual alma mater, which was preparing to launch a $10-million campaign that had been put on hold during the war. According to Cutlip (1965), "When the campaign to raise $10 million for the Harvard Endowment Fund was launched, it not only made fund-raising history but changed the course of American higher education, for Harvard was dramatically telling the nation and sister colleges that the old methods of financing higher education in America were passe" (p. 173).

Cutlip quoted Emerson as recalling that campaigns previous to the Harvard Endowment Fund were run by men who were "obliged to shoot almost entirely in the dark. . . . They knew in a general way that they were after money and the net result of their appeal usually was 'Please give us some money because we want it'" (p. 173). "Not so with the Jones-Duncan directed campaign," said Cutlip (p. 173), who stated:

> Efforts to obtain gifts were preceded by an intensive, *intelligent* publicity program documenting the service which the university . . . had furnished the nation. The education program made clear Harvard's pressing needs, as well as her opportunities for greater service, *if* the money were given to her. (pp. 173-174; italics added)

By November 1919, less than 1 year after the start of the Harvard Endowment Fund, $14.2 million had been raised, "and," according to Cutlip, "the big movement of organized giving to American education was under way" (p. 174). In that same month, Jones incorporated his commercial fund-raising firm.

It is clear that Jones was affected by the public information model championed by Bishop Lawrence and Ivy Lee. Cutlip said that Jones told his Harvard associates that "he sought to develop enthusiasm for giving to Harvard by dignified means, 'without rough and tumble methods'" (p. 174). Cutlip evaluated the approach used by Jones, saying, "He wisely saw that the publicity must reflect the nature of the institution and that donors must be shown reasons for giving" (p. 174).

When Jones founded his fund raising firm in November 1919, "to give counsel and service in organization and publicity to business houses, institutions of public, semi-public and private character, and to individuals" (Cutlip, 1965, p. 175), he built a staff composed primarily of former journalists like himself (e.g., George A. Brakeley, a Princeton graduate who had worked with Jones on the New York *Sun*). According to Cutlip, "The heavy journalism orientation of this eager young staff naturally resulted in heavy emphasis on the role of publicity in fund raising" (p. 176). This orientation differed sharply from that of the press agentry approach of other firms that grew out of the pioneer Ward firm. The latter came from the Y school of intensive, short, fund-raising drives during which publicity facilitated emotional giving (i.e., the press agentry model of fund raising).

Bishop Lawrence's approach to fund raising, the public information model, was oriented to facts and figures disseminated through the mass media of the day. The John Price Jones firm, with its journalistic orientation and Jones' penchant for research, combined the asymmetrical approach of the press agentry model with the dissemination of "true" facts from the public information model to formulate the two-way asymmetric model of fund raising.

As described in chapter 11, Jones—because of his journalism background—conceived his firm to be both a fund-raising and public relations business; but, although he put equal stress on both areas in seeking clients and accounts, the John Price Jones firm became best known and drew its principal income for its fund raising activities. Cutlip said, "Postwar America was ready for the commercial fund-raising expert; it was not as receptive to the need for the public relations expert" (p. 177). Although Grunig and Hunt (1984) credit the workings of the Creel Committee with the post-World War I establishment of new public relations firms, they fail to note the lack of success of those new firms as compared to the dramatic growth of public relations firms following World War II and the work of the Office of War Information. As Cutlip stated:

> The dramatic demonstrations of power staged by George Creel in his direction of the Committee on Public Information and by Ivy Lee and Charles Sumner Ward in the giant Red Cross fund drives had awakened great interest in the art of influencing public opinion through barrages of publicity. Yet the public relations counseling business grew slowly in the 1920's in sharp contrast to the tremendous boom in public relations practice that followed World War II. (p. 177)

As noted in chapter 11, Jones' senior vice president, Robert Duncan, insisted that public relations and fund raising were two separate fields, and he "never shared Jones's enthusiasm for building up the public relations side of the business" (Cutlip, 1965, p. 178). Keeping in mind that when founding the firm in 1919 Jones defined its purpose as giving counsel and service "in organization and publicity," it is clear that "organization"—the key describer of the Ward-Pierce-Y school—refers to the fund-raising function and "publicity" equates to public relations (p. 175). Regarding this relationship, Duncan said, "Organization is the heart of the business. . . . Although publicity is essential, organization bears the ultimate responsibility of producing the funds," (cited in Cutlip, 1965, pp. 178-179).

According to Curti and Nash (1965), Jones reported in 1919 that he had modified his views regarding the relative importance of publicity and organization and had decided that organization was the more important. Curti and Nash quoted Jones as saying, "Publicity provides a certain amount of mental ammunition that is shot at the mind and the heart by constant repetition; it makes a prospective giver think again and again of the question of giving, and gradually works upon his mind and his heart in such a way that he finally comes across" (p. 203). Jones added, "It is a scientific fact that advertising saves two-thirds of a salesman's time. The same truth applies to publicity in a campaign of this kind" (cited in Curti & Nash, 1965, p. 203).

As concluded in chapter 11, the role of public relations as it relates to the fund-raising function has been frozen in time (i.e., the earlier models of press agentry and public information are the ones that fund raisers use to define public relations). And, it can also be concluded here that the fact that commercial fund raising grew quicker than commercial public relations helped to institutionalize the earlier public relations models in fund raising.

According to Cutlip, the distinction between work in fund raising and in public relations became a perennial topic at the John Price Jones annual staff conference. At the 1935 staff conference, the question that eternally bothered Jones executives was raised: "Why, if we are equipped to conduct a public relations account, don't we have a few public relations clients?" (p. 179). One of the three answers provided by Jones executive Bayard F. Pope, Jr. was, he said, "Because we are regarded by the public as a fund-raising organization and because the public fails to see the similarity between the two types of work" (cited in Cutlip, 1965, p. 179).

Ketchum Inc., another successful fund-raising firm that still remains a leader in the field, was founded the same year as John Price Jones, but its beginning marked a much faster change in orientation. According to Cutlip, Ketchum Inc., "grew into one of the nation's largest fund-raising firms, though it had been initially organized as a public relations enterprise" (p. 168). Former publicists for the University of Pittsburgh, Carlton and George Ketchum quickly realized that there was more demand for help on fund raising than there was for public relations counsel. "Unlike Jones, they pulled back on public relations and concentrated on fund-raising campaign management," stated Cutlip (p. 177). As mentioned in chapter 11, there are two Ketchum firms today: a fund-raising consulting firm and a public relations and advertising firm.

Summarizing this point, the history of fund raising helps explain today's worldview of the relationship between fund raising and public relations. Journalists and publicists who started some of the earliest and most successful fund-raising firms in the United States believed that the public could not see a similarity between fund raising and public relations and that the demand for the former delegated the latter to a supportive role.

In addition to introducing research to fund raising, codifying procedures, and matching giving messages to attitudes and values of donor publics, John Price Jones also was the first fund-raising consultant to invest heavily in a strong central library. According to Cutlip (1965), "He undergirded fund appeals, from the early twenties on, with thorough research on the institution to be served, its degree of support, and the case to be presented in the fund appeal" (p. 183). Curti and Nash (1965) reported that Jones' fund-raising campaigns for Smith and five other women's colleges "began with careful planning, including a survey of the needs of the colleges and of the social and economic status of alumnae and other potential donors" (p. 204). According to these higher education scholars, "Special attention was given to the kind of publicity likely to be most effective in view of the traditions of the college and the psychology and values of the alumnae" (p. 204). Cutlip said, "In every endeavor he insisted upon pinpoint targeting and 'raised merry hell' about wasted motion" (p. 183). In all aspects, Jones typified the two-way asymmetric model of fund raising. According to Cutlip, Jones often asserted that "The fund raiser is entitled to take pride and satisfaction in his work. He serves a social need far beyond that served by a mere press agent or publicity man" (p. 255).

As stated in chapter 5, the technique of volunteer leadership truly evolved into its modern form under the two-way asymmetric model. According to Cutlip, the National Cathedral Campaign, although managed and directed by the Jones firm, was under "the nominal leadership" of chief volunteers General John J. Pershing and Senator George Wharton Pepper, who "provided a prestigious front for the Jones-directed campaign" (p. 285). Although the press agentry model used volunteer workers extensively and volunteer leaders frequently, it was the two-way asymmetric model developed by Jones that refined the psychological technique of placing prestigious volunteers in "starring roles" and of delegating the fund raiser to behind-the-scene direction. The benefits gained from volunteer figureheads, the hard lesson learned by Jones of not taking credit for raising gifts (as discussed in chapter 5), and the profit-motive incentive for commercial fund-raising firms to maintain a low profile in achieving "institutional success," have contributed to the fund-raising practitioner's generally accepted role in today's fund-raising process—that of the necessary, but "invisible" player.

The two-way asymmetric model, as practiced by Jones and other members of his firm, continued to exploit the power of volunteer leaders throughout its development. These leaders, however, were not always prestigious or of the type widely admired. For example, Cutlip reported that at the 1930 Annual Conference of the Jones staff, Vice President Duncan described how he used the power of an unpopular chairman to successfully complete a $1.25-million campaign for a midwestern hospital, explaining:

> For certain reasons there could be no newspaper publicity whatever. The entire activity had to be conducted quietly. Mr. Insull [Samuel Insull the notorious utilities manipulator], a great campaign leader, was Campaign Chairman, but out of the city most of the time. . . . The class of men whom we did want [for a Preferred Gifts Committee] who would do what Mr. Insull asked them to do were those financial men who handled the far-flung Insull security business. . . . Knowing that a certain house did most of the Insull financing, we conferred with the head of that house and, almost overnight, a splendid, though small, group of workers sprang into being. (cited in Cutlip, 1965, pp. 252-253)

The "group of workers" referred to by Duncan gave money personally and solicited other gifts, which were then announced at a luncheon, which resulted in Mr. Insull, the chairman, giving $800,000, or approximately 80% of the total raised up to that point. According to Cutlip, "The 'enlistment of a few effective workers' and polite business blackmail was an effective fund-raising technique even then!" (p. 253).

Finally, it must be noted that, like the press agentry model of fund raising, the two-way asymmetric model has been criticized historically. For example, Cutlip (1965) said, "Evidence of a deepening resentment of what John Price Jones called the 'scientific method of raising funds' began to appear in the mid-twenties and has grown into the crescendo of criticism of the never-ending list of money appeals we hear so frequently today" (p. 330).

Summarizing this discussion of the two-way asymmetric model of fund raising, this third-generation model first appeared in 1920 following World War I. The purpose of the model is to scientifically persuade giving, and the nature of communication is two-way, with unbalanced, or asymmetrical effects. As stated in Table 13.2, the two-way asymmetric model is dependent on strategic positioning with publics and uses formative research to shape communications. The success of this model is evaluated by the number of private dollars raised, often in relation to the cost of fund raising. The leading historical figure associated with this model is John Price Jones, whose fund-raising philosophy and activities are described above as evidence of the model's distinguishing characteristics.

It is hypothesized that 30% of all charitable organizations actively involved in fund raising today practice the two-way asymmetric model. It is further hypothesized that this model is predominately practiced by private colleges, private and public universities, hospitals and medical centers, and by most fund-raising consultants. This section turns now to the most recent model of fund raising, the two-way symmetric model.

The Two-Way Symmetric Model of Fund Raising

This book does not identify any leading historical figure as being associated with the most recent fund-raising model, the two-way symmetric model, which is a situation similar to that in public relations. Grunig and Hunt (1984) explained that the reason it is more difficult to trace the historic origins of the two-way symmetric model to any individuals is "because practitioners only now are beginning to practice the model" (pp. 41-42). As also discussed in the next section, this book concludes that the two-way symmetric model of fund raising is a very new phenomenon, emerging only in this decade. There is, however, some historical evidence of the model in the literature (i.e., symmetrical concepts can be identified in the history of fund raising).

For example, the fund-raising philosophy and practice of Harvard University in the second half of the 1800s under the presidency of Charles Eliot, as provided by Curti and Nash (1965), can be interpreted as early signs of the two-way symmetric model. Harvard, according to the authors, was open to change, unlike its peer institutions of the time. President Eliot, who believed that donors should express interest before being asked for a gift, based his success in fund raising on always having "his plans so clearly shaped that these would appeal to a man who might be interested" (Curti & Nash, 1965, p. 138). Curti and Nash described Eliot's approach to fund raising, saying:

> On occasion he pointed out to industrialists that a needed laboratory might well yield new knowledge highly useful to their businesses. For the most part, however, Eliot emphasized Harvard's contributions to public service, making clear what was wanted and why it was needed. (p. 138)

By engaging only those who expressed interest, by having the institution's formulated plans always available to share, by pointing out mutual benefits, and by emphasizing the concept of the public interest, Eliot was an extremely successful fund raiser. According to Curti and Nash (1965), gifts for three dormitories and a building for Harvard's law school came without any solicitations by Eliot or any of his officers. In addition, Harvard's endowment tripled between 1869 and 1878 and tripled again in the next 20 years under Eliot's leadership. Annual gifts for operating costs increased almost 150 times between 1869 and 1889.

Exhibiting a sense of social responsibility that would be considered rare even today, Eliot's successor, Abbott Lowell, did everything he could in the early 1900s to re-direct the largest gift in Harvard's history to the Massachusetts Institute of Technology (MIT) in order to avoid needless duplication of equipment and instruction in the field of engineering. According to Curti and Nash (1965), the income of a trust of approximately $20 million, established in 1903 by a bequest, was to go to Harvard to support engineering education. As MIT, which was in financial difficulties, already had an engineering school only a few miles away, Lowell devised a plan that would allocate most of the income from the trust to MIT "and thus serve the donor's intention more efficiently" (Curti & Nash, 1965, p. 149). Facing opposition from the Harvard alumni, Lowell only agreed to accept the gift when the Massachusetts Supreme Court declared in 1917 that a new institution would be established to receive the income if Lowell's plan was not dropped. Despite—or, as discussed later in the chapter on presuppositions, because of—his sense of social responsibility in fund raising, Lowell helped Harvard's endowment increase from $22 million in 1909 to $128.5 million when he retired in 1933. Harvard's fund-raising behavior under the presidencies of Eliot and Lowell appears to have contained symmetrical concepts.

Grunig and Hunt (1984) said that, historically, few public relations practitioners practiced the symmetric model, although many defined the function as such. As a result, these scholars said, educators have done the most to define how the two-way symmetric model should be practiced. It is argued here that the same situation exists for fund raising.

As summarized in Table 13.2, the purpose of the two-way symmetric model of fund raising is to reach mutual understanding. The nature of its communication is two-way between groups with balanced, or symmetrical effects. This characteristic is important in that the nature of communication for the other three models is graphically portrayed in Table 13.2 as source to receiver. The nature of communication for the two-way symmetric model, however, is group to group, which emphasizes its orientation to systems theory and the environmental interdependencies of donors and charitable organizations. Unlike the press agentry model of fund raising, which is dependent on the emotions of its publics, or the public information model, which is dependent on their enlightenment, the two-way symmetric model is dependent on congruency with its donor publics.

This most recent model uses formative research to balance the needs of the charitable organization and its donor publics (i.e., research is used to identify opportunities for private funding and to identify issues that the charitable organization is not addressing through donor relationships). The effectiveness of this model is evaluated by its contribution to enhancing and protecting organizational autonomy through the fund-raising process. As stated earlier, no leading historical figure is identified with the two-way symmetric model, although a few educators and senior practitioners currently are defining how such a model should be practiced. It is hypothesized that only 5% of all charitable organizations practice the two-way symmetric model of fund raising, primarily a few universities and some fund-raising consultants.

Similar to public relations, few fund-raising practitioners historically practiced the two-way symmetric model, although many defined the function as such. For example, Harold "Sy" Seymour helped establish two-way symmetrical policies for managing the National War Fund during World War II, although he actually practiced the two-way asymmetric model of fund raising throughout his career as a nationally known consultant and author. Cutlip (1965) said that a committee aided by Seymour set down four basic policies, including that "the fund would represent no single interest but would do its best to represent both the organizations seeking money and the Americans giving money," (p. 406). Describing him as "among the more candid of the veterans in this field," Cutlip later quoted Seymour as saying, "It is usually called 'high' pressure by those who oppose or dislike big fund-raising campaigns, especially by those innocents who still think that there is substantial nourishment to be found in 'quiet special gifts efforts'" (p. 485).

Cutlip provided another example of practitioners defining fund raising as two-way symmetric, but practicing a different model. Quoting the written history of the United Defense Fund, Cutlip said, "Fund-raising is basically a public relations operation. Be it a single organization or a federation, it is supported in direct ratio to the impact it, itself, makes on the public" (p. 503). Unfortunately, the United Defense Fund practitioners described asymmetrical and press agentry concepts when they go on to say that the support of a charitable organization will be dependent on "skillful interpretation of its program [and the] degree of emotional response it elicits" (p. 503).

According to Grunig and Hunt (1984), it was only after full-time faculty replaced part-time practitioners in the classroom that the two-way symmetric model of public relations was developed. Discounting the centers recently established for the study of philanthropy (which have shown little interest in fund raising), Brittingham and Pezzullo (1990) found that "no colleges or universities were identified with a scholarly program in fund raising or with . . . professors following a clear course toward the development of theory" (p. 85). Based on the public relations precedent and the status of fund-raising education, this chapter concludes that very few practitioners practice a two-way symmetric model of fund raising, and that until fund raising finds an "academic home" in public relations departments with full-time scholar-teachers, the symmetric model will remain an under-utilized and largely unknown model.

THE FOUR FUND-RAISING MODELS TODAY

Drawing from the preceding section and the earlier discussions of the fund-raising function, this chapter concludes by placing the four models of fund raising in a modern context. This section answers the research question: Given the four models of fund raising identified historically, what evidence can be found to substantiate the hypothesis that these four models continue to be used by organizations today? Based on the evidence provided in the fund-raising and philanthropy literature, this section hypothesizes that the press agentry model—the oldest model—is practiced by approximately 50% of today's charitable organizations that are actively engaged in fund raising. In addition, hypotheses are advanced as to what types of charitable organizations practice one of the four models predominately.

In response to his own question on how fund raisers persuade people to give generously, Payton (1987), said:

> Manipulation of emotion for various purposes is practiced on a national and even world-wide scale in our time. But it is at least as old a practice as the art of persuasion itself—indeed, it is one of the fundamentals of classical rhetoric. Philanthropy, after all, is the product of persuasion, not of logical demonstration. The abuses of rhetorical technique in a good cause are so familiar as to be commonplace. (p. 41)

Emphasizing his estimation of the predominant use of the press agentry model, Payton said, "Charity needs coercion—or at times seduction, or manipulation, or threat—to come into being" (p. 41). As Payton is described as the nation's "leading thinker in U.S. philanthropy" (Worth, 1989), his worldview of fund raising indicates that many, if not most, charitable organizations practice the oldest model of fund raising, the press agentry model.

In support of this worldview, Cutlip (1965) said that from the fund-raising firm started by Ward after World War I "came five of today's largest fund-raising organizations and scores of trained fund raisers" (p. 158). According to Cutlip, Ward and Pierce developed "the short-term fund drive that today is a fixed feature of Americans' civic lives" (p. 528). Cutlip cited Marts' estimate that the Ward-Pierce-Y school's method had brought in over $75 billion by 1960. In addition, Cutlip stated, "Use of the emotional rather than the education approach to getting money for popular philanthropy continues, though perhaps not to the same extent as was practiced in the early 1920's" (p. 236). Commenting again on the widespread use of emotion in modern fund raising, Cutlip said, "Nevertheless, tearful appeals, such as stories and photographs of pathetically crippled children, continue to be used in much of twentieth-century fund raising, and they remain a topic of fierce debate among social workers and fund raisers" (p. 21). Cutlip's comments bring to mind Jerry Lewis' annual Labor Day Telethon as a modern example of the press agentry model of fund raising. Finally, Cutlip said, "Today's high-powered, high-pressure campaign to raise money is here to stay" (p. 538).

Following Payton (1987) and Cutlip (1965), this section hypothesizes that the press agentry model is currently practiced by many charitable organizations and that it is predominant in national health and social agencies, and in religious organizations, which are the recipients of the majority of gift income. Curti (1958/1983) identified these charitable organizations closely with the press agentry model when he stated:

> The zest for organization and for "drives" has become increasingly characteristic of American behavior. Parenthetically, this zest owes much to . . . such religious organs as De Witt Talmage's *Christian Herald*, as anyone who reads the sensational appeals for sending street urchins to fresh air camps and the even more sensational appeals for disaster relief, can appreciate. In our own century the Red Cross and the proliferating number of organizations designed to stem mortality in tuberculosis, infantile paralysis, cancer and heart ailments have also designed unique campaigns for fund raising. . . . The Community Chest and United Givers are still more recent examples of both high-pressure salesmanship and of wide participating in giving more or less voluntarily. (p. 174)

Whitaker (1974) provided a modern example of the press agentry model and its use of coercion in his discussion of the fund-raising efforts by American Jews for the benefit of Israel. Noting that American Jews contributed between 75% and 80% of the $900 million originally raised for the settlement of Israel, Whitaker described the high pressure, public exposure of the card-calling dinner used to raise this money. Explaining that at such a function, people must say how much they are going to give when their name is called, Whitaker quoted a New York trustee who said:

> It was really a type of blackmail. It is still used today in a great deal of fund-raising, but it is most open in the Jewish world. . . . and that's how they raise funds for the UJA [United Jewish Appeal]. (p. 43)

Any discussion of the current use of the press agentry model of fund raising by religious organizations demands an example from the recent controversies surrounding televangelists. Calling these controversies "one of the most unseemly episodes in the history of religious philanthropy," Payton (1989) said,

"The so-called 'televangelists' seem to have exploited their followers by raising money that they then deflected to their own comfort and pleasure" (p. 65). The recent fund-raising behavior of Oral Roberts represents exploitation through the press agentry model. In 1987 Roberts said that God would "call [him] home" if he didn't raise $8 million for scholarships at Oral Roberts University Medical School ("Give & take," 1989b). Two years later after collecting $9 million, Roberts made a second appeal for $11 million from students at the university, saying that scandals in other ministries had caused a decline in monthly contributions and that creditors were threatening to dismantle his ministry and their university. According to a news article on the appeal ("Give & take," 1989b):

> During the service, Oral's son Richard, who serves as the university's executive vice present, laid a $100 bill at his mother's and father's feet. Then hundreds of students left checks, change, and bills on the stage. About $8,500 was collected, the university said. (p. A28)

Less than 6 months later, Roberts announced that he was closing the medical school ("Oral Roberts," 1989).

Two other examples from the fund-raising literature document the practice of the press agentry model of fund raising today. Groman (cited in Royer, 1989), founder of a marketing firm for charitable organizations, recommends that charitable organizations jazz up their publicity to grab the attention of baby-boomer donors. He suggested, for example, "that the Salvation Army hire Revlon girls to ring the bells next to charity buckets at Christmas time and coordinate a publicity blitz around them" (cited in Royer, 1989, p. 20). Stressing short-term dollar results that are characteristic of the press agentry model, Edwards (1989) stated:

> If you're in the business of acquiring money, you need to spend your time, energy, and resources on programs that will bring you the greatest return in the shortest time for the least investment. . . . That's why I spend 90 percent of my time and money raising major gifts—because that's where the money is. And why not go for the money? (p. 72)

In his study of 22 donors of $1 million or more and 1,000 fund-raising practitioners, Panas (1984), as referred to in chapter 5, developed factors or tenets that guide and shape the success of securing mega gifts. Most of these tenets can be related to the press agentry model of fund raising. For example, Panas' Tenet #3 for success, "Individuals give emotionally, not cerebrally," emphasizes that "giving is visceral," on which the press agentry model of fund raising is based (p. 172). In Tenet #12, "The decision to give is spontaneous,"

Panas again underlined the press agentry model's dependence on emotion. He said, "There is almost an immediate spark of electricity" (p. 176). Yet, he warned in Tenet #13 that commitment for a major gift is rarely made during the first visit to the donor, at which time fund raisers should spend most of their time "selling the drama, the power, and the excitement of the program" (p. 176). Describing the fund-raising staff of charitable organizations practicing the press agentry model, Panas said that a dynamic staff is "propelled with the zeal of a dedicated missionary," and that chief executive officers who do well at fund raising "thrive on it," and, "A few even lust for it" (pp. 182-183). His charge to fund raisers in Tenet #32 is an emotional challenge worthy of the press agentry model of public relations' leading historical figure, P. T. Barnum, when he stated, "There is no lack of money, only a lack of vision. It's there, all yours, for the asking" (p. 186).

In his description of Tenet #30, on strategically selecting the right person for making the call on the prospect, Panas (1984) said that women are handicapped in raising funds, which can be interpreted as using the press agentry model. He said that young women have difficulty soliciting widows and added, "Young, attractive women are not effective in soliciting large gifts from middle aged men" (p. 184).

Unlike other women, however, Panas said that nuns are very effective for calling on male and female prospects, but they are even more effective when they wear their habits. He praised a Mexican priest who wears his clerical vestments when soliciting funds in the United States even though in Mexico the same priest is not allowed to wear his robes outside the church. "That's smart fund raising!," claimed Panas (p. 185).

In his chapter on rethinking the capital campaign, Joel P. Smith (1981), former vice president for development at Stanford University, challenged the conventional wisdom of these "concentrated, full-throttled efforts to achieve predetermined dollar goals . . . during a specified period of time" (p. 60). His arguments provide evidence that such campaigns correlate to the press agentry model of fund raising as exemplified by the historic "whirlwind" campaigns" of the Ward-Pierce-Y school as described earlier. Challenging the assumptions that capital campaigns are virtually essential to a successful program, Smith said, "Finally, it is widely assumed that the enthusiasm and momentum of a campaign make it possible to set and to meet goals that could not otherwise be accomplished." The emotion of a campaign, as described by Smith, creates a dynamic that forces fund raisers "to hurry, to claim present commitments at the expense of the longer view, so that, again and again, the emphasis is on large numbers—large numbers now" (p. 65). In other words, regardless of the fund-raising model practiced by charitable organizations, when such organizations enter a capital-campaign mode, they generally assume a press agentry model of fund raising—one that is based on emotion with the purpose of propagandizing the cause.

According to Smith (1981), capital campaigns encourage neglect of his concept of gift utility, which is discussed more fully in chapter 14 on measuring the effectiveness of fund raising.   Basically, Smith charged that fund raisers, particularly those involved in capital campaigns, solicit and accept gifts for big-dollar goals rather than for what they contribute to organizational priorities and objectives. Smith said that gift utility gets short shrift in capital campaigns, as documented by campaign case statements that avoid hard choices and are composed of institutional wish-lists "commonly prefaced by a suitably platitudi-nous discussion of institutional merits and needs in the context of institutional history and nostalgia" (p. 66). According to Smith, the entire concept of capital campaigns "is significantly influenced by preoccupation with big numbers" (p. 66). As a result, Smith said, "fund raisers pursue additional and often cosmetic objectives, rather than the basic institutional needs" (p. 66).   Contrary to conventional wisdom that measures fund-raising success "by the frequency and magnitude with which colleges undertake capital campaigns—and meet their goals" (p. 60), Smith argued, "The probable result, instead, is haste and waste, a lot of relatively indiscriminate [sic] activity that may produce apparently impressive results. But when such results are more carefully analyzed, they can be soberly disappointing" (p. 65).

In support of Smith's argument, as was noted in chapter 2, Stanford University and Johns Hopkins University, as well as other institutions of higher education, have found that capital campaigns do not provide solutions to financial difficulties (e.g., in spite of its $1.1-billion campaign, Stanford announced a deficit for 1988–1989).   Interestingly, Smith left his fund-raising position at Stanford University shortly after his arguments against capital campaigns were published and before Stanford entered its record-breaking fund-raising efforts. In his arguments, he had predicted that a university would soon undertake a campaign with a goal of $1 billion and said that such a campaign would be perceived as greediness.

In support of Smith's prediction, an article in *The Chronicle of Philanthropy* ("Key departures," 1990) recently introduced the new term *mega-campaigns* to describe those capital campaigns of $1 billion or more. Reporting that the announced resignation of President Derek Bok has delayed Harvard University's "planned drive to raise at least $2-billion," the article stated the following:

> The large campaigns by major universities are expected to put pressure on non-profits around the country to increase the size of their own fund drives. That has

led many fund raisers to worry that such large goals will provoke questions about whether major universities are *needy or greedy*. (p. 5; italics added)

Following Smith (1981), this book argues here and in later chapters that the press agentry model, including the capital campaign, is less socially responsible and pragmatically less effective than the two-way symmetric model of fund raising. This argument is based on two important concepts: the utility of gifts in support of organizational goals, and fund raising's contribution to the enhancement and protection of organizational autonomy. Saying that fund raisers should discourage the notion that the success of a fund-raising program ought to be judged by a big number on the bottom line, Smith stated, "That fascination with larger and larger numbers is shortsighted and superficial; it ignores the entire subject of utility." It is added here that the press agentry model's single focus on dollar totals also ignores the entire concept of autonomy lost or gained through the fund-raising process. As discussed shortly, Smith advocated a practice of fund raising that involves symmetrical concepts that are related to the two-way symmetric model of fund raising.

The purpose of the public information model, it is recalled, is to disseminate information on needs to prospective donors. Panas (1984) argued against the effectiveness of the public information model in his Tenet #14, which states, "Do not sell the needs of the institution" (p. 177). According to Panas, "People do not give to needs, they give to opportunities" (p. 177). He refuted the public information model that is dependent on a rational donor public by saying, "Columns of statistics, financial statements, and historical facts may be very important for substantiation and background. But large donors appear unmoved by such minutiae and tedium. No unrestrained exhilaration in this sort of stuff!" (p. 173). However, one of the million-dollar donors interviewed by Panas said that although fund-raising literature has little impact on major donors, "it is important for smaller gifts" (p. 120). Reinforcing this viewpoint that the public information model likely is used by those charitable organizations that focus on unrestricted lower level gifts, Panas stated, "Campaign literature is certainly important. . . . It is probably effective for smaller gifts. But for the major donor, it will likely take something different to make the sale" (p. 121).

Steinberg (1987) developed a model of fund raising that appears to be extremely similar to the public information model identified in this chapter. He said, "Advertising is in many ways analogous to fund-raising" (p. 134). To obtain this analogy, Steinberg applied Ehrlich and Fisher's model of advertising to the fund-raising function and created a fund-raising model in which donors exchange gifts for factual fund-raising literature. In his model, donors are motivated to give, but are uncertain as to which charitable organizations have the most desirable characteristics in terms of type and quality of service and their efficiency in converting donations to that service. Fund-raising literature, which is significantly cheaper for prospective donors to obtain than the cost of gathering relevant information on their own, allows donors to make their gift decisions. According to Steinberg, "When fund-raising literature is truthful, information is traded for donations, and social allocations are likely to be improved" (p. 122). If fund-raising literature is not easily available, Steinberg said, donations go down.

As was previously noted, the nature of the public information model of fund raising is one-way, truthful communication. As with Steinberg's model, the public information model is dependent on a donor public that is highly enlightened (i.e., donors are prepared to make gifts once they decide who to give to). The identification of this model by a scholar of philanthropy lends some support to its existence today.

According to Milofsky (1987), grant-writing skills are particularly valuable for charitable organizations that seek federal and foundation funding. Explaining that people working in government agencies and foundations receive many proposals from organizations they know little about, Milofsky said, "To choose among them, they look to see whether proposals are technically sophisticated, sensitive to current policy issues, and appropriately concerned with fiscal and administrative controls so that accountability is ensured" (p. 287). As community colleges, for example, traditionally have acquired more government grants than private funds from the three sources of gifts, it is not surprising that they have fund-raising practitioners on staff who are competent in grant-writing skills (i.e., they generally practice a public information model of fund raising when they turn their attention to nongovernment sources of funds).

This chapter hypothesizes that the public information model is practiced by approximately 15% of all charitable organizations, primarily cultural organizations, public 2- and 4-year colleges, and conservation-wildlife organizations.

It is also hypothesized that the two-way asymmetric model is practiced at approximately 30% of all charitable organizations, primarily by private colleges and universities, hospitals–medical centers, public universities and by most fund-raising consultants. Panas (1984) summarized the two-way asymmetric model of fund raising and its purpose of scientific persuasion through research when he said:

> Individuals require their own needs to be met. Listen carefully. See how you can mold the needs of the potential donor to the opportunities of the proposed program. . . . The trick is in making certain that what they want most is what you want most. (p. 172)

Panas emphasized the role of feedback in the two-way asymmetric model even more simply in his Tenet #16, which is one word, "Listen." He later stated, "The most effective solicitor listens—and then moves directly to make the potential donor's dream one in the same with that of the institution" (p. 192).

The important role of research in the two-way asymmetric model of fund raising is emphasized by Panas (1984) in Tenet #56, "Research your prospect with finite care and painstaking attention" (p. 194). He said, "No detail is too small. What might appear to be an insignificant bit of information can often open the door to the mega gift" (p. 194). In his chapter, "Are You Dozing Through a Changing Market?", Panas compared fund raising to marketing cigarettes, toothpaste, and toys. He said that Colgate learned that the way to sell toothpaste was to promise beauty and romance and that donors want the same type of lofty aspirations. Panas said, "Large donors do not give to needy causes. . . . They give to dreams, to visions, to bold and imaginative ventures" (p. 116). Continuing his sales promotion analogy, Panas pointed out that not everyone who has the financial resources to give does so, and asked, "How do you find the 'right button'? And when you do, how do you most effectively push it?" (p. 9). He concluded by saying, "Don't sell what you want. Sell what they want" (p. 116).

Panas explained how the two-way asymmetric model of fund raising is a two-way communication process, but one that is designed to shape messages for the purpose of persuasion when he said:

> That doesn't mean at all that you have to settle for a designated gift that is not relevant to the mission of your organization or one that is not in keeping with the program of the campaign. Good marketing means helping the major donor want to share in your dream. This means proper interpretation and effective *persuasion*. (p.115)

It is important to note that the example of the two-way asymmetric model provided by Panas includes a perspective of fund raising as "good marketing." Brittingham and Pezzullo (1990) provided another example of this model with a marketing focus. Reviewing the research on donor motivation, they said:

> Knowledge of donors' behavior and motivation is critical to the practicing fund raiser. As input to the design of a *marketing* strategy, it can inform the choice of timing for solicitation and campaigns (economic considerations), the particular pitch (emotional versus collaborative ties), and the size of the request (group and organizational motivation and elasticity). (p. 33; italics added)

From these examples, we can conclude that the two-way asymmetric model fits comfortably with current perspectives of fund raising as a sales or marketing function, as discussed in chapter 5.

The presence of the two-way asymmetric model in modern fund-raising practice is verified by Cutlip (1965) when he stated, "The carefully organized campaign, with prestigious leaders in front and professional fund raisers behind, that carefully pinpoints prospects, organizes their solicitation, and build a psychological climate that *compels* people to give is now a fixture of American philanthropy" (p. 538; italics added).

As expected, there are relatively few examples in the literature of the practice of the two-way symmetric model of fund raising. Whitaker (1974) did provide evidence, however, that a few scholars advocate a symmetric model of fund raising. He quoted from the introductory chapter of an unfinished book written by Alan Gregg in 1953, stating:

> The best and most durable relationships develop when the giver and the receiver fully agree in their sense of values as to what needs to be done and the exceeding importance of that need. For a purpose thus shared, and in complementary contribution to a common cause, both donor and recipient can be and usually are grateful each to the other. The giver gives money, confidence, approval and responsibility; the receiver gives his time, his thought, his work, and sometimes risks his reputation in accepting the gift. (p. 202)

Discussing the interdependencies of universities with their various publics, including corporate donors, Ernst Benjamin (1989), general secretary of the American Association of University Professors, advanced symmetrical concepts as they relate to protecting institutional autonomy. For example, he said, "The advice I have for advancement officers is this: Throughout your work, emphasize the quality of education in the long run, not what we on campus can do for the business community, politicians, or students in the short run" (p. 11). Stressing the importance of negotiation in interdependent relationships, he stated:

> Finally, of course it will sometimes be compelling or advantageous to trade a little of our educational capital to business, the community, or the legislature. But when you must make such a trade, be tough about it. Be as tough as the other side is. (p. 11)

Lord (1983) advocated what appears to be the two-way symmetric model of fund raising when he stated, "It's essential to listen to the donor community. If we can find out what's on *their* minds and where *they're* going, we'll be in a strong position to shape our offering accordingly" (p. 11). Continuing this line of thought, Lord said that charitable organizations that are not "in tune" with donor publics may end up trying "to coerce people" (p. 11). He stated, "We may find ourselves trying to convince people how they *should* think and what they *should* do. It's much easier to relate our program to what people already want" (p. 11).

Unfortunately, Lord (1983) offered an illustration of his symmetrical approach that raises questions regarding organizational autonomy. Saying, "A little imagination and creativity can go a long way in 'making the match' between prospect and program" (p. 13), Lord related a story about a zoo that wanted to get a specific businessman interested in its building campaign. Because the businessman was interested in education and in projects that promoted free-enterprise values, the zoo's fund raisers proposed that he "invest" in an education department for young people that would teach them about animal societies and how the "basic principles of competition, cooperation, adaptation and survival were related to the children's own future in a free society" (p. 14). According to Lord, this creative match gave the entrepreneur an opportunity to invest in "the values that were most important to him" (p. 14). Although the donor got what he wanted and the zoo's fund raisers got what they wanted (i.e., more money toward their assigned campaign goals), there is some doubt that the gift contributed to the predetermined goals of the zoo. In fact, Lord's illustration may be viewed as a case of fund raising as a marketing function (as discussed in chapter 5), in which a charitable organization changed its offerings in order to attract private gifts. As Dressel (1980) stated:

> Only simultaneous and sympathetic interaction of an institution with society directed at maximizing the performance of the institution and its services to society can attain a conception of autonomy that benefits both the institution and its supporters. Since there is no unanimity either within the institution or the society it serves, this is a continuing process of interaction and negotiation. (p. ix)

As pointed out earlier, Smith (1981, 1982) advocated a practice of fund raising that contains symmetrical concepts in contradiction to the press agentry model of capital campaigns. For example, he said (1982), "Much of the art of fund raising lies in bringing about a match—sufficient but rarely perfect—between the legitimate preferences of donors and our own needs" (p. 36). Smith urged charitable organizations to reach an internal understanding of fund-raising needs, to translate those needs into fund-raising objectives, and then to match those objectives with the interest and preferences of donor prospects. Saying that automatic matches are rare, Smith urged fund raisers to "solicit donors' understanding and enthusiasm for those needs that have been 'certified' by the institution" (p. 36). In congruence with systems theory and the public relations theory of Grunig (e.g., in preparation; Grunig & Hunt, 1984), Smith said, "In doing that, we must understand that there is nothing wrong in donors having ideas of their own" (p. 36). Although he said that the viewpoint of donors as willful people who are trying to impose their own value systems on the recipients of their gifts is an exaggeration, Smith admitted, "But it is true that many potential donors have strong preferences about what they want to accomplish" (p. 36).

It is hypothesized that 5% or less of all charitable organizations practice the two-way symmetric model, probably a few private universities and a few consulting firms. In support of this hypothesis, David Dunlop (1987), director of capital gifts for Cornell University—a private university in New York—advocated a symmetrical approach to raising "ultimate" gifts (i.e., those truly major gifts that donors probably can give only once because of the substantial portion of resources they represent). For example, Dunlop stated:

> If we want to go beyond the annual and special gifts to the gifts that are of the greatest importance to the giver, we need to look beyond our own particular needs and campaigns and causes. We must look instead at the needs and interests of the giver and respond to those needs—even as we go about the business of serving our institution. (p. 13)

Saying that ultimate gifts are not based on what fund raisers do over a given year, but on what has happened over the last 25 or 30 years, Dunlop (1987) said, "Ultimate gift fund raising, then, depends on our ability to build and develop long-term relationships with a few special givers" (p. 10). Given the fact that Cornell launched a $1.25-billion capital campaign in 1990, it will be interesting to see how Dunlop's approach to fund raising survives the intense pressure of such short-term drives.

As discussed in chapter 16, further research on fund raising should include attempts to measure characteristics of the four fund-raising models at charitable organizations. By gathering data on the characteristics of these models, scholars will gain a better understanding of the fund-raising behavior of charitable organizations and how they practice fund raising differently. Such information will contribute to a better understanding of the benefits *and* costs of the various models (i.e., their effectiveness and efficiency).

With the dominance of the press agentry model in mind, the book now turns to chapter 14, in which theories of strategic public relations management are used to critique the current principles and practices of measuring fund-raising effectiveness by dollars raised.

Chapter 14

Measuring the Effectiveness of Fund Raising

This chapter uses the theories of strategic public relations as analytical tools for examining current principles and practices of measuring fund-raising effectiveness. In doing so, it responds to the research question: What is the relationship between current measurements of fund-raising effectiveness and the overall effectiveness of a charitable organization? Chapter 14 also answers a second and related question: Given the public relations concept of managing communication strategically, how *should* fund-raising effectiveness be measured? Based on Grunig's (in preparation) theories of strategic public relations, chapter 14 concludes that studies measuring fund-raising effectiveness are actually studies of efficiency, or productivity, which are based on the flawed assumption that fund raising contributes to organizational effectiveness when it provides indiscriminant dollars.

In contrast, this book argues that the primary purpose of fund raising is not to raise money for its own sake, but to help charitable organizations manage their environmental interdependencies with donor publics (i.e., to enhance and protect autonomy through the fund-raising process).

It is concluded here that fund raising can be most effective when integrated into the public relations function because such an integration allows the fund-raising function to be measured by its impact on organizational autonomy as it relates to all strategic publics to which the organization is accountable, including donors.

CURRENT STUDIES OF FUND-RAISING EFFECTIVENESS

This section reviews studies of fund-raising effectiveness that currently support the accepted practice of measuring effectiveness by dollars raised. Studies by Pickett (1977, 1981), Dunn (Dunn & Hutten, 1985; Dunn & Terkla, 1985; Dunn, Geronimo, & Adam, 1986), and Loessin and Duronio (1989; Duronio & Loessin, 1989; Loessin, Duronio, & Borton, 1986, 1988) are used to represent the major work in this area. This section concludes that a concentration on dollar–cost ratios and fund-raising potential is short-sighted and does not truly measure effectiveness as it relates to overall organizational goals. As Kanter and Summers (1987) stated:

> The significant questions about performance measurement are thus not technical but conceptual: not *how* to measure effectiveness or productivity but *what* to measure and how definitions and techniques are chosen and are linked to other aspects of an organization's structure, functioning, and environmental relations. (p. 158)

According to Duronio and Loessin (1989), "A general conceptual understanding of effectiveness in fund raising includes raising the most money you can with the least amount of expenditures and doing so in such a manner that enhances the likelihood both that current donors will continue their support and new donors will provide new support" (p. 3). Basically, the effectiveness of fund raising is evaluated by dollar totals and sometimes by cost–benefit ratios that divide the dollars raised by fund-raising expenses. Contrary to the second half of the conceptual understanding provided by Duronio and Loessin, little—if any—attention generally is paid to donor relations when it comes to measuring fund-raising effectiveness. As Dunn, Geronimo, and Adam (1986) said, "The simplest fund-raising achievement measures are (1) total dollars raised and (2) total dollars raised in relation to institutional expenditures" (p. 41).

The standard that is most often used in practice to evaluate the fund-raising performance of charitable organizations is the percentage increase in gift dollars as compared to the preceding year. Simply stated, an effective fund-raising department is one that generates more funds each year. As Loessin et al. (1986) explained, "While fund raising provides a support service for its host institution, the work is actually production- and market-oriented, and clearly entrepreneurial in nature, since *success is measured in terms of dollars generated*" (p. 55; italics added). At many institutions, such as the University of Maryland, neither fund-raising costs nor inflation is factored into the percentage increase, which helps ensure positive evaluation of fund-raising efforts. By way of comparison, General Electric determines a measure of efficiency, which it calls the level of productivity, by computing revenues after the effects of price increases have been removed and costs after discounting for the effect of inflation, and then dividing these "real" revenues by the "real" costs (Hutton, 1989).

Because gifts come from three primary external sources (i.e., individuals, corporations, and foundations), macrofactors such as tax climate, level of general economic health, corporate profits, and foundation payout regulations can affect fund-raising outcomes. In addition, meso-, or organizational, factors can affect outcomes (e.g., a scandal in the Athletic Department at a university), as can microfactors, such as vacancies in fund-raising positions. Explaining that "fund-raising results are easily affected by changes on the institutional level, as well as at the regional, state, and national levels," Loessin et al. (1986) said, "Factors that may affect the institution's relationship with major changes of donors can be altered practically overnight by such events as a stir among area ethnic groups; strikes, work stoppages, and plant closing; a winning (or losing) football team; or the retirement of a popular college president" (p. 59). Regardless of such uncontrollable factors, the effectiveness of fund-raising practitioners is generally measured by their ability to raise more dollars each year.

As mentioned in chapter 5, Brittingham and Pezzullo (1990) found in their review of research that along with analyses of donor behavior, "Studies that attempt to explain institutional effectiveness. ...seem to have dominated research in fund raising for the last 20 years" (p. 79). Regardless of this assessment, effectiveness of fund raising is still a relatively new research area with few completed studies, of which most are focused on fund raising for higher education. According to Duronio and Loessin (1989), the few studies on the effectiveness of fund raising "have as a common theme the effort to identify, define, and measure critical factors related to fund raising outcomes" (p. 7). In other words, scholars have concentrated their research efforts on helping colleges and universities increase the number of dollars they raise (i.e., their research has been administrative, rather than theoretical). Reviewing past studies of fund raising for higher education, Leslie and Ramey (1988) said that the research has emphasized "fund-raising strategies and performances of individual institutions" (p. 118). Earlier studies, these scholars said, dealt with efficiency of expenditures as it related to the quantity of gifts (i.e., an input–output approach).

As noted in chapter 11, there has been little agreement over what constitutes the costs of fund raising, primarily because of the communication objectives other than behavior with which fund raising concerns itself (e.g., awareness, understanding, and attitudes). Related to this confusion is the fact that there is little clarity on the part of fund-raising practitioners about the role of public relations in the fund-raising process. In February 1986, the Council for Advancement and Support of Education (CASE) received a grant from the Lilly

Endowment for a 3-year project that would develop uniform standards and definitions for reporting the expenses of fund raising. In September 1990, a report on the study was released, showing that the average college spends 16 cents to raise $1 ("It costs," 1990). The report also showed that the average college spent an additional 14 cents on alumni and public relations to raise that $1. By separating "direct fund-raising costs" from the rest of the functions in departments of institutional advancement, the study showed "a 525% return on the institution's fund raising investment" (p. 5).

Following the earlier input–output approach, according to Leslie and Ramey (1988), later studies on efficiency emphasized fund-raising potential, which seeks to "estimate empirically fund-raising potential for groups of universities" (p. 118). Regarding recent studies on fund-raising potential, Dunn, Terkla, and Secakusuma (1989) said that their own work is related to major research efforts by Pickett (1977, 1981) and Loessin et al. (1988) because all of these studies focus on "the relationship between institutional traits and fund-raising performance" (p. 54). Pointing to a common conclusion found in these research efforts, Dunn et al. said, "These studies all found that a substantial fraction of the variance in achievement seems to relate to characteristics that suggest institutional wealth" (p. 54).

Referred to by many as a landmark study, Pickett's (1977, 1981) study of fund-raising potential is generally thought to provide a more rigorous test for determining the effectiveness of fund raising than total dollars raised. Pickett (1977) reasoned that because total income from gifts failed to take potential into account, it would be possible to "confuse a 'fortunate' college with an 'effective' one" (p. 115). Loessin et al. (1986) explained this shift in recent research from dollar totals to fund-raising potential by saying, "Measuring effectiveness requires more than a simple review of bottom-line figures, more than a general comparison of this year's achievements with last year's, and more than a quick assessment of an individual institution's performance with its peers" (p. 56).

In his study, Pickett (1977, 1981) found that 69% of the variation in gift income between institutions could be explained by four independent variables: size (number of alumni), wealth (market value of endowment), prestige (cost of attendance), and quality (proportion of senior class planning to attend graduate school). Pickett used these four variables to calculate gift *potential*, which he then compared to actual gift income of a sample of private colleges, selecting half successful (overproductive) and half unsuccessful (underproductive) institutions. He then concluded that trustee leadership, a sense of institutional direction, and a commitment of a major effort to fund raising are the three important characteristics shared by those colleges and universities that surpassed their fund-raising potential. Pickett's work convinced other researchers that it was possible and desirable to make reliable estimates of fund-raising potential as a method for measuring effectiveness. It should be noted that Pickett changed his study from one on fund-raising *effectiveness* in his original 1977 dissertation to one of fund-raising *productivity* in his chapter in Pray's (1981) book. For example, Pickett (1981) concluded, "Policy makers should not evaluate fund-raising programs solely on the basis of the amount of gift income . . . evaluation should be based upon the *productivity* of the fund-raising program—that is the relationship between actual gift income and potential gift income" (p. 14; italics added).

Whether Pickett's (1977, 1981) evaluation method is a more rigorous test of effectiveness, or not, is beside the point. This book argues that his study, as well as those discussed here, measure the wrong unit of analysis (i.e., dollar totals as opposed to donor relations). Before turning to the next study, it must be emphasized that Pickett's study supports the conventional wisdom that the rich get richer (i.e., the variables he used to measure fund-raising potential can all be attributed to the size, wealth, and prestige of the institution). For example, number of alumni is a measurement of size, and endowment is a measurement of wealth. As observed by Dunn, et al. (1989), a common finding of the major research conducted on the effectiveness of fund raising is that the institutional traits most strongly related to fund-raising performance are those associated with the wealth of an institution. In other words, the variance in dollar totals between colleges and universities is explained largely by institutional variables that have little to do with fund-raising efforts. Yet, these researchers continue to assume that the effectiveness of fund raising can be measured best by a comparison of gift totals. As Brittingham and Pezzullo (1990) said, "[The] variables that have been used in some studies to predict effectiveness are more properly thought of as consequences or measures of effectiveness (e.g., size of the endowment). Knowing their association with effectiveness may improve one's understanding of effectiveness but add not a whit to one's ability to control it" (p. 19).

The fallacy of this assumption is emphasized by references in the literature of fund-raising effectiveness to the absence of a strong relationship between short-term fund-raising efforts and private dollars received. For example, Paton (1986) said, "The causal relationships between fund-raising efforts and giving are neither direct nor immediate" (p. 19). Dunn et al. (1986) stated, "The cash proceeds realized last year often represent development efforts of preceding years, especially with respect to bequests realized or large gifts that took years to solicit and years to pay out" (p. 43). Stressing the need for sustained efforts when raising ultimate gifts, Dunlop (1987) said, "If you count the numbers of givers based on when they happened to become givers, as opposed to looking at those who are developing relationships, you're not measuring the thing that really matters" (p. 11). Again, Paton said, "Experienced development officers understand that the results of new or very modest fund-raising programs or activities primarily reflect the *a priori* motivation [or willingness] of donor prospects to contribute, independent of efforts to cultivate their support" (p. 20). Finally, Loessin et al. (1986) stated:

> Economy and effectiveness in fund raising depend on a loyal and dependable funding base so that educational organizations can count on a certain amount of money each year. If an institution were to re-create every donor every year, operating costs would be prohibitive. (p. 59)

In summary, charitable organizations receive gifts that have little relation to short-term efforts to raise funds. Those that report large dollar totals each year are institutions that are generally regarded as large, rich, and prestigious. Therefore, measuring the effectiveness of fund raising by comparing dollar totals is generally misleading and, as is discussed in the next chapter on presuppositions, contributes to unrealistic expectations of fund-raising practitioners.

Dunn and Hutten (1985) studied financial data from academic years 1971–1972 to 1981–1982 on 34 selective private colleges and universities to determine if there were any consistent indicators of "success" in fund raising, which they defined as total private support and "support leverage," or the percentage represented by gifts in the institution's Educational and General (E&G) budget. The first definition of success, according to these researchers, tends to favor larger institutions, whereas the second favors smaller ones. The second definition is of particular interest in relation to the earlier chapter on systems theory because it actually measures the importance of donors in comparison to other sources of financial support for colleges and universities, which would indicate a degree of dependency on donors. In other words, support leverage, as measured by Dunn and Hutten, provides evidence of institutional vulnerability to external control by donors as described by Pfeffer and Salancik (1978). It has been noted that if a charitable organization does not have alternative sources from which to obtain a resource, it is more likely to exchange its autonomy to the external providers of that resource.

For their sample as a whole, Dunn and Hutten (1985) found that support leverage (i.e., the contribution of gifts toward the financial support of private institutions) decreased sharply during their study period, from 33.6% in 1971–1972 to 22.6% in 1981–1982. Because their findings showed that total private support—when adjusted for inflation—had risen only 2.2% over the 10-

year period, they speculated that the percentage decrease in support leverage resulted from rising enrollments/tuition and federal research support that kept pace or rose above inflation. In other words, the private colleges and universities studied by Dunn and Hutten grew more dependent on students and the federal government between 1971 and 1982 than on donors. Interestingly, enrollment was the most consistent predictor of support leverage, but in a negative sense (i.e., the smaller the institution, the more dependent it is on donors). As concluded in chapter 10, nonselective private colleges are more vulnerable to external control than private or public universities. Dunn and Hutten's findings support this conclusion, in that gifts to those private institutions with smaller enrollments (i.e., colleges as opposed to generally larger universities) represent a higher percentage of total financial support, which increases the vulnerability of those colleges to external control by donors.

In further support of this conclusion, Dunn et al. (1989) identified the 50 colleges and universities in the United States whose total income from gifts was the largest in proportion to their budget, averaged across a 7-year period. These researchers then ranked those institutions by their averages, which produced a listing of 49 private institutions, including 12 theological seminaries, and 1 public institution, Virginia Military Institute. Contrary to most institutional rankings related to fund raising, the top 50 institutions in fund-raising leverage tend to be small and relatively unknown colleges and universities (e.g., Harvey Mudd College, Webb Institute of Naval Architecture, Huntington College, Schreiner College, Hillsdale College, and Southwestern University—all of which are in the top 16 positions). Dunn, Terkla, and Secakusuma reported, "For the group as a whole, fund raising produced a median of 60 percent of institutional budget, with a range from about 178 percent to 46 percent" (p. 53). Although these researchers had found in the same study that the two variables of endowment and budget accounted for 65% of the variance in total gift income for those institutions—such as Harvard—that bring in the most private support, these same variables had a low and negative correlation with the top 50 institutions in fund-raising leverage. Discussing these results, the researchers said, "It appears that the fewer students an institution has, the lower its endowment, the more modest its budget, and the more scarce its alumni, the higher its fund-raising leverage is likely to be" (p. 55).

In their 1985 study, Dunn and Hutten found that three of their four variables, which measured "successful" fund raising, were significant and consistent predictors of total private support: The larger the enrollment, the higher the ratio of endowment-per-student, the greater the average alumni gift, then the higher the total private dollars raised. Their fourth variable, the percent of alumni who contribute, was not a significant predictor of either total private support or support leverage. Obviously, the first two significant variables can be directly related to institutional size and wealth—as discussed earlier—whereas the third significant variable can be interpreted as an indicator of institutional wealth and prestige. It should be noted, however, that the four variables studied only accounted for about 50% of the variance in fund-raising success. Interpreting the study's results, the researchers hypothesized that the balance of the variation "probably lies partly in factors that fund raisers can change only slightly in the long run, such as traditions of loyalty or alumni wealth" (p. 46). In other words, these scholars studying the effectiveness of fund raising attribute 50% of success to institutional traits that cannot be controlled by the fund-raising function and hypothesize that much of the remaining 50% also cannot be controlled by fund-raising efforts.

A follow-up study was conducted by Dunn and Terkla (1985) when they analyzed the fund-raising results of 20 major private universities—as opposed to private colleges *and* universities—over a 7-year period. The researchers used three independent variables—enrollment, operating budgets, and size of the alumni body—to predict dollar results. Again, enrollment and size of the alumni body are characteristics of institutional size, and an operating budget is a characteristic of institutional wealth. Dunn and Terkla said that whereas the earlier study of private colleges and universities had predicted only 50% of the variance in fund-raising success, the second study showed that the three variables predicted 80% of the variation in fund-raising success for universities. Dunn and Terkla's findings support the earlier conclusion of this book that private universities raise more private gift dollars than private colleges because of their size, wealth, and prestigious positions in the academic community. In further support of the conclusion that size, wealth, and prestige are major factors in number of dollars raised, Duronio and Loessin (1989) found that *private and public research universities*, which represented only 8.2% of the 575 institutions they studied, accounted for 53.4% of total private support.

Finally, Dunn and Terkla (1985) admitted that the variables they found to have predictive powers in the second study are of little value to fund raisers because they are institutional characteristics generally beyond the fund-raising department's control. The researchers concluded that, in their estimation, "the institutions with the best fund-raising records have two things to their credit: traditions of giving and patterns of family wealth among alumni" (p. 45). According to Dunn and Terkla, the fund-raising strategies suggested from their findings are "to work with alumni administrators to build traditions of loyalty and to work with admissions to create and reinforce patterns of family wealth in the student body" (p. 45). Although they admitted that the latter strategy has ethical and social implications, the researchers did not point out that by influencing the admissions process to create patterns of family wealth, the fund-raising function could be viewed as infringing on institutional autonomy and academic freedom on behalf of future and unknown donors (i.e., fund raising would diminish the right of the institution to determine its own admissions goals and the right of its faculty to determine who shall be taught).

Apparently, such action is not unknown. The University of Vermont (UVM), a public institution, recently acknowledged that out-of-state students from families with "development potential" are given special consideration for admissions ("Give & take," 1989d). Called the "Reggie Richkid" (p. A29) policy by a local newspaper, the practice of basing selection of students on their parents' wealth has been criticized by some UVM faculty members.

According to Duronio and Loessin (1989), who are well-known for their ongoing and active research program on evaluating the effectiveness of fund raising, size, wealth, and prestige have traditionally been associated with fund-raising outcomes. They stated, "Conventional wisdom maintains that higher levels of voluntary support are dependent upon higher amounts of these institutional resources" (pp. 11, 13). These practitioner-researchers at the University of Pittsburgh have found evidence that both supports the conventional wisdom for some types of colleges and universities and refutes it for others.

Duronio and Loessin (1989) examined the relationships of institutional factors of wealth, prestige, and size to fund-raising results (dollar totals) for 10 types of colleges and universities. The typology they used had two dimensions: (a) public/private designation of governance by (b) complexity of educational mission (i.e, research, doctoral, comprehensive, baccalaureate, and 2-year). The Pitt researchers found strong evidence that the "rich get richer," but they also found that this conventional wisdom was primarily true for a limited number of institutions: those that happen to be the best-known, with the most institutional resources, and with the highest dollar totals in private support. The purpose of their study, according to the researchers, "was to lay a foundation for future research by (a) describing how relationships of institutional characteristics and voluntary support outcomes differ by type of institution and by donor group; and (b) identifying institutions with effective fund raising programs, based on their levels of institutional resources" (p. 10). It also should be added that the Pitt researchers, like others, began their study with the unstated assumption that fund-raising effectiveness is synonymous with high dollar totals.

In an article reporting the results of this study, Loessin et al. (1988) said, "It is well known that some types of institutions have far greater potential for raising money than others" (p. 33). Supporting this fund-raising axiom, the Pitt researchers found that overall gift totals decrease as complexity of mission decreases (i.e., 2-year public and private colleges, which by mission can only offer an associate arts degree, raise significantly fewer private dollars than public and private research universities, which by mission offer baccalaureate, master's, and doctoral degrees). As stated earlier, Loessin, Duronio, and Borton reported that private and public research universities accounted for 53.4% of the total voluntary support included in their study. According to the researchers, however, "The fact that more complex institutions raise higher amounts does not necessarily mean that they are better fund raisers" (p. 33). They emphasized that dollar results tell nothing about how well the institution performed relative to its fund-raising potential.

The study reported by Loessin et al. (1988) showed that the range in the 3-year average of total private support at public research universities, such as the University of Minnesota and the University of Maryland, went from a high of about $54 million to a low of about $5 million, or a difference of approximately 980%, and that total support at public comprehensive universities ranged from a high of about $8 million to a low of approximately $71,000, or an 11,508% difference. The researchers hypothesized that "these wide differences within types might be that institutions at the higher level have greater institutional resources to employ in fund raising than those at middle or lower levels" (p. 34). In other words, rather than examining environmental variables that may have an impact on gift totals, the researchers hypothesized that differences in dollars raised within governance-and-mission-based types of institutions can be explained best by variables such as fund-raising expenditures (i.e., the more an institution spends on fund raising, the more it will raise; and the rate of return will remain steady until an institution matches the highest fund-raising outcomes of its peers). Their hypothesis, for example, fails to recognize long-term donor relations, or the impact that historical interdependencies may have on current fund-raising totals (e.g., Minnesota, which currently raises more than $50 million each year, was the first public institution to conduct a capital campaign in the late 1920s; Cutlip, 1965, whereas Maryland did not implement a fund-raising program until the late 1970s).

As related to their hypothesis, Loessin et al. (1988) reported that within certain types of institutions—specifically, private and public research and doctoral universities and private baccalaureate colleges—those with higher fund-raising results generally had greater institutional resources. However, the Pitt researchers failed to point out in their text that the correlation coefficients between fund-raising expenses (one of the four indicators of wealth) and total private support at private research and doctoral universities and at private baccalaureate colleges were, respectively, nonsignificant or low (.49). In fact, the only types of institutions that demonstrated even a medium relationship between fund-raising expenses and total private giving were public research and doctoral universities (.68) and private comprehensive universities (.79). In other words, although these researchers said that institutional resources predict higher gift totals for 5 of the 10 types of institutions of higher education (private and public research and doctoral universities and private baccalaureate colleges), they failed to emphasize that financial resources invested directly in fund raising have relatively little impact on increasing gift totals. That is to say, institutional characteristics are better predictors of fund-raising outputs than fund-raising efforts themselves, but the effectiveness of fund-raising practitioners is still measured by total dollars raised.

Loessin et al. (1988) reported that greater institutional wealth does not explain fund-raising success at the five types of educational institutions—particularly 2-year colleges—that are not private and public research and doctoral universities and private baccalaureate colleges. For example, at private 2-year colleges, three of the four indicators of wealth, including fund-raising expenses, have negative and nonsignificant correlation coefficients with total private support. From these findings the researchers concluded, "Institutions with the highest fund-raising results were not necessarily those with the greatest institutional resources" (p. 34). And they also concluded, "It is not useful to compare actual dollar results for a research university and a 2-year college, for instance, to tell which had a more successful year" (p. 33).

Loessin et al. (1988) said their findings show that when researchers look at higher education in general or at broad categories of institutions, they "find powerful evidence to support the conventional wisdom that a strong relationship exists between institutional wealth and fund-raising success" (p. 35). This is also true, they said, for those institutions with the most complex missions (i.e., research and doctoral universities), but the evidence is less powerful and less consistent for other types of educational institutions (e.g., private comprehensive universities or public baccalaureate colleges).

In order to help fund raisers move beyond simple gift totals as the measurement of effectiveness, the Pitt researchers outlined a procedure for identifying peer institutions on which to base fund-raising potential. They presented what is identified in the next chapter of this book as a pragmatic worldview of fund raising when they challenged fund raisers to transcend assumed limitations, saying, "Chances are good that somewhere an institution much like yours has . . . raised significantly more money" (p. 36).

Interestingly, Loessin et al. (1988) interjected a qualifier in their procedure for identifying peer institutions that emphasizes the need to go beyond dollar totals in measuring fund-raising effectiveness. Stressing that it is important for fund raisers to use their judgment in determining if fund-raising outcomes are in line with those of peer institutions, the Pitt researchers said, "You may know that this total is actually an appropriate level for your institution's history, current needs and goals, investment in fund raising, and *environmental position*" (p. 40; italics added).

As a follow-up to their 1987 study, Loessin and Duronio (1989) turned to qualitative methods to identify a model for fund-raising effectiveness. Significantly, this second study can be viewed more as a response to their qualifier as just stated than to their mixed findings regarding the conventional wisdom of institutional resources predicting fund-raising outcomes. In other words, these practitioner-researchers seem to have changed their direction in studying fund-raising effectiveness. For example, they said that the basic conclusion of their 1987 study was that "analysis of institutional characteristics alone does not explain why some institutions raise considerably more money in voluntary support than do other similar institutions" (pp. 1-2). Therefore, they stated:

> Given that this quantitative research raised as many questions as it answered, we thought about *other ways* to examine the concept of fund raising effectiveness. We decided to go to institutions with effective programs and to conduct in-depth qualitative analyses of how fund raising programs were carried out. (p. 2; italics added)

Although the Pitt researchers adopted new methodologies and different variables for studying effectiveness, they retained their basic assumption that fund-raising effectiveness is synonymous with dollars raised. As the sample for their qualitative study, they selected one institution from each of the 10 types at which "actual total dollars raised were higher than statistically predicted" (p. 2).

As a theoretical framework for their study, Loessin and Duronio (1989) developed a model for elements of fund-raising effectiveness from Gilley, Fulmer, and Reithlingshoefer's (1986) book, *Searching for Academic Excellence: Twenty Colleges and Universities on the Move and Their Leaders*. The 13 elements of the model are divided into two sections: one focusing on what the Pitt researchers called institutional environment, and the other focusing more specifically on the fund-raising function. For example, the four elements incorporated in institutional environment included the president's leadership and participation, and the degree that the fund-raising function and its chief development officer are perceived as being critical for achieving the mission of the institution. Included within the section of the fund-raising function were written program plans and accountabilities for all donor groups, commitment to the institution, and a closeness to and concern for the community and donors.

Following site visits to the sample of "over-productive" colleges and universities, Loessin and Duronio (1989) rated each element on a numerical scale from 1 to 4, with 4 signifying that the element was an outstanding characteristic of that institution. After the completion of 9 of the 10 site visits, the Pitt researchers concluded that closeness to the community and donors was the most significant element among those institutions that were successful in raising dollar totals greater than statistically predicted. Explaining this element that received the highest average ranking of 3.56 on the 4-point scale, Loessin and Duronio said that it represents "effective relations with [a] well-defined external community," and that it demonstrates "concern for [the] best interests of donors" (p. 5). The second highest average ranking was for presidential leadership, which after the 10th site visit surpassed closeness to community and donors for the top position as the most significant element in fund-raising effectiveness ("In college fund raising," 1989).

Discussing their early results, Loessin and Duronio (1989) said, "These preliminary data suggest that the model does contain elements that are definitely characteristic of institutions with effective fund-raising programs" (p. 8). In addition to closeness to community and donors and presidential leadership, three other elements had overall ratings in the "definite to outstanding" range (3.0 and above): institutional commitment to fund raising, represented by the number of fiscal and human resources allocated to that function and a focus by the institution on long-term fund-raising results; commitment to excellence, represented by the practitioners' focus on excellence and integrity in current and future fund-raising programs; and commitment to the institution, represented by practitioners' expressions of love, pride, and respect for the overall institution. It should be noted that two of the highest ranked elements were from the section on institutional environment and three were from the section focused on the fund-raising function.

More significantly, the five highest ranked elements for raising more private gifts than predicted emphasize the importance of environmental relationships (closeness to community and donors), involvement of senior management (presidential leadership), long-term results (institutional commitment), integrity in programming (commitment to excellence), and commitment to the institution. In other words, fund-raising effectiveness, as defined by Loessin and Duronio (1989), is dependent on organizational characteristics that can be related to theories of strategic public relations, as discussed in chapters 10 and 11. For example, Grunig (in preparation) stressed that behavioral objectives, such as

affecting a giving behavior, are rarely achieved on a short-term basis, but rather
are achievable over a longer term. Integrity, which is related to social
responsibility, is characteristic of the two-way symmetric model of fund raising,
and it is argued in the next chapter on presuppositions that this model is also
pragmatically more effective than the other three.

In their early report, Loessin and Duronio (1989) said that administrators who
want to strengthen fund-raising programs should concentrate on "improving
community and donor relationships" (p. 8), but upon completion of the 10th site
visit and the change in order of the top two elements, Loessin (cited in "In
college fund raising," 1989) stated:

> Many people assumed that presidential leadership was important to development
> programs. What is entirely new here is how important it is. It turns out to be not
> one of the factors, but by far the most important factor stimulating institutional
> advancement. (p. 4)

In fact, only one-tenth of 1% separated the two elements, and it can only be
assumed that Loessin stressed presidential leadership in his remarks because it
is more acceptable to the commonly held worldview of fund raising than the
concept of environmental relationships.

Finally, Loessin and Duronio (1989) pointed out that the three elements with
the lowest ratings indicate that there is an absence of written or formal planning
and evaluation processes at effective institutions. And, as a point of interest,
these researchers found that the support and involvement of trustees, leadership
of the chief development officer (who generally is highly paid), and the
perception that the chief development officer and the fund-raising function is
critical for achieving the institutional mission fell in the mid-range of elements
of fund-raising effectiveness (2.01 to 2.99).

Summarizing this section on studies of effectiveness, the effectiveness of fund
raising is viewed as synonymous with raising indiscriminant dollars at the highest
possible rate. Although in practice effectiveness is measured by percentage
increases in gift totals over previous years, research studies have concentrated on
cost–benefit ratios and more recently on fund-raising potential. An examination
of major work on fund-raising potential reveals that the institutional characteristics of size, wealth, and prestige account for half or more of the variance in gift
totals. Such institutional variables have little value for determining effectiveness
of fund raising because they are factors that cannot be controlled by fund-raising
departments.

In addition to using gift totals as the dependent variable in their studies, some
researchers have also used gift totals as a percentage of operating budget (i.e.,

fund-raising leverage). These researchers have found that institutional size and wealth generally have a negative correlation to fund-raising leverage, which supports this book's earlier conclusion that nonselective colleges—as opposed to research and doctoral universities—are more vulnerable to external control by donors. Studies on fund-raising effectiveness also have demonstrated that there is a wide range of variation in total dollars raised among similar institutions that are grouped by governance and mission (i.e., public–private and complexity of mission from 2-year colleges to research universities). These studies indicate that although much of this variation can be explained by institutional size, wealth, and prestige for those that are the biggest, the wealthiest, the best known, and who receive the most private support, the variables do not consistently explain variance in gifts for other types of institutions.

This inconsistency has led researchers to examine other elements of "effective" fund raising, and that research has produced findings showing that raising large amounts of dollars beyond those predicted by size, wealth, and prestige depends on presidential leadership and close relationships to and concern for the community and donors. These elements of effectiveness are related to theories of strategic public relations management (i.e., managing environmental inter-dependencies contributes to organizational effectiveness). This section concludes that a concentration on dollar-ratios of gifts and costs and fund-raising potential is short-sighted and does not truly measure effectiveness as it relates to overall organizational goals.

USING STRATEGIC PUBLIC RELATIONS ROOTED IN SYSTEMS THEORY TO EXPLAIN FUND-RAISING EFFECTIVENESS

The three methods of measuring the effectiveness of fund raising by annual percentage increases of total dollars, by cost–benefit ratios, and by the potential of the organization, ignore the difference between effectiveness and efficiency; ignore what the fund-raising function contributes to overall organizational effectiveness; and ignore how the fund-raising process can help a charitable organization enhance and protect autonomy. As Brittingham and Pezzullo (1990) noted, "Too much concern for the bottom line in fund raising discourages both fund raisers and other institutional officers from discussing the relationship between raising funds for institutional priorities versus increasing the overall amount of support raised" (p. 60).

As stated in earlier chapters, Grunig (e.g., in preparation) believes that the major goal of an organization is autonomy from its environment (e.g., the freedom to pursue its goals without interference). Moving down one level of abstraction, Grunig believes that organizations are interdependent with publics that can enhance or limit autonomy, and that public relations contributes to organizational effectiveness by helping organizations manage these interdependencies. Moving down one more level of abstraction, when public relations is managed strategically, its objectives are formulated in support of overall goals of the organization (i.e., public relations programs are designed to achieve communication objectives that support organizational goals). Therefore, a public relations department is effective when the outcomes of its programs help an organization achieve self-determined goals, when it helps an organization manage environmental interdependencies that may enhance or limit autonomy, and when it helps an organization maintain the degree of freedom that is necessary for the organization to pursue its goals without interference from the environment.

As concluded in earlier chapters, fund raising is a specialization of public relations that is defined in this book as donor relations. Therefore, the fund-raising function is effective, not when it raises greater amounts of private dollars, but when it raises gifts in support of organizational goals, when it effectively manages communication with those donor publics that may enhance or limit the autonomy of a charitable organization, and when it contributes to the organization's freedom to pursue its goals without interference. In support of this new approach to measuring the effectiveness of fund raising, this section first examines the concept of "gift utility" and how the purposes of restricted gifts can support or not support organizational goals. It then relates the utility of gifts to key concepts in theories of strategic public relations. It also discusses the difference between effectiveness and efficiency from the perspective of systems theory, and finally, the section draws from theories of strategic public relations and organizational behavior to present a normative theory of how fund-raising effectiveness should be measured.

It has been stated and alluded to throughout this book that, regardless of monetary level, not all gifts are of equal value to a charitable organization. For example, a gift of $5 million restricted to constructing a new chapel probably would not be considered as valuable as a $5-million gift in support of a new classroom building to a college that was experiencing increased enrollment. Nor, probably, would a gift of antique instruments with an estimated worth of $1 million (and a provision not to sell them) be considered by a symphony orchestra to be as valuable as a gift of $100,000 in support of salaries for musicians. Although such reasoning appears to be basic and logical, there are no provisions in current measures of the effectiveness of fund raising to account for such logic. While working for the College of Journalism at the University of Maryland, for example, I solicited and accepted a cash gift of $250,000 and a pledge for an additional $750,000 over the next 3 years in support of operating costs for the college's new journalism review. Because the journalism review was operating in deficit, the gift designated for operating costs was highly valued by the dean of the journalism school, but by fund-raising measures it paled in comparison to the $3-million appraised value of a daily newspaper's archives given to the college the year before—archives that continue to drain institutional funds for storage costs until a new wing on the library is opened. In short, the usefulness, or utility of gifts generally is not considered when evaluating fund-raising programs or fund-raising practitioners.

Joel Smith (1981, 1982), a fund-raising consultant who is a former college president and the former vice president for development and secretary of the board of trustees at Stanford University, is one of the few fund-raising practitioners who has challenged the conventional wisdom of measuring effectiveness of fund raising by total dollars raised. Smith (1981) said:

> How regrettable it is, then, that so many fund raisers and the institutional leaders who employ them are preoccupied by big numbers instead of promoting an understanding of which gifts are the most useful, which the least, and what is the approximate order of the many that fall between those extremes. (p. 64)

As discussed in chapter 13, Smith advanced a concept of gift utility, saying that fund raisers should "discourage the notion that the success of a fund-raising program ought to be judged by a big number on the bottom line" (p. 64).

Smith (1981, 1982) argued that the current superficial focus on dollar totals leads to fund-raising programs that are more random than rational. He advocated the adoption of institutional agendas to guide the solicitation and acceptance of gifts, particularly major gifts. According to Smith, institutional agendas are composed of organizational needs as determined by senior management (e.g., academic officers and financial planners for institutions of higher education) that have been translated into fund-raising objectives. In other words, Smith argued against raising gifts for the sake of dollar totals and argued for the concept of designing fund-raising programs that will achieve objectives in support of organizational goals. He stated, "Gifts should help accomplish the goals we have set for our institutions" (1982, p. 36).

Chapter 2 noted that the responsibility for fund raising has only recently moved out of the hands of senior managers and policymakers, such as presidents and trustees, to become internalized as a function of lay specialists. As discussed in that chapter, this evolution means that fund-raising decisions frequently are being made in isolation from overall management and financial planning. Smith (1981) emphasized the need to integrate fund raising into the overall management of charitable organizations when he said that fund-raising objectives must be ranked in their relative order of importance to the organization so that priorities are defined for all those who participate in the solicitation and acceptance of gifts. Stressing the short-sightedness of annual evaluations based on gift totals, as well as the need to combine fund raising with overall financial planning, Smith (1982) said, "Fund raising must be integrated with our other financial resources. We need a long-term financial plan that takes into account other sources of income—tuition, endowment income, and so on—as well as fund raising" (p. 35).

As discussed in chapter 5, unrestricted gifts are perceived by charitable organizations to have the highest value of all gifts because they can be used at the discretion of the organization's managers (i.e., in support of self-defined goals). What is less commonly found in the fund-raising literature is a recognition of the value of budget-relief gifts—those gifts restricted to purposes that are already factored into an organization's budget. Smith said unrestricted gifts, by definition, "have the highest utility of all gifts" (1981, p. 66), and he said "you don't need an institutional agenda to tell you that you can also use the functional equivalents of unrestricted money—that is, gift support for certain general fund expenditures you're going to have to make anyway (student aid, library, and so forth)" (1982, p. 36). Echoing Smith, Paton (1986) stated:

> Most fund raisers explicitly understand that different kinds of gift revenues have different value. Unrestricted giving has the highest utility, because this income can be used for any purpose. Restricted giving for purposes currently supported by unrestricted revenues from nondevelopment sources [for example, tuition revenues] has the next highest utility. This restricted giving releases unrestricted revenues from other sources for reassignment—the net effect is the same as for unrestricted giving. The utility of giving for other restricted purposes is a direct function of the priority of the specific purposes and the availability of alternative methods for financing them. (p. 35)

Although Paton (1986) said that understanding about the differential utility of different kinds of gifts is a fundamental consideration in justifying fund-raising *costs* (i.e., it costs more to raise unrestricted lower level gifts than major gifts), he claimed that when it comes to analyzing fund-raising *performance* "it is useful to ignore the distinction" between different types of gifts (p. 41). He explained, "Fund raisers can influence the distribution of gifts between these categories to some extent, asking donors for one kind of gift or another. It is the total dollars raised that is often of most interest" (p. 41). Paton—like other scholars—ignored the consequences of gifts such as those cited in chapter 2 that seem to support purposes far removed from the primary goals of the recipient organizations. He also ignored gifts that actually cost money to accept. For example, a recent article on fund-raising research ("Prospecting for alumni gold," 1988) said that Vanderbilt University is famous for having spent weeks soliciting a gift from the late Winthrop Rockefeller, who finally donated a herd of rare cattle worth thousands of dollars. Unfortunately, by the time the university found a buyer, the cattle had eaten as much food as they were worth.

Acknowledging that charitable organizations may have almost unlimited objectives, but must operate with limited means, Smith (1982) said that trade-off decisions are the essence of an institutional agenda. He stated:

> Sometimes the institutional agenda will tell us we need to refuse a proffered gift. That is difficult. But as I look back on 20 years of fund raising in American colleges and universities, I see far too many gifts that ended up costing too much. Gifts should not be costly. (p. 36)

It was noted in chapter 13 that Smith (1982) viewed fund raising as bringing about a match "between the legitimate preferences of donors and our own needs" (p. 36). In other words, Smith implied that fund raising is a social exchange that involves the enhancement and protection of autonomy as related to donor preferences and organizational need. He emphasized that fund-raising practitioners must look beyond dollar totals when measuring their true contribution to charitable organizations, stating:

> Sometimes a donor's preferences and purposes simply do not match ours. And then the honorable thing to do is to say no. I suspect that in the future, more frequently than in the past, we will find ourselves having to say no to a gift. (p. 36)

Because of their emphasis on haste and their preoccupation with big numbers, capital campaigns rarely promote the concept of gift utility (Smith, 1981). Smith advised charitable organizations, such as colleges and universities, to take a long-term approach to fund raising—one that is sustained and concentrates on the utility of gifts rather than large numbers. He then raised an inevitable question and responded to it, saying:

> Will that kind of sustained program yield as many dollars as campaigns? Maybe, maybe not. But the point I wish to make is that we ought to be asking a different question: Which pattern will provide more support year-in, year-out for the most important objectives of the institution? (p. 68)

In illustration of how the concept of gift utility can be used in fund raising, I recently negotiated a gift that involved changing its purpose in order to meet institutional needs, while still supporting the objectives of the corporate donor. A national grocery store chain decided that it needed to hire more business school graduates in the Mid-Atlantic region and approached the University of Maryland System to offer a gift of $40,000 that would help recruit employees.

Managers from the corporation were convinced that merit scholarships for junior and senior business majors were the best gift vehicle for reaching their stated objective. Three of Maryland's campuses accepted the corporate grants as offered, but I refused to accept the gift for scholarships on behalf of the business school at College Park.

After preliminary discussions with the appropriate faculty chairman, I pointed out that merit scholarships for juniors and seniors were not a priority for the business school because they could not be used for student financial aid or for recruiting merit scholars to the institution—the two traditional reasons for seeking private support for scholarships. Rather, the gift would simply pass from the corporate sponsor to individual students who had already decided to attend College Park's business school and who did not necessarily need the money to complete their education. I also pointed out that such gifts, in fact, have an economic cost to the school, which must administer them without receiving any direct benefit for the institution (i.e., staff and faculty time must be allocated to selecting qualified recipients, communicating with the corporate donor, transferring funds, and reporting). In short, the gift as offered would have little value to the institution in relation to its goals and would cost the institution resources if accepted, although it would increase fund-raising totals.

As an alternative, the faculty chairman and I suggested to the corporate prospect that it restrict its $20,000 gift to our school to underwrite three faculty fellowships and an unrestricted grant to the student marketing association. Because faculty salaries are a financial priority for the College Park business school, this grant would allow the recipients of the fellowships to receive summer stipends in addition to their regular salaries, which would increase their total income and provide summers free for research. In return, the faculty recipients would invite managers of the corporation to be guest lecturers in classes and at meetings of student organizations. When providing career advice to students, the faculty would ensure that consideration was given to the retail grocery business. No promises or guarantees could be made regarding recruitment, but faculty could assure the corporate sponsor that it would receive increased visibility as an employment option among the business students at College Park. In addition, the alternative purpose supported a relationship with faculty—not students—that could lead to faculty research projects and other industrial–university ventures.

Admitting that this was the first time the national corporation had ever been convinced to deviate from its scholarship strategy, corporate managers agreed to fund the alternative proposal and to evaluate the results of the relationship in comparison with gift programs at other institutions at the end of the year's funding period. Although it is possible that results may not satisfy the corporate donor or the faculty of the business school and that the relationship may not continue past the initial year, it is more probable that the scholarship gifts to the other three campuses will prove to meet donor needs, but be of little value to those institutions. In such cases, particularly at public institutions, it can be said that tax and tuition dollars are being drawn away from institutional objectives and allocated to subsidize the goals of external organizations. However, because the fund raisers at these other campuses generally are evaluated by the total dollars they raise, such considerations are of little interest or concern to them.

In relation to fund-raising goals, it should be added that 7 months after making its initial grant, the grocery store chain was asked for and pledged $150,000 toward the cost of a classroom in the new building under construction for the College Park business school. This second gift would seem to indicate a positive evaluation of the faculty fellowships and a desire to further develop the donor–recipient relationship.

There is little evidence in the fund-raising literature or practice that supports Smith's (1981, 1982) concept of gift utility or an approach to fund raising such as the one just described. One of the sparse references to utility of gifts recently was embedded in an article on increasing gift totals for colleges and universities ("Gifts to colleges appear," 1989), which reported that Duke University—which is currently conducting a $400-million campaign—planned to focus its fund-raising efforts in 1989–1990 on raising unrestricted gifts and "budget-relieving" gifts.

In the same token, there is little scholarly evidence that fund raising does not support organizational goals because the subject rarely has been examined. However, in his study of the fund-raising function at private liberal arts colleges, Shilling (cited in Rowland, 1983) posed the following research questions: (a) In what manner have the private liberal arts colleges sought to advance themselves toward their educational goals through the performance of the development function? and (b) To what extent does the performance of the development function in the private liberal arts colleges reflect, or to what extent is it consistent with, the concept of the liberal arts college? The conclusion of the study was that "there is little relationship between the performance of the development function in the private liberal arts colleges and the concept of a liberal arts education" (p. 48).

Finally, it should be mentioned that charitable organizations, particularly colleges and universities, are adopting fund-raising totals as measurements not only of their fund-raising effectiveness, but also of overall organizational

effectiveness.   For example, the University of Maryland at College Park
submitted a proposal in 1989 to the State of Maryland requesting enhancement
funding of $100 million.   A number of the accountability measures in the
proposal (i.e., indicators of successfully meeting stated objectives) are fund-
raising totals. In fact, the enhancement plan states that if the state provides $100
million, the institution will raise $50 million in support of enhancement
objectives as "proof" of the success of the enhanced programming.   In other
words, rather than measuring educational outcomes, the institution has chosen to
use gift totals as measurements of organizational effectiveness.   Kanter and
Summers (1987) explained:

> The focus in nonprofit organizations is likely to shift away from output to input.
> Rather than focus on results [delivery of services, attainment of goals], these
> organizations are likely to concentrate on resource attraction. . . . Thus, planning
> becomes more concerned with fund-raising or resource inputs than with service, in
> part because of the greater ease of measuring the former. (p. 163)

Yet, Hall (1988) argued that the utility of the goods and services provided by
charitable organizations—"education, health care, culture, and so on"—is not a
function of quantity but of quality (p. 41). He illustrated by saying, "The
measure of educational achievement is not how many students pass through the
classroom, but the success with which certain things are learned" (p. 41). Given
the evidence presented in this book, it can only be concluded that measuring the
overall effectiveness of charitable organizations by gifts is misleading and also
dangerous in that such organizations can become increasingly dependent on
donors to provide dollars, not for what those dollars add to organizational
operations, but because the dollars are viewed as indicators of effectiveness.

Grunig (in preparation) reviewed theories of organizational effectiveness "to
show why managed interdependence is the major characteristic of successful
organizations." Grunig found that effectiveness is most often measured by the
successful attainment of organizational goals; however, an organization requires
autonomy to set, pursue, and attain its goals. Theories from the sociology of
organizations suggest that an organization is most likely to be effective in
meeting such goals as profit, innovation, employee satisfaction, social responsibility, or survival if it successfully manages its interdependence with publics
that enhance or limit its autonomy. Grunig also used theories from the sociology
of organizations to explain the relationship between the public relations function
and the autonomy of organizations. According to Grunig (cited in "Computer
Chat," 1987):

> Public relations helps manage interdependence with publics by helping the
> organization communicate with those publics. If the organization uses an appropriate

PR model for a given public, it can achieve a communication objective such as awareness of a position. . . . Achieving one of these communication objectives helps the organization manage interdependence with the target publics that reduce the organization's autonomy. Maintaining autonomy . . . saves money. (pp. 30-31)

Complete autonomy may be the abstract goal of an organization, but the organization must settle for managed interdependence with its publics as a compromise. According to Grunig et al. (1986), organizations can manage interdependence with these publics by negotiating and cooperating with them or by dominating them. As discussed in chapter 6, an open-systems approach to organizational behavior, as developed by Katz and Kahn (1978), views organizations as living organisms that are dependent on their environment for survival and success. Katz and Kahn defined effectiveness as the ability of an organization to adapt to, manipulate, or fulfill expectations of the external environment. Therefore, if the fund-raising function helps a charitable organization manage its interdependence with donor publics, then the organization will lose less autonomy and will be more effective, and the fund-raising function will be effective because it has contributed to the overall effectiveness of the organization.

In relation to the concept of gift utility, we can conclude that gifts with high degrees of usefulness for a charitable organization will enhance autonomy (e.g., they will help an organization pursue its self-determined goals). In such cases, the fund-raising function contributes to organizational effectiveness by raising gifts in support of organizational goals. On the other hand, gifts that have little utility will limit autonomy because organizational goals will be displaced and/or internal resources will be reallocated to purposes other than those determined by the organization. The fund-raising function contributes to organizational effectiveness in such cases by refusing to accept gifts that are not in support of organizational goals (i.e., fund raising protects autonomy and _saves_ the charitable organization money). Finally, as discussed in chapter 11, fund raising can also protect autonomy and save a charitable organization money by identifying issues that are not being met through donor relations and bringing those issues to the attention of the organization's senior management. In other words, fund raisers can identify issues that may create conflict between a charitable organization and its donor publics and counsel managers to change organizational behavior in order to avoid conflict, which may cost the organization money.

Kramer (1980) lent support to this new approach for evaluating fund-raising effectiveness. In discussing presidential leadership, Kramer provided what this book advocates as a valid viewpoint of the effectiveness of fund-raising practitioners. Kramer said that academic leaders actually serve two purposes:

to be entrepreneurial and protective. He said they are expected to be entrepreneurs "seeking the financial and scholarly resources that will make excellence possible," and also are expected "to be protective of the institution and to buffer its values and academic assets against the damage that could be caused by an often indifferent, sometimes short-sighted, and occasionally hostile world" (p. 10). This dual purpose of academic leadership correlates with the double-edged sword concept raised in earlier chapters and is similar to the Janusian approach to fund raising advocated in chapter 16 (i.e., fund raisers need to realize that private support can both enhance an organization's autonomy by providing the means to pursue goals and can diminish organizational autonomy by displacing goals or the means to attaining them). Kramer concluded by saying, "Academic leaders are not considered successful unless they perform both the entrepreneurial and protective functions at least fairly well" (p. 10).

Discussing the difference between effectiveness and efficiency, Pfeffer and Salancik (1978) said that effectiveness is an external measure and is a question of sociopolitical support, whereas efficiency is a quantitative, internal measure of the ratio of resources used to output produced. They said, "Organizational effectiveness is an *external* standard of how well an organization is meeting the demands of the various groups and organizations that are concerned with its activities" (p. 11). Although effectiveness may be concerned with economic considerations (e.g., when colleges are criticized for rising tuition), it also reflects the perceived usefulness of what is being done.

The question, of course, is usefulness to whom? As noted in chapter 7, McConnell (1981) stated, "Accountability is still further complicated by a question of what special interests should be served and what should be put aside" (p.39). Focusing on colleges and universities, the discussion on the relationship of the federal government to research universities in chapter 7 pointed out that demands made and met by these institutions have resulted in criticism from congressional leaders and others that the "multiversities" are not effective teaching institutions. There even have been suggestions by legislators that minimum teaching loads should be tied to legislation appropriating funds for research. It can be concluded from this analogy that the perceived effectiveness of charitable organizations can be diminished by external funding if that funding creates an imbalance in organizational goals (i.e., some constituencies perceive ineffective performance in meeting some goals if external funding emphasizes one at the expense of the others).

In his opinion piece mentioned in chapters 1 and 2 on gifts that "have a hook on them," Boyer (1989) addressed the imbalance in curriculum that can result from private gifts to colleges and universities. He stated, "Giving can leave a campus unevenly supported. Science, engineering and business have always been pet projects, while programs in the social sciences and humanities often go begging" (p. 9-A). According to Dunn (1986), "Fund-raising dollars, though usually only fourth or fifth among the sources of revenue for colleges and universities, can have a disproportionate impact in shaping their programs" (p. 1). Much of this impact, he said, results from the attractiveness of certain academic programs or projects to donors. Dunn explained how an imbalanced curriculum results from private gifts by saying, "Projects that attract support go forward; those that do not, however deserving, are left in the starting blocks" (p. 1). As demonstrated earlier, Dunn is a leading scholar in the area of measuring the effectiveness of fund raising; however, he has limited his work to measuring the potential of institutions to raise more dollars, which does not address issues such as curriculum imbalance caused by fund raising.

As noted in chapter 6, Harvard University's president, Derek Bok (1982), admitted that the freedom of donors to select which academic programs they will support influences colleges and universities "in important ways" (p. 266). Yet, he said that although such influences are "troubling," they are "inevitable" because "universities have little choice in the matter" (p. 266). Reflecting a philosophy that equates effectiveness of fund raising with total dollars raised rather than the effect those dollars have on an organization's mission, Bok said, "Business schools will be better endowed than schools of education, while medical research will expand more rapidly than philosophy departments" (p. 266).

Such a philosophy, or worldview, on the financial imbalance caused by private gifts, may lead to an organization being perceived as effective by its donor publics, but may also cause the institution to be viewed as ineffective by other publics (e.g., faculty).

In seeking private support, therefore, charitable organizations should be concerned not so much with fund-raising potential, or the cost–benefit ratios of their fund-raising departments—the internal measurement of efficiency—but with the impact those private dollars will have on the perceived effectiveness of the institution as measured by the external and internal groups that are concerned with its activities (e.g, consumers, employees, legislators, and other donors). If gifts are raised in support of organizational goals, effectiveness should be increased; if gifts are accepted for purposes that overemphasize one of multiple goals, or for goals that are not a part of the institution's mission, effectiveness will decline.

Pfeffer and Salancik (1978) provided an anecdote about the frequent confusion between efficiency and effectiveness within charitable organizations, particularly institutions of higher education. Faced with declining financial support from the state legislature, the University of Illinois at Urbana–Champaign responded with a cost efficiency report (e.g., student–faculty ratios). The university made no attempt to assess its effectiveness as measured by the opinions and beliefs of its external publics, although later it attempted to stress how its achievements had helped the state. Erroneously, however, it used criteria important to the faculty rather than to external groups. "Thus," said Pfeffer and Salancik, "the university had followed many other organizations down the path of mistaking cost-efficiency for effectiveness" (p. 88).

Saying that strict financial measurements of performance are appropriate for organizations in the for-profit sector, Kanter and Summers (1987) said:

> But the "test" in nonprofits is different: these organizations have defined themselves not around their financial returns but around their mission, or the services they offer. They are organizations in which financial goals are subordinated to mission. (p. 154)

Using police departments as an example, the authors said that when effectiveness is defined as production rates (e.g., the number of tickets written) the measure of effectiveness creates quota systems. As a result they said, police workers may shape their work activities to improve their rates, without regard for their larger mission. According to Kanter and Summers, organizations must always be on guard against "letting a measurement system define the organization's purpose" (p. 156).

As demonstrated in the previous section, fund-raising effectiveness generally has been defined as efficiency, or rates of production (i.e., the number of dollars raised). This practice may force fund raisers to ignore their larger mission of supporting the goals of their organizations so that they can meet dollar quotas. Such a situation can be viewed as dangerous in relation to the fund raiser's boundary role in managing the organizations' interdependencies with donor publics. In the same vein, reliance on cost–benefit ratios to evaluate effectiveness of fund raising may pressure fund raisers to concentrate increasingly on major gifts because the cost ratio of producing these large gifts is much smaller and acceptable than the higher cost ratio traditionally incurred by broad-base, lower level gift programs. As the development of a broad base of donors was identified earlier in this book as a strategy recommended by Pfeffer and Salancik (1978) to avoid external control, it can be concluded that the conventional wisdom of measuring fund-raising effectiveness by cost–benefit ratios increases the potential for control by donors and a corresponding loss of autonomy of charitable organizations.

Because of multiple constituencies, or stakeholders, that have an interest in a charitable organization, Kanter and Summers (1987) said that none of the common ways of measuring performance can guide a charitable organization alone. The authors proposed that "acknowledgement of the realities of multiple constituencies and explicit attempts to develop multiple measures is the only sensible course" out of the dilemma (p. 155).

Pfeffer and Salancik (1978) outlined a procedure for assessing organizational effectiveness that helps organizations correctly identify external dependencies and their relative importance to the organization. This procedure "represents both a model of organizational behavior and a prescription for managing organizations to ensure their continued survival" (p. 89). According to Pfeffer and Salancik, "The first task in assessing external demands is to ascertain those groups or organizations that are relevant for the functioning of the focal organization or for a particular activity" (p. 84). They added, "The next step is to recognize that all may not be of equal importance. It becomes necessary to weight the relative power of the various groups" (p. 85). These scholars said that the third step in their model is "to determine the criteria or values by which each group evaluates the organization" (p. 85). Finally, Pfeffer and Salancik said information about the different groups and their values should be used to assess "potential reactions to activities or out-puts of the focal organization" (p. 86).

Pfeffer and Salancik's (1978) model is similar to the public relations procedure of benefit–cost analysis outlined by Grunig and Hunt (1984), which utilized a simplified form of linear programming to identify and weigh linkages to an organization's publics (e.g., enabling, functional, problem solving, constrained, and high–low involvement). The model is also similar to stakeholder analysis and the public-identification process outlined by Pavlik (1987) that includes the criteria or issues on which an external public evaluates the effectiveness of an organization (i.e., an organization's accountability). Pavlik outlined the four-step procedure recommended for organizations to define environmental publics: (a) identify publics that have a relationship with the organization; (b) evaluate those relationships, including the level of involvement with the organization; (c) identify the issues that are of concern to those publics; and (d) measure the power of those publics (i.e., money, resources, influence).

As explained in chapter 10, donors are only one of many publics that may be strategic to the survival and success of a charitable organization. Because of this, it was argued that donor relations should be incorporated within the public relations function so that environmental interdependencies can be managed effectively through a horizontal structure that can shift resources as strategic publics change.

In light of this critical point and the discussion in this chapter of the impact that gifts can have on charitable organizations, its donor publics, and its other strategic publics, chapter 14 concludes by proposing a normative, three-step process for measuring the effectiveness of fund raising. Following Pfeffer and Salancik (1978), Kanter and Summers (1987), Grunig (in preparation; Grunig & Hunt, 1984), and Pavlik (1987), it is recommended that fund-raising effectiveness be evaluated by: (a) measuring the impact of giving on the charitable organization (i.e., to what degree did gifts enhance or limit organizational autonomy?); (b) measuring the impact of giving on donors (i.e., to what degree did gifts satisfy the objectives of donors?); and (c) measuring the impact of giving on other strategic publics of the organization (i.e., to what degree did gifts help the charitable organization fulfill the expectations of key publics other than donors?). In support of such a process, Kanter and Summers stated:

> The ideal performance assessment system in a nonprofit organization would acknowledge the existence of multiple constituencies and build measures around all of them. . . . an explicit but complex array of tests of performance that balances clients and donors, board and professionals, groups of managers, and any of the other constituencies with a stake in the organization. (p. 164)

Such a balanced approach, according to these scholars, provides data to help the charitable organization know how it is doing on "any of the dimensions of performance with which an active constituency might be concerned" (p. 164).

In defense of this process, it is argued here that charitable organizations must maintain a degree of equilibrium with their environments (i.e., they must balance autonomy and accountability). If the fund-raising process is ignored in seeking such an equilibrium, or is allowed to cause imbalances, charitable organizations will be subject to increased threats to their autonomy. As Simon (1987) said, criticism of the third sector is "based on charges of insufficient accountability and responsiveness to the public at large" (p. 70). He pointed to charges of inefficiency, of fund-raising abuse and other frauds, and of "domination by the wealthy or by other elite groups" (p. 70). He concluded by saying, "With all the criticism comes a barrage of new governmental regulation" (p. 71). Kanter and Summers (1987) said that the ultimate test of performance for a charitable organization is whether representatives of society, starting with the Internal Revenue Service, believe it deserves its special status. Finally, Dressel (1980) stated, "The only justification for autonomy is performance in service of society that surpasses what would be achieved under regulation" (p. 96).

This chapter concludes, therefore, that the fund-raising function is effective, not when it raises greater amounts of private dollars, but when it contributes to a charitable organization's freedom to pursue its goals by effectively managing communication with those publics that may enhance or limit autonomy. Moving down one level of abstraction, when fund raising is managed strategically, its objectives are formulated in support of overall goals of the organization (i.e., gifts are raised not for their monetary level, but for their utility). To measure the effectiveness of fund raising at this lower level of abstraction, this section concludes by suggesting means of measurement that can be adopted by charitable organizations.

For example, a process can be adopted that evaluates the effectiveness of fund raising by both gift totals and gift utility. Fund-raising results can be compared to institutional priorities, assigning values to specific gifts in relation to their utility. In other words, unrestricted gifts would be valued greater than restricted gifts of the same amount, and restricted gifts designated for programs that had high priority for the organization would be assigned a greater value than restricted gifts of the same amount designated for low-priority programs. Similarly, budget-relief gifts, or those gifts restricted to purposes that were already factored into an organization's budget, would be assigned a high value. At the very least, charitable organizations can _subtract_ from gift totals those restricted gifts that have little utility for the organization and that cost an organization money by re-directing internal resources to support the purposes of such gifts. Low-priority gifts are not difficult to identify, particularly if the task is assigned to a committee that is representative of strategic internal publics and senior management. Such a process likely would remove from gift totals those major gifts restricted to purposes that are extraneous to the organization's mission, which would result in a "truer" picture of the effectiveness of fund-raising efforts.

In addition, charitable organizations can adopt a time frame longer than 12 months for evaluating the effectiveness of fund raising. As discussed earlier, annual reviews rarely measure the long-term effects of fund-raising programs. For example, it was pointed out by Dunlop (1987) that ultimate gifts result from long-term relationships between charitable organizations and prospective donors—relationships that span decades. It also was pointed out in chapter 11 that it generally takes an average of 3 years to raise a major gift. As major and ultimate gifts compose the majority of private support raised by many charitable organizations, particularly colleges and universities, it would seem logical to adopt a time period longer than 1 year for evaluating fund raising. Although charitable organizations may need to compile annual gift totals, this book recommends that the _effectiveness_ of fund-raising programs should be evaluated over a 3-year period and not on such annual compilations.

Finally, charitable organizations can adopt a means of measuring the _process_ of fund raising on which to also base their evaluation of that function's effectiveness. As Grunig and Hunt (1984) said, "Evaluations may either be 'process' or 'outcome' evaluations" (p. 183). Whereas outcome evaluations, such as the number of dollars raised, are based on the effects of fund-raising programs, process evaluations "ask whether a program is being administered effectively" (Grunig & Hunt, 1984, p. 183). Grunig and Hunt used AT&T as an example of an organization that utilized outcome evaluation to determine whether its public relations programs have had an effect and also used process evaluation to provide "continual measures of the effectiveness of a program and the performance of the people working in the program" (p. 183).

Describing the raising of major gifts as "the business of enhancing the prospect's relationship with the institution," Dunlop (1987) said, "So if you measure the dollars that happen to flow in during, say, 1987, you're not looking at the *process*. You're just totaling the cash register tape at the end of the process" (p. 11; italics added). Under Dunlop's management, the capital-gifts program at Cornell University tracks the involvement of donor prospects as a process evaluation of it programs and its fund raisers. According to Dunlop, "Our means of measurement is the number and type of contacts each of our top prospects has with the institution" (p. 11). He explained the value of process evaluation in fund raising by saying, "If we can monitor their experiences—and initiate additional experiences of the right sort at the right time—we can deepen that person's relationship with the institution. And the deeper that relationship, the more likely that person will eventually consider our institution for an ultimate gift" (p. 11).

Cornell's program qualifies contacts with prospective donors by the quality, quantity, frequency, and continuity of the contacts, which are planned by members of Dunlop's (1989) fund-raising staff, who he referred to as "moves managers" (p. 13). Furthermore, the program classifies contacts with prospective donors into two categories: foreground initiatives, which are activities planned with a specific prospect in mind (e.g., planning a private lunch with a prospective donor and faculty members); and background initiatives, which are activities or services planned for groups of people that may include one or more prospects (e.g., advisory councils and annual reports). A computer is used to store contact information on each prospective donor, and this tracking program allows Dunlop's department to generate monthly reports on the process leading up to each major gift. Such reports provide continual measurements of the effectiveness of fund-raising programs and of the performance of Cornell's fund raisers.

Following Grunig and Hunt (1984) and Dunlop (1987), this book recommends that charitable organizations adopt process evaluation as one means to measure the effectiveness of fund raising. Simple tracking systems that record the quantity, frequency, and continuity of fund-raising initiatives planned by the fund-raising department will provide a valid measurement of fund-raising effectiveness. In addition, a measurement of the *quality* of contacts with prospective donors, such as the one used at Cornell, will enhance such a process evaluation (e.g., a position on a university's board of trustees would be a contact of higher quality than participation in an alumni event). By measuring the agreed upon process of fund raising (i.e., research, cultivation, solicitation, and recognition), charitable organizations can move beyond dollar totals to evaluate the effectiveness of particular fund-raising programs and the performance of their fund-raising practitioners.

In summary, current principles of the effectiveness of fund raising concentrate on measuring the dollars raised, often in comparison to fund-raising potential and/or cost. Such a concentration on indiscriminant dollars ignores the concept of gift utility and the fact that gifts can enhance organizational autonomy by supporting self-determined goals or limit autonomy by displacing goals and/or the means to achieving those goals. Fund-raising practitioners contribute to organizational effectiveness when they solicit and accept gifts in support of organizational goals and when they refuse to accept gifts that would limit autonomy.

In addition, theories of strategic public relations reveal that fund raising is effective when it helps a charitable organization manage environmental interdependencies with donor publics that may threaten the organization's autonomy. By helping charitable organizations recognize such threats and respond to potential conflicts, fund raising supports the need of a charitable organization to maintain equilibrium with its environment.

Current measures of effectiveness prohibit fund raisers from contributing to organizational effectiveness as described here because their performance is measured not by what they contribute to organizational goals—including autonomy—but only by increased dollar amounts. In effect, charitable organizations are evaluating fund raising by internal measurements of efficiency rather than by external measurements of effectiveness. Such short-sightedness on the part of charitable organizations may lead to increased threats on their autonomy by members of their multiple constituencies. It is argued in this chapter that effectiveness of fund raising should be measured by the impact of gifts on the autonomy of the charitable organization, on the donor public, and on other strategic publics to which the organization is accountable. On a lower level of abstraction, this chapter recommends that charitable organizations measure the effectiveness of fund raising by assigning values to specific gifts in relation to their utility for the organization, by adopting a 3-year time period on which to measure effects, and by utilizing process evaluation to provide a continual measurement of the effectiveness of specific programs and the performance of fund-raising practitioners.

The wide gap between current principles of fund-raising effectiveness and the concepts of autonomy and accountability leads to a discussion of presuppositions about fund raising and the resulting argument that the two-way symmetric model of fund raising is pragmatically more effective, as well as being more ethical and socially responsible.

Chapter 15

Presuppositions About Fund Raising

The third and final chapter of Part IV uses Grunig's (1989a; Grunig & White, in preparation) presuppositions about public relations as an analytical tool to examine worldviews about the role of fund raising in society. Specifically, these presuppositions are used in this chapter to draw analogies that help explain why presuppositions about fund raising have led to misinterpretations of and unrealistic demands on the function, which threaten organizational autonomy. Whereas the four models of fund raising explain *how* charitable organizations practice fund raising in different ways, these presuppositions help to explain *why* these organizations select the models they practice.

This chapter argues that there are five worldviews based on different sets of presuppositions that shape the practice of fund raising: (a) pragmatic (its social role is to help charitable organizations raise money); (b) neutral (an objective view of fund raising that allows it to be observed as an object of study); (c) conservative (its social role is to maintain an elitist socioeconomic system); (d) radical (its role leads to social improvement and reform through the transformation of private dollars into public good); and (e) idealistic (its social role is to manage interdependence and conflict between charitable organizations and their donor publics).

Chapter 15 concludes that asymmetrical presuppositions (i.e., those presuppositions that support the pragmatic, conservative, and radical worldviews) generally have led to a dominance of asymmetrical models of fund raising today (i.e., the press agentry, public information, and two-way asymmetric models). This chapter argues that fund raising programs based on asymmetrical presuppositions promise powerful results for the potential good of the charitable organization, but they may not be as successful as generally claimed, they place unrealistic expectations on fund raisers that encourage unethical and socially irresponsible behavior, and they cost a charitable organization money.

It is further argued that charitable organizations should adopt the two-way symmetric model of fund raising, based on neutral and idealistic presuppositions, to effectively manage interdependencies with foundation, corporate, and individual donors.

As emphasized by Grunig (in preparation), the understanding of presuppositions (i.e., where theories come from and why there is conflict over them) is a critical, and often missing, step in building and applying theory. Grunig said that all theories are derived from presuppositions and that different presuppositions make up worldviews "about the nature of truth, of society, of right or wrong, or simply of how things work in the world." Grunig (1989a) said that unless scholars and practitioners recognize the effect of presuppositions, "they will blindly follow the prevailing worldview of the field" (p. 17).

Grunig (1989a) argued that the prevailing worldview of public relations is as a persuasive and manipulative function, and he recommended that such asymmetrical worldviews be replaced by a symmetrical view that sees the purpose of public relations as managing conflict and promoting understanding between an organization and its strategic publics.

Reflecting back to the discussion in chapter 7 on the relationship between the federal government and research universities, it is recalled that the impact of that resource dependency relationship on the recipient organizations was described by Lehecka (1968) as "a happening." Kerr and Gade (1981) and others expressed almost a shocked surprise at the changes brought about by federal research dollars.

Similarly, Salamon (1987) said that the lack of attention paid to the evolving dependency of all types of charitable organizations on government funding before the 1980s resulted from the distorted lenses through which scholars have viewed the problem, or in the terminology of this chapter, from *presuppositions*. He stated:

> [Scholars] have failed to appreciate the reality of extensive government-nonprofit relationships because of faults in the conceptual lenses through which they have been examining this reality. To come to terms adequately with the facts, therefore, it is necessary to reconfigure the lenses, not simply add more information. To do so, we must first examine what the existing lenses look like, and determine how they have distorted our view. It may then be possible to fashion an alternative body of theory with greater power to let us see what has been going on. (p. 108)

Echoing Salamon (1987), Schmidtlein (1973) said that conceptual frameworks limit perceptions of reality. He stated, "They serve as a lens through which the observer views phenomena. The properties of these conceptual lenses filter out, magnify, and distort facts, thus biasing the conclusions of the observer" (p. 30). This chapter is designed to examine the "existing lenses" through which fund raising is viewed and to determine how presuppositions have distorted the worldviews of fund raising in research and in practice. This examination is necessary as a final step in building a theory of donor relations that has greater power to, in Salamon's words, "see what has been going on."

Paraphrasing Salamon (1987), the problem of relating fund raising to its effect on organizational autonomy is not simply a result of lack of research. The reality of extensive private support has been too apparent for too long to accept this as an adequate explanation, especially because other aspects of donor relationships have been examined, such as donor motivations. As Salamon said, "That this reality was not perceived, or was perceived inappropriately, must therefore be attributed as much to a conceptual as to an empirical problem" (p. 108).

This book contends that, conceptually, fund raising has been misinterpreted and its impact on organizational autonomy has been ignored because of the presuppositions we bring to our understanding of that function. Presuppositions about fund raising have rarely—if ever—been discussed, and their influence generally has not been recognized. Following Grunig (1989a), this chapter argues that we must understand presuppositions if we are going to improve the ethical quality of fund raising, as well as its chance for success in resolving practical fund-raising situations.

According to Grunig (1989a), presuppositions consist of assumptions about the world and values attached to those assumptions. They define the problems researchers attempt to solve, the theories that are used in research, "and the extent to which the world outside a research community accepts the theories that result from research" (p. 18). Grunig (in preparation) said that at one time, scientific theory was looked at as free of values, that neutral explanations of how phenomena work, such as the process of public relations, could be expected. "Today," according to Grunig, "philosophers of science realize that theories are not value-free, that they cannot exist independently of the basic worldview of the people who develop or hold them." In other words, theories of fund raising reflect the worldviews, or different sets of presuppositions, of the scholars who develop them and the practitioners and others who hold them.

Grunig (1989a) maintained that presuppositions about the nature of public relations have steered research and theory in the field in a direction that he considers to be both ineffective and ethically questionable. As mentioned earlier, Grunig believes that public relations is dominated by the presupposition that "the purpose of public relations is to manipulate the behavior of publics for the assumed, if not actual, benefit of the manipulated publics as well as the organization" (p. 29). Similar to Grunig, this chapter argues that fund raising is dominated by the presupposition that the purpose of fund raising is to manipulate the behavior of donors for the potential benefit of the recipient organization and the assumed benefit of the donors.

Grunig (1989a) said that although practitioners often substitute the word "persuade" for "manipulate," he argued that "changing the word does not change the mindset" (p. 18). He also said that practitioners with a social conscience often convince themselves that manipulation benefits publics as well as the organizations, but he argued that the mindset remains the same. This mindset of public relations, according to Grunig, is the asymmetrical approach to public relations, and he suggested an alternative, the symmetrical approach, which has a different set of presuppositions and calls for a different kind of theory.

ASYMMETRICAL PRESUPPOSITIONS IN FUND-RAISING RESEARCH

Discussing the role that presuppositions play in the development of scientific theory, Grunig (1989a) called public relations one of the "least-developed communication domains" (p. 20). He said, "We have few theories because we have not defined the important problems in the domain" (p. 22). As discussed in chapter 1, Laudan (1977) said problems are the focal point of scientific thought, and theories are the end result. That chapter also noted that the prevalent view of fund raising is as a set of organizational problems concerned with raising more money, which has led to research on fund raising that is administrative in purpose rather than critical. Fund-raising scholars rarely see their field as a domain for theorizing, which is attributable to an absence of consensus on the important problems. Following Grunig (1989a), this chapter concludes that there are few theories about fund raising because scholars and practitioners have not defined the important problems in the domain. This conclusion is directly related to the dominant presupposition about the purpose of fund raising.

For example, it was documented in chapter 4 that previous research on fund raising reveals almost an obsession with the problem of identifying donor attitudes that predetermine a giving behavior. This preponderance of donor-attitude studies leads us to believe that the presuppositions held by fund-raising scholars includes the assumption that foundations, corporations, and individuals who hold positive attitudes about an organization will give money to it. Yet, most of the findings of those studies, as well as the work of communication researchers over the last 40 years, do not support such an assumption (i.e., positive attitudes are not a necessary *and* sufficient condition of a giving behavior).

Grunig (1989a) said that before theoretical problems can be resolved, scholars must solve domain problems (i.e., select the problems they want to solve). To do that, he said, scholars must understand where problems come from. And, he said, research traditions and extra-scientific worldviews provide presuppositions that identify research problems.

In the field of fund raising, unlike more mature fields, the presuppositions of practitioners have greatly influenced the selection of research problems. As noted by Carbone (1986) and Brittingham and Pezzullo (1990), most studies of fund raising have been conducted not by scholars, but by practitioner/graduate students who bring their worldviews from the practice of fund raising into the scholarly arena. Emphasizing this fact, the major research work on fund-raising effectiveness analyzed in chapter 14 was conducted by practitioners and administrators rather than full-time scholars; that is, Pickett (1977) and Loessin and Duronio (1989) are—or were at the time of their studies—fund-raising practitioners, and Dunn (Dunn & Hutten, 1985) is an administrator in institutional research. It is hypothesized that practitioner–scholars and the presuppositions they hold about fund raising have been responsible for identifying the search for "effectiveness" formulas and "the magic button," as described earlier, as important research problems, which has had a significant impact on shaping research in the field of fund raising.

In addition to determining the priorities of problems in a domain, presuppositions also influence which theories practitioners and scholars generally use and study (i.e., the selection of a theory is based on its compatibility with the selector's worldview). Grunig (1989a) said that the asymmetrical presuppositions of the press agentry, two-way asymmetric, and public information models of public relations have suggested attitude and behavior change, means of persuasive communication, and diffusion of innovations as relevant theories for public relations research. This chapter contends that similar asymmetrical presuppositions have influenced which theories have been used to study fund raising. This helps explain why, as pointed out in chapter 4, there is so much repetition of the "same" study on donor attitudes by different researchers without a cumulative body of findings. Practitioner/graduate students, because of the presuppositions they bring to their research, ignore or refuse to select the negative findings of previous research on donor attitudes as a basis for their own studies. Likewise, the limited and cognitive effects theories of communication have rarely been used in donor-attitude studies because they do not fit within the boundaries of worldviews held by most practitioners—worldviews that contain a priori assumptions about the powerful effects of communication.

It would appear that an extremely important presupposition to understand about fund raising—and the powerful influence it has on the practice and study of fund raising—is the generally held assumption that fund raising is effective when it raises the most dollars. As discussed in chapter 14, the parameters of this presupposition are simply income, cost, and potential, without any regard for other organizational concerns, such as gift utility (i.e., the importance of the purpose of the gift in relation to the goals of the organization) or long-term relationships with donor publics. The predominance of this presupposition in the study of fund raising is illustrated by the dependent variables most commonly used to measure the effectiveness, or "success" of fund-raising programs (i.e., total dollars raised, cost–benefit ratios, or potential).

Summarizing the discussion on fund-raising research, presuppositions influence both the problems that are selected for study in this domain and the theories that are used to study those problems. The dominant presupposition defines fund raising as the manipulation of donor publics for the potential benefit of the recipient organization and assumed benefits for the donors. This presupposition has focused research efforts on administrative research, rather than critical research, or as Grunig (1989a) said, "research designed to help the organization further its ends rather than to criticize the performance of the organization" (p. 34). Problems identified by this presupposition include positive attitudes as preconditions for giving and measuring the effectiveness of fund raising by total dollars raised. The dominant presupposition has determined that fund-raising researchers use theories of persuasion, attitude–behavior change, and cost–benefit ratios to study fund raising and has prevented them from using theories that may lead to a new understanding of this function, such as communication theories of cognitive effects or theories of institutional autonomy. Finally, the dominant presupposition about fund raising has hampered a consensus on the important problems defining this domain, which has led to an absence of theories on fund raising.

ASYMMETRICAL PRESUPPOSITIONS IN FUND-RAISING PRACTICE

According to Grunig (in preparation), "Presuppositions define the worldview of scholars *and* practitioners" (italics added). He said that the worldviews of practitioners, as well as their organizations, are made up of a priori assumptions that are not true but are assumed to be so based on their worldview. Saying that his four models of public relations represent the values, goals, and behaviors held or used by organizations, Grunig (1989a) collapsed his four models into two worldviews: asymmetrical and symmetrical. He defined the two-way symmetric model as a symmetrical worldview and the press agentry, public information, and two-way asymmetric model as an asymmetrical worldview. It should be noted that although Grunig had formerly defined the public information model as symmetrical in purpose, he now argues that the model—which provides objective, but incomplete information—has the effect of indirect manipulation of publics because it influences the action of others by controlling their access to and use of information. Therefore, Grunig said, it is de facto asymmetrical public relations.

Following Grunig (1989a), this section collapses the four models of fund raising into two worldviews and defines the press agentry, public information, and two-way asymmetric models as an asymmetrical worldview of fund raising. An asymmetrical worldview of fund raising, therefore, is represented by those models whose purposes are to publicize a cause that through emotion will manipulate publics into giving (the press agentry model); to disseminate incomplete information of needs to indirectly manipulate enlightened publics in making rational gift decisions (the public information model); or to persuade donor prospects to give through scientifically researched and designed messages (the two-way asymmetric model). The two-way symmetric model is defined as a symmetrical worldview of fund raising, which holds a purpose of matching institutional objectives with external interests to achieve mutual understanding between an organization and it donor publics. Although chapter 13 noted that this book represents the first time that Grunig's (1976, 1984; Grunig & Hunt, 1984)) four public relations models have been used to explain fund raising, the literature on fund raising and philanthropy has traditionally used the verbs, "to persuade" and "to match" when describing the fund-raising process (i.e., the dimension of asymmetrical and symmetrical is documented in the common terminology of fund raising).

According to Grunig (1989a), "When an organization, its dominant coalition, or its public relations practitioners hold an asymmetrical worldview, they presuppose that the organization knows best" (p. 32). It is further assumed by those holding an asymmetrical worldview that the public would benefit by cooperating with the organization, and "if dissident publics had 'the big picture' or understood the organization, these publics would willingly 'cooperate' with the organization" (Grunig, 1989a, p. 32). This point is important in that it explains why benefits to publics, including donors, are assumed and not actual in the dominant presuppositions about the purposes of public relations and fund raising as previously stated. In other words, an asymmetrical worldview of fund raising holds that the donor automatically benefits from giving because the recipient organization benefits (i.e., the fund-raising effects are unbalanced, or asymmetrical).

Grunig (1989a) reminded us that although an asymmetrical worldview may sound like a reasonable position, organizations holding such perspectives often expect publics to accept things such as pollution, dangerous products, discrimination, higher prices, and even warfare as a result of "cooperation." Similarly, charitable organizations holding asymmetrical worldviews of fund raising expect publics to accept strange things for their own good. Indeed, the commonly accepted definition of philanthropy as translating private resources into public goods assumes that charitable organizations know best. Even the labels assigned to two of the three categories of charities drawn from Douglas (1983) and discussed in chapter 3 indicate a know-best position (i.e., public good and positive externalities). Yet, there is much about fund raising that philosophically conflicts with such asymmetrical worldviews.

For example, in a recent opinion piece titled, "Fed Up With Charity," Bourque (1989) sharply criticized the marketing mindset that has desensitized him and perhaps other Americans to the multiple appeals of charitable organizations:

> You flay my conscience with the good health I enjoy, by telling me about the less fortunate. You jab at my capitalist instincts by enclosing unsolicited address labels, or a pencil, or a wooden object made by a handicapped person, counting on my sense of fairness to pay for the goods I've received; you attack me with a photo of a heart-rendingly beautiful girl-child whose dark eyes plead for rescue from poverty, starvation and ignorance. (p. 10)

Raising issues about the "stupid debates on the worthiness of one cause over another," the percent of gifts going to "administrative expenses," and the sleaze factor in fund-raising techniques such as sweepstakes, Bourque warned: "I'm realistic enough to recognize that there are bound to be a few con artists among you. But whatever your statements show, the competition for my dollar is leading most of you toward even more questionable fund-raising methods" (p. 10).

As discussed in Chapter 5, commercial solicitation firms have been the subject of increased government investigation and regulation in relation to the high percentage of gifts some of them command for administrative expenses. These firms also have been charged with unethical practices. For example, the Pennsylvania Chiefs of Police Association recently agreed to pay the State of Pennsylvania $150,000 in penalties because it knew the professional fund raiser it had hired was using deceptive methods ("Pa. police," 1989). The firm involved, Rainbow Associates, Inc., collected over $1.4 million for the association between 1987 and 1989 by telling donors to the association's magazine that fund-raising employees were police officers and that all the money would go to *local* police. The commercial solicitation firm got 65% of the funds and the nonlocal association got the rest. Such situations, it appears, are not uncommon. After contributing an average of $50 a year for a number of years to a fraternal organization of police that the phone solicitor only identified by its number, my husband discovered that he had been contributing to the pension fund of the airport police (i.e., officers who were not protecting our neighborhood as he assumed, but who were permanently stationed at an international airport approximately 20 miles away from our home).

In his chapter entitled, "The Cheats in Fund Raising," Cutlip (1965) said that some fund raisers "have taken advantage of the *huckstering* atmosphere of modern charity to make a personal fortune" (p. 450; italics added). Calling philanthropy "a playground for the unscrupulous," Cutlip said, "With the advent of America's twentieth-century surefire methods of fund raising and multibillion-dollar philanthropy, dishonest and wasteful fund raising has become a serious social problem" (p. 441). Illustrating his point, he said that the National Kids' Day Foundation, Inc. collected almost $4 million from 1948 to 1953 and spent the entire amount on fund-raising, promotion, and administrative services, with not one dollar ever going to the direct aid of a needy child. Cutlip said that careful scrutiny of the charitable organization revealed that "the Foundation's function was merely to promote the *idea* of aiding needy children" (p. 445).

In relation to a nationally recognized charitable organization, Cutlip (1965) said that the Disabled American Veterans Association (DAV) raised millions of dollars during the 1950s through mass mailings to car owners of key chains with the prospective donors' license plates number on them. According to Cutlip, only a few cents of each dollar given in return for the key chains ever went to assist veterans, and that net proceeds after deducting fund-raising and administrative costs in 1953 were 9%. Justifying the fact that the DAV spent approximately 91% of all gifts on administrative expenses, managers said that the purpose of the association was to encourage assistance for veterans, not to actually assist them.

Assuring us that ethical issues are still of concern today, Payton (1987) said, "The abuses of philanthropy are reported regularly in the press. Under the cloak of philanthropy it appears that some institutions have lost their integrity" (p. 43). Explaining the continuation of abuses, Payton (1988b) said, "The self-interest of donors is often lamented; less often heard is concern about the self-interest of recipients." However, Payton (1987) did mention that state governments are increasingly introducing legislation to regulate the fund-raising behavior of charitable organizations. He pointed out, for example, that one state regulation capped administrative expenses of fund raising at 25%, although that law was later overturned by the Supreme Court in 1989.

Turning from ethics to the issue of social responsibility, charitable organizations holding asymmetrical worldviews use fund raising to bring about what they consider to be socially desirable behaviors. As a result, pro-life organizations persuade and manipulate their donor publics to give money in order to stop abortions, whereas pro-choice organizations do the same in order to keep abortions available. Likewise, Handgun Control views giving money to stop the sale of handguns as a socially desirable behavior, whereas the National Rifle Association holds an entirely opposite viewpoint. Indeed, Douglas (1983) justified the existence of charitable organizations by claiming that the third sector takes over when social values are not common enough to be supported by government programs or cannot be supported economically through the marketplace (i.e., charitable organizations represent social values that do not meet the test of the ballot box or the marketplace). Douglas said, "But where social values diverge in ways that are, rather literally, tolerable, a voluntary Third Sector permits different and inconsistent social values to be pursued concurrently" (p. 146).

It is largely these different and inconsistent social values held by charitable organizations that make asymmetrical worldviews about fund raising philosophically inappropriate. This chapter argues that in addition to ethical considerations as outlined above, the very nature of charitable organizations demands that they practice the two-way symmetric model of fund raising in order to be socially responsible. As Douglas (1983) said, "A *voluntary* Third Sector enables those who want more [programs in support of a particular social value] to give more without *forcing* others to do the same" (p. 146; italics added). In other words, justification for the very existence of charitable organizations (i.e., voluntary association) demands that donor publics not be persuaded or manipulated through fund raising to give money.

From this discussion, it can be concluded that charitable organizations holding asymmetrical worldviews practice the press agentry, public information, or two-way asymmetric model of fund raising (i.e., asymmetrical fund raising). These models are less ethical and socially responsible than the two-way symmetric model. In particular, the "know-best" presupposition of an asymmetrical worldview tends to ignore the ethical abuses perpetuated in the name of transforming private resources into public goods. There is evidence that donors are becoming desensitized to fund-raising appeals from charitable organizations holding asymmetrical worldviews, and high administrative expenses for the fund-raising behavior of some of these organizations has led to increased dissatisfaction and government intervention. Finally, asymmetrical fund raising is inappropriate for charitable organizations that represent diverse social values (i.e., the persuasion and manipulation of donors through fund raising is not socially responsible for those organizations that exist in our democratic society for the very reason that they do not represent values held by the majority of, or even many, Americans).

FIVE WORLDVIEWS OF FUND RAISING

Saying that presuppositions begin with the role a function plays in society as perceived by its scholars and practitioners, Grunig and White (in preparation) described five worldviews of public relations. These five worldviews, which are based on presuppositions or assumptions about the social role of public relations, are used here to help explain the presuppositions that shape the practice and research of fund raising. They are pragmatic, neutral, conservative, radical, and idealistic.

Pragmatic Worldview of Fund Raising

According to Grunig and White (in preparation), a pragmatic worldview is held by many scholars and practitioners "who believe that public relations has no social role other than to help a client meet its objectives." This book contends that numerous fund-raising practitioners hold a worldview that is based on the pragmatic social role of fund raising. For example, Grunig and White said, "Practitioners with a pragmatic view of public relations usually see no need for codes of conduct or ethical standards because they may interfere with 'getting results' for a client." At the 1989 Mid-Atlantic District Conference of the Council for Advancement and Support of Education, William Pickett (1977, 1981) participated in a panel on the professionalism of fund raising. As mentioned in chapter 14, Pickett's (1977) dissertation on characteristics of effective fund-raising programs is highly regarded among fund-raising scholars and practitioners. His career in educational fund raising led to his current position as president of St. John Fishers College, and he is recognized as a senior fund-raising practitioner.

  After presenting characteristics of a profession and placing fund raising on a professional continuum, Pickett (1989) stated that he personally did not want fund raising to become a profession because it would get in the way of loyalty to an institution. Pickett added that the shrinking pool of available fund raisers and the skyrocketing salaries that have resulted in "job hopping" already hamper colleges' efforts to raise gifts and that professional norms would only make the situation worse. One of the characteristics of a profession is, what Grunig and Hunt (1984) called, "Serving Two Masters," (i.e., professional fund raisers would hold an allegiance to the organization for which they worked *and* an allegiance to the profession from which they gain their values and expertise) (p. 64). It is, therefore, highly likely that nonprofessional fund raisers would be more apt to stay at a particular institution than to leave for another fund-raising position (i.e., be more "loyal" to their employer). Although Pickett (1989) used the employment market for opposing professionalism in fund raising, he also may oppose such a move because professionals value peer recognition more importantly than evaluation by their superiors. In other words, as a college president *and* a practitioner–scholar who believes that fund-raising effectiveness should be measured by the amount of money fund raisers generate for their institutions, Pickett may oppose the introduction of professional norms because they would conflict with the self-serving dollar goals of a charitable organization.

Scholars and practitioners holding a pragmatic worldview assume that charitable organizations use fund raising to persuade or manipulate donors to give money for the potential benefit of the recipient organization and the assumed benefits of donors (i.e., presuppositions included in a pragmatic worldview are asymmetrical). Further discussion of this worldview is delayed until a comparison is made between asymmetrical worldviews and the idealistic, or symmetrical, worldview offered by Grunig and White (in preparation).

Neutral and Scientific Worldviews of Fund Raising

According to Grunig and White (in preparation), "Some social scientists take what they consider to be an objective view of public relations: it is a neutral practice that is to be observed as an object of study." With such a worldview, these scholars said, "Researchers can discover how practitioners view their social role and what their motivations are." In a sense, this book takes a neutral view of fund raising, in that it regards fund raising as an object that can be studied relatively objectively. But as Grunig and White warned, "An observer can never be free of his or her presuppositions."

As discussed in more detail later, the theory of donor relations developed in this book is rooted in the worldview of an idealistic social role for fund raising.

This "orientation," therefore, brings a priori assumptions to the book and infringes upon its pure neutrality. Regardless of the symmetrical presuppositions brought to the book, this chapter approaches fund raising from a neutral worldview in an attempt to discover how fund-raising practitioners view their social role. For that reason, the idealistic, or symmetrical, worldview is contrasted with asymmetrical worldviews (i.e., pragmatic, radical, and conservative).

Furthermore, this book approaches fund raising from a scientific worldview, in that it regards philanthropy and fund raising as objects that can be scientifically studied. As concluded in chapter 4, there has been little scholarly research on the role of fund raising in society and/or factors affecting the fund-raising behavior of charitable organizations. This chapter contends that the absence of research on fund raising is related to worldviews held by practitioners and scholars that are incompatible with a scientific worldview. In turn, these incompatible worldviews reveal how some fund-raising practitioners view their social role and what motivations underlie their behavior.

According to Schmidtlein (1973), a worldview that supports science "is by no means universally accepted" (p. 4). This higher education scholar provided four worldviews that are diametrically opposed to the scientific worldview (i.e., they are incompatible with science). When applied to fund raising, these worldviews help explain presuppositions about fund raising that are currently held by some scholars and practitioners.

The first worldview that disallows fund raising as an object of study is the assumption of a world of random or unpredictable events. Explaining this worldview, Schmidtlein said, "Analysis and control of events is impossible if phenomena behave in random ways" (p. 4). He added, "One must be content with accepting life as it comes and making peace with whatever circumstances arise" (p. 4). Evidence of this worldview is found in the fund-raising literature. According to Dunn (1986), "Fund raising is often viewed by its practitioners as an art, not a science. They may contend that development is not susceptible to analysis and management in the traditional sense" (p. 2). In his monograph on fund raising as a profession, Carbone (1989b) quoted an anonymous writer, who said, "Fund raising is a long series of miserable failures followed by a few brilliant successes . . . all of which were accidental" (p. 22).

The second worldview provided by Schmidtlein (1973) is the assumption of a predictable inanimate world inhabited by unpredictable humans. According to Schmidtlein, this worldview holds that humans "interpret events and react in complex ways that are not susceptible to prediction and control" (p. 6). He stated, "Social science, consequently, is impossible both in principle and in practice" (p. 6). An example of this worldview as it relates to fund raising is provided by Smith (1981), who saw human behavior as an unsatisfactory unit for rational analysis. He said, "No matter how hard we try to be analytical and systematic, we cannot gainsay the fact that ours is a profession based on transactions among human beings; for that reason, among others, it is impossible to subject the basic causal relationships in fund raising to rational analysis" (p. 61). Such a worldview, as well as the one just discussed, would discourage the scientific study of fund raising.

The third of Schmidtlein's four worldviews is the assumption of a world governed by metaphysical forces, which incorporates the religious views of fund raising found in much of the practitioner literature. Describing this worldview, Schmidtlein said, "Analysis is useless or illegitimate if it involves tinkering with the workings of some divine providence that is located outside the physical world known to man" (p. 4). In chapter 3, it was pointed out that the terms *philanthropy* and *charity* generally are used interchangeably, although the former traces its roots to a concept of community and the latter to religious concepts. Much of the fund-raising literature alludes to a metaphysical force that controls, or at least contributes to, donor relations. For example, Panas (1984) said, "Without question in the case of many donors, the motivating factor and the most compelling for giving would be a religious one" (p. 107). Describing one of the mega donors he interviewed for his study, Panas said, "When W. Clement Stone makes a gift, he feels that he is really doing the Lord's work, sharing his time, expertise, and wealth" (p. 107). Panas quoted Stone as saying, "A spiritual influence is always present in my giving. I feel that when I give, I am directed."

Panas supported the belief that giving away resources brings monetary returns back to donors. He quoted one of his other mega-donor subjects, Gerald Jennings, as saying, "The more we gave, the more we earned. . . . And frankly, we're afraid to stop. The Lord has been so good to us since we started giving" (p. 154). Underlining a metaphysical worldview of gift giving and getting, Panas said, "There is something bewildering about tithing. Mystifying, even forgetting the biblical admonitions, it appears true—life is like a wheel, what you give comes right back to you" (p. 154).

According to this assumption of a world governed by metaphysical forces, Schmidtlein (1973) said, "The task of analysis is to discover the externally ordained laws of the universe and to regulate activities in accordance with these laws" (p. 5). It is of little importance if these externally ordained laws conflict with observed reality because evil or sin may be responsible. Clearly, such a worldview would not support the scientific study of fund raising, and practitioners holding this worldview would reject the theory of donor relations developed in this book.

The fourth and final worldview provided by Schmidtlein (1973) is the assumption of a world of impressionistic values. Explaining this mindset, Schmidtlein said, "Analysis is illegitimate and dysfunctional if the true values in life result from the perception of events as totalities" (p. 5). Holders of such views, according to Schmidtlein, believe that too great an emphasis on the parts destroys one's appreciation for the larger whole. He said, "One should not seek understanding, only appreciation and sensation" (p. 5). Arguing that philanthropy is a First Amendment right, Payton (1987) said, "We should not let our legitimate concern about some silliness or even fraud obscure the enormous value of charitable activity dispersed throughout the population" (p. 45). In other words, some scholars and practitioners hold the worldview that the over-arching benefits that result from philanthropy (e.g., education for minorities, relief for disaster victims, and prevention of disease) should be appreciated without analyzing and seeking to understand the parts of philanthropy that may destroy one's appreciation for it.

Yet, as stated shortly, Payton (1988c) advocated a scientific approach to the study of philanthropy, one that would allow scholars to examine even its "warts." It is contended here that the presuppositions about a world of impressionistic value are to some degree responsible for the less than rigorous study of fund raising to date (e.g., the preponderance of studies on positive attitudes as indicators of a giving behavior and the absence of studies on the self-interest of recipient organizations). Quoting De La Rochefoucauls, Panas (1984) stated, "We would often be ashamed of our finest actions if the world understood all the motives which produce them" (p. 207). Such a worldview would not support the scientific study of fund raising.

In summary, worldviews that are incompatible with science, such as the four provided by Schmidtlein (1973), have contributed to the misconceptions and myths discussed in chapter 5 and have hampered previous efforts to understand the fund-raising function. This book approaches the subject of fund raising with a scientific worldview. Without a scientific perspective, Payton (1988c) said that fund raising will be delegated to a vocational status. In support of this book's approach, he stated:

> When we encourage academics to look critically at philanthropy, we must do so with a commitment to deal with the entire philanthropic tradition . . . warts and all. If we are not prepared to do so, we should back away from the academy. We should not encourage the study of philanthropy as a field of serious inquiry, but only as a form of training for careers in fund raising or fund-raising counselling. (p. 4)

Conservative and Radical Worldviews
of Fund Raising

Continuing with the five worldviews of public relations, Grunig (in preparation) said, "The conservative and radical presuppositions assume that organizational communication can have powerful effects on society." According to Grunig and White (in preparation), those scholars and practitioners who hold a conservative worldview see the social role of public relations as defending the interest of the economically powerful in order to maintain a system of privilege. A radical worldview, on the other hand, sees the role of public relations as leading to social improvement, reform, and change. Similarly, conservative and radical presuppositions assume that fund raising can be a powerful weapon against other social groups in maintaining a system of privilege (conservative) or in bringing about reforms (radical).

Presuppositions related to either of these two worldviews assume that charitable organizations use fund raising to manipulate foundations, corporations, and individuals to give money for the potential benefit of the recipient organization and the assumed benefit of the donor. In other words, such presuppositions are asymmetrical. Illustrating the conservative worldview, Whitaker (1974) summarized a common criticism of foundations and the fund raisers who—by soliciting and accepting grants from such donors—become a party to the criticism:

> Currently, their efforts are too often open to the criticism that they are principally used merely to lubricate the machinery of the status quo, for almost all the people who control foundations belong to segments of society whose privileges predispose them to be basically satisfied with its present structure—and indeed frequently have a vested interest in preventing any seriously radical reforms. (p. 215)

Supporting the existence of the conservative worldview, Cutlip (1965) quoted a mid-1950s fund-raising brochure from Gustavus Adolphus College in Minnesota:

> The private colleges of America are the bulwark of our free economy. If they are allowed to disintegrate for the lack of [private] support, government will have to assume the responsibility of educating all our youth. Therein lies grave danger of our way of life. (p. 517)

Curti (1958/1983) said that all of philanthropy has traditionally been criticized as a tool used to patch up short-comings in the capitalist system and "to preserve a status quo that did not deserve preservation" (p. 170). As noted in chapter 14, Simon (1987) said that one of the current criticisms of the third sector is charges of domination by the wealthy or other elite groups. He further stated, "This last set of charges asserts that here, even more than in the world of business, is to be found the last refuge of privilege" (p. 70).

Odendahl's (1990) book, *Charity Begins at Home*, provides scholarly support for these charges. As discussed in chapter 8, Odendahl argued that the charitable tax deduction has created a system that enables the upper classes of American society to use philanthropy to preserve the status quo. Summarizing Odendahl's argument, an article on this controversial book ("Philanthropy promotes," 1990) stated, "Philanthropy, far from aiding the poor and the disenfranchised, ultimately promotes the interests of the upper class, whose charitable dollars serve to preserve an elite constellation of social, cultural, and educational institutions" (p. A29).

In response, conservative critic Leslie Lenkowsky (cited in "Philanthropy promotes," 1990) said, "The problem with the left-wing critique of philanthropy [is that] it insists that the only proper purpose of giving is to help the poor, reduce inequality, or assist other fashionably disadvantaged groups, such as women" (p. A31). Lenkowsky said that Odendahl's book revealed more about her point of view than what the wealthy actually do with their money.

Indeed, Odendahl is a good example of a scholar who holds a radical worldview of philanthropy (i.e., she believes that the purpose of philanthropy is not to maintain a system of privilege, but to promote social improvement, reform, and change). In the concluding chapter of her book she called for reforms in tax laws and suggested ceilings on the federal charitable deduction and different categories for tax-exempt status.

On this opposite ideological side, Whitaker (1974) provided an illustration of foundation donors that can be used to point out the radical role of fund raising held by many practitioners and scholars. He said, "They possess the capacity, in microcosm, to criticize and suggest re-shapings of society" (p. 209). According to Curti (1958/1983), foundations have been criticized from both ideological sides for being conservative or radical. He said, "It is interesting to note that the first Congressional investigation of foundations on the eve of the first World War criticized them for alleged effects in consolidating an existing status quo and that the Reece committee in McCarthy's time damned them for the support they had presumably given to an Un-American collectivism" (p. 174).

The powerful effects that fund raising is assumed to have on society by those who hold a radical worldview is often supported by historical recitations of innovation, reform, and change brought about by philanthropy. As Whitaker (1974) stated, "Most public welfare provisions, including hospitals and schools for the poor, employment exchanges and adult education, as well as family planning and hostels for the homeless, were first pioneered by charities" (p. 73).

Reflecting on such historical evidence, it is easy to understand why many fund raisers adopt a worldview about the radical social role of fund raising. In relation to the earlier discussion on the worldview of impressionistic values, it also is easy to see that these two worldviews are compatible (i.e., the overarching benefits of charitable organizations outweigh the need for analyzing fund raising, which might destroy appreciation for the collective good these organizations provide). Illustrating this point, Broce (1986) said that the two most challenging realities facing fund raisers are that they always deal in the future and they are "always concerned with enriching the quality of the human condition" (p. 5).

As do their counterparts in public relations, many fund-raising practitioners who work for charitable organizations often assume that their "cause" is for the good of society (i.e., they work for the greater good). They rarely question the self-interest of their organization and the end often justifies the means. For example, senior practitioner and former vice president of institutional advancement at the University of North Carolina at Chapel Hill, Gary Evans (1989), provided a radical worldview of fund raising when he stated, "I prefer to think of what we do in development not as 'the business of raising money' but as a calling for service to a greater and nobler cause" (p. 7). Curti (1958/1983) explained such a worldview by saying, "In relieving class and group tensions and in facilitating the growth of social well-being, philanthropy has in a sense been equivalent for socialism" (p. 174).

Yet, a close examination of the fund-raising and philanthropy literature reveals that value judgments of which cause is greater, or more worthy, often "turns the waters murky." For example, "In 1969, the British people left a total of 988,000 lbs. for animal welfare to the Royal Society for the Prevention of Cruelty to Animals, compared with 334,000 lbs. to the National Society for the Prevention of Cruelty to Children" (Whitaker, 1974, p. 72). As Payton (1987) stated, "It is very difficult to understand that one's own good cause isn't necessarily someone else's" (p. 44).

It is a common fund-raising axiom that the neediest organizations are not necessarily the ones that attract support. As Panas (1984) said, "People do not give because there is a need. . . . donors run away from 'needs.' They hide from the institution that is not financially stable. Large donors give to heroic, exciting programs rather than to needy institutions" (p. 35). In support of Panas' conclusion, it was discussed in chapter 14 that the independent variables used by scholars to measure fund-raising effectiveness are institutional characteristics of wealth, which predict 50% or more of the variation in the amount of money raised by colleges and universities.

As previously pointed out, both the conservative and radical worldviews are asymmetrical. According to Grunig (in preparation), holders of conservative and radical worldviews "see public relations as a tool used in a war among opposing social groups." From the discussion of the worldviews about fund raising, we can adopt Grunig's use of game theory language and state that fund raising based on asymmetrical presuppositions is a "zero-sum game" (i.e., "one organization, group, or public gains and the other loses"). Grunig and White (in preparation) advocated an alternative worldview, the idealistic view, which is based on a set of symmetrical presuppositions.

Idealistic, or Symmetrical, Worldview of Fund Raising

According to Grunig (in preparation), "A symmetric worldview sees public relations as a nonzero-sum game in which competing organizations or groups both can gain if they play the game right." Grunig and White (in preparation) said that an idealistic worldview sees the social role of public relations as a mechanism by which organizations and publics manage their interdependence. Therefore, paraphrasing these public relations scholars, the idealistic worldview sees fund raising as a tool, not a weapon, by which charitable organizations and donor publics interact in a pluralistic system to manage their interdependence and conflict for the benefit of all. As does Grunig's theory, the theory of donor relations developed in this book fits within this idealistic framework. Again paraphrasing Grunig and White, fund raising should be practiced to serve the public interest, to develop mutual understanding between charitable organizations and their donor publics, and to contribute to the examination and solutions of societal issues.

It is assumed that fund-raising practitioners and scholars will find it difficult to understand or accept the theory of donor relations presented in this book. From the literature and observation of the fund-raising practice over the last 16 years as a practitioner, teacher, and scholar, there is little evidence that many practitioners or scholars work from idealistic, or symmetrical, presuppositions. Rather, the majority of fund raisers hold pragmatic, conservative, or radical worldviews—all of which are asymmetrical—that would lead them to reject the theory presented here. As Grunig and White (in preparation) explained, practitioners and scholars generally use and study only those theories that fit within the boundaries of their worldviews. For example, Rowland's (1977, 1983) definitions of institutional advancement (i.e., cultivating support for and developing understanding of institutional mission, goals, and needs) are based on asymmetrical presuppositions, which would not easily accommodate the theory of donor relations presented here.

More importantly in relation to the power-control theory discussed at the end of this chapter, many of the senior managers to whom fund raisers report would find an idealistic framework in conflict with their own presuppositions about fund raising (i.e., their organizational ideology or schema of fund raising is shaped by their pragmatic, conservative, or radical worldviews about raising private money). As discussed shortly, asymmetrical presuppositions held by members of the dominant coalition will determine that fund raisers practice a fund-raising model based on such presuppositions.

As stated earlier, this book concludes that fund-raising programs based on symmetrical presuppositions are more ethical and socially responsible than asymmetrical fund raising. As is demonstrated next, this book also concludes that, pragmatically, symmetrical fund raising is also more successful because it enhances and protects organizational autonomy. That is to say, the purpose of fund raising is not to raise money, but to help charitable organizations manage their interdependencies with donor publics, which contributes to their effectiveness.

During their 6-year study on excellence in public relations, the research team headed by Grunig (in preparation) and sponsored by the foundation of the International Business Communicators Association (IABC), plans to test and support its hypothesis that public relations programs based on symmetrical presuppositions are not only more ethical and socially responsible, but are also characteristic of excellent departments of public relations. In other words, the public relations researchers hope to prove pragmatically that symmetrical public relations programs are more successful than asymmetrical ones. The IABC researchers based their hypothesis on their literature review, which showed that symmetrical communications programs are successful more often than asymmetrical ones and contribute more to organizational effectiveness. According to Grunig (1989a), under-utilization of the two-way symmetric model of public relations and the failure of the asymmetrical models to resolve conflict and contribute to organizational effectiveness provides some support for the success of the two-way symmetric model.

The fund-raising literature also provides similar evidence (i.e., the under-utilization of the two-way symmetric model of fund raising and the failure of the predominant asymmetrical models lend support for the pragmatic value of the two-way symmetric model). For example, fund-raising programs based on asymmetrical presuppositions promise powerful results for the good of their organizations, raising billions of dollars each year. Yet, individually, many of the fund-raising campaigns have failed to reach their dollar goals. As related in the chapter on fund-raising models, Cutlip (1965) provided examples of numerous failures and frequent ethical abuses of the press agentry model (e.g., the 1919 Red Cross fund for $25 million that failed dismally and set off a wave of bitter criticism). Curti (1965) reported that in 1923 John Price Jones, the historical figure associated with the two-way asymmetric model of fund raising, conducted a survey of fund-raising campaigns for colleges and universities. Of the 109 institutions that responded to his survey, 64 had conducted campaigns since the end of World War I, and of that number only 36 (56%) had reached their dollar goal.

Not surprisingly, there is little information available on the failure to meet campaign or annual fund-raising goals—quite unlike the barrage of publicity on announcements for campaigns and multimillion gifts that was presented earlier in this book. However, a recent membership career survey (NSFRE, 1988) reported that at least 35.8% of the fund raisers who belong to the National Society of Fund Raising Executives say they did not meet their fund-raising goals in each of the last 5 years. It should be noted that the percentage of failure reported was originally 63.1%, but the analysts adjusted the figure for those who had been in the field less than 5 years and for those who did not respond (i.e., if respondents answered "no" to the question on successfully meeting goals, but had not worked in fund raising for more than 5 years, or if respondents did *not* answer the question, they were removed from the analysis; thereby, increasing the proportion reported as successful). The general percentage of failure also may be higher because there is obviously a great deal of pressure to present a winning side in fund raising (i.e., fund raisers are evaluated on the total dollars raised for their organization even if factors beyond their control contribute to failure).

In his study of fund raisers who belong to the three major professional associations, NSFRE, CASE, and NAHD, Carbone (1989b) found that a "frequent complaint is 'unrealistic expectations' and lack of 'understanding the appropriate role of development officers'" (p. 29). As recalled from chapter 2, an anonymous fund-raising practitioner in Carbone's study said, "In general, organizations tend to have unrealistic expectations of their development professionals" (p. 29). Carbone said that such complaints suggest that dollar goals are being imposed on many fund raisers by their organizations.

Finally, a recent dissertation reviewed in CASE *Currents* (Goldman, 1989) found that fund-raising campaigns with goals of at least $10 million conducted in the last 10 years by public doctoral universities correlated with fund-raising *failure*. According to the reviewer, the book's author "suggests that institutions that conduct campaigns are seeking a quick fix in lieu of establishing a true 'history' of development activities" (p. 57). The reviewer displayed the predominant asymmetrical worldview of fund raising when she dismissed such a suggestion by saying, "It's more likely that the negative correlation simply reflects the temporary drop in gifts that often follows the close of a campaign" (p. 57).

Based on the discussion here, this chapter concludes that asymmetrical presuppositions create unrealistic expectations of the fund-raising function. Supporting this conclusion, Panas (1984) provided a charge to fund raisers that can be viewed as one based on asymmetrical presuppositions when he said, "Those that will succeed will be the courageous, the innovative, the aggressive. What will be required is creative and strategic planning—a do-something attitude that expects the impossible, and achieves it" (p. 16). Summarizing this point, asymmetrical presuppositions suggest that charitable organizations can achieve powerful results through fund raising. There is evidence, however, that programs based on these presuppositions are not necessarily successful. In addition, the powerful results promised by asymmetrical presuppositions about fund raising encourages charitable organizations to behave in unethical and socially irresponsible ways.

In an article on institutional integrity, Charles E. Lawson (1988), who is the chairman and chief executive officer of Brakeley, John Price Jones, Inc., warned, "In this era of ever increasing goals, comprehensive campaigns and extended campaigns, many institutions are becoming increasingly vague and somewhat misleading in reporting the always essential *success* of their fund-raising efforts." As pointed out in the earlier discussions on capital campaigns, charitable organizations recently have been criticized for "adopting" accounting policies that appear to border on the unethical in order to ensure fund-raising success. For example, senior administrators, volunteers, and fund raisers at the University of Maryland have adopted a policy that will count the *total value* of bequests as gifts toward its current capital campaign, even though bequests are not irrevocable and those that are not changed may not be received until decades after the "successful" closing of the campaign.

One bequest in which I personally was involved totaled almost $2 million for the business school at College Park. By campaign policy, the bequest was counted the same as a $2-million pledge, even though the 72-year-old donor, who played tennis twice a week, threatened to change his will whenever something displeased him about the university—which was almost as frequent as his tennis games. Taking such considerations into account, some charitable organizations count bequests on a sliding scale determined by the age of the donor and/or on a standardized percent of value, which acknowledges that not all bequests are received.

Also related to the "essential success" of capital campaigns, donors generally do not realize that campaign goals are not entirely "new" money, but rather that annual projections of gift income are a substantial portion of the announced goal. For example, of the $200-million goal established for the University of Maryland System, it has been estimated that during the campaign period, which ends June 1993, approximately $120 million would "come in" without an announced campaign, not adjusted for inflation. Of the approximately $80 million remaining of the goal, it is estimated that approximately $50 million will be generated by the routine fund-raising activities of the six new campuses that were added to the System after the start of the advance stage of the campaign. Yet, the campaign literature and messages treat the campaign goal as if it were new money that otherwise could not be expected.

Gifts-in-kind also tend to misrepresent the "success" of capital campaigns. For example, 10.3% of the $125 million raised toward the University of Maryland Campaign as of March 1990 consisted of gifts-in-kind, although such gifts rarely are related to those areas of need defined at the beginning of a campaign as justification for undertaking such a major fund-raising effort ("Campaign comments," 1990). In other words, although the University of Maryland had launched a $200-million campaign ostensibly to meet urgent needs for endowment, faculty support, and capital projects, more than $12.5 million of the total raised at the end of the third year of the 6-year campaign was non-cash gifts, such as books, equipment, and the $3-million newspaper archives described earlier in Chapter 14.

Finally, one third ($42.8 million) of the University of Maryland's campaign total at the halfway point of the campaign consisted of pledges (13.2%), planned gifts (10.8%), and gifts-in-kind (10.3%), such as those just described ("Campaign comments," 1990). Although charitable organizations may differ in their accounting policies, it is safe to say that, generally, the "success" of capital campaigns cannot be interpreted as dollars readily available for meeting organizational needs.

In her study of colleges and universities conducting or having just completed capital campaigns with goals of more than $100 million, Bornstein (1989) found that 90% of the responding institutions counted pledges in campaign totals, some with payment periods as high as 10 years. Of particular relevance to this discussion, 31% of the respondents in Bornstein's study "counted payments against pledges to prior fund-raising campaigns" (p. 15). In other words, one third of these colleges and universities have accounting policies that allow a donor's payments on a pledge to be counted in the "success" of one campaign, although the donor's original pledge had also been counted toward the "success" of a previous campaign.

A majority (59%) of the institutions in Bornstein's (1989) study included bequest expectancies, revocable trusts, or both in their totals. Although some of the respondents said they selectively counted only a very few such gifts toward campaign goals, the fact remains that bequests and revocable trusts, which can be changed by a donor at any time and are transformed into resources for the charitable organization only at the time of the donor's death, are counted by a number of capital campaigns today even though the "gift" may not be realized for 30 or 40 years. As Alexander (1990) stated, "Crediting millions of dollars to a campaign based on an unrealized bequest can be a total *distortion* of how much money was actually raised" (p. 26; italics added).

Bornstein (1989) also reported that about one fourth of the institutions in her study counted either or both state and federal funds, which, by definition, are not gifts. A former fund raiser for Johns Hopkins University told me that accounting practices such as those described here largely were responsible for the "success" of the $100-million campaign "completed" by Hopkins in 1976, which was referred to in chapter 2. As this senior fund raiser said, "We counted everything."

Such accounting abuses, according to Alexander (1990), are directly attributable to the "unrealistic size of goals" for today's capital campaigns. In his opinion piece on this issue, he said, "The prevailing trend to conduct ever-larger campaigns creates a sometimes overwhelming burden on fund raisers. And therein lies the potential—sometimes the demand—for abuse" (p. 26). Addressing the fact that some colleges and universities count the full value of a life-insurance policy even though the donor may be only 50 years old, Gearhart (cited in "Lax rules," 1990), said, "To portray a campaign as successful which has done nothing more than count will expectancies and verbal pledges is, in my opinion, contrary to everything that higher education is about" (p. 8).

On the subject of counting insurance policies toward campaign goals, Alexander (1990) told the following story:

> I know of a development officer whose campaign was short of the goal. So he purchased a $1-million term life-insurance policy on himself, declared victory in the campaign, and shortly thereafter got another job. Needless to say, he also let the policy lapse. (p. 26)

Alexander pointed out yet another accounting abuse that is commonly used when trying to meet an unrealistically high goal: "recapturing" gifts, or counting funds received years before the campaign began. He said, "One major state university, which set its goal specifically to surpass the goal of a rival university, recaptured five years' worth of gifts in order to count several large gifts toward the new campaign" (p. 27). Going back to the issue of "new money," which was raised earlier in this discussion, Alexander said, "The greatest danger in all of these accounting abuses is that the amount of new money actually raised is only a small fraction of the goal. Yet the publicity generated by the 'success' of the record-breaking campaign tells a very different story" (p. 27). He concluded by saying, "Consequently, these record-breaking campaigns are not always yielding the actual funds necessary to meet the high expectations raised by campaign publicity" (p. 26).

In short, fund raising based on asymmetrical presuppositions may *not* be as successful in raising dollars as generally claimed. In addition, the unrealistic expectations placed on fund raisers by the asymmetrical worldviews held by their senior managers encourages practices that can be viewed as unethical and socially irresponsible. Finally, as discussed in the preceding chapter and below, asymmetrical fund raising can *cost* an organization money.

Asymmetrical fund-raising programs can lead to loss of autonomy, and, therefore, detract from organizational effectiveness. The literature provides sparse, but powerful support for the adoption of Smith's (1981, 1982) concept of gift utility, with warnings to practitioners that asymmetrical fund raising can *cost* an organization money, rather than saving money through the protection and enhancement of autonomy. For example, Lawson (1988) said:

> "Enlightened opportunism" should not become the driving force of any organization. As difficult as it may be for the enthusiastic fund raiser, some gifts should not be accepted. The ramifications of soliciting and accepting a gift that compromises an institution's mission could undermine future support for years to come. (p. 60)

According to Curti and Nash (1965), the "cost" of accepting gifts is not a recently discovered phenomenon. They quoted Dr. Abraham Flexner, a member of Carnegie's General Education Board, college trustee, and philanthropist, who in 1930 criticized colleges and universities for accepting gifts "for costly but dubious innovations that drained funds from more basic needs" (p. 165). Curti and Nash said, "Admitting the delicacy of refusing a gift for some object that might prove a drain, Flexner nevertheless indicted educational leaders for failing to enlighten givers, for accepting gifts they could not in fact afford to take" (p. 165). Providing an argument that is still valid today, Flexner (cited in Curti & Nash, 1965) stated:

> It is a thousand pities that of this vast total so much has been applied to poor and unworthy purposes. . . . No American University president of recent years has

fearlessly hewed to the line, accepting money for general and important purposes—the central disciplines, the accepted and necessary professions—and refusing to accept special gifts which almost invariable make the university poorer and weaker, rather than richer and better. For almost every activity once undertaken grows, and as it grows, needs further support. The asset of today becomes a liability tomorrow. (p. 165)

As pointed out in chapter 2, a gift that becomes a liability is in actuality an infringement on organizational autonomy (i.e., the cost to support one thing, precludes an organization from doing something else). Yet fund raisers, who negotiate these gifts, are often outside the dominant coalition that prioritizes organizational programs and needs.

Illustrating this common isolation, the vice president of administration at the University of Maryland at College Park wrote a memorandum to the vice president of institutional advancement in 1988 questioning the lack of congruency between the fund-raising goals of the university's current capital campaign and the capital plans the public institution had submitted to the state government. He was particularly distressed that a new building for the business school was slated for construction, but no fund-raising opportunities for naming all or part of that building were in the fund-raising plan, whereas $10 million for renovating and expanding the journalism building was listed as a fund-raising goal, but the journalism building had not been designated as a capital improvement priority for the university.

As discussed in chapter 14, Smith (1981, 1982) presented a compelling argument on the need for generating "institutional agendas" to direct fund-raising efforts. According to Smith (1982):

We in the fund-raising business sometimes lose sight of an important fact: Some gifts are more important than others. How do we tell which are the most valuable to our institutions and which are the least? Unless we have [an institutional agenda], our fund-raising programs are going to be more random than rational. (p. 37)

Smith's (1981, 1982) concepts of institutional agendas and gift utility demonstrate that asymmetrical fund raising can cost charitable organizations money. Symmetrical presuppositions, on the other hand, suggest more realistic programs and goals for fund raising than asymmetrical ones.

Symmetrical fund-raising programs often succeed and make the charitable organization more effective by helping it manage interdependencies with donors that provide threats to and opportunities for the organization. In addition, ethical considerations and the issue of social responsibility provide strong philosophical arguments against fund-raising programs grounded in asymmetrical presuppositions.

DETERMINING THE FUND-RAISING MODEL

The importance of presuppositions in the research and practice of fund raising is further increased by explanations of why organizations choose the public relations models they practice. Grunig (in preparation) has suggested a power-control theory to explain why organizations practice different models of public relations. Conclusions arrived at earlier in this book indicate that this power-control theory also explains why charitable organizations practice different models of fund raising, even when the model they use is not the most appropriate one for their environment.

Early theories of interorganizational relationships, such as the theory of contingency (Lawrence & Lorsch, 1967), predicted that environmental forces, such as market demand, would determine the structure and communication behavior of an organization. According to such theories, organizations would adopt an organizational structure and communication system that best helped them manage their environmental relationships, or interdependencies. According to Grunig (in preparation), "Extensive research, however, has failed to show a strong relationship between the nature of an organization's environment and the models of public relations it practices." Although researchers at the University of Maryland tried for nearly 15 years to explain the choice of public relations models by examining the effects of organizational structure and the joint effect of environment and structure, none of the variables were very successful in predicting which model would be used by an organization. Grunig and Grunig (1989) concluded, "We have found consistently that organizations do not practice the kind of public relations that our theories argue, logically, would be best in their environments" (p. 29).

According to Grunig (1989a), organizations use models in two ways: First, they function as situational strategies for use with different publics and problems; and second, the "presuppositions of the models function as part of an organization's ideology" (p. 31). Grunig said that the dominant coalition, or the organization's power elite, identifies strategic publics in the environment as the target for public relations, then turns the problem over to the public relations director and "dictates to the director which model would be an appropriate strategy" (p. 31). Grunig said, "Which model the dominant coalition chooses depends on whether that model fits with organizational culture and whether the public relations director has the expertise to carry out the model" (p. 31).

Elaborating, Grunig (in preparation) advanced a power-control theory that is more powerful than environmental or structural theories in explaining why organizations practice public relations in the way they do. He said, "A power-control theory states that organizations behave in the way they do—in our case they choose the public relations programs they do—because the people who have power in an organization choose that behavior." One of the seven factors influencing the choice of a model by those in power is the schema for the function, which Grunig said "describes the mindset for—the presuppositions about—public relations that are dominant in an organization." Based on Grunig's power-control theory, this chapter concludes that charitable organizations may not choose the most appropriate fund-raising model for their environment because the choice is made by the dominant coalition, which is influenced by its presuppositions about fund raising. Furthermore, few charitable organizations practice the two-way symmetric model because their worldview of fund raising does not include that model.

In other words, the power of presuppositions to influence the model of fund raising practiced by charitable organizations is threefold. As demonstrated earlier in this chapter, presuppositions influence the selection of research problems and the theories that are used to study those problems. As also demonstrated in this chapter, they define the worldviews held by fund-raising practitioners, who express these worldviews through their day-to-day activities. And, finally, presuppositions define the mindset held by members of the dominant coalition, who select the organization's strategic publics and the strategy for communicating with them. As Grunig (1989a) summarized, "Now that ideology and culture have come to the fore as critical predictive variables, the presuppositions of the models take on great importance" (p. 31). He concluded by saying, "To change the way organizations practice public relations, therefore, we must change the dominant presuppositions about public relations" (p. 31).

It can be stated similarly that to change the way charitable organizations practice fund raising, we must change the dominant presuppositions about fund raising. Given that the predominant presuppositions are asymmetrical, which create unrealistic demands, encourage unethical and socially irresponsible behavior, and support fund-raising programs that are pragmatically less effective than symmetrical ones, it would seem imperative for scholars and practitioners to address the conceptual problem of presuppositions about fund raising. Without discussion of presuppositions and recognition of their influence, charitable organizations will continue to blindly follow the field, which may lead to increased regulation and loss of autonomy to government and to donors.

In summary, presuppositions influence the research and practice of fund raising. Asymmetrical presuppositions that make up the prevalent worldviews on fund raising have led to a focus on administrative research that concentrates on problems such as identifying positive attitudes as predictors of giving behavior and measuring fund-raising effectiveness by the total dollars raised. Because there has not been agreement on the important problems of fund raising, there are few theories of fund raising and a research domain has failed to form. The selection of theories to study administrative problems reflect asymmetrical presuppositions in that theories such as persuasion and attitude–behavior change are selected for their ability to deal with fund raising as the manipulation of donors for the benefit of the recipient organization. In addition, some commonly held worldviews hamper the study of fund raising as an object of scientific analysis.

In practice, asymmetrical presuppositions influence the placement of unrealistic demands on the fund-raising function and encourage unethical and socially irresponsible behavior, which, in turn, may lead to increased government regulation. This chapter concludes that many practitioners hold one of the three worldviews of fund raising as serving a pragmatic, conservative, or radical social role, which are asymmetrical worldviews. It further concludes that fund-raising programs based on asymmetrical presuppositions may not be as successful in raising large amounts of dollars as generally thought and that the concept of gift utility demonstrates how such programs can cost charitable organizations money.

Finally, a power-control theory of public relations explains how the asymmetrical presuppositions held by the senior managers of charitable organizations influence the selection of inappropriate models of fund raising. Chapter 15 concludes that symmetrical presuppositions about fund raising are desirable and that charitable organizations should adopt the two-way symmetric model of fund raising to effectively manage external interdependencies with foundation, corporate, and individual donors. It is predicted, however, that the theory of donor relations developed in this book—a theory that advocates the adoption of the two-way symmetric model—will not be well received by scholars, practitioners, and senior managers because of the asymmetrical worldviews of fund raising they hold.

Completing this final step in building a theory of donor relations, the book turns to Part V and the final chapter to draw together the conclusions of the preceding sections, to discuss a major problem with the theory developed, and to explore future research directions.

PART V

A THEORY OF DONOR RELATIONS: CONCLUSIONS AND DIRECTIONS FOR FUTURE RESEARCH

Concluding the book, chapter 16 draws together the major conclusions to capsulize the theory of donor relations developed through the step-by-step process of this critical analysis. A set of propositions is expounded from the theory to guide the behavior of fundraising practitioners and to help them solve the problems they face. The overall approach recommended is that fund raisers take on what Cameron (1984/1986) described as Janusian thinking and what Grunig and Stamm (1979) term *hedging* (i.e., holding two contradictory cognitions at the same time). In other words, fund raising can facilitate accountability while providing outstanding benefits to charitable organizations and—at the same time—fund raising can be a powerful threat to organizational autonomy. According to Janusian thinking, which is named after the Roman god who looks in two directions at the same time, the resolution of the apparent contradiction is what leads to major breakthroughs in insight (Cameron, 1984/1986).

This final chapter also explores future directions for research in response to the question: How can future research shape, revise, and improve a theory of donor relations? Both quantitative and qualitative studies are suggested.

Chapter 16

Conclusions and Directions for Future Research

THE THEORY OF DONOR RELATIONS

In relation to the background of the problem prompting this book, fund raising—as an ongoing set of activities managed by internal specialists—is a new function for charitable organizations in our society. This newness has two important implications. Fund-raising programs today are managed and executed by practitioners who are largely outside the dominant coalition of their organizations with little responsibility for setting policy or managing overall finances. This specialization and separation of the fund-raising function have resulted in a narrow focus whereby fund raising is generally measured by dollars raised rather than by what the function contributes to the overall success of the charitable organization. Second, fund raising—as a specialized organizational function—developed during an era of expansionism in the third sector when few questions were raised about limiting organizational focus. As a result, restricted gifts that were solicited and received for purposes beyond traditional program-ming were rarely viewed as detracting from organizational goals because missions were broadly interpreted and could generally accommodate new programs in response to donor wishes. Today, economic factors have led charitable organizations to the conclusion that they can no longer be all things to all people and that they must focus on selective goals. These organizations, however, have not reached a congruency between their fund-raising behavior and their limited resources to support selective goals. Major gifts, which are primarily restricted in purpose, are being increasingly solicited and received, and a number of these gifts are for purposes that appear questionable in relation to selective goals.

The increasing number of major gifts and the increasing amount of fund-raising activity raises the issue of autonomy and the fact that some gifts, by purpose or conditions of the donor, can infringe on the right of a charitable organization to control its own goals and operations. The solicitation and acceptance of a gift clearly involves two-way considerations. Donors frequently expect and are given the power to determine—in varying degrees—the goals and the means of pursuing the goals of charitable organizations, including colleges and universities. In short, fund raising is a new organizational function that solicits and accepts gifts that may *not* support pre-determined organizational goals and that may, in fact, lead to a loss of organizational autonomy.

In relation to definitions, a lack of clarity, misinterpretations, and generalizations have created confusion in the literature and have distorted our understanding of the fund-raising function. Different types of gifts are not well-defined, although gifts to charitable organizations consist essentially of annual gifts and major gifts, which are unrestricted or restricted in purpose. Some practitioners and scholars use charity and philanthropy interchangeably, but there is little consensus on what actually constitutes a philanthropic or charitable act. Furthermore, the failure to differentiate charitable organizations by legal and political concepts has contributed to the confusion about the fund-raising function and misconceptions about donor motivation. By concisely defining charitable organizations as public good, positive externalities, and eleemosynary, the theory of donor relations clarifies the fact that gifts may be, but most often are not, made for altruistic reasons. Also, this theory holds that charity best describes fund raising for and fund-giving to those organizations that are primarily eleemosynary, and that philanthropy best describes fund raising for and fund-giving to those organizations whose goods and services are defined as positive externalities or public goods (e.g., universities, churches, and public television). Finally, theoretical and operational links between fund raising and public relations have been ignored in previous research because fund-raising scholars and practitioners have utilized definitions of public relations that differ from those definitions currently being advanced by public relations scholars.

Research on charitable organizations has largely been ignored by scholars in academic disciplines until recently. Added to that absence of research, fund raising—an important function within these organizations—has been ignored, or limited, as a research subject historically and within the current and growing body of literature on philanthropy. The relatively few studies on educational fund raising have been primarily administrative in purpose with very few introspective studies or basic studies that lead to theory building. In short, research on fund raising is sparse and generally of poor quality. It receives little scholarly attention as a serious subject of study. There is little evidence that would support fund raising as a separate paradigm, as defined by Kuhn (1962). In addition, an absence of consensus on the important problems in the field is interpreted as evidence that fund raising has failed to become a research domain, as defined by Laudan (1977). Fund raising is an anomaly, yet there is a great need for research on fund raising that can be used by practitioners to solve problems and guide their behavior.

There are a number of flawed assumptions underlying current principles of fund raising. Although scholars and practitioners propagate the view that gifts provide flexible funding, major gifts have historically been restricted as to their purpose and current giving statistics document that approximately 80% of all private dollars to American colleges and universities are restricted. Although charitable organizations, including colleges and universities, expanded their donor base after World War I in response to criticism about dependencies on a small number of donors, the current emphasis on capital campaigns and major gifts has led to increased dependencies on those few donors who are capable of making mega or ultimate gifts. The myth of unrestricted gifts and the myth of a broad base of donors, have hidden the fact that an increased focus on donors of major gifts can affect the autonomy of charitable organizations.

The myth of the volunteer solicitor and its corollary, the myth of the invisible fund raiser, can be attributed primarily to the historical evolution of the fund-raising function and to the self-interests of commercial fund-raising firms that do not solicit money as part of their consulting service. In contrast to current principles that assume volunteers are critical to the solicitation of gifts and that the role of fund-raising practitioners is to manage the process behind the scenes, evidence shows that internal fund raisers do solicit major gifts today. The acceptance of these myths has hidden the fact that lay administrators, rather than chief policymakers, are currently responsible for managing and executing the solicitation and acceptance of gifts that may or may not support organizational goals.

Perspectives of fund raising as a sales or marketing function are inappropriate for an understanding of an organizational behavior dealing with donor motivations that encompass more than the *quid pro quo* of the marketplace. Such perspectives are likely to lead to loss of organizational autonomy by relinquishing control to donors or by bringing about increased government regulation, including changes in the tax deduction of gifts and the tax-exempt status of charitable organizations. Explanations of fund raising as a function that deals primarily with altruistic behavior by donors is also rejected. Donor–recipient relationships include the presence of direct benefits for the donor, although by legal definition, a gift must first be charitable in purpose (i.e., it must contribute to the public good). Approaching private giving as a complicated economic and sociopolitical decision, the theory of donor relations differentiates between relationships with donors of lower level unrestricted gifts and those of major restricted gifts, concluding that the latter inherently involves negotiation because such gifts generally are restricted in purpose.

Systems theory explains the relationship between charitable organizations and donors as environmental interdependencies, contrary to conventional wisdom, which views these relationships as benevolent, business, or pseudo relations. These fund-raising interdependencies constitute an ongoing exchange process that requires management and negotiation by the charitable organization so that it can protect and enhance its autonomy.

The resource dependence perspective incorporated within the theory of donor relations holds that organizations are shaped and constrained by their relationships with external sources of needed resources. Relationships with donors who provide private funding (i.e., foundations, corporations, and individuals) represent external resource dependencies that may infringe on the charitable organization's power to determine and pursue its own goals. Control lost or gained through negotiations with these providers of resources largely is determined by the vulnerability of the recipient organization, which, in turn, is determined by the extent to which an organization has come to depend on certain types of exchanges. Charitable organizations strive to stabilize external dependencies on donors through joint ventures and cooptation, but these strategies require that some degree of organizational control be forfeited.

The norm of reciprocity, which is also incorporated in the theory developed in this book, requires that a charitable organization return some benefits to its donors. Although charitable organizations are dependent, to some degree, on external sources for private funding, these sources are dependent on the recipient organizations for some unspecified benefits that differ from situation to situation and from organization to organization. The noneconomic value of gifts and reciprocal benefits are determined by the perception of the actors involved in the exchange process, and the most common situation is one in which one party gives something more or less than that received. The negotiations involved in such exchanges of gifts are critical to the amount of control a charitable organization abdicates in the process.

As an exchange relationship, fund raising can be viewed as a process in which a charitable organization seeks to exchange the social, economic, and political benefits it possesses for private funds from donors; and the power of each relative to the other affects the outcome. The theory of social and power exchange provides five conditions that lead to an imbalance of power in fund raising. A charitable organization may have:

1. strategic resources to induce a donor,
2. alternative sources for the gift,
3. the power to coerce the donor,
4. the ability to get along without the gift, or
5. no alternative but to comply with the donor's wishes.

This theory also provides a hierarchy of reciprocal benefits that a charitable organization can use in a social exchange involving gifts from donors: gratitude, approval, services, material rewards, and compliance. These concepts are incorporated into the theory of donor relations.

The theory of donor relations holds that charitable organizations sacrifice some of their autonomy by managing interdependence with groups and organizations in their environment; but by doing so, they reduce the risk of losing even more autonomy. Using the recognized four linkages between an organization and its environment, donors are defined as an enabling public that provides necessary resources for charitable organizations. As fund raisers are often the actors in social-exchange relationships with donors, it is necessary that these practitioners learn the vital skills of negotiation.

Emphasizing these points, the major goal of charitable organizations is to maximize autonomy from their environments, which may be limited by interdependent relationships with donors. These organizations face a double-edged sword: In order to enhance their autonomy, they must seek gifts to support their organizational goals, but in so doing, they risk losing autonomy by accepting gifts that may limit their power to determine goals and the means of pursuing them. By managing interdependence with donors through their fund-raising function, charitable organizations sacrifice some of their autonomy, but reduce the risk of losing even more. If interdependencies with donors are not managed or are ignored (i.e., donor relations are not recognized as potential sources of external control) fund raising may lead to a greater loss of organizational autonomy.

The concept of institutional autonomy is defined as *substantive* in nature (i.e., the power of a college or university to determine its own goals and programs) and *procedural* (i.e., the power of an institution to determine the means by which its goals and programs will be pursued). Absolute autonomy is neither possible nor desirable for charitable organizations, including colleges and universities, because all public and private funding involves some loss, and society extends autonomy to these special organizations because it believes that society benefits from such action (i.e., all charitable organizations are accountable to society).   Therefore, discussion of autonomy must focus on the nature and extent of autonomy required for effective operation of the organization and on the charitable organization's fulfillment of its responsibilities to society.

Major gifts from foundations, corporations, and individuals have in the past and can in the future limit the autonomy of charitable organizations. Rather than being dissimilar, the three sources of private support have much in common. Although there are many such organizations, relatively few foundations and corporations make most of the gifts to charitable organizations. In relation to colleges or universities, relatively few foundations, corporations, and individuals provide most gift dollars. The majority of gift dollars to higher education from all three sources of private support is directed to a very small percentage of institutions (i.e., major research and doctoral universities). The motivations of corporate, foundation, and individual donors can best be understood as neither benevolent nor villainous, but rather within the context of environmental interdependencies.   Whereas foundations and corporations are dependent on colleges and universities largely for employees and research, individuals seek reciprocal benefits that range from gratitude to compliance and that vary from situation to situation.

Contrary to conventional wisdom, the hundreds or thousands of individuals who contribute to any one charitable organization are not equal in their ability to influence the organization; rather those individuals who can provide mega or ultimate gifts are extremely powerful in their exchange relationships with recipient organizations. Higher education traditionally attracts gifts from the small percentage of American individuals who control a great deal of the wealth (i.e., poor people rarely give to colleges and universities). Failure to differentiate charities with positive externalities, such as colleges and universities, from eleemosynary charities, such as CARE, has led to flawed assumptions in previous studies about individual giving to higher education. The increasing number and size of capital campaigns by colleges and universities have made these institutions more dependent on a small pool of individuals who can provide the lead gifts necessary to ensure the success of a campaign, regardless of the actions of thousands of lower level donors who provide the bulk of the *number* of gifts.

Unlike foundations, corporations make gifts generally, not because they are required to by law, but because doing so supports their proclaimed "enlightened self-interest," and their role as socially responsible corporations. That is to say, corporations make gifts both to acquire needed resources, such as technical knowledge and skilled labor, and to increase their autonomy by improving their public standing and the business climate in which they operate. Like foundations, corporations generally prefer to support projects and specific programs (i.e., their gifts are usually restricted in purpose). Major gifts from foundations, corporations, and individuals can, individually, affect the substantive and procedural autonomy of charitable organizations. Major and lower level gifts from corporations, foundations, and individuals also can infringe on organizational autonomy collectively (i.e., a perception of what will appeal generally to donors can cause a charitable organization to change its behavior in a way that is incongruent with self-determined goals and objectives).

Three major assumptions of the theory of donor relations are:

1. *All* sources of donors—foundations, corporations, and individuals—have potential for infringing on the autonomy of charitable organizations through their gifts;

2. *All* types of charitable organizations—even those eleemosynary charities most closely related to altruistic gifts—are vulnerable to losing autonomy during the process of raising private gifts;

3. *All* gifts (i.e., major gifts, individually and collectively, and lower level gifts, collectively) have potential to affect organizational autonomy negatively.

Four-year public and 2- and 4-year nonselective, private colleges may be the most vulnerable to compliance in the solicitation and acceptance of gifts. Resource dependencies with donors exist to varying degrees at all colleges and universities, but strategies to avoid external control are not equally available to these institutions; rather, some institutions, such as 4-year public and nonselective private colleges are probably more vulnerable than large and wealthy public and private research and doctoral universities.

Like public relations, fund raising is a boundary role, responsible for helping charitable organizations manage their interdependencies with donor publics. As such, fund-raising practitioners are responsible for the continuing interaction and negotiation with donors that determine the degree of autonomy lost or gained through the solicitation and acceptance of gifts.

Given the fact that fund raisers are lay administrators who are highly paid, in great demand, change jobs frequently, are generally young, and are often inexperienced, there is some doubt about their ability to protect the central mission of a charitable organization through the fund-raising process. In short, fund raising as currently practiced can increase the vulnerability of a charitable organization to external control.

In addition, fund raising contributes to the vulnerability of charitable organizations because it causes such organizations to de-emphasize or ignore strategic publics other than donors that may threaten or enhance the organization's autonomy. Grunig's (e.g, in preparation; Grunig & Grunig, 1989; Grunig & Hunt, 1984) theory holds that public relations contributes to organizational effectiveness by identifying strategic publics in the organization's environment that affect or are affected by the behavior of the organization as it relates to strategic issues. Grunig (in preparation) said that excellent public relations departments (i.e., those that will help organizations achieve their goals) are structured horizontally so that an organization can reallocate staff and resources as strategic publics change. Fund raising, with its one-dimensional focus on donor publics, supports managers in subjectively choosing an environment that may exclude strategic publics that have the power to infringe on organizational autonomy. Those charitable organizations that have subsumed public relations under fund raising, or have created separate departments for the two functions, have added further to their vulnerability by emphasizing donor publics over other strategic publics, even in situations in which such an emphasis is inappropriate and dangerous.

On a macro- and mesolevel, therefore, fund raising should be approached as a part of the public relations function of charitable organizations because such a perspective helps to protect and enhance the autonomy of these organizations. The primary purpose of fund raising is not to raise money, but—as a part of public relations—to enhance and protect organizational autonomy by effectively managing communications between a charitable organization and the donor publics in its environment.

On the microlevel, the generally accepted process of fund raising consists of four steps: research, cultivation, solicitation, and recognition—which the theory of donor relations holds as a process similar to that used in public relations. Fund raising is a public relations specialization that requires—at some point—a communication objective of affecting behavior in the short term, but it also can maximize long-term behavioral changes by selecting short-term cognitive effects for the majority of its programs. Current fund-raising practices and axioms support the proposition of this theory that fund raising is basically a communication function.

Finally, the techniques used by fund raising provide little, if any, differentiation between the fund-raising and public relations functions, and the selection of techniques is based on the same communication objectives for fund raising, as it is for public relations (e.g., whereas annual giving is primarily built on mass communication techniques, solicitation of major gifts requires the same interpersonal communication that the public relations manager is advised to use in legislative relations or in dealing with activist publics).

A few corporate public relations practitioners are providing evidence that the giving of money, appropriately managed by the public relations function, can significantly contribute to corporate goals of social responsibility, as well as to more pragmatic goals related to economic and sociopolitical benefits. In addition, these practitioners demonstrate that public relations can utilize donor relationships to help corporations enhance and protect autonomy. Fund raising—the other side of the philanthropic coin—also should be incorporated into the pubic relations function in order to maximize its contribution to organizational effectiveness. Donor relationships, managed by public relations practitioners, can enhance the autonomy of charitable organizations by raising gifts in support of overall goals and protect autonomy from donors who seek to control such organizations.

Historically, four models of fund raising have been identified: press agentry, public information, two-way asymmetric, and two-way symmetric. All four of the historical models of fund raising are still in practice today, and it is hypothesized that 50% of all charitable organizations predominantly practice the press agentry model, 15% practice the public information model, 30% practice the two-way asymmetric model, and only 5% practice the newest model, the two-way symmetric. The last model, which is more socially responsible and pragmatically more effective than the three older models, will remain under-utilized and largely unknown until fund raising finds an academic home in public relations departments with full-time scholar-teachers.

The purpose of the press agentry model is to propagandize a cause. The nature of communication for this model is one-way, with truth not being an essential factor, and communication being dependent on emotions. Little research is conducted by its practitioners, and fund-raising results are evaluated by dollar totals and the number of donors. The leading historical figures associated with this model are Charles Sumner Ward, Lyman Pierce, and their YMCA associates. It is hypothesized that the press agentry model is practiced at national health and social service agencies, as well as at most religious organizations.

The purpose of the public information model of fund raising is to disseminate information on needs of a charitable organization. Whereas the press agentry model depends on emotions, the public information model relies on "enlighten-ment" (i.e., the model requires a rational, intelligent, and compassionate donor public). The nature of communication is one-way and in contrast to the press agentry model, truth is important although information is incomplete. Little research is conducted by practitioners using this model aside from research on prospective donors and on mailing lists. The leading historical figures associated with this model are Bishop William Lawrence and Ivy Lee. It is hypothesized that the public information model is practiced at cultural organizations, public colleges, and conservation/wildlife organizations.

The purpose of the two-way asymmetric model of fund raising is to scientifically persuade donors to give, and the nature of communication is two-way, with unbalanced, or asymmetrical, effects. The two-way asymmetric model depends on strategic positioning with publics and uses formative research to shape communications. The success of this model is evaluated by the number of private dollars raised, often in relation to the cost of fund raising. The leading historical figure associated with this model is John Price Jones. It is hypothesized that this model is predominately practiced by private colleges, private and public universities, hospitals and medical centers, and by most fund-raising consultants.

The purpose of the two-way symmetric model of fund raising is to reach mutual understanding. The nature of its communication is two-way between groups with balanced, or symmetrical, effects. Unlike the press agentry model of fund raising, which is dependent on the emotions of its publics, or the public information model, which is dependent on their enlightenment, the two-way symmetric model is dependent on congruency with its donor publics. This most recent model uses formative research to balance the needs of the charitable organization and its donor publics (i.e., research is used to identify opportunities for private funding and to identify issues that the charitable organization is not addressing through donor relationships). The effectiveness of this model is evaluated by its contribution to enhancing and protecting organizational autonomy through the fund-raising process. No leading historical figure is identified with the two-way symmetric model, although a few educators and senior practitioners currently are defining how such a model should be practiced. It is hypothesized that only 5% of all charitable organizations practice the two-way symmetric model of fund raising, primarily a few universities and some fund-raising consultants.

Regardless of the fund-raising model practiced by charitable organizations, such organizations generally assume a press agentry model of fund raising when they enter a capital-campaign mode—one that is based on emotion with the purpose of propagandizing the cause.

Current principles of the effectiveness of fund raising concentrate on measuring the total dollars raised, often in comparison to fund-raising potential and/or cost. Such a concentration on indiscriminant dollars ignores the concept of gift utility and the fact that gifts can enhance organizational autonomy by supporting self-determined goals or limit autonomy by displacing goals and/or the means to achieving those goals. Fund-raising practitioners contribute to organizational effectiveness when they solicit and accept gifts in support of organizational goals and when they refuse to accept gifts that would limit autonomy. In addition, fund raising is effective when it helps a charitable organization manage environmental interdependencies with donor publics that may threaten the organization's autonomy. By helping charitable organizations recognize such threats and respond to potential conflicts, fund raising supports a charitable organization's need to maintain equilibrium with its environment.

Current measures of effectiveness prohibit fund raisers from contributing to organizational effectiveness, as just described, because their performance is measured not by what they contribute to organizational goals—including autonomy—but only by increased dollar amounts. In effect, charitable organizations are evaluating fund raising by internal measurements of efficiency rather than by external measurements of effectiveness. Such short-sightedness on the part of charitable organizations may lead to increased threats on their autonomy by members of their multiple constituencies.

The theory of donor relations advocates a normative, three-step process for measuring the effectiveness of fund raising. It recommends that fund-raising effectiveness be evaluated by: (a) measuring the impact of giving on the charitable organization (i.e., to what degree did gifts enhance or limit organizational autonomy?); (b) measuring the impact of giving on donors (i.e., to what degree did gifts satisfy the objectives of donors?); and (c) measuring the impact of giving on other strategic publics of the organization (i.e., to what degree did gifts help the charitable organization fulfill the expectations of key publics other than donors?). Moving down one level of abstraction, the theory recommends that charitable organizations measure the effectiveness of fund raising by assigning values to specific gifts in relation to their utility for the organization, by adopting a 3-year time period on which to measure effects, and by utilizing process evaluation to provide a continual measurement of the effectiveness of specific programs and the performance of fund-raising practitioners.

Presuppositions influence the research and practice of fund raising. Asymmetrical presuppositions that make up the prevalent worldviews on fund raising have led to a focus on administrative research that concentrates on problems such as identifying positive attitudes as predictors of giving behavior and measuring fund-raising effectiveness by the total dollars raised. The selection of theories to study administrative problems reflects asymmetrical presuppositions in that theories such as persuasion and attitude–behavior change are selected for their ability to deal with fund raising as the manipulation of donors for the benefit of the recipient organization. Other worldviews that are commonly held reject the study of fund raising because it is not an object that can be scientifically analyzed (e.g., the giving and getting of gifts is controlled by metaphysical forces).

In practice, asymmetrical presuppositions result in unrealistic demands on the fund-raising function and encourage unethical and socially irresponsible behavior, which, in turn, may lead to increased government regulation. Many practitioners hold one of the three worldviews of fund raising as serving a pragmatic, conservative, or radical social role, which are asymmetrical worldviews. But fund-raising programs based on asymmetrical presuppositions may not be as successful in raising large numbers of dollars as generally thought, and the concept of gift utility demonstrates how such programs can actually cost charitable organizations money. A power-control theory of public relations explains how the asymmetrical presuppositions held by the senior managers of charitable organizations influence the selection of inappropriate models of fund raising.

Symmetrical presuppositions about fund raising are desirable, and charitable organizations should adopt the two-way symmetric model of fund raising to effectively manage external interdependencies with foundation, corporate, and individual donors. It is predicted, however, that the theory of donor relations developed in this book—a theory that advocates the adoption of the two-way symmetric model—will not be well received by scholars, practitioners, and senior managers because of the asymmetrical worldviews of fund raising they hold.

The theory of donor relations, which reorients fund raising within the paradigm of public relations, provides a fuller understanding of the fund-raising function—one that promises to help fund-raising practitioners and their charitable organizations carry out this important function more effectively and solve the problems presented at the beginning of this book. The following are propositions that are drawn from the theory.

The theory of donor relations encourages practitioners to:

- recognize the tensions inherent in the interdependencies of an organization with its donor publics;
- consider potential loss of autonomy as a primary factor in negotiating the purposes and conditions of major gifts and in planning annual giving programs for lower level gifts;
- calculate and communicate the gift-utility *cost* involved in accepting every gift;

- implement and evaluate everyday decisions with a keen awareness of their role in and influence on organizational autonomy;
- prioritize fund-raising programs and activities by institutional agendas;
- decline gifts that are inappropriate to the organization's goals or that will limit the organization's means to pursue its internally determined goals (i.e., gifts that "cost" too much to accept);
- evaluate the results of fund-raising programs, not by dollar totals or by interorganizational comparison, but by how much the programs contributed to organizational effectiveness; and
- research, plan, execute, and evaluate fund-rasing activities with the understanding that donors are not an organization's only public (i.e., in dynamic environments, organizational problems change and strategic publics may also change so that donors may at times be less important than other publics of the organization; for example, legislators, faculty, or students).

In conclusion, the theory of donor relations helps charitable organizations and their fund-raising practitioners recognize the trade-offs inevitably associated with private sources of financial support. In most cases, efforts by donors to externally control charitable organizations will not be covert or even intentional, but may still lead organizations to change in unanticipated ways. Recognition of this basic proposition can be considered essential to the future well-being and survival of charitable organizations. Addressing the difficulty produced by external sources of financing, Powell and Friedkin (1987) said, "The forces of change often work quietly, and frequently it is not until too late that the organization recognizes that its legitimacy has been eroded and its purpose neglected" (p. 191).

DIRECTIONS FOR FUTURE RESEARCH

This section outlines suggestions for future research. It must first be repeated from earlier chapters, however, that a major problem of the theory of donor relations developed in this book is its low probability of acceptance by scholars and practitioners. It was noted in the chapter on presuppositions that the asymmetrical worldviews on fund raising held by practitioners, scholars, and members of the dominant coalition of charitable organizations will not support their acceptance of a theory that advocates symmetrical concepts. Illustrating the predominant asymmetrical worldview, Panas (1984) quoted a college president who describes fund raising as "the art of plucking the goose to obtain the largest amount of feathers, with the least possible amount of hissing," (p. 84). In counter-argument to the anticipated resistance, this book defends the necessity of a symmetrical approach to fund raising. Following Grunig's (1989a) conclusion about asymmetrical public relations, it is asserted that the asymmetrical models of fund raising largely have been unsuccessful in managing interdependencies with donors, whereas the two-way symmetric model, which has been under-utilized, promises greater effectiveness, as well as a higher degree of ethics and social responsibility.

As documented throughout this book, the necessity for a new approach to fund raising—one that is based on symmetrical presuppositions—is apparent from the perspective of ethics and social responsibility. According to a recent article ("Charities advised," 1989), Independent Sector, which represents 650 foundations and nonprofit organizations, created a committee to devise a code of ethics to guide nonprofit organizations "because of growing governmental and public concern about dishonest fund-raising practices by some non-profit groups" (p. 18).

This same article stated, "Public confidence in charities appears to be dwindling, and charity officials seem to be greatly worried about it" (p. 18). Reporting on the October 1989 annual meeting of the Independent Sector, the article stated that when asked how many thought the public perception of charities was worse today than 5 years ago, all but 12 of the 450 nonprofit and foundation managers attending a session on ethics raised their hands. When asked what they thought most threatened the nonprofit sector, the same audience shouted out words such as "arrogance," "profiteering," "lack of accountability," "irrelevance," and "public cynicism," ("Charities advised," 1989, p. 18).

Addressing the need to curb abuses of fund-raising techniques, an attorney general of Connecticut is quoted as saying, "Some charities think they have an absolute right to survive, not just an opportunity, and they think they can do whatever they have to to survive" ("Charities advised," 1989, p. 18). She continued, "If there isn't already a serious erosion in public confidence in fund raising, the time is ripe for that erosion to occur" (p. 18). In his opinion piece criticizing fund raising, which was cited earlier in chapter 15, Bourque (1989) stated:

> In my view, many of you have sold your souls to computerized mass marketing. You may have to endure the damnation of an oversaturated and increasingly cynical market. . . . I trust in your good intentions, but your methods make me feel like a mark to be processed by slick professionals who have learned to milk the public cow. If I'm in any way representative, my deteriorating attitude bodes ill for your future. (p. 10)

On the national level, a 1990 survey by the Roper Organization found that Americans feel they are being bombarded by charitable appeals and that they are more skeptical about the worthiness of charitable organizations ("Baby boomers, 1990). Based on a sample of approximately 2,000 men and women 18 years and older, the poll reported that nearly "90% of Americans said they were being overwhelmed by requests for donations" (p. 13). In addition, 70% of those polled said they were finding it more difficult to determine whether charities were legitimate.

Drawing from discussions in previous chapters, a brief overview of current trends in regulations supports this book's contention that asymmetrical models of fund raising have eroded public confidence and that charitable organizations stand to lose high degrees of autonomy to government if current practices continue. In 1986, the members of the National Association of Attorneys General approved a model law to regulate the activities of fund raisers ("Attorneys general," 1986). The proposed law would require all charitable organizations, including colleges and universities, to register, pay fees, file annual financial reports in each state where they solicit gifts, and to disclose what percentage of contributions would go to cover fund-raising costs to all prospective donors.

In 1989, the lead paragraph of an article on charity fraud ("States modify laws," 1989) stated, "In what one state charity regulator termed an 'unheard of' flurry of activity, lawmakers in a least nine states have passed legislation this year aimed at cracking down on misleading solicitations for charity" (p. 1). One of those states was Oregon where charitable organizations that were formerly exempt from registration requirements, such as hospitals, educational institutions, university foundations, and nursing homes, were required to file information under that state's new law.

As it turned out, actually 13 states enacted major new legislation governing fund raising in 1989, and approximately 15 states currently have pending legislation that would affect fund-raising practice ("Proposed legislation," 1990). More than 20 states have proposed or passed laws instituting taxes for charitable organizations that have traditionally enjoyed tax-exempt status from real estate, sales, and state and local taxes (Lyddon, 1990). Hardest hit so far have been YMCAs and nonprofit hospitals, both of which have been criticized for neglect of their charitable mission ("Responding to criticism," 1989).

The IRS recently stepped up its surveillance of benefits related to gifts, warning charitable organizations and their fund raisers that they have a responsibility for informing donors of the portion of gifts that can be deducted from federal income tax (AAFRC, 1988b). In the summer of 1989, high-ranking officials of the U.S. Postal Service and the Federal Trade Commission

(FTC) suggested that Congress expand the authority of the FTC to all nonprofits, including charitable organizations ("Colleges are nervous," 1989). The proposed legislation was prompted by a Congressional hearing in July 1989 on deceptive fund-raising practices (AAFRC, 1989b). Significantly, the hearing occurred as the Justice Department was investigating whether some colleges were violating federal antitrust laws in the way they set tuition and award financial aid, and as the U.S. Post Office was preparing to levy fines and penalties against numerous charitable organizations for using nonprofit postal rates to mail material on profit-making activities, such as selling insurance policies to alumni ("Colleges are nervous," 1989).

The commercialization of fund raising through cause-related marketing has prompted growing attention, such as the reforms proposed in 1990 for the Illinois charitable-solicitation law that would set strict new conditions on "commercial co-ventures"—marketing campaigns by for-profit businesses that are tied to charitable solicitations" ("State charity," 1990, p. 23).

Most significant, federal legislators enacted a "floor" on charitable deductions in 1990 as a means of easing the federal deficit ("3 percent floor," 1990). It is recalled from chapter 2 that the government loses about $13 billion a year in revenues because of deductions taken for charitable gifts.

According to Gurin and Van Til (1989), "The basic philosophical rationale of the deduction is that giving should not be taxed because, unlike other uses of income, it does not enrich the disburser" (p. 6). Although these fund-raising experts claimed that broad public support exists for the charitable tax deduction, they said, "Nonetheless, it should be noted that the deduction acts as a government subsidy" and that "some groups advocate the repeal of the charitable deduction" (p. 7).

Finally, many fear that the current emphasis by fund raisers on the tax-shelter aspects of planned gifts will raise the ire of legislators and bring about detrimental changes in the federal tax laws (Sharpe, 1989). Denouncing the promotion of gifts primarily as tax shelters, the group of planned-giving officers mentioned in chapter 5 ("Fund raisers assail," 1989) stated, "Unless these issues are addressed by the charitable community in a prompt and constructive fashion, the misguided efforts of those for-profit promoters who seek to subvert the charitable tax deduction as a tax shelter could cause a Congressional and public-opinion backlash that will seriously undermine the future of philanthropy" (pp. 1, 12).

From this and from earlier discussions of eroding public confidence and increased government intervention, it is clear that all charitable organizations are facing a crisis regarding their fund-raising behavior.

This crisis overrides predicted objections to the theory of donor relations developed in this book. In other words, this book presents a departure from conventional wisdom and a dilemma for fund-raising scholars and practitioners who hold asymmetrical worldviews; be that as it may, current conditions demand that underlying assumptions be re-examined and that a new approach to fund raising—one based on symmetrical presuppositions—be considered as a viable alternative. As quoted earlier in chapter 15, Grunig (1989a) said that we cannot change the practice until we change the presuppositions about the function. It is hoped that rather than being a weakness, the departure of this book from current approaches will be the beginning step in that direction.

In relation to future research directions, this section suggests that the theory of donor relations developed in this book offers a fruitful and largely untilled field of study. For example, both quantitative and qualitative methods should be utilized to study the degree of organizational autonomy lost or gained through the fund raising process. A quantitative study measuring the loss or enhancement of autonomy would provide statistical evidence in support or disproof of the central concept of this theory. In anticipation of such a future study, some sample indicators have been developed to measure the effect of fund raising on the institutional autonomy of American colleges and universities and are presented here.

#1   To what degree would you say your fund-raising appeals are related to the published mission statement of your institution?

☐ Appeals are strongly related to mission statement.

☐ Appeals are moderately related to mission statement.

☐ Appeals are weakly related to mission statement.

☐ Appeals are generally not related to mission statement.

#2   To what extent can you reiterate the programs offered by your institution and the total resources it requires to carry out its mission?

☐ I can generally summarize all programs and required resources.

☐ I can generally summarize most.

☐ I can generally summarize some.

☐ I generally can summarize a few.

☐ I generally cannot summarize the programs and resources.

#3 Hypothetically speaking, do you think your institution would agree to alter its stated mission in order to attract a particular major gift?

[ ] Never under any circumstances.

[ ] Possibly under certain circumstances.

[ ] Probably if it were the right circumstances.

[ ] Highly likely if the circumstances were right.

#4 In your opinion, has any organization that you have represented as a fund raiser altered its stated mission in order to attract a particular gift?

[ ] No

[ ] Yes

If you answered "no," please skip to question #6; if you answered "yes," please continue with #5.

#5 Which of the following situations best describe the relationship between a particular major gift and the change in institutional mission that you referred to in #1? (In the case of multiple gifts, indicate the appropriate answer for gift #1, gift #2, etc.)

[ ] Donor funded some or all costs of mission change that had previously been evaluated as desirable by organizational management.

[ ] Donor's gift helped determine which of two equally desirable directions would be followed by the organization.

[ ] Donor's gift stimulated discussion on several mission options, but final decision was an internal one, not related to gift.

[ ] Donor's gift was directly responsible for modifying or changing some aspect of the organization's mission.

[ ] None of the above.

#6 Does your institution have policies to control the acquisition of charitable gifts; for example, what can and can not be accepted, or what potential costs of administrating the gift's purpose must be covered by the gift?

☐ My institution has a comprehensive written policy that is reviewed periodically and strictly enforced.

☐ My institution has a brief written policy statement that is supplemented by a strong oral tradition of fund-raising standards.

☐ My institution does not have a policy, but fund raisers are expected to abide by a professional code of ethics.

☐ My institution does not have a policy because each fund raiser is responsible for judging gifts on a case-by-case basis.

#7 Does your institution have policies to control the recognition of charitable gifts; for example, what is the minimum gift necessary to name a faculty professorship, or when is it appropriate to distribute free football tickets to donors?

☐ My institution has a comprehensive written policy that is reviewed periodically and strictly enforced.

☐ My institution has a brief written policy statement that is supplemented by a strong oral tradition of fund-raising standards.

☐ My institution does not have a policy, but fund raisers are expected to abide by a professional code of ethics.

☐ My institution does not have a policy because each fund raiser is responsible for judging gifts on a case-by-case basis.

#8 Which of the following "forms of recognition" do you as a fund raiser view appropriate for different levels of giving? (Check as many as you believe appropriate.)

Forms of Recognition	_$10,000_	_$100,000_	_$1 million_
Board of Advisors/Visitors Membership			
Salaried Position with Institution			
Athletic Event Tickets			
Plaques/Awards			
Participation in Personnel/ Program Decisions			
Recognition Dinners			
Named Scholarships/Faculty Positions			
Named Buildings			

Forms of Recognition	*$10,000*	*$100,000*	*$1 million*
Increased Information Sharing			
Special Library/Facility Privileges			
Gift Society Club Membership			
Trusted Counselor Role			
Personal Attention for Students of Friends/Relatives			
Special Privileges for Friends/Relatives			
VIP Treatment at Institutional Events			
Special Consideration as Vendors of Products and Services			
Special Consideration for Recruiting Employees			
Weighted Opinions on Operational Decisions			

#9 Of the total private dollars raised by your institution last year, approximately what percentage were given as unrestricted and/or undesignated for purpose or program?

☐ 100% of total private dollars raised last year.

☐ 75% of total private dollars

☐ 50% of total private dollars

☐ 25% of total private dollars

☐ 10% of total private dollars

☐ 9% or less or total private dollars raised last year.

#10 In comparison, what percentage of the **number** of total gifts raised by your institution last year were unrestricted and/or undesignated gifts?

☐ 100% of total number of gifts raised last year.

☐ 75% of total number of gifts

☐ 50% of total number of gifts

☐ 25% of total number of gifts

☐ 10% of total number of gifts

☐ 9% or less or total number of gifts raised last year.

In addition to this type of quantitative study, case studies of representative institutions of the different Carnegie Committee categories, which recently have received a mega or ultimate gift, would provide valuable data on negotiating autonomy at different types of institutions from the perspectives of the key administrators, including the fund raisers, the major donors, and members of other strategic publics of the institutions. In his agenda for research on fund raising, Carbone (1986) called for research on case studies that would examine the effect of major gifts on the priorities and operations of colleges and universities.

Now that a theory of fund raising has been developed around the concept of organizational autonomy, such case studies would be more meaningful in understanding the effect of such gifts. For example, in M. Hall's (1989) study of centralized and decentralized fund-raising structures at American doctorate-granting and research universities, 47% of the fund raisers reported that a major gift had, in the past, caused a significant shift in the academic priorities of an academic unit at their institution. Of these respondents, 94% said that the shift in priorities caused by a major gift was readily accepted by the academic unit, while slightly more (95%) said that it was readily accepted by the central administration of the university. Such responses previously would have contributed little to our understanding of fund raising. In view of this book, such responses would signal a need for much deeper probing of the autonomy lost or gained in the situations referred to by Hall's respondents.

Quantitative and qualitative studies to measure fund-raising behavior at all types of charitable organizations would be a logical step in testing the theory's power to generalize beyond higher education. In addition, studies should be designed to test the existence of the four models of fund raising presented in this book. Indicators developed by Grunig (e.g., 1976, in preparation) could be modified for such studies, and multivariate statistical techniques could be utilized to identify the four models. It is also suggested that an introspective study on the organizational relationship between the fund-raising and public relations functions be undertaken as a follow-up to the study cited earlier in chapters 10 and 11 that focused solely on members of the Public Relations Society of America (PRSA) who worked for educational and cultural organizations (Kelly, 1989b). Such a study may provide evidence of encroachment of public relations by fund raising practitioners and the impact of structural variables on the effectiveness of the organization.

Regarding fund-raising effectiveness, it is suggested that studies be undertaken to examine the concept of gift utility and its relationship to organizational effectiveness. Case studies would be particularly valuable in the early stages of documenting how excellent fund-raising departments add to organizational effectiveness as defined by the theory of donor relations.

In relation to current research, this book supports introspective studies on fund raising, such as the work being done by Carbone (1987) on the professionalism of fund raising. Rather than supporting fund raising as a profession, however, it is hypothesized that such studies will provide evidence that fund raising is a vocation which, in isolation from public relations, presents a danger to charitable organizations. In support of such future studies, Carbone found that only 45% of fund raisers at educational institutions rated "the adoption of a code of ethics and the imposition of sanctions against those who violate it," (p. 14) as very important. Gary Quehl, who recently left his position as president of the Council for Advancement and Support of Education, said that most fund raisers are perceived as "technicians who know how to bring home the bacon," (Ernest, 1989, p. 1). In his foreword to Carbone's (1986) monograph on an agenda for fund-raising research, Payton said that it is only out of courtesy that he assumes most senior fund raisers are not technicians. He stated, "Technicians are also indifferent to purpose, but focus instead on process and technique. They tend to know everything about a subject except what it is for," (p. 8).

Broom and Dozier's (1986) theory on public relations roles and their differentiation between managers and technicians could be used in future introspective studies of fund raising to document how much fund-raising practitioners contribute to organizational effectiveness, which may prove to be relatively little. In other words, although Gilley, Fulmer and Reithlingshoefer (1986) described the development officer as one of three new "power brokers" (p. 81) who are emerging on American campuses, Broom and Dozier's theory may prove that most fund raisers are technicians who have little representation in the dominant coalition of charitable organizations, including colleges and universities.

Finally, this book argues that much more research in public relations needs to encompass the fund-raising function. For example, the theory of donor relations suggests that the ability of the public relations function to contribute to the effectiveness of charitable organizations is greatly influenced by the fund-raising function. In view of its findings, therefore, this book has extended the theory of excellence currently being tested in the field by the IABC team of public relations researchers headed by Grunig (in preparation). Excellent public relations departments in charitable organizations, it is hypothesized, will have incorporated the fund-raising function within that department in order to effectively manage communication with all of the organizations' strategic publics, including donors.

With the shift in the public relations paradigm provided by this book, future studies of public relations must recognize fund raising both as a factor in public relations effectiveness and as a specialization of public relations. As pointed out in chapter 4, the PRSA Body of Knowledge Task Force (1988) has opened the research door to studying fund raising as a function of public relations, categorizing it with more traditional specializations, such as community relations and investor relations. Scholars conducting basic and applied research in public relations need to turn their attention to this new specialization.

In conclusion, the theory of donor relations promises to expand and enhance the field of public relations, to provoke controversy in the field of fund raising, and to provide scholars with multiple opportunities for future research. More importantly, the theory offers answers to the important problems described in the beginning chapters of this book and provides practitioners and charitable organizations with new concepts to guide their fund-raising behavior and help them be more effective in an ethically and socially responsible manner.

References

AAUP president goes head to head with a critic of the professorate. (1989, April 19). *The Chronicle of Higher Education*, pp. A17, A19.

Administrators' pay up 5.3 pct. in year, outpacing inflation. (1989, February 15). *The Chronicle of Higher Education*, pp. 1, A15.

After Rockefeller Center, Westmar College. (1990, February 26). *Newsweek*, p. 71.

Alabama Ethics Commission faults Auburn fund raiser. (1989, April 12). *The Chronicle of Higher Education*, p. A31.

Albert, D. (1985/1986). The organizational context of the American research university. In M. W. Peterson (Ed.), *ASHE reader on organization and governance in higher education* (3rd ed., pp. 79-110). Lexington, MA: Ginn Press.

Alexander, A. S. (1988, March). Understanding the philanthropic partnership: Why corporations give. CASE *Currents*, pp. 12-14, 16.

Alexander, G. D. (1990, January 23). Unrealistic goals for major capital campaigns are leading to dangerous accounting abuses. *The Chronicle of Philanthropy*, pp. 26-27.

Almanac. (1990, September 5). *The Chronicle of Higher Education.*

Altbach, P. G., & Berdahl, R. O. (Eds.). (1981). *Higher education in American society*. Buffalo, NY: Prometheus Books.

American Association of Fund-Raising Council (AAFRC) Trust for Philanthropy. (1987). *Giving USA: Estimates of philanthropic giving in 1986 and the trends they show*. New York: Author.

American Association of Fund-Raising Council (AAFRC) Trust for Philanthropy. (1988a, May/June). Philanthropy's "resiliency" hailed by AAFRC leaders. *Giving USA Update*, pp. 6-7.

American Association of Fund-Raising Council (AAFRC) Trust for Philanthropy. (1988b, November/December). IRS reviews premiums and awards for tax-deductibility status. *Giving USA Update*, p. 3.

American Association of Fund-Raising Council (AAFRC) Trust for Philanthropy. (1989a, January/February). Glossary and notes. *Giving USA Update*, p. 10.

American Association of Fund-Raising Council (AAFRC) Trust for Philanthropy. (1989b, May/June–July/August). Ethical versus fraudulent fund raising: A synopsis by the AAFRC. *Giving USA Update*, pp. 1, 11.

American Association of Fund-Raising Council (AAFRC) Trust for Philanthropy. (1989c). *Giving USA: The annual report on philanthropy for the year 1988*. New York: Author.

An ambitious Texas philanthropist aims at creating a $5-billion foundation. (1989, February 7). *The Chronicle of Philanthropy*, p. 6.

An appeal to donors' desire to be important. (1989, July 11). *The Chronicle of Philanthropy*, pp. 13-15.

Andrews, F. E. (1953). *Attitudes toward giving*. New York: Russell Sage Foundation.

Annual survey: State laws regulating charitable solicitations. (1989, January/February). *Giving USA Update*, pp. 3-10.

Arnove, R. F. (1980). Introduction. In R. F. Arnove (Ed.), *Philanthropy and cultural imperialism: The foundations at home and abroad* (pp. 1-23). Boston, MA: G. K. Hall.

At $79,300 average salary of top fund raisers at private colleges in East found to be highest. (1986, November 26). *The Chronicle of Higher Education*, pp. 23, 25.

Attorneys general propose a "model" law to regulate the activities of fund raisers. (1986, December 17). *The Chronicle of Higher Education*, pp. 25, 28.

Baby boomers give generously to charities, survey finds, but their willingness to do volunteer work is questioned. (1990, July 24). *The Chronicle of Philanthropy*, pp. 1, 13.

Baldridge, J. V., Curtis, D. V., Ecker, G. P., & Riley, G. L. (1986). Alternative models of governance in higher education. In M. W. Peterson (Ed.), *ASHE reader on organization and governance in higher education* (3rd ed., pp. 11-27). Lexington, MA: Ginn Press. (Original work published 1977)

Barnes & Roche Newsletter. (1989, June). pp. 1-4.

Barton Gillet Letter. (1989, September-October).

Baskin, O. W., & Aronoff, C. G. (1988). *Public relations: The profession and the practice* (2nd ed.). Dubuque, IA: Wm. C. Brown.

Baumol, W. J. (1975). Business responsibility and economic behavior. In E. S. Phelps (Ed.), *Altruism, morality, and economic theory* (pp. 45-56). New York: Russell Sage Foundation.

Behavioral science—The future [Editorial]. (1988, October 3–9). *PR Week*, p. 6.

Benjamin, E. (1989, July/August). Let faculty be faculty. CASE *Currents*, pp. 8-11.

Berdahl, R. O. (1971). *Statewide coordination of higher education*. Washington, DC: American Council on Education.

Berdahl, R. O., & Altbach, P. G. (1981). Higher education in American society: An introduction. In P. G. Altbach & R. O. Berdahl (Eds.), *Higher education in American society* (pp. 1-9). Buffalo, NY: Prometheus Books.

Bernays, E. L. (1952). *Public relations*. Norman, OK: University of Oklahoma Press.

Bintzer, H. R. (1981). The many uses of professional counsel. In F. C. Pray (Ed.), *Handbook for educational fund raising* (pp. 216-223). San Francisco, CA: Jossey-Bass.

Blakely, B. E. (1985, July/August). Mutual support: Without more advancement for researchers, we won't see more research in advancement. CASE *Currents*, p. 64.

Blau, P. M. (1986). *Exchange and power in social life* (rev. ed.). New Brunswick, NJ: Transaction Books.

Body of Knowledge Task Force of the PRSA Research Committee. (1988). Public relations body of knowledge task force report. *Public Relations Review*, *14*(1), 3-40.

Bok, D. (1982). *Beyond the ivory tower: Social responsibilities of the modern university*. Cambridge, MA: Harvard University Press.

Bolnick, B. R. (1975). Toward a behavioral theory of philanthropic activity. In E. S. Phelps (Ed.), *Altruism, morality, and economic theory* (pp. 197-223). New York: Russell Sage Foundation.

Boorstin, D. J. (1983). From charity to philanthropy. In B. O'Connell (Ed.), *America's voluntary spirit: A book of readings* (pp. 129-141). New York: The Foundation Center. (Original work published 1963)

Bornstein, R. (1989, January). Adding it up. CASE *Currents*, pp. 12-17.

Botan, C. H., & Hazelton, V. (1989). *Public relations theory*. Hillsdale, NJ: Lawrence Erlbaum Associates.

Boulding, K. E. (1973). *The economy of love and fear: A preface to grants economics*. Belmont, CA: Wadsworth.

Bourque, J. (1989, September 4). Fed up with charity. *Newsweek*, p. 10.

Boyer, E. L. (1989, August 19). When gifts for universities have a hook in them. *The Philadelphia Inquirer*, p. 9-A.

Brittingham, B. E., & Pezzullo, T. R. (1990). *The campus green: Fund raising in higher education*, ASHE-ERIC Higher Education Report No. 1. Washington, DC: George Washington University, School of Education and Human Development.

Broce, T. E. (1986). *Fund raising: The guide to raising money from private sources* (2nd ed.). Norman, OK: University of Oklahoma Press.

Broom, G. M., & Dozier, D. M. (1986). Advancement for public relations role models. *Public*

Relations Review, 12(1), 37-56.

Brossman, W. R. (1981). The central importance of large gifts. In F. C. Pray (Ed.), *Handbook for educational fund raising* (pp. 69-72). San Francisco, CA: Jossey-Bass.

B-schools get a global vision. (1989, July 17). *Fortune,* pp. 78, 80, 85-86.

Burke, K. E. (1985, March 11). *Capital campaigns.* Unpublished paper, University of Maryland, College Park, MD.

Burke, K. E. (1988). *Institutional image and alumni giving.* Unpublished doctoral dissertation, University of Maryland, College Park, MD.

Burns, T., & Stalker, G. M. (1961). *The management of innovation.* London: Tavistock.

Cal. regents halt pay of convicted ex-chancellor. (1989, August 2). *The Chronicle of Higher Education,* p. A2.

Cal. State U. decides against accepting gift. (1990, September 12). *The Chronicle of Higher Education,* p. A32.

Calabresi, G. (1975). Comment. In E. S. Phelps (Ed.), *Altruism, morality and economic theory,* (pp. 30-34). New York: Russell Sage.

Cameron, K. S. (1986). Organizational adaptation and higher education. In M. W. Peterson (Ed.), *ASHE reader on organization and governance in higher education* (3rd ed., pp. 409-427). Lexington, MA: Ginn Press. (Original work published 1984)

Campbell, D. A. (1989, June). Second to none: If you've asked the right giver for the right amount, your lead gift will lead the way. CASE *Currents,* pp. 22-26.

Campaign comments: An update for fund raisers. (1990, June). (Available from the Office of University Relations, University of Maryland System, Elkins Building, 3300 Metzerott Road, Adelphi, MD 20783.)

Cantor, B., & Burger, C. (Ed.). (1984). *Experts in action: Inside public relations.* New York: Longman.

Cantor, B., & Burger, C. (Ed.). (1989). *Experts in action: Inside public relations* (2nd ed.). New York: Longman.

Carbone, R. F. (1986). *Agenda for research on fund raising* (Monograph No. 1). College Park, MD: University of Maryland, Clearinghouse for Research on Fund Raising.

Carbone, R. F. (1987). *Fund raisers of academe* (Monograph No. 2). College Park, MD: University of Maryland, Clearinghouse for Research on Fund Raising.

Carbone, R. F. (1989a, January 23). *Professionalism of fund raising.* Session at the CASE District III Conference, Pittsburgh, PA.

Carbone, R. F. (1989b). *Fund raising as a profession.* (Monograph No. 3). College Park, MD: University of Maryland, Clearinghouse for Research on Fund Raising.

Carnegie, A. (1983). The gospel of wealth. In B. O'Connell (Ed.), *America's voluntary spirit* (pp. 97-108). New York: The Foundation Center. (Original work published 1889)

Carnegie Committee for the Improvement of Teaching. (1982). *The control of the campus: A report on the governance of higher education.* Lawrenceville, NJ: Princeton University Press.

Carnegie's "gospel of wealth," 100 years later. (1989, June 27). *The Chronicle of Philanthropy,* pp. 5, 8.

Center for the study of philanthropy: Research awards program. (1989, February 7). *The Chronicle of Philanthropy,* p. 24.

Charitable giving by Americans topped $100-billion last year, but donations to education fell slightly. (1989, June 14). *The Chronicle of Higher Education,* pp. A29, A31.

Charities advised to offer meaningful work to business leaders. (1989, October 31). *The Chronicle of Philanthropy,* p. 18.

Chief fund raiser resigns at Auburn U. after 6 months of controversy. (1989, May 17). *The Chronicle of Higher Education,* pp. A33-A34.

Chrysler's Iacocca, class of '45, brings verve to Lehigh U. fund-raising drive. (1987, December 2). *The Chronicle of Higher Education,* pp. 1, A30-A31.

Cialdini, R. B. (1987, January). What leads to yes: Applying the psychology of influence to fund raising, alumni relations, and PR. CASE *Currents,* pp. 48-51.

Coldren, S. L. (1982). *The constant quest: Raising billions through capital campaigns.* Washington, DC: American Council on Education.

Colleges are nervous as Congress weighs moves to stop deceptive fund-raising practices. (1989, September 27). *The Chronicle of Higher Education,* p. A28.

Colleges get more aggressive in quest for major gifts from individual donors. (1987, May 13). *The Chronicle of Higher Education,* pp. 39, 41.

Colwell, M. A. C. (1980). The foundation connection: Links among foundations and recipient organizations. In R. F. Arnove (Ed.), *Philanthropy and cultural imperialism: The foundations at home and abroad* (pp. 413-452). Boston, MA: G. K. Hall.

Columbia U. opens campaign to raise $1.15-billion; Cornell is said to prepare for a $1.25-billion drive. (1990, October 3). *The Chronicle of Higher Education*, pp. A33-A34.

Community colleges contributions. (1989, November/December). CASE *Currents*, p. 38.

Company may pull gifts from Ind. county. (1989, June 27). *The Chronicle of Philanthropy*, p. 6.

Computer chat links IABC study leaders. (1987, March). *IABC Communication World*, pp. 29-31.

Continuing education: Training resources for your rookies. (1989, July/August). CASE *Currents*, pp. 30-31.

Corporate-gift plan approved by panel. (1989, July 25). *The Chronicle of Philanthropy*, pp. 24-25.

Corporate gifts called investment, not impulse. (1987, September 30). *The Chronicle of Higher Education*, p. A28.

Corporate philanthropy in the 1990s. (1989, January 23). Session at the CASE District III Conference, Pittsburgh, PA.

Corson, J. J. (1968). Public service and higher education: Compatibility or conflict? In C. G. Dobbins & C. B. T. Lee (Eds.), *Whose goals for American higher education?* (pp. 83-90). Washington, DC: American Council on Education.

Council for Aid to Education. (1988). *Voluntary support of education 1986-1987*. New York: Author.

Council for Aid to Education. (1989). *Voluntary support of education 1987-1988*. New York: Author.

Crable, R. E., & Vibbert, S. L. (1986). *Public relations as communication management*. Edina, MN: Bellwether Press.

Curti, M. (1957). The history of American philanthropy as a field of research. *American Historical Review, 62*, 352-363.

Curti, M. (1965). Foreword. In S. M. Cutlip, *Fund raising in the United States: Its role in America's philanthropy* (pp. xi-xiv). New Brunswick, NJ: Rutgers University Press.

Curti, M. (1983). American philanthropy and the national character. In B. O'Connell (Ed.), *America's voluntary spirit* (pp. 161-179). New York: The Foundation Center. (Original work published in 1958)

Curti, M., & Nash, R. (1965). *Philanthropy in the shaping of American higher education*. New Brunswick, NJ: Rutgers University Press.

Cutlip, S. M. (1965). *Fund raising in the United States: Its role in America's philanthropy*. New Brunswick, NJ: Rutgers University Press.

Cutlip, S. M., & Center, A. H. (1952). *Effective public relations*. Englewood Cliffs, NJ: Prentice-Hall.

Cutlip, S. M., Center, A. H., & Broom, G. M. (1985). *Effective public relations* (6th Ed.). Englewood Cliffs, NJ: Prentice-Hall.

Dalessandro, D. (1989, June). By the numbers: An inside look at the arduous but vital process of setting your campaign's goal and length. CASE *Currents*, pp. 16-21.

Dannelley, P. (1986). *Fund raising and public relations: A critical guide to literature and resources*. Norman, OK: University of Oklahoma Press.

Diamond jubilee: Advancement's founding field looks back on 75 eventful years. (1988, February). CASE *Currents*, pp. 17-29.

Dilenschneider, R. L. (1989). Foreword. In B. Cantor (Ed.), *Experts in action: Inside public relations* (2nd ed., pp. 1-4). New York: Longman.

Dittman, D. A. (1981). Criteria for judging staff size and functions. In F. C. Pray (Ed.), *Handbook for educational fund raising* (pp. 226-231). San Francisco, CA: Jossey-Bass.

Dobbins, C. G., & Lee, C. B. T. (Eds.). (1968). *Whose goals for American higher education?* Washington, DC: American Council on Education.

Douglas, J. (1983). *Why charity? The case for a third sector*. Beverly Hills, CA: Sage.

Dowling, J. H. (1988, November 14-20). No definition needed. *PR Week*, p. 10.

Dressel, P. L. (1980). *The autonomy of public colleges*. San Francisco: Jossey-Bass.

Drucker, P. (1964). *Concept of the corporation*. New York: North American Library.

Drugstore chain unveils plan to donate up to 5 pct. of its receipts to local charities. (1989, April 18). *The Chronicle of Philanthropy*, p. 14.

Drunk-driving foes accept big gifts from alcoholic-beverage producers. (1989, July 25). *The Chronicle of Philanthropy*, pp. 1, 12-14.

Duke may not accept $20-million gift. (1987, February 11). *The Chronicle of Higher Education*, p. 29.

Dunlop, D. R. (1987, May). The ultimate gift. CASE *Currents*, pp. 8-13.

Dunn, J. A. (Ed.). (1986). *Enhancing the management of fund raising*. San Francisco, CA: Jossey-Bass.

Dunn, J. A., Geronimo, D., & Adam, A. (1986). Comparative studies of fund-raising performance. In J. A. Dunn (Ed.), *Enhancing the management of fund raising* (pp. 39-53). San Francisco, CA: Jossey-Bass.

Dunn, J. A., & Hutten, L. R. (1985, September). Private fund raising over time. CASE *Currents*, pp. 45-47.

Dunn, J. A., & Terkla, D. G. (1985, September). Research update. CASE *Currents*, p. 45.

Dunn, J. A., Terkla, D. G., & Secakusuma, P. (1989, September). Fund raising's top 100. CASE *Currents*, pp. 50-55.

Dunn, S. W. (1986). *Public relations: A contemporary approach*. Homewood, IL: Irwin.

Duronio, M. A., & Loessin, B. A. (1989). *Fund raising outcomes and institutional characteristics in ten types of higher education institutions*. Unpublished paper, University of Pittsburgh, Pittsburgh, PA.

Duryea, E. D. (1981). The university and the state: A historical overview. In P. G. Altbach & R. O. Berdahl (Eds.), *Higher education in American society* (pp. 13-33). Buffalo, NY: Prometheus Books.

Duryea, E. D. (1986). Evolution of university organization. In M. W. Peterson (Ed.), *ASHE reader on organization and governance in higher education* (3rd ed., pp. 165-197). Lexington, MA: Ginn Press. (Original work published 1973)

Edwards, A. H. (1989, April). Go for the gold. CASE *Currents*, p. 72.

Encyclopædia Britannica (Micropædia Vol. 7). (1979). Chicago: Encyclopædia Britannica, Inc.

Energetic board chairman uses skills that built Burger King to help U. of Miami dominate Southern Florida fund raising. (1989, September 5). *The Chronicle of Philanthropy*, pp. 4-7.

Ernest, E. (1989, January 24). CASE national sets a new course for professionals. *Confluence*, p. 1. (Available from CASE, 11 Dupont Circle, Washington, D.C. 20006.)

Escalating costs force private research universities to scale back academic, administrative operations. (1989, August 16). *The Chronicle of Higher Education*, pp. A21-A22.

Etzioni, A. (1986). Administrative and professional authority. In M. W. Peterson (Ed.), *ASHE reader on organization and governance in higher education* (3rd ed., pp. 28-35). Lexington, MA: Ginn Press. (Original work published 1964)

Evans, G. A. (1989, March). The cornerstone of education. CASE *Currents*, pp. 6-9.

Fate of tax proposal worries non-profits. (1990, October 2). *The Chronicle of Philanthropy*, p. 31.

Ferguson, M. A., Doner, L., & Carson, L. (1986). Using persuasion models to identify givers. *Public Relations Review*, *12*(3), 43-50.

$15-million gift returned by Utah U. (1989, September 19). *The Chronicle of Philanthropy*, p. 6.

Fisher, J. L. (1985, September). Keeping our place at the academic table. CASE *Currents*, pp. 11-14.

Foundation created by a self-made millionaire supports private colleges and universities that have bold outlooks. (1989, July 19). *The Chronicle of Higher Education*, pp. A21-A22.

Fowler, G. L. (Ed.). (1989). *Journalism Abstracts, 26*. Columbia, SC: Association for Education in Journalism and Mass Communication.

Franz, P. J. (1981). Trustees must lead by example. In F. C. Pray (Ed.), *Handbook for educational fund raising* (pp. 161-166). San Francisco, CA: Jossey-Bass.

Freeman, D. K. (1987, June). Ethical considerations in fund raising. *Fund Raising Management*, pp. 72-77.

Freire, P. (1970). *Pedagogy of the oppressed*. New York: Seabury Press.

Frick, J. W. (1981). The development officer as educator. In F. C. Pray (Ed.), *Handbook for educational fund raising* (pp. 279-281). San Francisco, CA: Jossey-Bass.

Fund drives get bigger, broader: 65 college goals top $100-million. (1987, September 2). *The Chronicle of Higher Education*, pp. A72-A76.

Fund raisers assail planners who push gifts as tax shelters and take big finder's fees. (1989, October 3). *The Chronicle of Philanthropy*, pp. 1, 12,

Gardner, J. W. (1983). Foreword: The independent sector. In B. O'Connell (Ed.), *America's voluntary spirit* (pp. ix-xv). New York: The Foundation Center.

GE bucks crowd, increases giving. (1988, March/April). *Giving USA Update*, pp. 2-3.

Geier, L. E. (1981). Public relations as an arm of development. In F. C. Pray (Ed.), *Handbook for educational fund raising* (pp. 203-210). San Francisco, CA: Jossey-Bass.

Gifts to colleges appear to be on the way up, after first decline in more than 10 years. (1989, September 6). *The Chronicle of Higher Education*, pp. 1, A27.

Gifts to colleges off 3.5 pct.; cutback by alumni blamed. (1989, May 3). *The Chronicle of Higher Education*, pp. 1, A30-A31.

Gilley, J. W., Fulmer, K. A., & Reithlingshoefer, S. J. (1986). *Searching for academic excellence: Twenty colleges and universities on the move and their leaders.* New York: American Council on Education and Macmillan.

Give & take. (1987, February 25). *The Chronicle of Higher Education*, p. 31.

Give & take. (1989a, March 29). *The Chronicle of Higher Education*, p. A27.

Give & take. (1989b, April 12). *The Chronicle of Higher Education*, p. A28.

Give & take. (1989c, April 19). *The Chronicle of Higher Education*, p. A29.

Give & take. (1989d, November 1). *The Chronicle of Higher Education*, p. A29.

Give & take. (1990, July 16). *The Chronicle of Higher Education*, p. A29.

Goldberg, P. B. (1989, February 21). Corporate philanthropy is fragile, but it can be a voice for change. *The Chronicle of Philanthropy*, pp. 23-24.

Goldman, R. (1989, November/December). Public interest [Review of *An assessment of factors related to successful fund raising at public, doctorate-granting universities*]. *CASE Currents*, p. 57.

Gonser Gerber Tinker Stuhr. (1986, March). The role of public relations in a comprehensive development program. *Bulletin*, pp. 1-4. (Available from Author, 105 West Madison, Chicago, Il 60602.)

Gould, S. B., (1968). A New objective. In C. G. Dobbins & C. B. T. Lee (Eds.), *Whose goals for American higher education?* (pp. 221-230). Washington, DC: American Council on Education.

Gouldner, A. W. (1960). The norm of reciprocity: A preliminary statement. *American Sociological Review, 25*(2), 161-178.

Grunig, J. E. (1976). Organizations and public relations: Testing a communication theory. *Journalism Monographs, 46.*

Grunig, J. E. (1984). Organizations, environments, and models of public relations. *Public relations research & education, 1*(4), 6-29.

Grunig, J. E. (1989a). Symmetrical presuppositions as a framework for public relations theory. In C. Botan & V. Hazelton (Eds.), *Public relations theory.* Hillsdale, NJ: Lawrence Erlbaum Associates.

Grunig, J. E. (1989b). Sierra club study shows who become activists. *Public Relations Review, 15*(3), 3-24.

Grunig, J. E. (1989c). Publics, audiences and market segments: Segmentation principles for campaigns. In C. T. Salmon (Ed.), *Information campaigns: Managing the process of social change* (pp. 197-226). Newbury Park, CA: Sage.

Grunig, J. E. (in preparation). Communication, public relations and effective organizations: An overview of the book. In J. E. Grunig (Ed.), *Excellence in public relations and communication management: Contributions to effective organizations* (working project).

Grunig, J. E. (Ed.). (in preparation). *Excellence in public relations and communication management: Contributions to effective organizations* (working project).

Grunig, J. E., Dozier, D. M., Ehling, W. P., Grunig, L. S., Repper, F. C., & White, J. (1986). *In search of excellence in public relations and communication management: A proposal for research on the contribution of public relations to organizational effectiveness.* San Francisco, CA: International Association of Business Communicators (IABC) Foundation.

Grunig, J. E., & Grunig, L. A. (1988, November). *The strategic approach to publics and issues related to increased competition in health care.* Paper presented to the Commission on Public Relations, Speech Communication Association, New Orleans, LA.

Grunig, J. E., & Grunig, L. S. (1989). Toward a theory of the public relations behavior of organizations: Review of a program of research. In J. E. Grunig & L. S. Grunig (Eds.), *Public Relations Research Annual* (Vol. 1, pp. 27-63). Hillsdale, NJ: Lawrence Erlbaum Associates.

Grunig, J. E., & Hickson, R. H. (1976). An evaluation of academic research in public relations. *Public Relations Review, 2*(1), 31-43.

Grunig, J. E., & Hunt, T. (1984). *Managing public relations.* New York: Holt, Rinehart & Winston.

Grunig, J. E., & Stamm, K. R. (1979). Cognitive strategies and the resolution of environmental issues: A second study. *Journalism Quarterly, 56*, 715-726.

Grunig, J. E., & White, J. (in preparation). Assumptions about communication and public relations: How they affect the theories chosen by researchers and practitioners. In J. E. Grunig (Ed.),

Excellence in public relations and communication management: Contributions to effective organizations (working project).

Grunig, L. A. (1986, August). *Activism and organizational response: Contemporary cases of collective behavior.* Paper presented to the Public Relations Division, Association for Education in Journalism and Mass Communication, Norman, OK.

Gurin, M. G. (1989). Introduction. In M. G. Gurin & J. Van Til, *Understanding philanthropy: Fund raising in perspective.* (Available from AAFRC, 25 West 43rd Street, New York, NY 10036.)

Gurin, M. G. (1990, October 16). Joint fund-raising ventures with business are making philanthropy too commercial. *The Chronicle of Philanthropy,* pp. 36-37.

Gurin, M. G., & Van Til, J. (1989). *Understanding philanthropy: Fund raising in perspective.* (Available from AAFRC, 25 West 43rd Street, New York, NY 10036.)

Hackman, J. D. (1985/1986). Power and centrality in the allocation of resources in colleges and universities. In M. W. Peterson (Ed.), *ASHE reader on organization and governance in higher education* (3rd ed., pp. 310-326). Lexington, MA: Ginn Press.

Haire, J. R. (1981). Voluntary support in the 1980s. In T. M. Stauffer (Ed.), *Competition and cooperation in American higher education* (pp. 139-145). Washington, DC: American Council on Education.

Hall, M. R. (1989). *The decentralization of institutional advancement activities at research and doctorate granting colleges and universities.* Unpublished doctoral dissertation, University of Maryland, College Park, MD.

Hall, P. D. (1987). A historical overview of the private nonprofit sector. In W. W. Powell (Ed.), *The nonprofit sector: A research handbook* (pp. 3-26). New Haven, CT: Yale University Press.

Hall, P. D. (1988). Private philanthropy and public policy: A historical appraisal. In R. L. Payton, M. Novak, B. O'Connell, & P. D. Hall, *Philanthropy: Four views* (pp. 39-72). New Brunswick, NJ: Social Philosophy and Policy Center and Transaction Books.

Hall, S. (1980). Cultural studies: Two paradigms. *Media, culture and society, 2,* 57-72.

Hampton, C. (1989, May). First-class stewardship. CASE *Currents,* pp. 59-61.

Hansmann, H. (1987). Economic theories of nonprofit organization. In W. W. Powell (Ed.), *The nonprofit sector: A research handbook* (pp. 27-42). New Haven, CT: Yale University Press.

Harcleroad, F. F. (1981). Private constituencies and their impact on higher education. In P. G. Altbach & R. O. Berdahl (Eds.), *Higher education in American society* (pp. 199-218). Buffalo, NY: Prometheus Books.

Harvard title for sale? (1987, November 23). *Newsweek,* p. 35.

Hedgepeth, R. C. (1989, January). *Funding the cost of fundraising for the public university.* Paper presented at CASE District VII Conference, Boston, MA.

Hobba, D. S. (1976, April). *Oklahoma higher education: A state plan for the 1970s, revision and supplement.* Oklahoma City: Oklahoma State Regents for Higher Education.

Hopkins delays academics surcharge. (1988, April 17). *The Sun,* p. 8B.

Hopkins president leaving a mixed legacy. (1990, June 24). *The Sun,* pp 1B, 4B.

Hopkinson, D. (1989, May). Thanks for everything. CASE *Currents,* pp. 55-57.

Horton, T. R. (1981). Corporate support of higher education. In T. M. Stauffer (Ed.), *Competition and cooperation in American higher education* (pp. 149-158). Washington, DC: American Council on Education.

House panel to weigh federal regulation of charity appeals. (1989, March 21). *The Chronicle of Philanthropy,* pp. 1, 21.

Howe, F. (1985, March/April). What you need to know about fund raising. *Harvard Business Review, 63*(2), 18-21.

Hsia, H. J. (1988). *Mass communications research methods: A step-by-step approach.* Hillsdale, NJ: Lawrence Erlbaum Associates.

Hunter, T. W. (1968). The million dollar gift. *College and University Journal, 7*(4) 21-38.

Hutton, C. (1989, March 27). Inside the mind of Jack Welch. *Fortune,* pp. 38-50.

If charities were given more unrestricted funds, more socially useful work would get done. (1989, October 3). *The Chronicle of Philanthropy,* p. 36.

Ill. charges cancer group with fund-raising fraud. (1989, July 11). *The Chronicle of Philanthropy,* pp. 29, 31.

"In" box. (1987, December 9). *The Chronicle of Higher Education,* p. A15.

In college fund raising, president's role is found more important than planning. (1989, July 25). *The Chronicle of Philanthropy,* pp. 4, 10.

Independent Sector. (1988). *Research in progress: 1986–1987, A national compilation of research projects on philanthropy, voluntary action, and not-for-profit activity.* Washington, DC: Author.

Insider. (1989a, March 21). *The Chronicle of Philanthropy*, p. 5.

Insider. (1989b, July 25). *The Chronicle of Philanthropy*, p. 6.

It costs the average college 16 cents to raise a dollar—a 525% return. (1990, September 4). *The Chronicle of Philanthropy*, pp. 5, 10.

Jacobson, H. K. (1986). Toward a network: Problems and opportunities in fund raising research. In R. F. Carbone, *An agenda for research on fund raising* (pp. 37-40). College Park, MD: Clearinghouse for Research on Fund Raising.

Jacobson, H. K. (1987, January). Bringing theory closer to practice. *CASE Currents*, pp. 61-62.

Jencks, C. (1987). Who gives to what? In W. W. Powell (Ed.), *The nonprofit sector: A research handbook* (pp. 321-339). New Haven, CT: Yale University Press.

Jimmy Carter on innovative grant making; creativity for the small foundation; drop in corporate philanthropy; high profile for the environment; and more. (1989, April 18). *The Chronicle of Philanthropy*, pp. 5, 8.

Johnson, D. B. (1973). The charity market: Theory and practice. In A. A. Alchian (Ed.), *The economics of charity: Essays on the comparative economics and ethics of giving and selling, with applications to blood* (pp. 63-88). London: The Institute of Economic Affairs.

Kanter, R. M., & Summers, D. V. (1987). Doing well while doing good: Dilemmas of performance measurement in nonprofit organizations and the need for a multiple-constituency approach. In W. W. Powell (Ed.), *The nonprofit sector: A research handbook* (pp. 154-166). New Haven, CT: Yale University Press.

Karl, B. D. (1982/1983). Corporate philanthropy: Historical background. In B. O'Connell (Ed.), *America's voluntary spirit: A book of readings* (pp. 377-383). New York: The Foundation Center.

Katz, D., & Kahn, R. L. (1978). *The social psychology of organizations* (2nd ed.). New York: Wiley.

Katz, S. N. (1987). Foreword. In D. N. Layton (Ed.), *Philanthropy and voluntarism: An annotated bibliography* (pp. ix-x). New York: The Foundation Center.

Kelly, K. S. (1979). *Predicting alumni giving: An analysis of alumni donors and non-donors of the College of Journalism at the University of Maryland.* Unpublished master's thesis, University of Maryland, College Park, MD.

Kelly, K. S. (1988). Development: A specialization of public relations. *Educational and Cultural Organizations Section Monograph, 2*(3). (Available from the Public Relations Society of America, 33 Irving Place, New York, NY 10032.)

Kelly, K. S. (1989a). *Study of the relationship between public relations and fund raising in educational and cultural organizations.* Unpublished paper, University of Maryland, College Park, MD.

Kelly, K. S. (1989b, Winter). PR and fund raising in E&CO: Symbiotic or Diametric? *The Tattler*, pp. 3-6. (Available from the Public Relations Society of America, 33 Irving Place, New York, NY 10032.)

Kelly, K. S. (1990). *The treatment of fund raising in leading public relations texts.* Manuscript submitted for publication.

Kerr, C. (1972). *The uses of the university.* New York: Harper & Row.

Kerr, C., & Gade, M. (1981). Current and emerging issues facing American higher education. In P. G. Altbach & R. O. Berdahl (Eds.), *Higher education in American society* (pp. 111-129). Buffalo, NY: Prometheus Books.

Key departures seen delaying Harvard as universities plan mega-campaigns. (1990, June 12). *The Chronicle of Philanthropy*, p. 5.

Kochevar, J. A. (1989, April 17). Damned if we do [Letter to the editor]. *Newsweek*, pp. 19-20.

Kotler, P. (1972). *Marketing management: Analysis, planning, and methodology* (2nd ed.). Englewood Cliffs, NJ: Prentice-Hall.

Kotler, P. (1982). *Marketing for nonprofit organizations* (2nd ed.). Englewood Cliffs, NJ: Prentice-Hall.

Kramer, M. (1980). *The venture capital of higher education: The private and public sources of discretionary funds.* San Francisco, CA: The Carnegie Foundation for the Advancement of Teaching.

Kuhn, A. (1979). *Unified social science.* Homewood, IL: Dorsey.

Kuhn, T. S. (1962). *The structure of scientific revolutions.* Chicago: University of Chicago Press.

Lane, F. S., Levis, W. C., & New, A. L. (1989, June). *Funding fund raising report.* New York: City University of New York Baruch College, Department of Public Administration.

Lang, K., & Lang, G. E. (1983). The new rhetoric of mass communication research: A longer view. _Journal of Communication, 33_(3), 128-140.

Laudan, L. (1977). _Progress and its problems_. Berkeley: University of California Press.

Lawrence, P. R., & Lorsch, J. W. (1967). _Organization and environment_. Homewood, IL: Irwin.

Lawsuit charges man was fired for refusal to give to United Way. (1989, March 21). _The Chronicle of Philanthropy_, pp. 5, 11.

Lawson, C. E. (1988, Winter). Institutional integrity: A prerequisite for philanthropic support. _NSFRE Journal_, pp. 59-61.

Lax rules for counting gifts seen harming fund raising's image. (1990, July 24). _The Chronicle of Philanthropy_, pp. 8-9.

Layton, D. N. (1987). _Philanthropy and voluntarism: An annotated bibliography_. New York: The Foundation Center.

Lee, C. B. T. (1968). Whose goals for American higher education. In C. G. Dobbins & C. B. T. Lee (Eds.), _Whose goals for American higher education?_ (pp. 1-15). Washington, DC: American Council on Education.

Leet, R. K. (1989, June 27). Charities should learn a lesson from business and aim their pitches only at those who care. _The Chronicle of Philanthropy_, p. 36.

Lehecka, R. (1968). No university should become "a happening." In C. G. Dobbins & C. B. T. Lee (Eds.), _Whose goals for American higher education?_ (pp. 97-100). Washington, DC: American Council on Education.

Leslie, L. L., & Ramey, G. (1988). Donor behavior and voluntary support for higher education institutions. _The Journal of Higher Education, 59_(2), 115-132.

Lesly, P., Budd, J., Cutlip, S., Lerbinger, O., & Pires, M. A. (1987, April 11). _Report of Special Committee on Terminology_. (Available from the Public Relations Society of America, 33 Irving Place, New York, NY 10032.)

Levy, R., & Oviatt, F., Jr. (1989). Corporate philanthropy. In B. Cantor (Ed.), _Experts in action: Inside public relations_ (2nd ed., pp. 126-138). New York: Longman, Inc.

Life- and health-insurance companies to give $16.2-million for AIDS education and services. (1989, April 4). _The Chronicle of Philanthropy_, p. 7.

Link to religion called significant for fund raisers. (1989, March 21). _The Chronicle of Philanthropy_, pp. 1, 8-9.

Loessin, B. A., & Duronio, M. A. (1989, May). _A model for fund raising effectiveness_. Paper presented at the Annual Forum, Association for Institutional Research, Baltimore, MD.

Loessin, B. A., Duronio, M. A., & Borton, G. L. (1986). Measuring and expanding sources of private funding. In J. A. Dunn (Ed.), _Enhancing the management of fund raising_ (pp. 55-68). San Francisco, CA: Jossey-Bass.

Loessin, B. A., Duronio, M. A., & Borton, G. L. (1988, September). Questioning the conventional wisdom. _CASE Currents_, pp. 33-40.

Lord, J. G. (1983). _The raising of money: Thirty-five essentials every trustee should know_. Cleveland, OH: Third Sector Press.

Lowenberg, F. M. (Ed.). (1975). _Professional components in education for fund raising_. New York: Council on Social Work Education.

Lowengard, M. (1989, October). Community relations: New approaches to building consensus. _Public Relations Journal_, pp. 24-30.

Lyddon, I. W. (1990, September). Tax exemption—Who should have it, who should get it, who should keep it? _NSFRE News_, p. 2.

MacIsaac, C. R. (1970). _Attitudes of donors at selected institutions of higher education_. Unpublished doctoral dissertation, University of Michigan, Ann Arbor, MI.

Major domo of Penn's billion-dollar campaign. (1990, October 16). _The Chronicle of Philanthropy_, pp. 7, 20-21.

Major gifts to higher education. (1989, May 10). _The Chronicle of Higher Education_, p. A30.

Major gifts to higher education. (1990, November 28). _The Chronicle of Higher Education_, p. A33.

Making the case for a good cause. (1989, April). _CASE Currents_, p. 14.

Many environmental groups turn to corporations to supplement their gifts from individual donors. (1989, February 21). _The Chronicle of Philanthropy_, pp. 4-7.

McCarty, D. J., & Young, I. P. (1981). Stress and the academic dean. In P. G. Altbach & R. O. Berdahl (Eds.), _Higher education in American society_ (pp. 269-285). Buffalo, NY: Prometheus Books.

McConnell, T. R. (1981). Autonomy and accountability: Some fundamental issues. In P. G. Altbach & R. O. Berdahl (Eds.), _Higher education in American society_ (pp. 35-53). Buffalo, NY:

Prometheus Books.

McKean, R. N. (1975). Economics of trust, altruism, and corporate responsibility. In E. S. Phelps (Ed.), *Altruism, morality, and economic theory* (pp. 29-44). New York: Russell Sage Foundation.

Milofsky, C. (1987). Neighborhood-based organizations: A market analogy. In W. W. Powell (Ed.), *The nonprofit sector: A research handbook* (pp. 277-295). New Haven, CT: Yale University Press.

Minds of Maryland: The campaign for the University of Maryland System. (1989, March). (Available from the Office of University Relations, UM System, Elkins Building, 3300 Metzerott Road, Adelphi, MD 20783.)

Minn. charities said to get 33 pct. of money collected by fund raisers. (1989, June 27). *The Chronicle of Philanthropy*, pp. 21-22.

Mintzberg, H. (1983). *Power in and around organizations*. Englewood Cliffs, NJ: Prentice-Hall.

"Misunderstandings" and "deviations from policy" found in an investigation of the fund-raising office at Berkeley. (1987, July 8). *The Chronicle of Higher Education*, pp. 19-20.

Moos, M. (1981). *The post-land grant university: The University of Maryland report*. (Available from the Office of University Relations, UM System, Elkins Building, 3300 Metzerott Road, Adelphi, MD 20783.)

More partnerships to boost technology sought for academe. (1989, April 19). *The Chronicle of Higher Education*, pp. A21-A23.

Mount Holyoke, Smith, and Wellesley in "friendly" competition to establish new fund-raising standards for women's colleges. (1989, April 5). *The Chronicle of Higher Education*, pp. A29-A30.

Muelder, W. G. (1978). Empowerment and the integrity of higher education. In D. B. Robertson (Ed.), *Power and empowerment in higher education* (pp. 1-24). Lexington: The University Press of Kentucky.

Nadel, M. V. (1990). *Nonprofit hospitals: Better standards needed for tax exemption* (GAO/T-HRD-90-45). Washington, DC: United States General Accounting Office, Human Resources Division.

Nason, J. W. (1981). Presidents and governing boards. In P. G. Altbach & R. O. Berdahl (Eds.), *Higher education in American society* (pp. 253-268). Buffalo, NY: Prometheus Books.

National Society of Fund Raising Executives (NSFRE). (1988, Winter). Profile: 1988 NSFRE membership career survey. *NSFRE Journal*, pp. 20-42.

National Society of Fund Raising Executives (NSFRE). (1989, Summer). Annual report. *NSFRE Journal*, pp. 33-44.

National Society of Fund Raising Executives (NSFRE) Institute. (1986). *Glossary of fund-raising terms*. (Available from Author, 1101 King Street, Suite 3000, Alexandria, VA 22314.)

Negotiations resume on Perot's $70-million gift to U. of Texas. (1987, September 2). *The Chronicle of Higher Education*, p. A78.

New tobacco alliance. (1989, February 13). *Newsweek*, p. 20.

Nielsen, W. A. (1985). *The golden donors: A new anatomy of the great foundations*. New York: E. P. Dutton.

Nielsen, W. A. (1990, May 1). Self-interest is not the whole story of philanthropy. *The Chronicle of Philanthropy*, pp. 35-36.

1988's gifts barely keep pace with inflation. (1989, January 24). *The Chronicle of Philanthropy*, pp. 1, 8).

Non-profit hospitals step up campaigns, hire more fund raisers. (1989, July 25). *The Chronicle of Philanthropy*, p. 5.

Non-profit sector is now a "hot topic" for researchers in several fields. (1985, April 10). *The Chronicle of Higher Education*, p. 18.

O'Connell, B. (1983). *America's voluntary spirit: A book of readings*. New York: The Foundation Center.

O'Connell, B. (1987). *Philanthropy in action*. New York: The Foundation Center.

Odendahl, T. J. (1990). *Charity begins at home: Generosity and self-interest among the philanthropic elite*. New York: Basic Books.

Olasky, M. N. (1987). *Corporate public relations: A new historical perspective*. Hillsdale, NJ: Lawrence Erlbaum Associates.

Olcott, W. (1990, October). Novel way to say thanks. *Fund Raising Management*, p. 8.

Olson, M. (1965). *The logic of collective action: Public goods and the theory of groups*. Cambridge, MA: Harvard University Press.

"Opportunism" seen in education ventures between U.S., Japan. (1990, May 30). *The Chronicle of Higher Education*, pp. 1, A25-A26.

Oral Roberts says he will close his medical school and hospital. (1989, September 20). *The Chronicle of Higher Education*, p. A2.

Pa. county acts to alter tax status of college buildings. (1990, March 28). *The Chronicle of Higher Education*, p. A27.

Pa. police unit concedes appeals were deceptive. (1989, May 30). *The Chronicle of Philanthropy*, p. 25.

Panas, J. (1984). *Megagifts: Who gives them, who gets them.* Chicago: Pluribus Press, Inc.

Paton, G. J. (1986). Microeconomic perspectives applied to development planning and management. In J. A. Dunn (Ed.), *Enhancing the management of fund raising* (pp. 17-38). San Francisco, CA: Jossey-Bass.

Pavlik, J. V. (1987). *Public relations: What research tells us.* Newbury Park, CA: Sage.

Pay gap widens among fund raisers as colleges pursue high-priced "stars." (1987, July 29). *The Chronicle of Higher Education*, pp. 21-22.

Payton, R. L. (1981). Essential qualities of the development officer. In F. C. Pray (Ed.), *Handbook for educational fund raising* (pp. 282-284). San Francisco, CA: Jossey-Bass.

Payton, R. L. (1987). American values and private philanthropy; Philanthropic values; A philanthropic dialogue. In K. W. Thompson (Ed.), *Philanthropy: Private means, public ends, 4* (pp. 3-20, 21-46, 123-136). Lanham, MD: University Press of America.

Payton, R. L. (1988a). *Philanthropy: Voluntary action for the public good.* New York:American Council on Education and Macmillan.

Payton, R. L. (1988b). Philanthropy in action. In R. L. Payton, M. Novak, B. O'Connell, & P. D. Hall, *Philanthropy: Four views* (pp. 1-10). New Brunswick, NJ: Social Philosophy and Policy Center and Transaction Books.

Payton, R. L. (1988c, March/April). Philanthropy in academia: Making the "non-subject" real. *Giving USA Update*, pp. 4-5.

Payton, R. L. (1989, Summer). Philanthropy and education. *NSFRE Journal*, pp. 64-65.

Pearson, R. A. (1989). *A theory of public relations ethics.* Unpublished doctoral dissertation, Ohio University, Athens, OH.

Perkins, J. (1966). *The university in transition.* Princeton, NJ: Princeton University Press.

Petitioners oppose Utah name change. (1989, July 26). *The Chronicle of Higher Education*, p. A26.

Pfeffer, J., & Salancik, G. R. (1978). *The external control of organizations: A resource dependence perspective.* New York: Harper & Row.

Philanthropy is . . . . (1988, November/December). *Giving USA Update*, pp. 1-2.

Philanthropy promotes the interests of the wealthy and does little to aid the poor, a scholar argues. (1990, April 18). *The Chronicle of Higher Education*, pp. A29-A31.

Phillips, G., & Richter, J. (1989, July 11). Should fund raisers risk their pay on the chance that a volunteer will bring in a big gift? *The Chronicle of Philanthropy*, p. 33.

Pickett, W. L. (1977). *An assessment of the effectiveness of fund raising policies on private undergraduate colleges.* Unpublished doctoral dissertation, University of Denver, Denver, CO.

Pickett, W. L. (1981). Prerequisites for successful fund raising. In F. C. Pray (Ed.), *Handbook for educational fund raising* (pp. 11-14). San Francisco, CA: Jossey-Bass.

Pickett, W. L. (1989, January 23). *Professionalism of fund raising.* Session at the CASE District III Conference, Pittsburgh, PA.

Pidgeon, W. P. (1989, September 5). Saving lives is important enough to merit financial aid from the brewing industry [Letter to the editor]. *The Chronicle of Philanthropy*, p. 29.

Pires, M. A. (1989, April). Working with activist groups. *Public Relations Journal*, pp. 30-32.

Postal inspectors open criminal investigation of controversial fund-raising firm. (1989, August 8). *The Chronicle of Philanthropy*, pp. 23, 27.

Powell, W. W. (Ed.). (1987). *The nonprofit sector: A research handbook.* New Haven, CT: Yale University Press.

Powell, W. W., & Friedkin, R. (1987). Organizational change in nonprofit organizations. In W. W. Powell (Ed.), *The nonprofit sector: A research handbook* (pp. 180-192). New Haven, CT: Yale University Press.

Pray, F. C. (1981). Fund raising past and present; Faculty as development colleagues; Traditional roles for volunteers and changing emphases; The president's role in administrative leadership; Trends in institutional resource management; The three joys of educational development. In F. C. Pray (Ed.), *Handbook for educational fund raising* (pp. 1-6, 140-142, 179-181, 189-191, 389-400, 401-403). San Francisco, CA: Jossey-Bass.

Prestigious positions on charitable boards now require much more time and effort. (1988, January 7). *The Wall Street Journal*, p. 31.

Preston, L. E. (1981). Corporate power and social performance: Approaches to positive analysis. In L. E. Preston (Ed.), *Research in corporate social performance and policy* (Vol. 3, pp. 1-16). Greenwich, CT: Jai Press.

Private health clubs assail tax exemptions of "yuppie" YMCA's with fancy facilities. (1989, May 30). *The Chronicle of Philanthropy*, pp. 1, 20, 22-23.

PRJ's fourth annual salary survey. (1989, June). *Public Relations Journal*, pp. 17-21.

Professors taking on important roles in raising funds for their institutions. (1987, March 18). *The Chronicle of Higher Education*, pp. 34-35.

Proposed legislation reflects concerns about unethical fund-raising practices. (1990, June). *NSFRE News*, pp. 1, 12.

Prospecting for alumni gold. (1988, September 5). *Newsweek*, pp. 66-67.

Public broadcasting acts to assure integrity. (1988, March 23). *The Chronicle of Higher Education*, p. A3.

Public colleges make gains in soliciting contributions. (1989, April 26). *The Wall Street Journal*, p. B1.

Public Relations Society of America. (1989). *Eligibility guidelines.* (Available from Author, 33 Irving Place, New York, NY 10032).

Ray, F. P. (1981). Research and cultivation of prospective donors. In F. C. Pray (Ed.), *Handbook for educational fund raising* (pp. 81-92). San Francisco, CA: Jossey-Bass.

Re, E. D. (1968). Education in the nation's service. In C. G. Dobbins & C. B. T. Lee (Eds.), *Whose goals for American higher education?* (pp. 91-93). Washington, DC: American Council on Education.

Reagan Years: Profound changes for philanthropy. (1988, October 25). *The Chronicle of Philanthropy*, pp. 1, 19-20, 22-23.

"Reparations" or tainted money? Women's groups face dilemma over Playboy's grants. (1989, January 24). *The Chronicle of Philanthropy*, pp. 4, 6-7.

Research centers on philanthropy, volunteerism, and non-profit organizations. (1989, February 21). *The Chronicle of Philanthropy*, p. 17.

Responding to criticism, non-profit hospitals look for ways to demonstrate that they are indeed charitable institutions. (1989, November 28). *The Chronicle of Philanthropy*, pp. 20-22.

Robbins, S. P. (1987). *Organization theory: Structure, design, and applications* (2nd ed.). Englewood Cliffs, NJ: Prentice-Hall.

Rowland, A. W. (Ed.). (1977). *Handbook of institutional advancement.* San Francisco, CA: Jossey-Bass.

Rowland, A. W. (1983). *Research in institutional advancement: A selected, annotated compendium of doctoral dissertations.* Washington, DC: Council for Advancement and Support of Education.

Rowland, A. W. (1986). *Research in institutional advancement: Addendum.* Washington, DC: Council for Advancement and Support of Education.

Royer, M. (1989, Summer). Please give generously, okay? *NSFRE Journal*, pp. 17-20.

Rozell, M. J. (1987). Corporate philanthropy and public policy: A search for normative guidelines. In K. W. Thompson (Ed.), *Philanthropy: Private means, public ends* (Vol. 4, pp. 91-107). Lanham, MD: University Press of America.

Rudney, G. (1987). The scope and dimensions of nonprofit activity. In W. W. Powell (Ed.), *The nonprofit sector: A research handbook* (pp. 55-64). New Haven, CT: Yale University Press.

Rudolph, F. (1962). *The American college and university: A history.* New York: Alfred A. Knopf.

Rusk, H. A. (1984). Fund raising. In B. Cantor (Ed.), *Experts in action: Inside public relations* (pp. 262-272). New York: Longman.

Salamon, L. M. (1987). Partners in public service: The scope and theory of government-nonprofit relations. In W. W. Powell (Ed.), *The nonprofit sector: A research handbook* (pp. 99-117). New Haven, CT: Yale University Press.

Salem College agrees to a merger with Teikyo University of Japan. (1989, August 9). *The Chronicle of Higher Education*, p. A3.

Schmidtlein, F. A. (1973, May). *An examination of the environment and processes of organizational decision-making: Some assumptions and their implications.* Unpublished qualifying paper, School of Education, University of California, Berkeley, CA.

Seymour, H. J. (1966). *Designs for fund raising: Principles, patterns, techniques.* New York: McGraw-Hill.

Sharpe, R. F. (1989, September 19). An invasion of greedy tax-shelter promoters is threatening to harm charitable giving. *The Chronicle of Philanthropy*, p. 40.

Shell, A. (1989, July). Cause-related marketing: Big risks, big potential. *Public Relations Journal*, pp. 8, 13.

Shoemaker, D. (1989, April. Two for the price of one. CASE *Currents*, pp. 46-50.

Silberg, C. A. (1987, October 28). *Factors associated with the philanthropic behavior of major donors: A proposal for a research study*. Unpublished doctoral proposal, University of Maryland, College Park, MD.

Simon, J. G. (1987). Research on philanthropy. In K. W. Thompson (Ed.), *Philanthropy: Private means, public ends* (Vol. 4, pp. 67-87). Lanham, MD: University Press of America.

Smith, H. W. (1988, March). Business Sense: The underpinnings of today's corporate-campus relationships. CASE *Currents*, pp. 6-10.

Smith, J. P. (1981). Rethinking the traditional capital campaign. In F. C. Pray (Ed.), *Handbook for educational fund raising* (pp. 60-68). San Francisco, CA: Jossey-Bass.

Smith, J. P. (1982, September). Setting fund-raising priorities. CASE *Currents*, pp. 34-37.

Smythe, D., & Van Dinh, T. (1983). On critical and communication research: A new critical analysis. *Journal of Communication, 33*(3), 117-127.

Some foundations try new solutions for an old problem: Whether to help non-profit groups meet operating costs. (1989, June 27). *The Chronicle of Philanthropy*, pp. 4-6.

Speech Communication Association. (1984). Policy. *Critical studies in mass communication, 1*(1).

Spencer, L. M. (1968). The research function and the advancement of knowledge. In C. G. Dobbins & C. B. T. Lee (Eds.), *Whose goals for American higher education?* (pp. 54-66). Washington, DC: American Council on Education.

State, charity officials battle over Illinois fund-raising law. (January 23, 1990). *The Chronicle of Philanthropy*, pp. 23-24.

State laws governing charitable solicitations. (1990, June 12). *The Chronicle of Philanthropy*, p. 33.

States modify laws on fund raising to crack down on charity fraud. (1989, August 8). *The Chronicle of Philanthropy*, pp. 1, 24-25.

Steinberg, R. (1987). Nonprofit organizations and the market. In W. W. Powell (Ed.), *The nonprofit sector: A research handbook* (pp. 118-138). New Haven, CT: Yale University Press.

Strategic giving: Sharp focus lets corporations link philanthropy to the bottom line, instead of just "giving money away." (1987, December 21). *pr reporter*, pp. 1-2.

Surge in gifts by individuals pushes private aid to colleges to $7.4-billion. (1987, May 13). *The Chronicle of Higher Education*, pp. 1, 40-41.

Tax fallout may be expensive for colleges, their staffs, and students. (1990, October 10). *The Chronicle of Higher Education*, p. A27.

Texans delay gift to Harvard after plan offering them special status is revealed. (1987, November 25). *The Chronicle of Higher Education*, pp. 1, A26.

Thompson, K. W. (Ed.). (1987). *Philanthropy: Private means, public ends* (Vol. 4). Lanham, MD: University Press of America.

Thompson, R. L. (1989, January 23). *Creating the right environment for the giving of major gifts*. Session at CASE District III Conference, Pittsburgh, PA.

3 percent floor set for deductions. (1990, December). *Fund-Raising Management*, p. 10.

To get clout, get results. (1988, November/December). CASE *Currents*, pp. 24, 26-28.

Tolbert, P. S. (1985/1986). Institutional environments and resource dependence: Sources of administrative structure in institutions of higher education. In M. W. Peterson (Ed.), *ASHE reader on organization and governance in higher education* (3rd ed., pp. 327-338). Lexington, MA: Ginn Press.

Trachtman, L. E. (1987, September). Where advancement fails. CASE *Currents*, pp. 11-13.

24-pct. turnover rate found for administrators; some officials are surprised by survey results. (1989, March 29). *The Chronicle of Higher Education*, pp. A13-A14.

U. of Rochester cancels admission of employee of a Kodak competitor. (1987, September 9). *The Chronicle of Higher Education*, pp. 1, A30.

U. of Rochester readmits employee of Kodak competitor. (1987, September 16). *The Chronicle of Higher Education*, pp. 1, A34.

UM enters fund-raising marathon. (1988, October 9). *The Sun*, pp. 1G, 6G.

Useem, M. (1987). Corporate Philanthropy. In W. W. Powell (Ed.), *The nonprofit sector: A research handbook* (pp. 340-359). New Haven, CT: Yale University Press.

U.S. funds for colleges and universities: The top 100 institutions in total federal obligations for fiscal 1986. (1987, December 9). *The Chronicle of Higher Education*, p. A22.

Vaughan, R. (1988, February 17). *The influence of alumni on the legislative process.* Unedited transcript of speech presented at CASE Columbus II Colloquium, Columbus, OH.

Venables, P. (1978). *Higher education developments: The technological universities 1956-1976.* London: Faber & Faber.

Walker, A. (1988). *The public relations body of knowledge.* New York: Foundation for Public Relations Research and Education.

Wallenfeldt, E. C. (1983). *American higher education: Servant of the people or protector of special interests?* Westport, CT: Greenwood Press.

Weaver, W. (1967/1983). Pre-Christian philanthropy. In B. O'Connell (Ed.), *America's voluntary spirit: A book of readings* (pp. 5-10). New York: The Foundation Center.

Webster's Seventh New Collegiate Dictionary. (1967). Springfield, MA: G. & C. Merriam.

Weick, K. E. (1986). Educational organizations as loosely coupled systems. In M. W. Peterson (Ed.), *ASHE reader on organization and governance in higher education* (3rd ed., pp. 42-60). Lexington, MA: Ginn Press. (Original work published 1976)

What lies ahead? (1989, Winter). *NSFRE Journal,* pp. 24-28.

Whitaker, B. (1974). *The philanthropoids: Foundations and society.* New York: William Morrow.

White, A. H. (1986). *The charitable behavior of Americans: Management summary.* Washington, DC: Independent Sector.

Wilkerson, G. S., & Schuette, A. W. (1981). Elements of annual giving program. In F. C. Pray (Ed.), *Handbook for educational fund raising* (pp. 26-34). San Francisco, CA: Jossey-Bass.

Wilson, L. (1968). Foreword. In C. G. Dobbins & C. B. T. Lee (Eds.), *Whose goals for American higher education?* (pp. vii-ix). Washington, DC: American Council on Education.

Wilson, R. (1989, February 10). *Equal employment opportunity in higher education: An historical perspective.* Speech presented at the Conference on Equity, University of Maryland, College Park, MD.

Winship, II, A. L. (1984). *The quest for major gifts: A survey of 68 institutions.* Washington, DC: Council for Advancement and Support of Education.

Wolfenden, J. (1968). British University Grants and Government Relations. In C. G. Dobbins & C. B. T. Lee (Eds.), *Whose goals for American higher education?* (pp. 206-215). Washington, DC: American Council on Education.

Wood, E. W. (1989). The four r's of major gift solicitation. *reid report* (141), pp. 1, 6. Pasadena, CA: Russ Reid Company.

Worth, M. J. (1989, March). The philosophy of philanthropy [Review of *Philanthropy: Voluntary action for the public good*]. CASE *Currents,* p. 43.

Yarmolinsky, A. (1983). The foundation as an expression of a democratic society. In B. O'Connell (Ed.), *America's voluntary spirit: A book of readings* (pp. 345-354). New York: The Foundation Center. (Original work published 1961)

Ylvisaker, P. N. (1987). Foundations and nonprofit organizations. In W. W. Powell (Ed.), *The nonprofit sector: A research handbook* (pp. 360-379). New Haven, CT: Yale University Press.

Young, C. J. (1981). Interests and motives of nonalumni givers. In F. C. Pray (Ed.), *Handbook for educational fund raising* (pp. 73-76). San Francisco, CA: Jossey-Bass.

Author Index

Subject Index